張謇与近代上海

ZHANGJIAN YU
JINDAI SHANGHAI

南通市档案馆◎编

广西师范大学出版社
GUANGXI NORMAL UNIVERSITY PRESS
·桂林·

张謇与近代上海
ZHANGJIAN YU JINDAI SHANGHAI

出版统筹：肖爱景
责编编辑：雷锋莉
责任校对：李　静
责任技编：伍智辉
封面设计：徐俊霞　俸萍利［广大迅风艺术］

图书在版编目（CIP）数据
张謇与近代上海 / 南通市档案馆编. -- 桂林 :
广西师范大学出版社，2024. 8. -- ISBN 978-7-5598-7212-8
Ⅰ. K825.38；K295.1
中国国家版本馆 CIP 数据核字第 2024U4H440 号

广西师范大学出版社出版发行
（广西桂林市五里店路 9 号　邮政编码：541004
网址：http://www.bbtpress.com）
出版人：黄轩庄
全国新华书店经销
广西广大印务有限责任公司印刷
（桂林市临桂区秧塘工业园西城大道北侧广西师范大学出版社集团有限公司创意产业园内　邮政编码：541199）
开本：787 mm × 1 092 mm　1/16
印张：19.5　　　　字数：322 千
2024 年 8 月第 1 版　　2024 年 8 月第 1 次印刷
定价：88. 00 元

张謇（1853—1926）

unesco

Regional Committee

The United Nations Educational, Scientific and Cultural Organization

certifies the inscription of

Archives of the Initial Dasheng Spinning Factory (1896-1907)

Nantong Municipal Archives

China

on the

Memory of the World Committee for Asia and the Pacific Regional Register

Kwibae Kim
Chair
MOWCAP

26 November 2022
Date

Jo Hironaka
Advisor/Chief of Unit
Communication & Information
UNESCO Bangkok

UNESCO Memory of the World Committee for Asia and the Pacific (MOWCAP)

“大生纱厂创办初期档案（1896—1907）”入选《世界记忆亚太地区名录》证书

编委会

前 言

南通市档案馆馆藏的近万卷大生档案，吸引了众多境内外的学者来查阅和研究。大生档案是比较系统地反映张謇创办大生纱厂的过程，以及以棉纺织业为核心，开办盐垦、交通、金融、贸易等企业，并在企业获利基础上，通过自身捐助和倡导社会资金投入，在南通兴办教育和慈善事业的历史记录。其中“大生纱厂创办初期档案（1896—1907）”于 2022 年入选《世界记忆亚太地区名录》。张謇在南通探索早期现代化的实践，引起了社会的瞩目，南通一度有模范城市的美誉。

大生档案就其形成的主体而言，主要是大生驻沪办事机构（由于名称多次变更，一般称之为大生沪所）形成的档案。大生沪所创立于 1896 年，彼时大生纱厂尚在筹备之中，初名为大生上海公所，负责采购机器物料、汇兑银洋、报税领照、与江海关交涉等事宜。1897 年下半年，大生上海公所迁出暂寓的广丰洋行，搬入天主堂街 31 号的春裕成，并改称大生沪帐房。1907 年大生纱厂第一次股东大会，决议将大生沪帐房改名为大生驻沪事务所，取得与会计、考工、营业、庶务等四所同等的地位。

大生沪所是张謇将大生纱厂，以及之后创办的一系列企事业单位与上海紧密联系起来的纽带。随着南通现代化进程的推进，大生沪所甚至成为南通在上海的窗口。大生沪所有效地加强了南通与上海之间的资金、人才、信息的交流，这对于南通接受上海的辐射，充分依托上海这个中国的经济和文化中心，承接来自上海的先进生产方式，汲取沪上的先进文化，有着不可估量的贡献。

在此基础上，张謇在上海开辟码头，开通沪通之间定期的轮船航班。在张謇多年的奔走下，天生港自开商埠，江海关在南通设立分关，极大地便利了南通及周边地区的商贸活动。这些举措使得南通与上海之间建立起更加密切的联系。

上海同时也是张謇的一所社会学校。机器生产、新式教育都是新生事物，从传统科举中走出来的张謇，对此能够驾轻就熟，除了天生对新事物敏感外，勤于观察、学习，又善于吸收、融合是主要原因。得风气之先的上海，为张謇提供了很多范本。上海诞生了中国第一家机器棉纺织工厂——上海机器织布厂，毁于大火的上海机器织布厂后来重建为华盛纺织总厂。华盛纺织总厂是张謇筹备大生纱厂时期主要的学习和借鉴对象，连企业的合同、工资标准都愿意提供给大生纱厂参考。

南洋公学由盛宣怀于 1896 年在上海创办，第二年南洋公学师范院正式开学上课，揭开了中国师范教育的序幕。南洋公学还设有译书院，1903 年曾请官方颁布版权保护的告示。南洋公学的首任总理何嗣焜是张謇多年的密友，译书院首任院长张元济跟张謇志同道合，他们对于张謇日后兴办教育、开设翰墨林书局应该有启迪作用。

上海中西交汇的特点，决定了张謇得到的启示是多元的。慈善是张謇在南通着力布局的公益事业，上海开埠之后，不仅慈善组织迅速增多，而且也出现一些与中国传统慈善运作方式不同的模式，这些特色对张謇是有启发作用的。宁波帮的代表人物叶澄衷创办的怀德堂，是对企业困难员工进行抚恤的内部互助性慈善机构，经费来源一方面是叶澄衷旗下各商号共同筹集的洋 2 万元，另一方面是企业员工捐助——每人每天献出一文钱，多助不限。张謇对此大为赞赏，认为怀德堂的善举值得记录和流传下去，让更多人知晓。张謇在南通倡议设立的新育婴堂，充分吸收了天主教耶稣会在徐家汇设立的土山湾孤儿院教养结合的方法，在育婴堂建筑上也吸取了土山湾孤儿院的经验。

张謇探索现代化的思想，是在不断的学习和实践中形成并演进的，上海无疑也是张謇现代化思想的孵化地和催生地。还是以慈善为例，1901 年张謇所作《上海怀德堂记》是研究其慈善思想形成的重要文献。张謇引用《诗经·小雅》“伐木丁丁，鸟鸣嘤嘤”，紧跟这句的是“出自幽谷，迁于乔木。嘤其鸣矣，求其友声。相彼鸟矣，犹求友声”。张謇认为天下没有人能不依靠别人的帮助而成事，得到别人的帮助事成后，只能与人共苦，不能与人同甘，也就是不能让别人分享成果，不得人心。在阐述了人与人之间互助、知恩图报的必要性后，张謇以《周礼》为例，认为中国的礼制中很早就对孤独鳏寡人群有抚恤制度。再谈到欧洲，凡是为国效力致残的，国家会给予终身补助；而为国捐躯的，国家会赡养其遗孀和孩子，以鼓舞士气。张謇认为，其实中国的古训里也有这样的思想，而叶澄衷对欧洲的有关抚恤的情况比较了解，借鉴了欧洲的有关做法，在致富之后，设立怀德堂，有与员工同甘共苦之意。

如果说南通是张謇探索富强之道的小舞台的话，那么上海无疑就是张謇展示家国情怀的大舞台。立宪运动、南北议和，张謇在其中发挥了独特的作用。张謇主持吴淞开埠，入股《申报》，支持复旦公学、震旦学院、吴淞商船专科学校、江苏省立水产学校、中国公学等学校，在上海近代史上留下了深深的印记。

本书以南通市档案馆馆藏大生档案为基础，结合征集到的相关档案，试图透过档案人的视角，通过档案来展示编者心目中的张謇与上海之间的联系。由于档案无法覆盖所有的方面，所以本书只能就着现有的档案展开，因此有很多地方无法涉及，或者无法深入。如果把张謇与上海这个课题视作一本厚重的史书，那么本书只不过是翻开了扉页。我们的本意是为研究者探赜索隐、钩深致远提供帮助。

张謇与上海这个既有历史价值又有现实意义的话题，某种意义上讲，探讨的是近代南通与上海的关系。晚清民初南通的迅速崛起，无疑是由于张謇的主导和引领，但依托的是当时的经济中心上海。上海的技术转移、资金流入、人才支持、物料输入，是张謇在南通探索早期现代化的核心支撑。张謇时代的南通，在经济和文化上主动接轨上海，其经验在长三角区域一体化发展的当下，依然有其借鉴意义。在厘清基本史实的基础上，探究沪通融合的缘由、方式和进程，摸索沪通两地之间互动的规律，有助于南通在上海这个龙头的带动下，在长三角区域一体化发展国家战略中更好地发挥作用。

目录

『上海一部分事最繁重』
——设立沪所

张謇与上海的关系，以 1895 年为界，之前是观察和学习阶段，之后则是张謇把上海视作自己施展抱负的舞台的阶段。如果说南通是其实业基地，并因实业的发展带动教育和公益慈善事业的进步，进而促进南通的早期现代化，那么南通的进步和发展，就给了张謇足够的自信和资历，使他得以在上海这个巨大的舞台上展示。

青少年时代的张謇对上海的认知，与其父亲张彭年有密切的关系。张彭年身处海门常乐，当年这个地方既不滨江也不临海，更不是因盐而兴的集镇，其实很闭塞。但是张彭年是个头脑灵活、善于进取的商人，他的见识远超乡人，为家庭带来大量的外部信息，特别是来自上海的新鲜故事。

张謇的《述训》里提及，张彭年先是有瓦屋 5 间、草屋 3 间，后来又陆续添建了房屋。张彭年初有田 20 余亩[1]，后来有所增加，还兼营瓷器，算是比较富裕。张彭年还是一个爱读书的人，“先君子营柳西草堂二楹，有书八椟，题以‘自随’”，较早的时候就有 8 个木柜的书籍。张彭年具体有哪些书，我们不得而知。但从张彭年晚年喜欢研究徐光启的《农政全书》看，他务实而喜钻研。张謇日后在给儿子张孝若的信里说：“儿宜自勉于学，将来仍当致力于农，此是吾家世业”，不得不说是受张彭年的影响。

1848 年至 1850 年间，连年灾害，张彭年借钱外出做生意，“附舟至上海，转商于宁波”，从海门坐上小船到上海，再赶往宁波。去宁波，很有可能是采购瓷器，因为宁波是中国的瓷业中心之一。这里的核心在于张彭年需要在上海中转。那时的上海已经于 1843 年开埠，正逐渐发展为中国最大的城市，外国商品和技术纷纷涌入，中西文化在此碰撞和交融。上海的繁华必然给久居乡间的张彭年带来心灵的冲击，望子成龙的他也

1　1 亩 ≈ 666.67 平方米。

一定会跟张謇讲述所闻所见。张彭年经常性地来到上海，尤其是他娶了张謇的母亲金夫人后，曾“岁半外出，一切经纪皆吾母手自厘绪”，一年中有一半时间在外经营，家里的事都是由金夫人打理。

1876 年 3 月 14 日，张謇曾在吴淞搭乘家中购买碗的船回海门，由此可见张彭年的瓷器生意达到了一定规模，而且经营稳定，已经不需要自己直接去上海接运。

书报也是张謇与上海间接接触的媒介，《申报》是一个例证。《申报》1872 年 4 月 30 日在上海创刊，1949 年 5 月 27 日停刊，是近代中国发行时间最长的报纸。《申报》是张謇了解时事、掌握新知的来源之一。1895 年前的张謇日记，至少有 7 处阅读《申报》的记录，其中 3 次是在海门，最早是在 1884 年 5 月 16 日，张謇在海门通过《申报》，“知吾军有调防奉天之讯”，此处“吾军”指吴长庆所率的淮军。能在海门乡间读到《申报》，张謇显然有稳定的获取渠道，凭张謇的家庭条件和张彭年的开明程度，长期订阅也有可能。《申报》扎根上海，必然把沪上新闻不断带给张謇，长年累月阅读下来，上海已然是个熟悉的城市了。

百闻不如一见。创办大生纱厂之前，张謇有很多机会来到上海。关于上海的经历，张謇在日记里一般只是记载生活起居和人际往来情况，几乎没有对上海的经济和文化状况发表看法。事实上，繁华的上海滩对于身处偏僻乡村的张謇而言，视觉和心理冲击力不会小。这种冲击不仅仅影响中国其他地区的人，也影响东瀛人。1867 年 2 月 19 日，日本的涩泽荣一等人乘坐的“阿尔菲”号靠岸上海，上海街道上煤气灯和电线杆让涩泽荣一的内心受到震撼。1895 年张謇从筹办大生纱厂开始，始终把上海作为其发展南通各项事业的资金、技术和人才的主要来源地，绝不是心血来潮。

张謇不仅看到上海生机勃勃的一面，认为“上海为全国商业中枢”，也体察到上海丑陋黑暗的一面。1878 年 2 月 20 日，张謇从海门坐船到上海，当晚住在永安街太古昌洋行，季瀛洲邀请他看戏。第二天，张謇上街购买扇袋、手巾、笺纸等物品。季瀛洲在兆荣里置酒请客，之后泾县胡㦤斋相邀至朱雪卿、王素娥词史处。张謇目睹湖北涂某，湖南周某、陈某等人花天酒地，一夜用掉番钱70余枚，感慨“贫家终岁作苦，所得讵有此耶”。1920年秋，张謇倡导设立的淮海实业银行开设上海分行，张謇拟写了对员工的训词，他提醒员工“沪之地，人聚、财聚而恶聚之海也”，劝勉大家要忠于职守，遵守规则，勤奋工作。“人聚、财聚而恶聚之海”这句话，反映了张謇对那时上海的认知。

如果要推举一个张謇与上海紧密联系的典型标志，非大生沪所莫属。早在大生纱厂筹办时期，1896年的上半年，张謇团队就设立了大生上海公所，负责采购机器物料、汇兑银洋、报税领照、与江海关交涉等事宜。之后大生上海公所名称多次变更（通称大生沪所或沪所），地址屡次变更，但在大生系统中的地位不断上升，发挥的作用愈发显著。

先有大生沪所，后有南通大生纱厂的厂房，可见上海在张謇心目中的重要程度。沪所如同一根纽带，将张謇的事业与上海紧紧联系在一起。张謇时代的沪所，随着大生事业的发展而逐步壮大，从最初寄寓在其他公司内，到在九江路建筑起气派的南通大厦。南通和上海两地的信息、资金、人员、物资，通过沪所进行交换和流动，使沪所一定意义上成为南通在上海的窗口。张謇作为社会名流，与沪上诸多人士有交往，也加入了许多社会团体，沪所也成为张謇在上海进行社会活动的场所。

张謇（1853—1926），出生于江苏海门常乐镇，清末状元、实业家、教育家，被誉为爱国企业家的典范、民营企业家的先贤和楷模。1895 年在南通筹建大生纱厂，1899 年 5 月 23 日大生纱厂开车纺纱。以大生纱厂为基础，张謇在南通建成以棉纺织业为主，涵盖盐垦、金融、交通等行业的工业体系。张謇在兴办实业的同时，倡导并赞助教育，从事慈善和公益事业，是中国早期现代化的开拓者。

大生馬頭

大生纱厂是丁忧在家的张謇受两江总督张之洞的委任筹办的。南通的土壤和气候条件适宜种植棉花。南通是著名的棉产区，又是土布的出产区。就地设立纱厂，既靠近棉花这个原材料市场，企业生产的棉纱又能就近销售。张謇坦言兴办纱厂是“为中国利源计”，他为创办的纱厂取名“大生”，来源于《易经》中的“天地之大德曰生”。

遵辦通海紗絲廠稟稿 光緒二十一年十二月初八日

爲遵辦通海紗絲廠擬章懇請通詳定案事

竊職等承通州前翰林院修撰張集諭承准

南洋大臣張照會開欽奉

諭旨飭令招商多設織布織綢等局以收利權查通州爲產棉最盛之區近年繭絲亦漸暢旺亟應推廣紗布繭絲各項商務惟必有公正紳士協同地方官員董率其間方能奏效應請總理通海一帶商務妥議章程由該商等稟由地方官核定舉辦並邀集紳富剴切勸導厚集股本早覩厥成等因職等竊維通海土產棉花鄉人以紡織爲生計近

通海紗絲廠章程 一

來外洋紡織機器盛行洋紗洋布銷售日廣本紗土布去路滯減鄉人窮極思變購用洋紗參織大小布疋線帶以致洋紗倒灌內地日甚一日查計現在通海兩境每日可銷洋紗二十大包已合機器一萬錠之數若寖增不已不出十年必盡變爲洋紗之布民間膏血耗奪無形不塞涓涓將有流爲江河之勢今蒙

諭旨飭辦官紳勸導所以爲民生計者至周職等復公同展轉議勸擬在通州城西唐家閘地方水口近便之處建立機廠擬名大生先辦紗機二萬錠以本地所出之花用本地習紡之工即以紡成之紗銷行本地及鄰近州縣運脚省

1896年1月26日，潘华茂、郭勋、樊芬、沈燮均、刘桂馨、陈维镛等6位筹办纱厂的董事，联名向张之洞上奏《遵办通海纱丝厂禀稿》。通海纱丝厂是大生纱厂的初名，《遵办通海纱丝厂禀稿》除了提及创办企业的由来、在唐家闸建厂的设想、集股的办法外，还附有通海大生纱丝厂的章程，共7条。章程第6条特别提出：“定购机器点收装运及陆续添购煤炭物料、汇兑银洋、出售纱丝、投税领照诸事，均在上海，其与道署、税关交涉甚夥，拟立公所一处，由厂派人经理，刊刻戳记，以昭凭信，文曰‘奏办通海大生纱丝厂上海公所记’”。

應用煤炭油火等件無論外洋辦來購自上海皆須照完關稅向例照內河章程用子口單分運今通州至上海江路徑直內河繞從蘇常鎮揚異常迂曲而廠中所用之物又異常重大繁瑣擬自備平底大板駁船數號隨時僱小火輪拖帶由吳淞出口應請變通舊章已稅之物至江海北關復驗轉運通州照洋商例不加捐稅並請飭道隨時給發護照以免途中關卡留難其小火輪出口護照亦請由道於前項給照之時一併發給輪回即銷續運雇輪再請道照註明通海大生紗廠運料字樣以杜蒙混

一定購機器點收裝運及陸續添購煤炭物料匯兌銀洋出售紗絲投稅領照諸事均在上海其與道署稅關交涉甚夥擬立公所一處由廠派人經理刊刻戳記以昭憑信文曰

奏辦通海大生紗絲廠上海公所記

一通海河港淤淺路徑窄狹機器重大之件搬運不易設有阻碍之處請准本廠自行疏通墊補

一通海無保險火政尤要請准廠中用自來水電氣燈

通州直隸州正堂汪批

候會同海門廳據情轉詳摺存

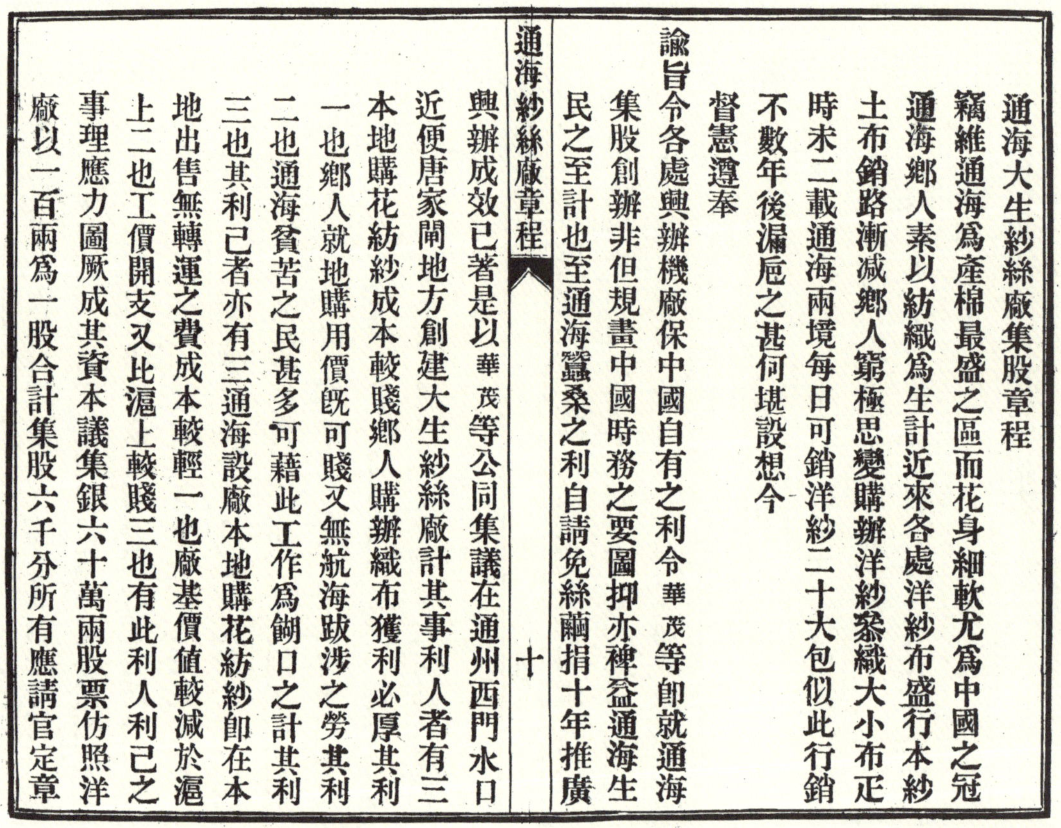

通海大生紗絲廠集股章程

竊維通海爲產棉最盛之區而花身細軟尤爲中國之冠通海鄉人素以紡織爲生計近來各處洋紗布盛行本紗土布銷路漸減鄉人窮極思變購辦洋紗參織大小布疋時未二載通海兩境每日可銷洋紗二十大包似此行銷不數年後漏卮之甚何堪設想今

督憲遵奉

諭旨令各處興辦機廠保中國自有之利令華 茂等即就通海集股創辦非但規畫中國時務之要圖抑亦裨益通海生民之至計也至通海蠶桑之利自請免絲繭捐十年推廣

通海紗絲廠章程 十

興辦成效已著是以華 茂等公同集議在通州西門水口近便唐家閘地方創建大生紗絲廠計其事利人者有三本地購花紡紗成本較賤鄉人購辦織布獲利必厚其利一也鄉人就地購用價既可賤又無航海跋涉之勞其利二也通海貧苦之民甚多可藉此工作爲餬口之計其利三也其利己者亦有三通海設廠本地購花紡紗即在本地出售無轉運之費成本較輕一也廠基價值較減於滬上二也工價開支又比滬上較賤三也有此利人利己之事理應力圖厥成其資本議集銀六十萬兩股票仿照洋廠以一百兩爲一股合計集股六千分所有應請官定章

1938年夏，陈维镛之子陈葆初在上海编辑《影印创办大生纱厂禀稿暨招股章程原稿》。陈葆初在跋中介绍说：章程内加刊“上海公所暂寓四马路广丰洋行内”之红色戳记，所谓上海公所即最初大生在沪之接洽机关，而广丰洋行即沪股要人潘丈鹤琴所供职之洋行也。

程稟由地方官轉詳
督憲已蒙批准具
奏在案茲擬集股章程七條具列於後
一集股本規銀六十萬兩分作六千股每股一票計規銀
一百兩凡各紳商願入股者一在上海本公所一在通
州萬昌福莊一在海門孫廣源莊三處認購自州廳出
示本廠登報開辦之日起以兩月爲期期滿截止收股
分四次第一次簽名時付銀二十五兩第二次本年六
月底付銀二十五兩第三次七月底機器運到時付銀
二十五兩每次隨給收照第四次八月底採辦棉花時

上海公所暫寓四
馬路廣豐洋行內

付銀二十五兩至第四次付銀之時將前三次收照繳
還兑換股票領取息摺其官息按長年八釐卽從領票
之日起息
一股票內須載明入股人籍貫姓名遇有遺失由本人具
稟州憲備案一面刊登申滬各報十日後領取息銀之
期另立保單由本廠補給股票以免轇轕倘有股票轉
售向本廠換票簽名以及遺失補給者每張貼紙筆費
銀三錢
一股本無論大小以本廠股票爲憑如簽名之後到期無
銀交出卽應註銷另招不准虛懸

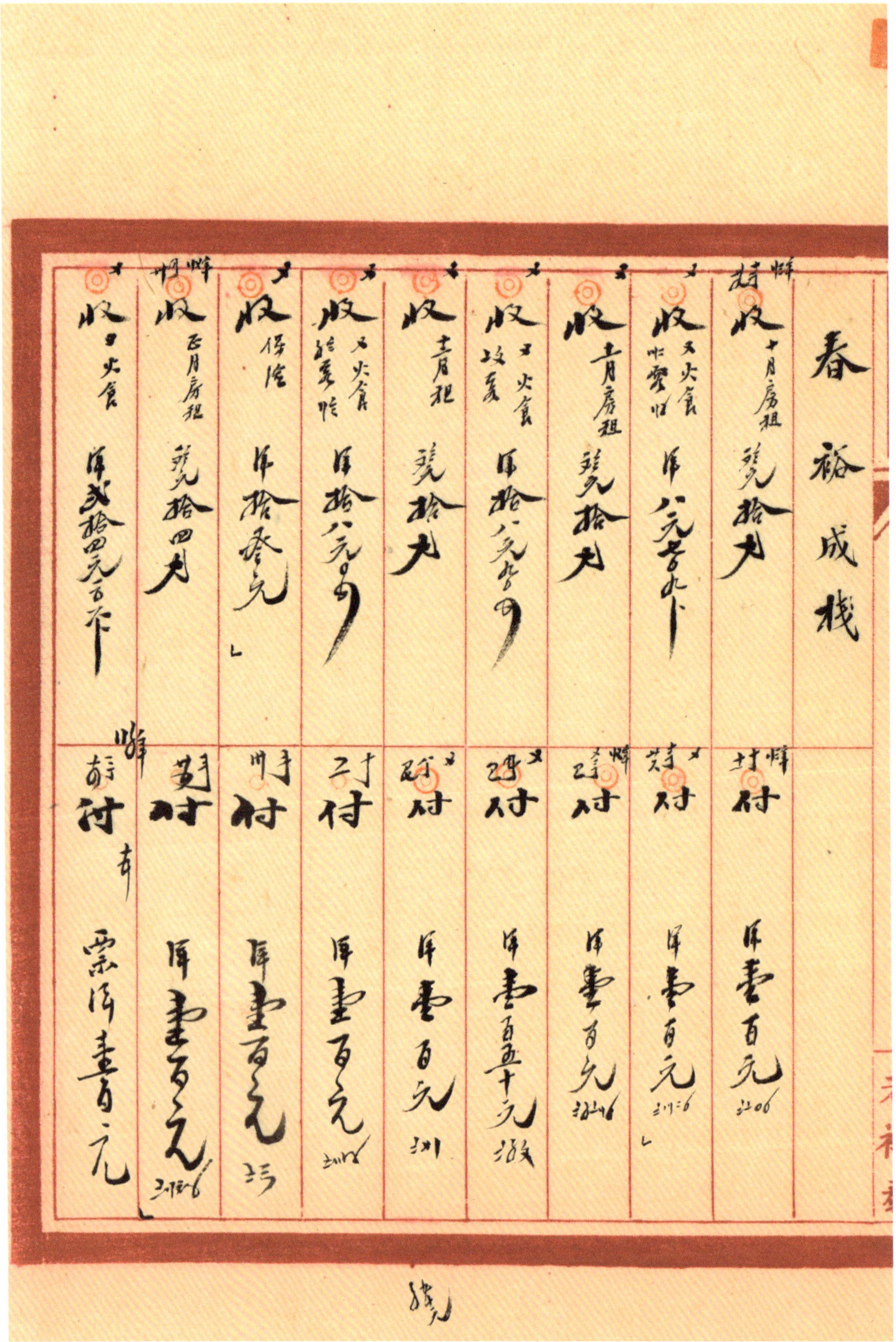

大生沪所《总录》中支付给春裕成的账目（部分）。1897 年下半年，大生上海公所迁出暂寓的广丰洋行，搬入天主堂街，借春裕成栈办公，改名大生沪所，一直到 1899 年农历五月才再次迁址。

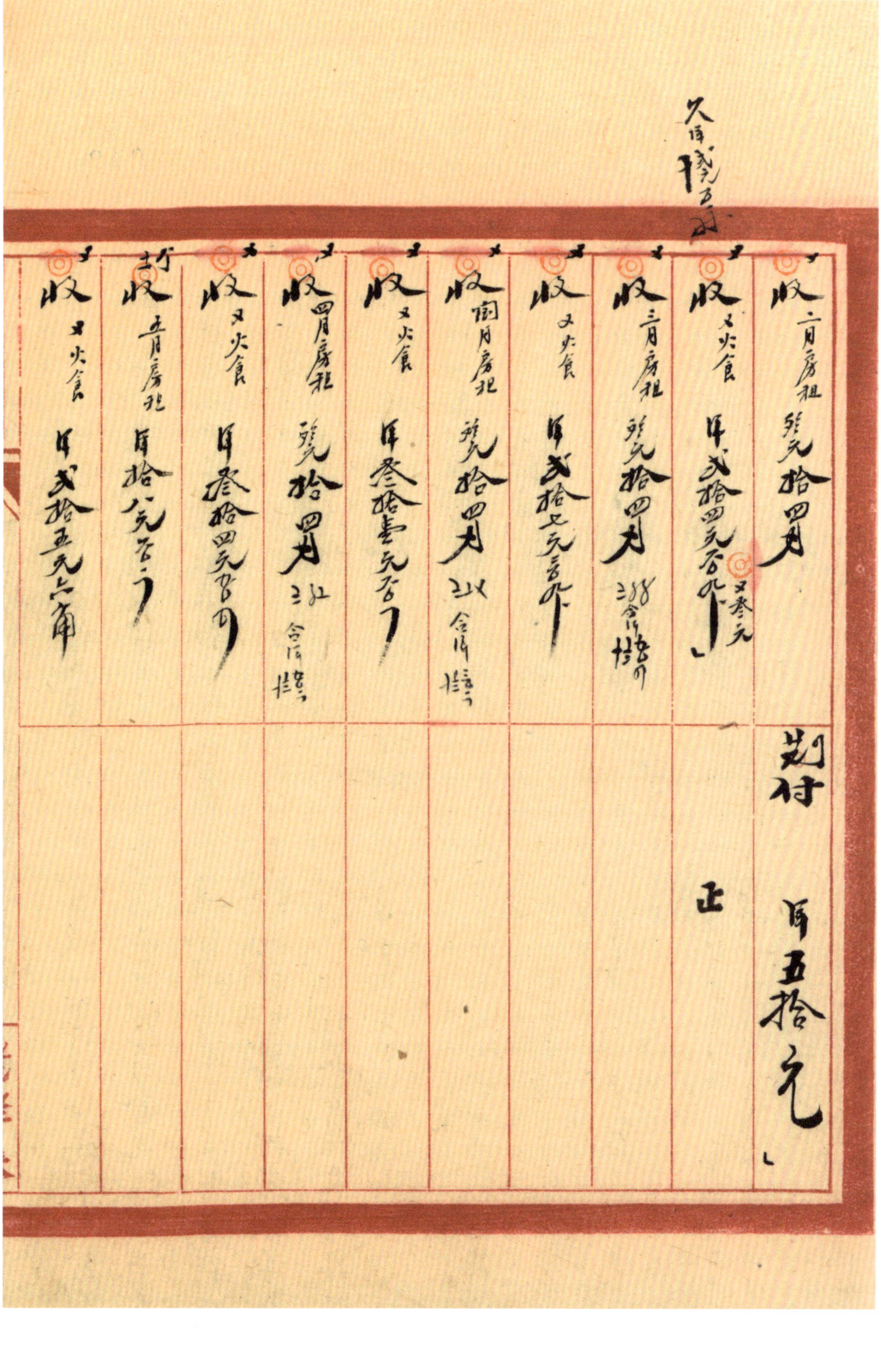
收 二月房租
收 又火食
收 三月房租
收 又火食
收 閏月房租
收 又火食
收 四月房租
收 又火食
收 五月房租
收 又火食
劃付 洋五拾元
正

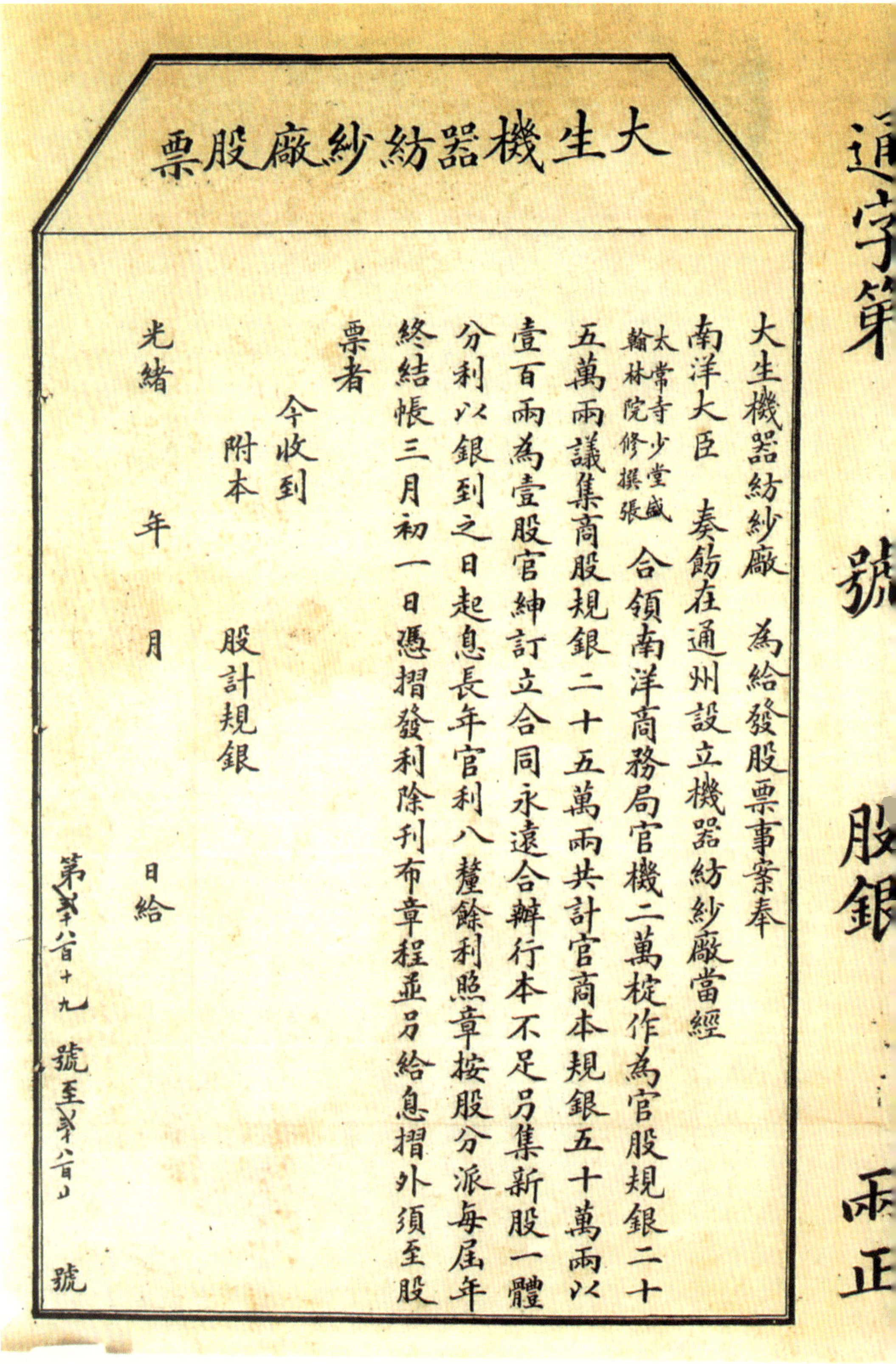

大生機器紡紗廠股票

大生機器紡紗廠　為給發股票事案奉
南洋大臣　奏飭在通州設立機器紡紗廠當經
太常寺少堂盛
翰林院修撰張　合領南洋商務局官機二萬錠作為官股規銀二十
五萬兩議集商股規銀二十五萬兩共計官商本規銀五十萬兩以
壹百兩為壹股官紳訂立合同永遠合辦行本不足另集新股一體
分利以銀到之日起息長年官利八釐餘利照章按股分派每屆年
終結帳三月初一日憑摺發利除刋布章程並另給息摺外須至股
票者
今收到
附本　股計規銀
光緒　年　月　日給
第　號至　號

通字第　號　股銀　兩正

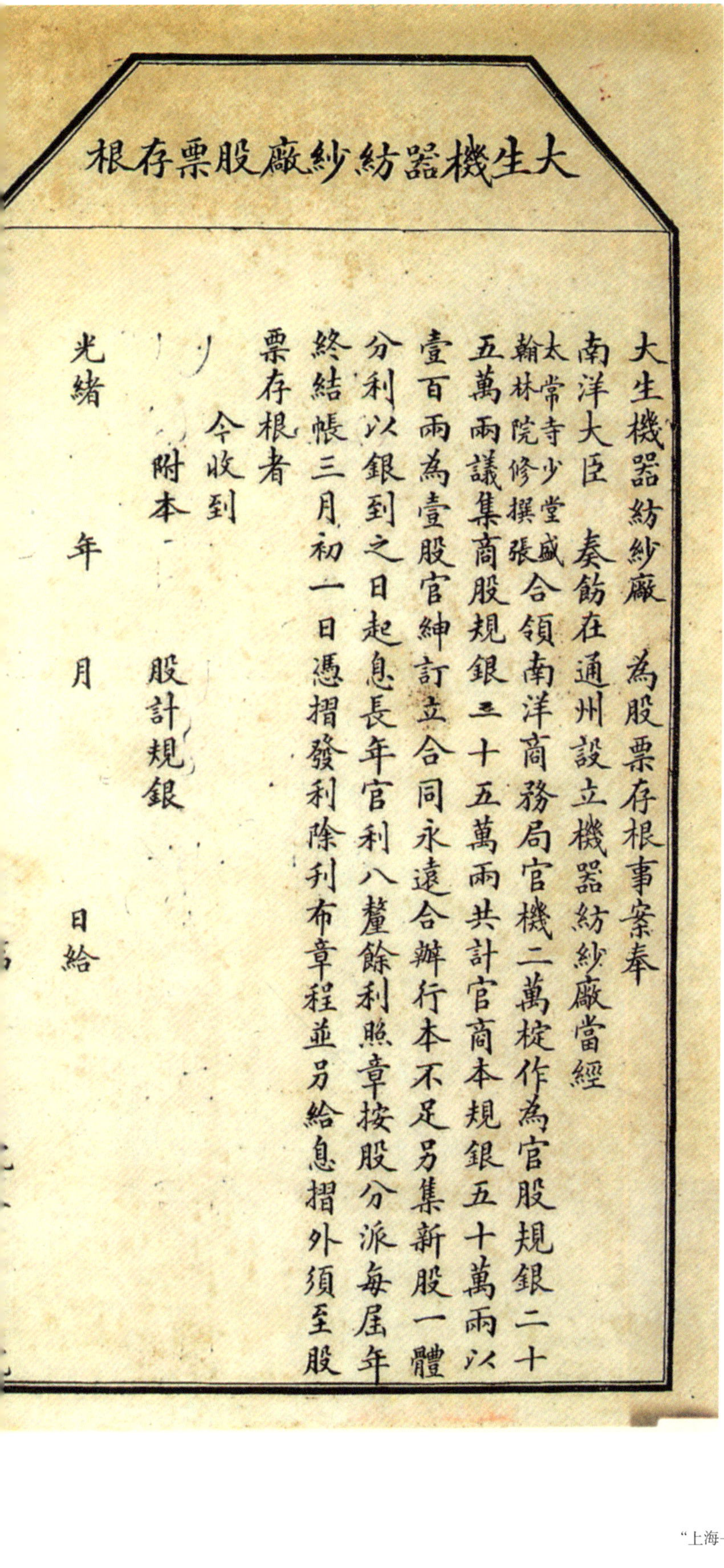
大生機器紡紗廠股票存根

大生機器紡紗廠　為股票存根事案奉
南洋大臣　奏飭在通州設立機器紡紗廠當經
太常寺少堂盛
翰林院修撰張
合領南洋商務局官機二萬錠作為官股規銀二十
五萬兩議集商股規銀二十五萬兩共計官商本規銀五十萬兩以
壹百兩為壹股官紳訂立合同永遠合辦行本不足另集新股一體
分利以銀到之日起息長年官利八釐餘利照章按股分派每屆年
終結帳三月初一日憑摺發利除利布章程並另給息摺外須至股
票存根者
今收到
附本　股計規銀
光緒　年　月　日給

大生纱厂创办初期向社会募集资金发行的股票及其存根（编号为2819至2820号）。通过大生沪所，来自上海或者通过上海转运的物料被源源不断地运往南通，资金和技术也由上海注入南通，大生沪所成为大生纱厂启动的重要引擎。

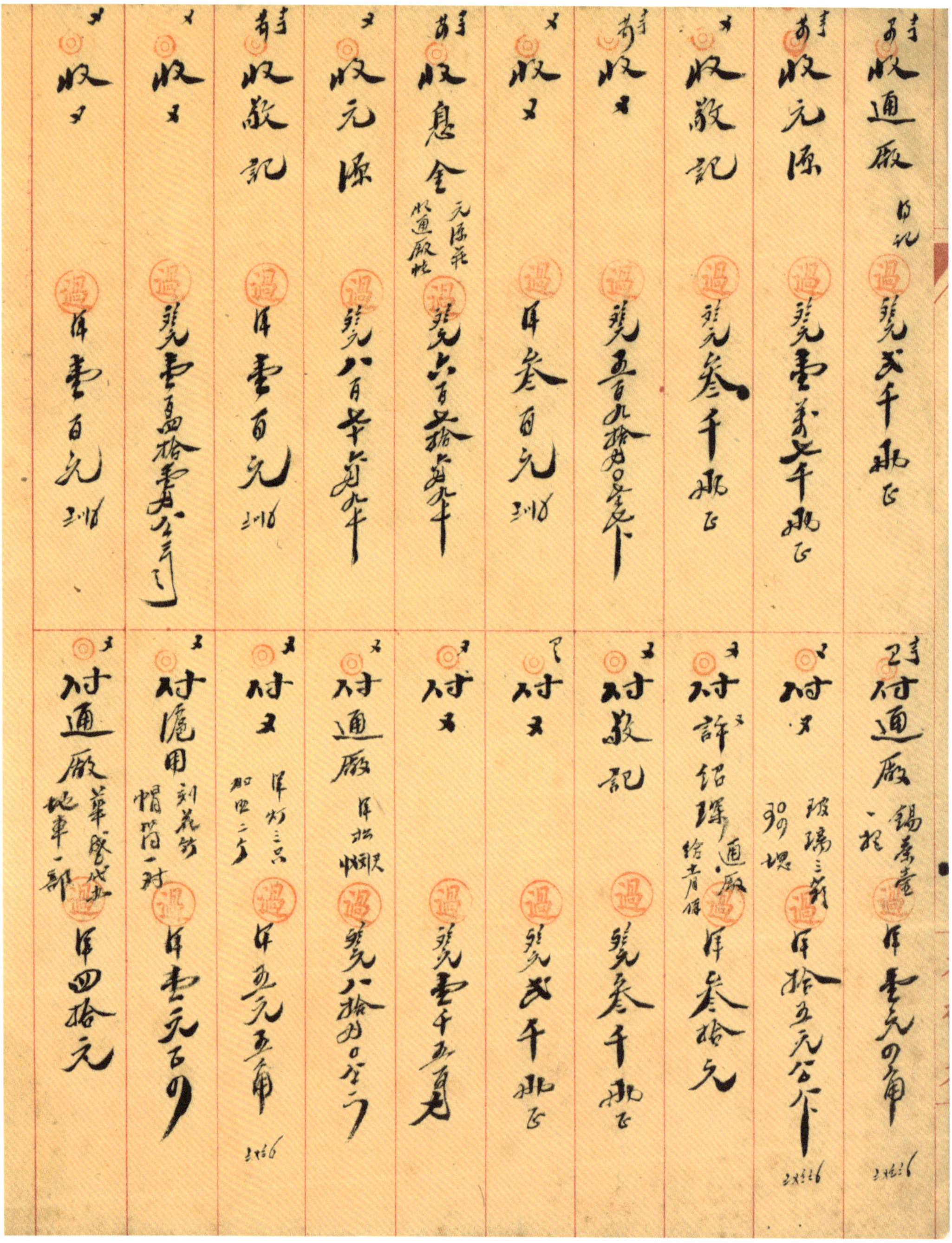

1897 年大生沪所的流水账（局部）。

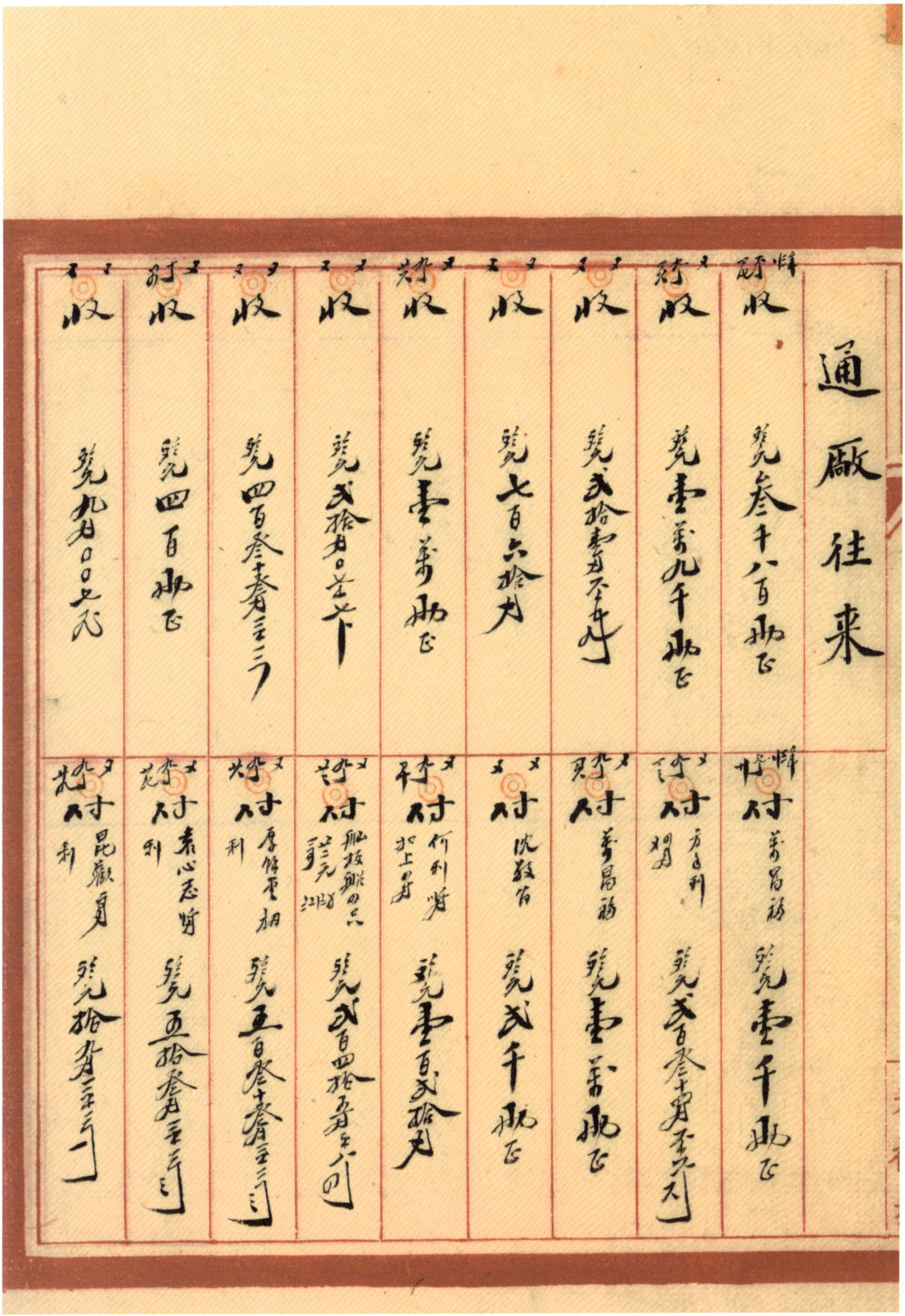

1897 年大生沪所《各往来》中，记载大生纱厂在上海经营活动的收支账（部分）。

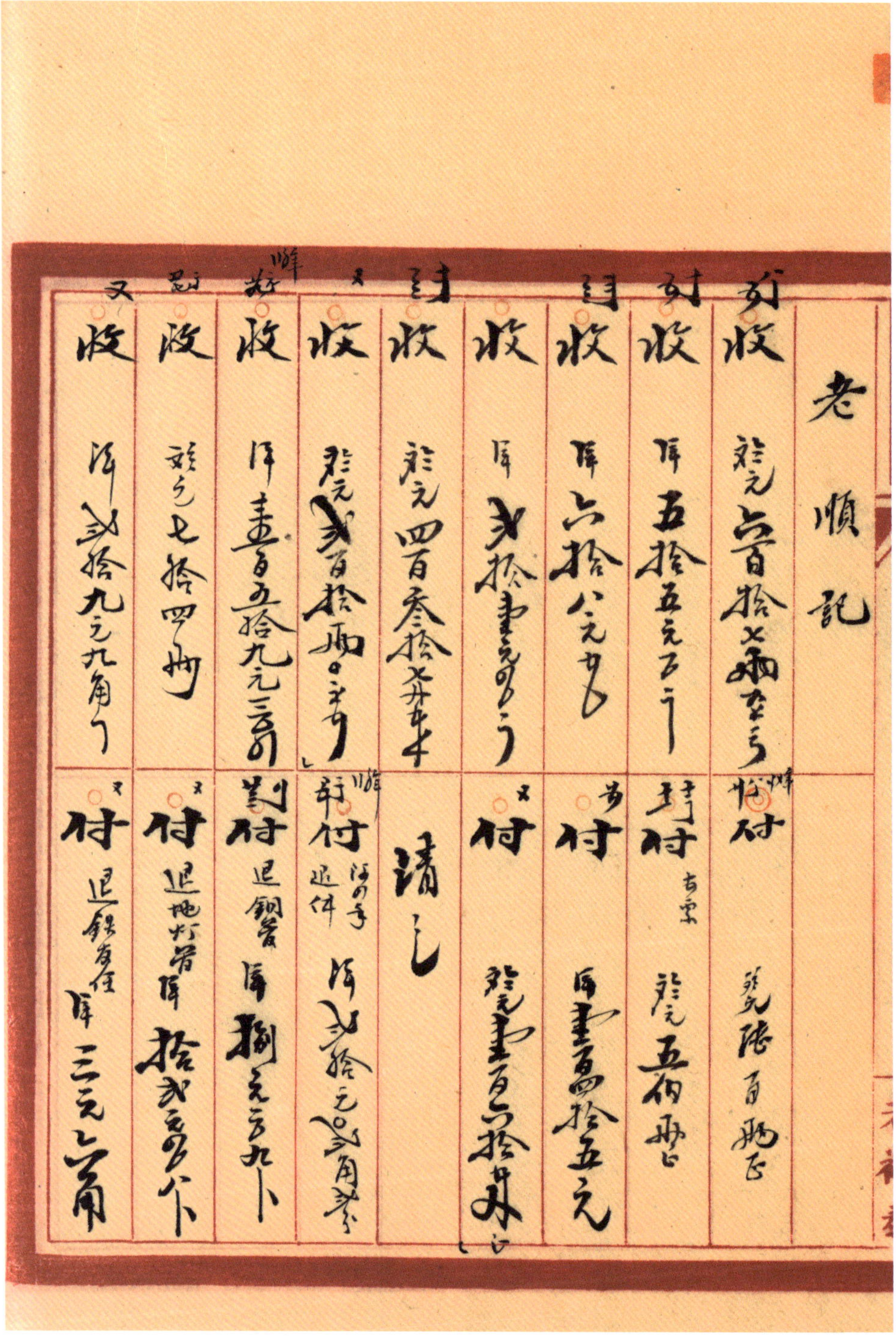

1897 年大生沪所《总录》中，向老顺记采购物资的账目（部分）。

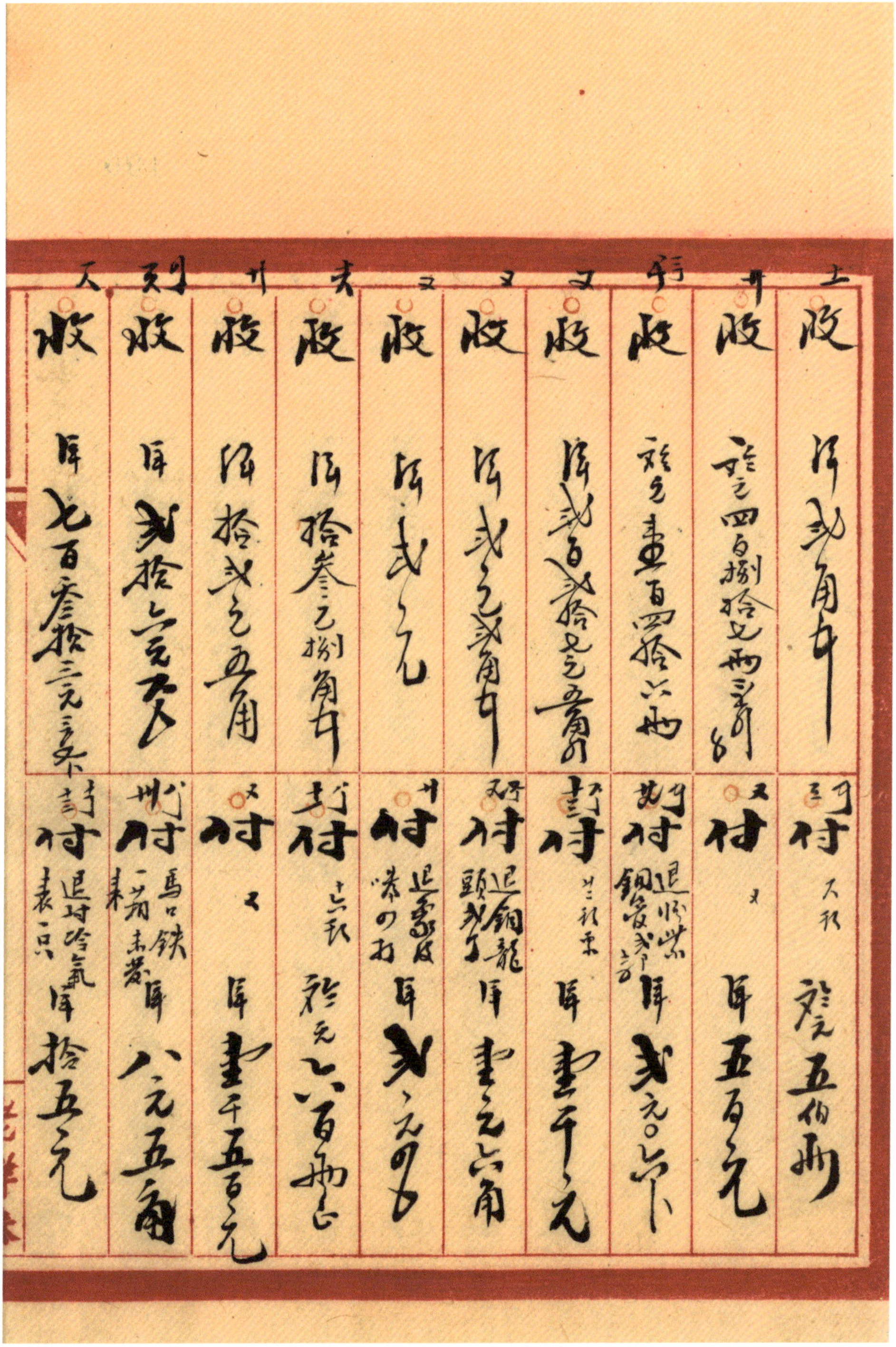

護照

為

右照給金長順船主收執

光緒貳拾肆年拾壹月　日給

十一

關

須至護照者

1898 年 12 月 23 日，江海关给大生纱厂运输煤炭的船主金长顺颁发的护照。

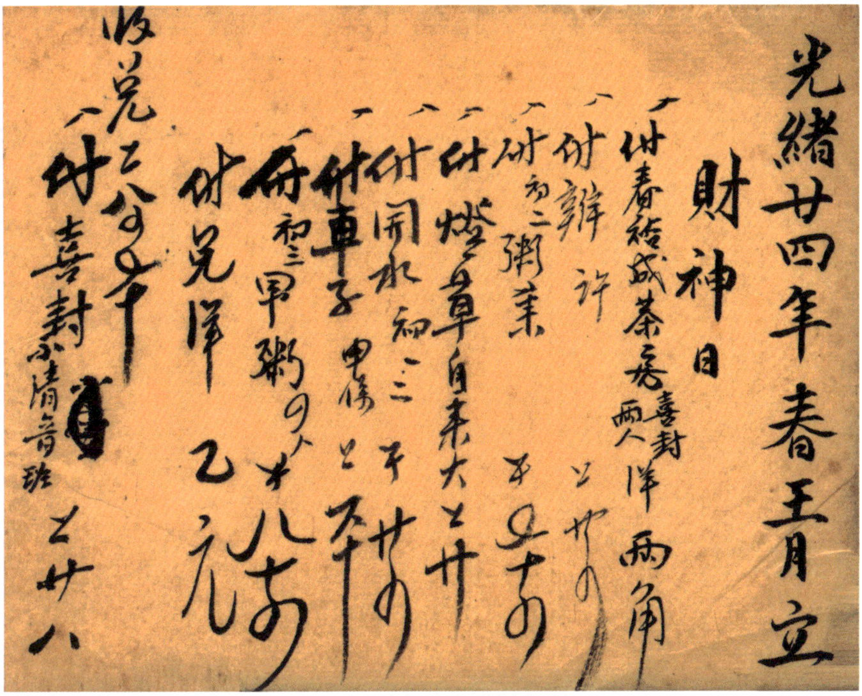

1898 年大生沪所《日抄》(局部)。

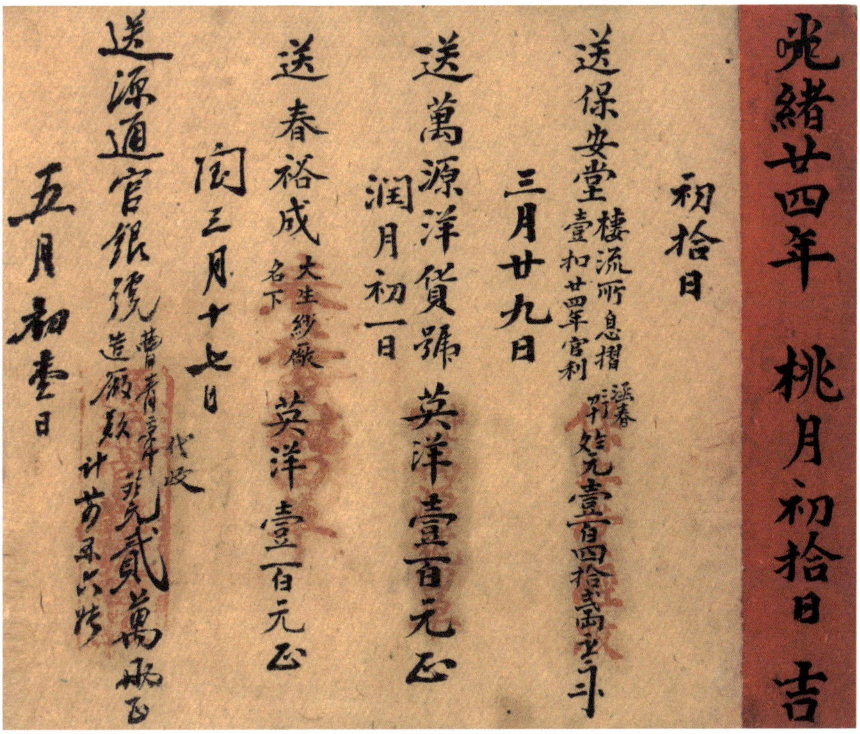

1898 年大生纱厂送银回单(部分)。

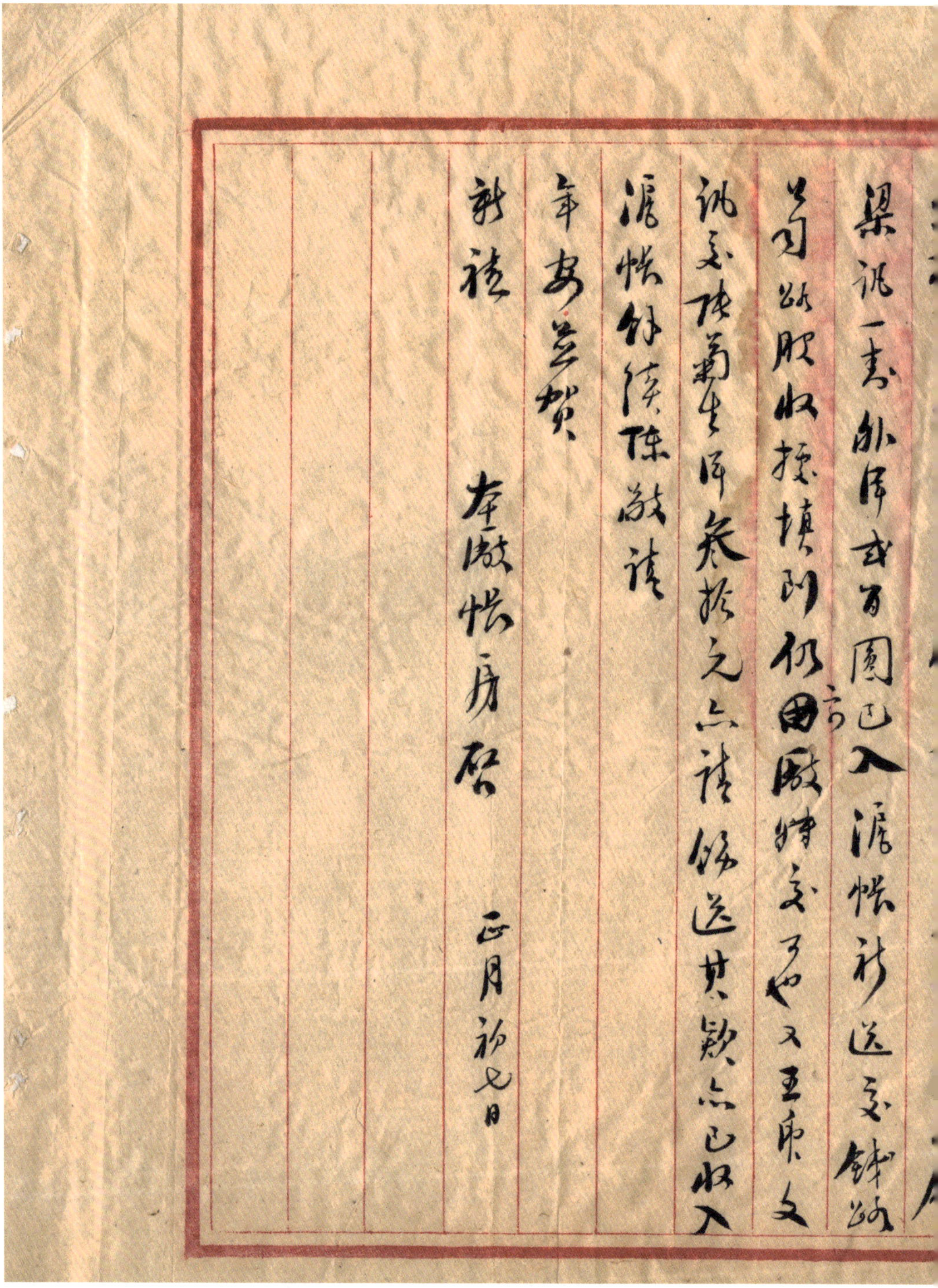

1907 年 2 月 19 日大生纱厂帐房致大生沪所的信函，是目前所见最早的大生号信。号信是大生沪所与大生相关企业联系的一种方式，以年为单位编流水号。

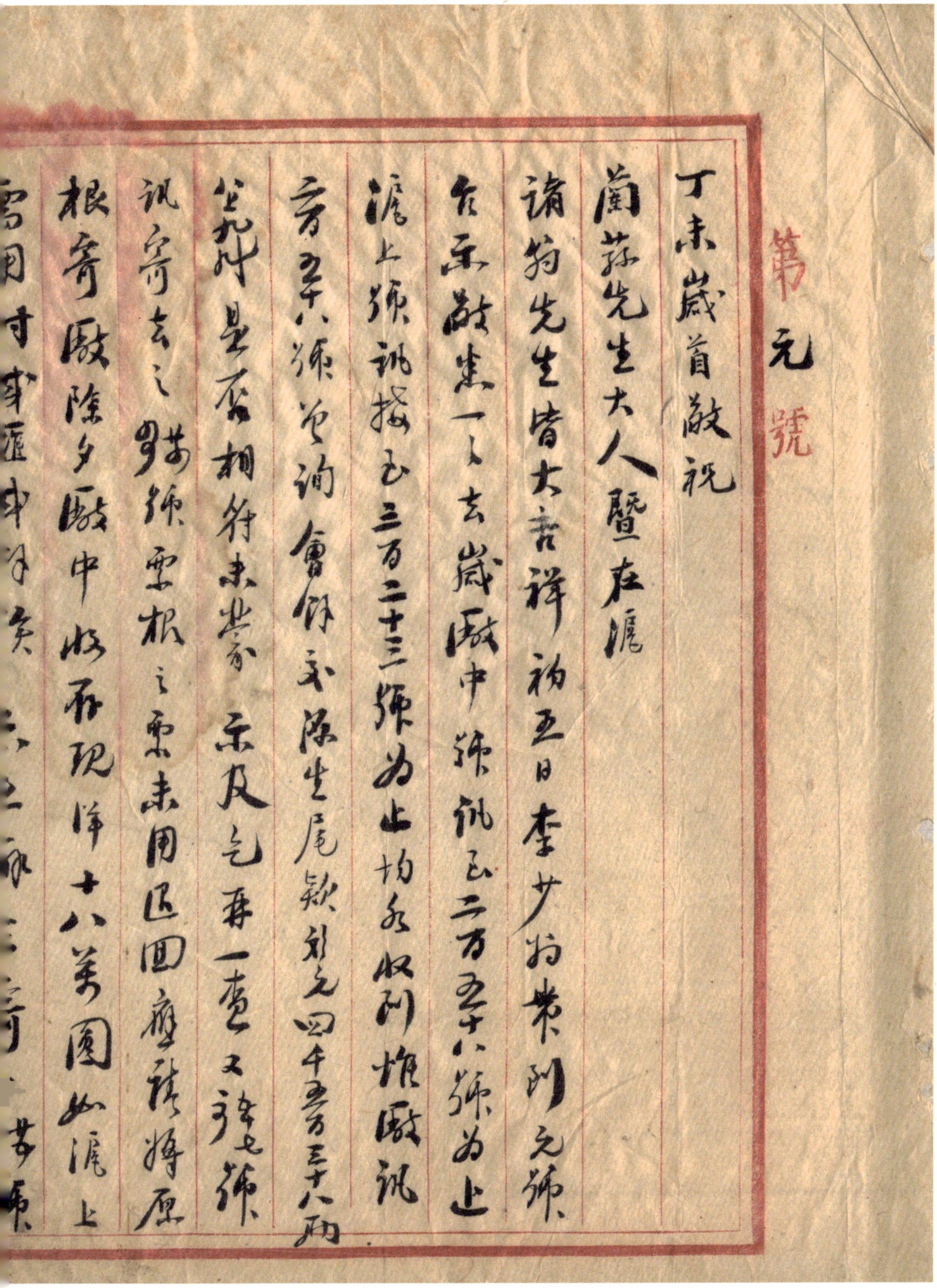
第元號

丁未歲首敬祝
蘭蓀先生大人暨在滬
諸翁先生皆大吉祥 初五日李少翁帶到兄號
台示敬悉一一 去歲敝中號訊已二万五千六號為止
滬上號訊接至三万二十三號為止 均已收到 惟敝訊
前五千八號內詢會館[illegible]源生尾款 [illegible]四千[illegible]三千八兩
是否相符 [illegible] 示及兌來一票 又號七號
訊寄去之[illegible]號要根之票 未用退回 應請將原
根寄敝 除敝中收存現洋十八萬圓 如滬上

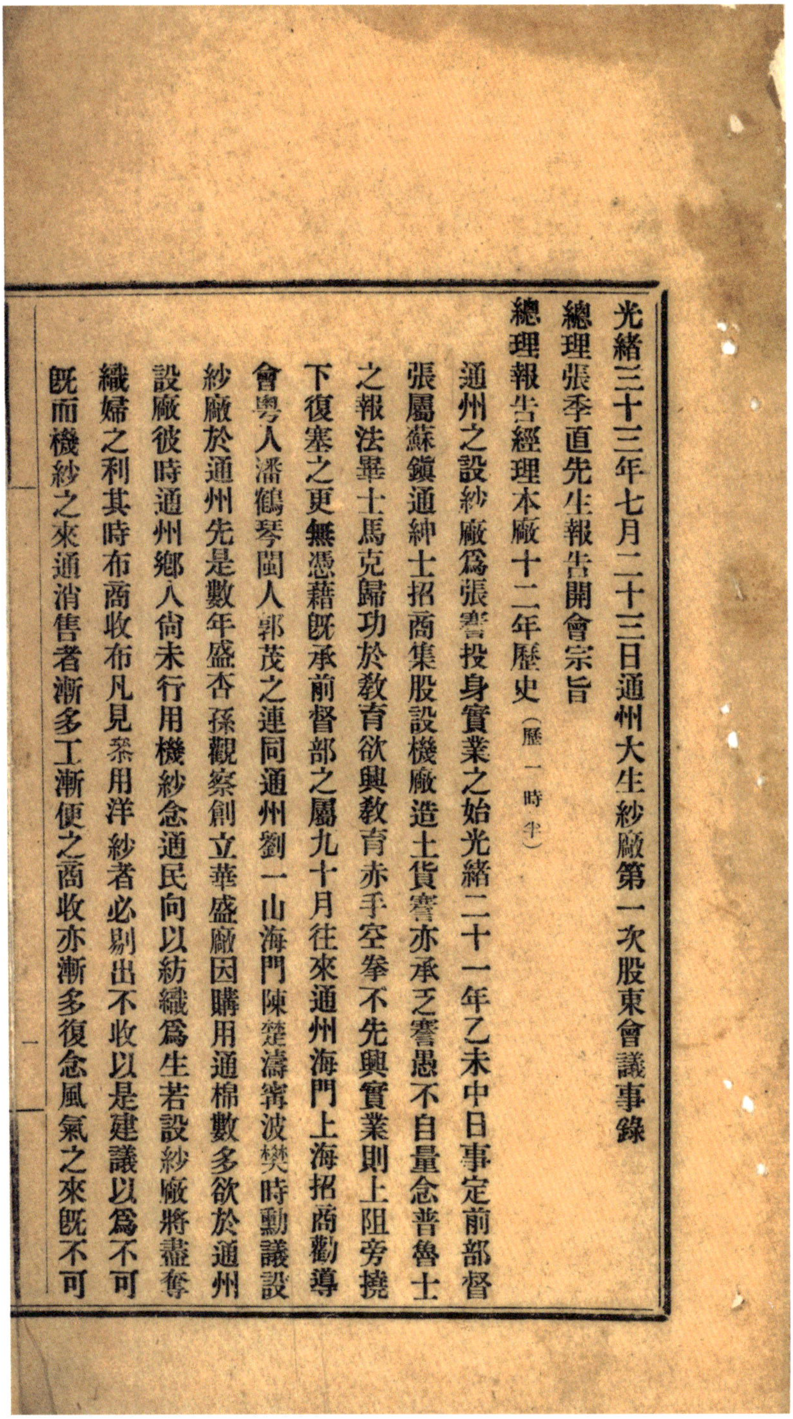
光緒三十三年七月二十三日通州大生紗廠第一次股東會議事錄
總理張季直先生報告開會宗旨
總理報告經理本廠十二年歷史（歷一時半）
通州之設紗廠爲張謇投身實業之始光緒二十一年乙未中日事定前部督
張屬蘇鎮通紳士招商集股設機廠造土貨謇亦承乏謇愚不自量念普魯士
之報法畢士馬克歸功於教育欲興教育赤手空拳不先興實業則上阻旁撓
下復塞之更無憑藉既承前督部之屬九十月往來通州海門上海招商勸導
會粵人潘鶴琴閩人郭茂之連同通州劉一山海門陳楚濤甯波樊時勳議設
紗廠於通州先是數年盛杏孫觀察創立華盛廠因購用通棉數多欲於通州
設廠彼時通州鄉人尚未行用機紗念通民向以紡織爲生若設紗廠將盡奪
織婦之利其時布商收布凡見紮用洋紗者必剔出不收以是建議以爲不可
既而機紗之來通消售者漸多工漸便之商收亦漸多復念風氣之來既不可

1907年8月31日至9月1日，大生纱厂召开第一次股东会，认为“上海一部分事最繁重”，决定将驻沪帐房改名为驻沪事务所，并取得与会计、考工、营业、庶务等四所同等的地位。

可據昨日所議即爲定論或者通融辦理俟查帳員查明後再議　劉厚生君言昨日鄭蘇堪君提議將無限制無法律之大生廠改爲有限制有法律之公司經衆股東贊成股東贊成之時即有限公司成立之時是今日已爲實行時代不得謂之過渡時代議長所言難表同情衆股東決議不得再議

議長宣告議案第三條公司原有四所董事現擬改名會計考工營業庶務四所每所設所長一員由總理協商董事局委託任用所長以下各職員隸於會計所者爲會計員餘類推均由總理選用上海一部分事最繁重本有駐滬帳房應改名駐滬事務所設所長一員多數認可

議長宣告議案第四條總理有事離公司應由總理於四所長中隨時委託一人暫代總理職務多數認可　劉旭初君請挽留協理　鄭蘇堪君言張叔儼君已被舉董事協理似可暫時不舉以後本公司重大之事由董事局會同總理議決尋常之事由各所長關白總理自行議決衆皆贊成

十七

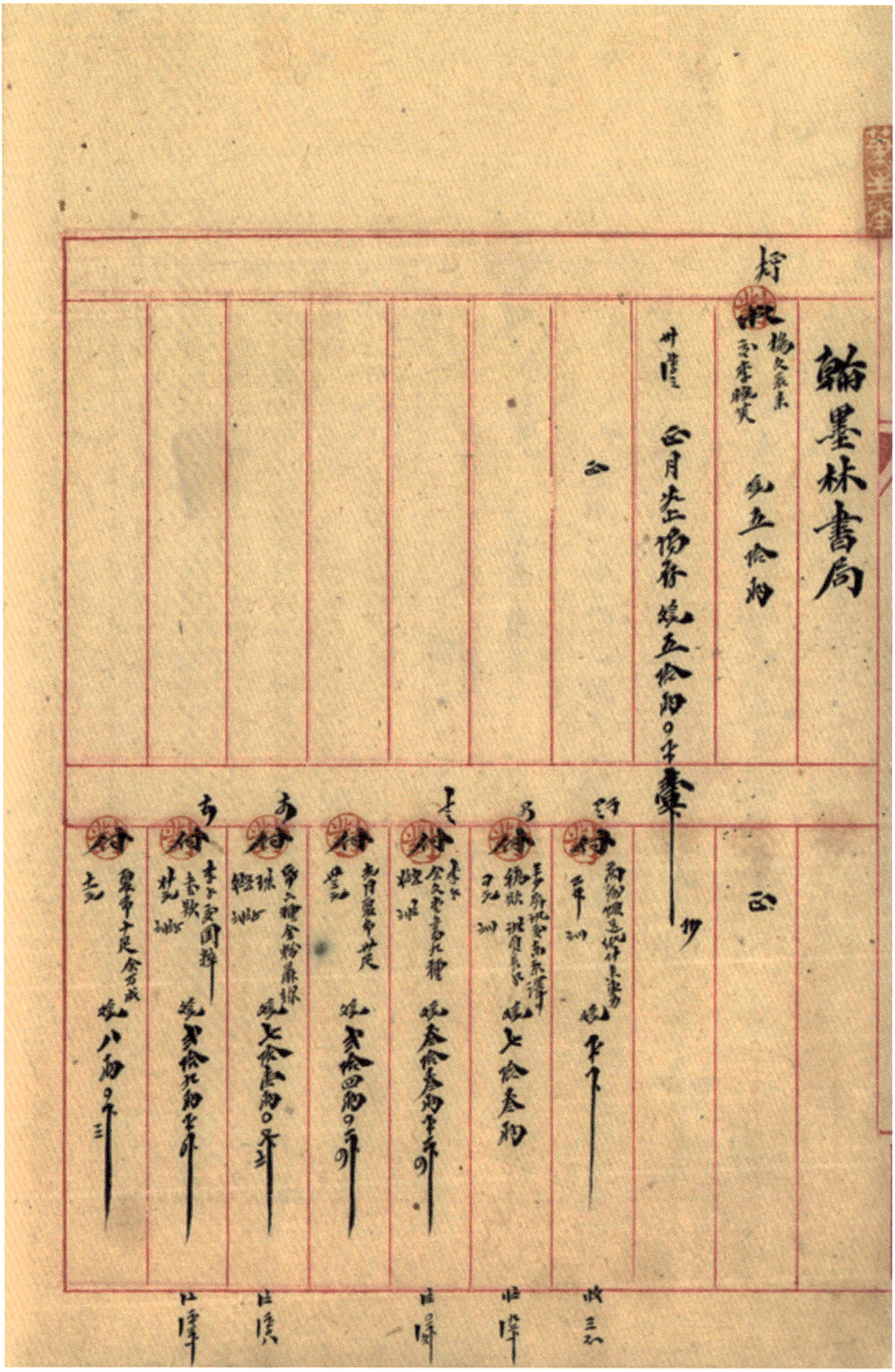

1907 年大生沪所代理翰墨林书局上海事务的账册。

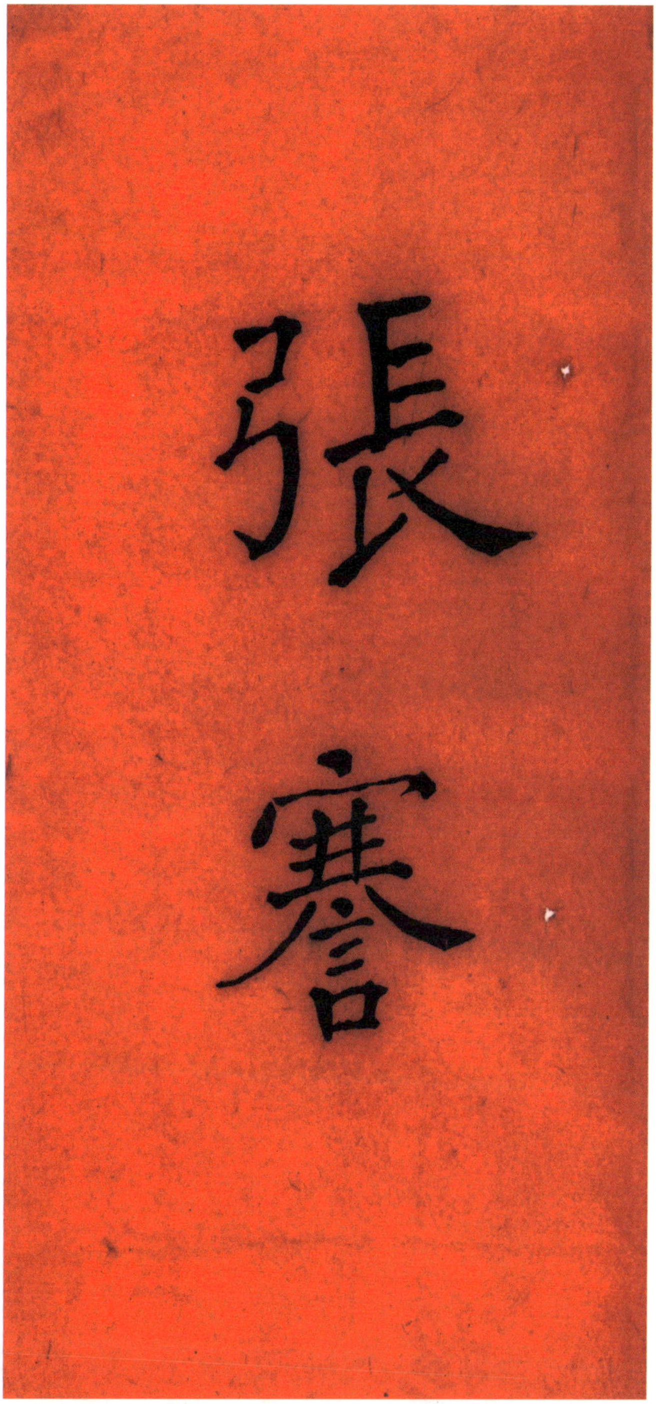
張
謇

大生沪所保存的张謇名片。大生沪所还是张謇在上海从事各种社会活动的基地，大到从事立宪运动、东南互保，小到与各界名流交往、社会考察、鬻字等，沪所都尽心尽责地做好保障工作。

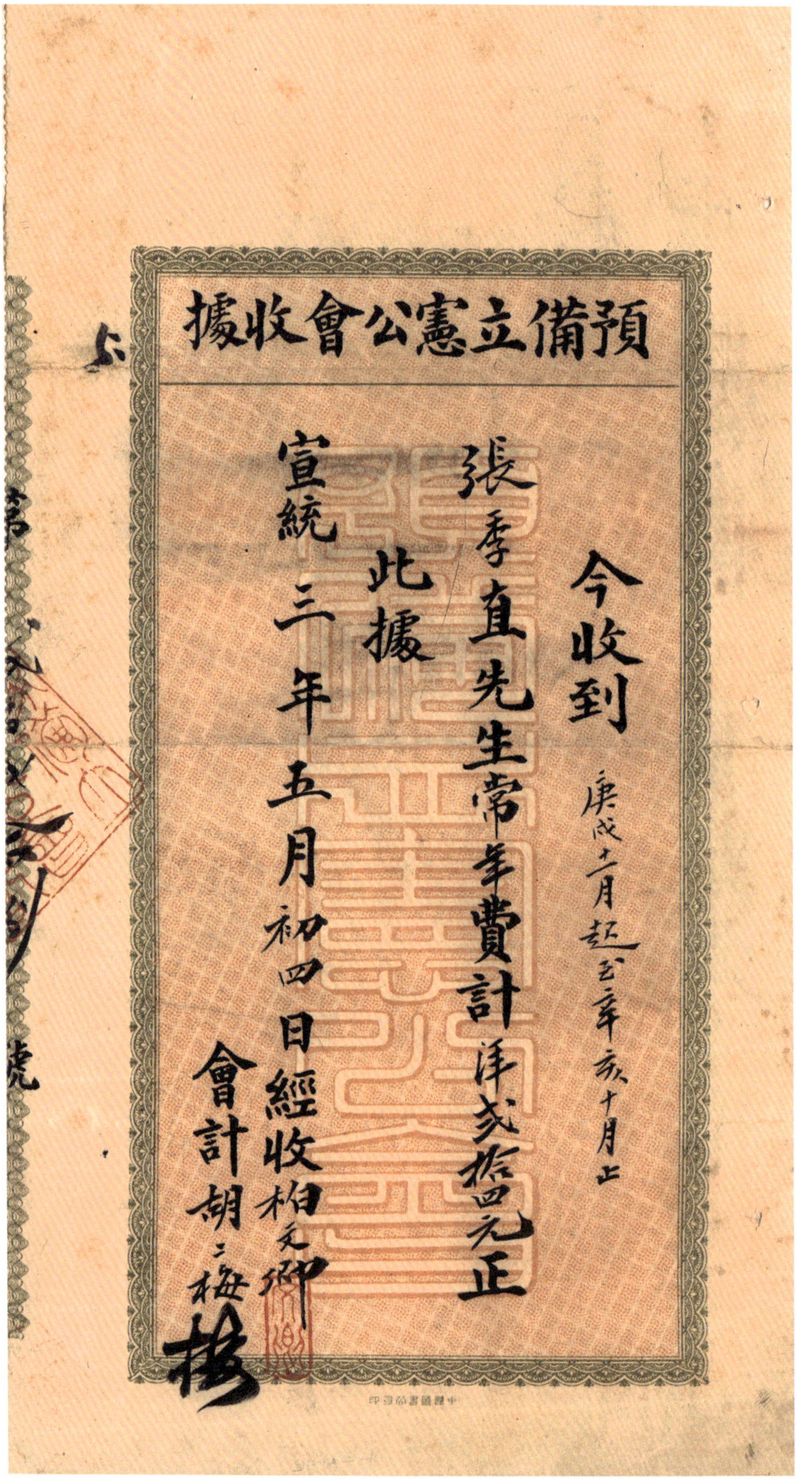
預備立憲公會收據

今收到

張季直先生常年費計洋弍拾四元正

庚戌十一月起至辛亥十月止

此據

宣統三年五月初四日經收柏文卿

會計胡二梅

1911 年 5 月 31 日，预备立宪公会出具的张謇缴纳常年费的收据。

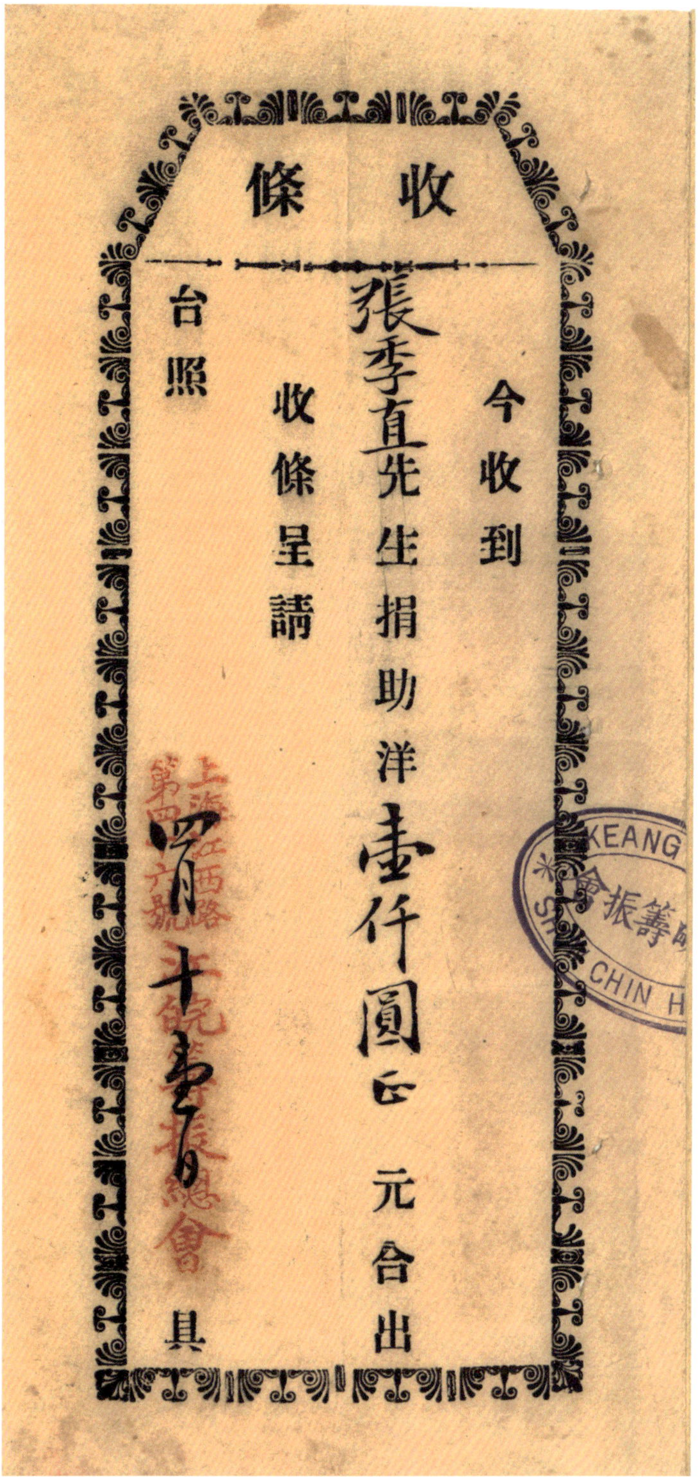
收條
今收到
張季直先生捐助洋壹仟圓正 元合出
收條呈請
台照
具
江皖籌振總會
KEANG
CHIN H

江皖筹振总会出具的张謇赞助洋 1000 元收据。

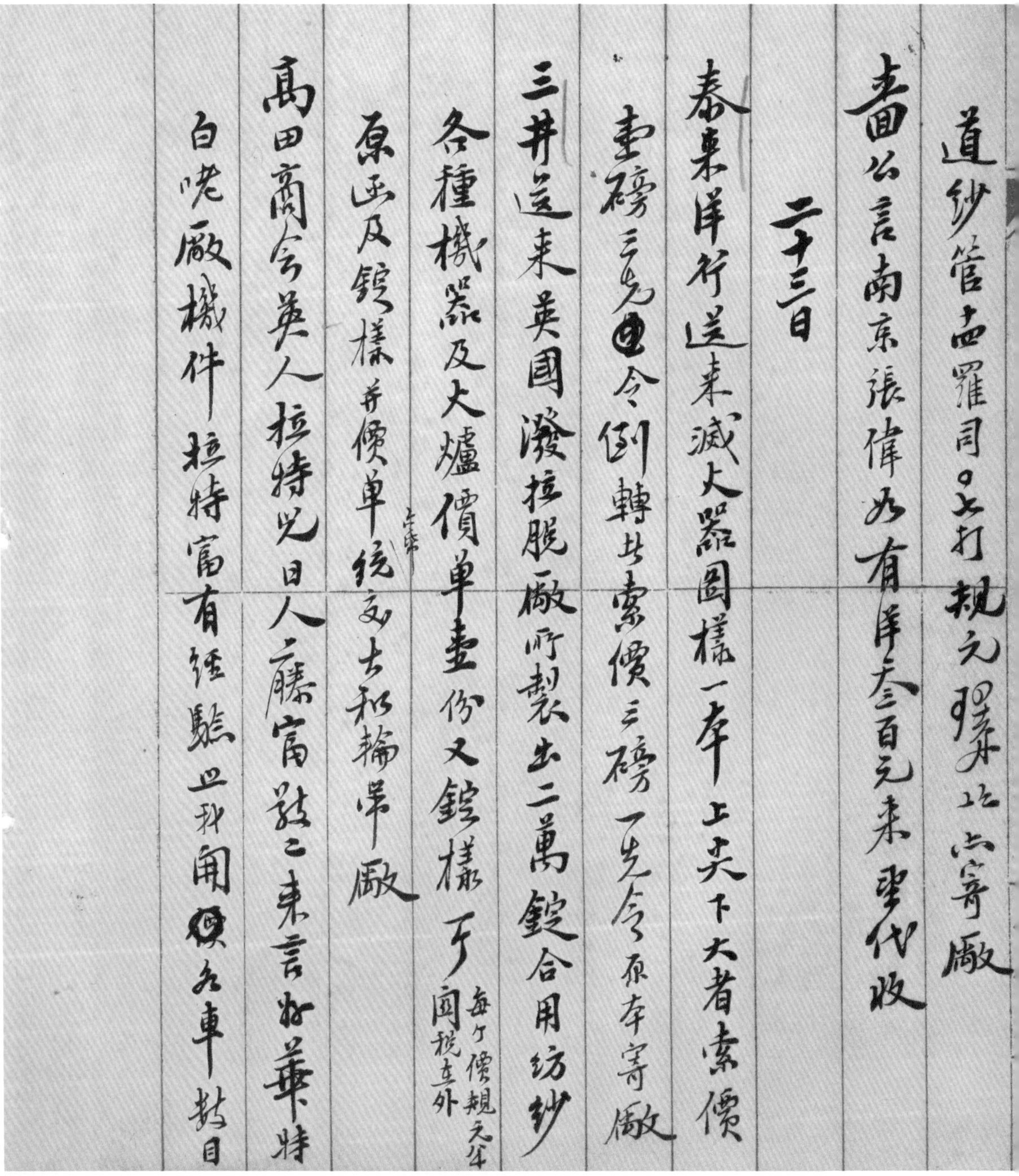

1913 年 2 月 28 日，大生沪所所长吴寄尘记载的为张謇在上海修裱字画的情况。

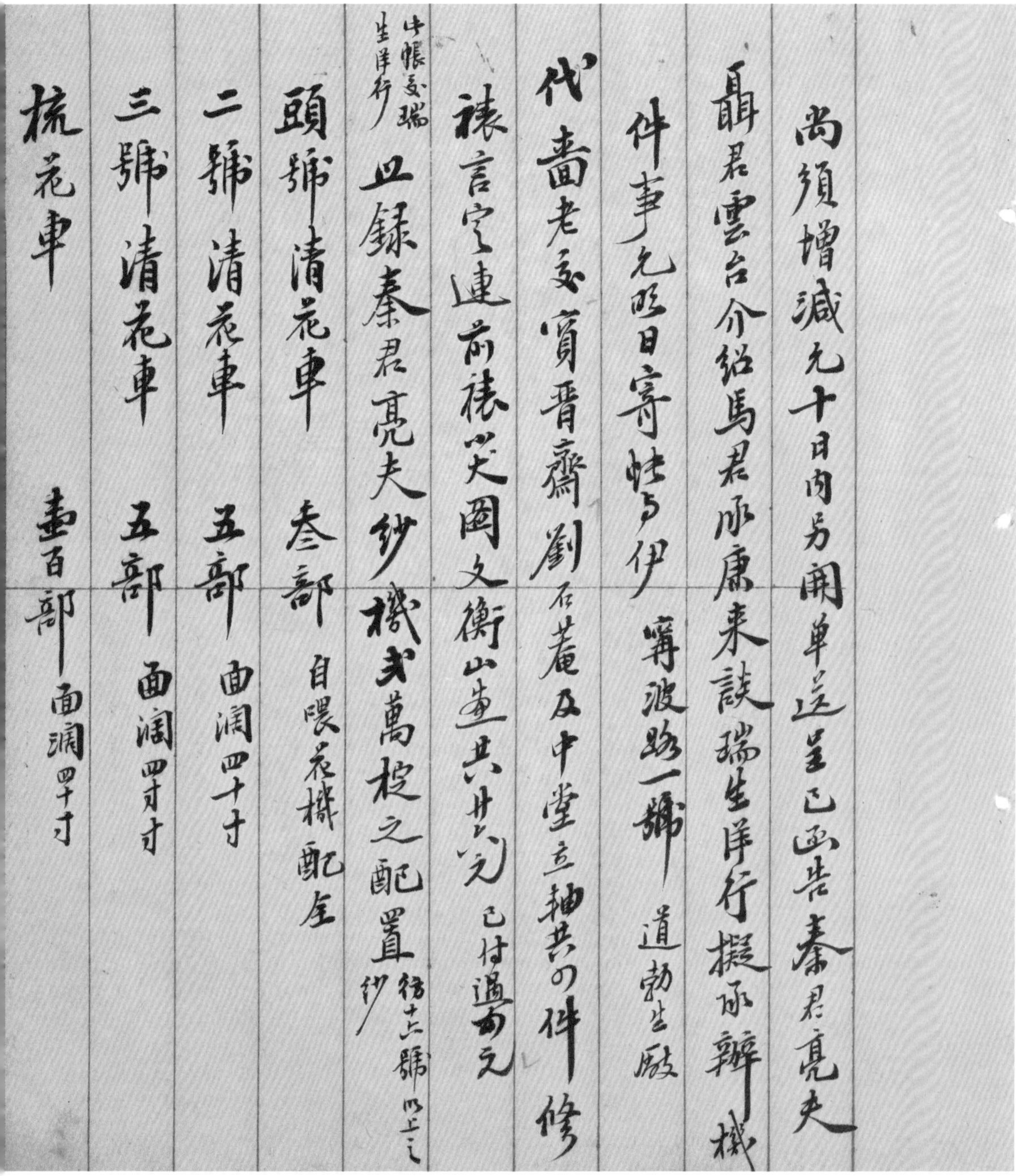
尚須增減兄十日内另開單送呈已函告秦君亮夫
聶君雲台介紹馬君承康來談瑞生洋行擬承辦機
件事兄明日寄快函伊 寧波路一號 道勃生啟
代畫老兄寶晉齋劉石菴及中堂立軸共四件修
裱言定連前裱笑圖文衡山畫共廿六元 已付過兩元
中帳交瑞生洋行
四錠秦君亮夫紗機弍萬枝之配置 紡十六支以上之紗
頭號清花車 叁部 自喂花機配全
二號清花車 五部 面闊四十寸
三號清花車 五部 面闊四寸寸
梳花車 壹百部 面闊四十寸

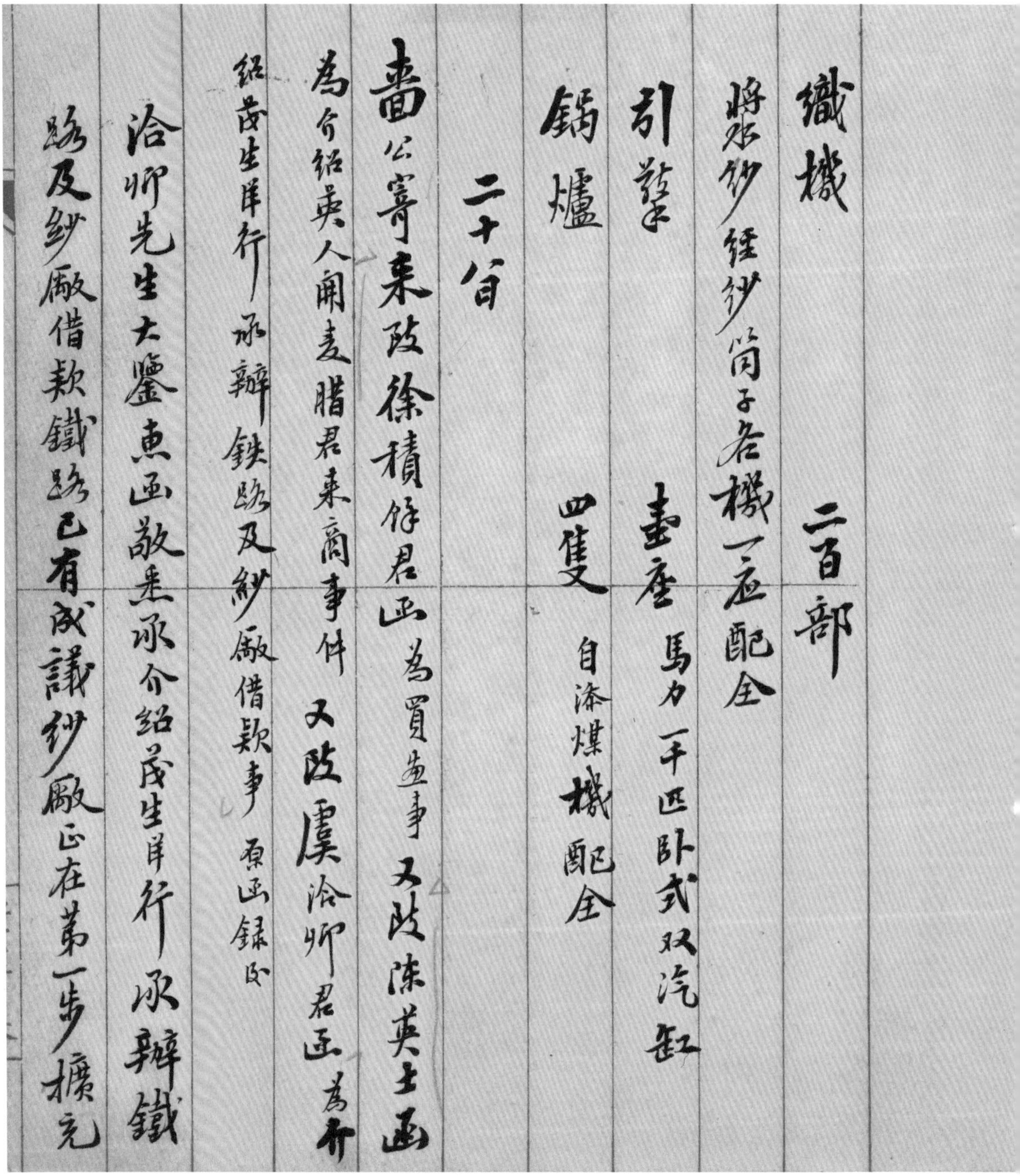

織機 二百部
漿紗 經紗 筒子 各機 一應配全
引擎 壹座 馬力一千匹臥式雙汽缸
鍋爐 四隻 自添煤機配全
二十日
嗇公寄來致徐積餘君函 為買地事 又致陳英士函
為介紹英人開麦腊君來商事件 又致虞洽卿君函 為介
紹茂生洋行承辦鐵路及紗廠借款事 原函錄後
洽卿先生大鑒 惠函敬悉 承介紹茂生洋行承辦鐵
路及紗廠借款 鐵路已有成議 紗廠正在第一步擴充

1913 年 3 月 5 日，吴寄尘抄录的张謇致虞洽卿的函。

之時除已有定本外尚須添招新股第一步既即續

謀第二步之進行該行如願借款承辦條件合宜亦

可磋商昨王君覲宸至滬帳房適值鄙人回通須已屬

帳房吳寄塵君至該行接洽矣

晉生洋行四川路五十三號總買辦虞[illegible]黃修皇　機器房王朝

聘覲宸

瑞生洋行開來杭州通益公紗廠購定布機清單

計開　交帳寄廠

織布機　寬四十寸　式拾座　共計美洋[illegible]元

布機式拾座應用皂邊撐皮帶皮緒皮柏布梳棕扣鉤

等共計備用布機零件百分之四分　美洋[illegible]元

BUILDING

南通大厦旧址。南通大厦位于上海九江路22号（现230号），毗邻河南南路，地块面积1226平方米，以每月九八规元800两的价格从上海永庆公司租来。从租地、建筑到出租、运营，具体工作由大生沪所操作，牵头负责的是吴寄尘。投资方则是专门为建造南通大厦而成立的上海南通房产公司。南通大厦落成后，1920年5月18日，大生沪所搬进前楼的二层楼办公。

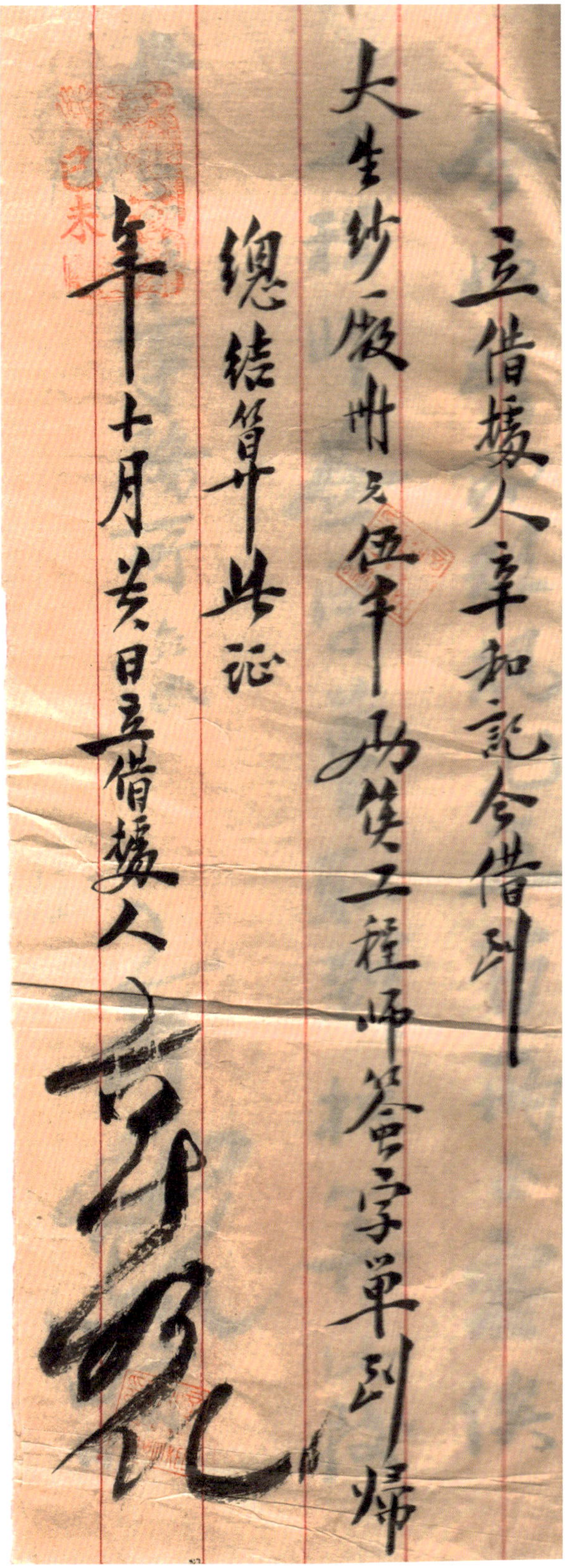
立借據人辛和記今借到
大生紗廠規元伍千兩憑工程師簽字單到歸
總結算此証
年十月廿六日立借據人
辛和記
己未

1919年12月17日，南通大厦的建筑承包商辛和记收到部分工程款后出具的收条。

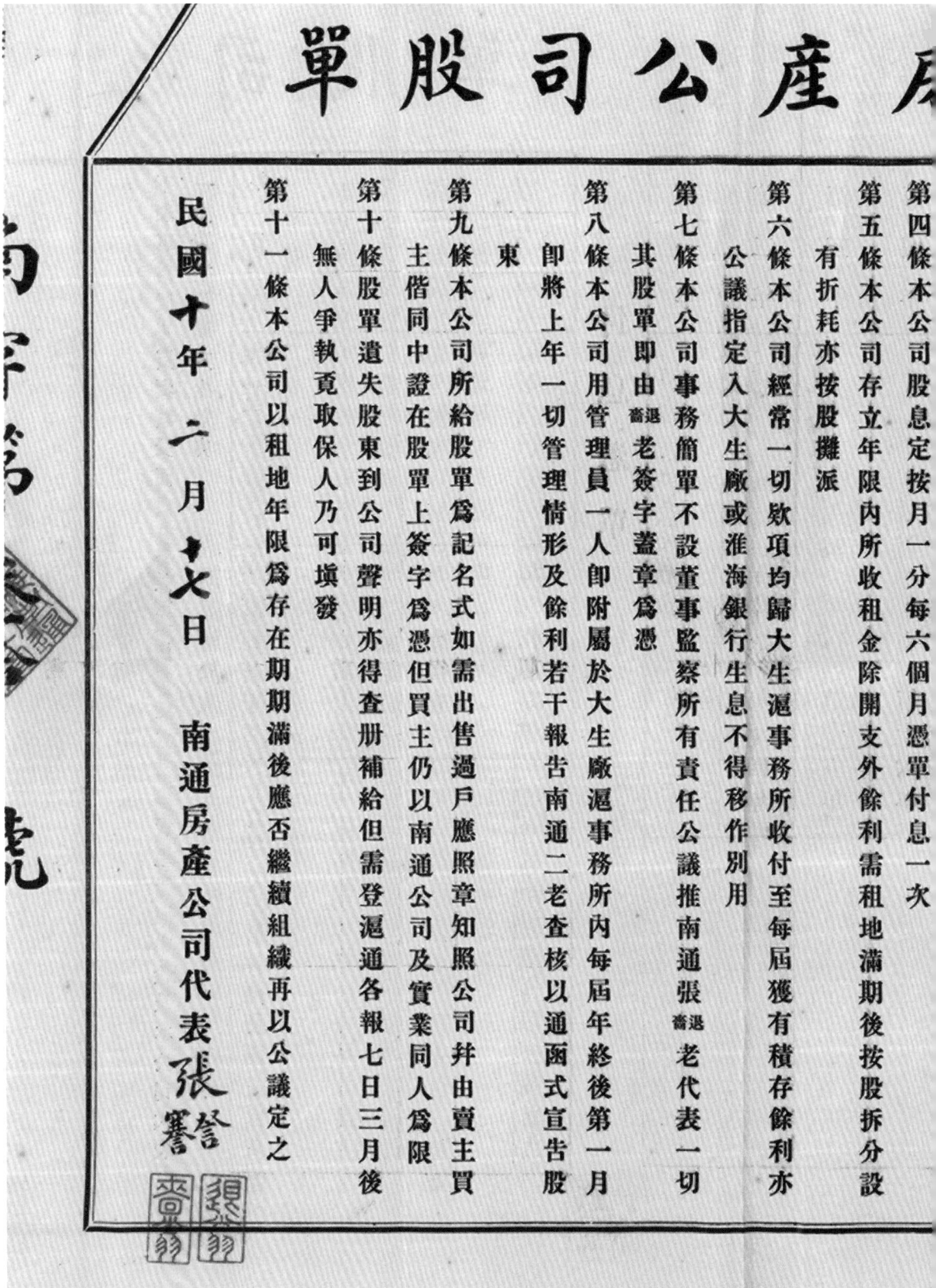
房產公司股單

第四條本公司股息定按月一分每六個月憑單付息一次
第五條本公司存立年限內所收租金除開支外餘利需租地滿期後按股拆分設
有折耗亦按股攤派
第六條本公司經常一切款項均歸大生滬事務所收付至每屆獲有積存餘利亦
公議指定入大生廠或淮海銀行生息不得移作別用
第七條本公司事務簡單不設董事監察所有責任公議推南通張嗇退老代表一切
其股單即由嗇退老簽字蓋章爲憑
第八條本公司用管理員一人即附屬於大生廠滬事務所內每屆年終後第一月
即將上年一切管理情形及餘利若干報告南通二老查核以通函式宣告股
東
第九條本公司所給股單爲記名式如需出售過戶應照章知照公司并由賣主買
主偕同中證在股單上簽字爲憑但買主仍以南通公司及實業同人爲限
第十條股單遺失股東到公司聲明亦得查冊補給但需登滬通各報七日三月後
無人爭執覓取保人乃可填發
第十一條本公司以租地年限爲存在期期滿後應否繼續組織再以公議定之

民國十年二月十七日

南通房產公司代表張謇簽

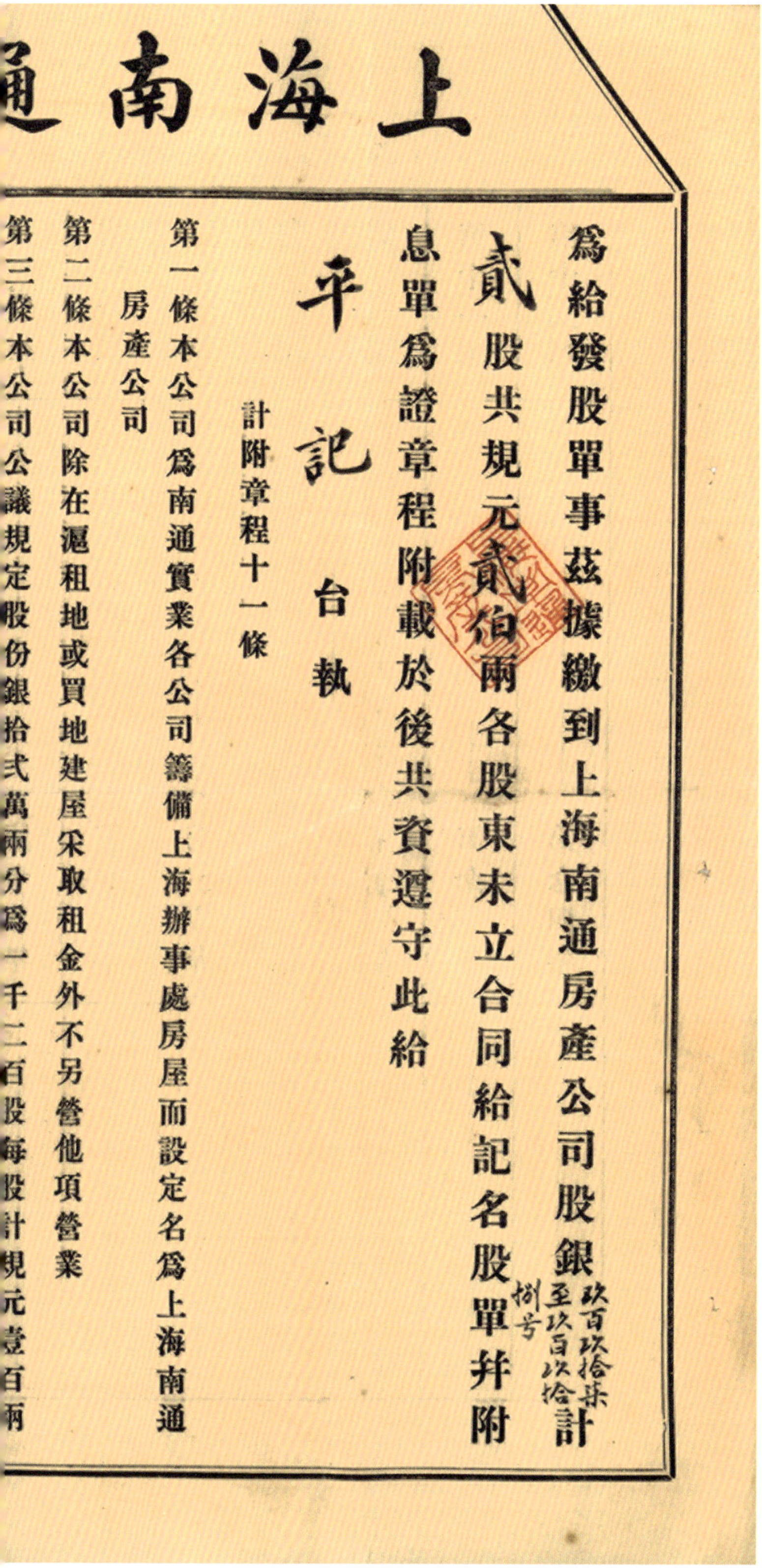
上海南通

爲給發股單事茲據繳到上海南通房產公司股銀玖百玖拾柒至玖百玖拾捌號計
貳股共規元貳佰兩各股東未立合同給記名股單幷附
息單爲證章程附載於後共資遵守此給
平記　台執
計附章程十一條
第一條本公司爲南通實業各公司籌備上海辦事處房屋而設定名爲上海南通房產公司
第二條本公司除在滬租地或買地建屋采取租金外不另營他項營業
第三條本公司公議規定股份銀拾弍萬兩分爲一千二百股每股計規元壹百兩

1921年2月17日上海南通房产公司股单的正反面。

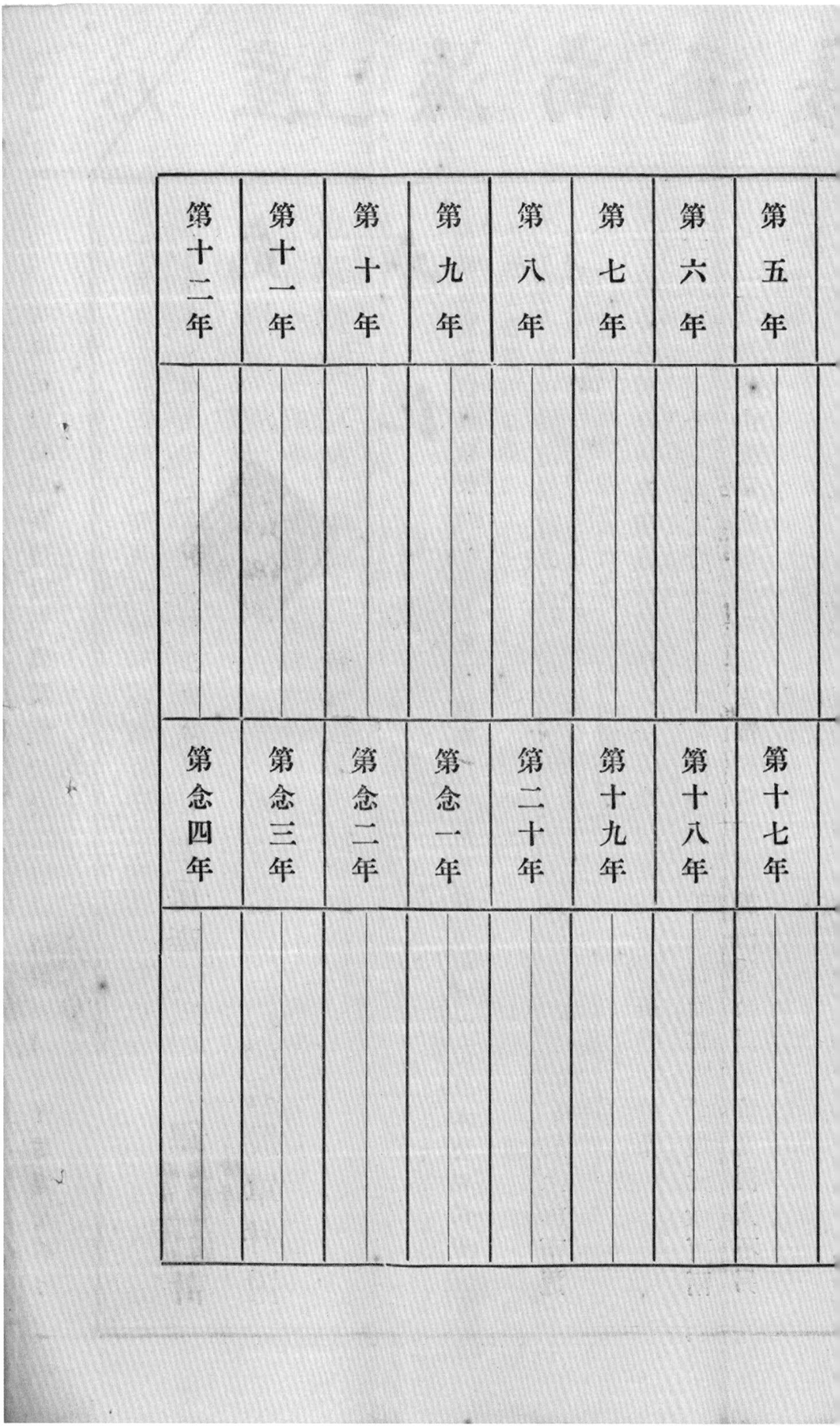

第五年	第六年	第七年	第八年	第九年	第十年	第十一年	第十二年
第十七年	第十八年	第十九年	第二十年	第念一年	第念二年	第念三年	第念四年

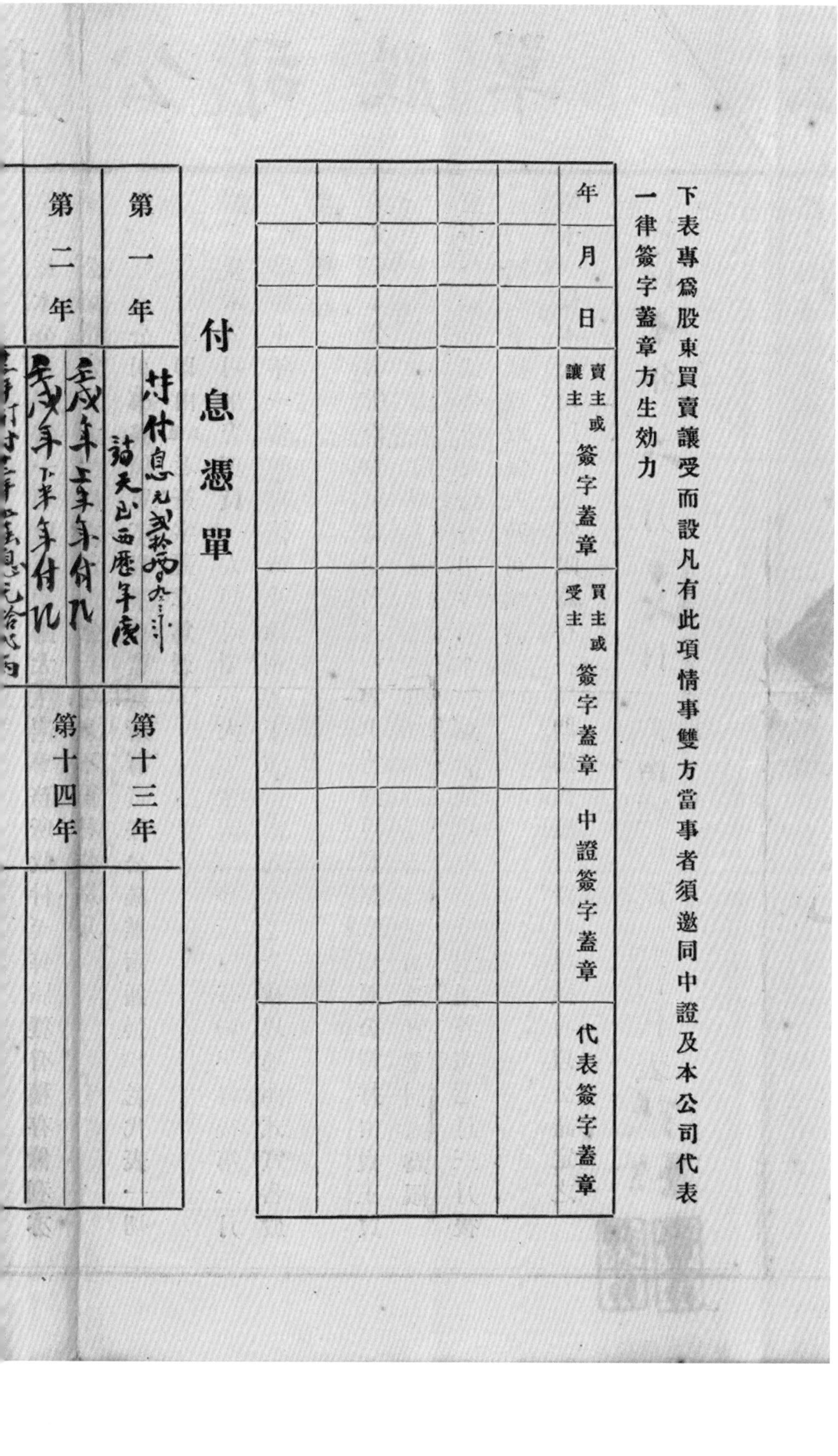

下表專爲股東買賣讓受而設凡有此項情事雙方當事者須邀同中證及本公司代表一律簽字蓋章方生効力

年	月	日

賣主或讓主簽字蓋章	買主或受主簽字蓋章	中證簽字蓋章	代表簽字蓋章

付息憑單

第一年	第二年
付息元貳拾[illegible] [illegible]	[illegible]戌年上半年付訖 [illegible]戌年下半年付訖 [illegible]
第十三年	第十四年

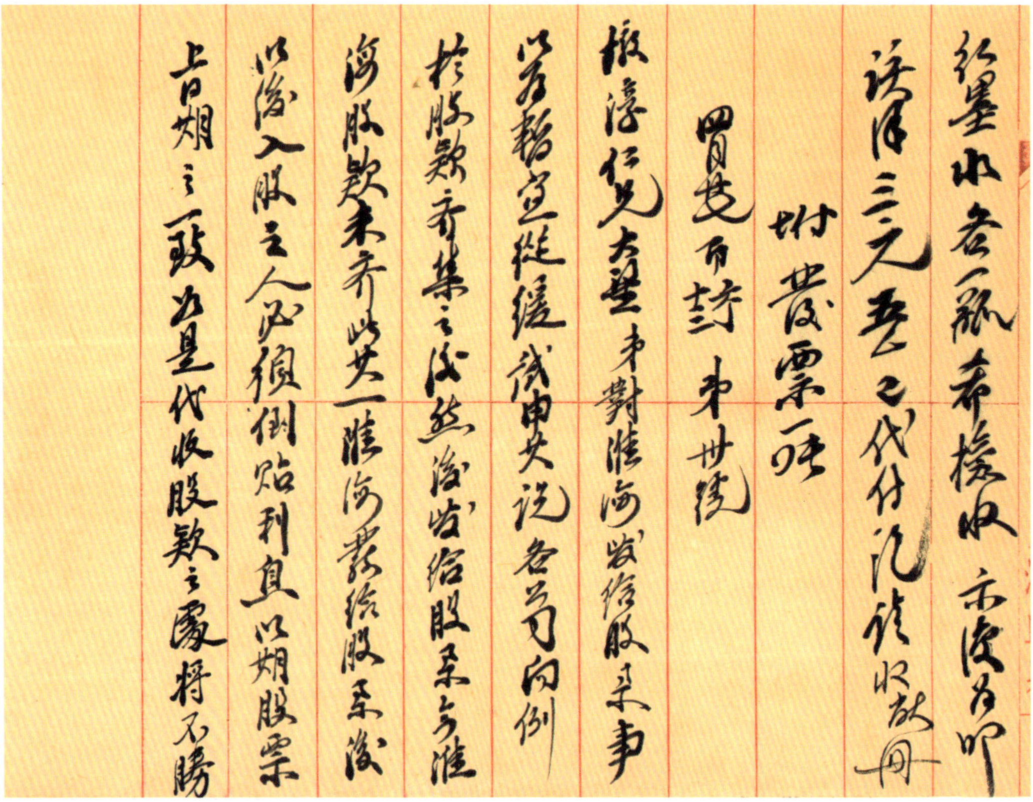

1920 年大生沪所致淮海实业银行的第 30 号号信，涉及沪所代发淮海实业银行股票事宜。1920 年淮海实业银行筹建时(淮海实业银行上海分行位于南通大厦的一楼)，在上海设立筹备处，其实就是由沪所代理部分筹备事宜。沪所作为大生系统在上海的窗口，不仅是已有企事业单位在上海的联络处，也是新创立单位的助推器。

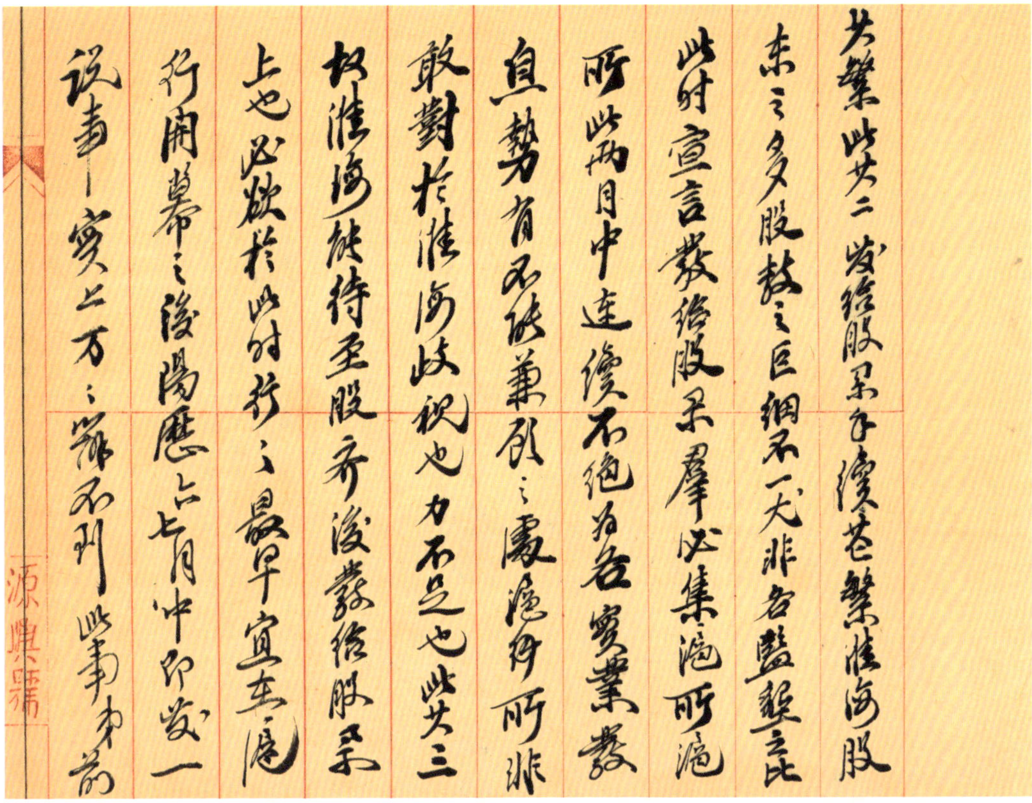
其繁。此其二。發給股票手續甚繁，淮海股
東之多，股數之巨，細不一式，非各鹽棧處
此時宣言發給股票，群必集滬所，滬
所此兩月中連續不絕，為各處業務
自有勢有不能兼顧之處，滬所所非
敢對於淮海收紀也，力不足也。此其三
故淮海能待至股齊後發給股票
上也。必欲於此時行之，最早宜在滬
行開幕之後，陽曆六七月中印發一
說者一實亡方之辦不到，此事本前

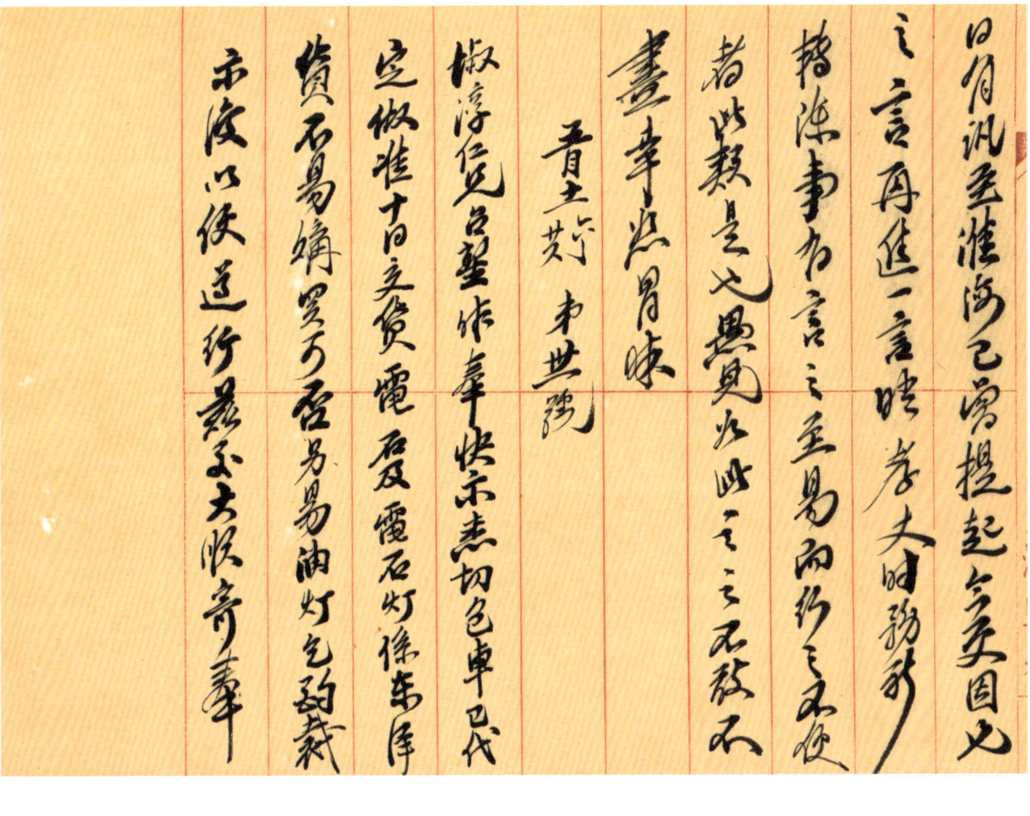
日有訊至淮海，已嘗提起，今又因之
之言，再進一言。時孝丈時務新
機，滬事方言之至易，而行之不使
者此類是也。愚見如此，云云，不敢不
盡，幸恕冒昧。
青士兄　弟世璐
敝淳仁兄名墾作章，快示悉，切色單已代
定做，准十日交貨。電石及電石燈係東洋
貨，不易購買，可否易易油燈，乞酌裁
示復，以便遵行。慈丈收齋章

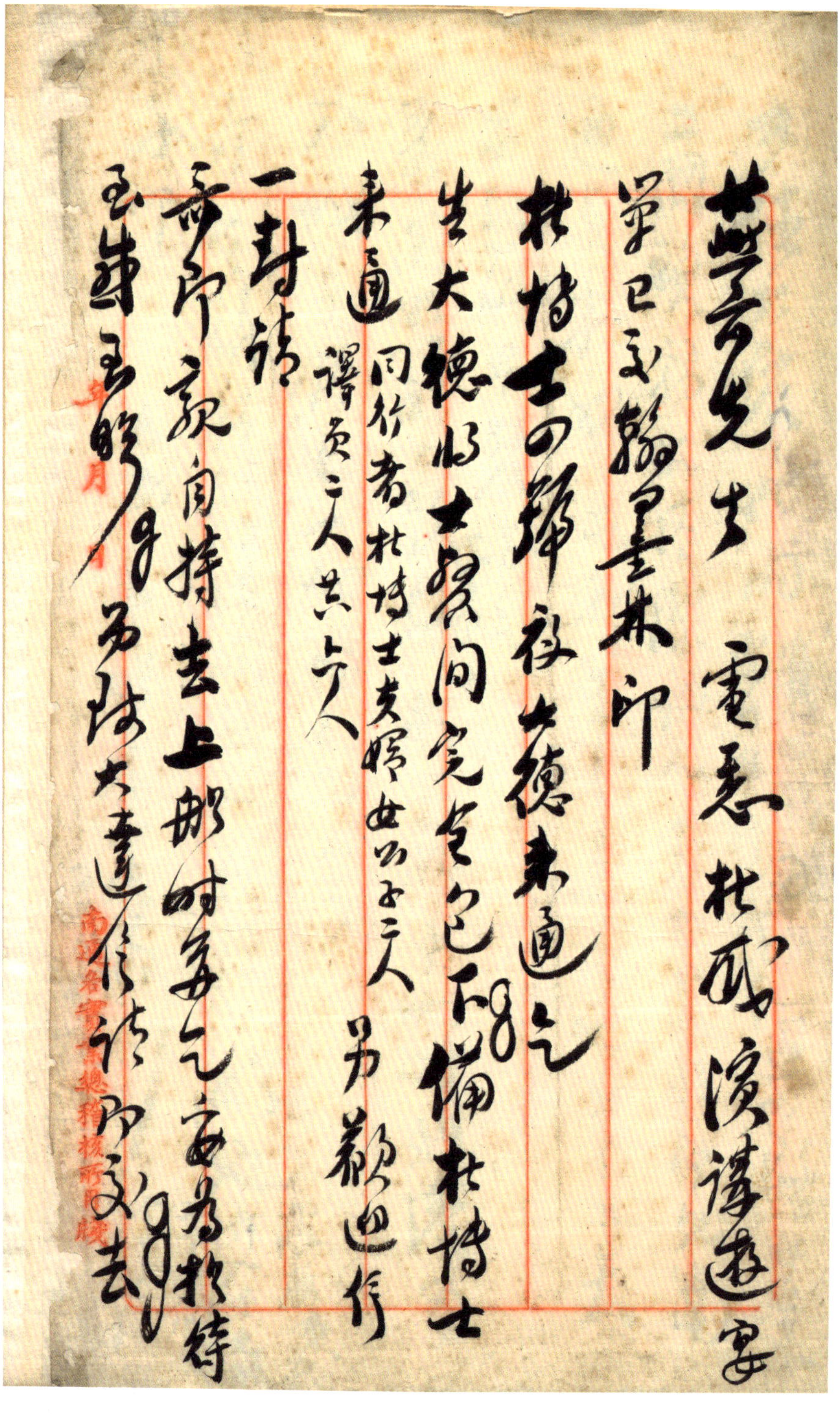

1920年5月31日，张謇儿子张孝若就杜威赴南通事宜致大生沪所沈燕谋的函。

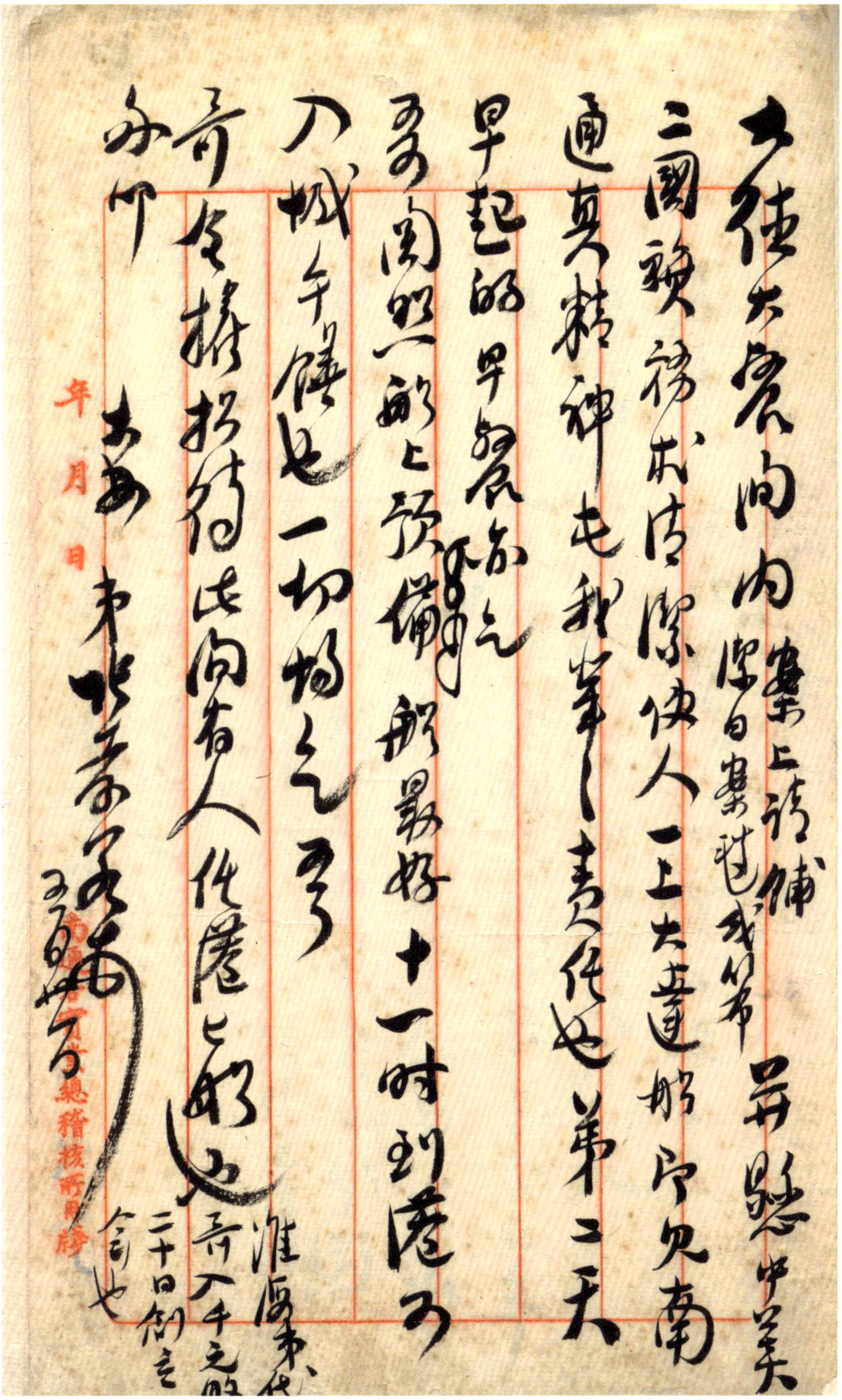
年 月 日
總稽核所用牋

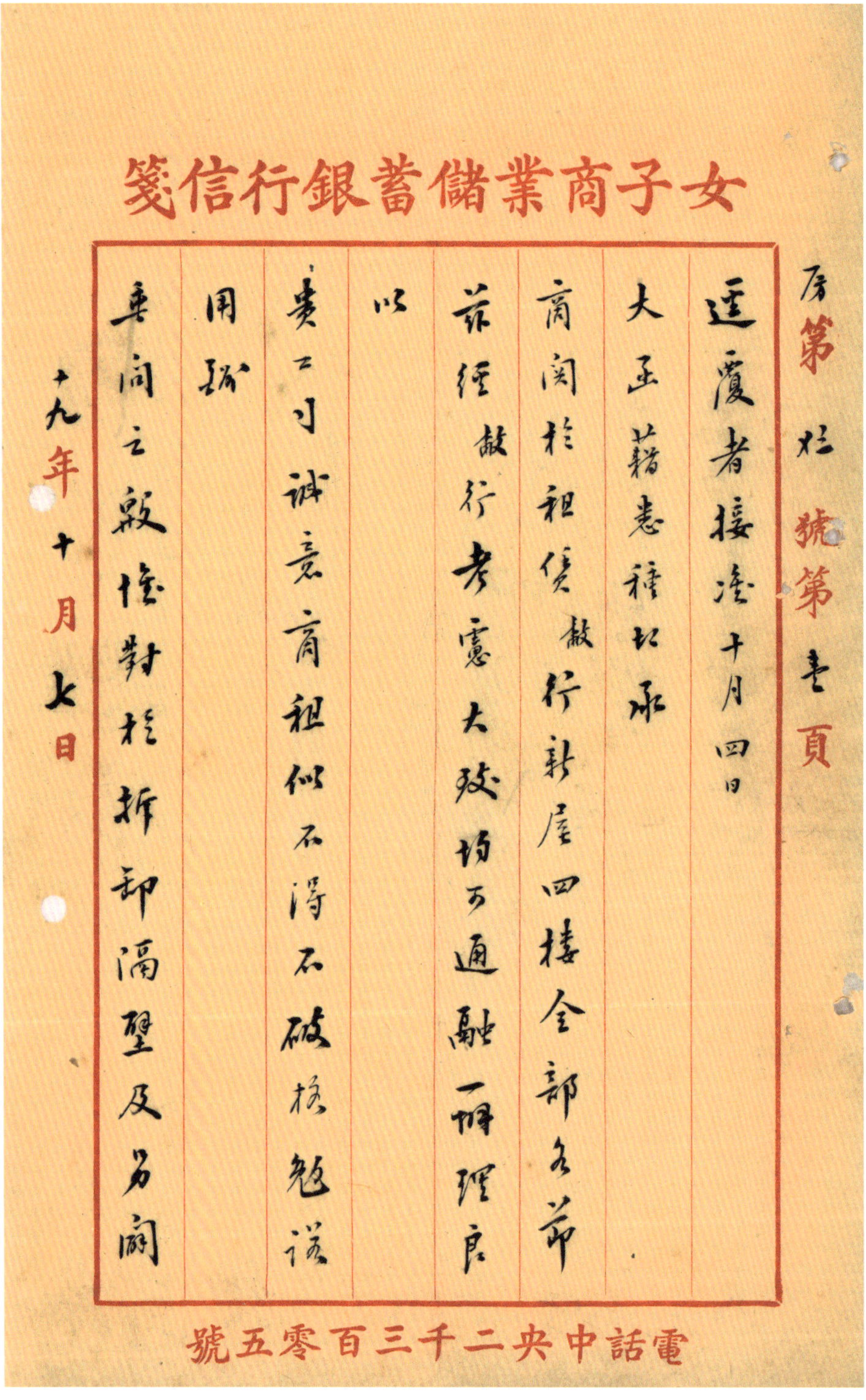
女子商業儲蓄銀行信箋

房第　灶　號第　壹　頁

逕覆者接准十月四日
大函藉悉種切承
商閱於租賃　敝行新屋四樓全部各節
前經　敝行考慮大致均可通融辦理良
以
貴方誠意商租似不得不破格勉從
因擬
惟向之敘情對於拆卸隔壁及另闢

十九年十月七日

電話中央二千三百零五號

1930 年 10 月 7 日，上海女子商业储蓄银行有关出租南京路保安坊房屋事宜致大生沪所的函。

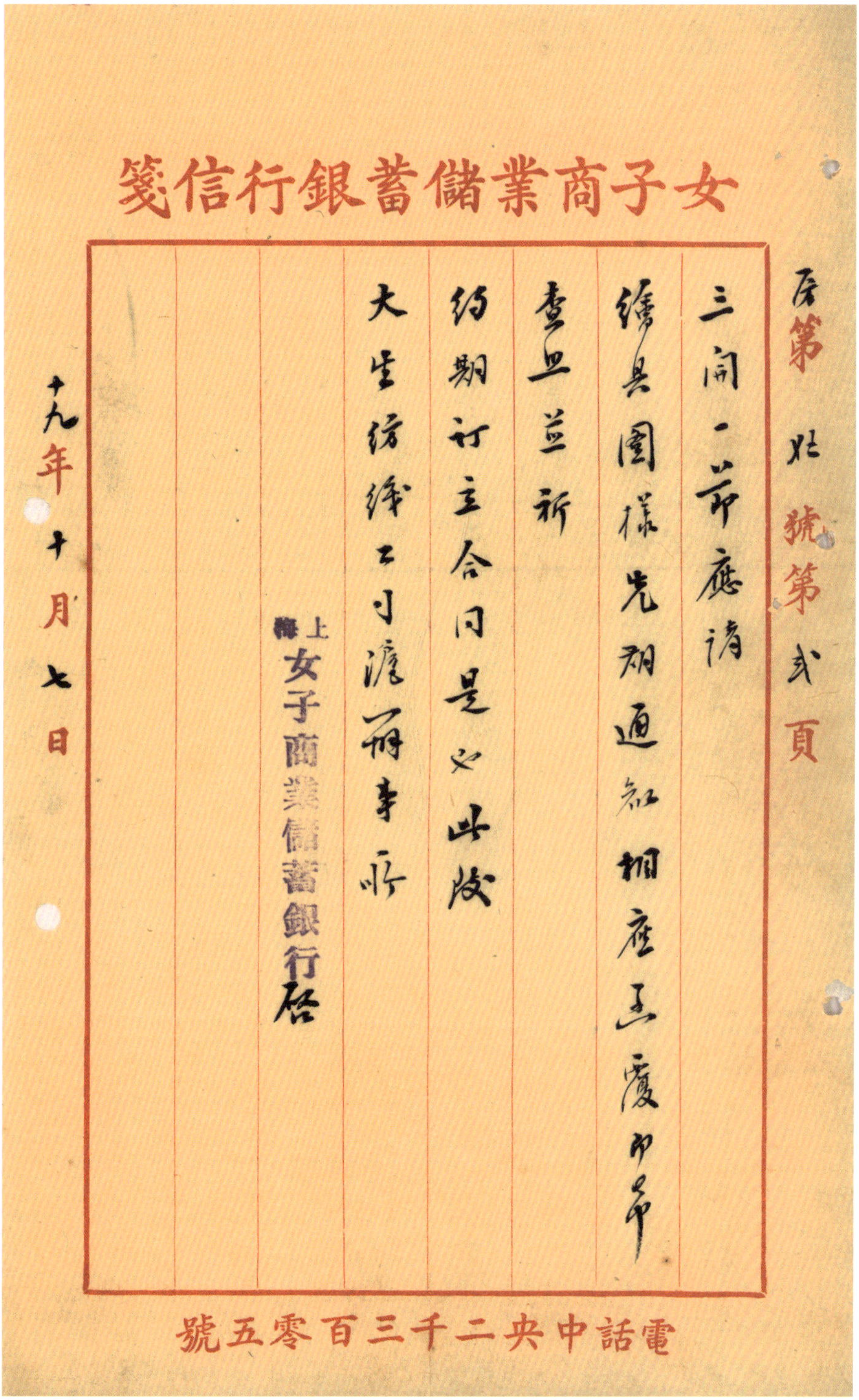
女子商業儲蓄銀行信箋

第　號第貳頁

三間一節應請

繡具圖樣先期通知相應函達即希

查照並祈

約期訂立合同是荷此致

大生紡織公司滬辦事處

上海女子商業儲蓄銀行啓

十九年十月七日

電話中央二千三百零五號

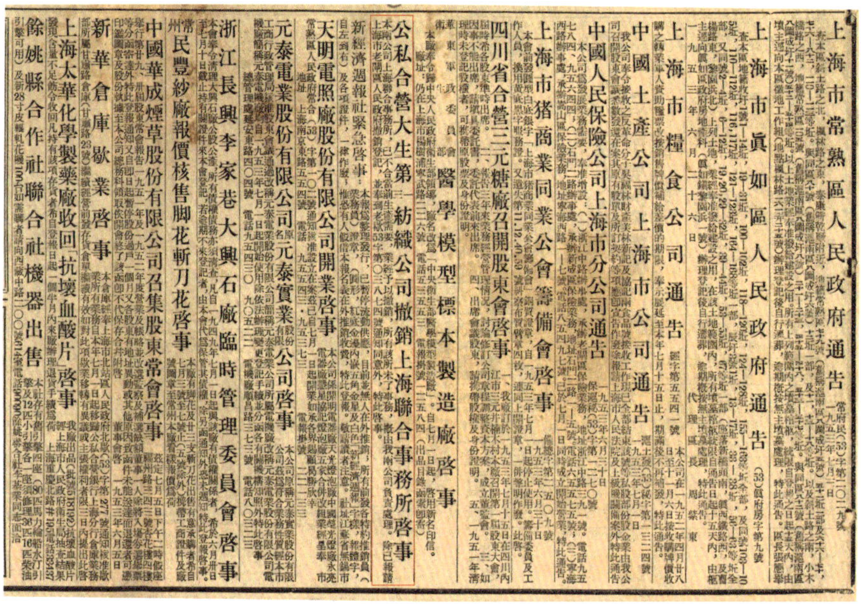

上海市常熟區人民政府通告

上海市眞如區人民政府通告

上海市糧食公司通告

中國土產公司上海市公司通告

中國人民保險公司上海市分公司通告

上海市猪商業同業公會籌備會啓事

四川省合營三元糖廠召開股東會啓事

醫學模型標本製造廠啓事

公私合營大生第一三紡織公司撤銷上海聯合事務所啓事

新經濟週報社緊急啓事

天明電照廠股份有限公司開業啓事

元泰電業股份有限公司元泰實業公司啓事

浙江長興李家巷大興石廠臨時管理委員會啓事

民豐紗廠報價核售脚花斬刀花啓事

中國華成煙草股份有限公司召集股東常會啓事

新華倉庫歇業啓事

上海太華化學製藥廠收回「抗壞血酸片」啓事

餘姚縣合作社聯合社機器出售

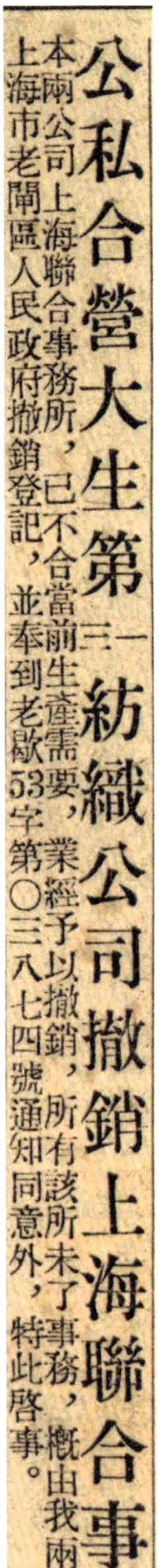

公私合營大生第一三紡織公司撤銷上海聯合事務所啓事

本兩公司上海聯合事務所，已不合當前生産需要，業經予以撤銷，所有該所未了事務，概由我兩公司負責處理。除已報請上海市老閘區人民政府撤銷登記，並奉到老歇53字第〇三八七四號通知同意外，特此啓事。

1953 年 7 月 3 日，上海市委机关报《解放日报》刊登《公私合营大生第一、三纺织公司撤销上海联合事务所启事》：“本两公司上海联合事务所，已不合当前生产需要，业经予以撤销，所有该所未了事务，概由我两公司负责处理。除已报请上海市老闸区人民政府撤销登记，并奉到老歇 53 字第 03874 号通知同意外，特此启事。”（局部图见右）

『沪地为万国竞争之场、商战之冲』

——借道沪上

张謇在创业伊始，客观上就融入世界经济发展的潮流中。美国学者斯文·贝克特的著作《棉花帝国》提到，到了19世纪末，欧洲以外的其他国家，面对进口棉纺织品对国内手工业的压力，有着建立工业经济的愿望，巴西、日本、中国和其他国家的政治家和资本家寻求用国内生产取代进口的办法。《棉花帝国》随后以张謇作为中国的例子：张謇对大量棉纱和棉布进口表示关切，特别在1895年《马关条约》允许建立外商独资棉纺厂的规定之后，他主张国内工业化，并且付诸实际行动，在自己的家乡南通建立了纺纱厂。

仲伟民在《棉花帝国》的中文序里评述，棉花产业不仅是工业革命的摇篮、杠杆和跳板，而且在现代世界的形成过程中，主导了世界贸易。与茶叶、鸦片、咖啡、糖、瓷器等商品的生产和贸易相比，只有棉织品才是真正全球性的商品，只有棉织品才引致了生产与加工环节持续不断的技术革新，只有棉织品能够调动全世界的资本、土地和劳动力。大生纱厂生产的原料是棉花，出品是棉纱，市场在已经对外开放的区域，由此面对的竞争是全球性的，想要生存和发展，必须具备世界眼光，全球视野。

张謇创办大生纱厂时，充分依托当时中国最大的城市，也是与世界接轨程度最深的上海。按照《海关十年报告（1912—1921）》的说法，“上海一直紧随着遍及全球每个角落的现代世界经济的消长盛衰而上下起伏”。大生纱厂所需的资金、物料、技术和人才，南通都匮乏，张謇自然而然把目光投向上海——当时的中国只有上海全部具备这些生产要素。1909年张謇在回复陈伯陶有关筹议江南工科大学事宜时提到，“沪地为万国竞争之场、商战之冲”。通过上海，张謇连接了世界，采用外国先进的设备、管理经验，聘用外国工程师，选送学生赴日本工厂学习，对大生纱厂乃至南通的发展起到关键作用。

上海是连接世界和中国的桥梁，是对外贸易的中心，大生纱厂可以通过洋行或者华商贸易公司，采购到机器及修配用零部件、动力设备所需的燃料煤炭、照明设备等，甚至可以通过上海的渠道直接跟日本的华商建立联系，购置棉纱筒管。与张謇共同筹办大生纱厂的六位董事中，潘华茂、郭勋是买办，樊芬为宁波帮代表人物，都是上海经济实力雄厚、人脉广泛、营商经验丰富的商人。张謇的本意是借助沪董的力量，以上海为中心吸纳社会资金。尽管由于不同原因，三位沪董先后退出大生纱厂的筹办，但张謇不改初衷。大生纱厂最初的股本构成中，占比最大的是以官府的纺纱机器折价的官股，这批机器曾长时间搁置在黄浦江边。

张謇起草于1897年、定稿于1899年10月的《厂约》，是大生纱厂早年的企业管理制度。《厂约》开宗明义大生纱厂的设立是“为通州民生计，亦即为中国利源计”。《厂约》明确规范大生纱厂总理（厂长）和各董事（分管业务的负责人）的职权、员工薪水的标准、余利的分配以及各部门的章程，是研究中国民族企业经营管理的重要文献。1923年张謇在《大生纱厂股东会建议书》里提及：“大生一厂之设，在前清未有商部之前，一切章程皆采诸上海各厂，而加以斟酌。”大生纱厂筹备的时候，上海已经建有中外纱厂，张謇派负责基建和设备安装的高清去考察。外资纱厂保密措施比较严格，中资纱厂中，华盛纺织总厂总办盛宙怀“遇有咨访，必具首尾见告”，1898年2月，大生纱厂从华盛纺织总厂借阅9份工程合同做参考。大生档案中还保存着大生纱厂从华盛纺织总厂抄录来的工资标准。规章是企业运行的准则，大生纱厂从一开始就吸取了上海纱厂的经验。

张謇事业的起点是大生纱厂。大生纱厂的成功，使得张謇有财力去实现他的理想，也使得张謇获得更多的社会声望，进而施展他的抱负。在张謇的倡导下，一系列的配套产业也陆续在通海地区投资设立。以棉纺业为核心的产业链逐步形成，以资本为纽带的大生企业集团日益壮大起来。在发展实业的基础上，张謇在南通兴办教育和慈善事业，许多理念来自上海。

1898年10月20日，正在上海为大生纱厂筹办事宜四处奔波的张謇，应好友何嗣焜的邀请抽空到南洋公学进行了一次考察。南洋公学于1896年春创办，是盛宣怀继1895年设立天津中西学堂（后改名为北洋大学堂）后开办的又一所新式学校。张謇到访时，时任南洋公学总理的何嗣焜陪同他参观了正在建设中的校舍。在考察过程中，张謇还同南洋公学的监督、美国人福开森，以及应邀而来的日本人辻武雄、伊藤贤道进行了有益的交流。辻武雄当时就职于江苏两级师范学堂，而伊藤贤道为杭州日文学堂的总理。这次南洋公学之行，其实是何嗣焜策划的一次“教育思想碰撞会”，为张謇此后从事教育实践提供了咨询交流的机会。张謇日后在南通兴办、倡导的教育事业，也是从师范开端，进而拓展到小学、中学、大学，与盛宣怀的教育理念有异曲同工之处。

新育婴堂是张謇在南通兴办慈善的开端，是张謇在创办大生纱厂获得成功，顺利开设通州师范学校之后，改良南通社会的又一举措。在婴儿抚养方面，张謇与同人努力摒弃旧育婴堂的各种陋习，吸取了上海土山湾孤儿院的育婴经验。1906年，张謇在《南通新育婴堂募捐启》里讲到，“开办一载，活婴千余，成效昭然矣”。还借鉴上海土山湾孤儿院，采取慈善和半工半读相结合的模式。南通新育婴堂以女婴为多，孤儿7岁送入幼稚园，聪颖的孩子之后送入女师附小，毕业后升入女师继续学习，女师毕业生应该具备自立的能力。其他孤儿则进入女工传习所或女子蚕桑讲习所学习技艺，日后以此谋生。这样的教育方式，使得孤儿既具备基本的文化知识，又有一门足以养家糊口的技艺。

张謇认为“立国由于人才，人才出于立学，此古今中外不易之理”。人才对于张謇所创事业的兴起和发展，都起到关键的作用。通过学校进行人才培养是有周期的，也不可能完全符合实际需求，张謇以全球眼光，从国内外广揽人才，尤其注重聘用外国技术人员，以弥补自身的不足。

1914年张謇在《规画度量衡说帖》里提到："吾财用缺乏则取资于外国，人才缺乏则取资于外国（技师到后，即于制造所附设一度量衡检定传习所，养成检定之人）。彼以其资本、学术供吾之用，吾即利用其资本、学术以集吾事。为行政计，似无便于此。"在张謇看来，哪个方面人才缺乏，都可以借助国外的力量，引进国外人才，达到促进事业发展的目的。张謇聘请的外国专家，很多来自上海。

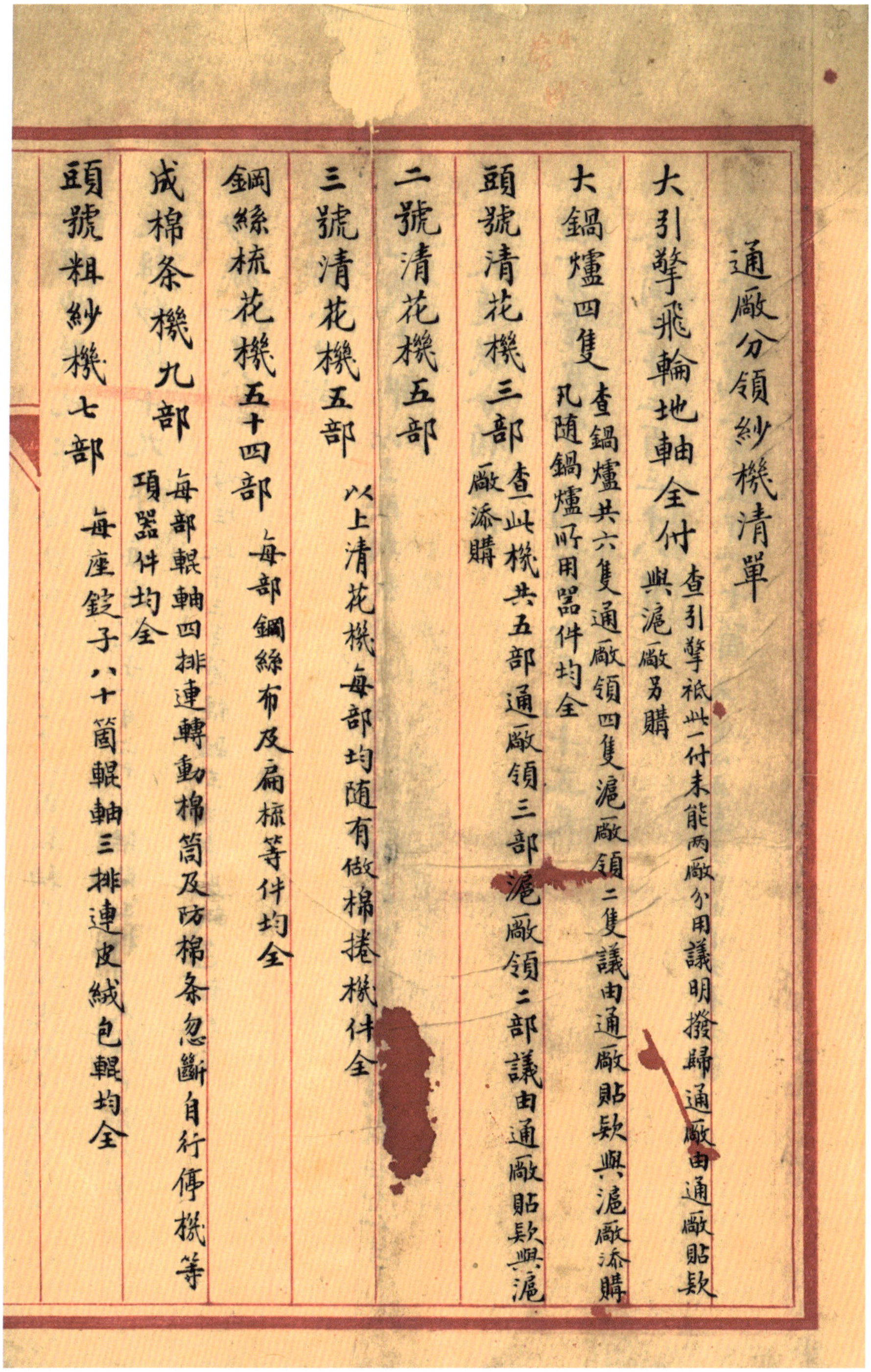
通廠分領紗機清單

大引擎飛輪地軸全付　查引擎祇此一付未能兩廠分用議明撥歸通廠由通廠貼款與滬廠另購

大鍋爐四隻　查鍋爐共六隻通廠領四隻滬廠領二隻議由通廠貼款與滬廠添購凡隨鍋爐所用器件均全

頭號清花機三部　查此機共五部通廠領三部滬廠領二部議由通廠貼款與滬廠添購

二號清花機五部

三號清花機五部　以上清花機每部均隨有做棉捲機件全

鋼絲梳花機五十四部　每部鋼絲布及扁梳等件均全

成棉條機九部　每部輥軸四排連轉動棉筒及防棉條忽斷自行停機等項器件均全

頭號粗紗機七部　每座錠子八十箇輥軸三排連皮絨包輥均全

通厂分领纱机清单（局部）。1897 年 8 月 11 日，张謇与盛宣怀签订《通沪纱厂合办约款》，约定双方各自领取 2 万余锭瑞记纱机，各作价 25 万两，分别在唐家闸和浦东开设工厂。

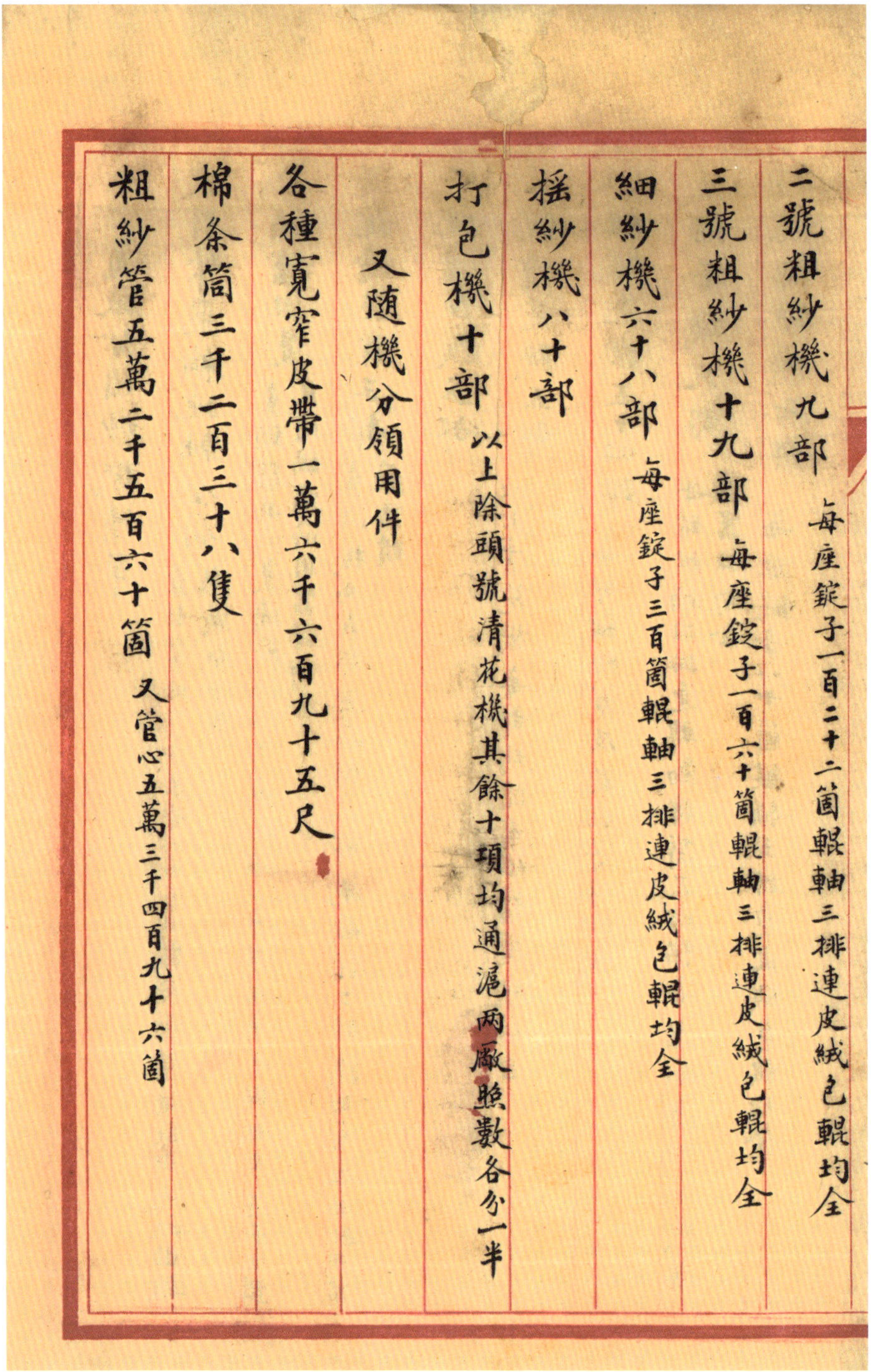

二號粗紗機九部 每座錠子一百二十二箇輥軸三排連皮絨包輥均全

三號粗紗機十九部 每座錠子一百六十箇輥軸三排連皮絨包輥均全

細紗機六十八部 每座錠子三百箇輥軸三排連皮絨包輥均全

摇紗機八十部

打包機十部 以上除頭號清花機其餘十項均通滬兩廠照數各分一半

又隨機分領用件

各種寬窄皮帶一萬六千六百九十五尺

棉條筒三千二百三十八隻

粗紗管五萬二千五百六十箇 又管心五萬三千四百九十六箇

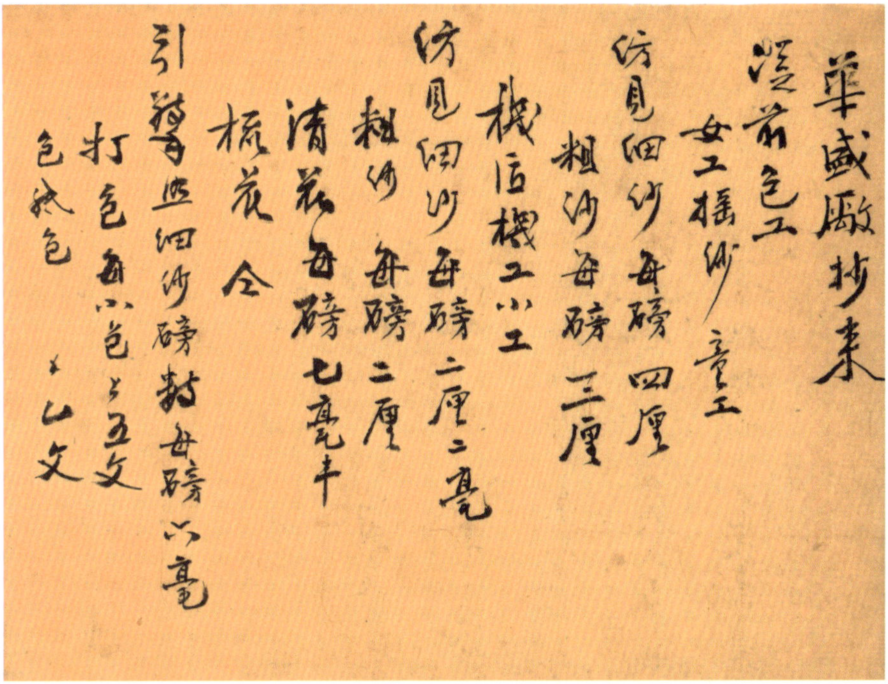

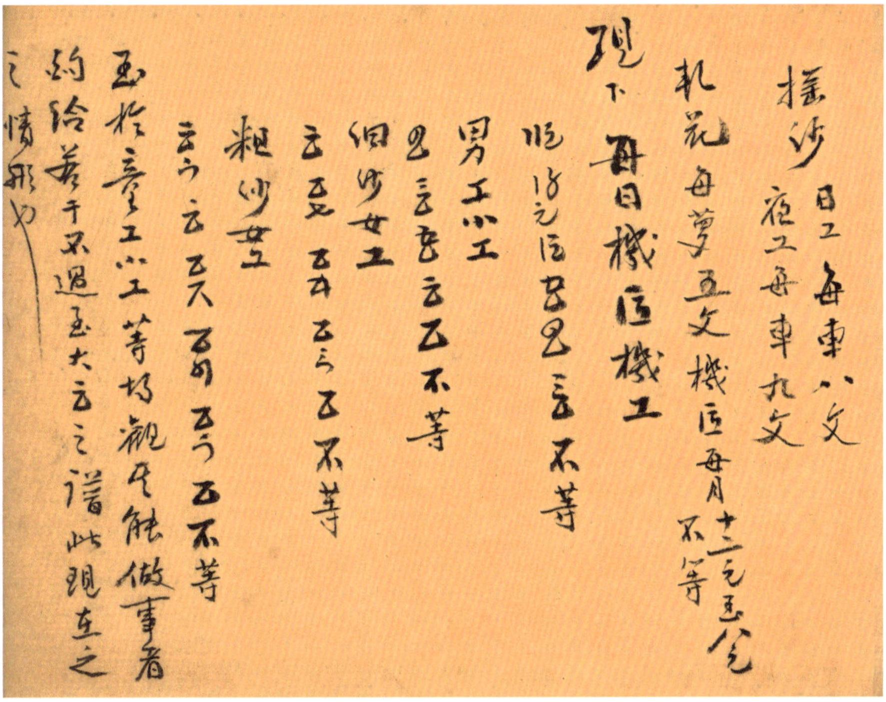

大生纱厂从华盛纺织总厂抄来的工资标准。

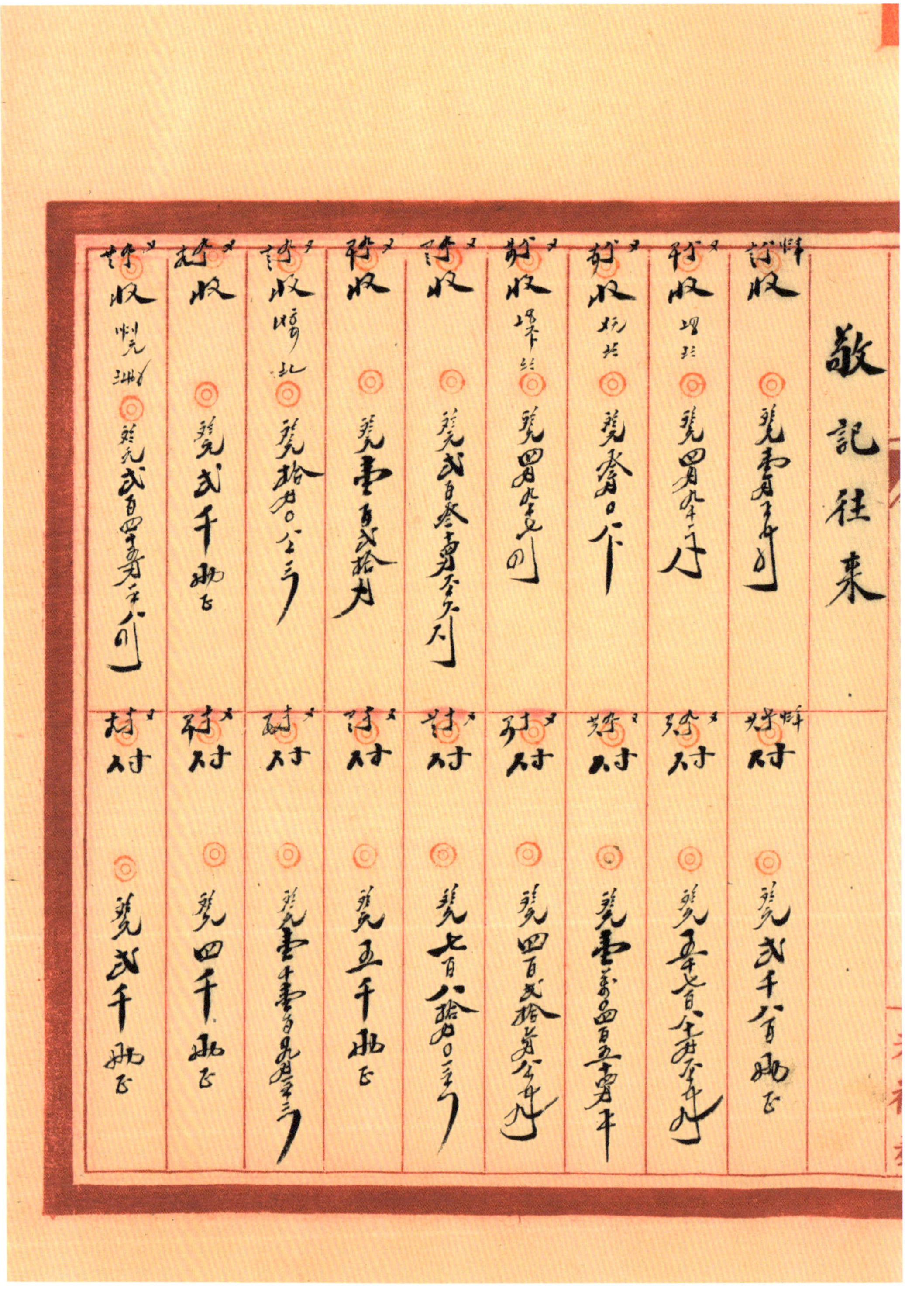

1897 年大生沪所《各往来》中记录的与沈敬夫经营的布庄经济往来的账目。

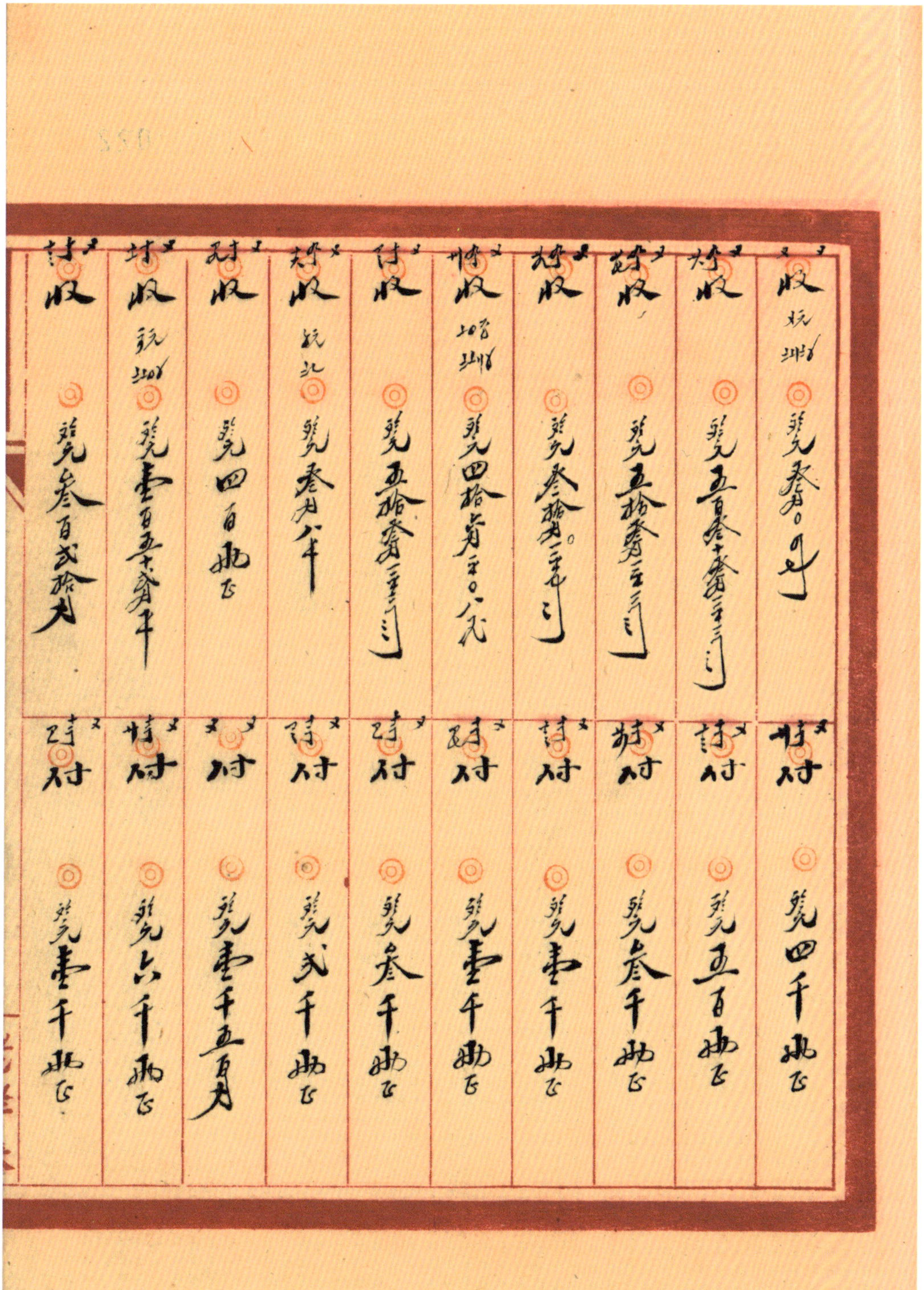

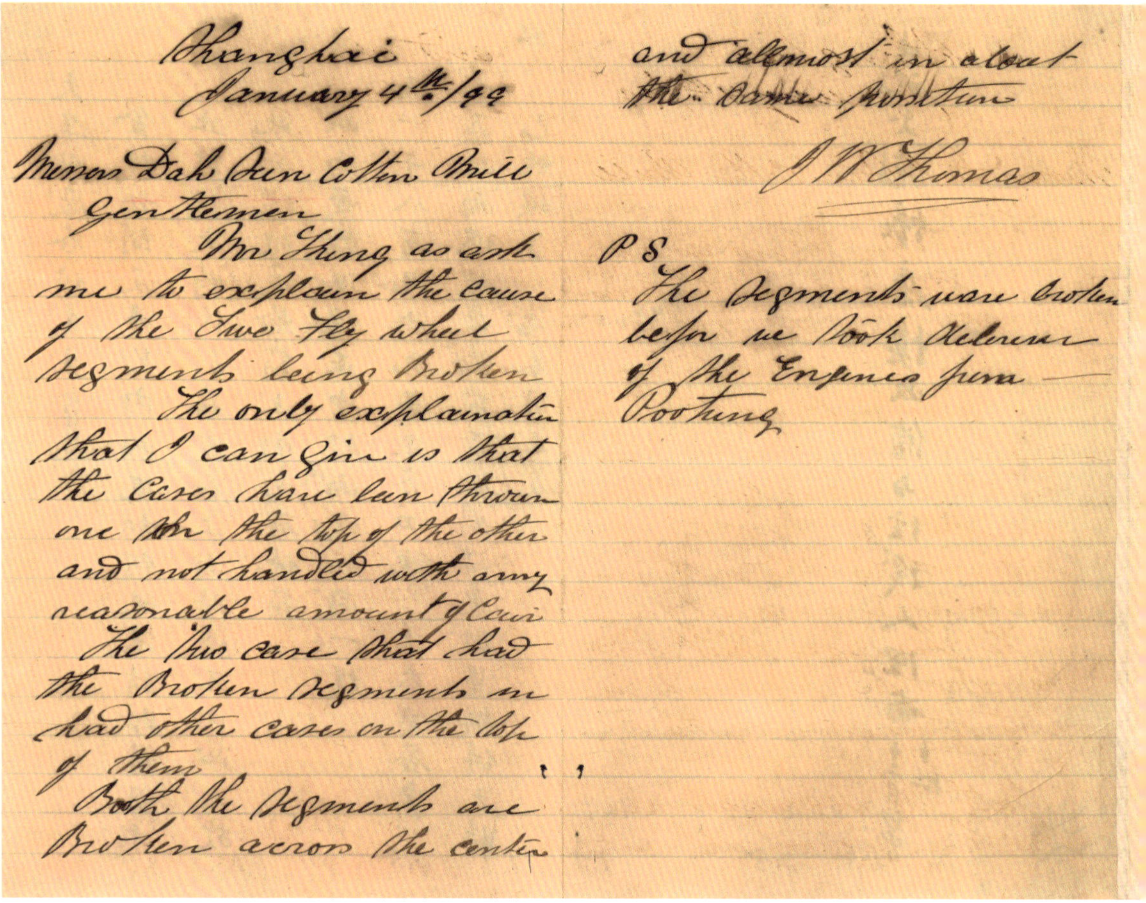

Shanghai
January 4th/99

Messrs Dah Sun Cotton Mill
Gentlemen
Mr Shing as ask me to explain the cause of the Two Fly wheel segments being Broken
The only explanation that I can give is that the cases have been thrown one on the top of the other and not handled with any reasonable amount of Care
The two case that had the Broken segments in had other cases on the top of them
Both the segments are Broken across the center and almost in about the same position

J W Thomas

P S
The segments were broken befor we took delivery of the Engines fera — Pootung

1899 年 1 月 4 日，大生纱厂装配纺纱机器的英国工程师汤姆斯给大生沪所的英文信，以及沪所的中文译件。信中解释两块飞轮损坏原因系压损。

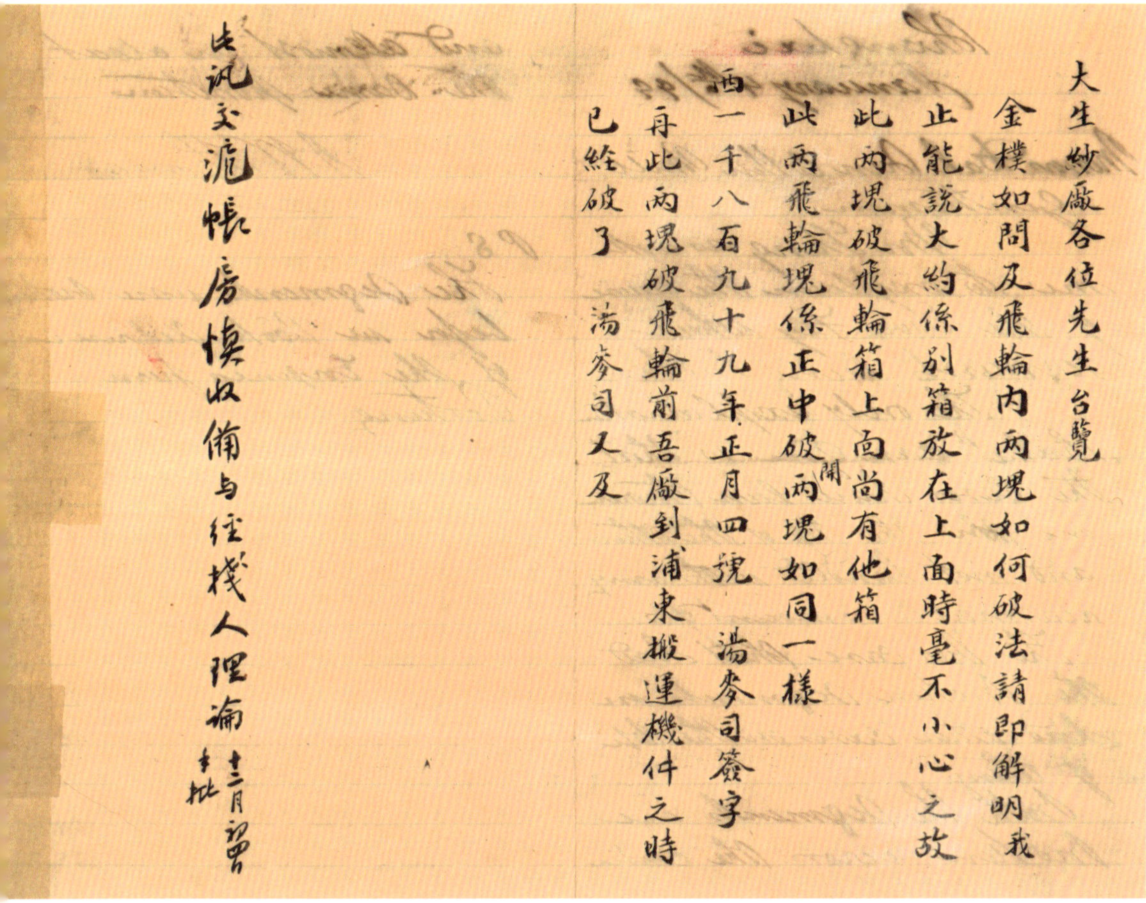

大生紗廠各位先生台覽
金樸如問及飛輪内兩塊如何破法請即解明我
止能說大約係別箱放在上面時毫不小心之故
此兩塊破飛輪箱上面尚有他箱
此兩飛輪塊係正中破開兩塊如同一樣
西一千八百九十九年正月四號 湯參司簽字
再此兩塊破飛輪前吾廠到浦東搬運機件之時
已經破了 湯參司又及

此訊交滬帳房慎收備与經棧人理論 十二月初四 手批

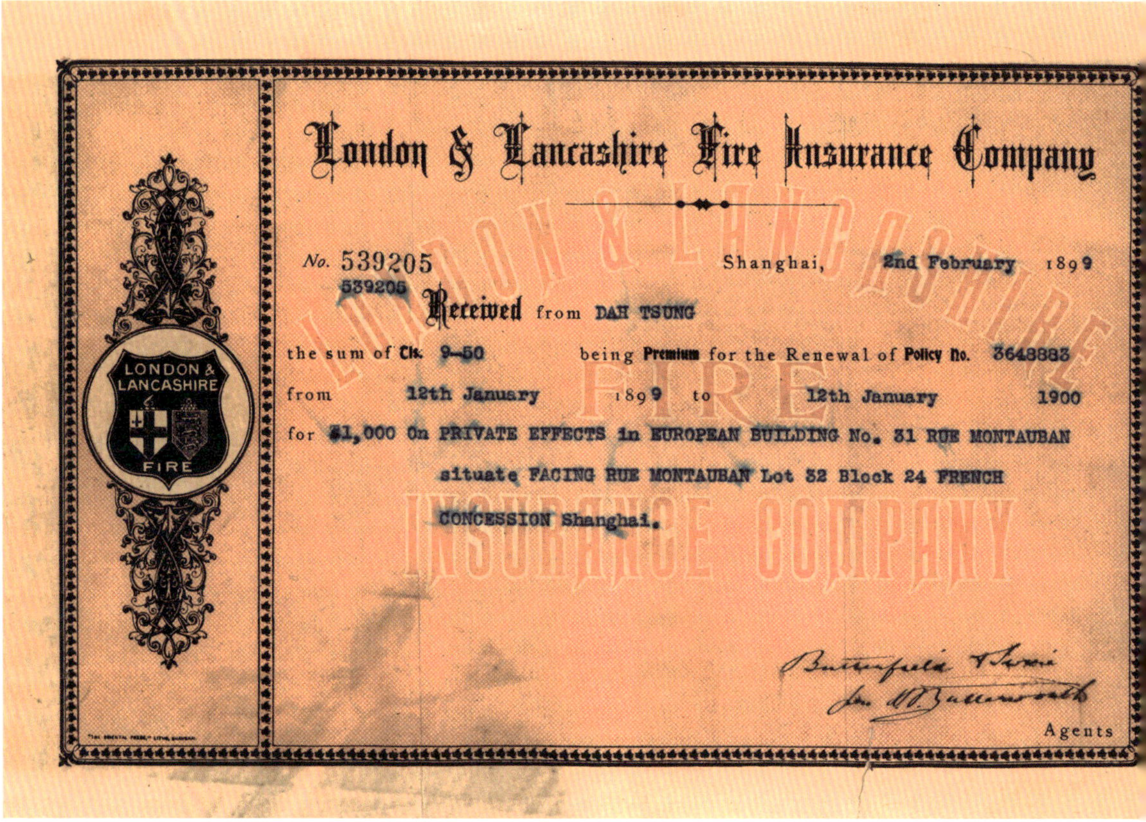

London & Lancashire Fire Insurance Company

No. 539205 Shanghai, 2nd February 1899

539205

Received from DAH TSUNG

the sum of Cts. 9-50 being Premium for the Renewal of Policy No. 3643883

from 12th January 1899 to 12th January 1900

for $1,000 On PRIVATE EFFECTS in EUROPEAN BUILDING No. 31 RUE MONTAUBAN

situate FACING RUE MONTAUBAN Lot 32 Block 24 FRENCH

CONCESSION Shanghai.

Agents

LONDON & LANCASHIRE
FIRE
LONDON & LANCASHIRE
FIRE
INSURANCE COMPANY

1899 年 2 月 2 日，伦敦暨兰开夏郡火险公司出具的大生沪所保险单。

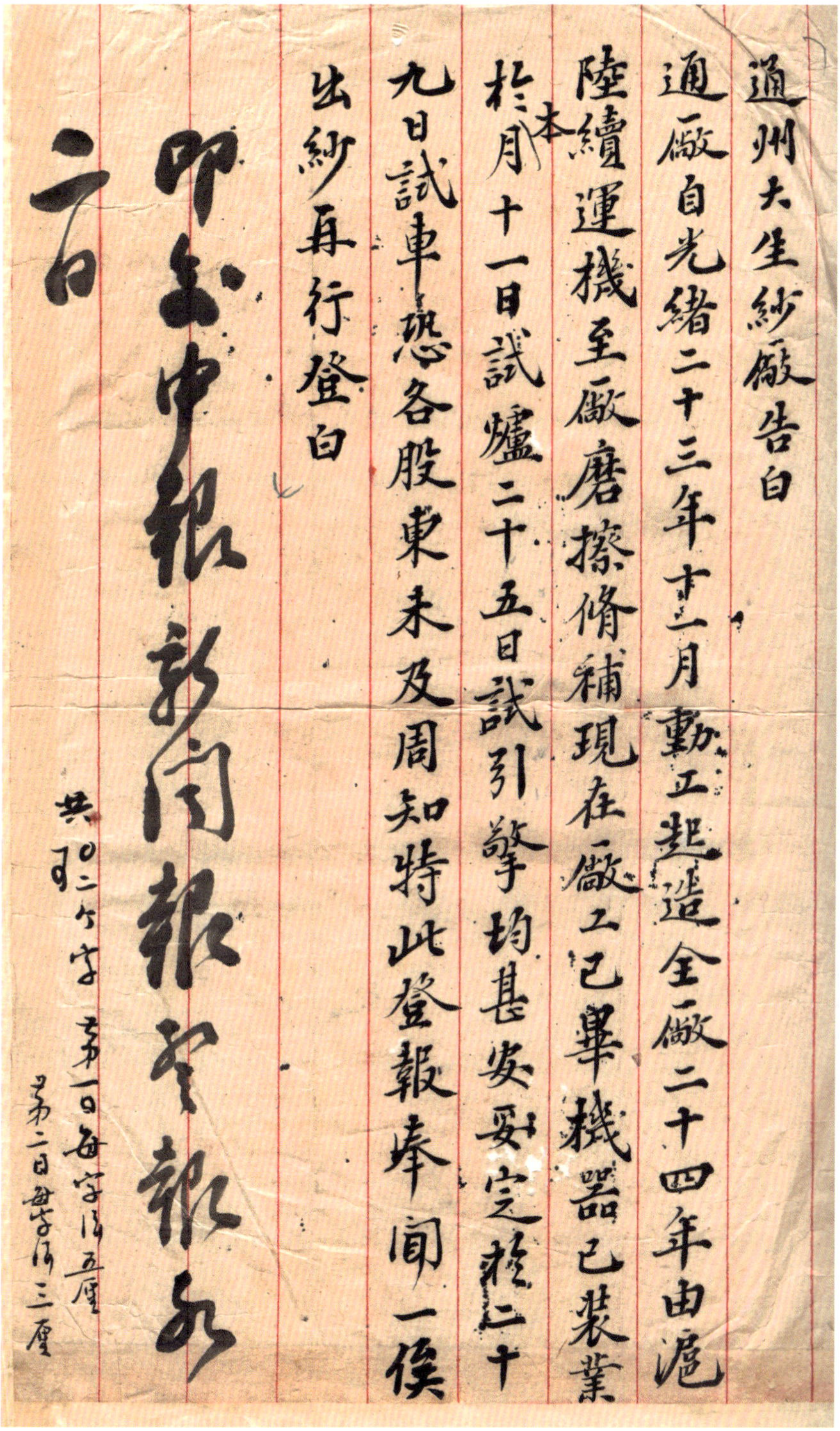
通州大生紗廠告白

通廠自光緒二十三年十二月動工起造全廠二十四年由滬陸續運機至廠磨擦修補現在廠工已畢機器已裝業於本月十一日試爐二十五日試引擎均甚安妥定於二十九日試車懇各股東未及周知特此登報奉聞一俟出紗再行登白

即登申報新聞報要報各二日

共約二分字 第一日每字價五厘 第二日每字價三厘

1899 年大生纱厂正式开车前，在《申报》《新闻报》刊登《通州大生纱厂告白》的文字底稿。

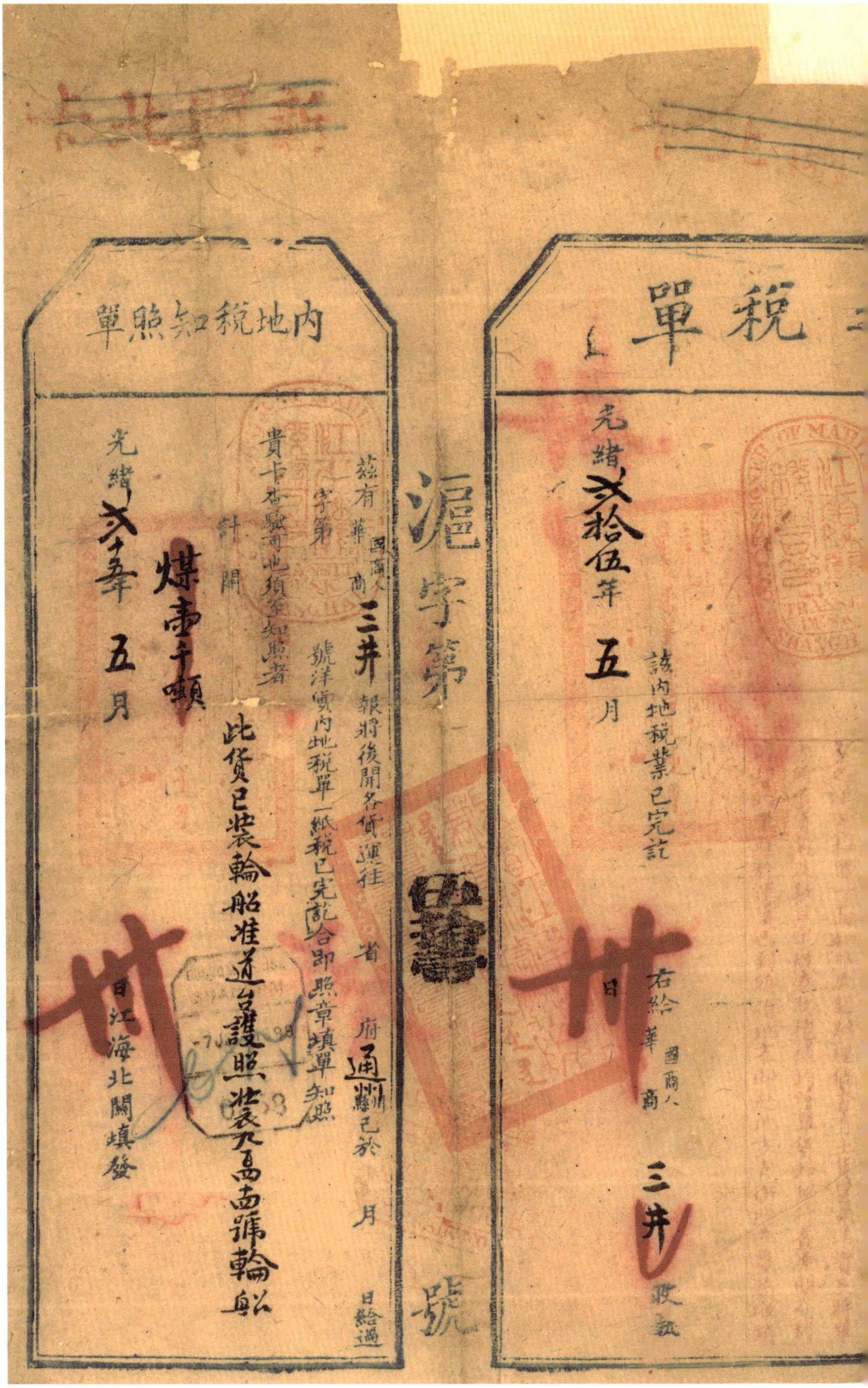
内地税知照单
兹有华商 三井 报将后开各货运往 省 府 通州 已於 月 日给过
字第 号洋货内地税单一纸税已完讫合即照章填单知照
贵卡查验前地须至知照者
计开
煤壹千吨
光绪二十五年 五月 日
江海北关填发
税单
沪字第 号
光绪贰拾伍年 五月 日
该内地税业已完讫
右给华商 三井 收执

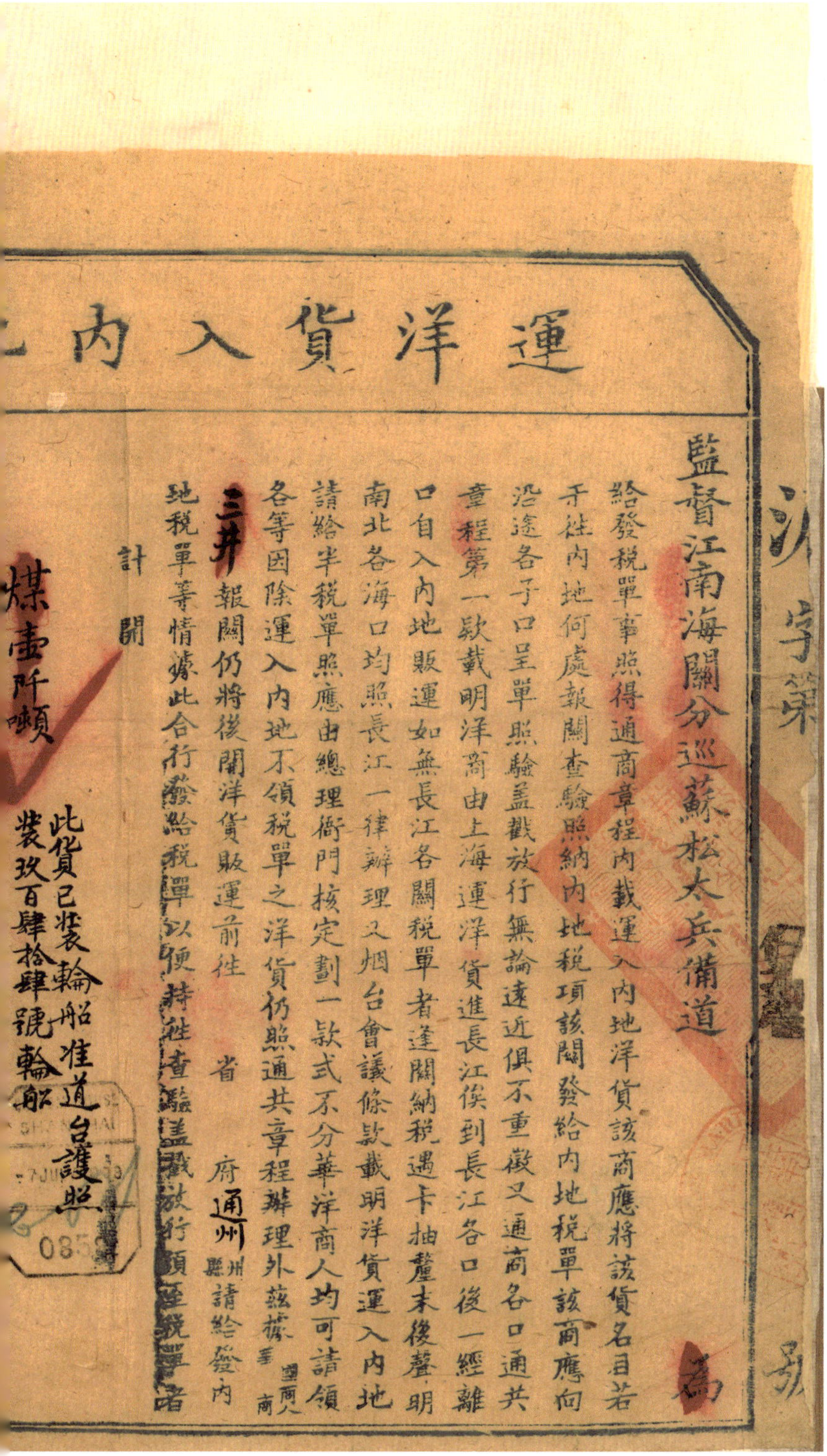
運洋貨入内

沪字第　號

監督江南海關分巡蘇松太兵備道　為

給發税單事照得通商章程内載運入内地洋貨該商應將該貨名目若干往内地何處報關查驗照納内地税項該關發給内地税單該商應向沿途各子口呈單照驗蓋戳放行無論遠近俱不重徵又通商各口通共章程第一款載明洋商由上海運洋貨進長江俟到長江各口後一經離口自入内地販運如無長江各關税單者逢關納税遇卡抽釐末後聲明南北各海口均照長江一律辦理又烟台會議條款載明洋貨運入内地請給半税單照應由總理衙門核定劃一款式不分華洋商人均可請領各等因除運入内地不領税單之洋貨仍照通共章程辦理外兹據

三井報關仍將後開洋貨販運前往　省　府　通州　請給發内地税單等情據此合行發給税單以便持往查驗蓋戳放行須至税單者

計開

煤壹阡噸

此貨已裝輪船准道台護照

裝玖百肆拾肆號輪船

1899 年 7 月 7 日，江海关颁发给三井洋行的从上海运送1000吨煤到大生纱厂的运洋货入内地之税单。

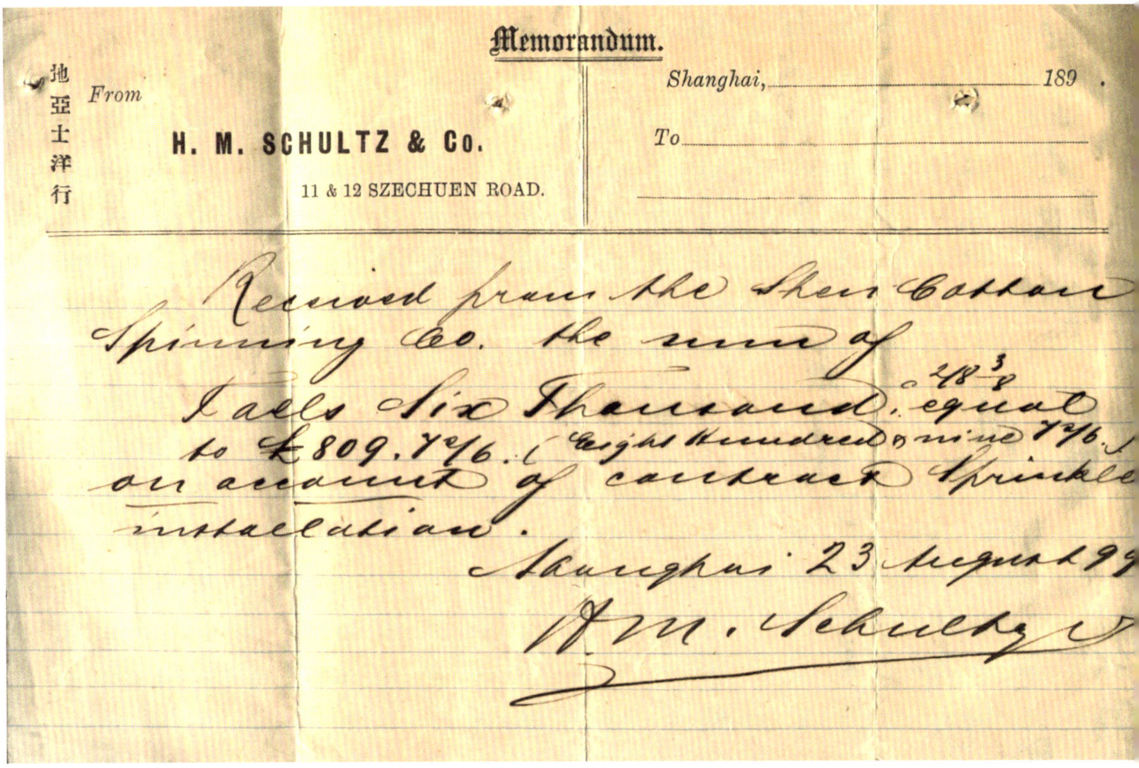

Memorandum.

地亞士洋行 From

H. M. SCHULTZ & Co.

11 & 12 SZECHUEN ROAD.

Shanghai, ... 189 .

To

Received from the Shen Cotton Spinning Co. the sum of Taels Six Thousand. @ 2/8 3/8 equal to £809.7s/6. (eight hundred & nine 7s/6.) on account of contract Sprinkler installation.

Shanghai 23 August 99

H. M. Schultz & Co.

1899 年 8 月 23 日，地亚士洋行出具的大生纱厂支付灭火器、飞锭款项的收条。

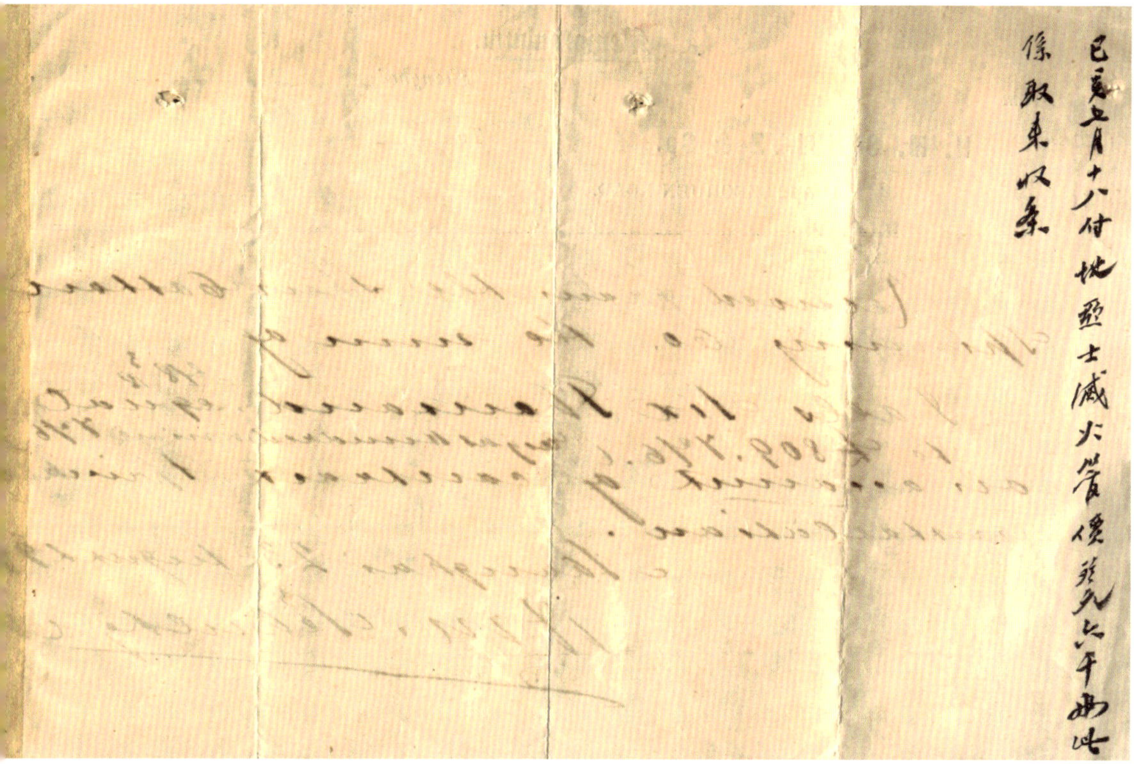

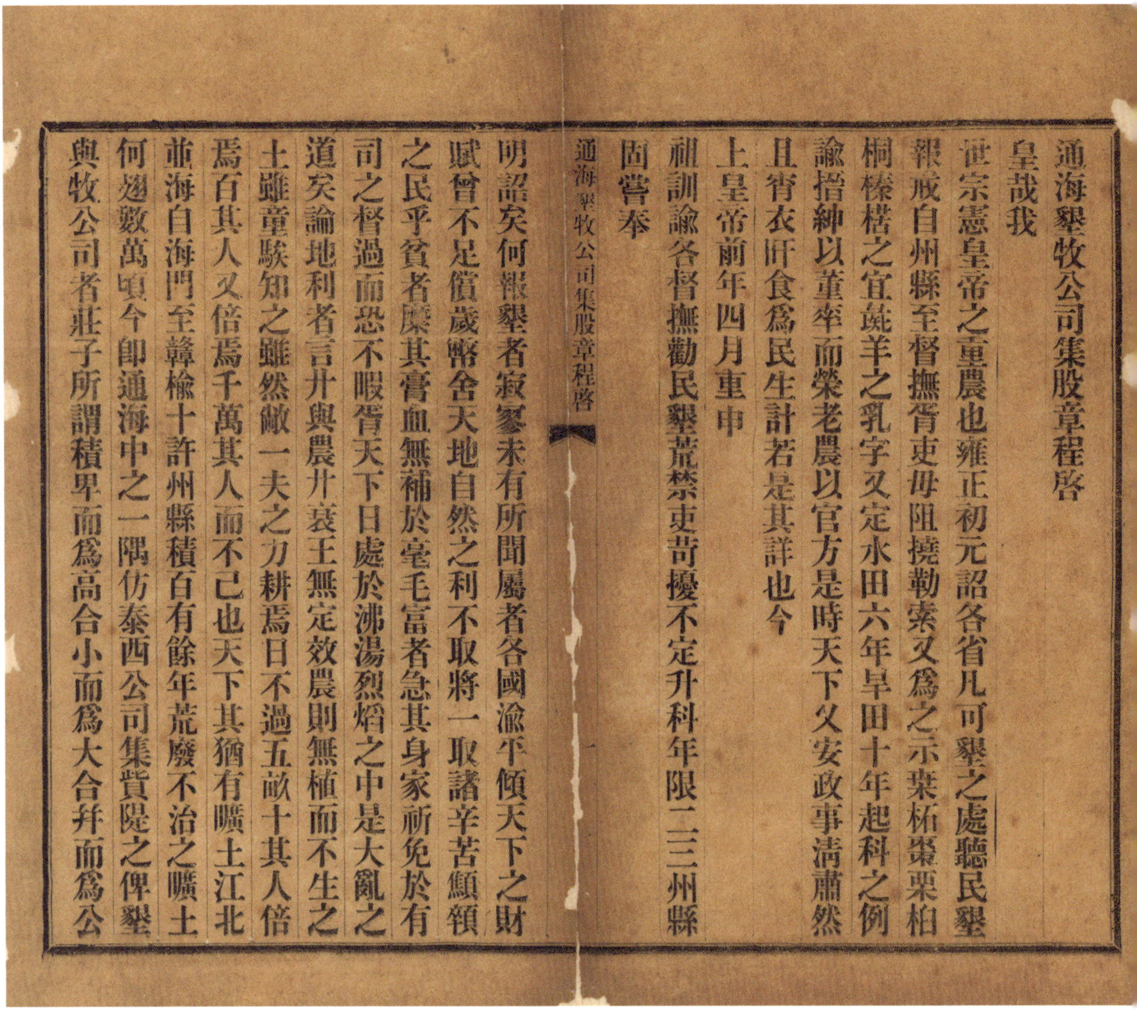

通海墾牧公司集股章程啓
皇哉我
世宗憲皇帝之重農也雍正初元詔各省凡可墾之處聽民墾
報戒自州縣至督撫胥吏毋阻撓勒索又爲之示桑柘棗栗柏
桐榛楛之宜畜羊之乳字又定水田六年旱田十年起科之例
諭搢紳以董率而榮老農以官方是時天下乂安政事清肅然
且宵衣旰食爲民生計若是其詳也今
上皇帝前年四月重申
祖訓諭各督撫勸民墾荒禁吏苛擾不定升科年限二三州縣
固嘗奉
明詔矣何報墾者寂寥未有所聞屬者各國淪平傾天下之財
賦曾不足償歲幣舍天地自然之利不取將一取諸辛苦顛頷
之民乎貧者糜其膏血無補於毫毛富者急其身家祈免於有
司之督過而恐不暇胥天下日處於沸湯烈焰之中是大亂之
道矣論地利者言井與農井衰王無定效農則無植而不生之
土雖童騃知之雖然畝一夫之力耕焉日不過五畝十其人倍
焉百其人又倍焉千萬其人而不已也天下其猶有曠土江北
並海自海門至韓楡十許州縣積百有餘年荒廢不治之曠土
何翅數萬頃今即通海中之一隅仿泰西公司集貲隄之俾墾
與牧公司者莊子所謂積卑而爲高合小而爲大合并而爲公

通海墾牧公司集股章程啓 一

《通海垦牧公司集股章程启》(局部)。大生纱厂开车后经营顺利，在张謇的倡导下，一系列的配套产业在通海地区陆续投资设立，以棉纺业为核心的产业链逐步形成，这些产业依然把上海作为主要的集资地。1901 年 6 月 16 日，张謇与汤寿潜、李审之、郑孝胥、罗振玉等人发布《通海垦牧公司集股章程启》，采用股份制方式集资设立农业公司。

之道也西人凡公司之業雖隣敵戰爭不能奪甚願天下凡有大業者皆以公司為之通海於天下此墾牧之地於通海皆九牛之一毛也不以一毛自餒而積之而已矣搢紳倡先抑亦懍憲皇帝之訓乎謹舉章程告我同志

第一曰申意意有四一務使曠土生財齊民擴業一為國家增歲入之貲收本富之利一儲通海小學堂農學堂經費一務使公司獲最優之利庶他州縣易於興起

第二曰建本興工築隄之始即擇千畝之地立農學堂延日本農科教習采日本農會章程斟酌試辦講求墾牧之事備公司任用亦即為他州縣儲才

第三曰畫界此次擬興墾牧之荒灘通境北止三補三補緊接二補之東二補之北即東十五總墾塗為倒岸河下游滙水之澤凡八十頃十九畝蘆葦特盛今議墾務自於丁蕩三十總內築隄種草暫以墾塗草供其采買俟丁蕩三十總草產足用再墾墾塗故暫不入此次畫界之內從二補大圩東北角向東卯酉綫迤至新港西止二補界河南止蒿枝港蒿枝港闢自光緒四年係按民竈界河順水勢而趨東北查照嘉慶十年廳州分司會勘詳定及道光元年竈民控請三補各案海精卑長泰外接漲新灘均歸三補所謂接漲新灘今蒿枝港即在其地照案從民竈界河卯酉綫直量凡二補以東之蒿枝港全在通境而陸先墩圩外蒿枝港南岸側尙有竈地西狹東寬長如邪幅二十餘里直至海濱惟此為通海精地分界而當若築隄之界不得不就蒿枝港顯然形勢以分南北東止圖畫可隄處虛綫海境北止蒿枝港西若迤南止陸先墩袁家圩狼蘇營兵田陳惠坡陸亮臣南北楊香圃倪愷張時蔚陸春源王家富等

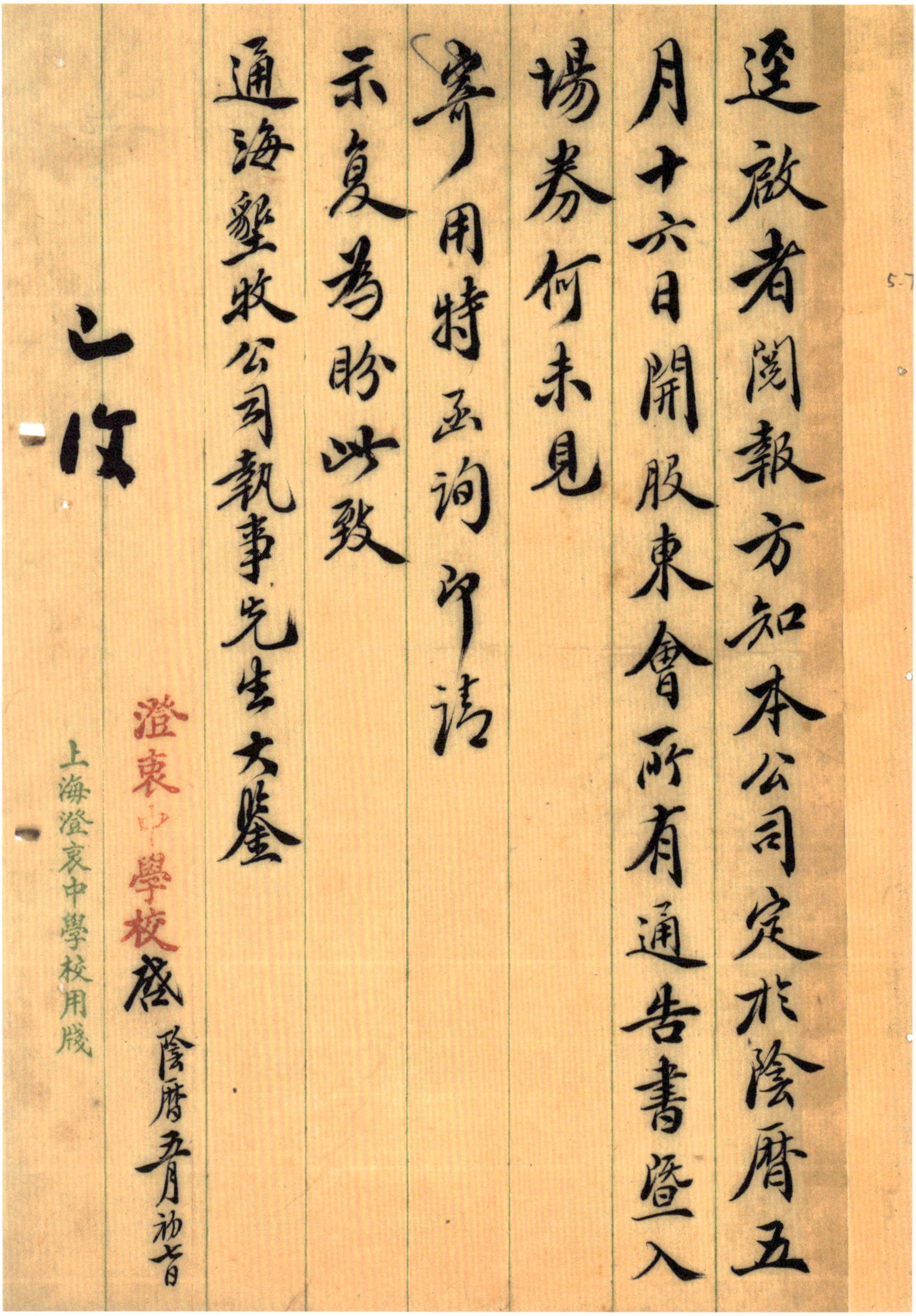

逕啟者閱報方知本公司定於陰曆五月十六日開股東會所有通告書遵入場券何未見寄用特函詢即請示復為盼此致

通海墾牧公司執事先生大鑒

澄衷中學校啟 陰曆五月初七日

上海澄衷中學校用箋

澄衷中学致通海垦牧公司询问股东会议召开事宜的函。上海澄衷中学为通海垦牧公司股东。

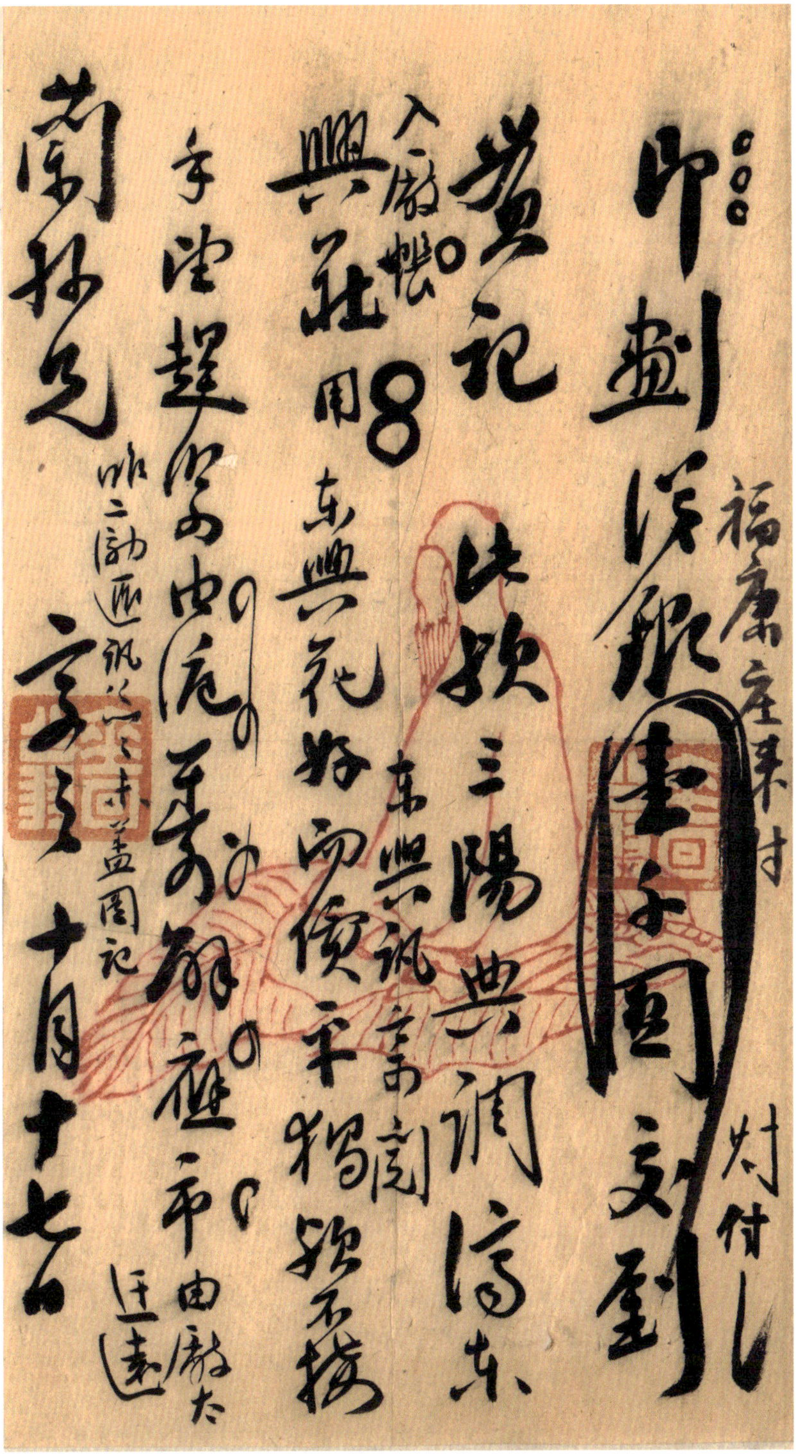

张謇给大生沪所主任林兰荪划拨资金的便条。大生沪所既是大生系统企业与上海金融界联系的纽带和桥梁，也负责资金的收付。

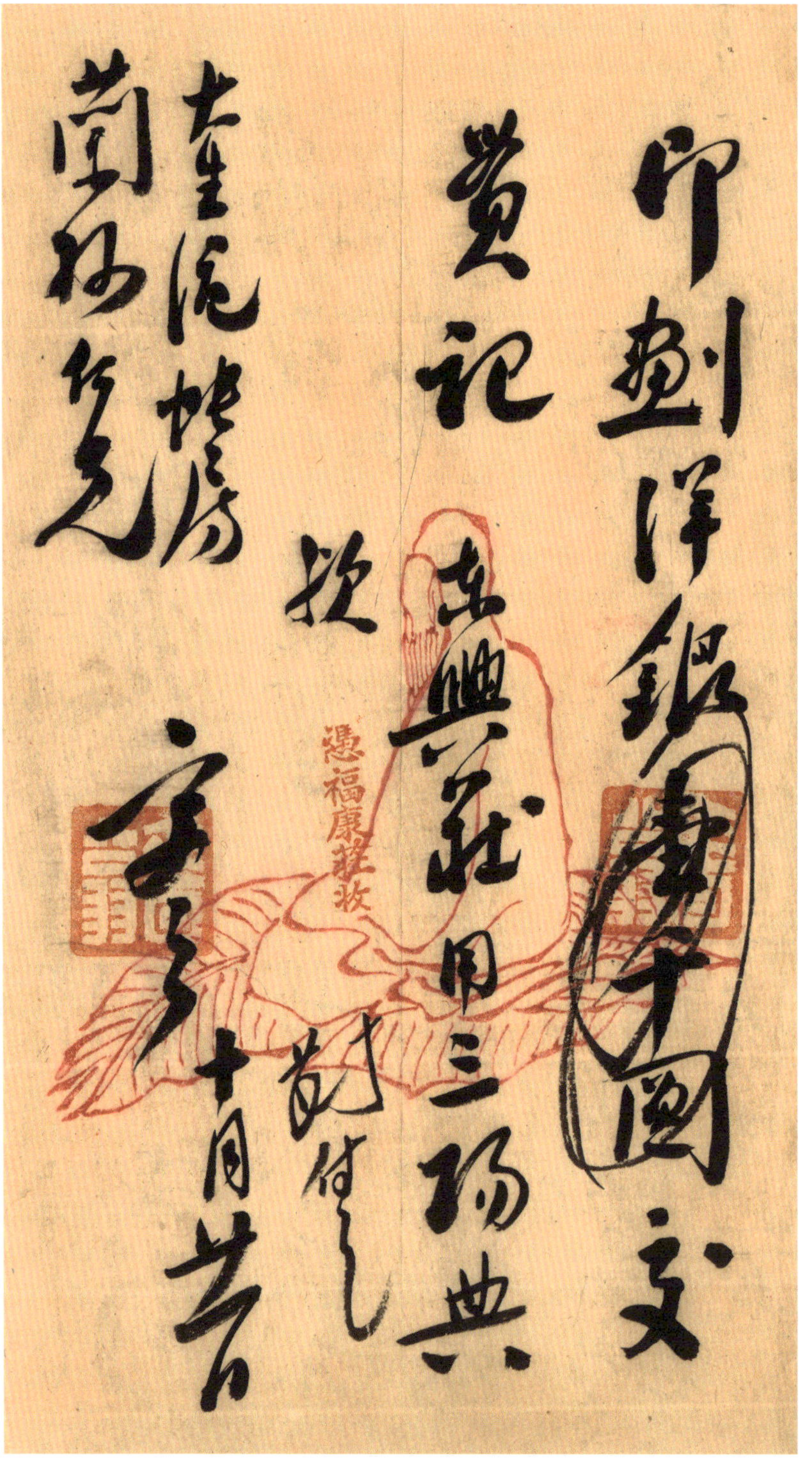

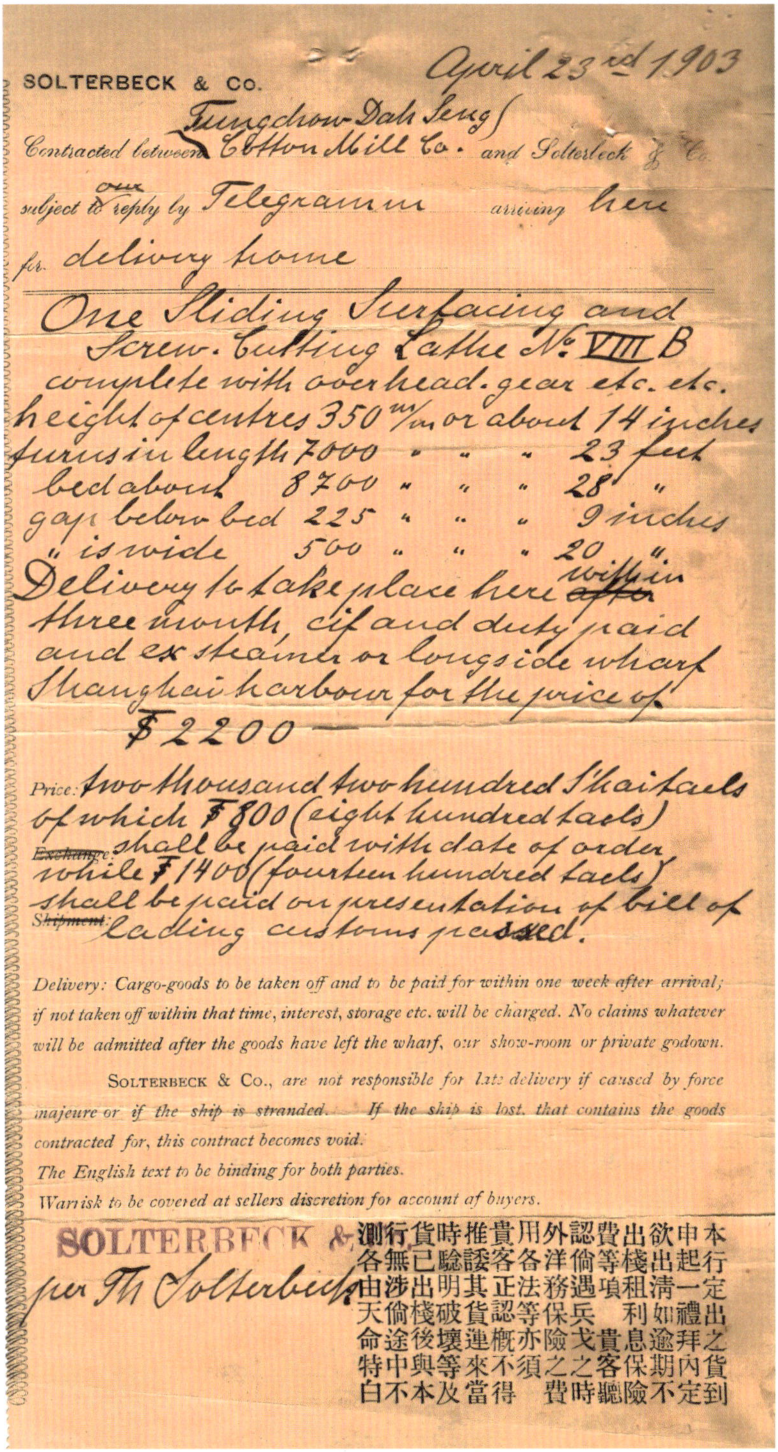

April 23rd 1903

SOLTERBECK & CO.

Tungchow Dah Seng
Contracted between Cotton Mill Co. and Solterbeck & Co.
subject to our reply by Telegramm arriving here
for delivery home

One Sliding Surfacing and
Screw-Cutting Lathe No VIII B
complete with overhead gear etc. etc.
height of centres 350 m/m or about 14 inches
turns in length 7000 " " " 23 feet
bed about 8700 " " " 28 "
gap below bed 225 " " " 9 inches
" is wide 500 " " " 20 "
Delivery to take place here ~~after~~ within
three month, cif and duty paid
and ex steamer or longside wharf
Shanghai harbour for the price of
₮2200 —

Price: two thousand two hundred S'hai taels
of which ₮800 (eight hundred taels)
~~Exchange:~~ shall be paid with date of order
while ₮1400 (fourteen hundred taels)
shall be paid on presentation of bill of
~~Shipment:~~ lading customs passed.

Delivery: Cargo-goods to be taken off and to be paid for within one week after arrival; if not taken off within that time, interest, storage etc. will be charged. No claims whatever will be admitted after the goods have left the wharf, our show-room or private godown.

SOLTERBECK & CO., *are not responsible for late delivery if caused by force majeure or if the ship is stranded. If the ship is lost, that contains the goods contracted for, this contract becomes void.*

The English text to be binding for both parties.

Warrisk to be covered at sellers discretion for account of buyers.

SOLTERBECK &

per M Solterbeck

本行定出之貨到申起一禮拜內定欲出清如逾期不出棧租利息保險費等項　貴客聽認倘遇兵戈之時外洋務保險之費用各法等亦須　貴客正認槪不得推諉其貨運來當時驗明破壞等及貨已出棧後與本行無涉倘途中不測各由天命特白

1903 年 4 月 23 日，大生纱厂向苏达伯洋行（SOLTERBECK）订购一台车床的合同。

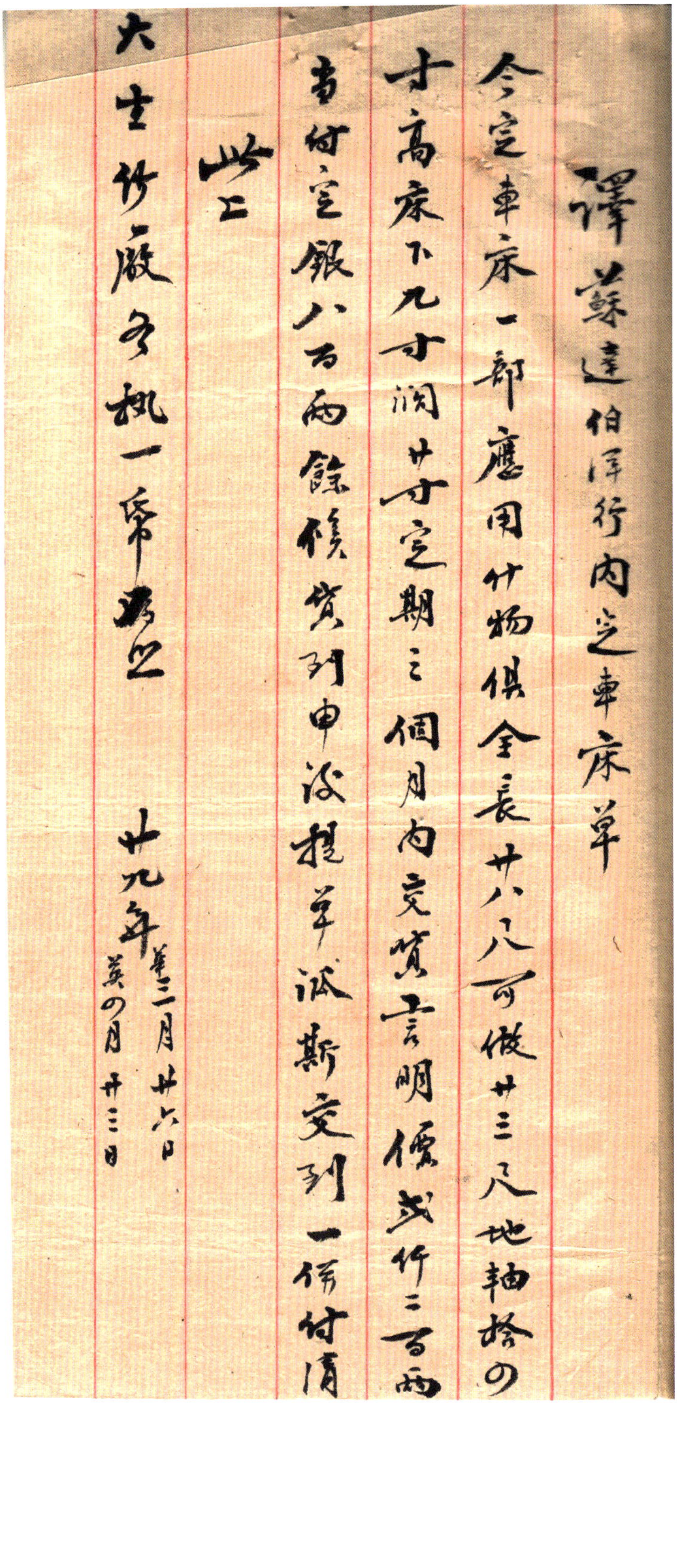
譯蘇達伯洋行內定車床單

今定車床一部應用什物俱全長廿八尺可做廿三尺地軸檯の
寸高床下九寸潤廿寸定期三個月内交貨言明價銀弍仟二百兩
當付定銀八百兩餘俟貨到申後提單試斯交到一併付清
此上
大生紗廠台執一紙存照

廿九年華二月廿六日
英の月廿三日

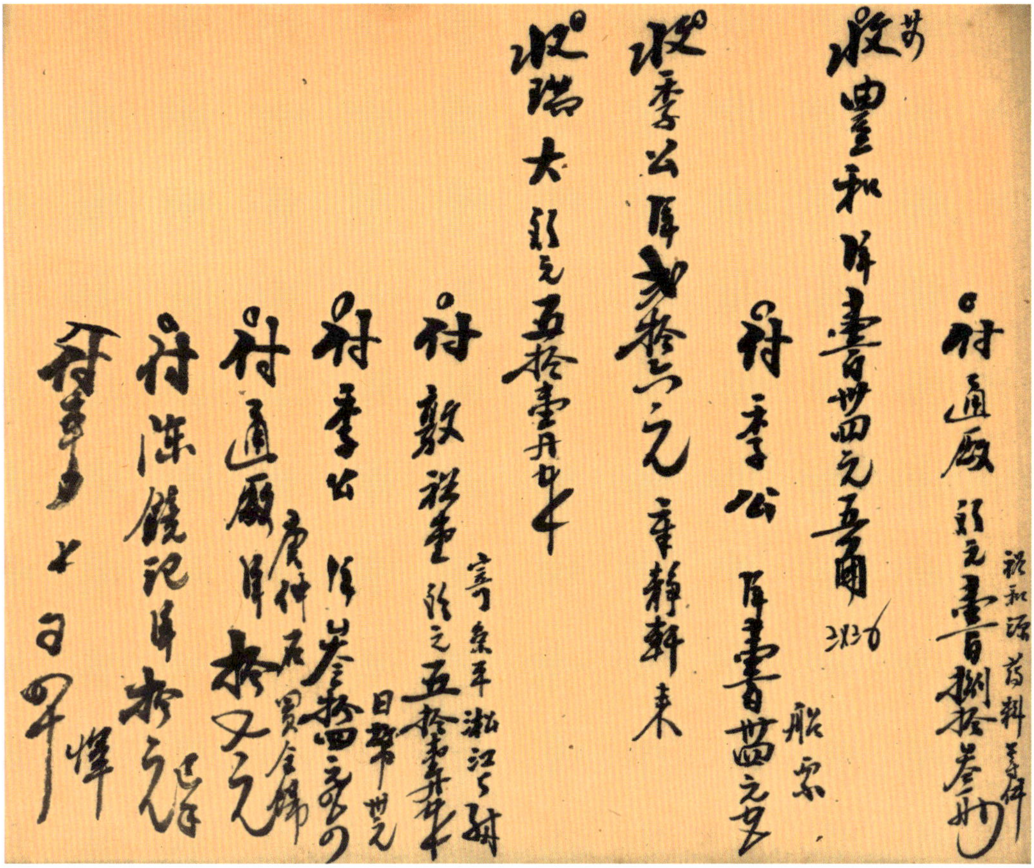

大生沪所流水账中记载的张謇赴日考察前在上海的一些活动。1903 年张謇赴日考察，开阔了视野。

癸卯東游日記
通州張謇自題

1903年，张謇自日本考察回国后整理出版的《癸卯东游日记》扉页。

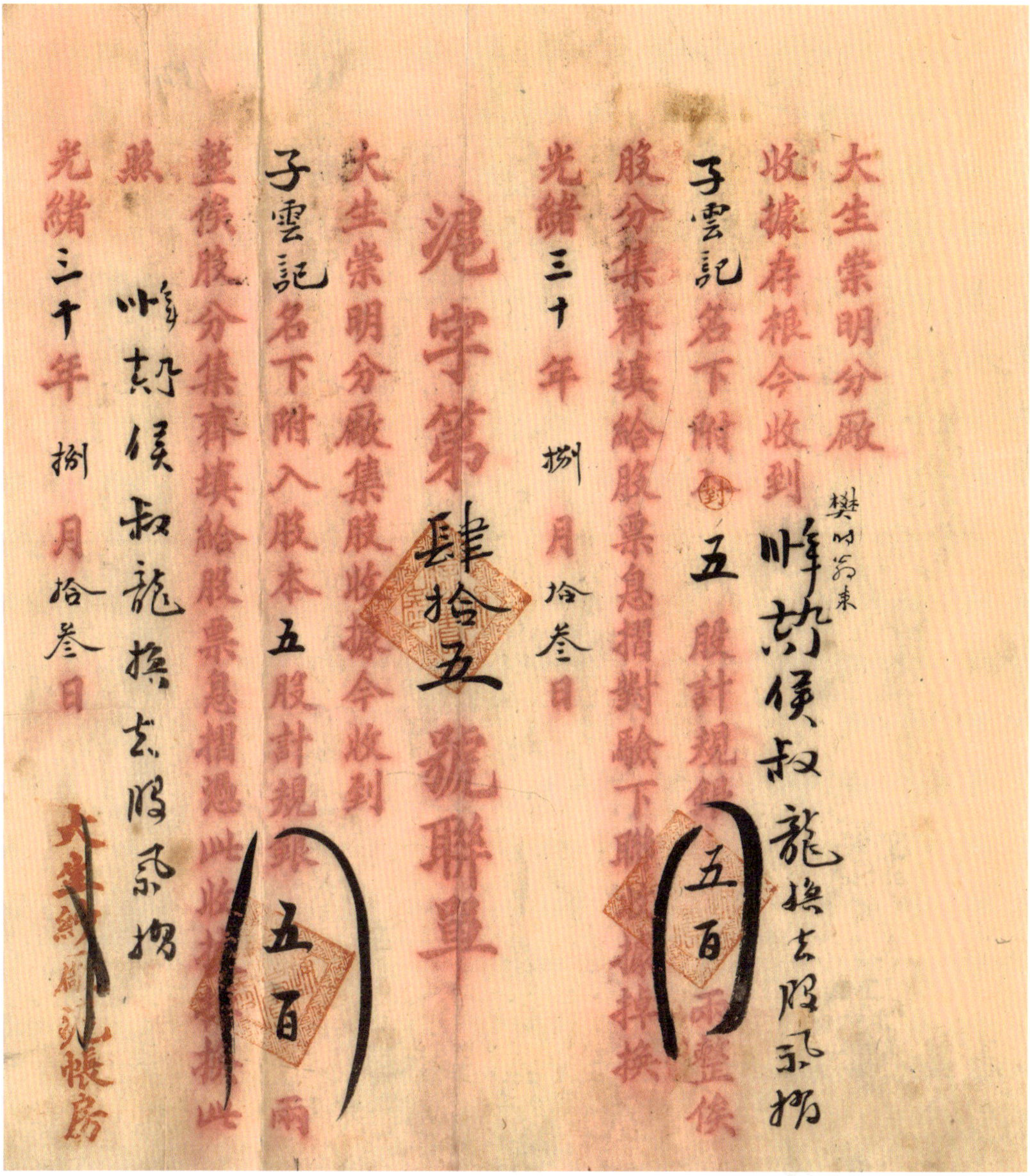

大生崇明分廠
收據存根今收到
子雲記名下附入 五 股計規銀 五百 兩整候
股分集齊填給股票息摺對驗下聯收據掉換
光緒三十年捌月拾叁日

滬字第肆拾五號聯單

大生崇明分廠集股收據今收到
子雲記名下附入股本 五 股計規銀 五百 兩
整候股分集齊填給股票息摺憑此收據掉換此
據
光緒三十年捌月拾叁日
大生紗廠帳房

1904年9月22日，大生沪所出具的收到子云记入股大生分厂股金银500两的收据。大生分厂是张謇继大生纱厂之后，在棉纺织业方面的进一步拓展。

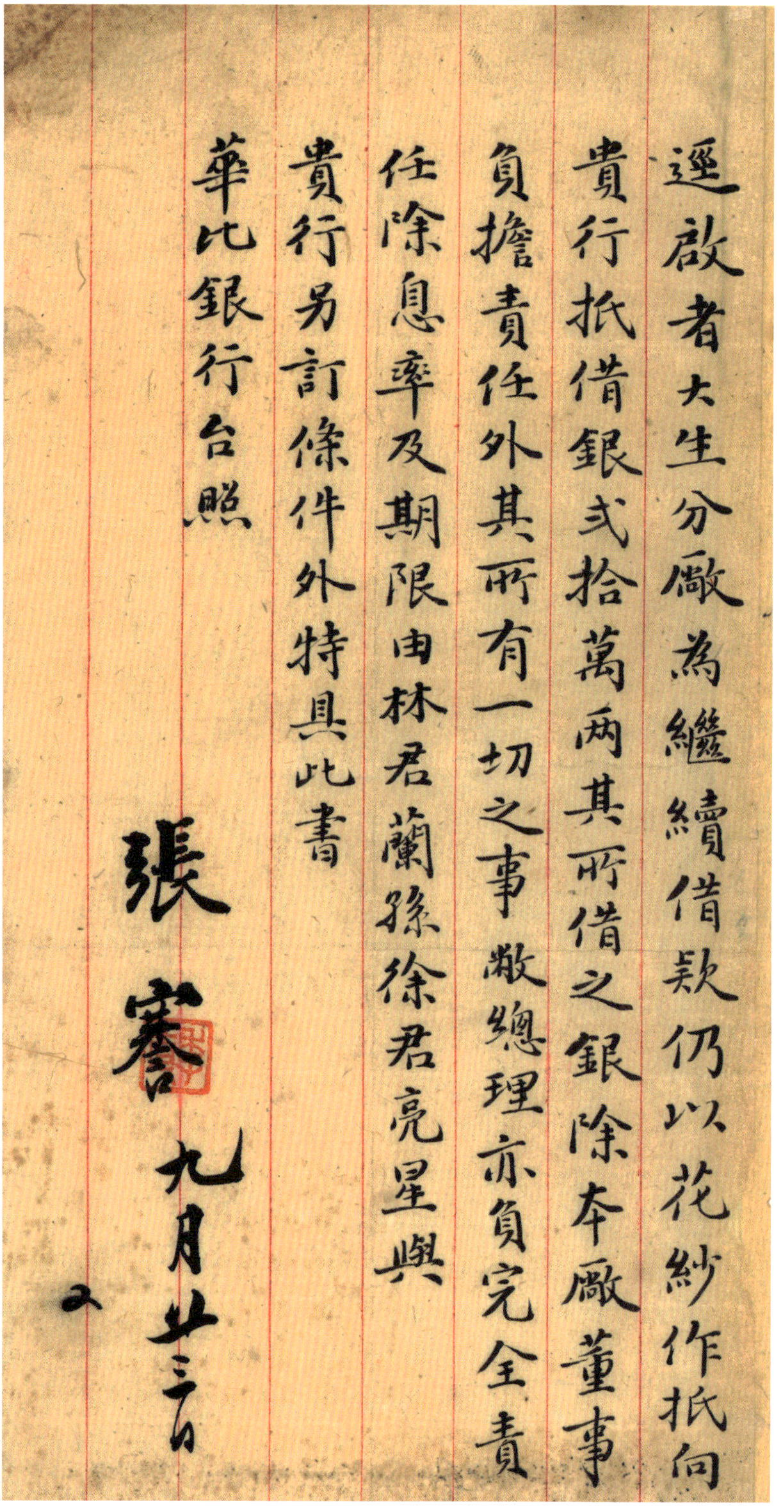

逕啟者大生分廠為繼續借款仍以花紗作抵向
貴行抵借銀式拾萬兩其所借之銀除本廠董事
負擔責任外其所有一切之事敝總理亦負完全責
任除息率及期限由林君蘭孫徐君亮星與
貴行另訂條件外特具此書
華比銀行台照
張謇 九月廿三日

张謇就大生分厂抵押借款事宜给华比银行的函。

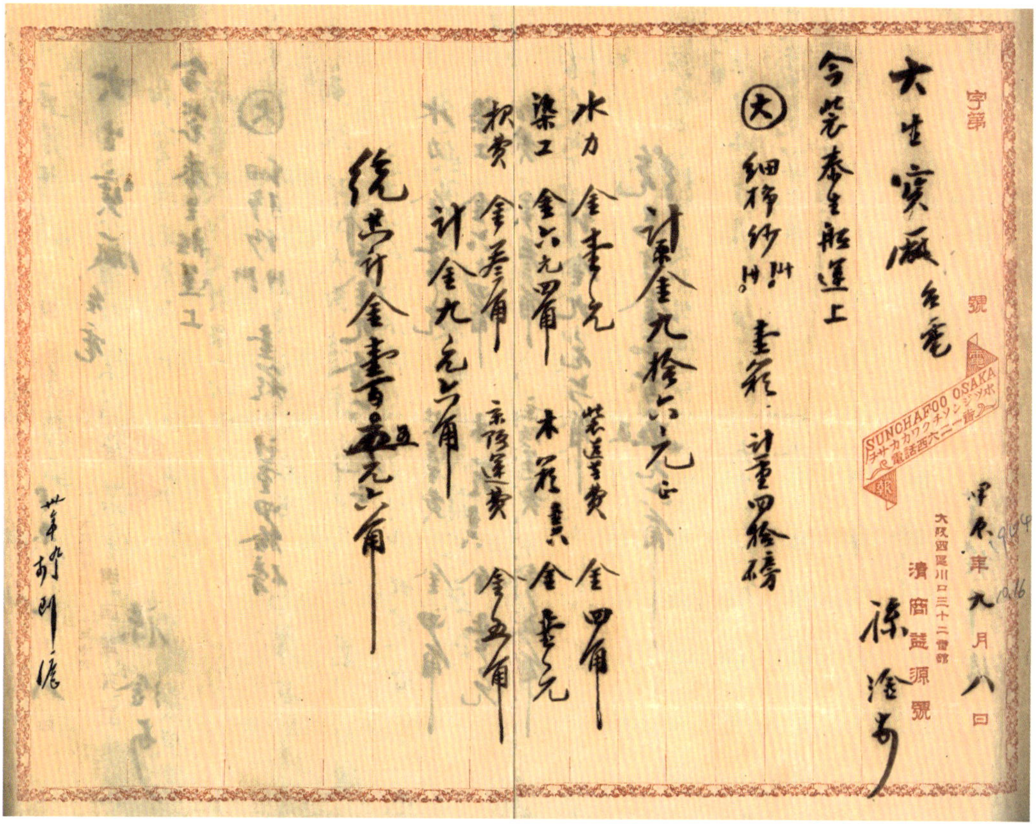
字第 號
大生實廠 台鑒
今裝春生船運上
(大) 細棉紗卅 壹箱 計重四拾磅
計洋金九拾六元正
水力 金壹元 裝運費 金四角
染工 金六元四角 木箱費 金壹元
稅費 金叁角 京阪運費 金五角
計金九元六角
統共計金壹百五元六角
甲辰年九月八日
SUNCHAFOO OSAKA
大阪西區川口三十二番館
清商益源號
孫淦

1904 年 10 月 16 日，旅日华商孙淦致函大生纱厂（沪所），条列其经营的益源慎商行出售的一箱细棉纱的价格。

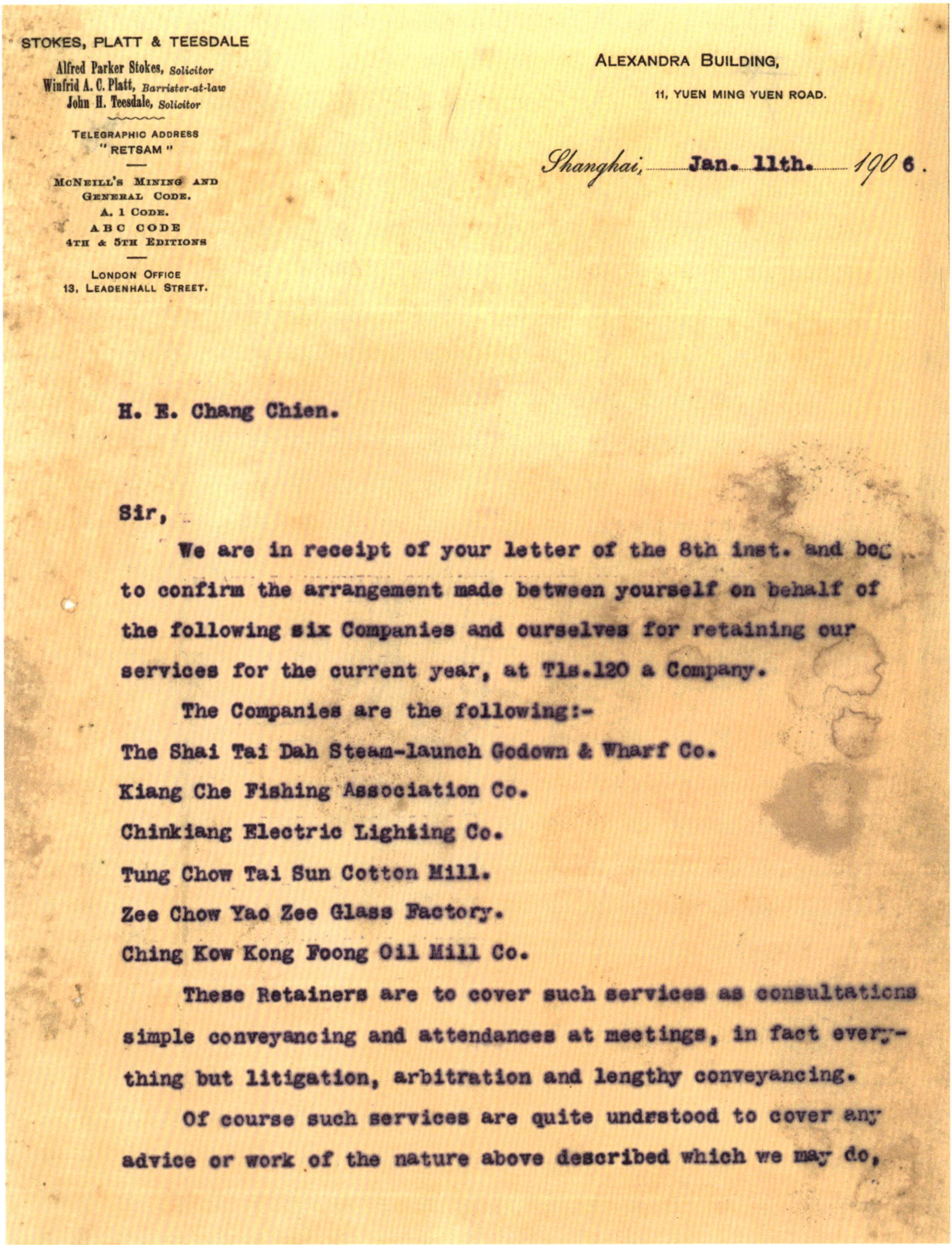

STOKES, PLATT & TEESDALE
Alfred Parker Stokes, Solicitor
Winfrid A. C. Platt, Barrister-at-law
John H. Teesdale, Solicitor

TELEGRAPHIC ADDRESS
"RETSAM"

McNEILL'S MINING AND GENERAL CODE.
A. 1 CODE.
ABC CODE
4TH & 5TH EDITIONS

LONDON OFFICE
13, LEADENHALL STREET.

ALEXANDRA BUILDING,
11, YUEN MING YUEN ROAD.

Shanghai, Jan. 11th. 1906.

H. E. Chang Chien.

Sir,

We are in receipt of your letter of the 8th inst. and beg to confirm the arrangement made between yourself on behalf of the following six Companies and ourselves for retaining our services for the current year, at Tls.120 a Company.

The Companies are the following:-

The Shai Tai Dah Steam-launch Godown & Wharf Co.
Kiang Che Fishing Association Co.
Chinkiang Electric Lighting Co.
Tung Chow Tai Sun Cotton Mill.
Zee Chow Yao Zee Glass Factory.
Ching Kow Kong Foong Oil Mill Co.

These Retainers are to cover such services as consultations simple conveyancing and attendances at meetings, in fact everything but litigation, arbitration and lengthy conveyancing.

Of course such services are quite undrstood to cover any advice or work of the nature above described which we may do,

1906 年 1 月 11 日，英籍律师哈华托致函张謇，同意担任大生纱厂、江浙渔业公司等单位的法律顾问。

2.

whether for you, Mr. Chou Chok Joon and Mr. Fan Tsze Shoon or any other gentlemen in connection with the business of the above six Companies.

If you wish us to advise you in regard to your private business, we shall be happy to do so for the present without any charge, though if it shouldhappen that you require our advice to any great extent, we can no doubt subsequently come to some special arrangement thereanent.

As we have made by this arrangement a reduction of our usual fees in consideration of these Companies having just started business, you will no doubt agree to consider this arrangement as a temporary one for a year. Any new arrangement at the expiration of such year can no doubt be easily fixed up between us.

Trusting that this arrangement will be satisfactory to all parties,

We are, Sir,

Yours faithfully,

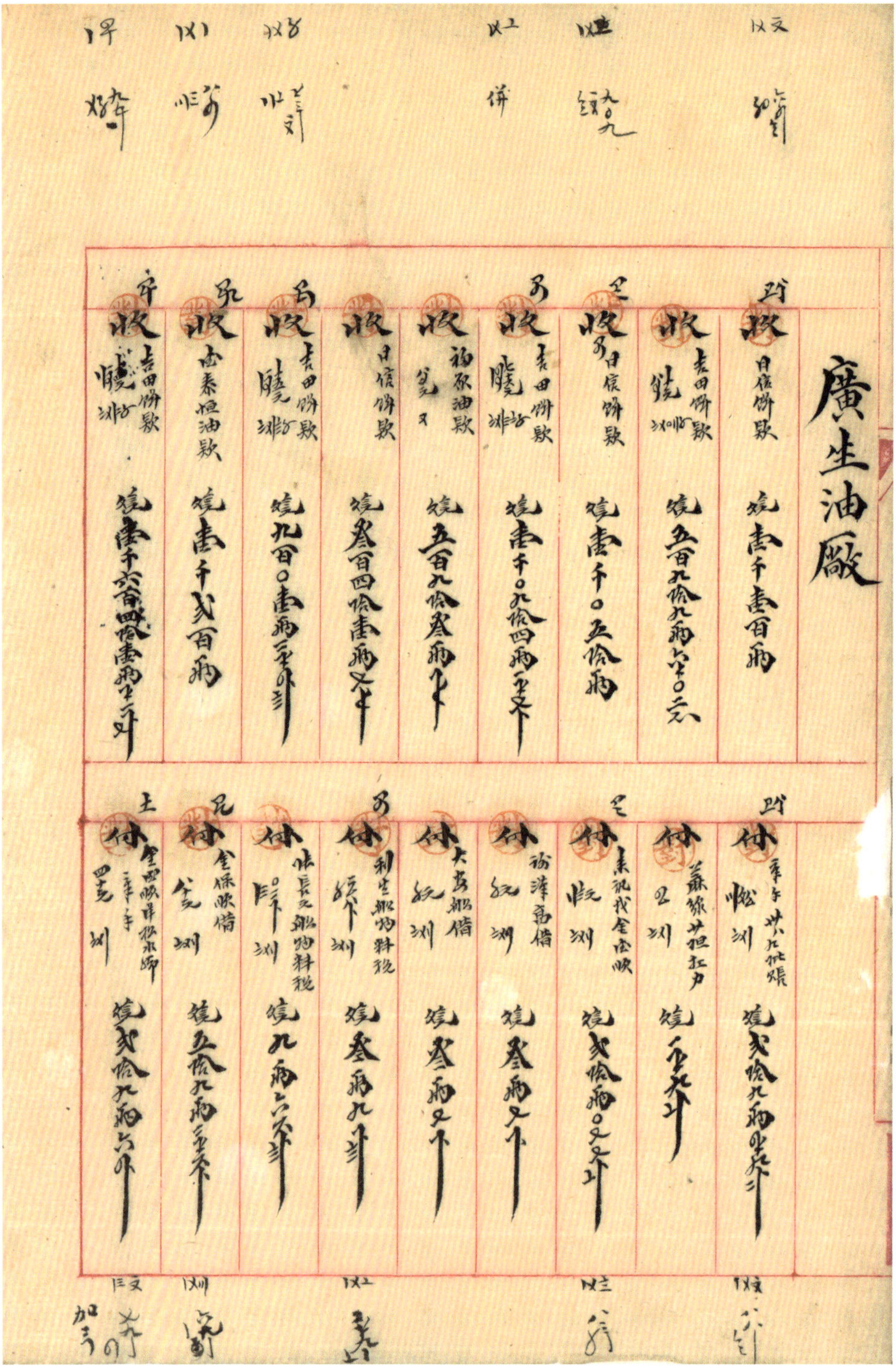
廣生油廠
收 日信餅款 洋壹千壹百兩
收 吉田餅款 洋五百九拾九兩
收 日信餅款 洋壹千〇五拾兩
收 吉田餅款 洋壹千〇九拾四兩
收 裕泰油款 洋五百九拾叁兩
收 日信餅款 洋叁百四拾壹兩
收 吉田餅款 洋九百〇壹兩
收 由泰恒油款 洋壹千弍百兩
收 吉田餅款 洋壹千六百四拾壹兩

1907 年大生沪所代理的广生油厂账目。

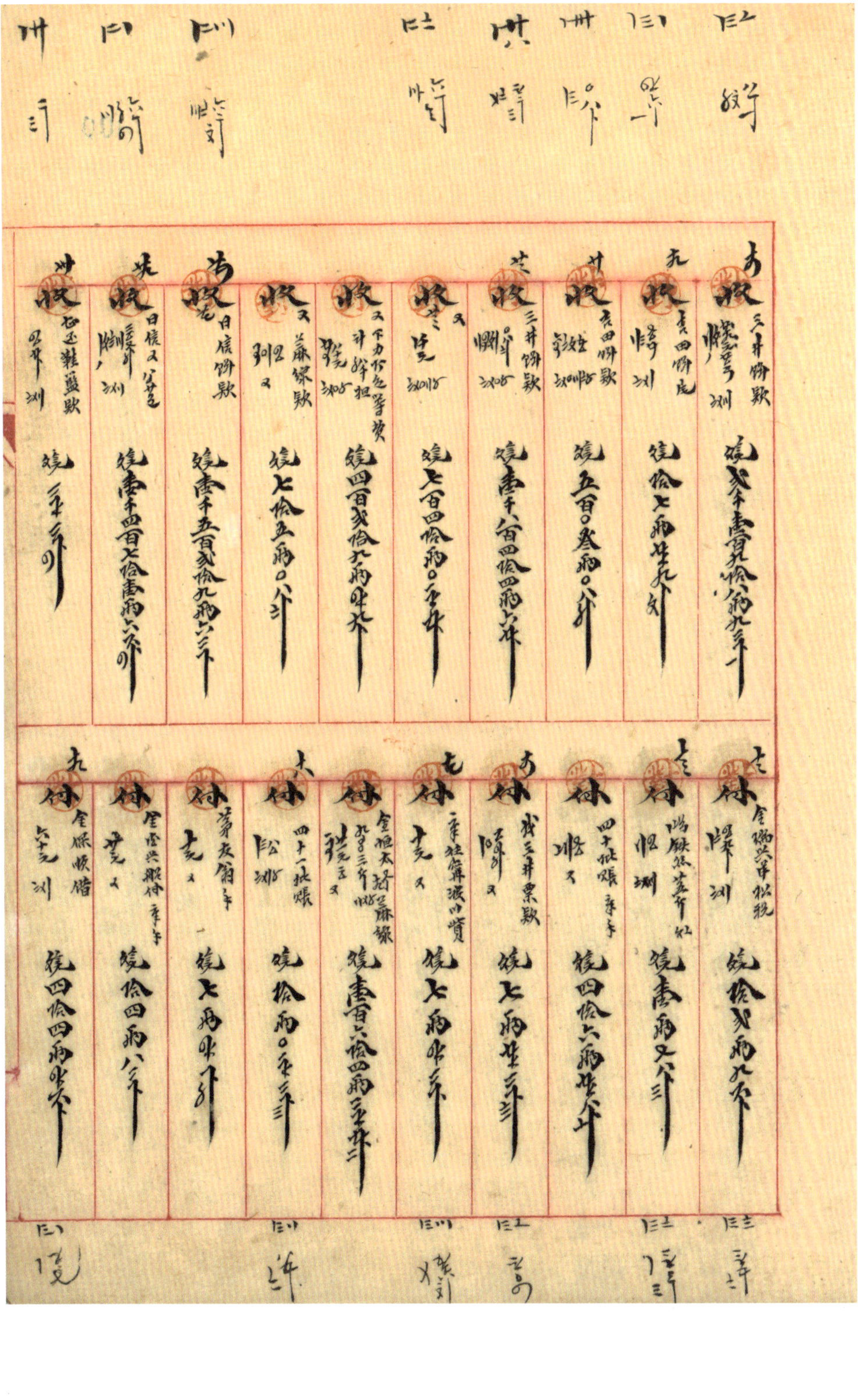

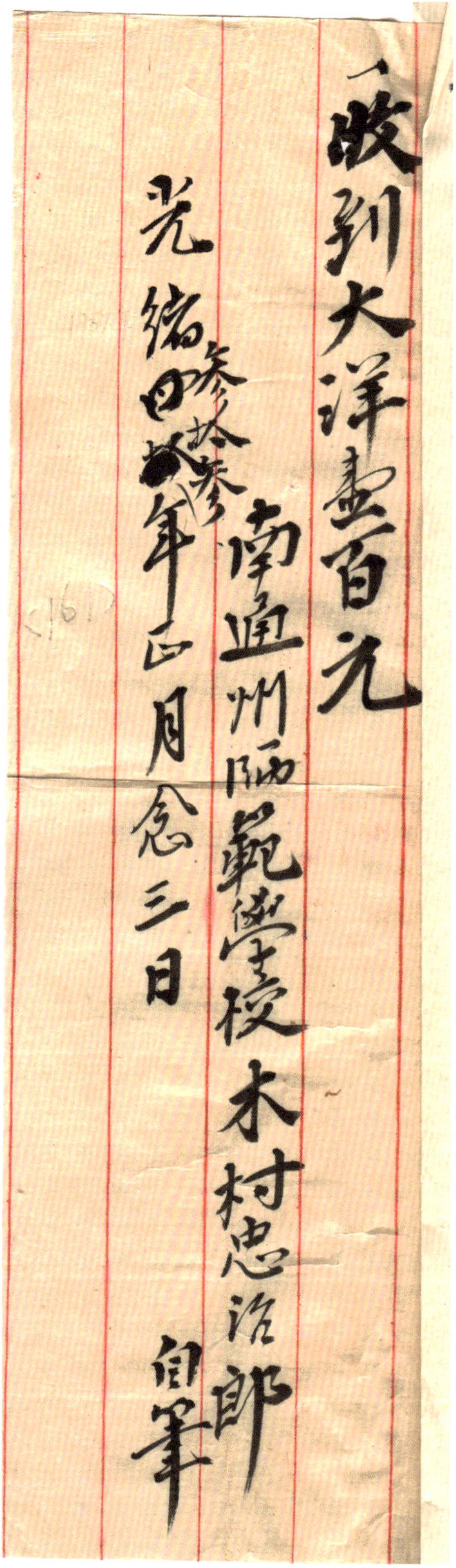
收到大洋壹百元
南通州師範學校木村忠治郎
光緒叁拾叁年正月念三日
自筆

1907 年 3 月 7 日，通州师范学校的日籍教师木村忠治郎在大生沪所领取洋 100 元的收条。

1907 年，大生沪所代理通州女子师范学校购置物件的账目。

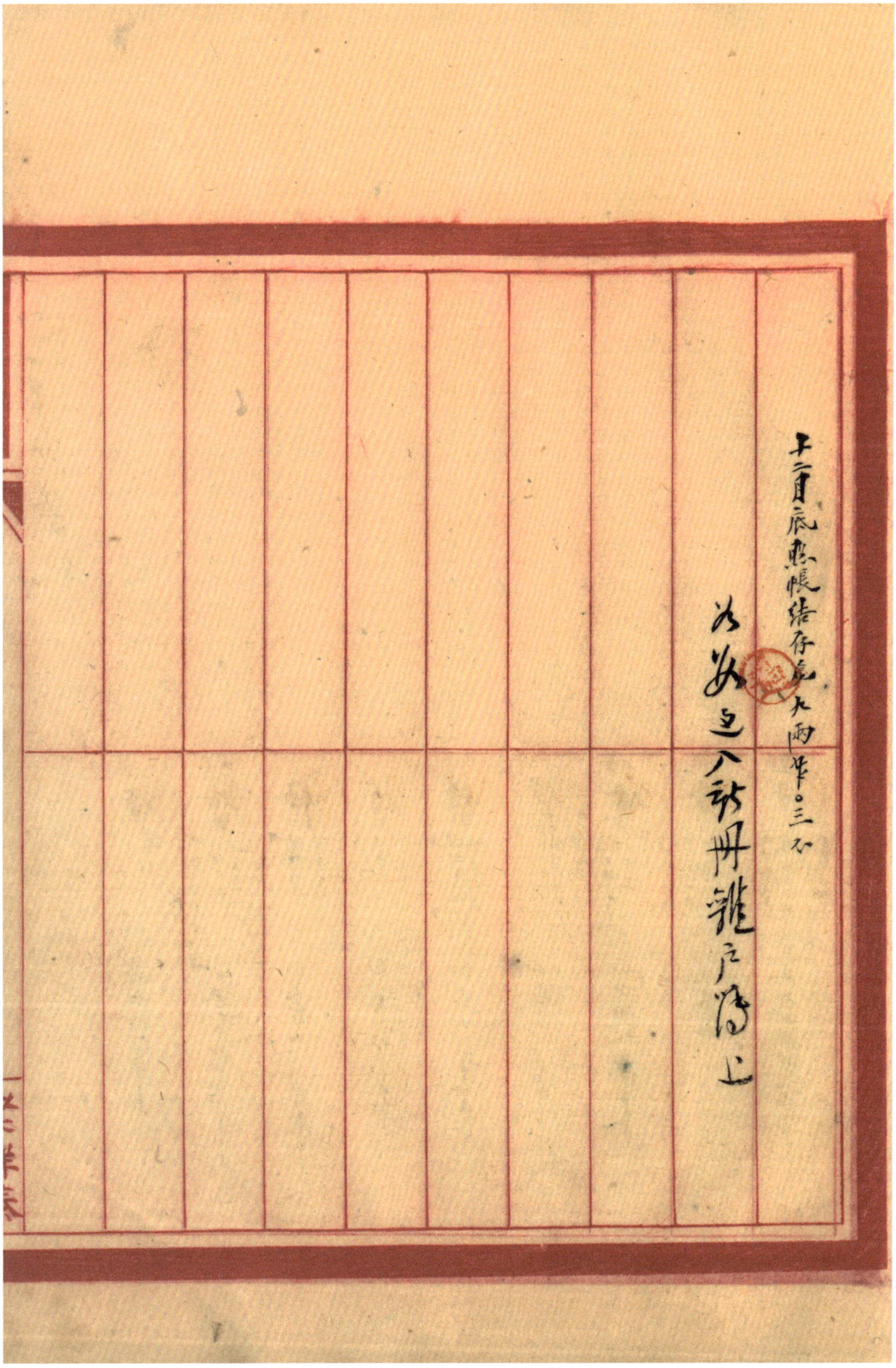

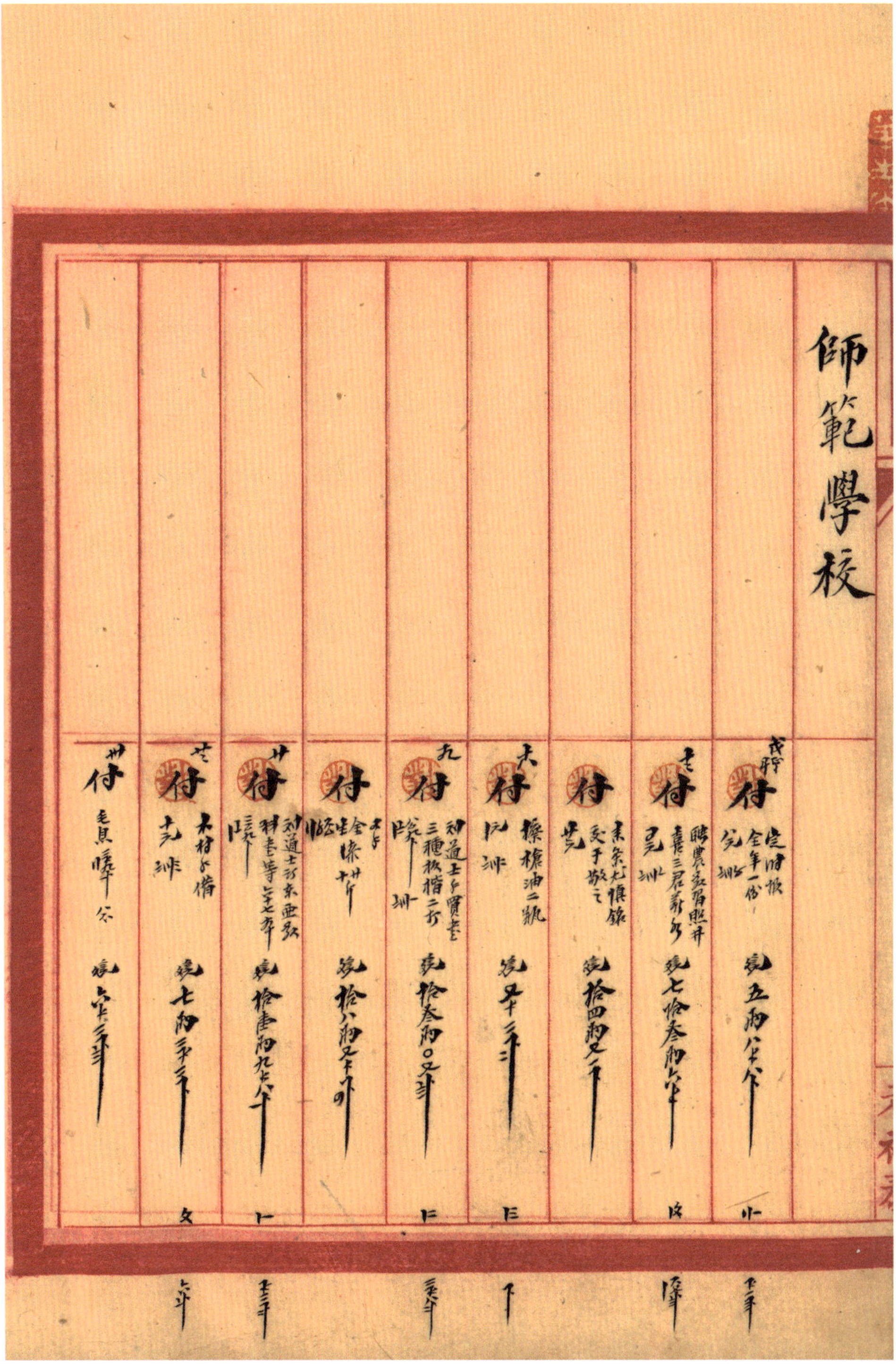

1907年，大生沪所代理通州师范学校办理庶务的账目。

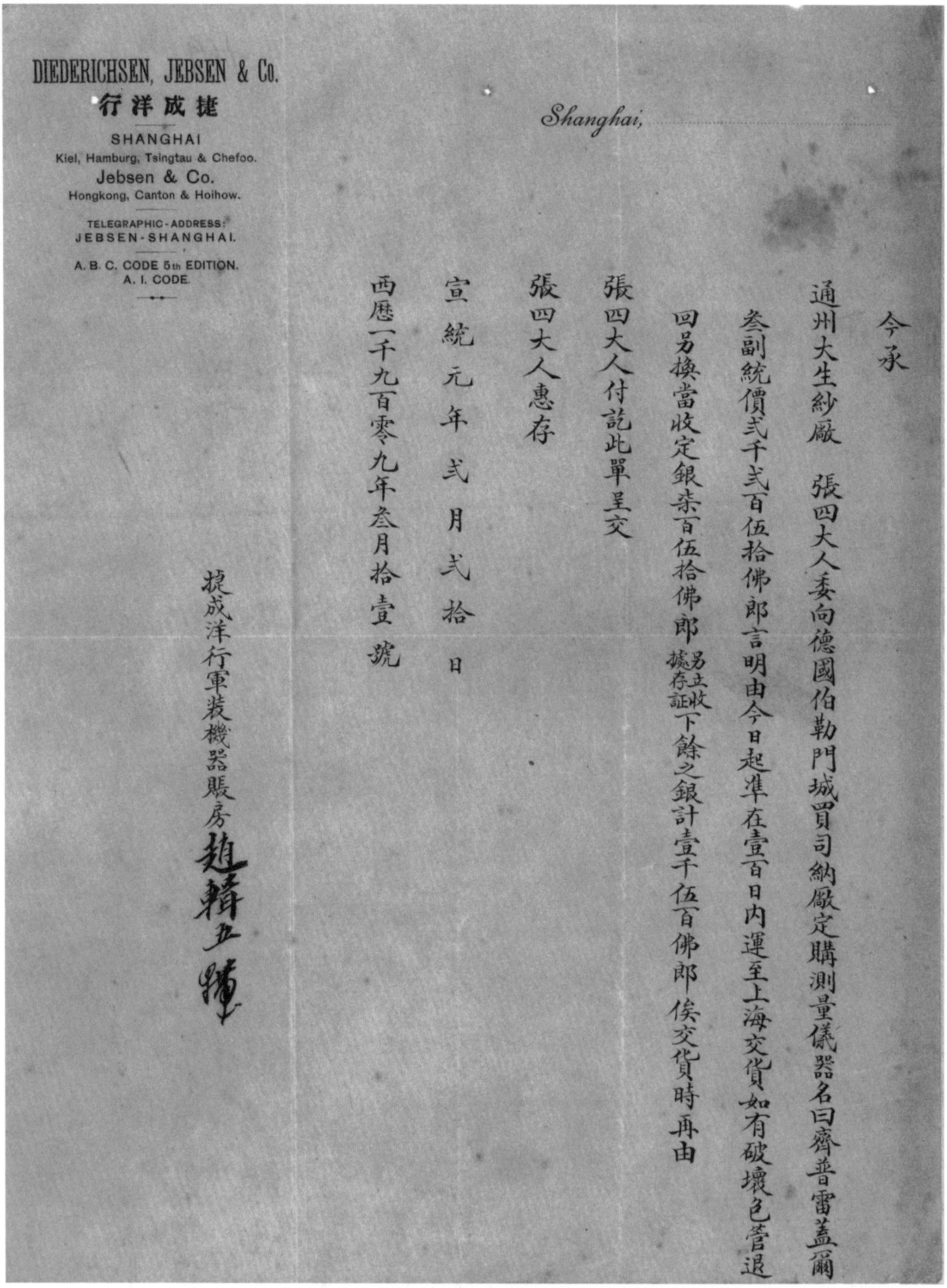
DIEDERICHSEN, JEBSEN & Co.
捷成洋行
SHANGHAI
Kiel, Hamburg, Tsingtau & Chefoo.
Jebsen & Co.
Hongkong, Canton & Hoihow.
TELEGRAPHIC-ADDRESS:
JEBSEN-SHANGHAI.
A. B. C. CODE 5th EDITION.
A. I. CODE.

Shanghai,

今承
通州大生紗廠　張四大人委向德國伯勒門城買司納廠定購測量儀器名曰齊普雷蓋爾叁副統價弍千弍百伍拾佛郎言明由今日起準在壹百日内運至上海交貨如有破壞包管退回另換當收定銀柒百伍拾佛郎另立收據存証下餘之銀計壹千伍百佛郎俟交貨時再由
張四大人付訖此單呈交
張四大人惠存
宣統元年弍月弍拾日
西歷一千九百零九年叁月拾壹號
捷成洋行軍装機器賬房趙輯五謹

1909 年 3 月 21 日，张謇委托捷成洋行购买测绘仪器的合同。

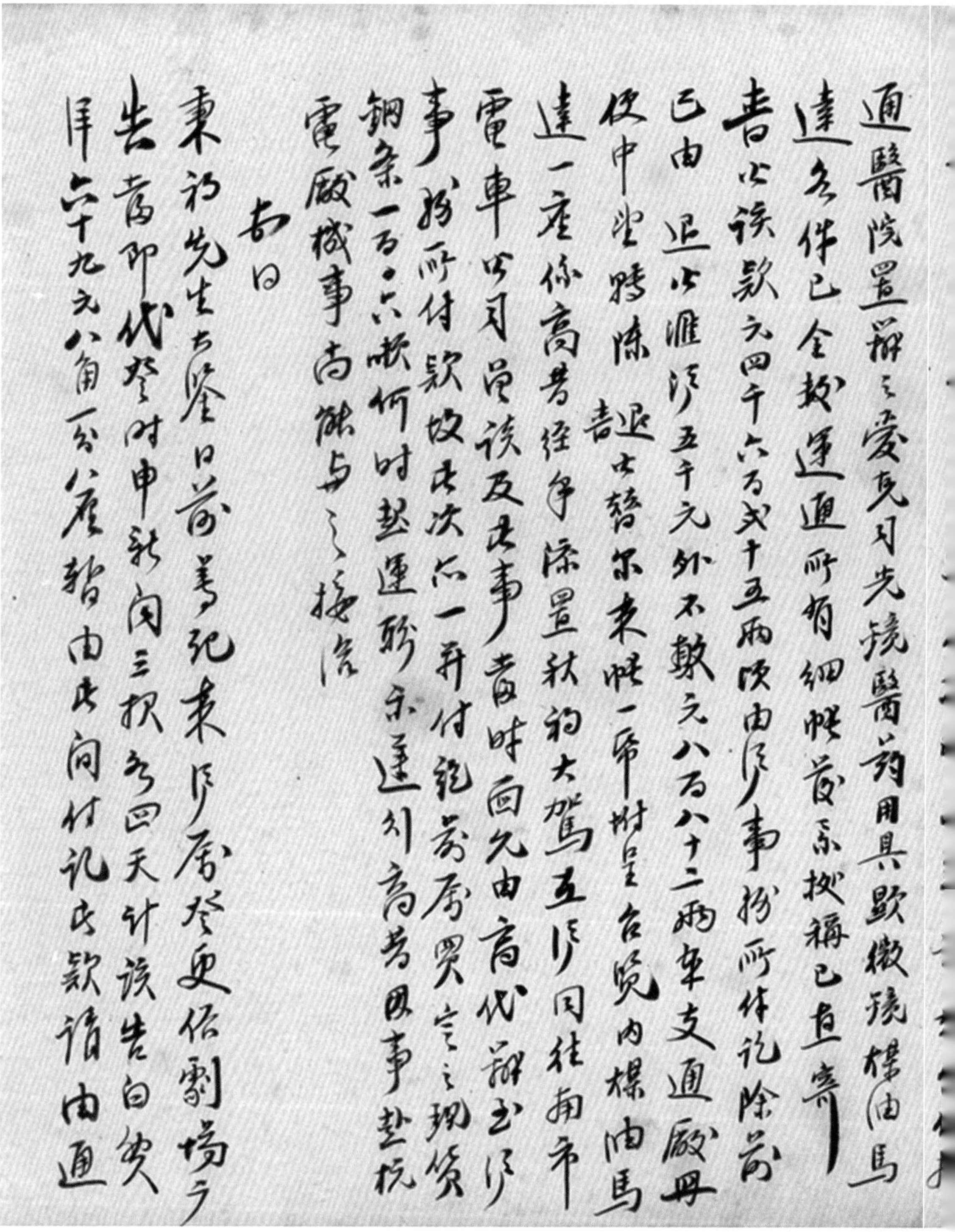

1919 年 11 月 7 日，大生沪所所长吴寄尘给徐广镕的为南通医院购置 X 光机、显微镜、煤油马达等件的信函留底。

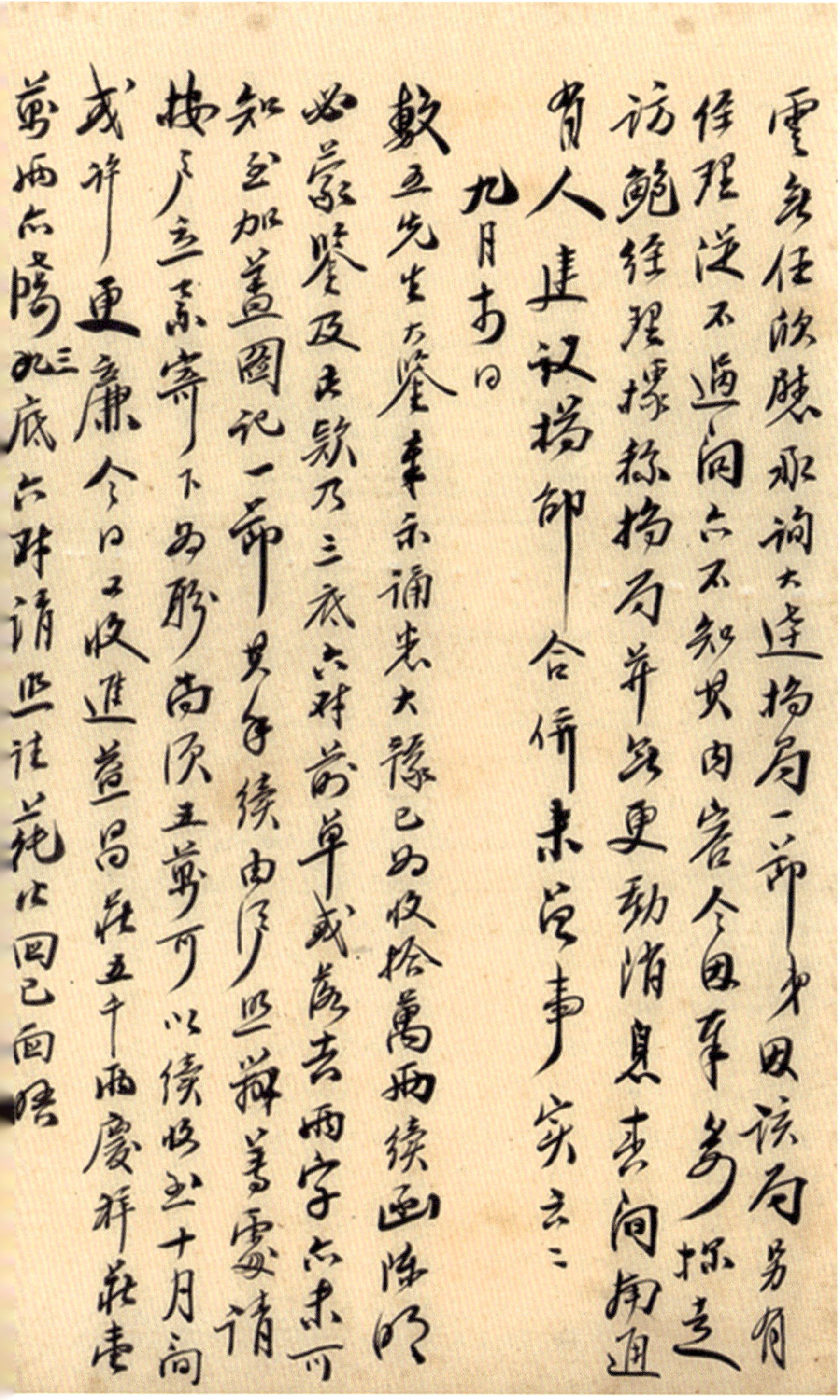
電悉。任欣購取詢大達揚局一節，業因該局另有
條理，從不過問，亦不知其內容。今因革參探達
訪，鮑經理據稱揚局并無更動消息，亦向揚通
貴人建議揚部，合併未宜事實云云。
九月十四日
敷五先生大鑒：奉示誦悉。大豫已如收拾，萬兩續匯。除照
必蒙鑒及。去款乃三底六對，前單載簽名兩字，亦未可
知。並加蓋圖記一節，其手續由□照辦著，要請
接之。立票寄下，如股尚須五萬，可以續收。並十月向
成祥、更康今日亦收進，蓋昌莊五千兩，慶祥莊壹
萬兩，亦照九三底、六對請照往莊收回，已面晤

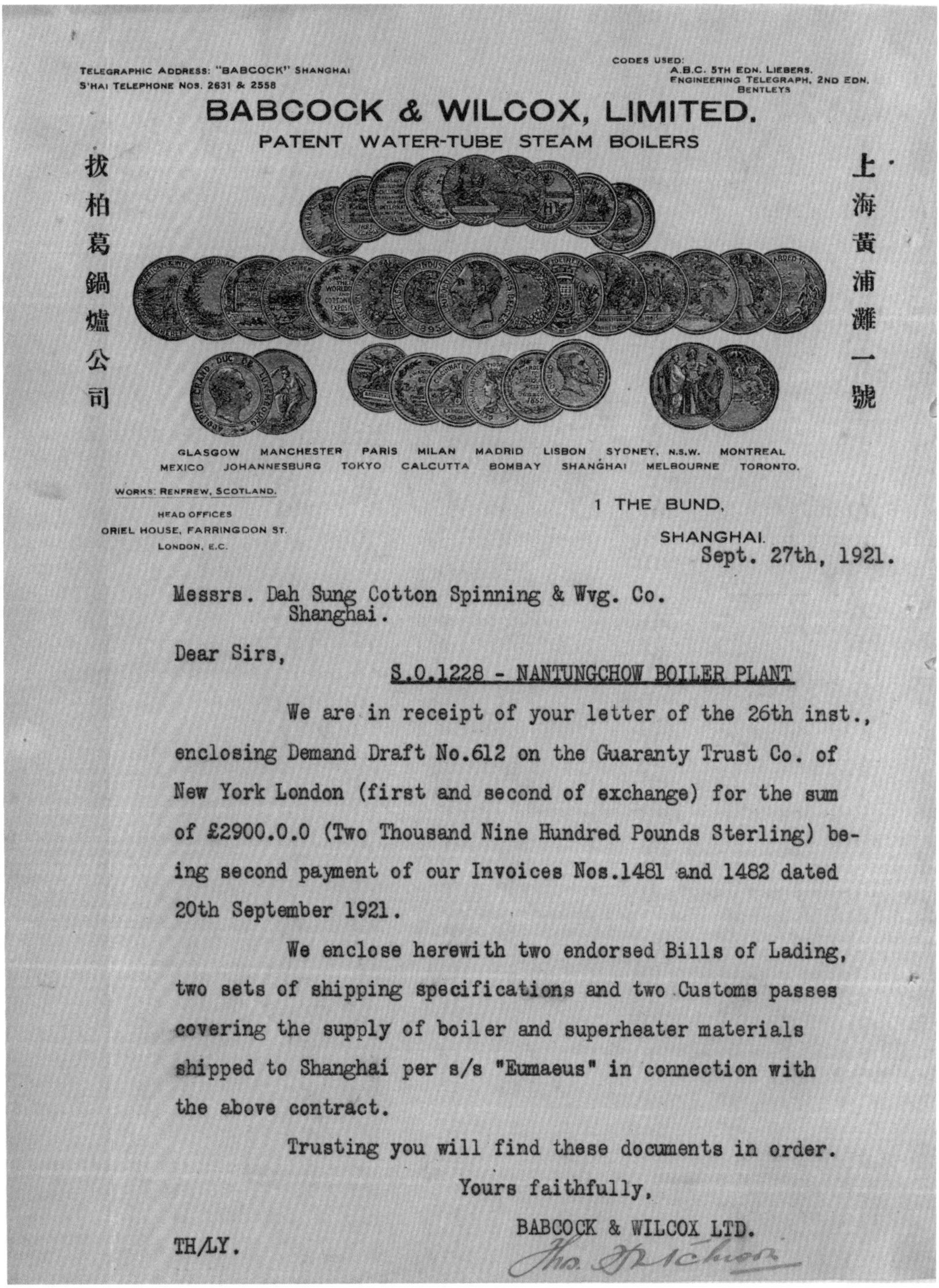

TELEGRAPHIC ADDRESS: "BABCOCK" SHANGHAI
S'HAI TELEPHONE NOS. 2631 & 2558

CODES USED:
A.B.C. 5TH EDN. LIEBERS.
ENGINEERING TELEGRAPH, 2ND EDN.
BENTLEYS

BABCOCK & WILCOX, LIMITED.

PATENT WATER-TUBE STEAM BOILERS

拔柏葛鍋爐公司

上海黃浦灘一號

GLASGOW MANCHESTER PARIS MILAN MADRID LISBON SYDNEY, N.S.W. MONTREAL
MEXICO JOHANNESBURG TOKYO CALCUTTA BOMBAY SHANGHAI MELBOURNE TORONTO.

WORKS: RENFREW, SCOTLAND.

HEAD OFFICES
ORIEL HOUSE, FARRINGDON ST.
LONDON, E.C.

1 THE BUND,
SHANGHAI.
Sept. 27th, 1921.

Messrs. Dah Sung Cotton Spinning & Wvg. Co.
Shanghai.

Dear Sirs,

S.O.1228 - NANTUNGCHOW BOILER PLANT

We are in receipt of your letter of the 26th inst., enclosing Demand Draft No.612 on the Guaranty Trust Co. of New York London (first and second of exchange) for the sum of £2900.0.0 (Two Thousand Nine Hundred Pounds Sterling) being second payment of our Invoices Nos.1481 and 1482 dated 20th September 1921.

We enclose herewith two endorsed Bills of Lading, two sets of shipping specifications and two Customs passes covering the supply of boiler and superheater materials shipped to Shanghai per s/s "Eumaeus" in connection with the above contract.

Trusting you will find these documents in order.

Yours faithfully,

BABCOCK & WILCOX LTD.

TH/LY.

1921 年 9 月 27 日，拔柏葛锅炉公司致大生沪所有关锅炉和过热器付款事宜的函。

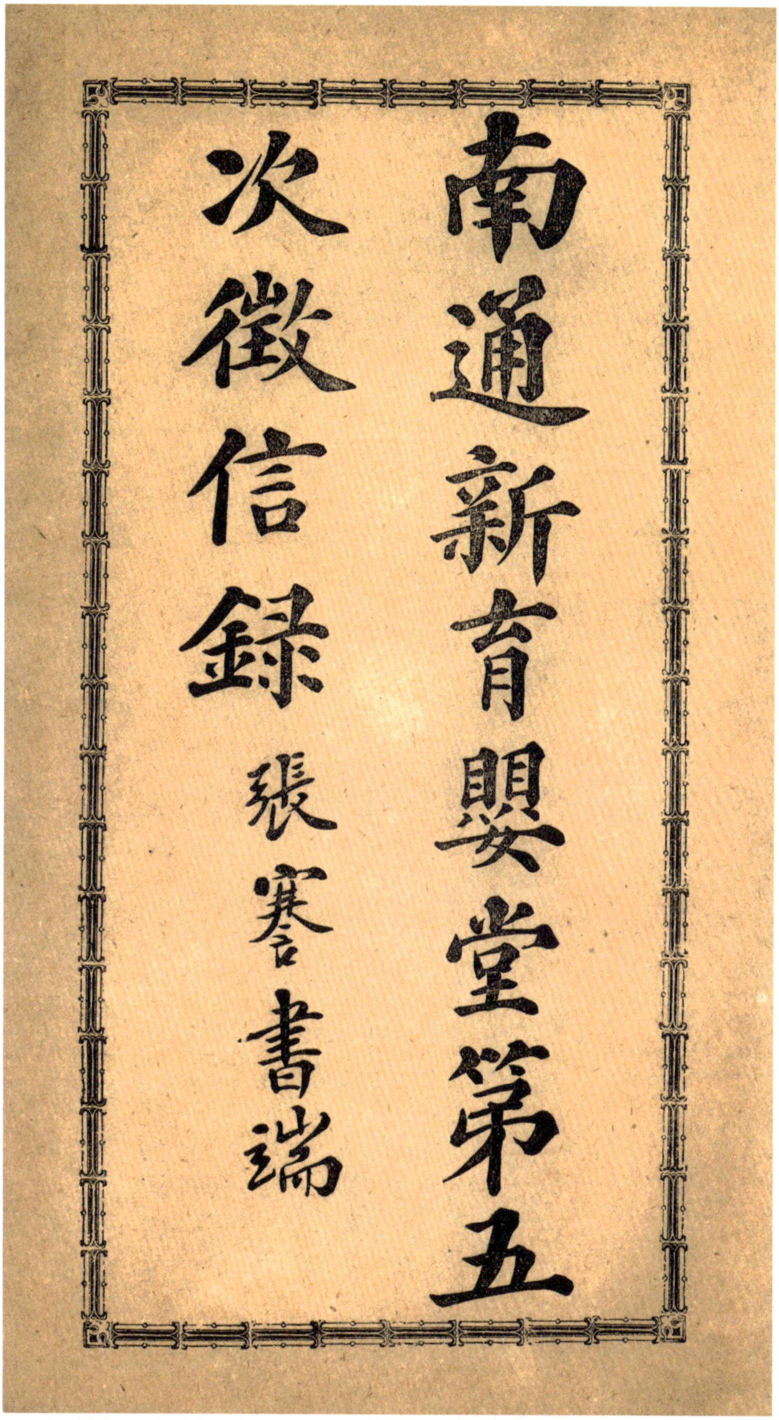
南通新育嬰堂第五次徵信錄
張謇書端

《南通新育婴堂第五次征信录》封面。南通新育婴堂是张謇在南通创办的第一个慈善机构。

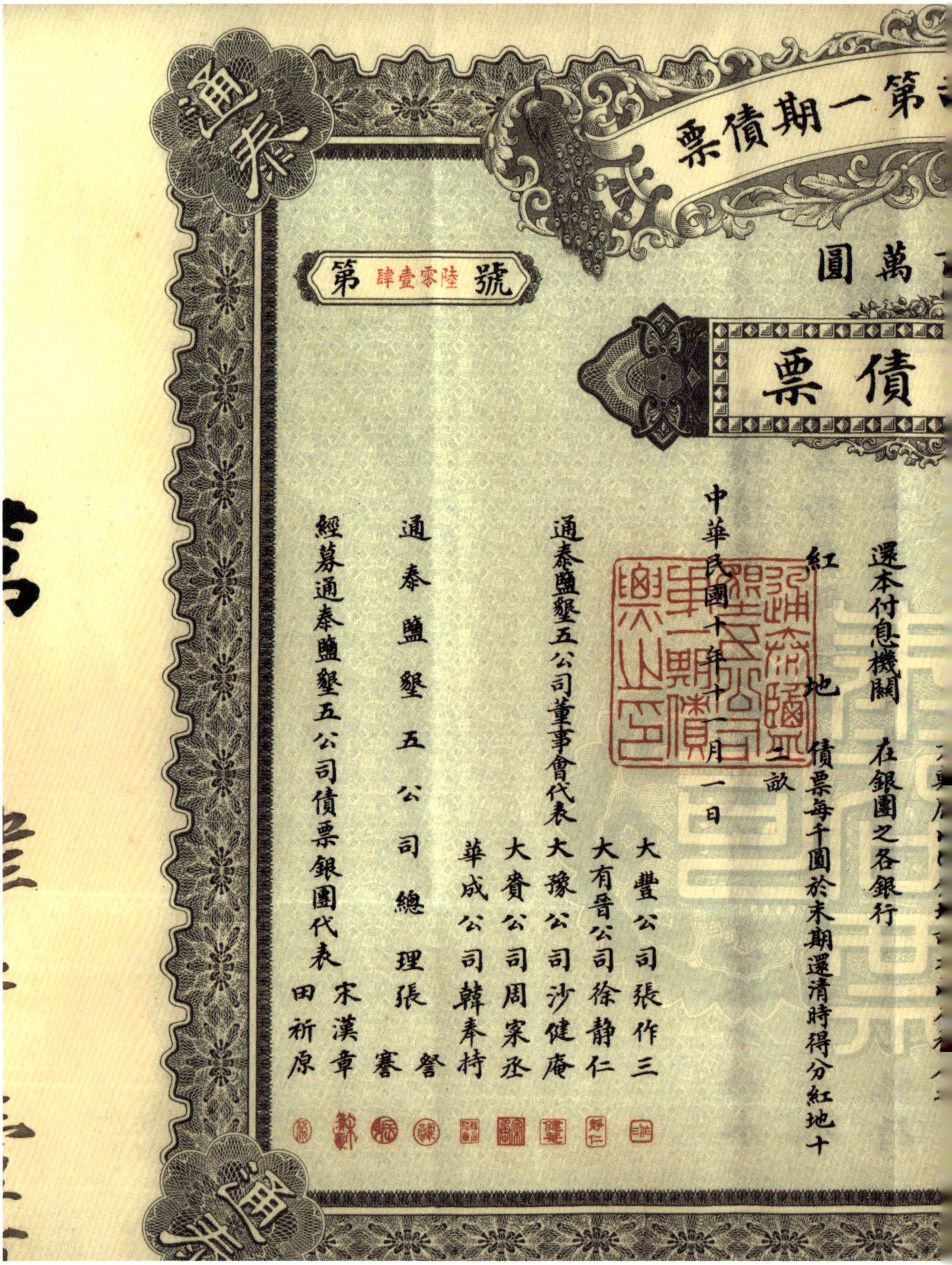
通泰
第一期債票
萬圓
第肆壹零陸號
債票
還本付息機關 在銀團之各銀行
債票每千圓於末期還清時得分紅地十二畝
中華民國十年十一月一日
通泰鹽墾五公司董事會代表
大豐公司張作三
大有晉公司徐靜仁
大豫公司沙健庵
大賚公司周家丞
華成公司韓奉持
通泰鹽墾五公司總理張謇 張詧
經募通泰鹽墾五公司債票銀團代表
宋漢章
田祈原

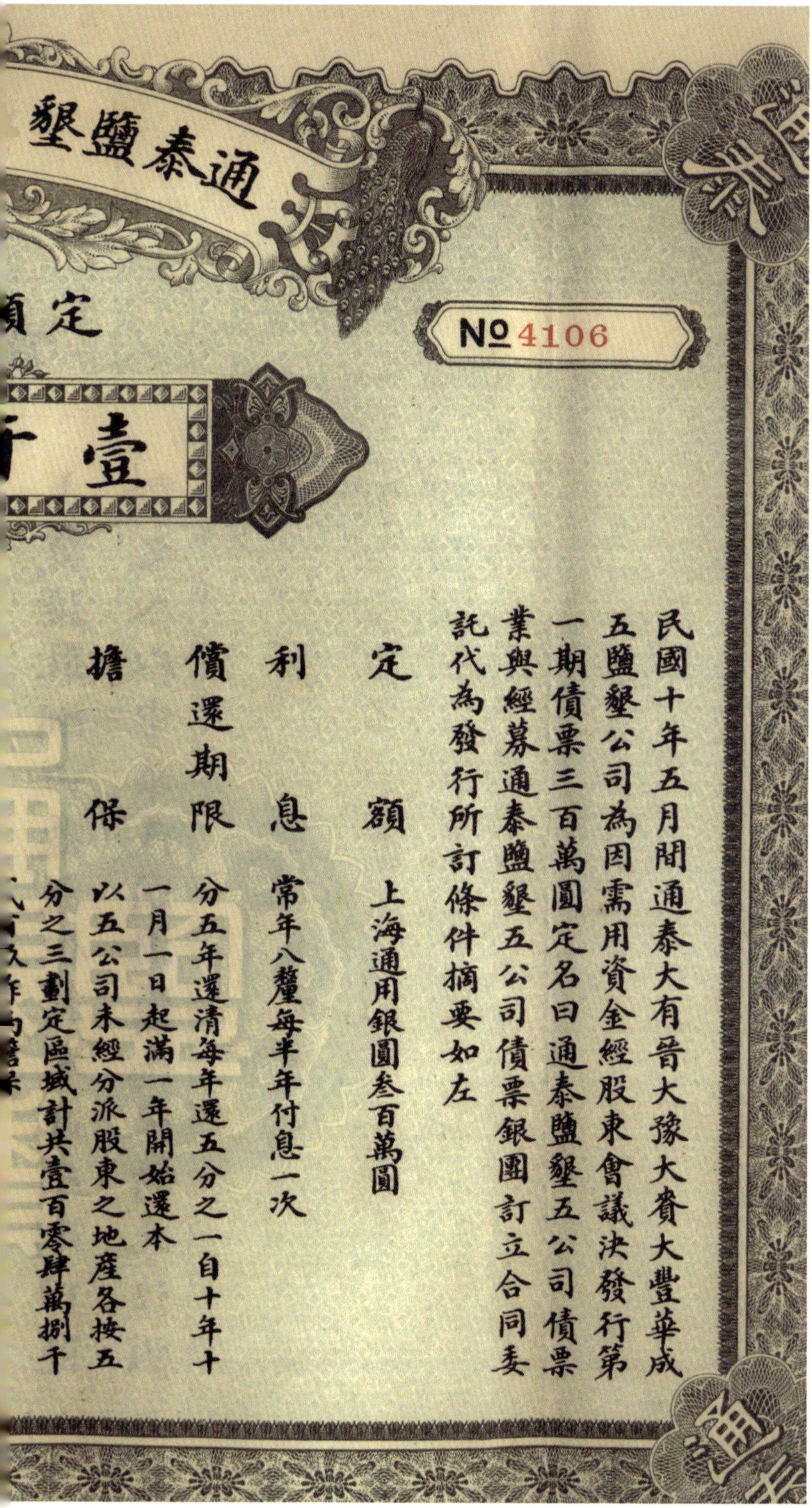
通泰鹽墾
定
№4106
壹
民國十年五月間通泰大有晉大豫大賚大豐華成五鹽墾公司為因需用資金經股東會議決發行第一期債票三百萬圓定名曰通泰鹽墾五公司債票銀團訂立合同委託代為發行所訂條件摘要如左
定額 上海通用銀圓叁百萬圓
利息 常年八釐每半年付息一次
償還期限 分五年還清每年還五分之一自十年十一月一日起滿一年開始還本
擔保 以五公司未經分派股東之地產各按五分之三劃定區域計共壹百零肆萬捌千

1921 年 11 月 1 日，通泰盐垦五公司第一期债票，这是中国历史上第一个企业债票。

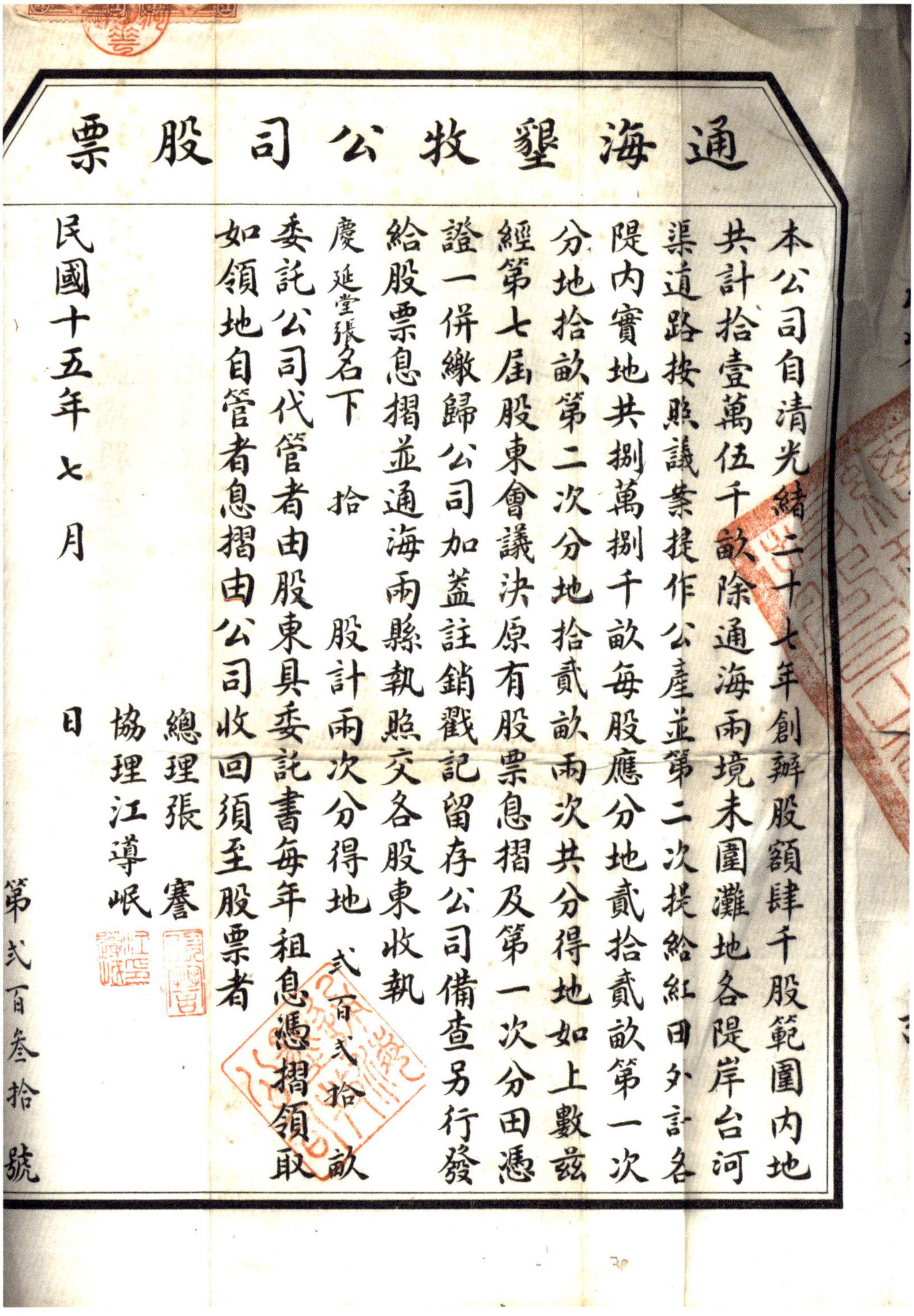
通海墾牧公司股票

本公司自清光緒二十七年創辦股額肆千股範圍內地共計拾壹萬伍千畝除通海兩境未圍灘地各隄岸台河渠道路按照議案提作公產並第二次提給紅田外計各隄內實地共捌萬捌千畝每股應分地貳拾貳畝第一次分地拾畝第二次分地拾貳畝兩次共分得地如上數茲經第七屆股東會議決原有股票息摺及第一次分田憑證一併繳歸公司加蓋註銷戳記留存公司備查另行發給股票息摺並通海兩縣執照交各股東收執

慶延堂張名下 拾 股計兩次分得地 貳百貳拾畝

委託公司代管者由股東具委託書每年租息憑摺領取

如領地自管者息摺由公司收回須至股票者

總理張謇

協理江導岷

民國十五年七月 日

第貳百叁拾號

1926 年通海垦牧公司股票。

大生第一紡織公司
藍印魁星
開設在南通縣
機器反手棉紗
DAH SUNG COTTON SPINNING & WEAVING CO., Ltd., NANTUNG

大生第一纺织公司“蓝印魁星”商标。

大生第一紡織公司副廠
金印魁星
開設在南通縣
機器順手棉紗
DAHSUNG COTTON SPINNING & WEAVING CO.Ltd., NANTUNG

大生第一纺织公司副厂“金印魁星”商标。

堆金
積玉

大生会计档案里的吉语“堆金积玉”。

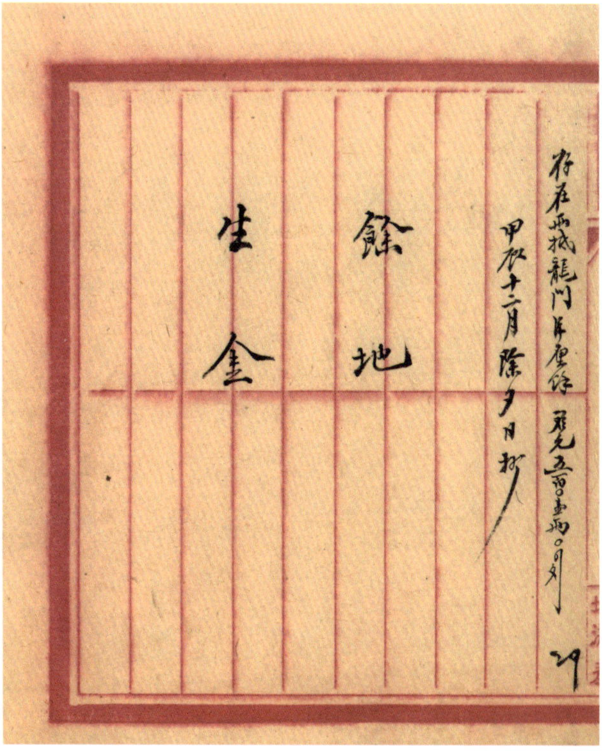
餘地
生金

大生会计档案里的吉语“余地生金”。

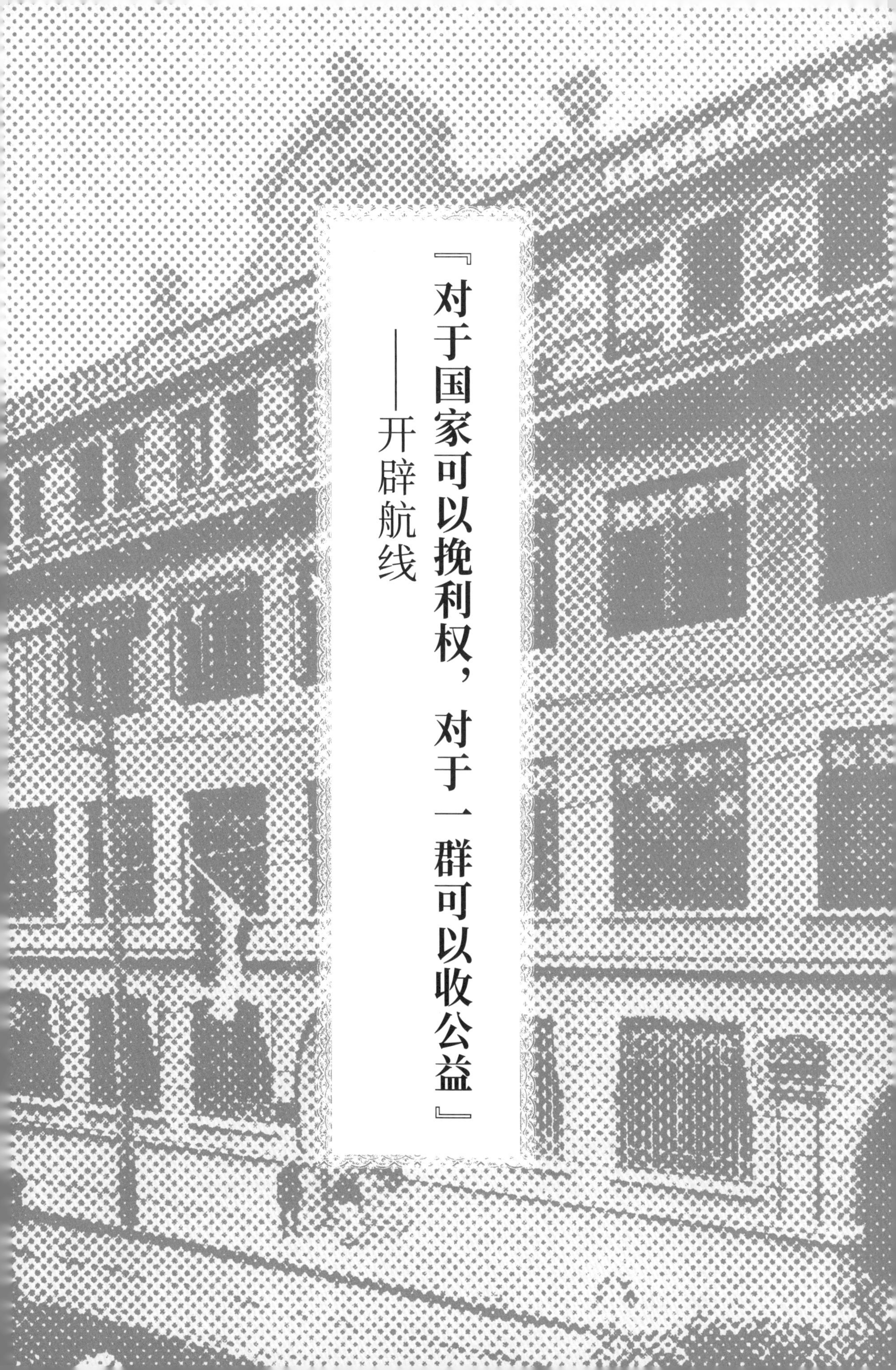

『对于国家可以挽利权，对于一群可以收公益』

——开辟航线

1905年，张謇在创办天生港大达轮步公司时，呼吁社会各界踊跃入股。张謇指出，创办航运公司，“对于国家可以挽利权，对于一群可以收公益”，就是通过投资既可以帮助国家争取经济上的权益，也是为社会做贡献。张謇先后在上海创办大生轮船公司和上海大达轮步公司，并通过在南通设立大达内河轮船公司、天生港大达轮步公司等航运企业，加强了南通与上海的经济和社会联系，有效地促进了区域的现代化进程。

大生纱厂筹办时期，需要从上海运送大量的机器和物料到南通，依靠的是水路运输。从目前掌握的史料看，官机是通过两江总督刘坤一所派的兵轮经长江运到天生港，再由小轮驳运到唐家闸。1897年12月1日的《申报》第5版，刊登《通州大生纱厂告白》，其中有：“机器由南洋派威靖兵轮船装运通州，业于本月十八日开运。”其他物件，则通过大生纱厂雇佣的民船运载。

1899年5月23日，大生纱厂开工纺纱。不久张謇请示刘坤一，大生纱厂准备租用专船。张謇告诉刘坤一，大生纱厂的官机由于锈蚀严重，根据英国工程师汤姆斯的意见，需要添置和更换的部件，价值至少七八万元。由于大生纱厂初创，资金紧张，不能一下子全部添购，只能分批从上海购进。而每一单购货，从订单寄出到收到物件，耗时都需要十天，甚至半个月。原因在于租赁的民船装货需要三天，等候涨潮开行有时需要两三天甚至五六天，等候海关查验需要七八天，辗转迟延，拖了大生纱厂的后腿。

张謇的解决方案是大生纱厂自备一条小轮船。大生纱厂租用宁波帮商人朱葆三的“济安”小轮船，改名为“大生”。“大生”轮从上海经内河往苏州，从常熟的浒浦过长江。因为租金昂贵，所以张謇希望能够参照开平矿务局运煤船搭客的惯例，让“大生”轮在运送物料经过浒浦的时候顺道搭载来往的客商，用水脚来贴补租金。张謇承诺“大生”轮接受厘局的查验，不夹带物料之外的私货，也不在南通的芦泾港逗留搭客，以免与招商局、太古洋行和怡和洋行这三家在芦泾港上下客的轮船发生纠葛。刘坤一认为大生纱厂“系官商合办，事关便商利运，应照准行”。

1900年农历五月，大生纱厂交给朱葆三股银5000元，按照约定，朱葆三应该在六月上旬将船开到上海修理，七月上旬开行通州、常熟、海门等地。之后不知何故，朱葆三在宁波将轮船转售，导致“济安”股东的不满，引发诉讼。张謇又通过刘坤一转饬宁波道台，才了结案件。迟至1901年的农历四月，轮船抵沪。由于停久失修，船身受损，再加船上物件缺失，导致修补费用增加。南通方面续入股银7000元，朱葆三方面作为沪股共入股2万元，通沪合计股本3.2万元。

1901年农历五月，“大生”轮开始行驶。大生档案里保存着当月张蕴卿、施星舫承揽“大生”轮在浒浦搭客的业务合同。按照合同，张蕴卿、施星舫负责筹资建造洋棚、购置划船，对上下船的客商妥为照料。不久“大生”轮不再走浒浦和通州，专门航行于上海和海门之间。此举招致一些股东的不满，认为与原先的约定不符。他们认为，通沪之间一天之内来不及行驶这个说法是不能成立的，招商局、太古洋行、怡和洋行、信安公司的轮船不就是这样走的吗？再说走浒浦的时候，“大生”轮的搭客也不少，如果按照约定来，即使亏本股东也没什么意见。

引起南通方面股东不满的，除了“大生”轮擅自改变线路外，还有其他一些原因。“大生”轮在上海修理时，“未经公议，又未公估，用费3000数百金之多，与原约之数增出，恐有不符”。原来约定的2000元修船费用，结果最后变为3000多元。南通股东认为，船从购定到抵沪，延迟了一年时间，其间增加的修理费应该由朱葆三承担。另外，按照原议，船到上海之前的200元燃料费、3个月人工费，不应该由公司负责。而最大的问题在于，朱葆三提供的“大生”轮1901年农历五月到年底的账簿，南通股东认为“未有总结，眉目不清，照帐[1]代核不符300余金”。

双方矛盾的解决，以南通股东接受朱葆三的建议，七折购买沪股而告终。从1902年8月4日（光绪二十八年七月初一）开始，“大生”轮由南通股东专办。因此，1913年5月出版的《通州兴办实业章程》收录的大生轮船公司的账略，1902年8月4日前是单独列出的，第一届账略时间为“光绪二十八年七月初一至十二月底”，第二届为“光绪二十九年（1903）正月初六开班至十二月底”，最后收录的是第八届“宣统元年（1909）正月至十二月底”。另据1921年南通大生第一纺织公司第二十三届账略，收到“大生”轮船股息“规银一千二百二十一两三钱六分”，说明至少在1921年大生轮船公司还是一个独立核算的企业。

1904年张謇与李云书等人在上海筹建上海大达轮步公司。上海大达轮步公司是张謇在上海最早兴办的企业。1904年，张謇在给南洋大臣《请设上海大达轮步公司公呈》中提及，上海浦西黄浦江岸，北自虹口，南到十六铺，凡是能够建造码头的地方，除了招商局码头外，均被洋商占据，黄浦江上桅杆林立，舳舻相继，上面飘扬的大多数是外国旗帜。十六铺往南至江海大关一带，处于华界，是建设码头的理想地带。张謇等人发起，在十六铺至老太平码头一带购地建筑轮步，同时建造栈房。

上海大达轮步公司开辟的至南通和扬州的航线，便利了南通及周边地区与上海的人财物交流，也有助于南通更快更多地接受来自上海的经济与文化辐射。上海大达轮步公司是张謇长江航运蓝图的核心，其配套

1 “帐”即“账”，本书图注、引文与图片保持一致，仍用“帐”。

工程是南通建立天生港大达轮步公司，并推动天生港自开商埠。开埠，是提升南通地位、促进南通及周边地区发展的战略措施。而前提条件之一，是南通与上海之间有着固定的航班。这套组合拳是建立在南通实业有一定基础之上的，是高水平规划南通开放发展的举措。

张謇通过创办系列航运公司，为大生系统的企业经营提供了便利，更是在社会层面将南通与上海等经济发达地区紧密联系起来，并通过上海这个中国的对外贸易中心和国际航运中心与世界相沟通。

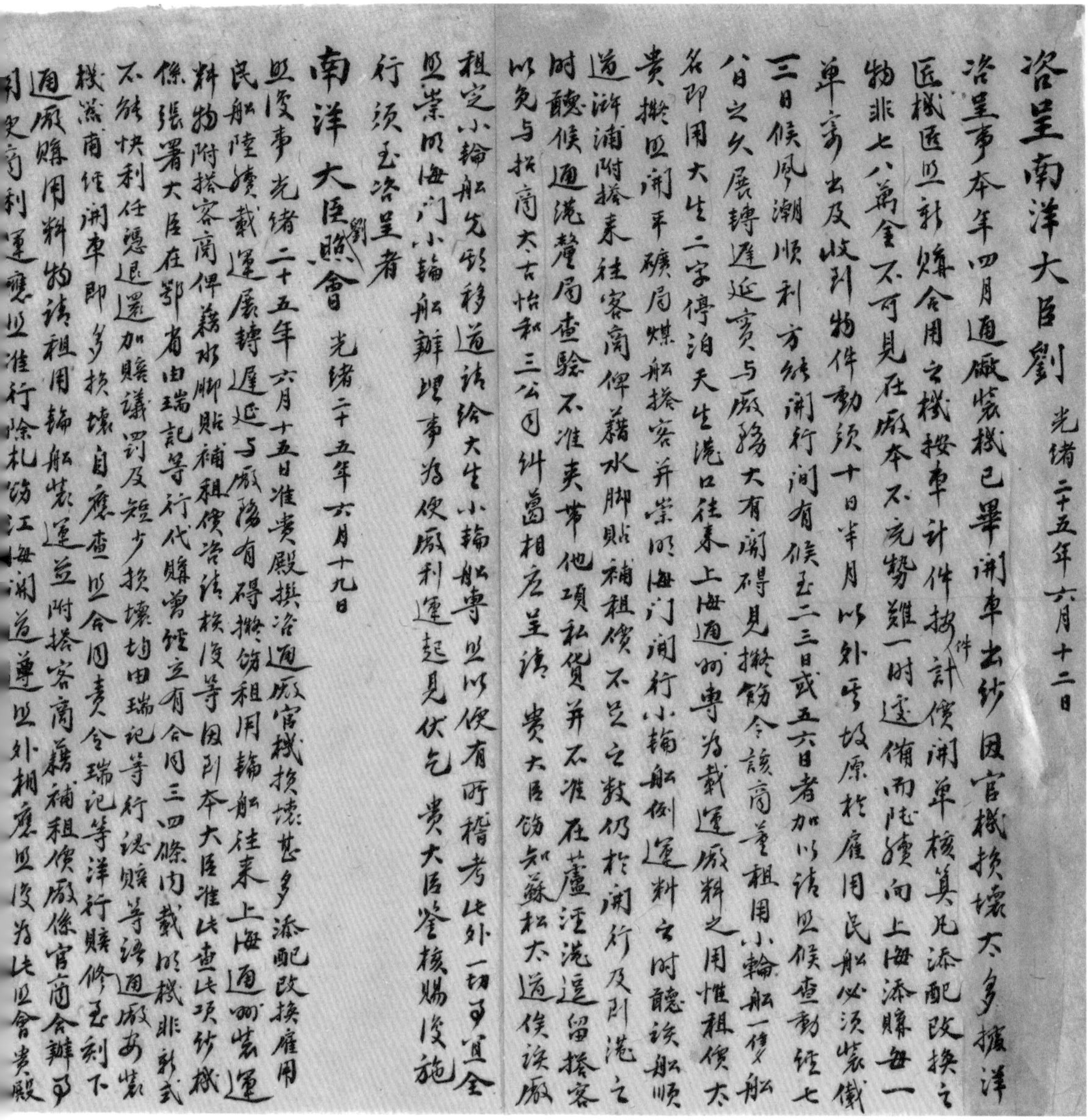

咨呈南洋大臣劉 光緒二十五年六月十二日

咨呈事本年四月通廠紗機已畢開車出紗因官機損壞太多擬洋匠機匠照新定合用之機按車計件擬件計價開單核算凡添配改換之物非七八萬金不可見在廠本不充勢難一時遽備而陸續向上海添購每一單寄出及收到物件動須十日半月以外故原於雇用民船必須紗機三日候風潮順利方能開行間有候至二三日或五六日者加以請照候查動經七八日之久展轉遲延實與廠務大有關礙見擬飭令該商董租用小輪船一隻船名即用大生二字停泊天生港口往來上海通州專為載運廠料之用惟租價太貴擬照開平礦局煤船搭客并崇明海門開行小輪船例運料之時聽該船順道沿浦附搭來往客商俾藉水脚貼補租價不足之數仍於開行及到港之時聽候通港釐局查驗不准夾帶他項私貨并不准在蘆涇港逗留搭客以免與招商太古怡和三公司糾葛相應呈請貴大臣飭知蘇松太道俟該廠租定小輪船先行移道請給大生小輪船專照以便有所稽考此外一切事宜全照崇明海門小輪船辦理事為便廠利運起見伏乞貴大臣鑒核賜准施行須至咨呈者

南洋大臣劉照會 光緒二十五年六月十九日

照復事光緒二十五年六月十五日准貴殿撰咨通廠官機損壞甚多添配改換雇用民船陸續載運展轉遲延與廠務有礙擬飭租用輪船往來上海通州裝運料物附搭客商俾藉水脚貼補租價咨請核復等因到本大臣准此查此項紗機係張署大臣在鄂省由瑞記等行代購曾經立有合同三四條內載明機非新式不能快利任憑退還加賠議罰及短少損壞均由瑞記等行認賠等語通廠安裝機器開車即多損壞自應查照合同責令瑞記等洋行賠修至剎下通廠購用料物請租用輪船裝運並附搭客商藉補租價廠係官商合辦事[illegible]史商利運應照准行除札飭江海關道遵照外相應照復為此照會貴殿

1899 年 7 月 19 日，张謇致南洋大臣刘坤一函，拟租用小轮行驶于上海与南通之间；7 月 26 日，刘坤一照会张謇，同意施行。

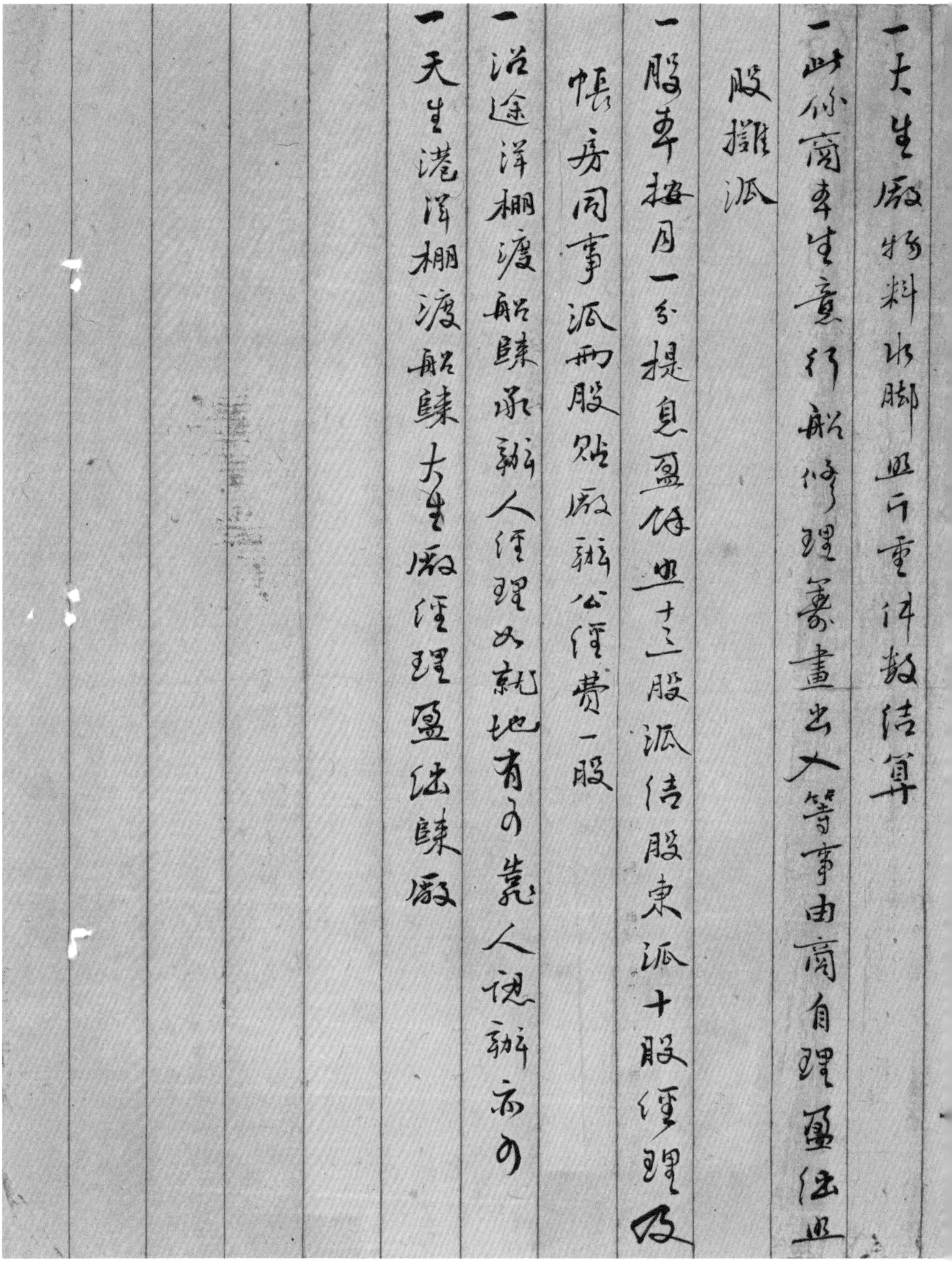

一大生廠物料水脚照斤重件數結算

一此係商本生意行船修理籌畫出入等事由商自理盈絀照

股攤派

一股本按月一分提息盈餘照十三股派給股東派十股經理及

帳房同事派兩股貼廠辦公經費一股

一沿途洋棚渡船躉承辦人經理如就地有可靠人諉辦亦可

一天生港洋棚渡船躉大生廠經理盈絀躉廠

《合办上海至通州天生港轮船草议合同》。

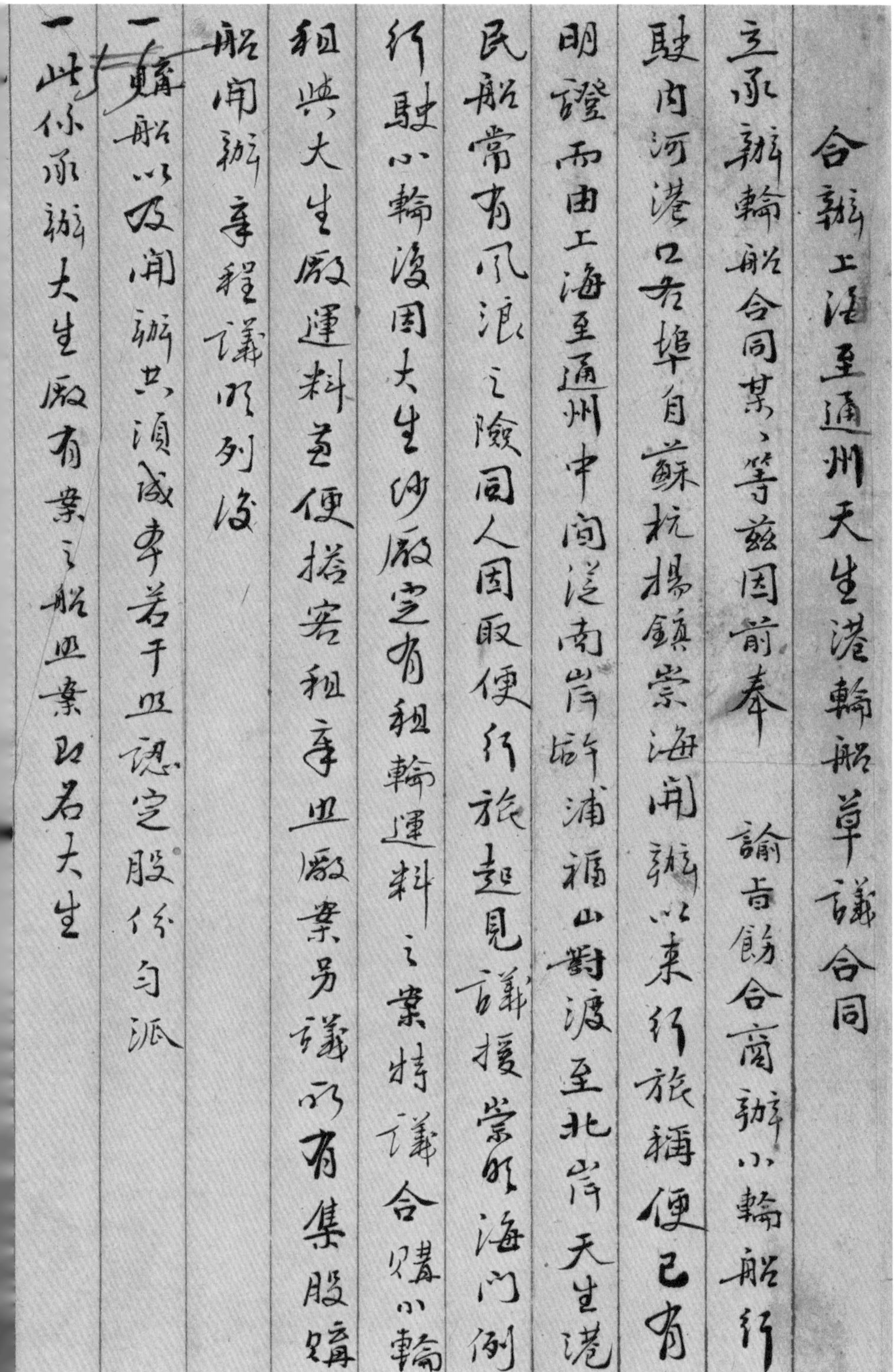
合辦上海至通州天生港輪船草議合同

立承辦輪船合同某某等茲因前奉
諭旨飭合商辦小輪船行駛內河港口各埠自蘇杭揚鎮崇海開辦以來行旅稱便已有明證而由上海至通州中間從南岸許浦福山對渡至北岸天生港民船常有風浪之險同人因取便行旅起見議援崇明海門例行駛小輪復因大生紗廠定有租輪運料之案特議合購小輪租與大生廠運料並便搭客租率照廠案另議所有集股購船開辦章程議明列後

一購船以及開辦共須成本若干照認定股份勻派

一此係承辦大生廠有案之船照案即名大生

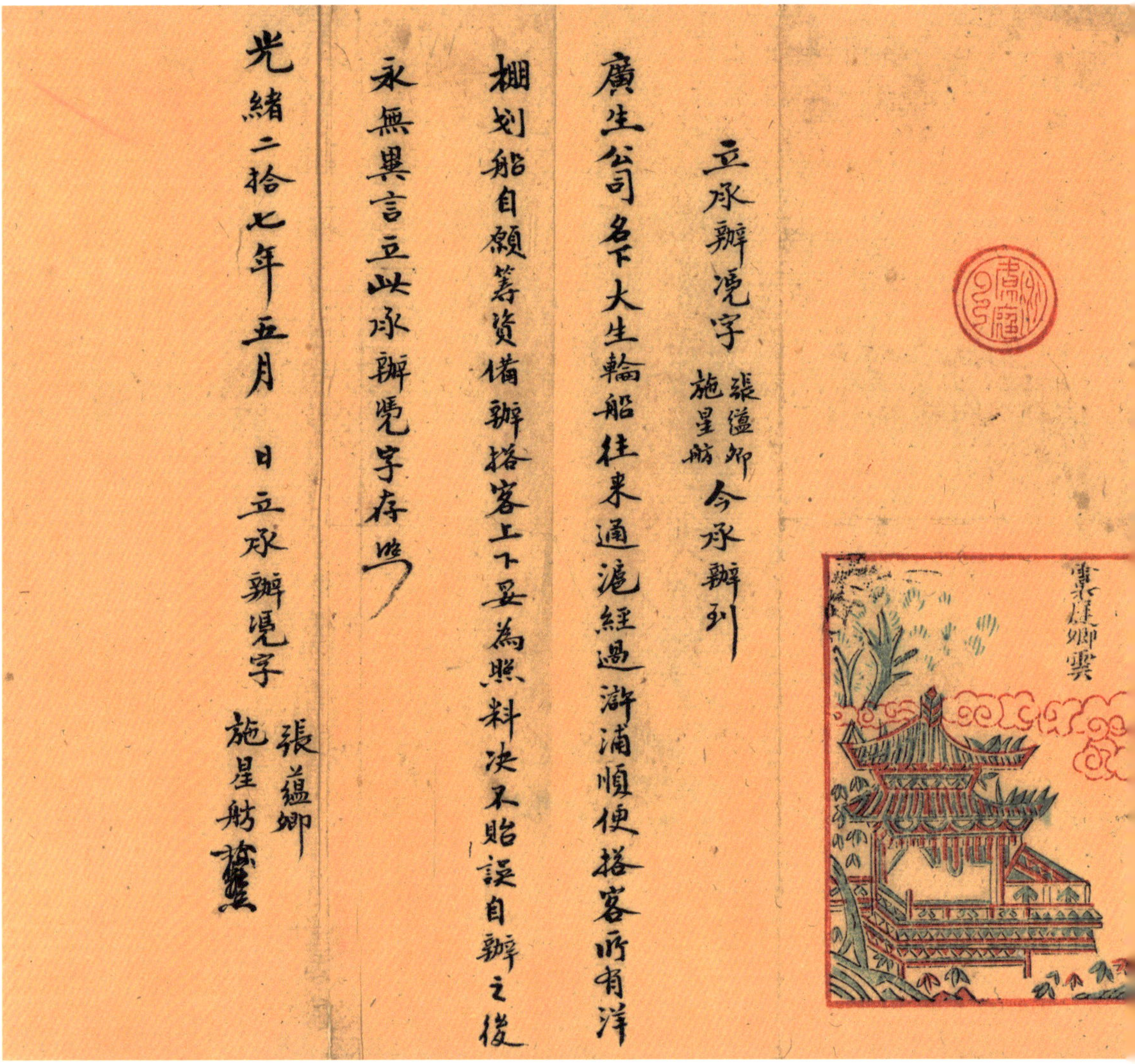

立承辦凴字 張蘊卿 施星舫 今承辦到
廣生公司名下大生輪船往来通滬經過滸浦順便搭客所有洋
棚划船自願籌資備辦搭客上下妥為照料决不貽誤自辦之後
永無異言立此承辦凴字存照
光緒二拾七年五月　日立承辦凴字 張蘊卿 施星舫

1901 年 6 月，张蕴卿、施星舫承办“大生”轮船在浒浦码头上下客业务的合同。

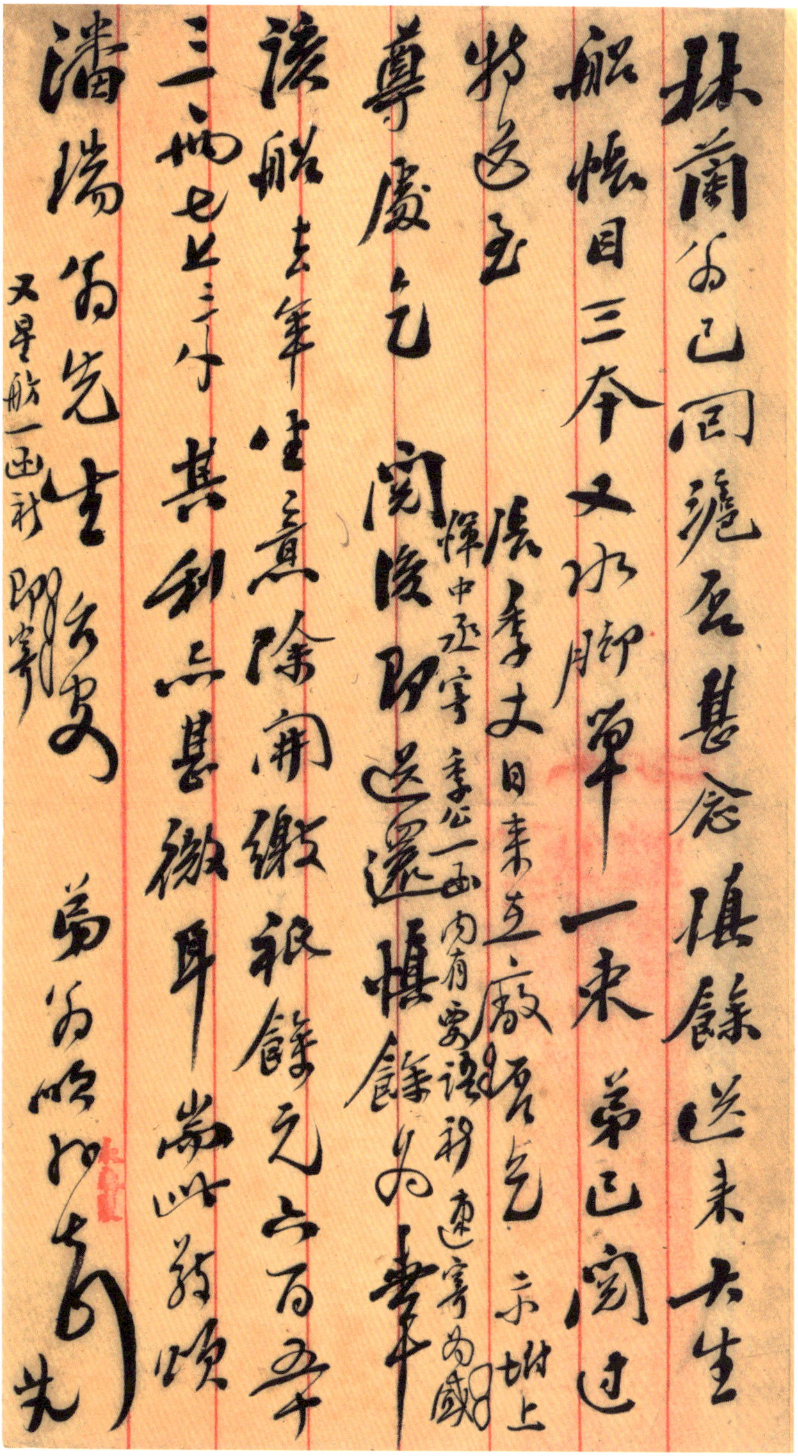

翁顺孙致函大生沪所潘瑞徵，告知送来“大生”轮船三本账本和一批水脚单。

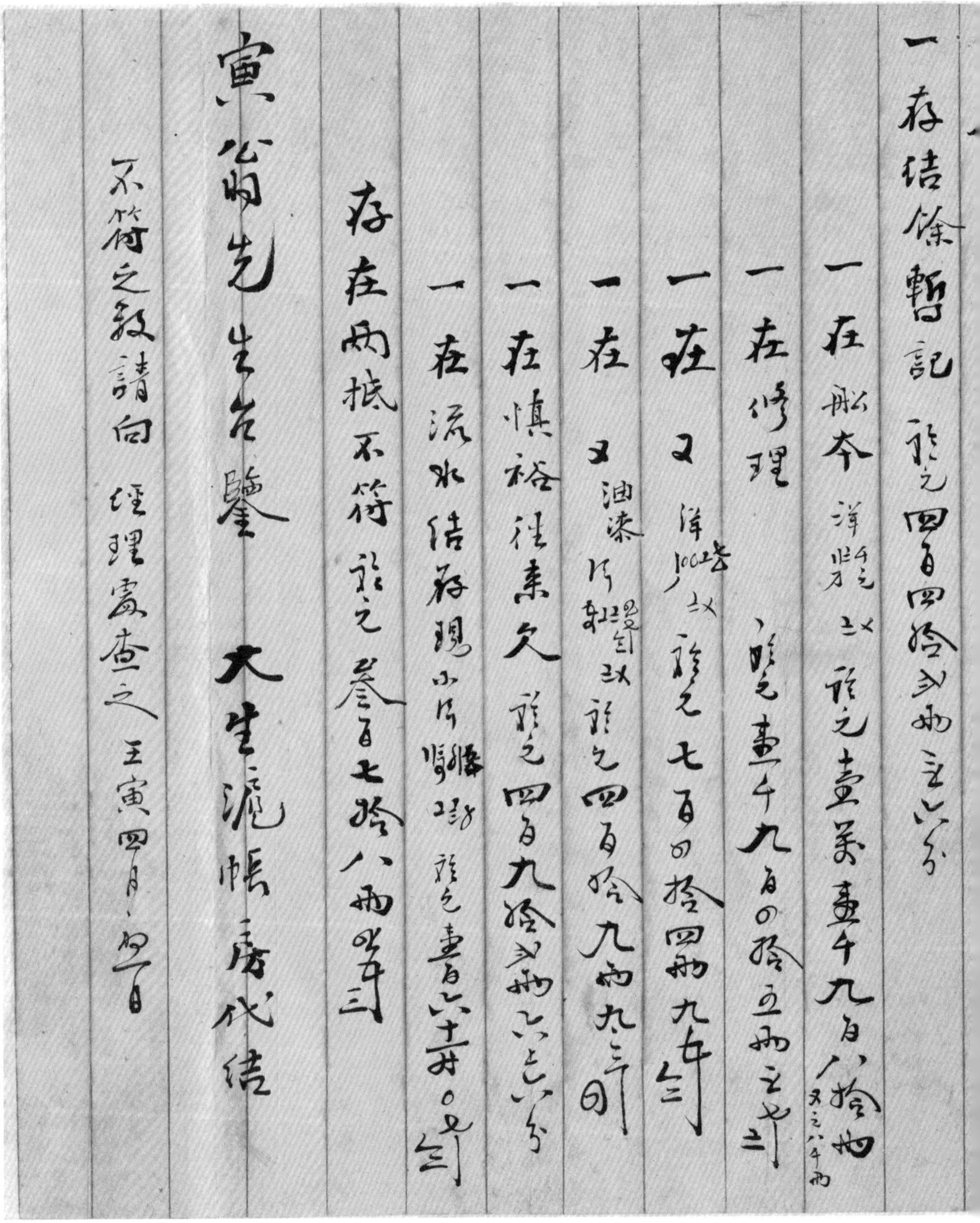

1902 年 5 月 8 日，大生沪所对朱葆三方面提供的账本进行核账的清单。

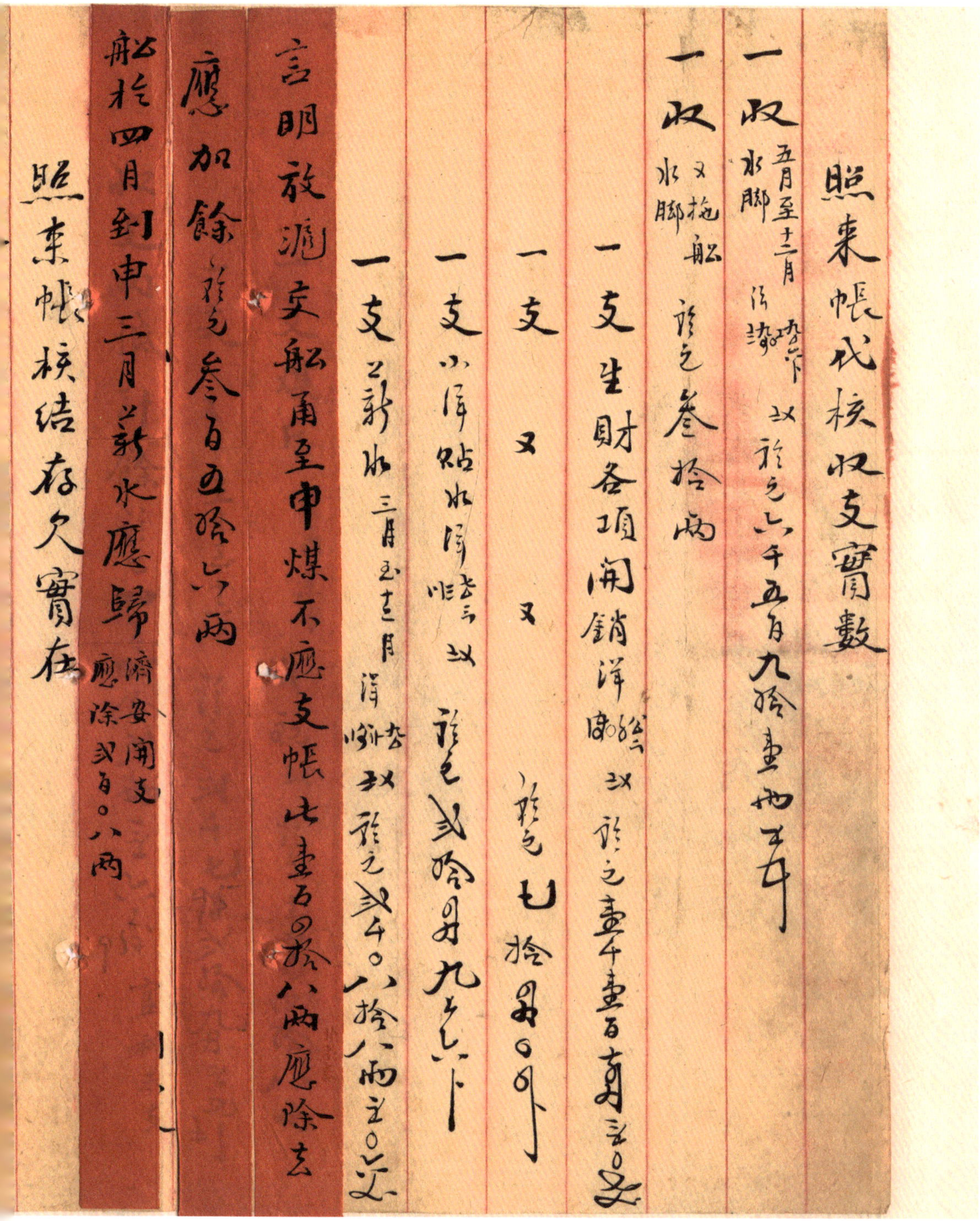
照来帳代核收支實數
一收水脚五月至十二月[illegible] 計規元六千五百九拾壹兩[illegible]
一收又拖船水脚 規元叁拾兩
一支生財各項開銷洋[illegible] 計規元壹千壹百[illegible]
一支又又 規元七拾[illegible]
一支小洋貼水洋[illegible] 計規元貳拾[illegible]九[illegible]
一支正薪水三月至十二月洋[illegible] 計規元貳千〇八拾八兩[illegible]
言明放滬交船甬至申煤不應支帳七[illegible]八兩應除去
應加餘規元叁百五拾六兩
船於四月到申三月薪水應歸濟安開支 應除貳百〇八兩
照来帳核結存欠實在

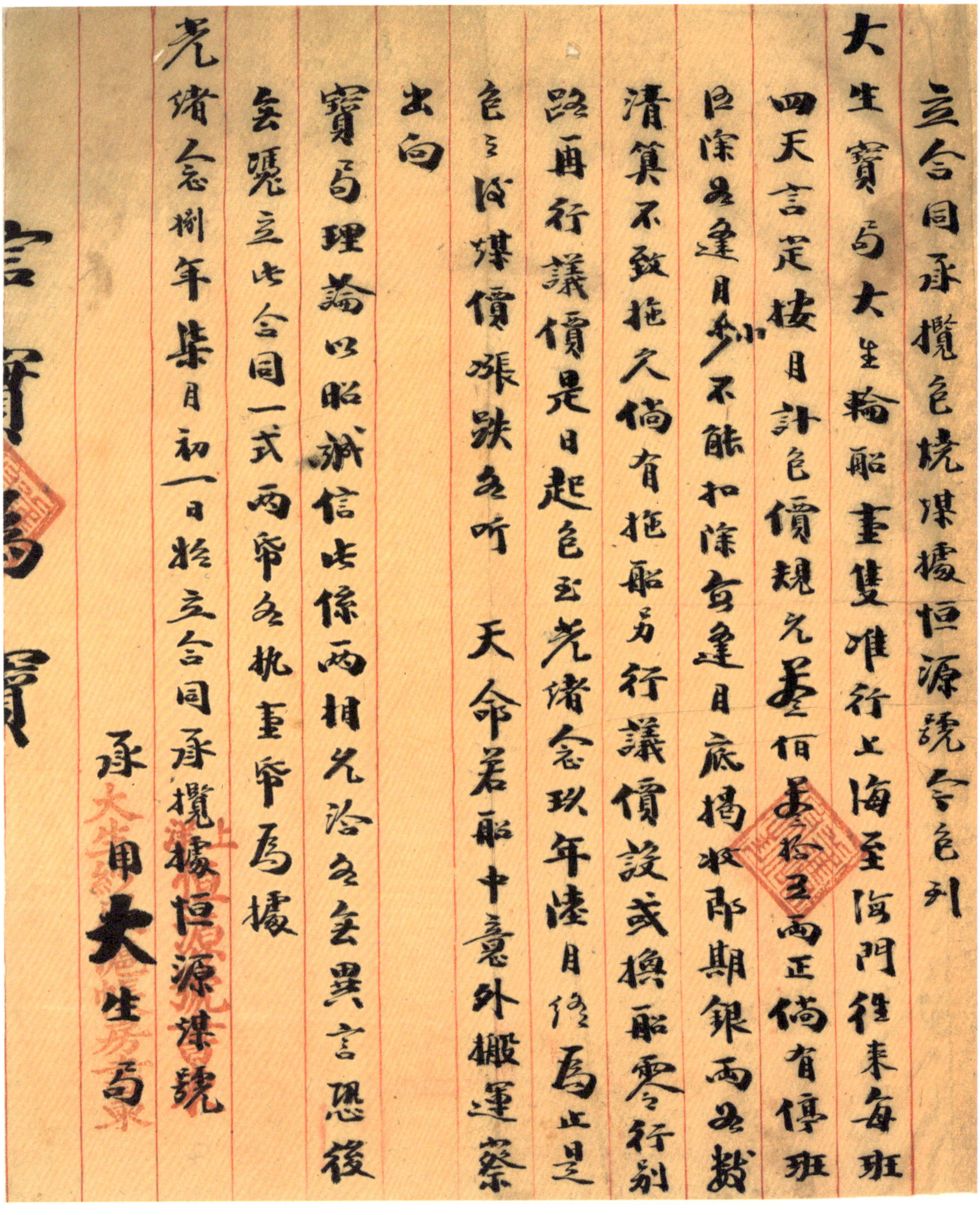
立合同承攬包燒煤據恒源號今包到
大生寶局大生輪船壹隻准行上海至海門往來每班
四天言定按月計包價規元叁佰叁拾叁兩正倘有停班
日除每逢月杪不能扣除每逢月底揭收即期銀兩無欵
清算不致拖欠倘有拖船另行議價設或換船零行別
路再行議價是日起包至光緒念玖年陸月終為止是
包之後煤價漲跌無所 天命若船中意外搬運察
出向
寶局理論以昭誠信此係兩相允洽各無異言恐後
無憑立此合同一式兩帋各執壹帋為據
光緒念捌年柒月初一日給立合同承攬據恒源煤號
承甲大生局

1902 年 8 月 4 日，恒源煤号与大生轮船公司签订的供煤协议。

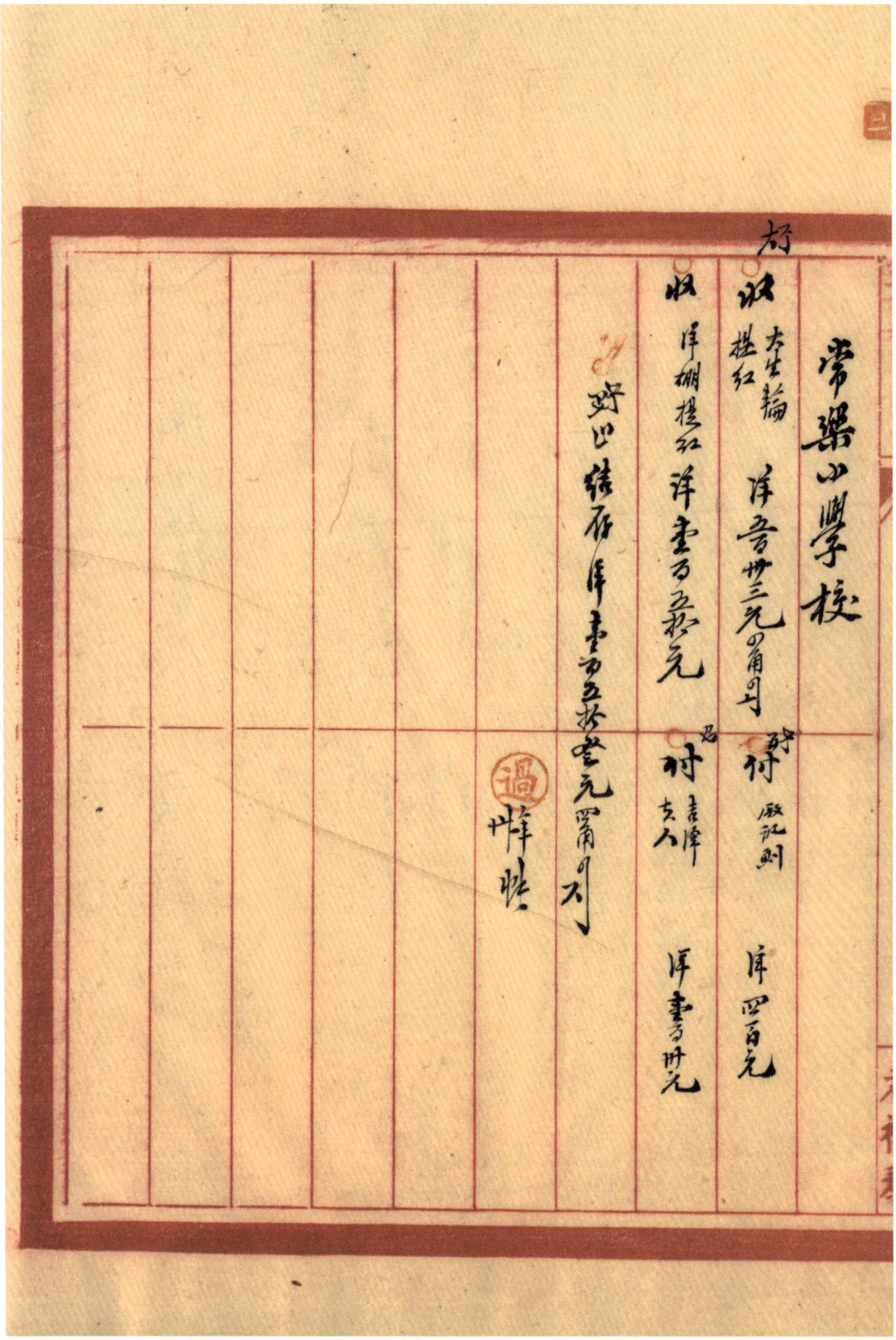

常樂小學校

1904 年大生沪所《总录》中，记载大生轮船公司通过分红的形式，赞助海门常乐小学校洋 533 元 4 角 4 分 6 厘。

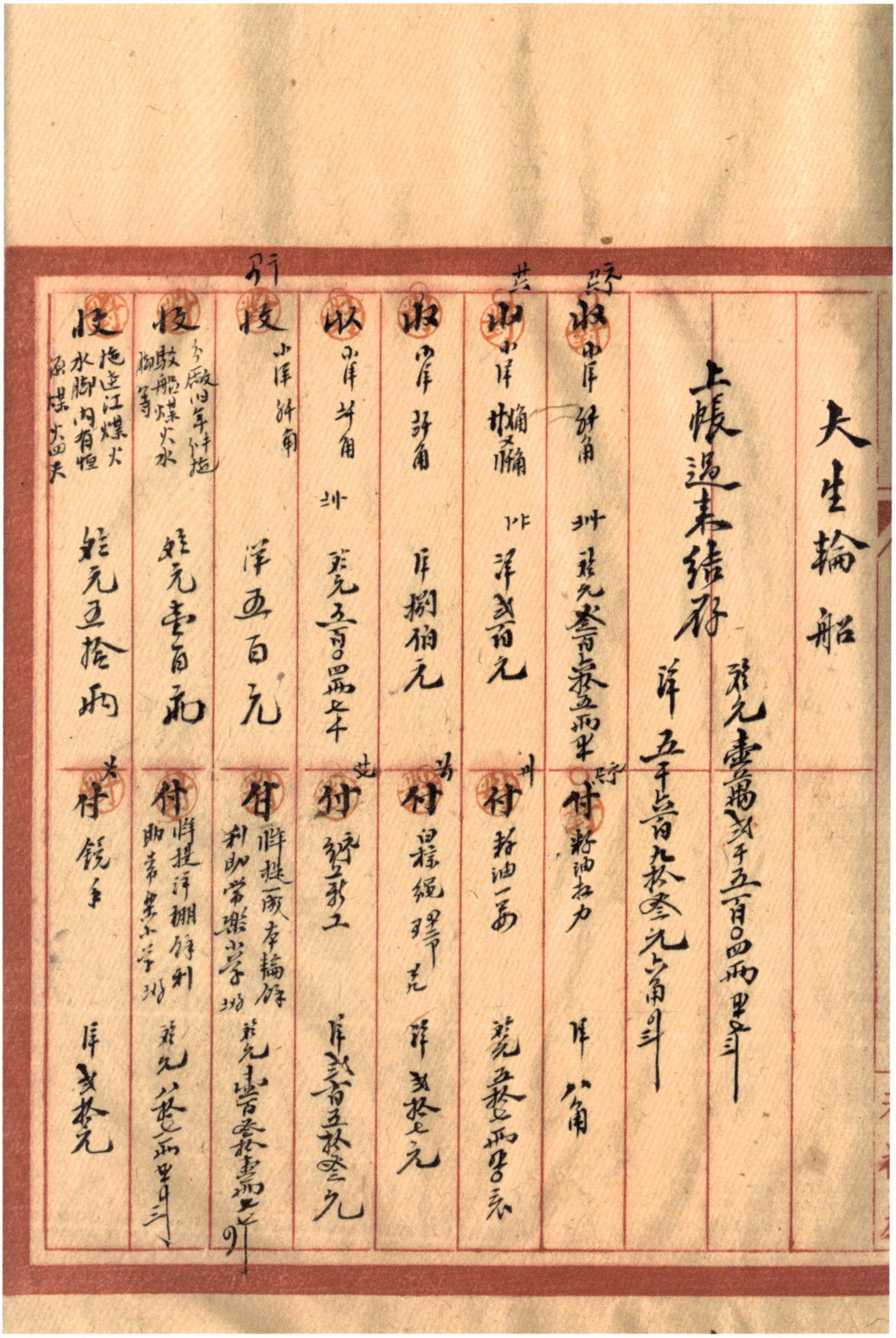

1905 年大生沪所《各户》中，大生轮船公司的收支账（局部）。

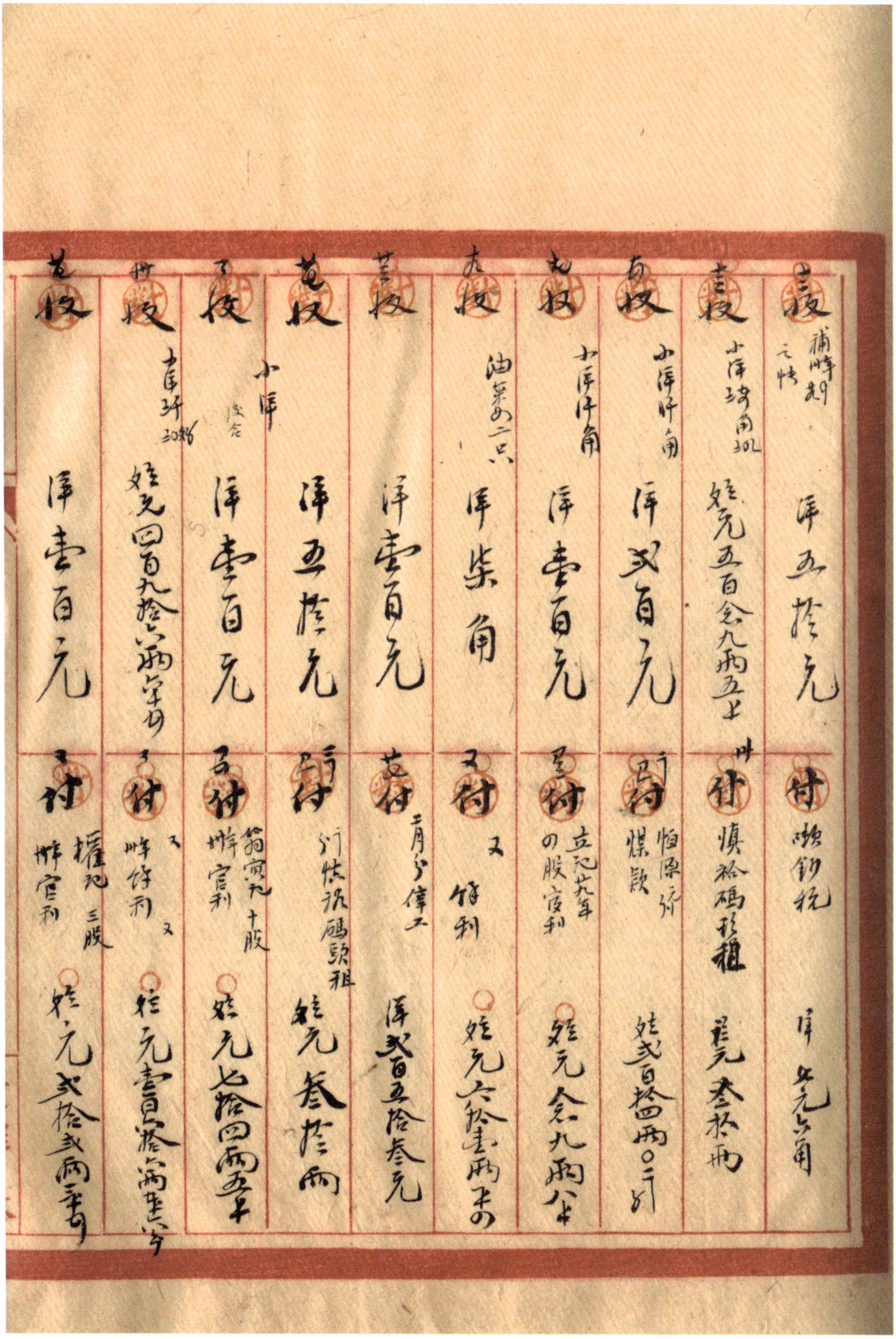

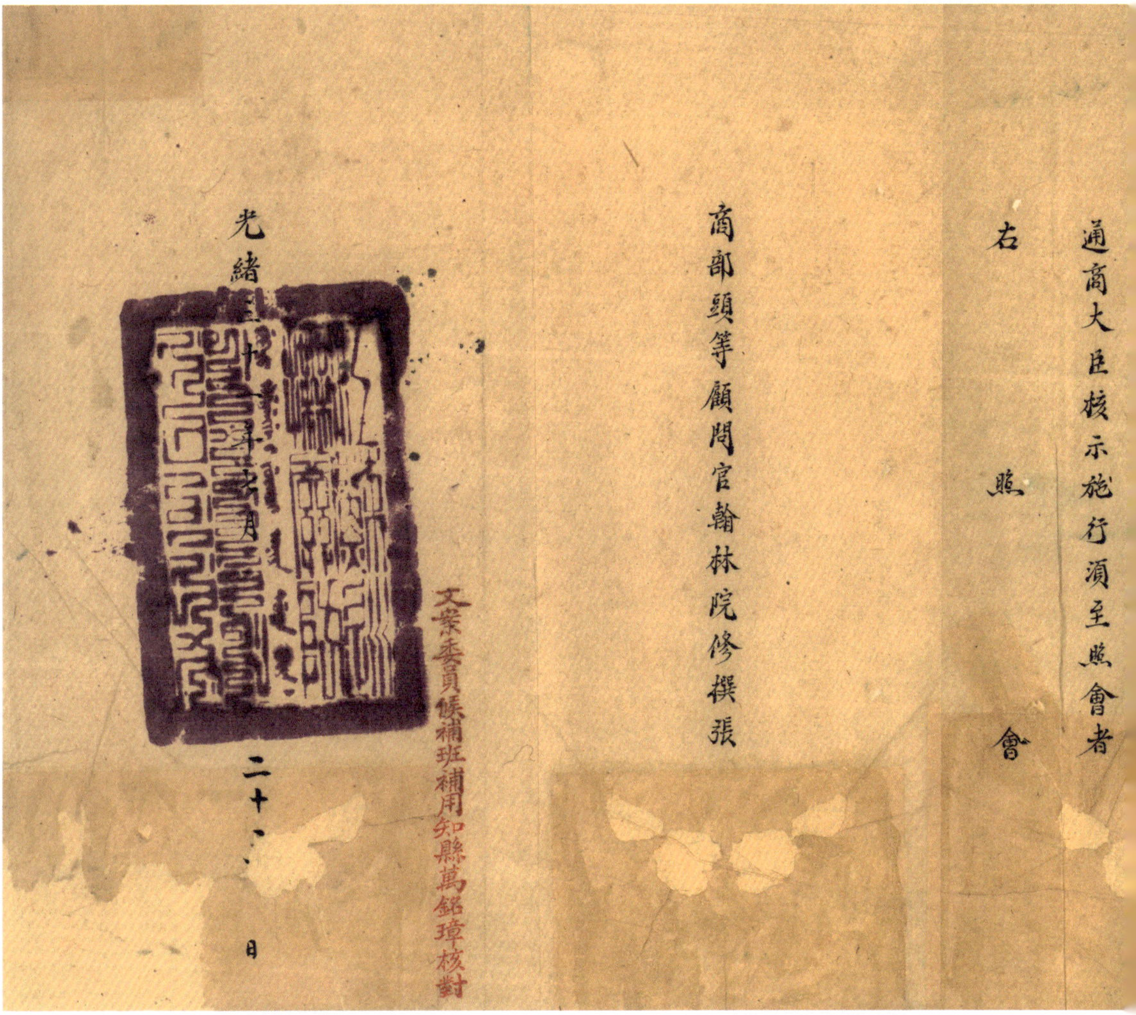
通商大臣核示施行須至照會者
右
照
會
商部頭等顧問官翰林院修撰張
光緒三十一年七月
二十三
日
文案委員候補班補用知縣萬銘璋核對

1905 年 8 月 23 日，江苏巡抚为集股创设大达轮步有限公司准予立案给张謇的照会。

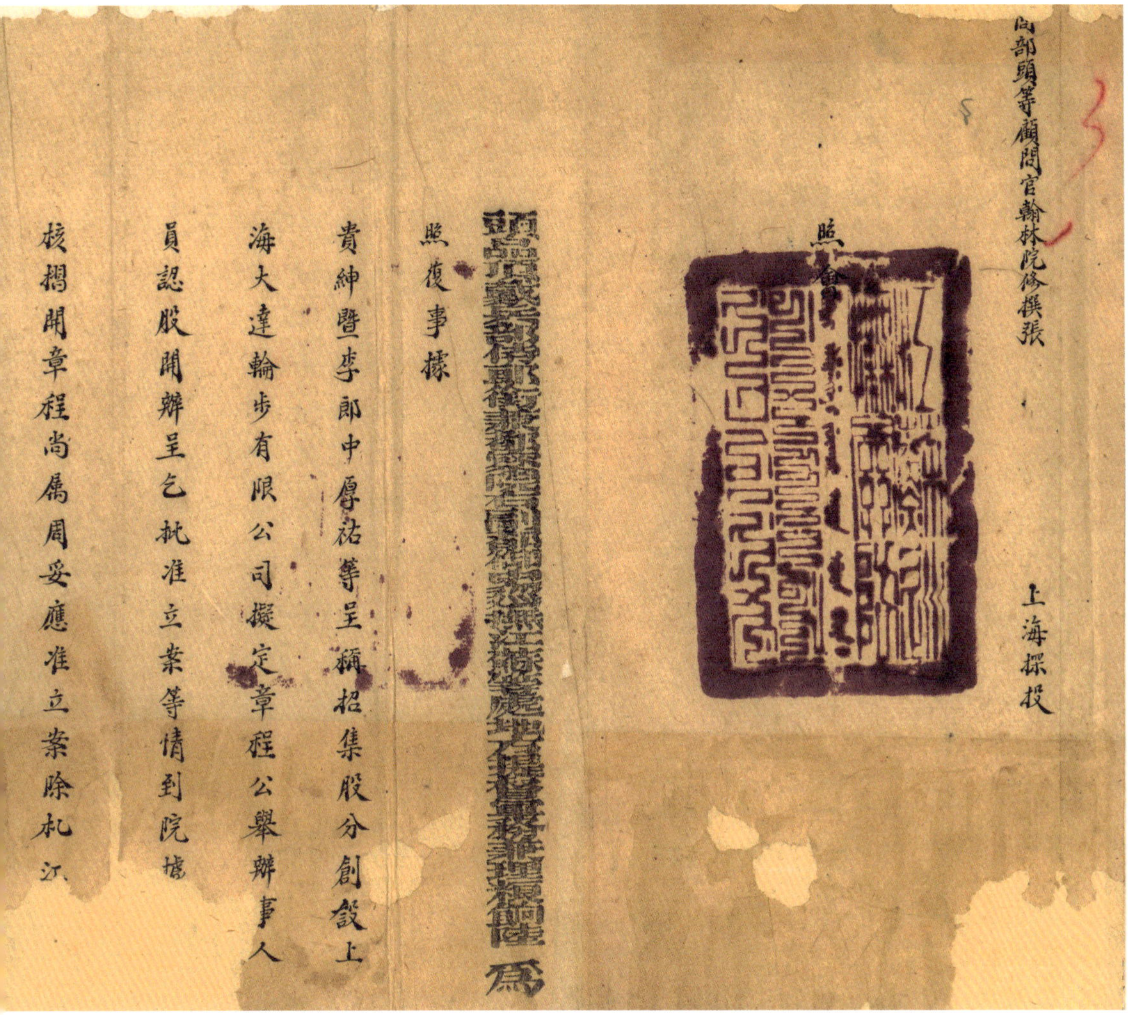
商部頭等顧問官翰林院修撰張
上海探投
照會
頭品頂戴[illegible]為
照復事據
貴紳暨李郎中厚祐等呈稱招集股分創設上
海大達輪步有限公司擬定章程公舉辦事人
員認股開辦呈乞批准立案等情到院據
核揭開章程尚屬周妥應准立案除札江

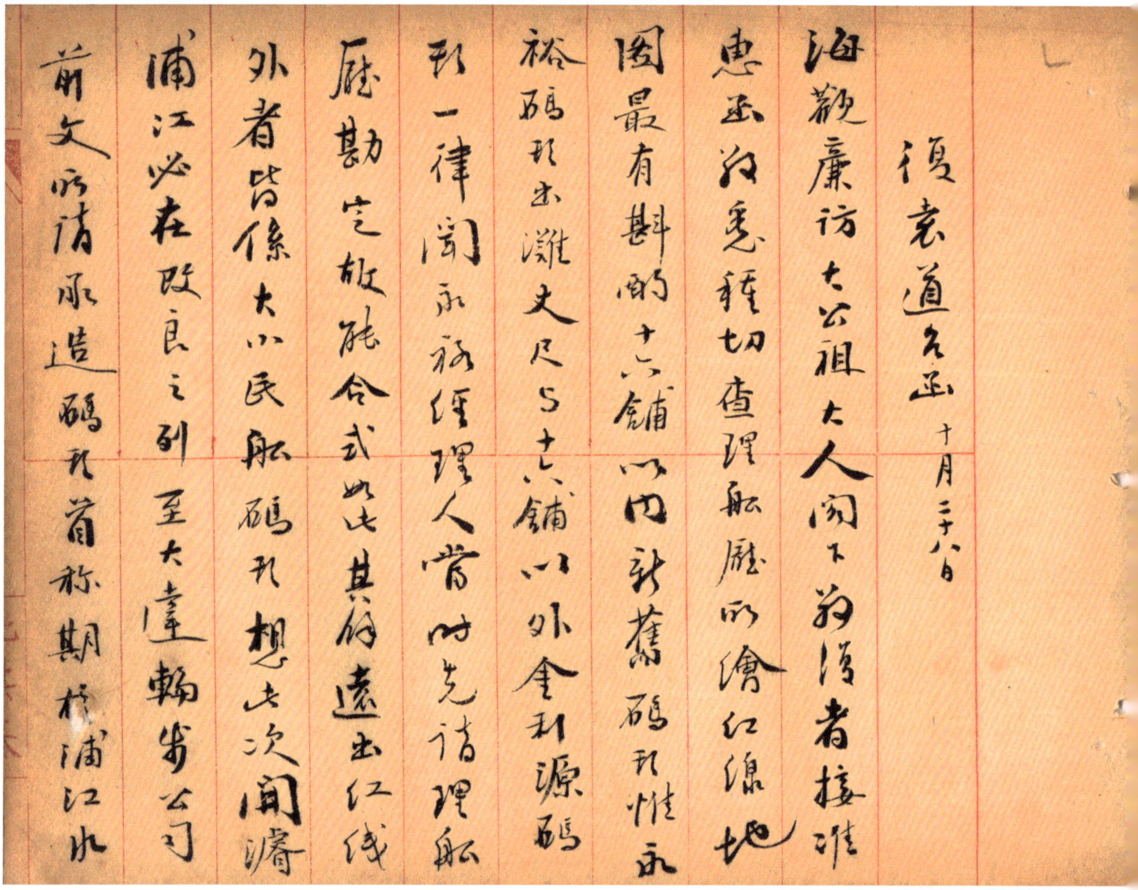

復袁道台函　十月二十八日
海觀廉訪大公祖大人閣下[illegible]者接准
惠函，以[illegible]須切查理船廳所繪紅線地
圖最有斟酌。十六鋪以內新舊碼頭惟永
裕碼頭出灘丈尺與十六鋪以外金利源碼
頭一律，聞[illegible]稅務司經理人當時先請理船
廳勘定，故能合式。其餘遠出紅線
外者，皆係大小民船碼頭。想此次開濬
浦江，必在改良之列。至大達輪步公司
前文所請承造碼頭，首稱期於浦江水

1905 年 11 月 24 日，张謇致上海道台关于在上海十六铺南建造大达码头事宜的函（抄件）。

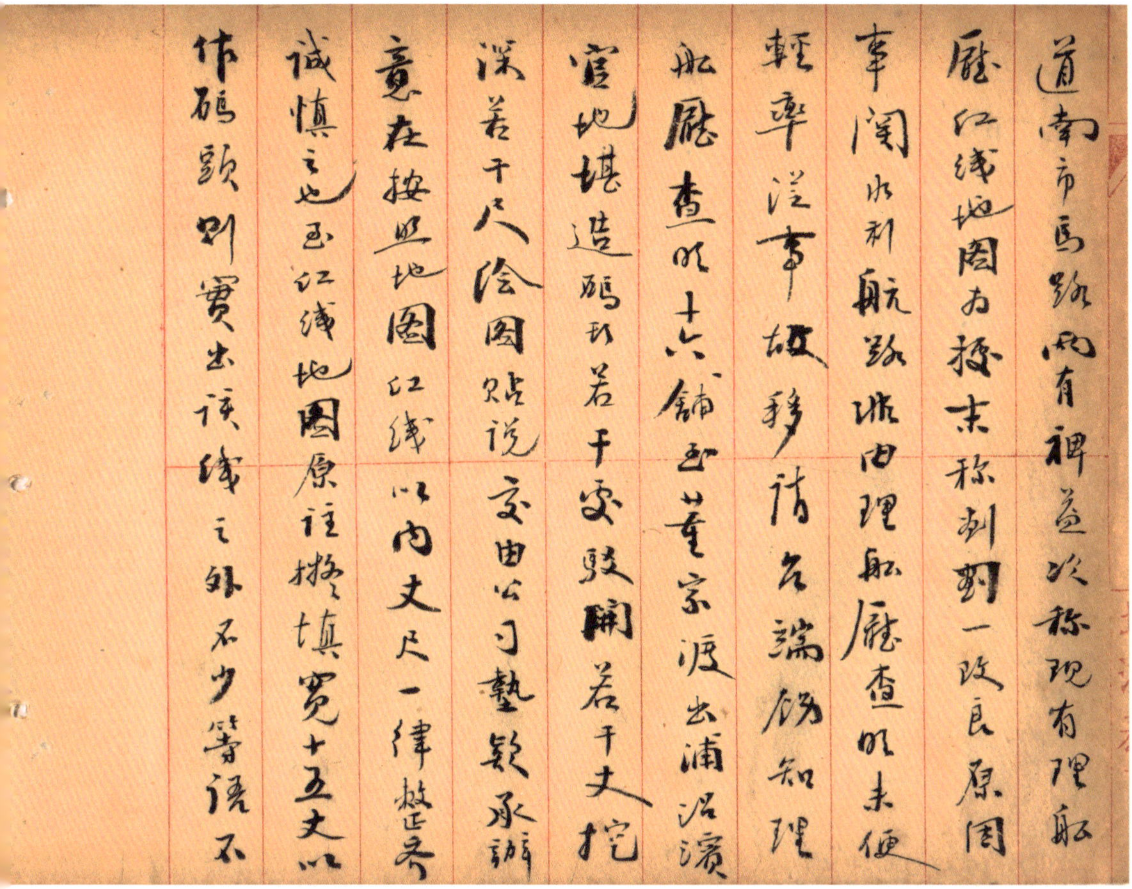
道南市馬路兩旁有碑並此称現有理船
廳红线地图为接末称划一段良原因
事関水利航路非由理船廳查明未便
輕率從事故移請台端飭知理
船廳查明十六舖至董家渡出浦沿濱
官地堪造碼頭若干安駁擱若干丈挖
深若干尺绘图貼说交由公司塾款承辦
意在按照地图红线以内丈尺一律整齐
誠慎之也至红线地图原注擬填寬十五丈以
作碼頭則實出該線之外不少等語不

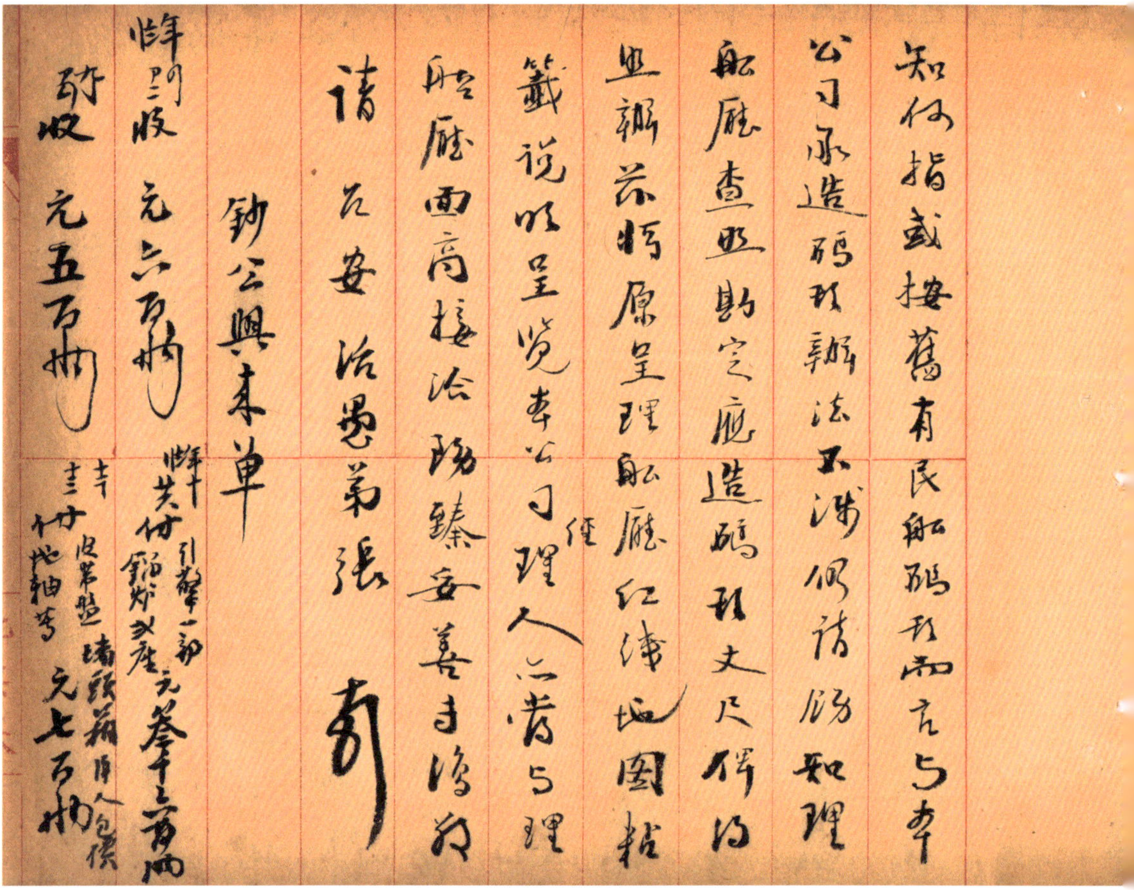
知係指或接舊有民船碼頭而言，与本
公司承造碼頭辦法不悖，仍請飭知理
船廳查照勘定，應造碼頭丈尺，俾得
照辦。茲將原呈理船廳紅綫地圖粘
籤說明呈覽。本公司經理人之責与理
船廳面商接洽，務臻妥善。專此敬
請 台安。治愚弟張 謇
鈞公興來單

1907 年 6 月 20 日，公兴机器船厂收到“大生”轮船修理费的收据。

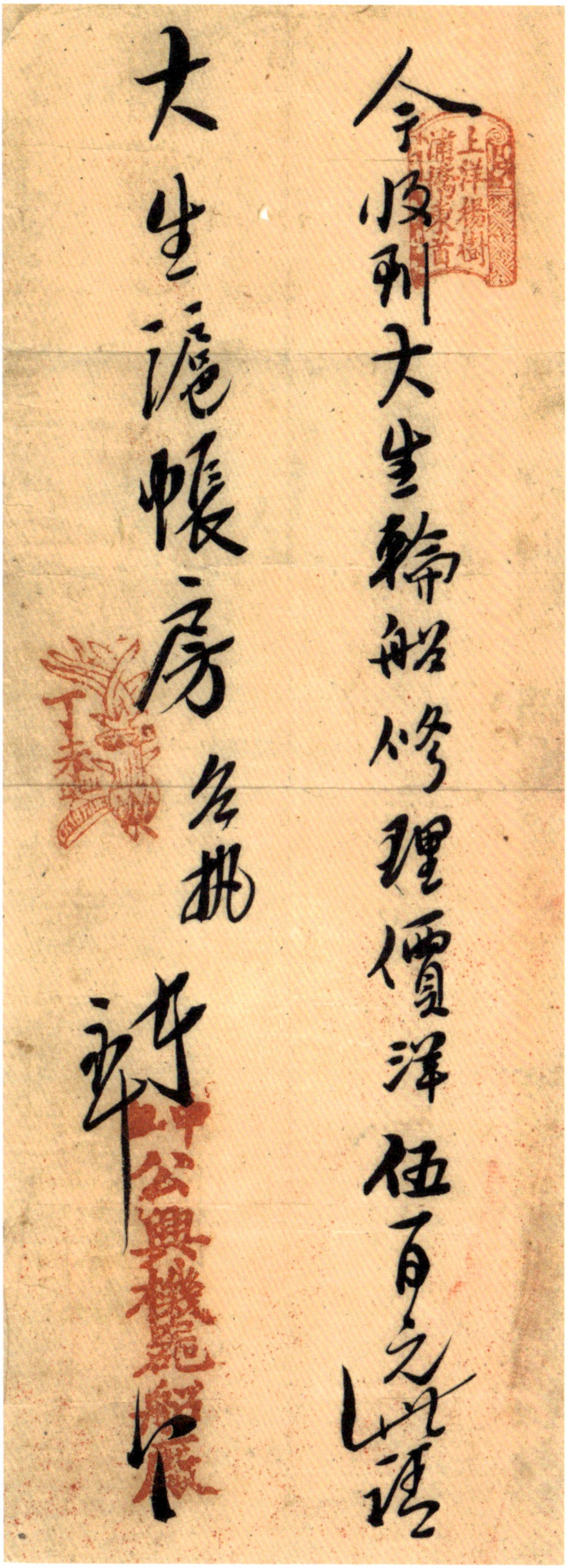
今收到大生輪船修理價洋伍百元
大生滬帳房 名擡
上洋楊樹浦橋東首
公興機器船廠

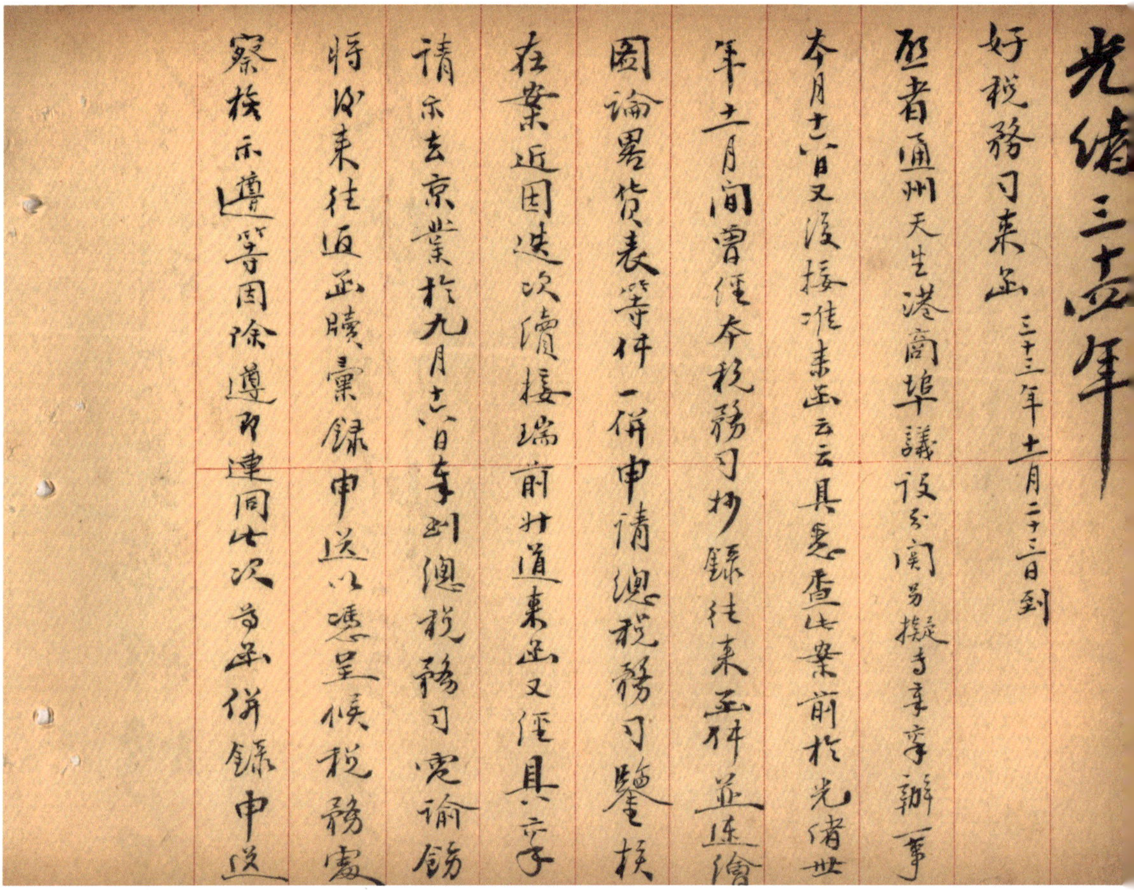

1907 年 12 月 27 日，大生沪所收到的江海关税务司致上海道台关于天生港自开商埠事宜的函（抄件）。

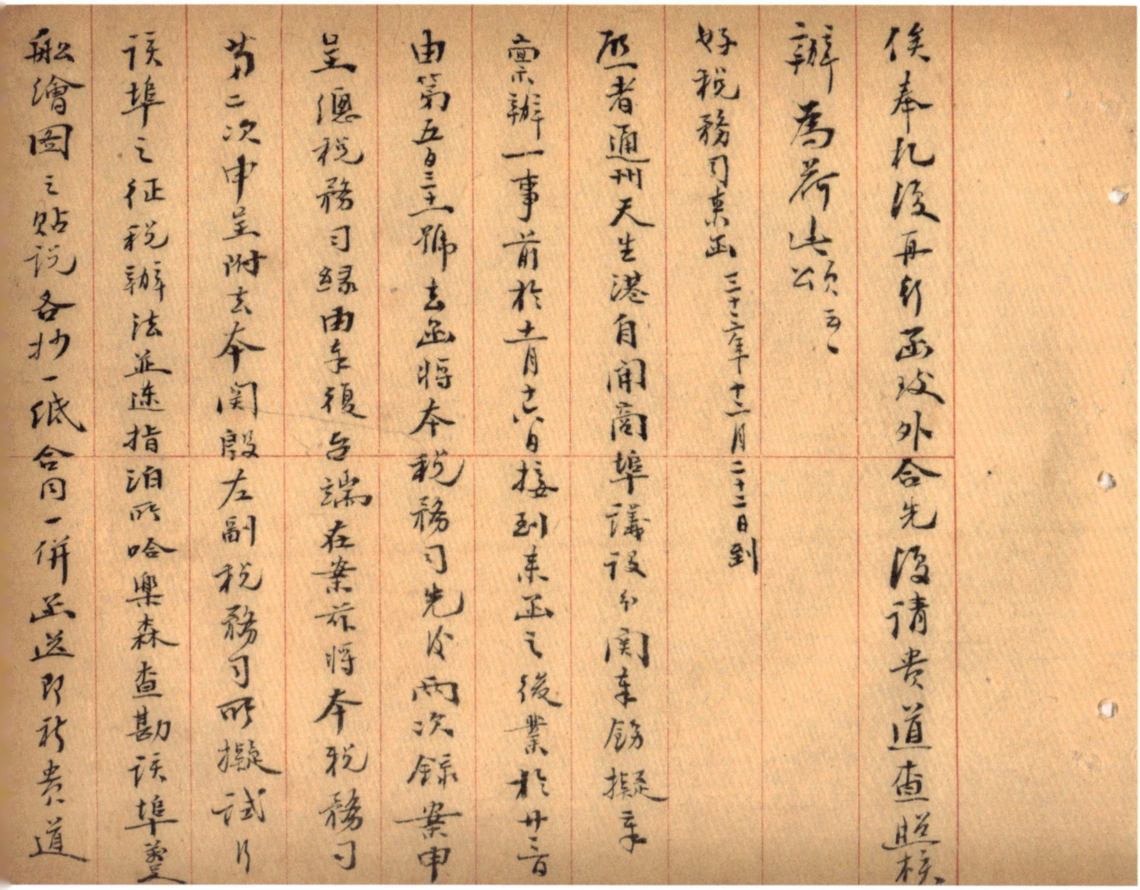

俟奉札後再行函致外合先復請貴道查照核
辦為荷此頌日祉
好稅務司來函 三十二年十二月二十二日到
逕者通州天生港自開商埠議設分關業飭擬章
稟辦一事前於十一月廿六日接到來函之後業於廿三日
由第五百三十號去函將本稅務司先後兩次錄案申
呈總稅務司緣由奉復在案茲將本稅務司
第二次申呈附去本關段左副稅務司所擬試行
該埠之征稅辦法並述指泊所哈樂森查勘該埠暨
所繪圖之貼說各抄一紙合同一併函送即祈貴道

位于天生港的江海关南通分关。

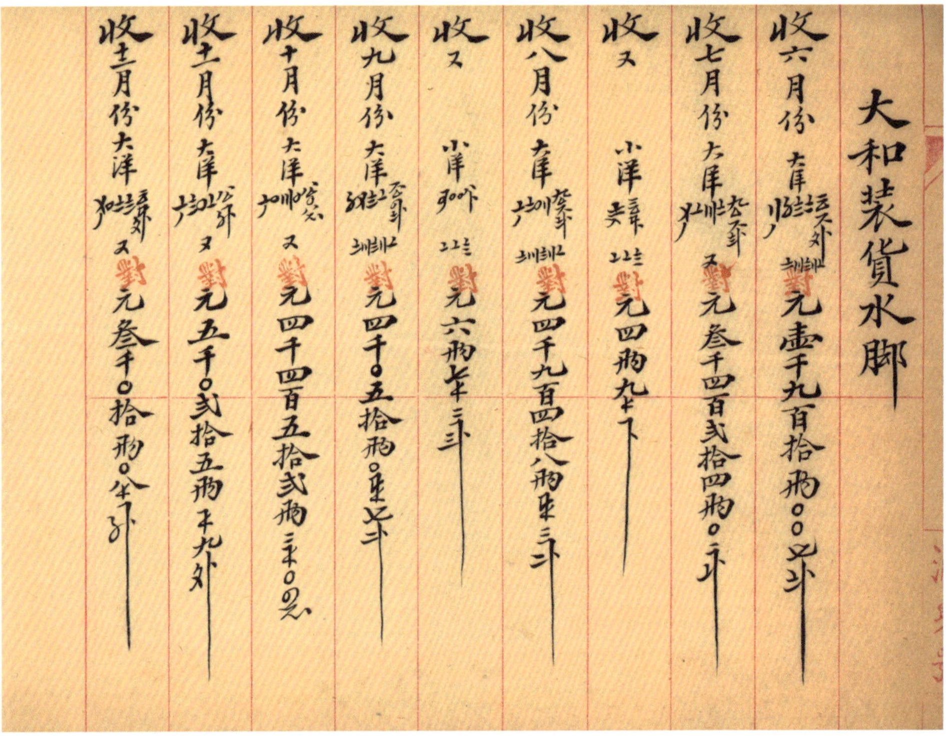

大和裝貨水脚

收六月份大洋 對元壹千九百拾兩○○

收七月份大洋 對元叁千四百弍拾四兩○

收又小洋 對元四兩

收八月份大洋 對元四千九百四拾八兩

收又小洋 對元六兩

收九月份大洋 對元四千○五拾兩

收十月份大洋 對元四千四百五拾弍兩

收十一月份大洋 對元五千○弍拾五兩

收十二月份大洋 對元叁千○拾兩○

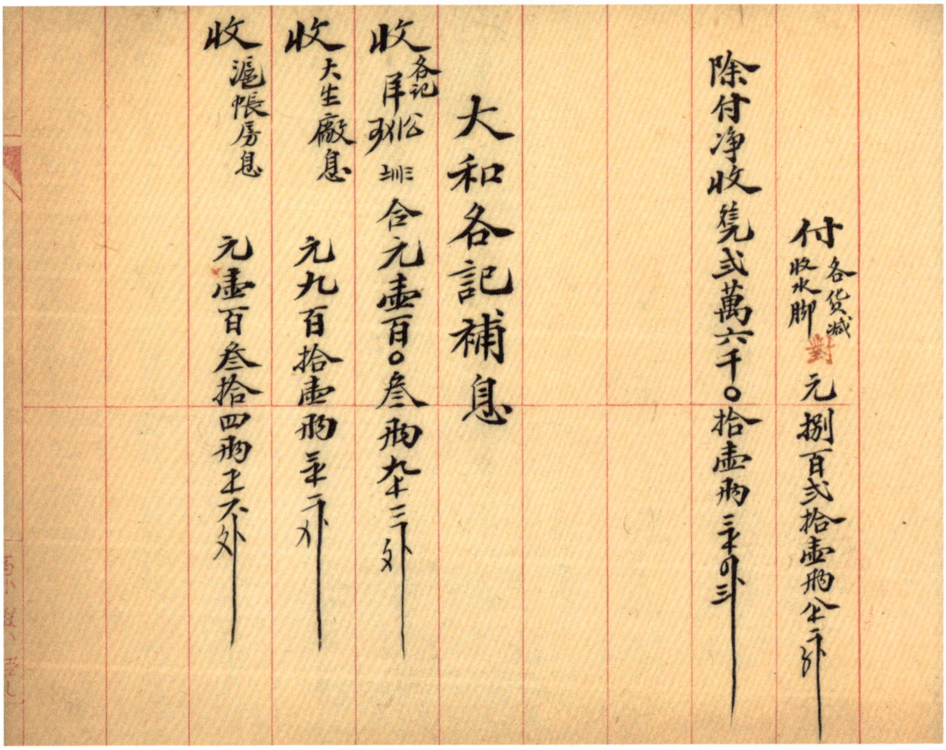

付各貨減收水脚 對元捌百弍拾壹兩

除付淨收規元弍萬六千○拾壹兩

大和各記補息

收各記洋 合元壹百○叁兩

收大生廠息 元九百拾壹兩

收滬帳房息 元壹百叁拾四兩

1908 年，上海大达轮步公司“大和”轮船账略底册（局部）。

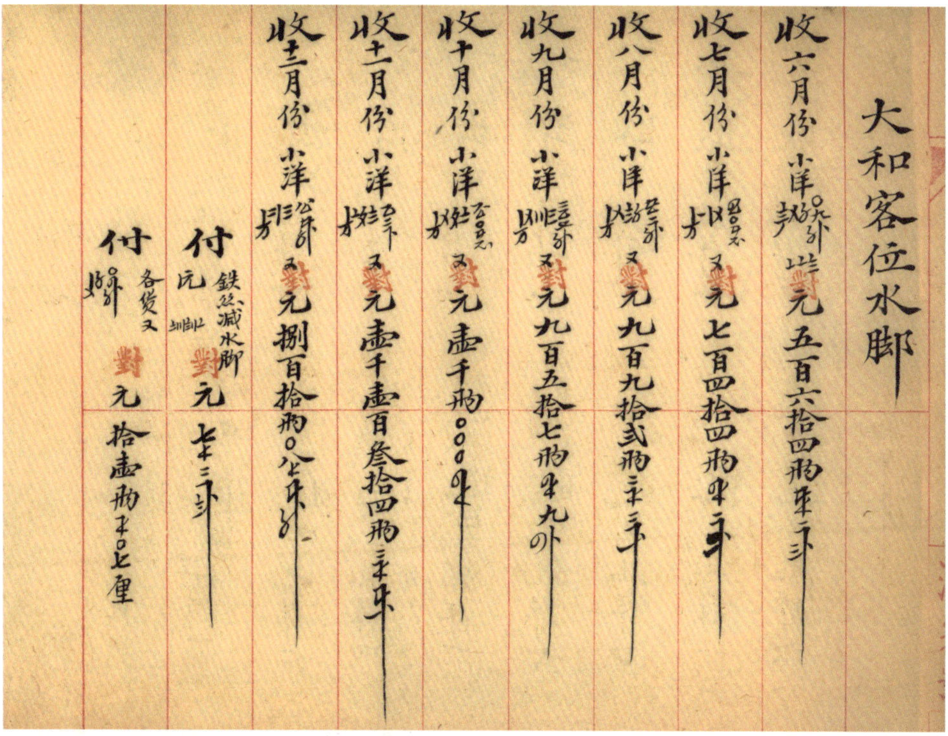
大和客位水脚
收六月份 小洋 对 元五百六拾四两
收七月份 小洋 对 元七百四拾四两
收八月份 小洋 对 元九百九拾贰两
收九月份 小洋 对 元九百五拾七两
收十月份 小洋 对 元壹千两
收十一月份 小洋 对 元壹千壹百叁拾四两
收十二月份 小洋 对 元捌百拾两
付 铁丝、减水脚 对 元
付 各货又 对 元拾壹两

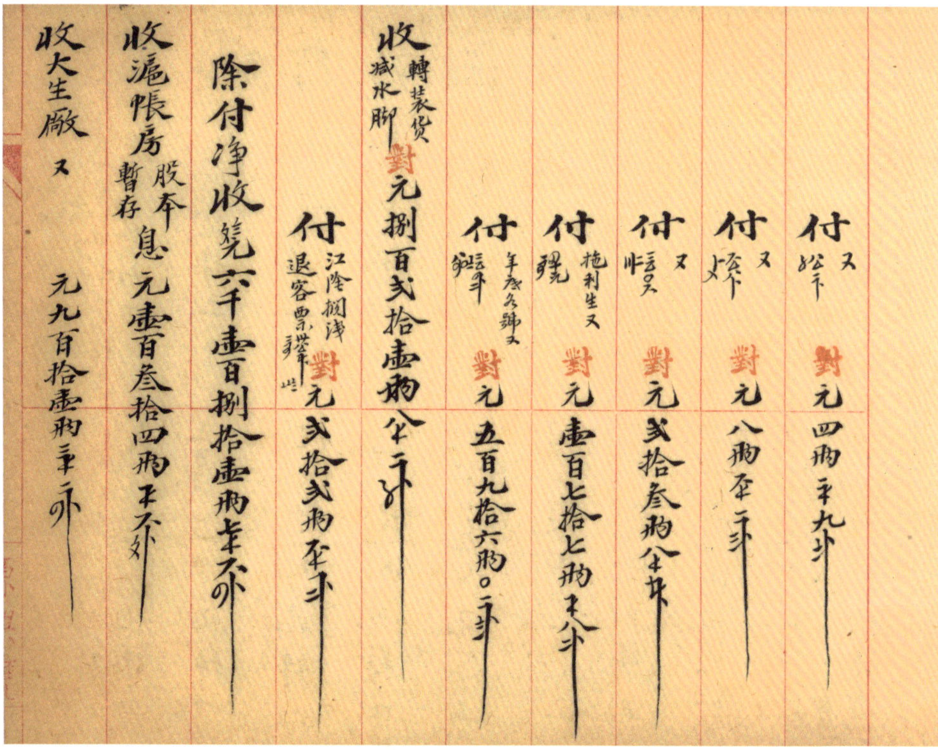
付又 对 元四两
付又 对 元八两
付又 对 元贰拾叁两
付 拖利生又 对 元壹百七拾七两
付 年底各轮又 对 元五百九拾六两
付 江阴搁浅 退客票 对 元贰拾贰两
收 转装货 减水脚 对 元捌百贰拾壹两
除付净收 元六千壹百捌拾壹两
收沪帐房 股本 暂存 息 元壹百叁拾四两
收大生厂 又 元九百拾壹两

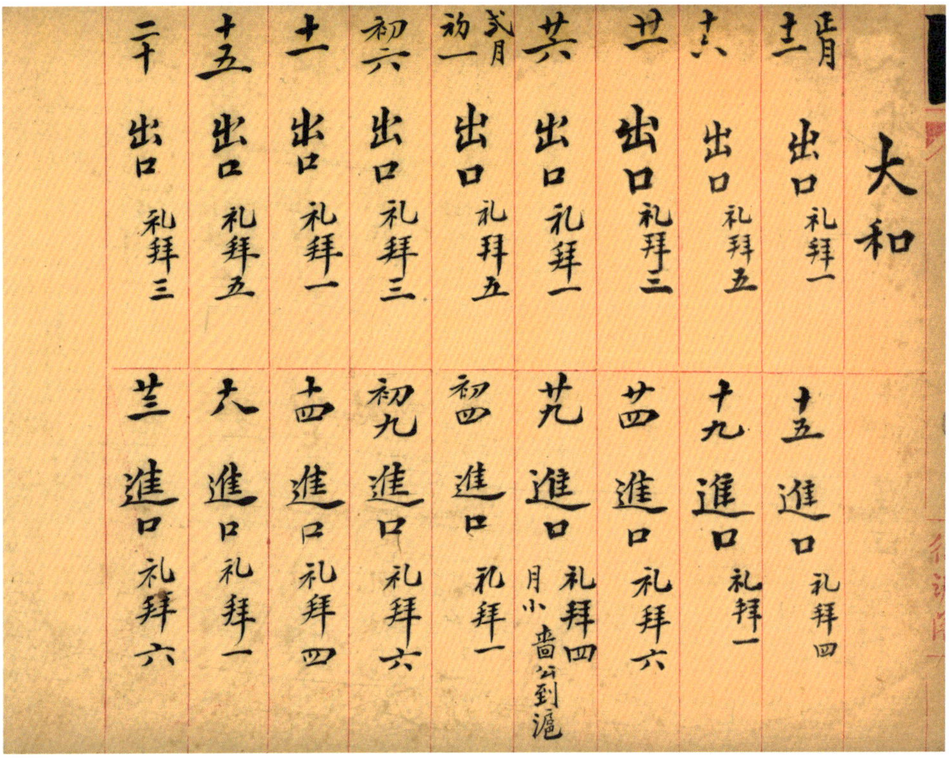
大和
正月十二 出口 礼拜一
十六 出口 礼拜五
廿一 出口 礼拜三
廿六 出口 礼拜一
二月初一 出口 礼拜五
初六 出口 礼拜三
十一 出口 礼拜一
十五 出口 礼拜五
二十 出口 礼拜三
十五 進口 礼拜四
十九 進口 礼拜一
廿四 進口 礼拜六
廿九 進口 礼拜四 月小 嗇公到滬
初四 進口 礼拜一
初九 進口 礼拜六
十四 進口 礼拜四
十八 進口 礼拜一
廿三 進口 礼拜六

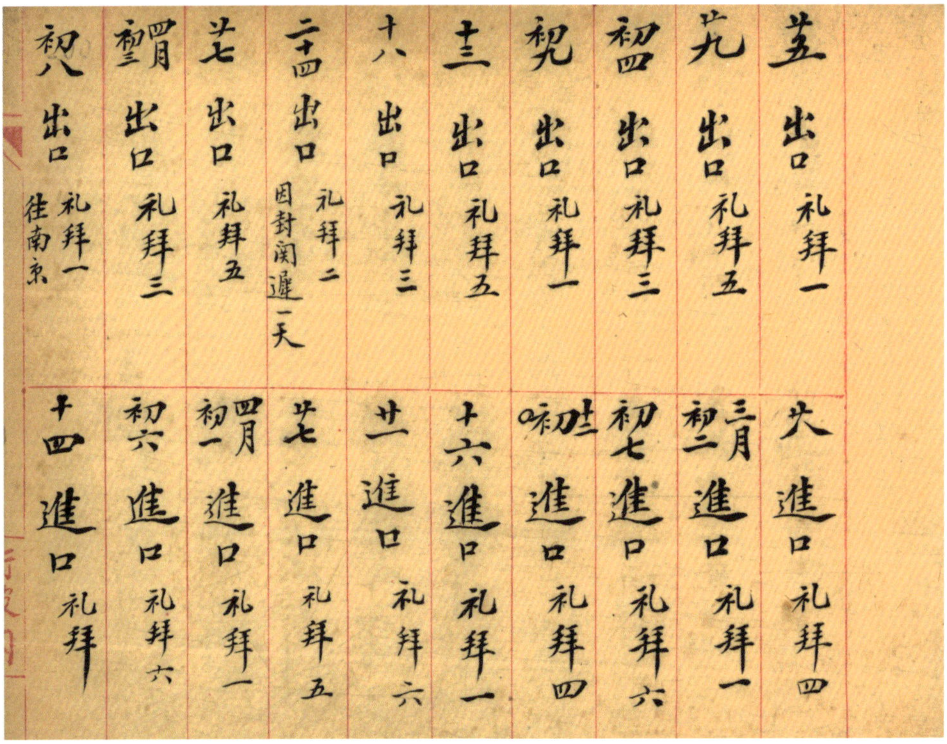
廿五 出口 礼拜一
廿九 出口 礼拜五
初四 出口 礼拜三
初九 出口 礼拜一
十三 出口 礼拜五
十八 出口 礼拜三
二十四 出口 礼拜二 因封関遲一天
廿七 出口 礼拜五
四月初三 出口 礼拜三
初八 出口 礼拜一 往南京
廿八 進口 礼拜四
三月初二 進口 礼拜一
初七 進口 礼拜六
十二 進口 礼拜四
十六 進口 礼拜一
廿一 進口 礼拜六
廿七 進口 礼拜五
四月初一 進口 礼拜一
初六 進口 礼拜六
十四 進口 礼拜

1910 年，上海大达轮步公司“大和”轮船班期（局部）。

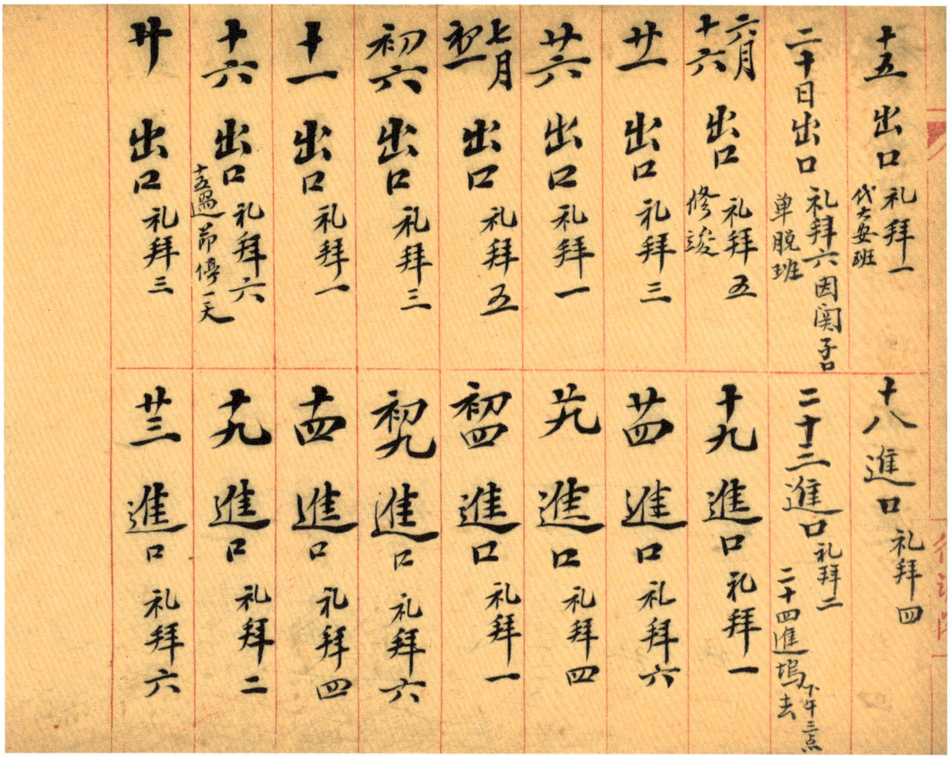
十五 出口 礼拜一 代大安班
二十日 出口 礼拜六 因関子口 单脱班
六月 十六 出口 礼拜五 修竣
廿一 出口 礼拜三
廿六 出口 礼拜一
七月 初一 出口 礼拜五
初六 出口 礼拜三
十一 出口 礼拜一
十六 出口 礼拜六 十五過節停一天
廿一 出口 礼拜三
十八 進口 礼拜四
二十三 進口 礼拜二 二十四進塢去 下午三点
十九 進口 礼拜一
廿四 進口 礼拜六
廿九 進口 礼拜四
初四 進口 礼拜一
初九 進口 礼拜六
十四 進口 礼拜四
十九 進口 礼拜二
廿三 進口 礼拜六

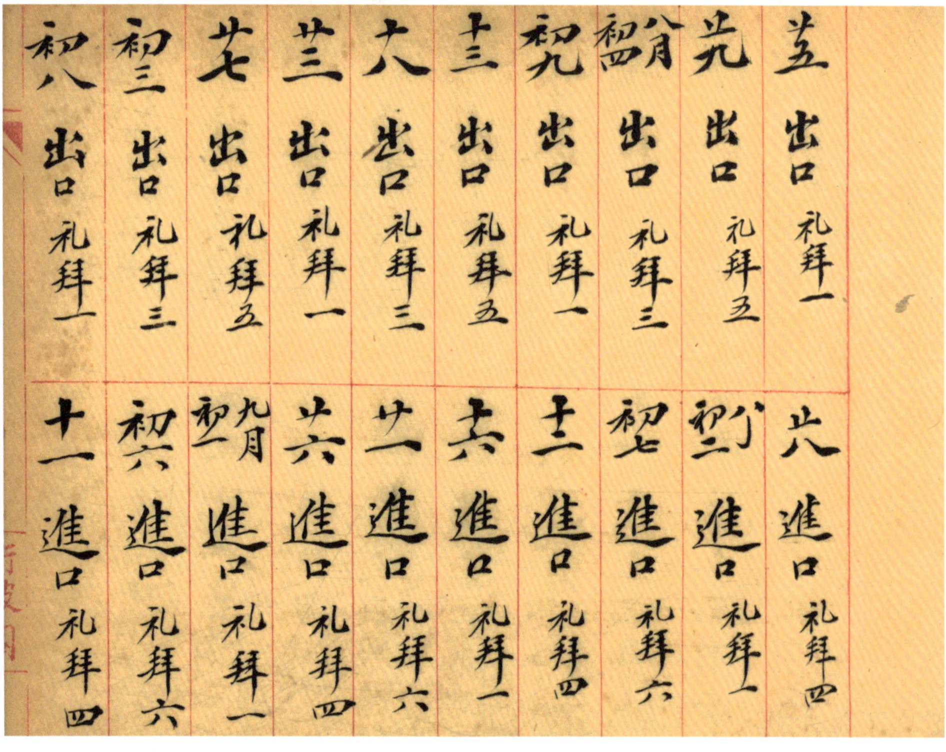
廿五 出口 礼拜一
廿九 出口 礼拜五
八月 初四 出口 礼拜三
初九 出口 礼拜一
十三 出口 礼拜五
十八 出口 礼拜三
廿三 出口 礼拜一
廿七 出口 礼拜五
初三 出口 礼拜三
初八 出口 礼拜一
廿八 進口 礼拜四
八月 初二 進口 礼拜一
初七 進口 礼拜六
十二 進口 礼拜四
十六 進口 礼拜一
廿一 進口 礼拜六
廿六 進口 礼拜四
九月 初一 進口 礼拜一
初六 進口 礼拜六
十一 進口 礼拜四

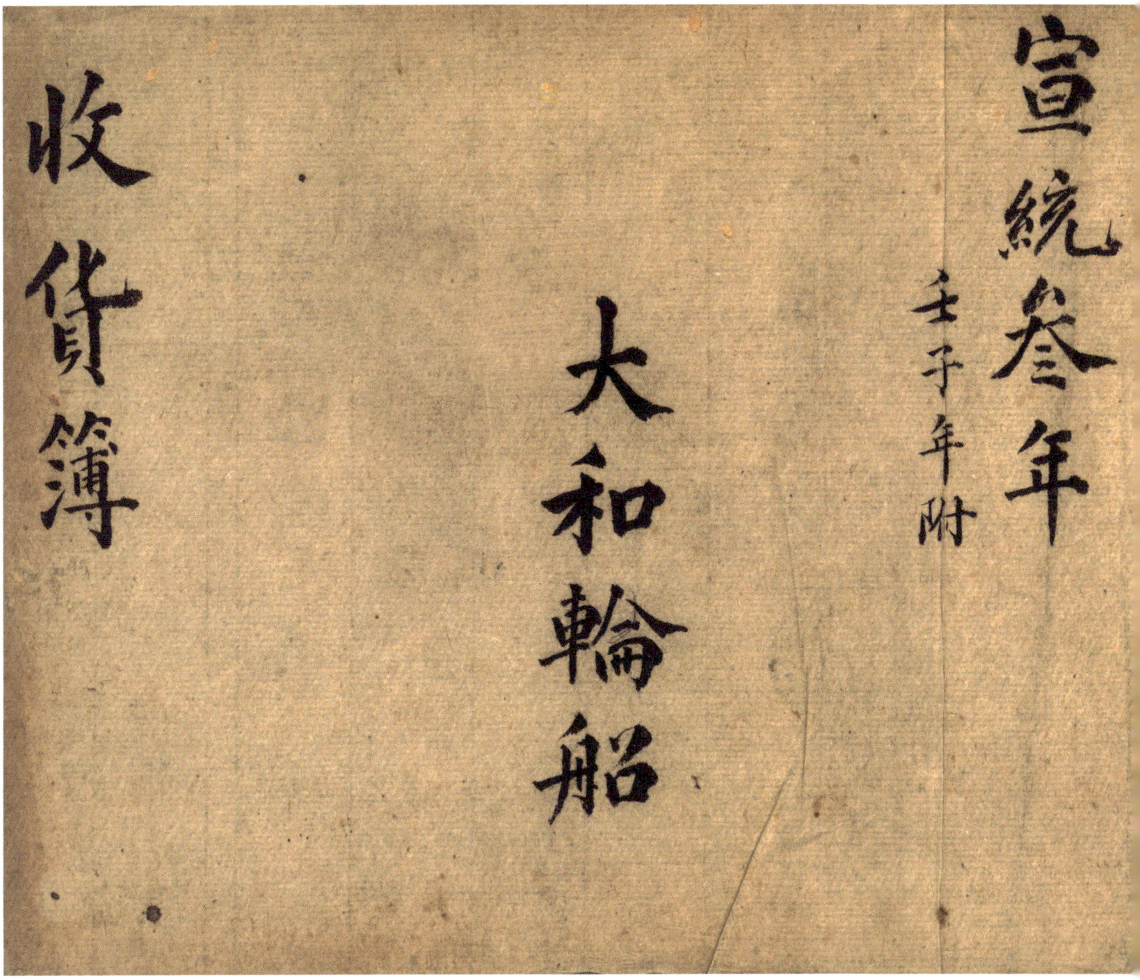
宣統叁年
壬子年附
大和輪船
收貨簿

1911 年，上海大达轮步公司“大和”轮船收货簿（局部）。

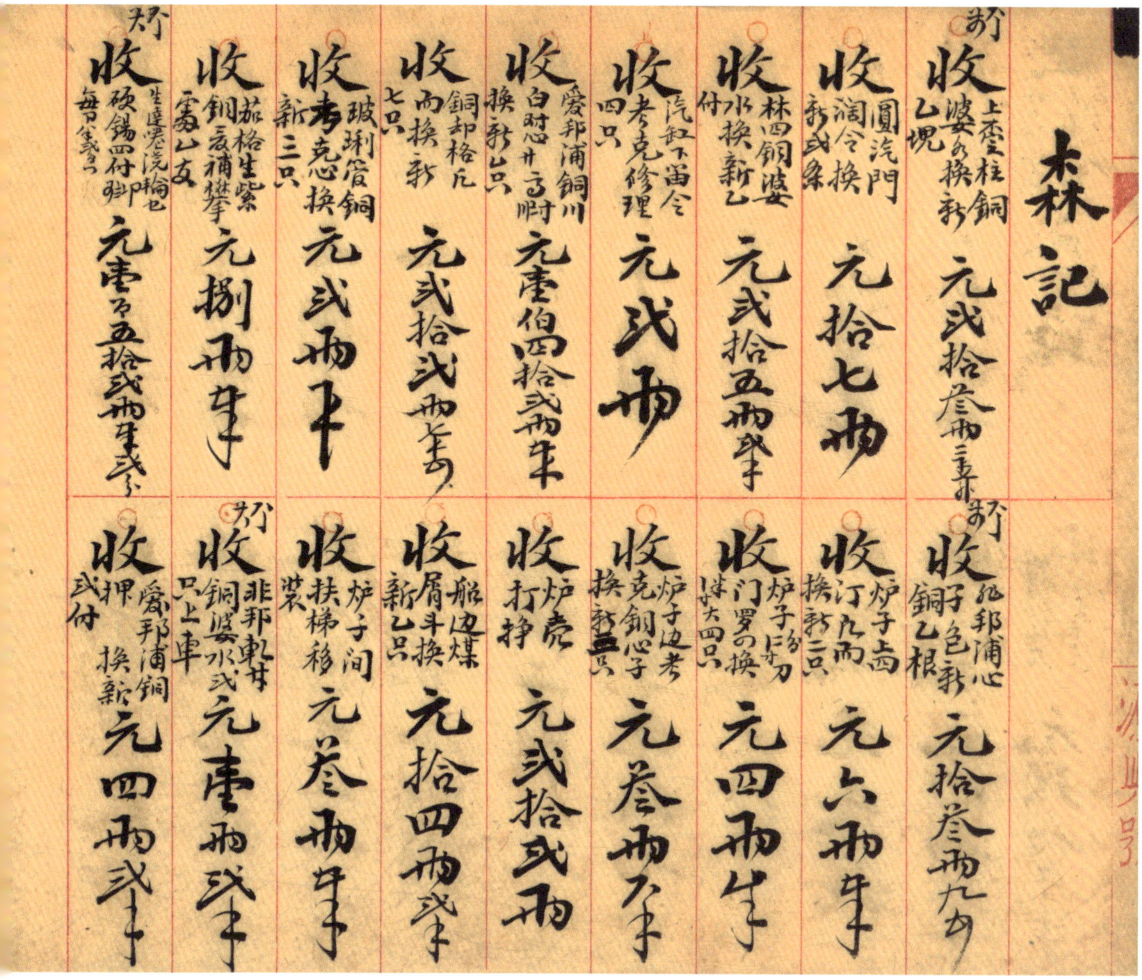

森記

收上壓柱銅婆々換新乙塊 元弍拾叁两三五

收圓汽門潤令換新弍条 元拾七两

收林四銅婆水換新乙付 元弍拾五两半

收汽缸下留令考克修理四只 元弍两

收愛邦浦銅川白対心廾乙吋換新乙只 元壹伯四拾弍两半

收銅卸格瓦兩換新七只 元弍拾弍两五

收玻璃管銅考克心換新三只 元弍两半

收旅格生紫銅皮補攀 元捌两半

收生達浮心汽輪乜硬錫四付每付 元壹百五拾弍两半

收紅邦浦心子色新銅乙根 元拾叁两九五

收炉子齒汀九両換新三只 元六两半

收炉子下各刀门罗の換 元四两半

收炉子边考克銅心子換新三只 元叁两半

收炉虎打掙 元弍拾弍两

收船边煤眉斗換新乙只 元拾四两半

收炉子间扶梯移装 元叁两半

收非邦軋廾銅婆水弍只上車 元壹两弍半

收愛邦浦銅押弍付換新 元四两弍半

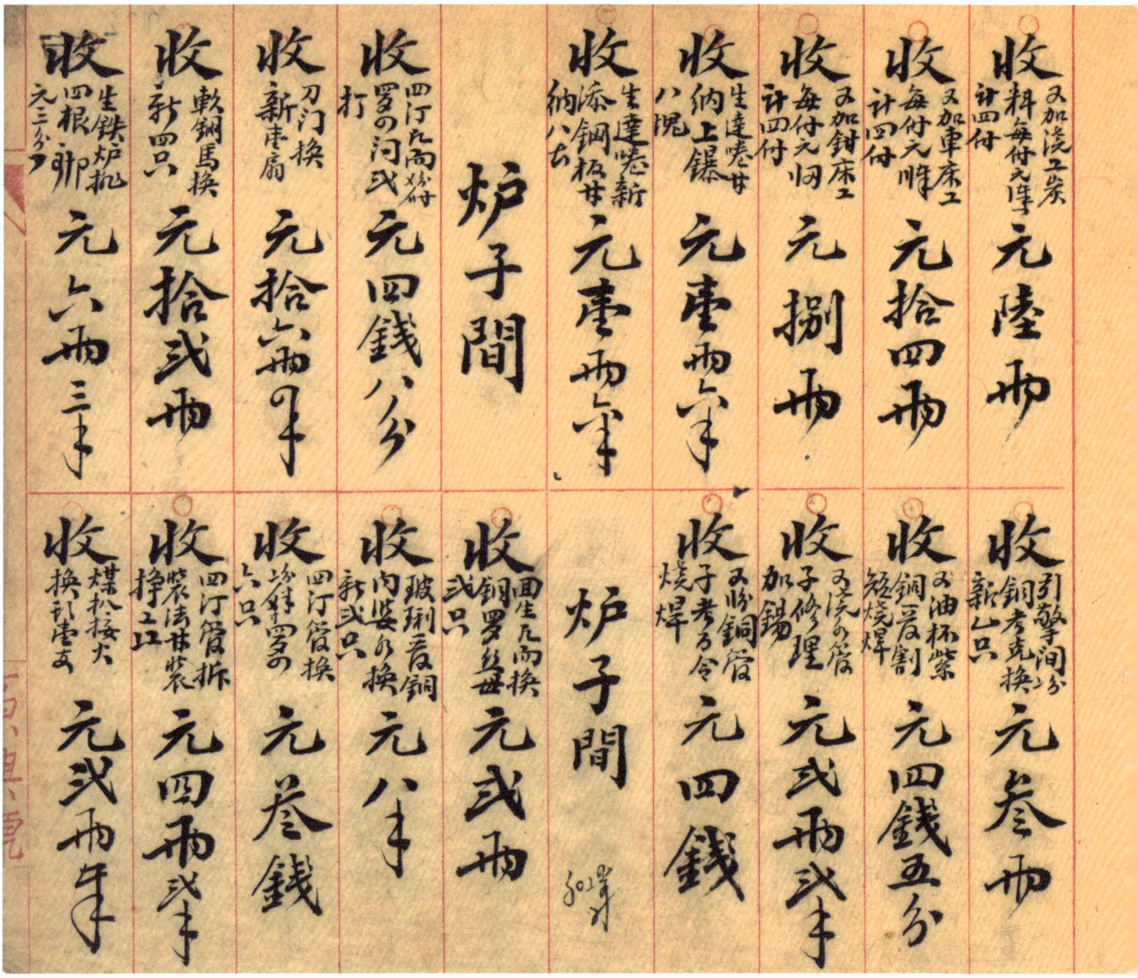
收 又加浇工炭 料每付元準 計四付 元陸兩
收 又加車床工 每付元聯 計四付 元拾四兩
收 又加鉗床工 每付元叼 計四付 元捌兩
收 生達喨廿 納上鏍 八梘 元壹兩六年
收 生達喨新 添銅板廿 納八去 元壹兩六年
炉子間
收 四汀元兩箹 罗的河式 打 元四錢八分
收 刀汀換 新車扁 元拾六兩四年
收 軋銅馬換 新四只 元拾弐兩
收 生鉄炉批 四根邦 元三分 元六兩三年
收 引擎间分 銅考克換 新六只 元叁兩
收 又油杯紫 銅管割 絡燒焊 元四錢五分
收 又浇的管 子修理 加錫 元弐兩弐年
收 又喉銅管 子考乃令 燒焊 元四錢
炉子間
收 四生元兩換 銅罗盘毋 弐只 元弐兩
收 玻琍管銅 內要的換 新弐只 元八年
收 四汀管換 箹彝罗的 六只 元叁錢
收 四汀管拆 浆法甘浆 掙工仕 元四兩弐年
收 煤朳接火 換引壹支 元弐兩年

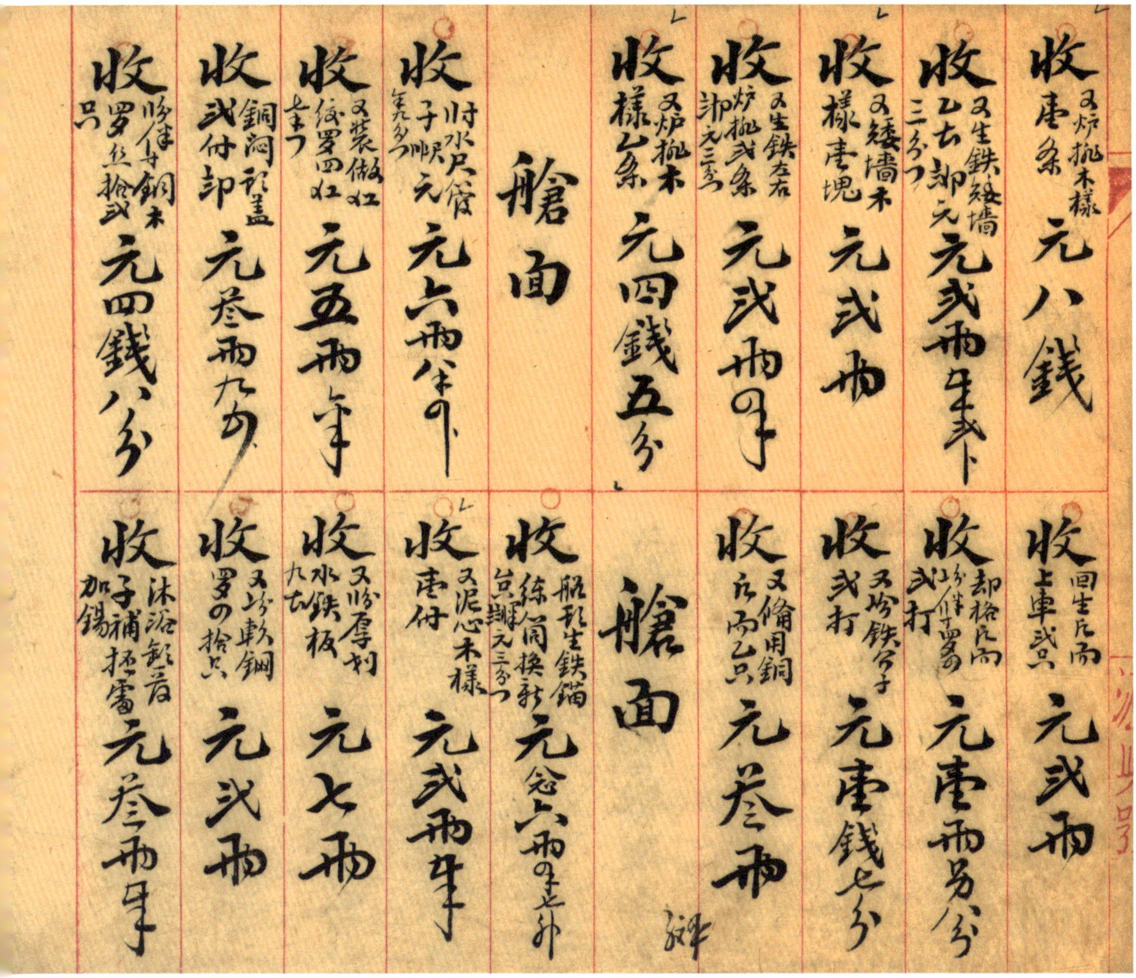

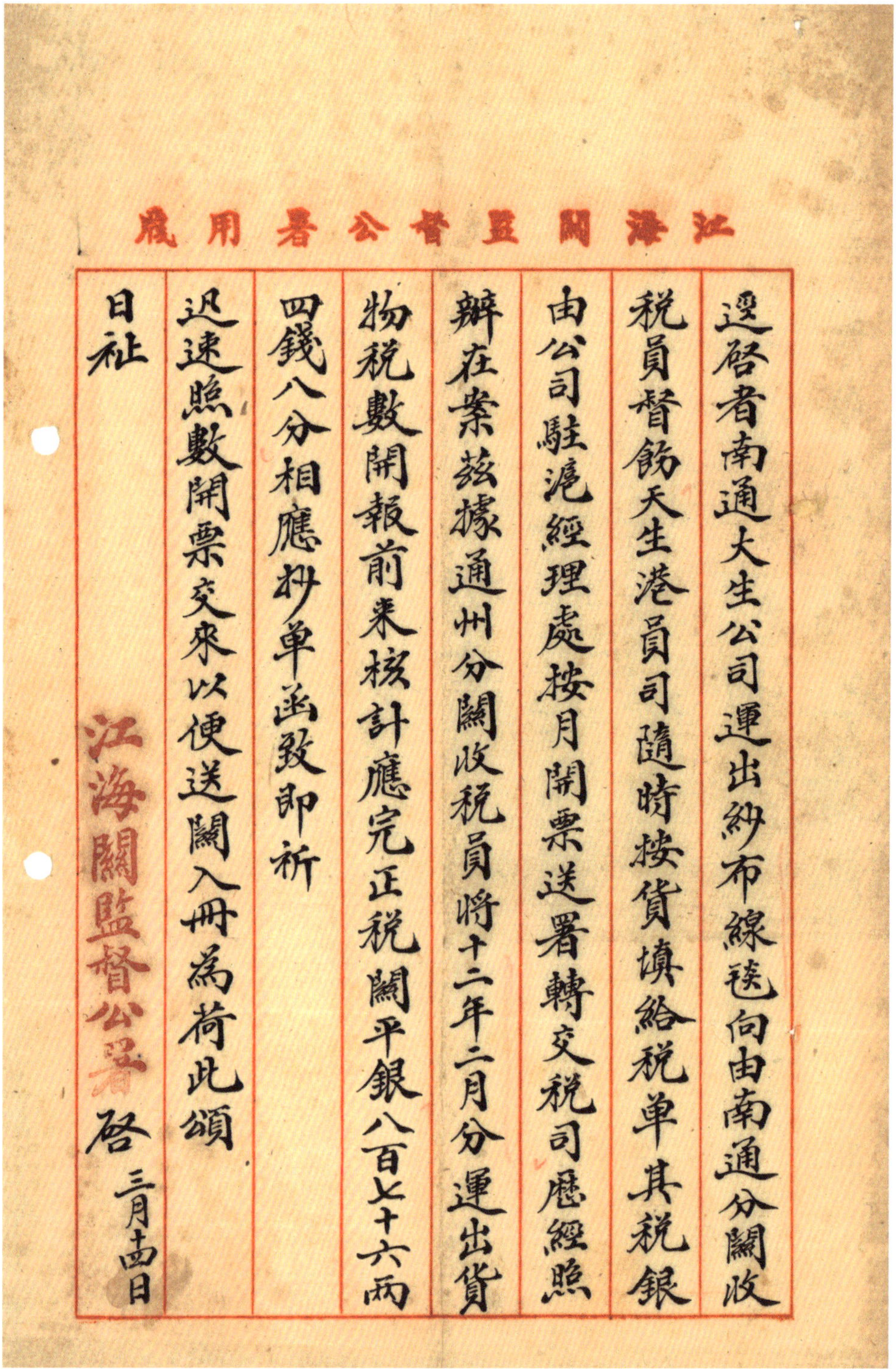

江海關監督公署用箋

逕啓者南通大生公司運出紗布線毯向由南通分關收稅員督飭天生港員司隨時按貨塡給稅單其稅銀由公司駐滬經理處按月開票送署轉交稅司歷經照辦在案茲據通州分關收稅員將十二年二月分運出貨物稅數開報前來核計應完正稅關平銀八百七十六兩四錢八分相應抄單函致即祈迅速照數開票交來以便送關入冊為荷此頌

日祉

江海關監督公署啓 三月十四日

1923 年 3 月 14 日，江海关监督公署致大生沪所的关于缴纳大生纱厂税银的函。

『多一学堂，未始无益』——助学申城

张謇与上海的教育界关系密切。1905 年，江苏省教育会在上海成立，张謇长期担任会长。江苏省教育会“以研究本省学务之得失，图学界之进步”为宗旨。江苏省教育会作为一个民间教育团体，在推动包括上海在内的江苏地区的新式教育的发展上，弥补了教育行政部门的不足，起到了独特的作用。

张謇的名字还与上海的不少学校联系在一起，如复旦公学、震旦学院、吴淞商船专科学校、江苏省立水产学校、中国公学等。张謇对于复旦公学和震旦学院的支持很有代表性。

震旦学院由马相伯始创于 1903 年，1905 年因与总教习南从周在教务问题上产生意见分歧，马相伯率学生出走，另创复旦公学，震旦学院陷于停顿。张謇认为“多一学堂，未始无益”，而且认为复旦公学“系中国自办学堂，更责无旁贷，必合力图成，与教会乐与人为善之宗旨，当不相背”。因此张謇一方面应耶稣会之请，担任震旦学院的董事，支持震旦的复校工作（1905 年 3 月 22 日，张謇日记记载：“徐汇故震旦学院请为董事，复支其学事，许之。”张謇与李平书、姚子让等人合组校董会，帮助震旦学院于 8 月正式复课），另一方面为复旦公学的开办奔走。3 月 25 日，张謇、王清穆、曾铸等多位士绅在上海一品香酒店集议，吁请马相伯主持复旦校务、讨论筹资办学事宜，同时考虑暂借吴淞陆军公所的空房先行办学。张謇和王清穆随即给两江总督周馥等发电报，得到周馥的赞同。周馥指示上海道与军方洽商，获得军方的支持。3 月 29 日张謇“为震旦已散学徒筹款得万元”。之后。张謇、曾铸、严复、熊希龄等人应马相伯之邀，担任复旦公学的校董。9 月 14 日，复旦公学在吴淞举办开学典礼。11 月 22 日，张謇邀请刚从广西来到上海的郑孝胥参观复旦公学，陪同参观的还有陈宝琛、王季樵、赵凤昌等人。复旦公学在吴淞办学一直到 1911 年。

张謇也是中国公学的坚定支持者。1905 年底，日本政府根据清政府的要求，颁布《关于准许清国人入学之公私立学校之规程》，取缔中国留学生的政治活动，剥夺中国留学生的言论、集会、结社、居住等自由，大批留日学生被迫回国。1906 年 1 月，13 省的归国留日学生代表在上海开会，决定自办学校，定校名为中国公学。两江总督端方答应每月资助中国公学 1000 两，并拨吴淞炮台湾海军衙门西六万多平方米官地作为校址。1908 年 9 月 13 日，中国公学开董事会，张謇被推举为董事会会长（总董）。张謇在任内多方筹款以维持中国公学的运作。1912 年，张謇率中国公学的董事，与北洋政府财政部多次交涉，要求把前清上海道蔡乃煌存放在比利时驻沪领事馆的源丰润等户抵押的房产、股票，交中国公学充作经费。

张謇还是吴淞商船学校和江苏省水产学校设校的倡导者，以及两所学校的创办人之一。1905 年，张謇就创办江浙渔业公司事宜咨呈商部，提及未来的五项工作，其中就有在江浙渔业公司附近建立水产、商船两个学校的设想，“选渔业各小学校毕业学生，聪明而体弱者令学水产，其强壮者令学驾驶”。

同年张謇的《呈南洋大臣议略》，设想水产学校讲授捕鱼器具的制作，以及养鱼、腌鱼、冰鱼、晒鲞的技艺；而商船学校学生在校两年练习驾船。张謇认为“水产学校兴则关系渔利，商船学校兴则关系海权。二者利民居三之一，利国居三之二”。

鉴于江浙渔业公司才在吴淞设立初等小学校，学生毕业后方可升入拟议中的水产学校，张謇决定先办商船学校。张謇感慨英国、德国、日本等国家都设有专门的大学培养航运人才，不仅仅是与商务，也同海军有密切的联系。中国长期缺乏航运人才，轮船公司里的驾驶和机务人员都由外国人支配，不但利权受损，也无法造就本国人才。世界商战惨烈，如果要确保主权，并且辅助海军，非创设商船学校不可。据 1907 年 7 月 17 日《申报》刊登的张謇致上海道台瑞澂的信中可知，“基址已于四月初一日开工填筑”。1907 年 5 月 12 日，张謇利用已经筹集的资金开始商船学校的地基建设。在张謇的努力下，江苏省水产学校于 1912 年设立，1913 年获得吴淞炮台湾复旦公学原校址土地建设新校区。

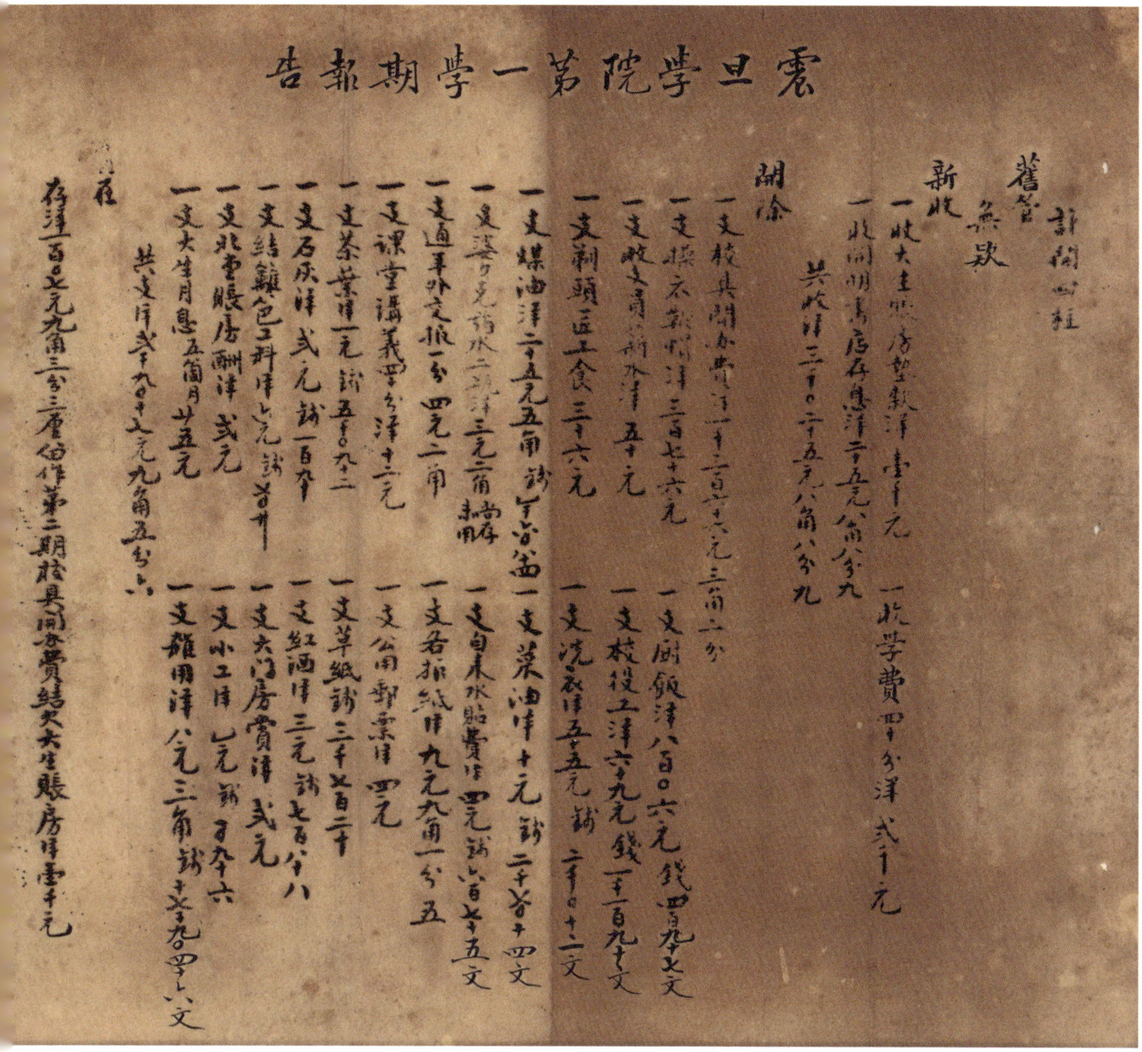

震旦學院第一學期報告

計開四柱

舊管　無款

新收

一收大生滬所墊款洋壹千元

一收開明書店存息洋二十五元八角八分九

共收洋三千〇二十五元八角八分九

一收學費四十八分洋貳千元

開除

一支校具開辦費洋一千二百六十六元三角二分

一支操衣靴帽洋三百七十六元

一支[illegible]薪水洋五十元

一支剃頭匠工食三十六元

一支煤油洋二十五元五角　錢[illegible]

一支燈火茶水二項洋三元二角（尚存未用）

一支通年外交報一分四元二角

一支課堂講義四分洋十二元

一支茶葉洋一元　錢五千〇九十二

一支石灰洋貳元　錢一百六十

一支結籠包工料洋七元　錢三百廿

一支北京賬房酬洋貳元

一支大生月息五個月廿五元

共支洋貳千九百十五元九角五分六

一支廚飯洋八百〇六元　錢四百九十七文

一支校役工洋六十九元　錢一千一百九十七文

一支洗衣洋五十五元　錢二千〇十二文

一支菜油洋十元　錢二千六百十四文

一支自來水貼費洋四元　錢六百七十五文

一支名擬紙洋九元九角一分五

一支公用郵票洋四元

一支草紙錢三千七百二十

一支紅酒洋三元　錢七百八十八

一支大門房賞洋貳元

一支小工洋七元　錢三百六十六

一支雜用洋八元三角　錢十七千九百四十六文

存

存洋一百〇七元九角三分三厘留作第二期校具開辦費　結欠大生賬房洋壹千元

《震旦学院第一学期报告》。报告中提到大生沪所垫款洋 1000 元。

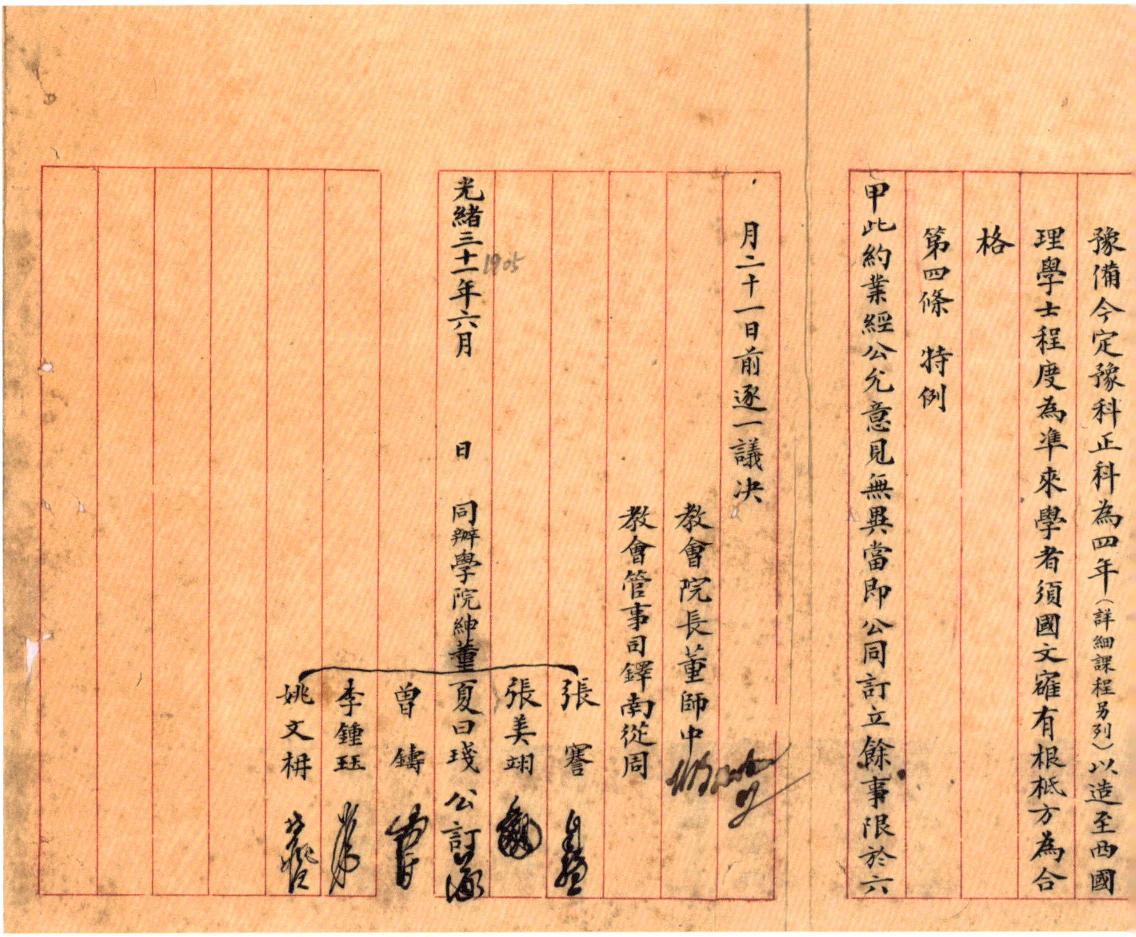
豫備今定豫科正科為四年（詳細課程另列）以造至西國
理學士程度為準來學者須國文確有根柢方為合
格
第四條 特例
甲此約業經公允意見無異當即公同訂立餘事限於六
月二十一日前逐一議決
教會院長董師中
教會管事司鐸南從周
光緒三十一年六月 日 同辦學院紳董
張謇
張美翊
夏日琖 公訂
曾鑄
李鍾珏
姚文枏

光绪三十一年（1905）六月，张謇等人签署的《震旦学院开办约》。

震旦學院開辦約

第一條　公任校員

甲凡教會之院長及管事之司鐸與此次同辦學院紳董統為本校校員

乙凡學務上對於院外之交涉校員公同具名

丙校員有同等之權嗣後學院中有重要事由校員公同議決

丁校員分任本院之義務凡籌備校舍擔任教課由教會之院長管事之司鐸任之凡籌備校具擔任庶務管理學生由紳董任之

第二條　辦事權限

甲校員於紳董中公推一員辦理庶務庶務校員對於學生有管理之責任

乙管理上有院章所未及詳備者庶務校員得便宜施行

丙院章課程由校員公同議定後院章由庶務校員實行他校員只可隨時稽察課程由院長司鐸揀派教員實行如須更改仍當由校員公議

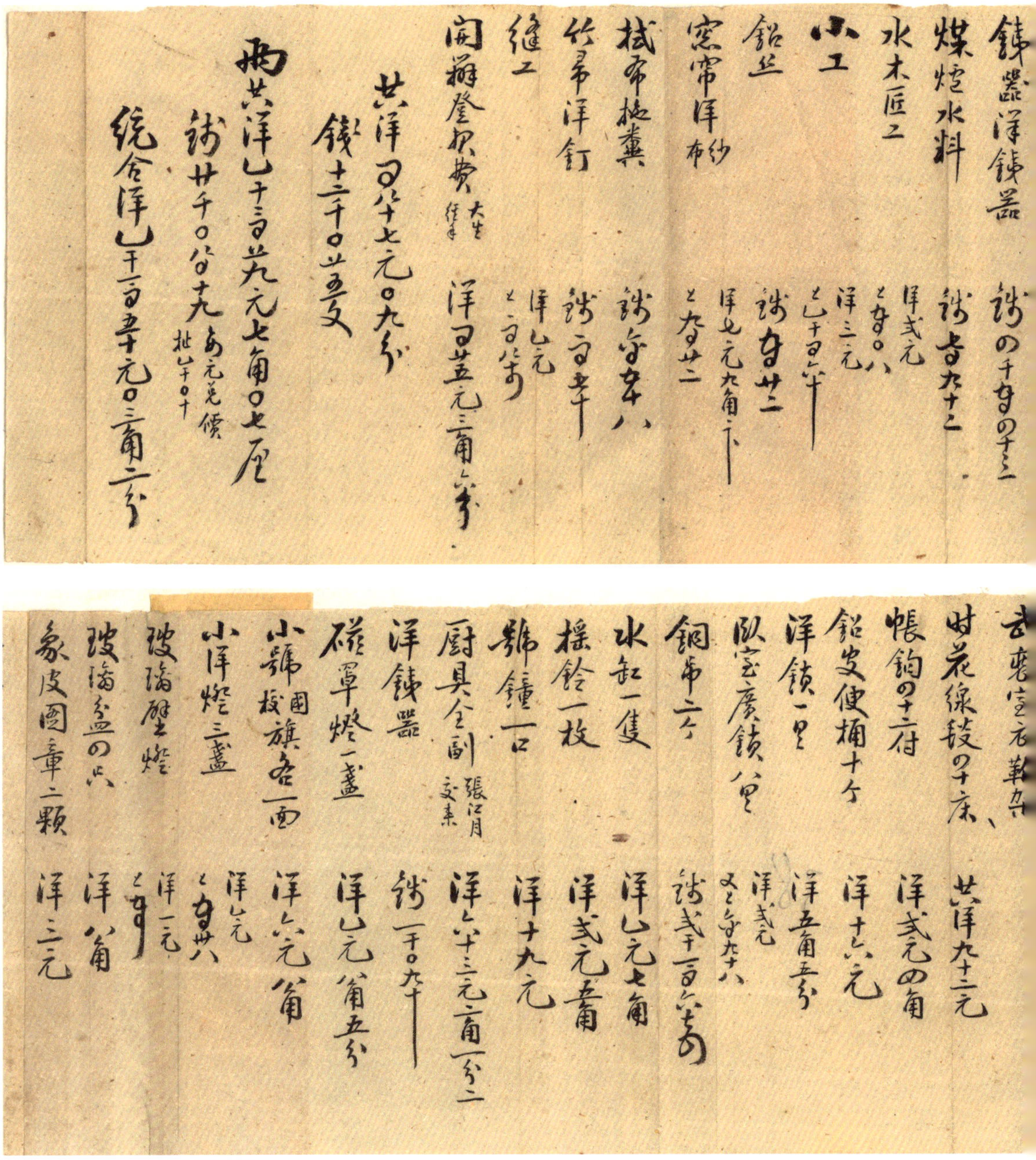

大生沪所代震旦学院支付开办费用清单。

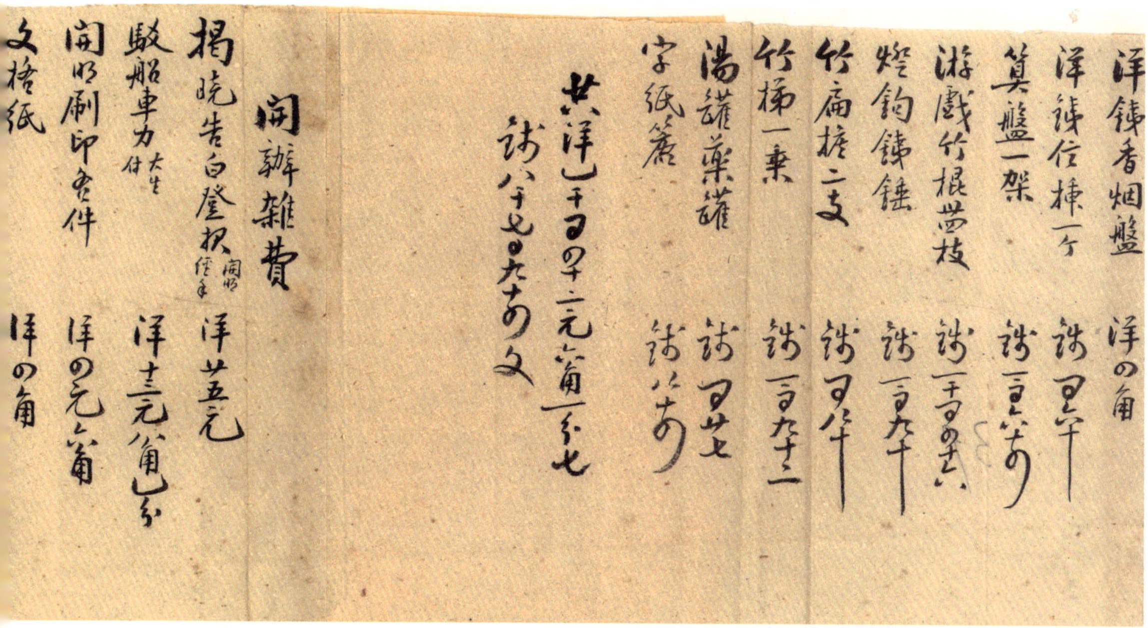

洋鐵香烟盤　洋〤角
洋鐵作棟一个　錢〤〥〸
算盤一架　錢〢〣〤〥
游戲竹根茵枝　錢一千〥〤〦
烟鈎鐵錘　錢〢〥〸
竹扁擔二支　錢〥〸
竹梯一乘　錢〢〨十二
湯罐藥罐　錢〥〤七
字紙簏　錢〤〥
共洋〡千〥〥二元〥角〡分七
錢〤〥〢〤文
開辦雜費
揭曉告白登報 開學 招考　洋廿五元
駁船車力 大生 付　洋十三元〥角〡分
開學刷印告件　洋〤元二角
文憑紙　洋〤角

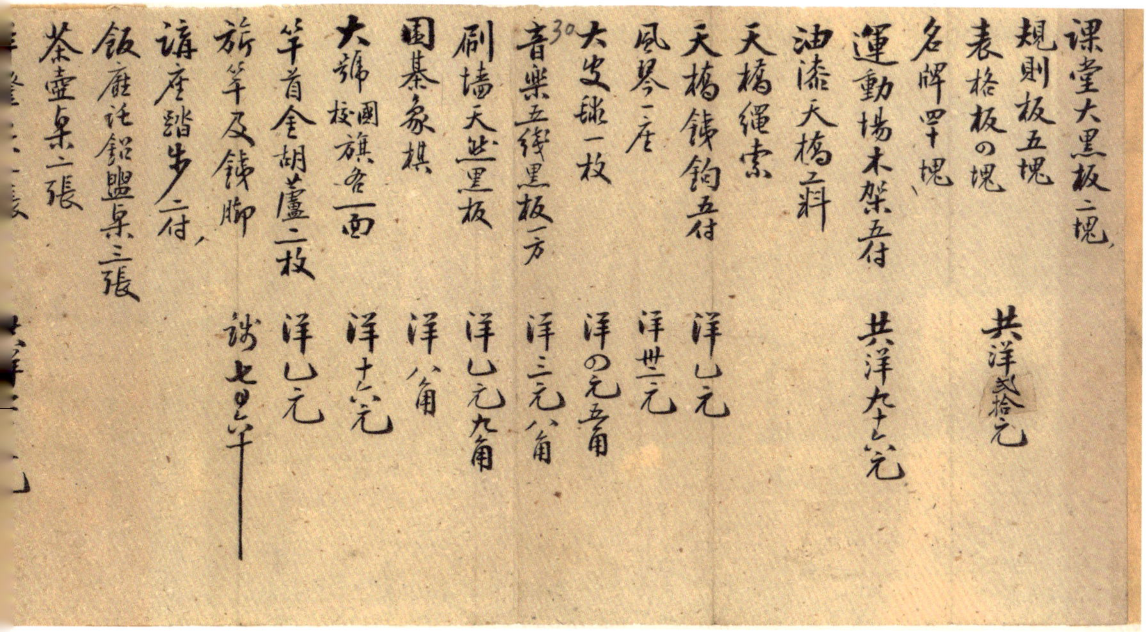

課堂大黑板二塊
規則板五塊
表格板〤塊
名牌〥塊　共洋貳拾元
運動場木架五付
油漆天橋木料　共洋〤十二元
天橋繩索
天橋鐵鈎五付　洋〡元
風琴二座　洋卅二元
大皮球一枚　洋〤元五角
音樂五線黑板一方　洋三元〥角
刷牆天然黑板　洋〡元九角
圍棊象棋　洋〥角
大旗校旗國旗各一面　洋十二元
竿首金胡蘆二枚　洋〡元
旗竿及鐵脚　錢七〤〥
講座踏步二付
飯廳託鉛盤桌三張
茶壺桌二張

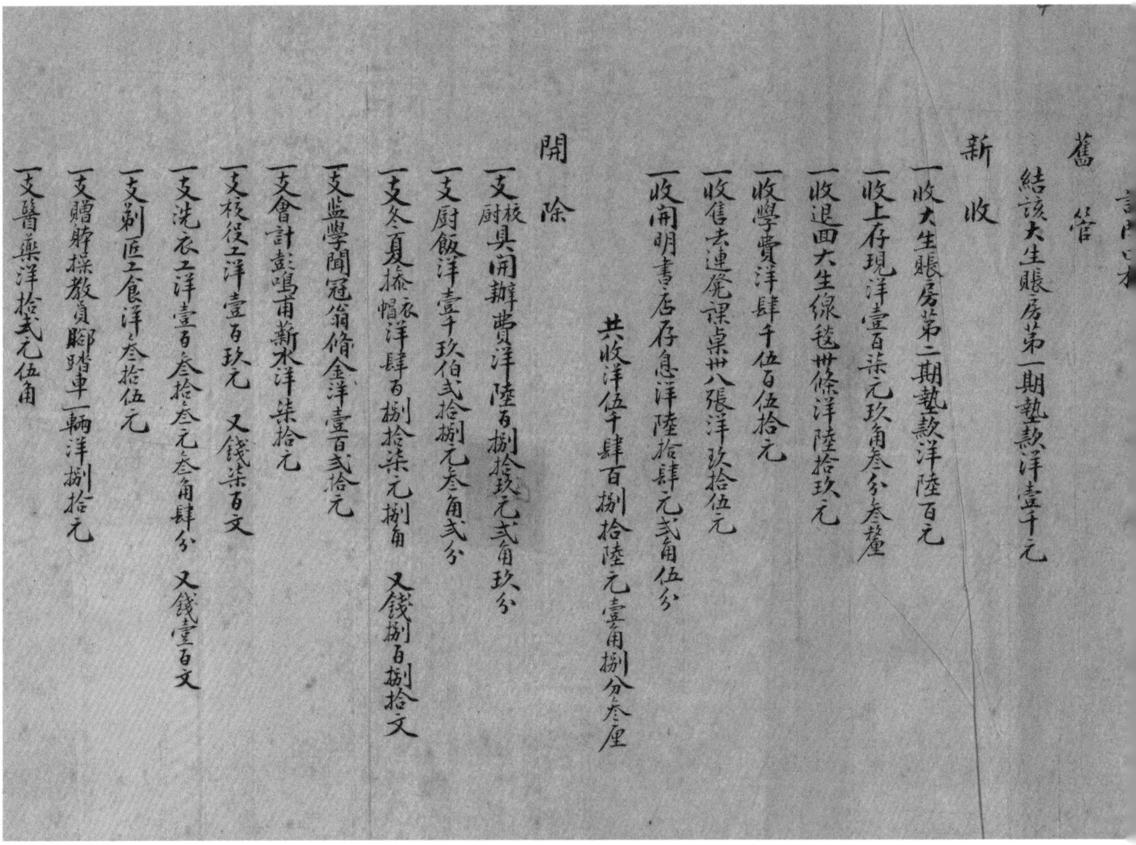

舊管

結該大生賬房第一期墊款洋壹千元

新收

一收大生賬房第二期墊款洋陸百元
一收上存現洋壹百柒元玖角叁分叁釐
一收退回大生綠毯卅條洋陸拾玖元
一收學費洋肆千伍百伍拾元
一收售去連凳課桌卅八張洋玖拾伍元
一收開明書店存息洋陸拾肆元弍角伍分

共收洋伍千肆百捌拾陸元壹角捌分叁厘

開除

一支校廚具開辦費洋陸百捌拾玖元弍角玖分
一支廚飯洋壹千玖伯弍拾捌元叁角弍分
一支冬夏操衣帽洋肆百捌拾柒元捌角 又錢捌百捌拾文
一支監學關冠翁脩金洋壹百弍拾元
一支會計彭鳴甫薪水洋柒拾元
一支校役工洋壹百玖元 又錢柒百文
一支洗衣工洋壹百叁拾叁元叁角肆分 又錢壹百文
一支剃匠工食洋叁拾伍元
一支贈體操教員腳踏車一輛洋捌拾元
一支醫藥洋拾弍元伍角

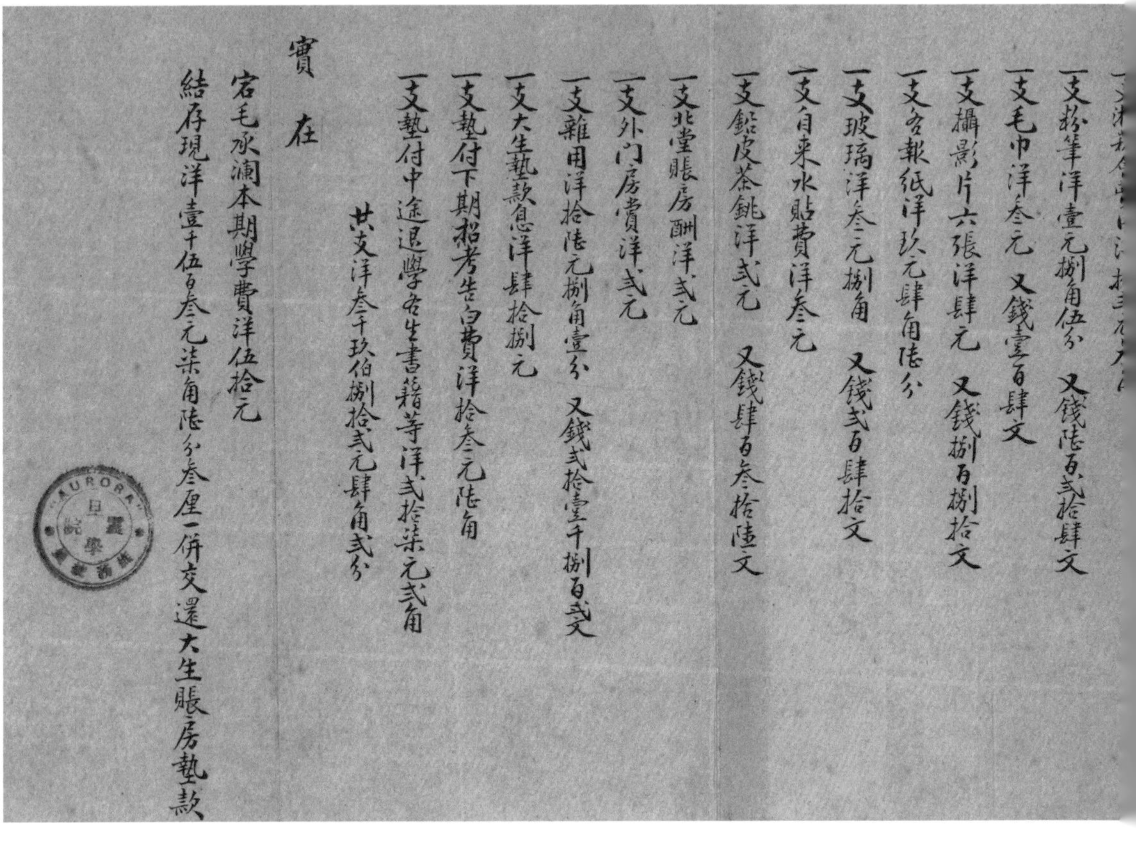
AURORA
震旦學院

一支粉筆洋壹元捌角伍分 又錢陸百弍拾肆文
一支毛巾洋叁元 又錢壹百肆文
一支攝影片六張洋肆元 又錢捌百捌拾文
一支各報紙洋玖元肆角陸分
一支玻璃洋叁元捌角 又錢弍百肆拾文
一支自來水貼費洋叁元
一支鉛皮茶銚洋弍元 又錢肆百叁拾陸文
一支北堂賬房酬洋弍元
一支外门房賞洋弍元
一支雜用洋拾陸元捌角壹分 又錢弍拾壹千捌百文
一支大生墊款息洋肆拾捌元
一支墊付下期招考告白費洋拾叁元陸角
一支墊付中途退學各生書籍等洋弍拾柒元弍角

共支洋叁千玖伯捌拾弍元肆角弍分

實在

宕毛承瀾本期學費洋伍拾元
結存現洋壹千伍百叁元柒角陸分叁厘一併交還大生賬房墊款

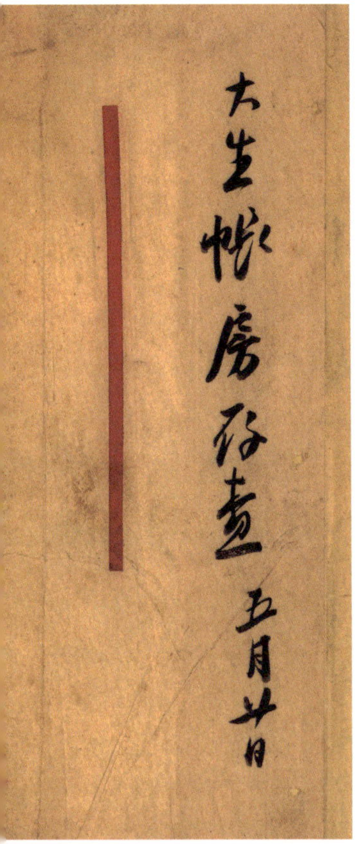
大生帐房存查 五月廿日

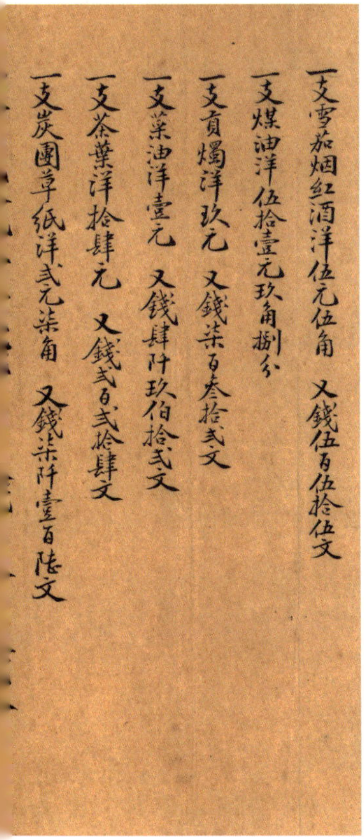
一支雪茄烟红酒洋伍元伍角 又錢伍百伍拾伍文
一支煤油洋伍拾壹元玖角捌分
一支貢燭洋玖元 又錢柒百叁拾弍文
一支菜油洋壹元 又錢肆阡玖伯拾弍文
一支茶葉洋拾肆元 又錢弍百弍拾肆文
一支炭團草纸洋弍元柒角 又錢柒阡壹百陸文

《震旦学院第二期收支报告》。报告提到大生沪所在第一期垫款洋1000元的基础上，垫款洋600元。

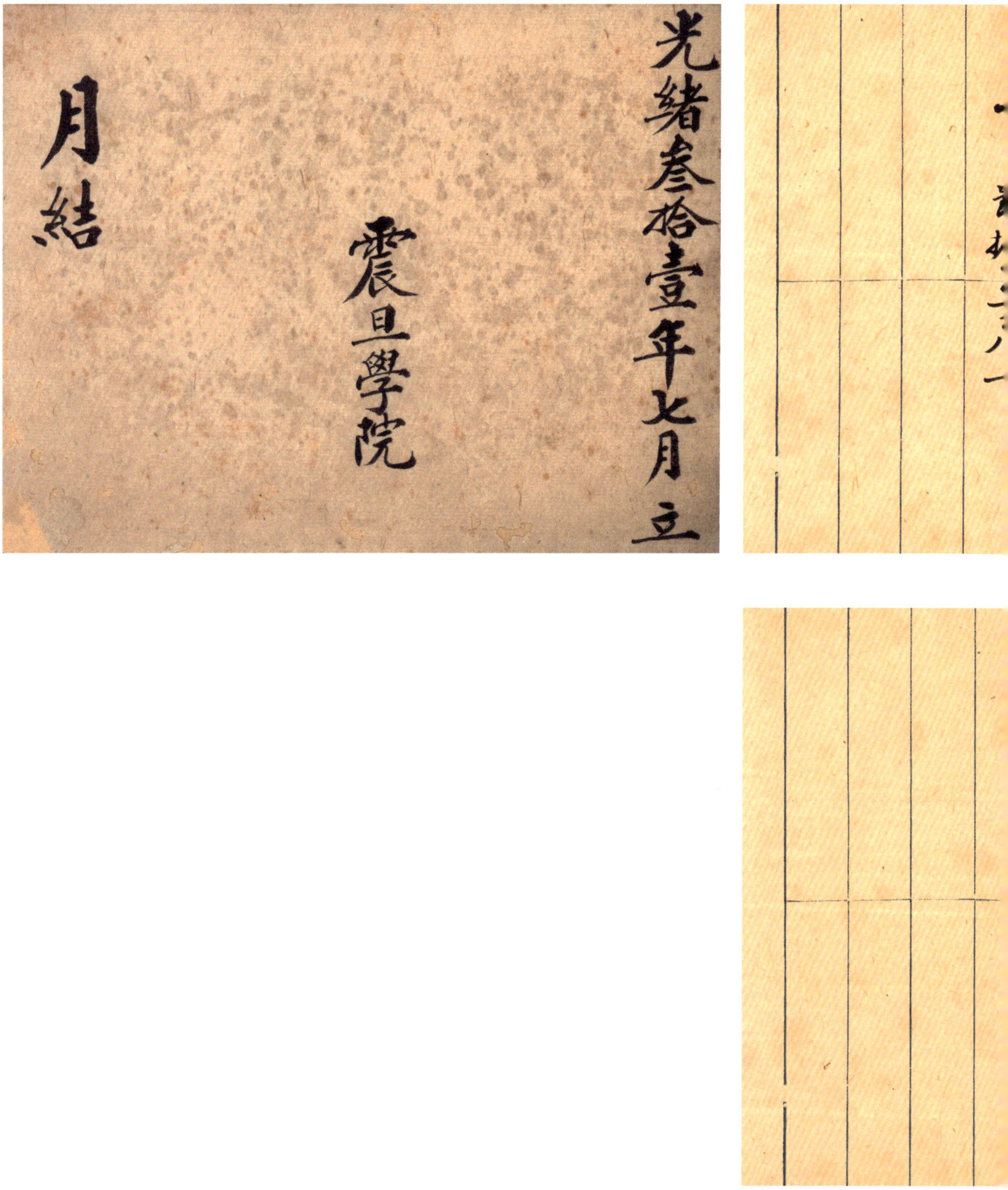
光緒叁拾壹年七月立
震旦學院
月結

1905 年，大生沪所代震旦学院记账的《月结》(局部)。

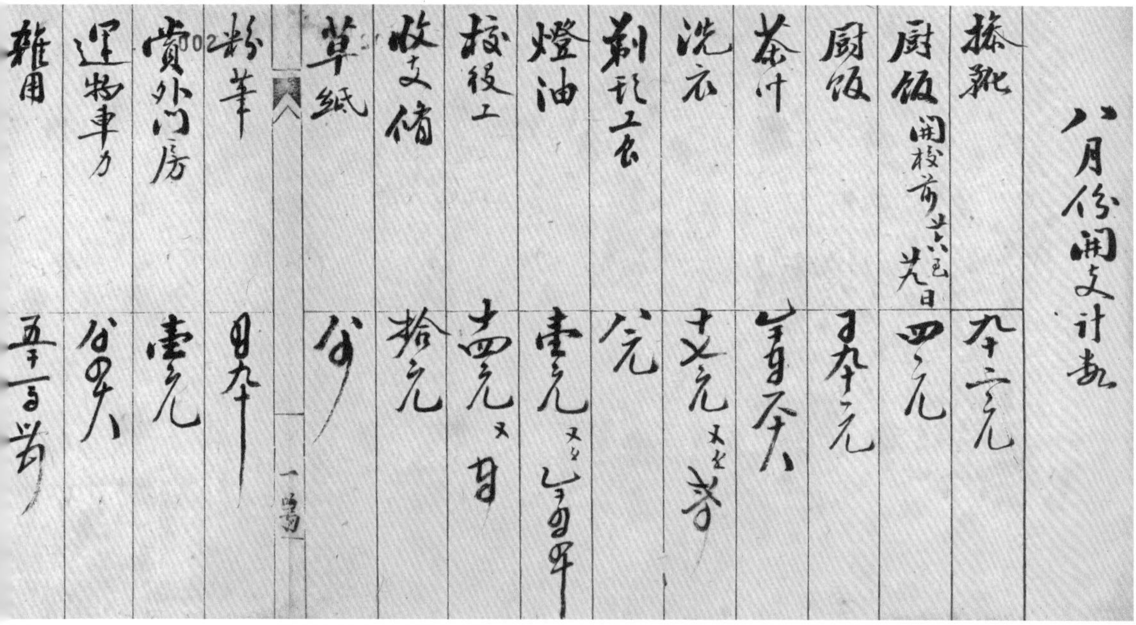

八月份用支计数

搽靴

厨饭 开校前

厨饭

茶叶

洗衣

剃头工衣

灯油

校役工

收支借

草纸

粉笔

赏外门房

运物车力

杂用

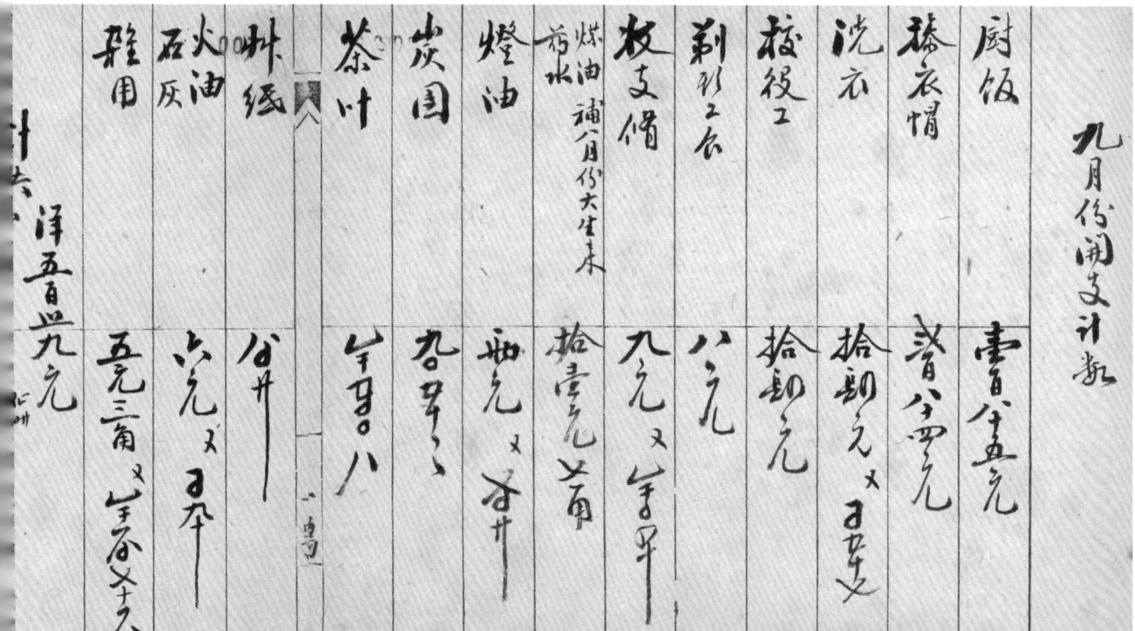

九月份用支计数

厨饭

搽衣帽

洗衣

校役工

剃头工衣

收支借

煤油 补八月份大生来 药水

灯油

炭团

茶叶

草纸

火油 石灰

杂用

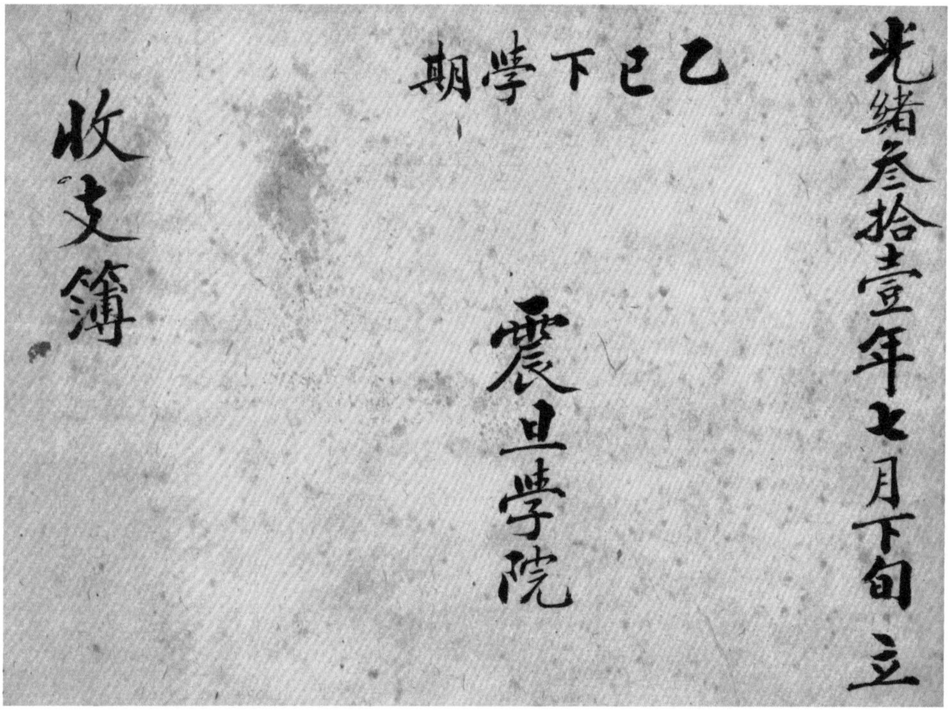
光緒叁拾壹年七月下旬 立
乙巳下學期
震旦學院
收支簿

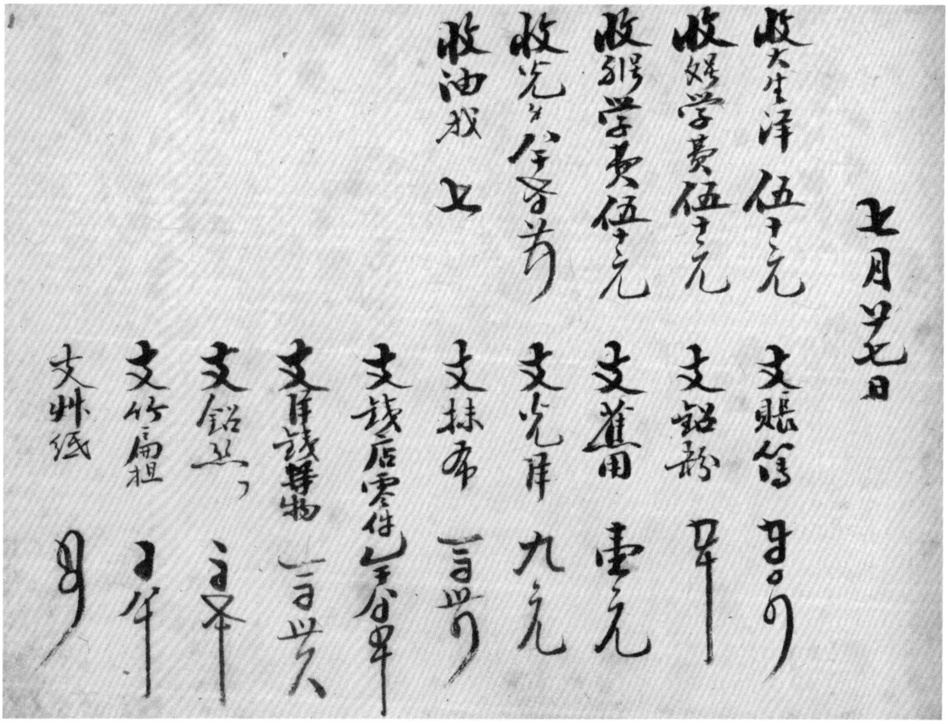

乙巳年（1905）下学期，大生沪所代震旦学院记账的《收支簿》(局部)。

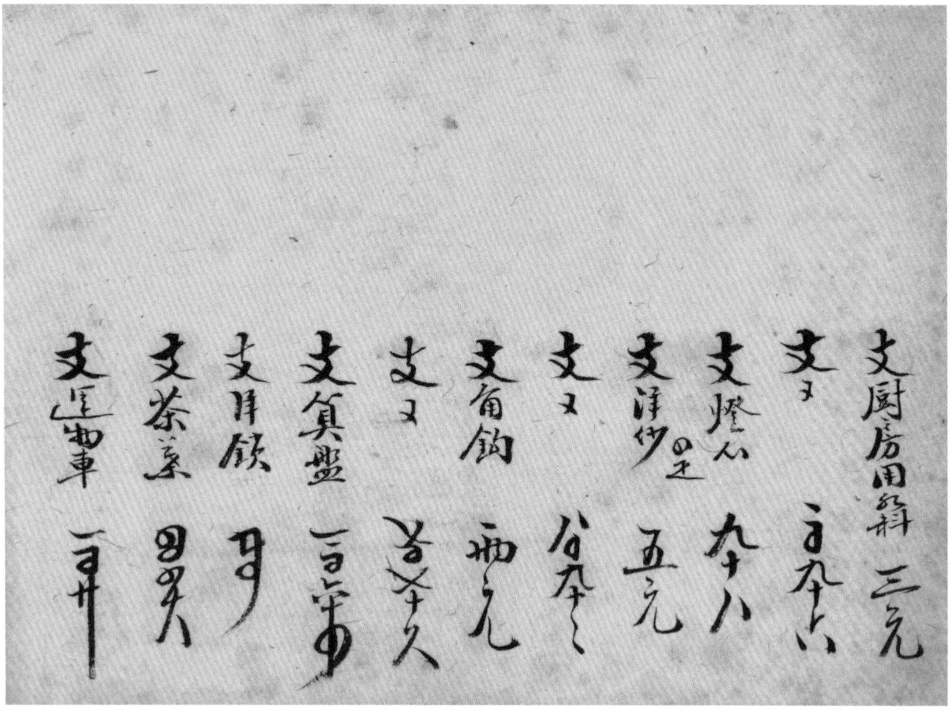
支廚房用料 三元
支燈火
支角鉤 两元
支算盤
支茶菜

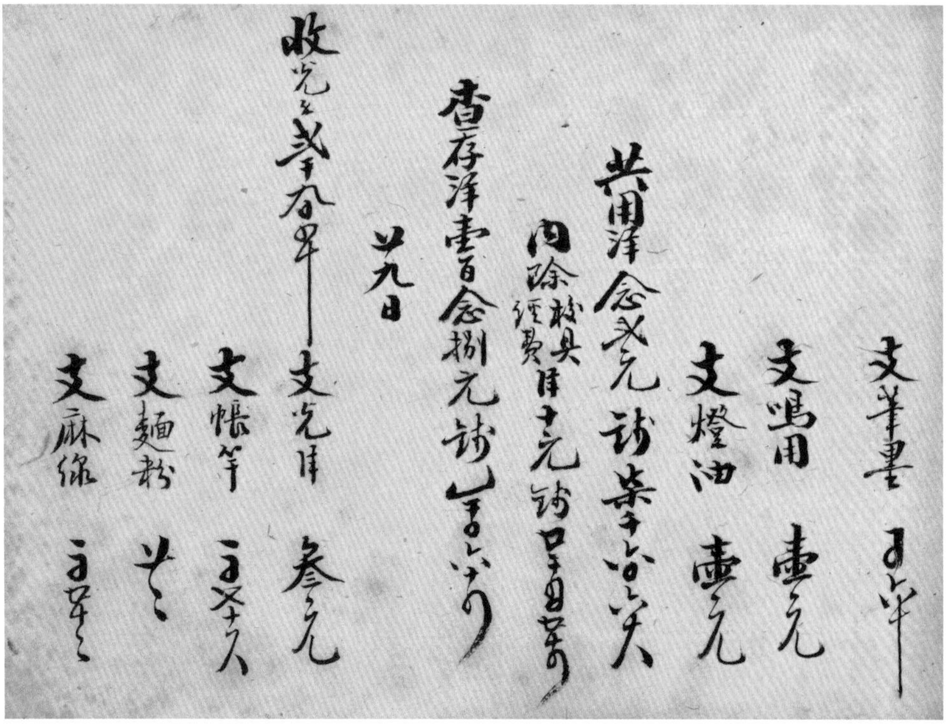
支筆墨
支燈油 壹元
查存洋壹百念捌元
廿九日
支光洋 叁元
支帳竿
支麵粉
支麻繩

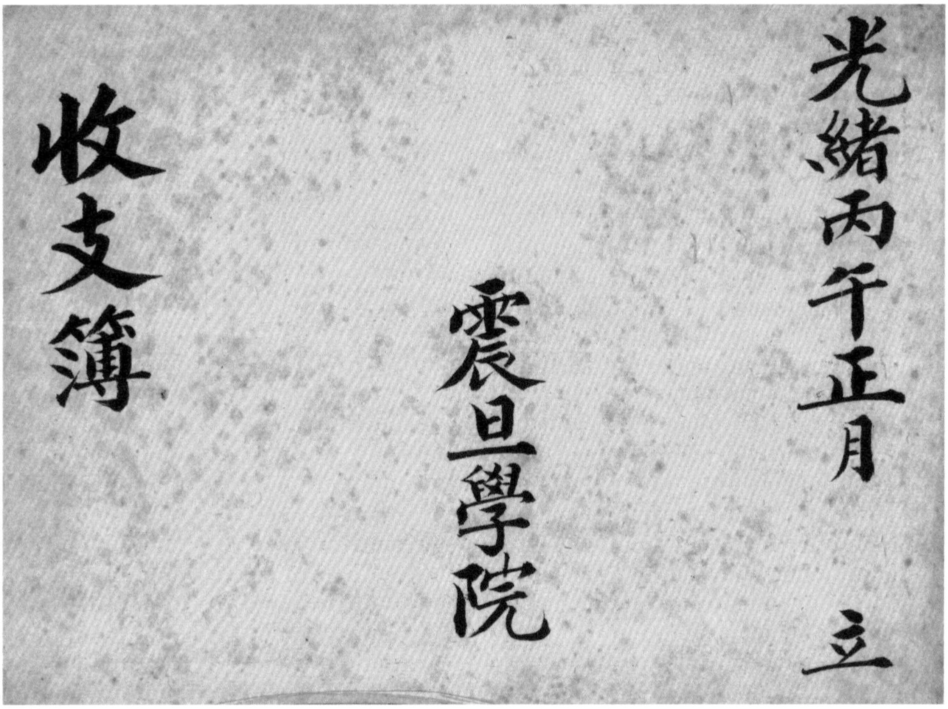
光緒丙午正月　立

震旦學院

收支簿

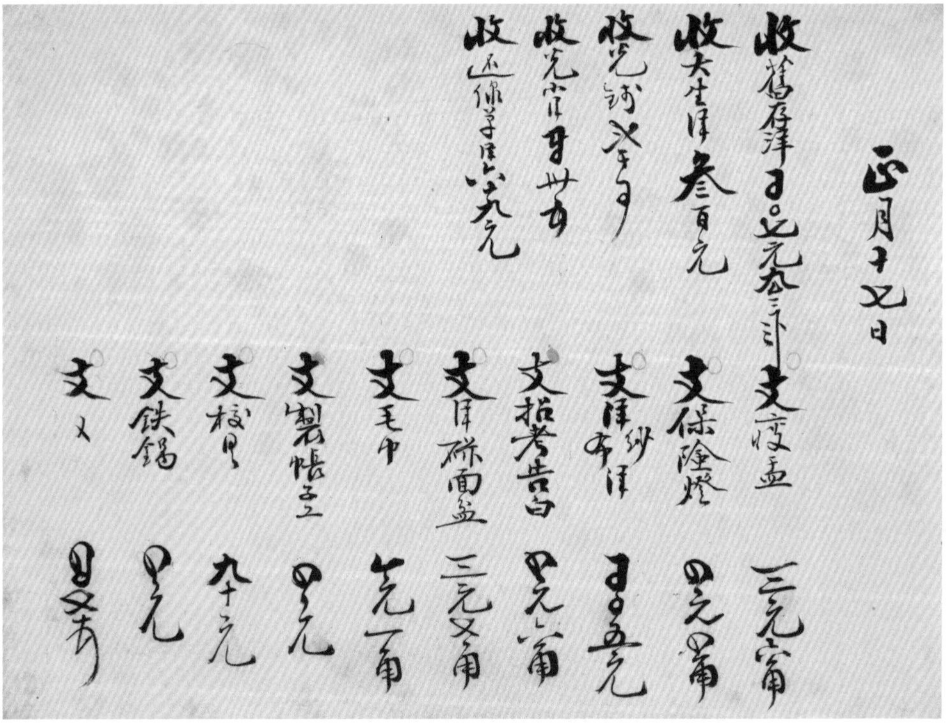

丙午年（1906），大生沪所代震旦学院记账的《收支簿》（局部）。

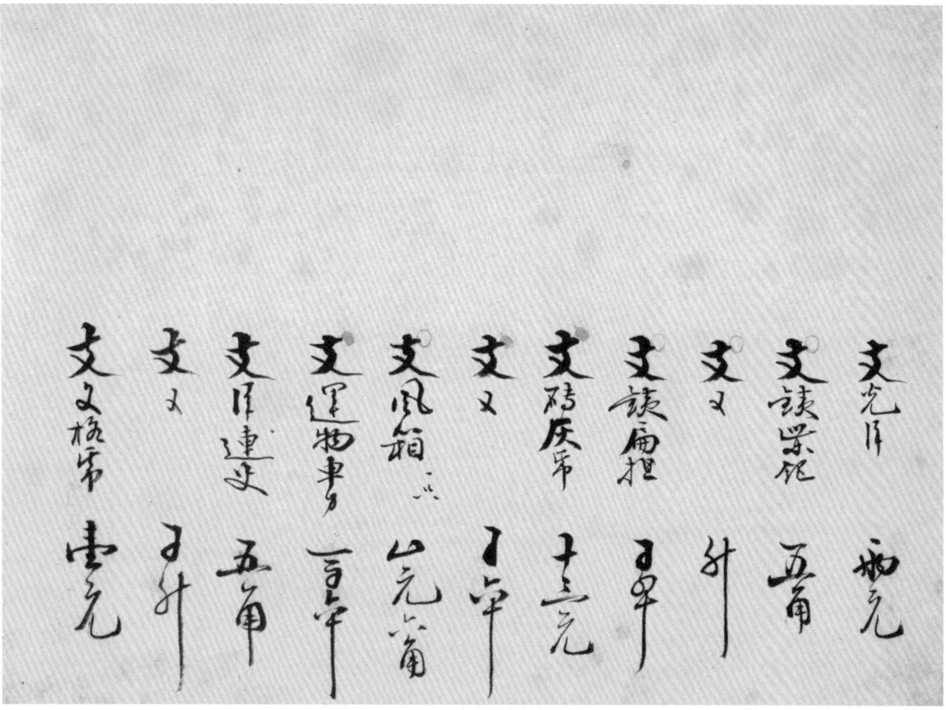

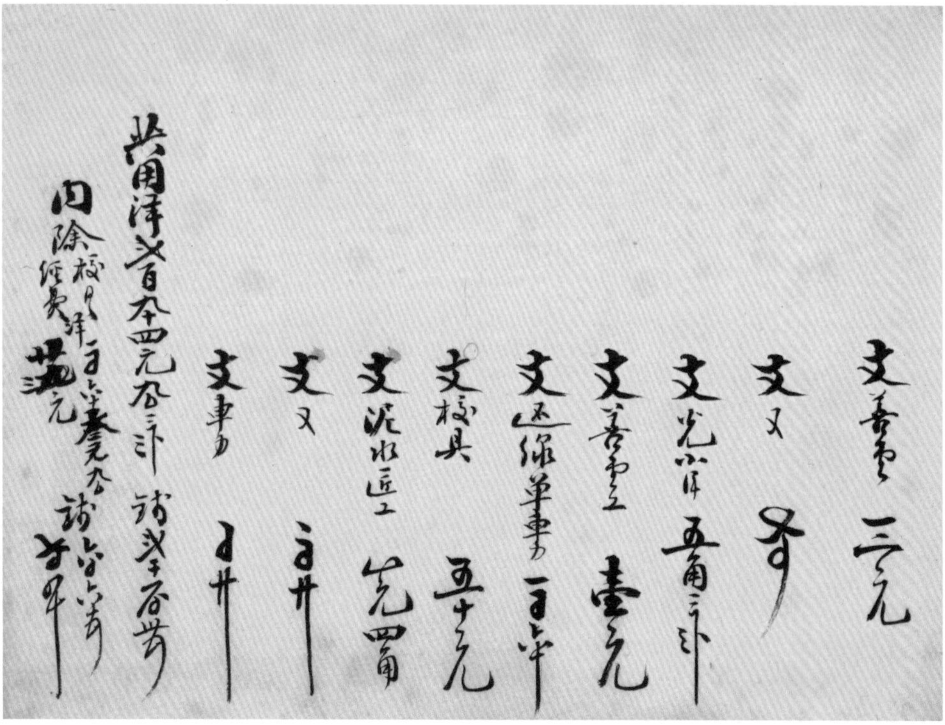

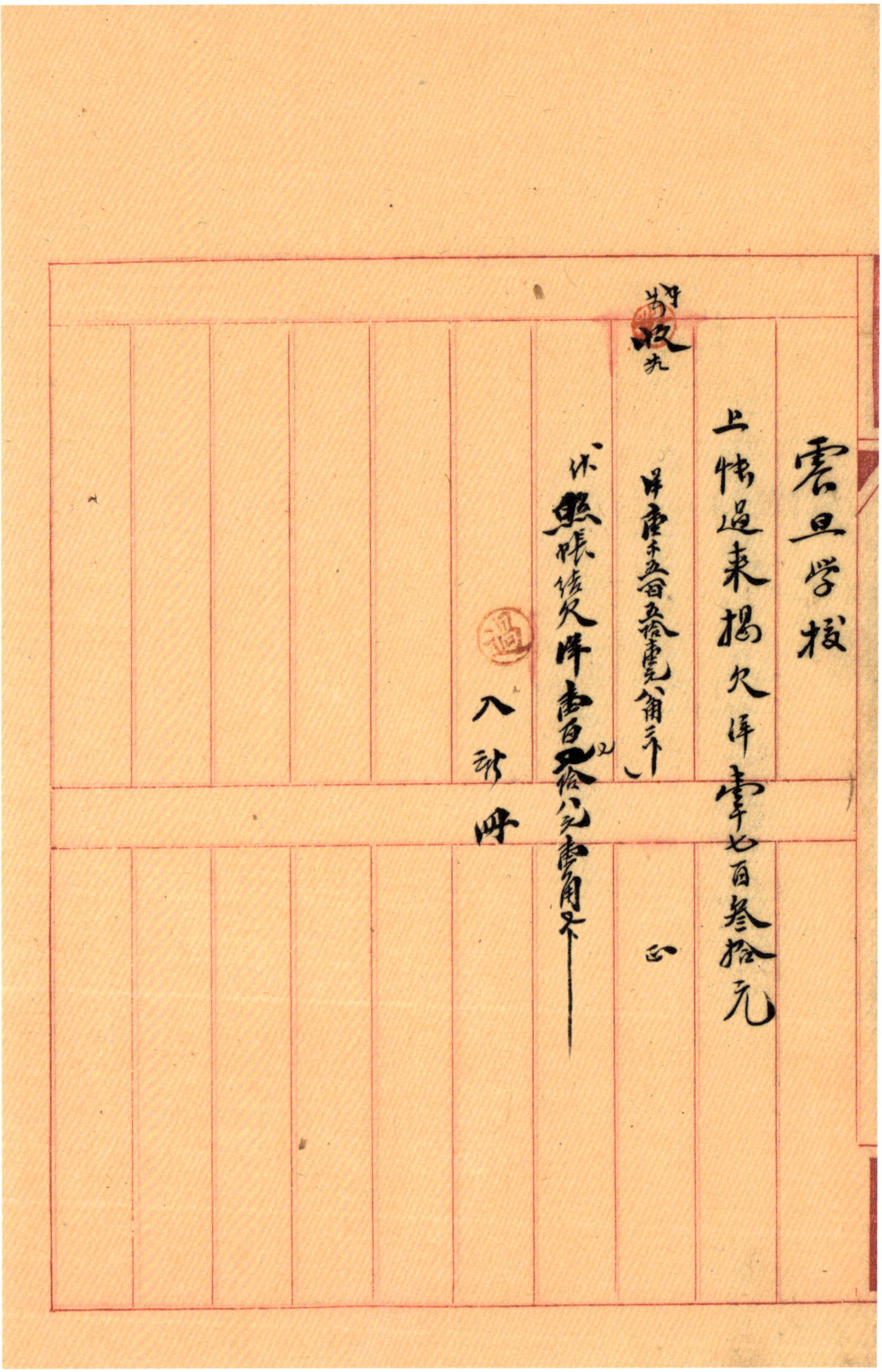
震旦学校
上帐過来揭欠洋壹千七百叁拾元

1906 年大生沪所《总录》中的震旦学院分项。

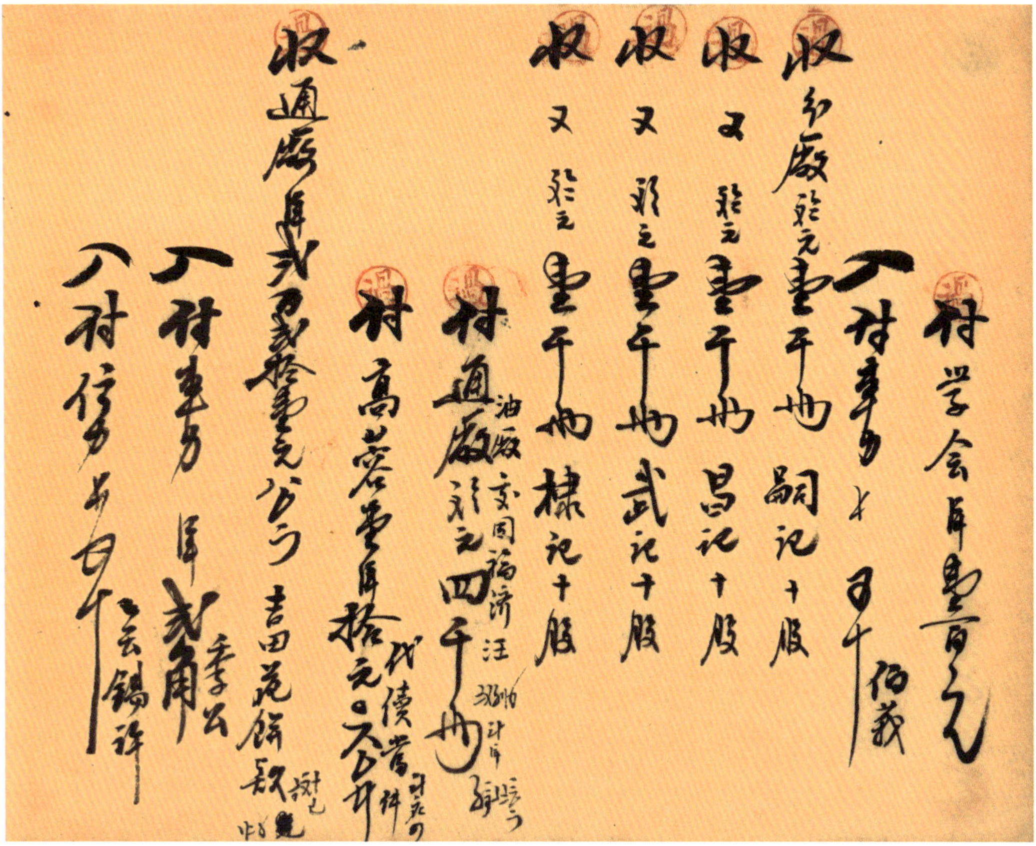

1906 年 6 月 13 日，大生沪所付江苏省教育总会洋 100 元的流水账。

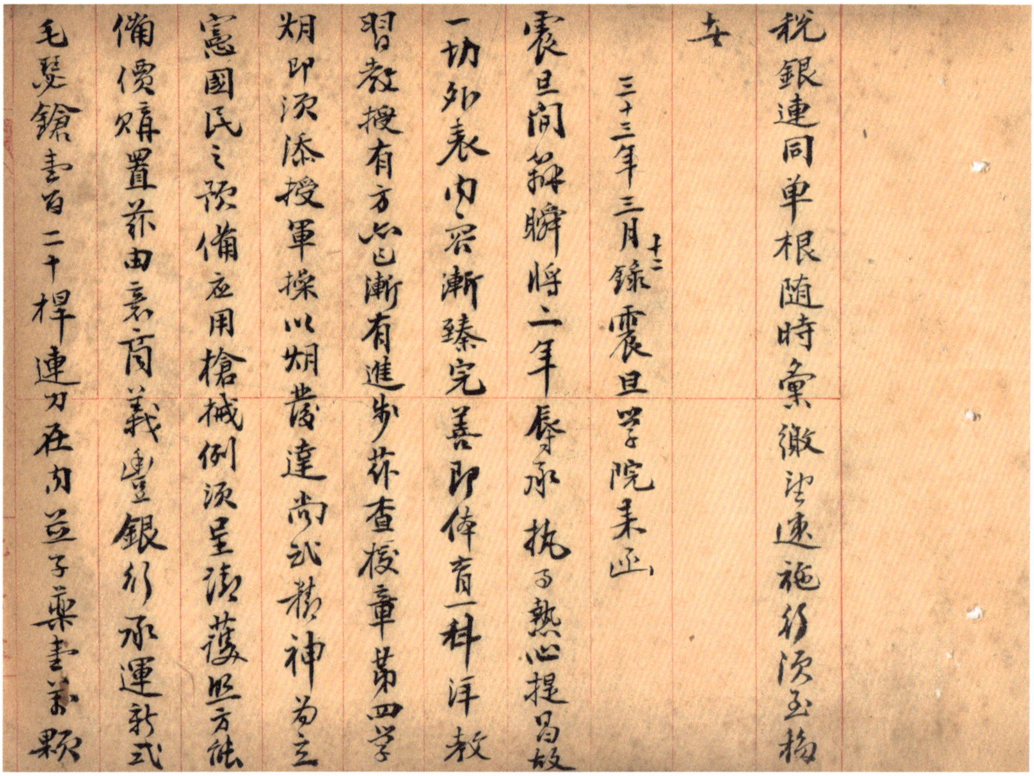

税銀連同單根隨時彙繳望速施行須至禱

安

三十三年三月十三錄震旦學院來函

震旦開辦將二年參承執事熱心提倡故

一切外表内容漸臻完善即体育一科洋教

習教授有方亦已漸有進步茲查校章第四學

期即須添授軍操以期養成尚武精神為立

憲國民之預備應用槍械例須呈請護照方能

備價購置茲由意商義豐銀行承運新式

毛瑟鎗壹百二十桿連刀在内並子藥壹萬顆

震旦学院通过意大利义丰银行购置毛瑟枪120杆、子弹1万颗，用于学生军操课。震旦学院请求张謇协助办理申请护照事宜，1907年4月24日，张謇致函上海道台瑞澂，希望这批枪弹能够顺利通关。

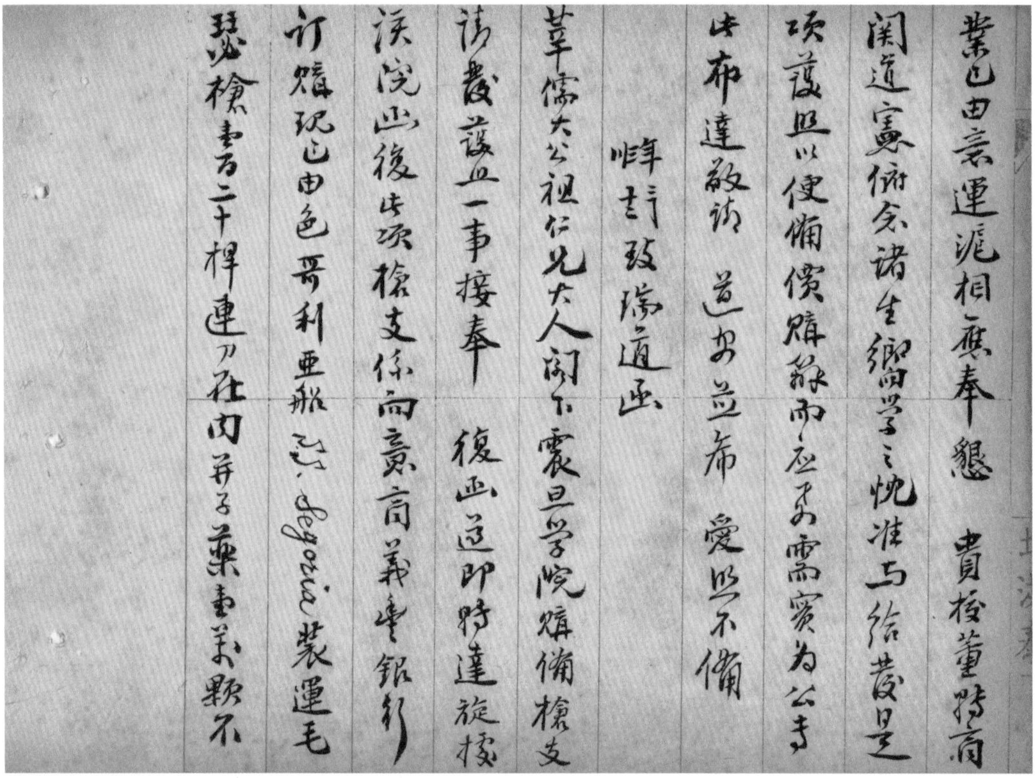

業已由袁運滬，相應奉懇 貴校董特商
關道憲俯念諸生嚮學之忱，准與給發是
項護照，以便備價購辦，而應要需，實為公幸。
此布，達敬請 道安，並希 愛照不備
附封致瑞道函
莘儒大公祖仁兄大人閣下：震旦學院購備槍支
請發護照一事，接奉 復函，送即特達。旋接
該院函復，此項槍支係向意商義豐銀行
訂購，現已由色哥利亞 Segovia 裝運毛
瑟槍壹萬二千桿，連刀在內，並子藥壹萬萬顆，不

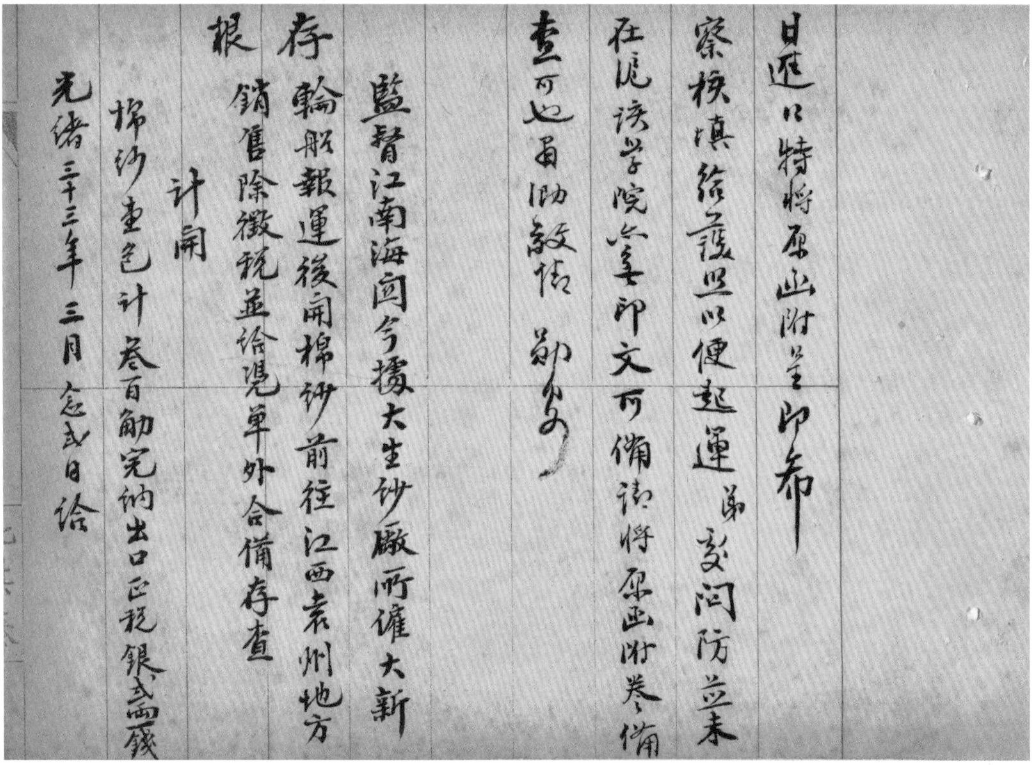

日進口，特將原函附呈，即希
察核填給護照，以便起運。弟處關防並未
在滬，該學院公牘印文可備，請將原函附卷備
查可也。肅此，敬請 勛安
監督江南海關今據大生紗廠所僱大新
存 輪船報運後開棉紗前往江西袁州地方
根 銷售，除徵稅並給憑單外，合備存查
計開
棉紗壹包，計叁百觔，完納出口正稅銀貳兩錢
光緒三十三年三月廿貳日給

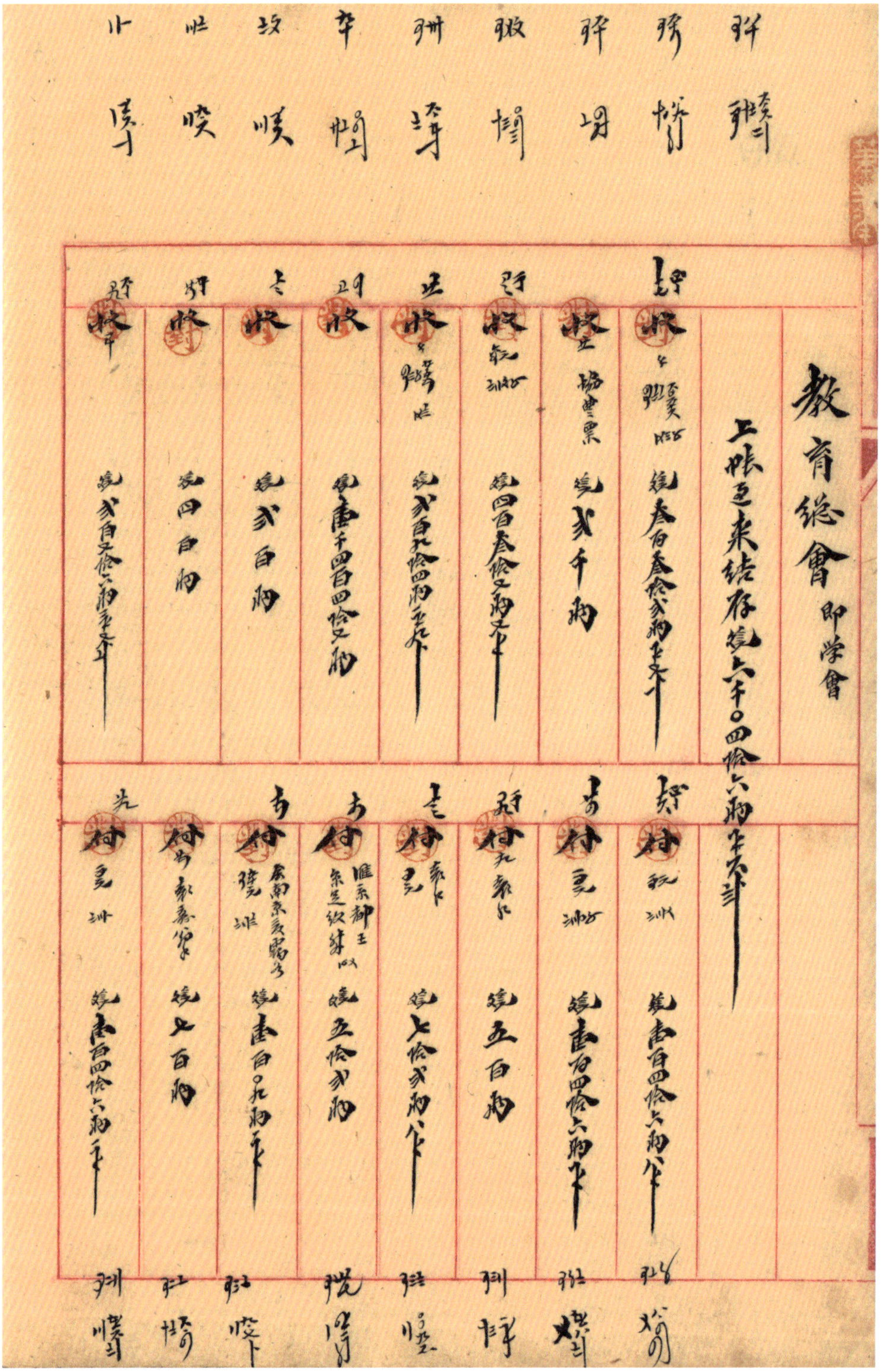
教育總會
即学會

1907 年大生沪所《同人、杂户总登》中的江苏省教育总会分项。

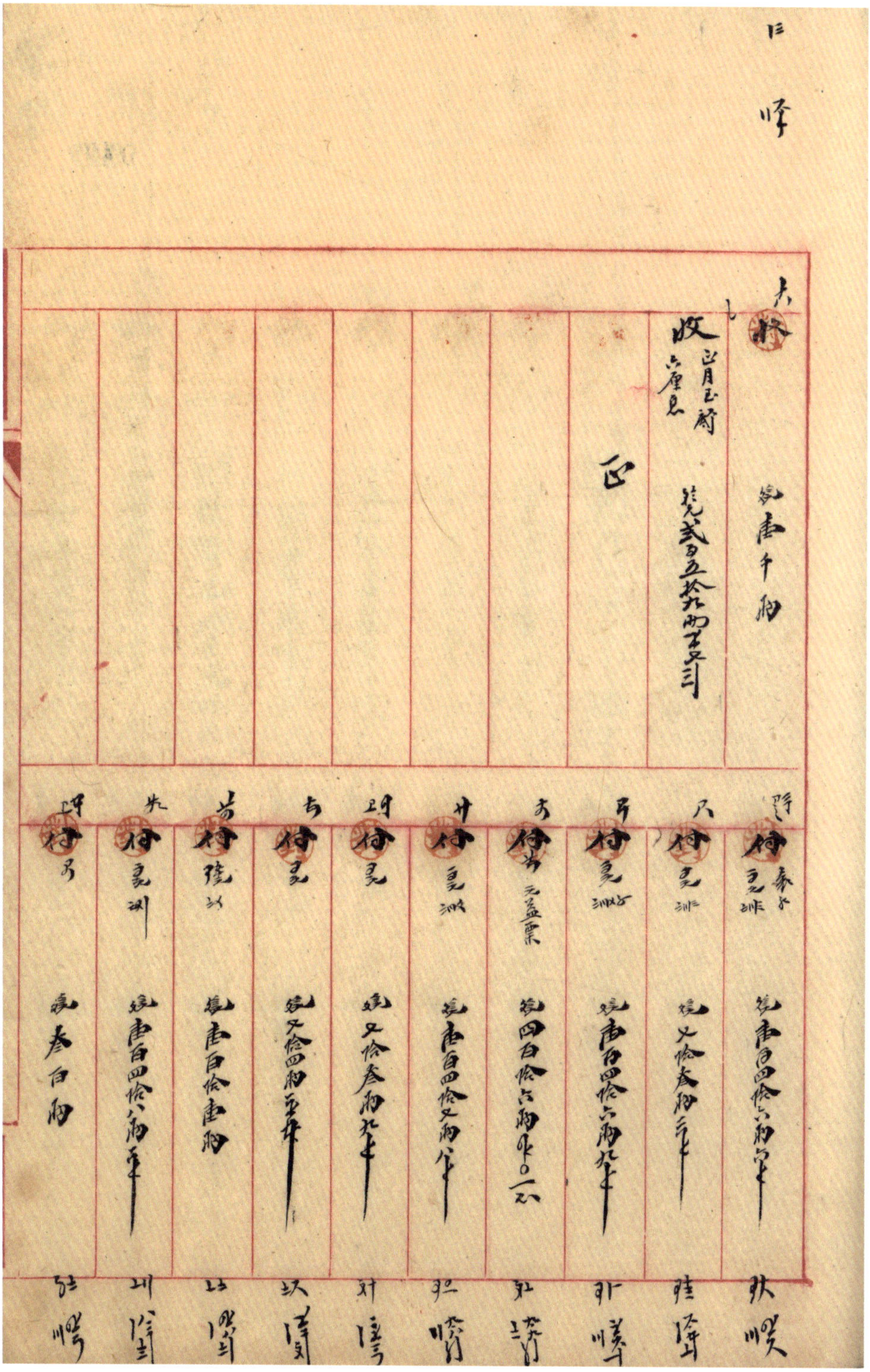

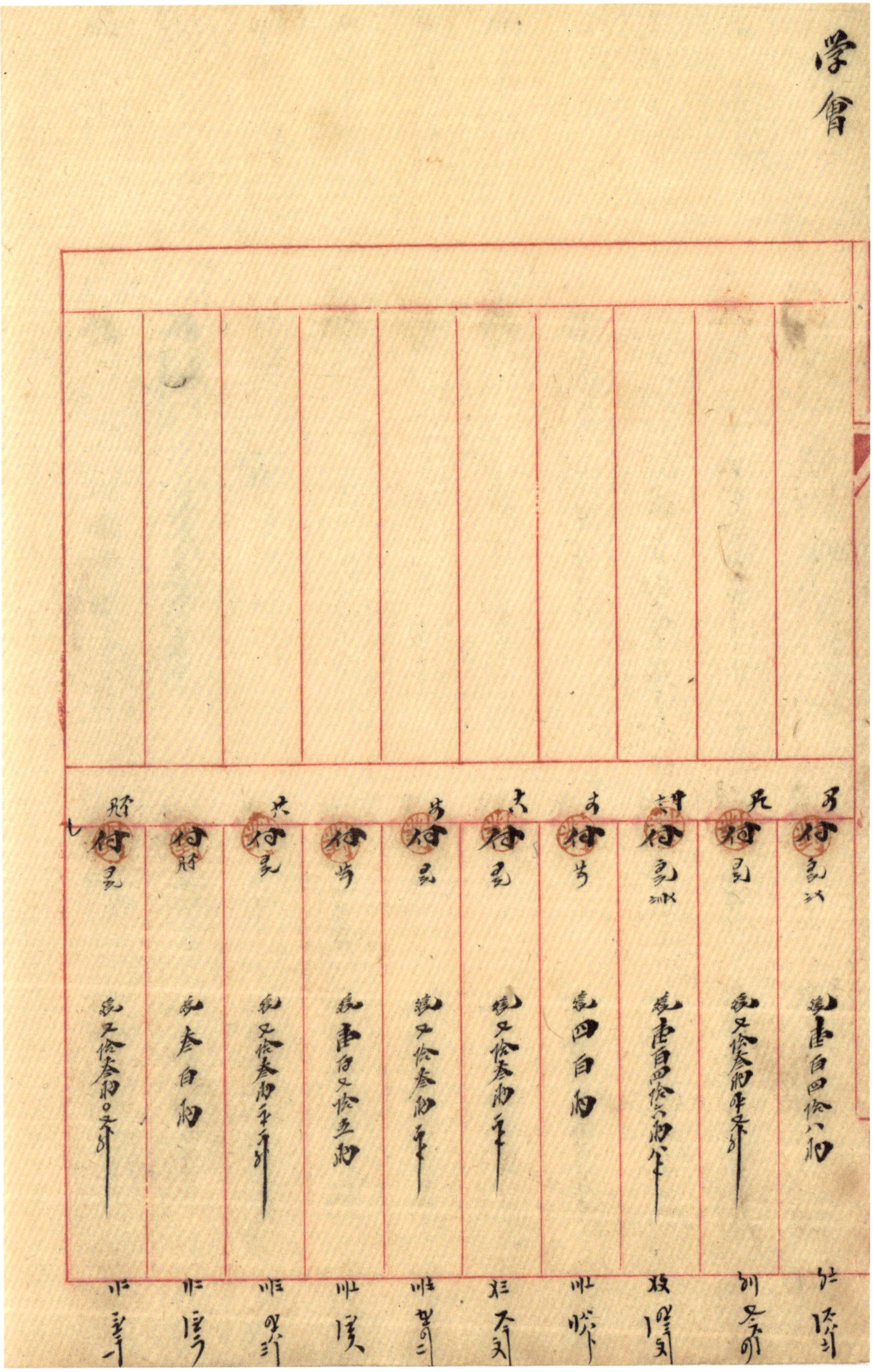
学會

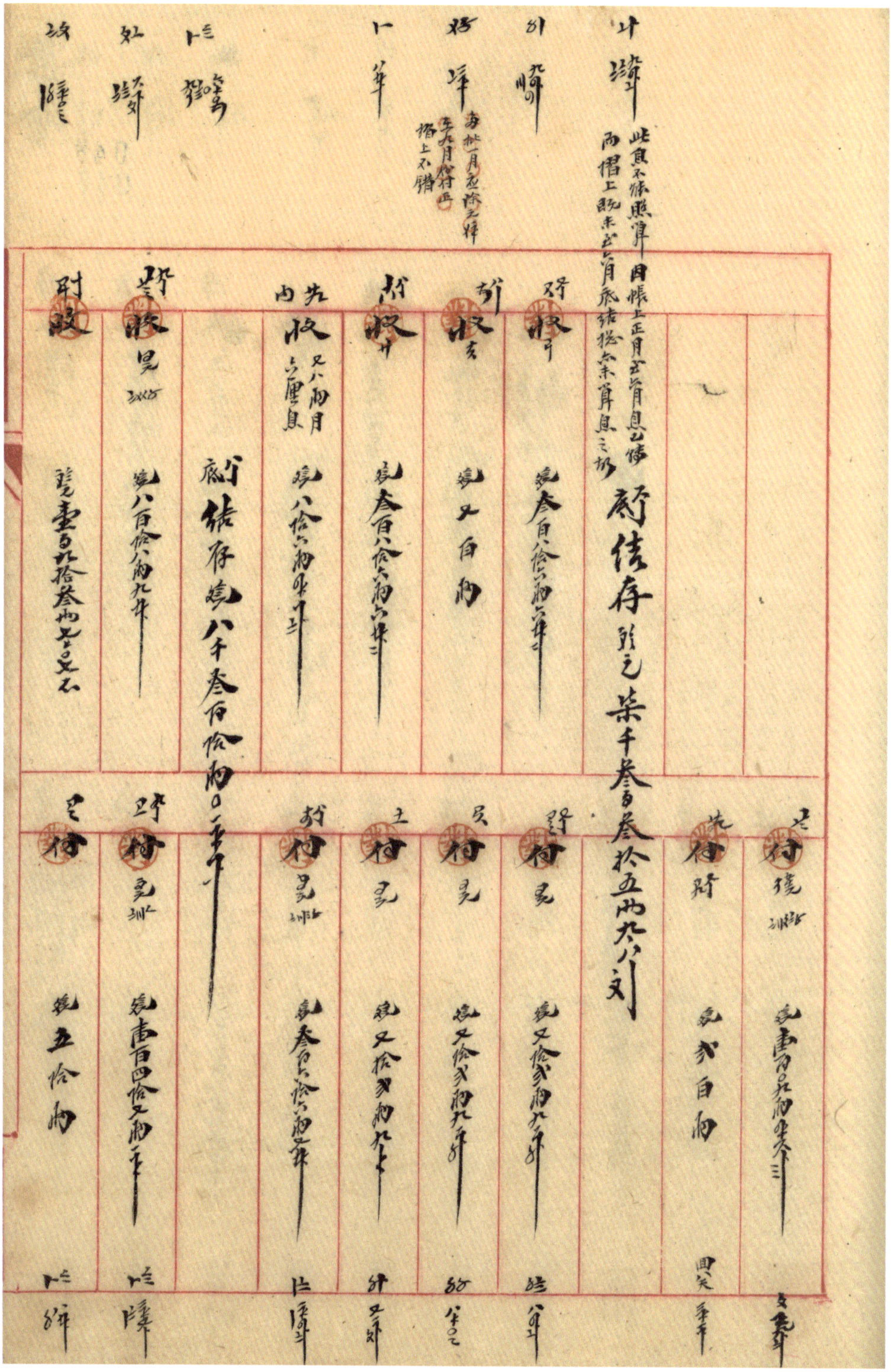

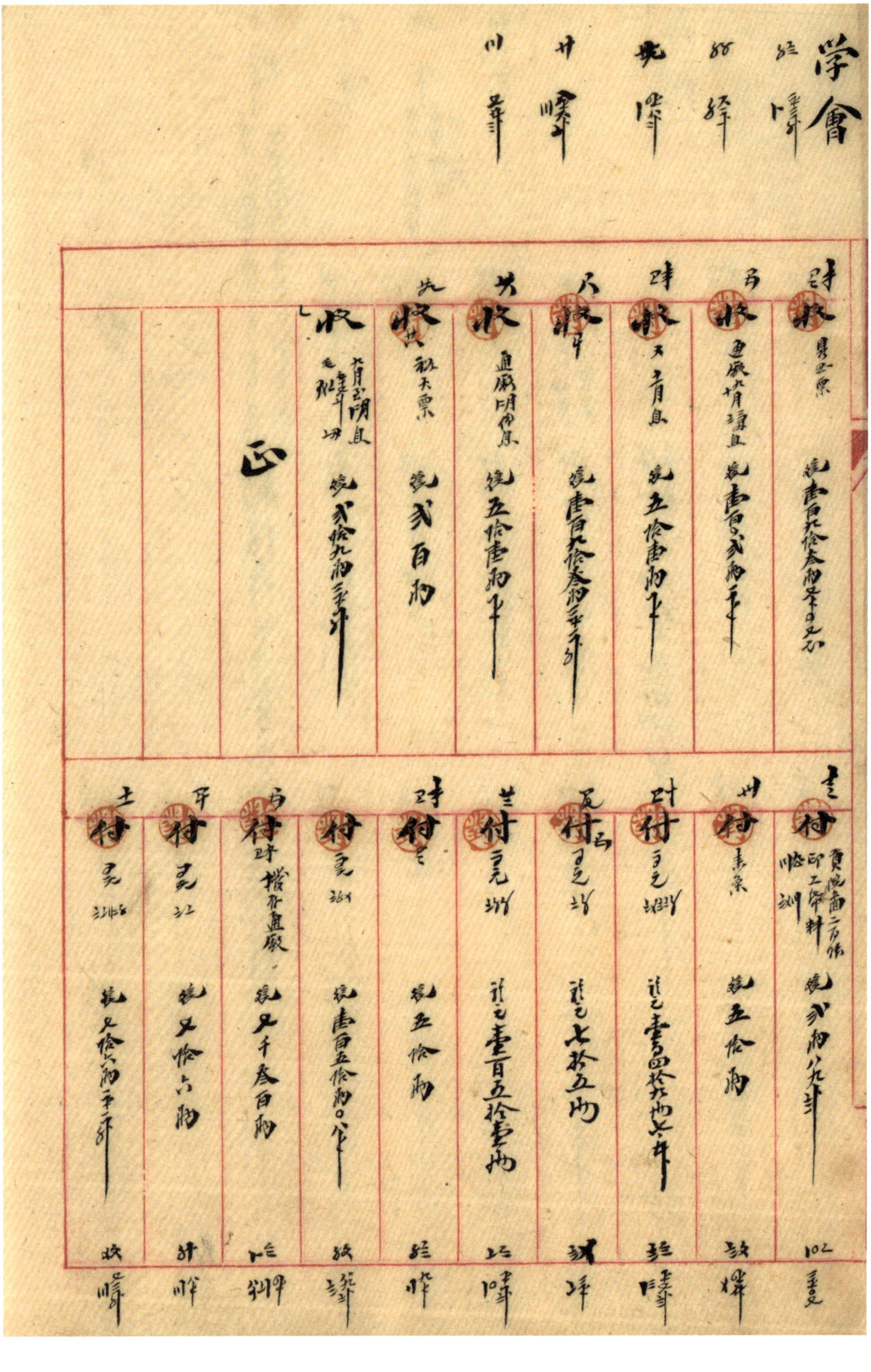

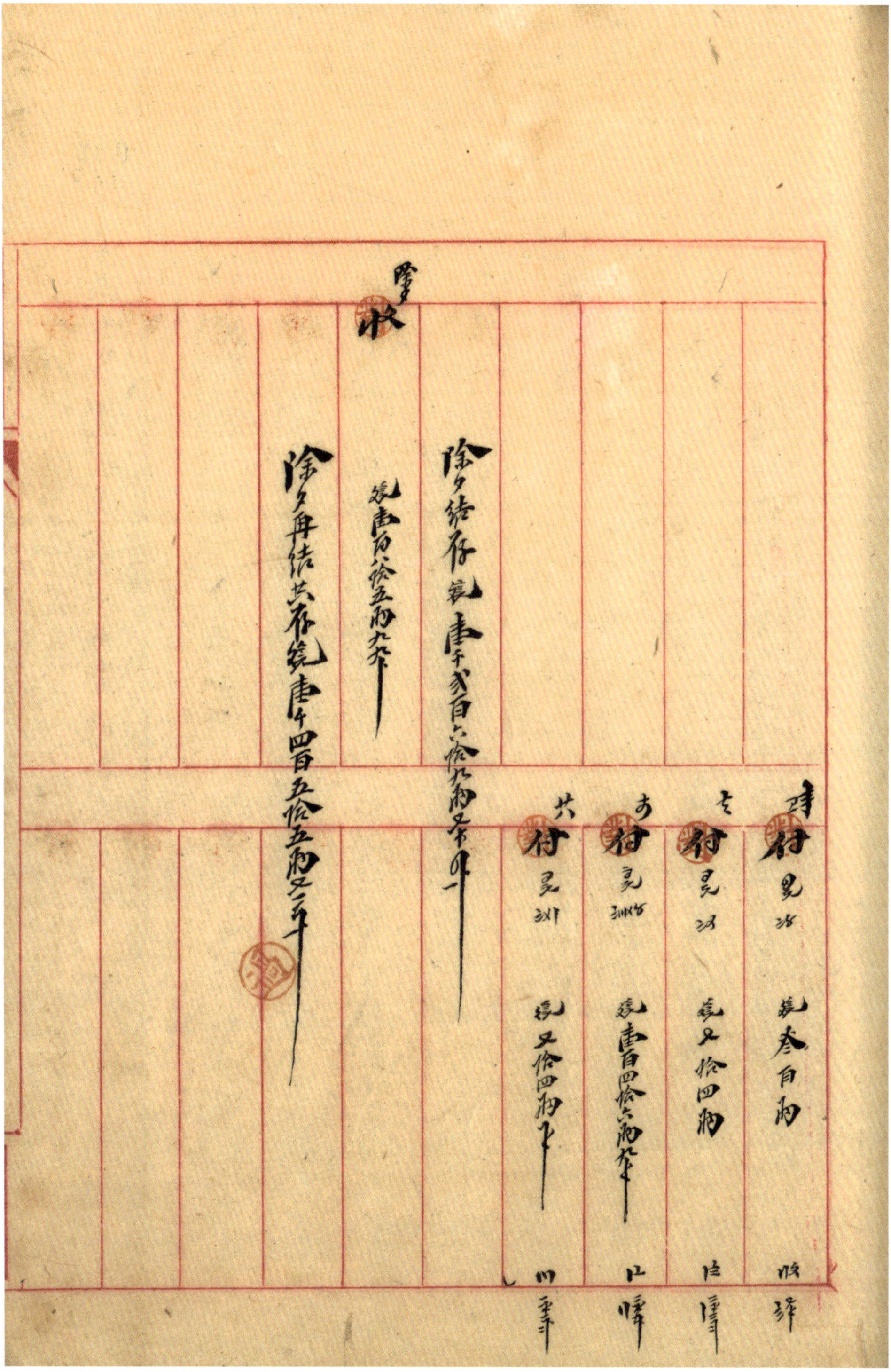
付 银叁百两
付 银五拾四两
付 银壹百四拾六两
付 银五拾四两
除夕结存银壹千贰百六拾九两
除夕收
银壹百六拾五两
除夕再结共存银壹千四百五拾五两

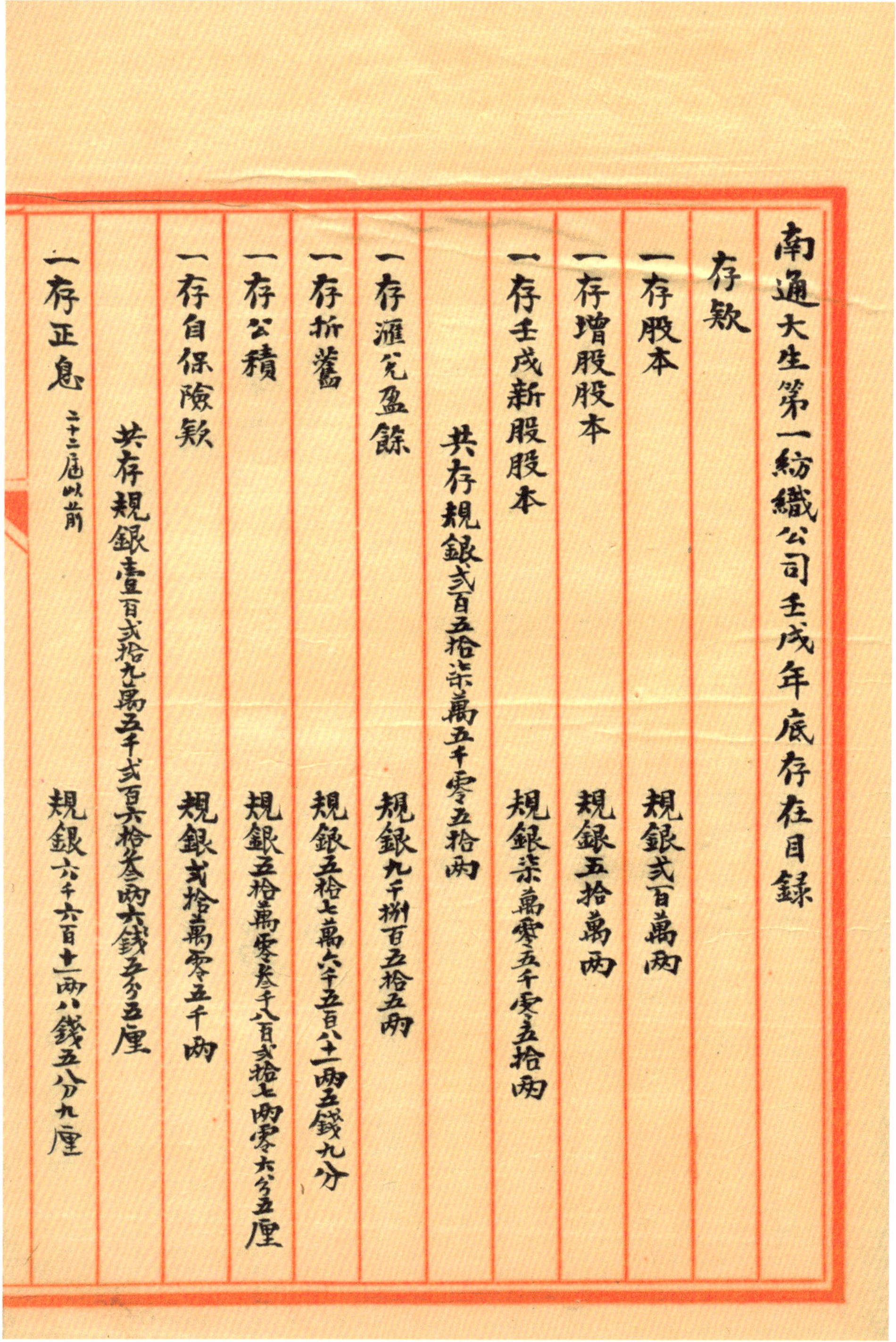
南通大生第一紡織公司壬戌年底存在目録

存欵

一存股本 規銀弍百萬兩

一存增股股本 規銀五拾萬兩

一存壬戌新股股本 規銀柒萬零五千零五拾兩

共存規銀弍百五拾柒萬五千零五拾兩

一存滙兑盈餘 規銀九千捌百五拾五兩

一存折舊 規銀五拾七萬六千五百八十一兩五錢九分

一存公積 規銀五拾萬零叁千八百弍拾七兩零六分五厘

一存自保險欵 規銀弍拾萬零五千兩

共存規銀壹百弍拾九萬五千弍百六拾叁兩六錢五分五厘

一存正息 二十二屆以前 規銀六千六百十一兩八錢五分九厘

1922年大生第一纺织公司的目录，震旦学院的旧欠依然没有还清。

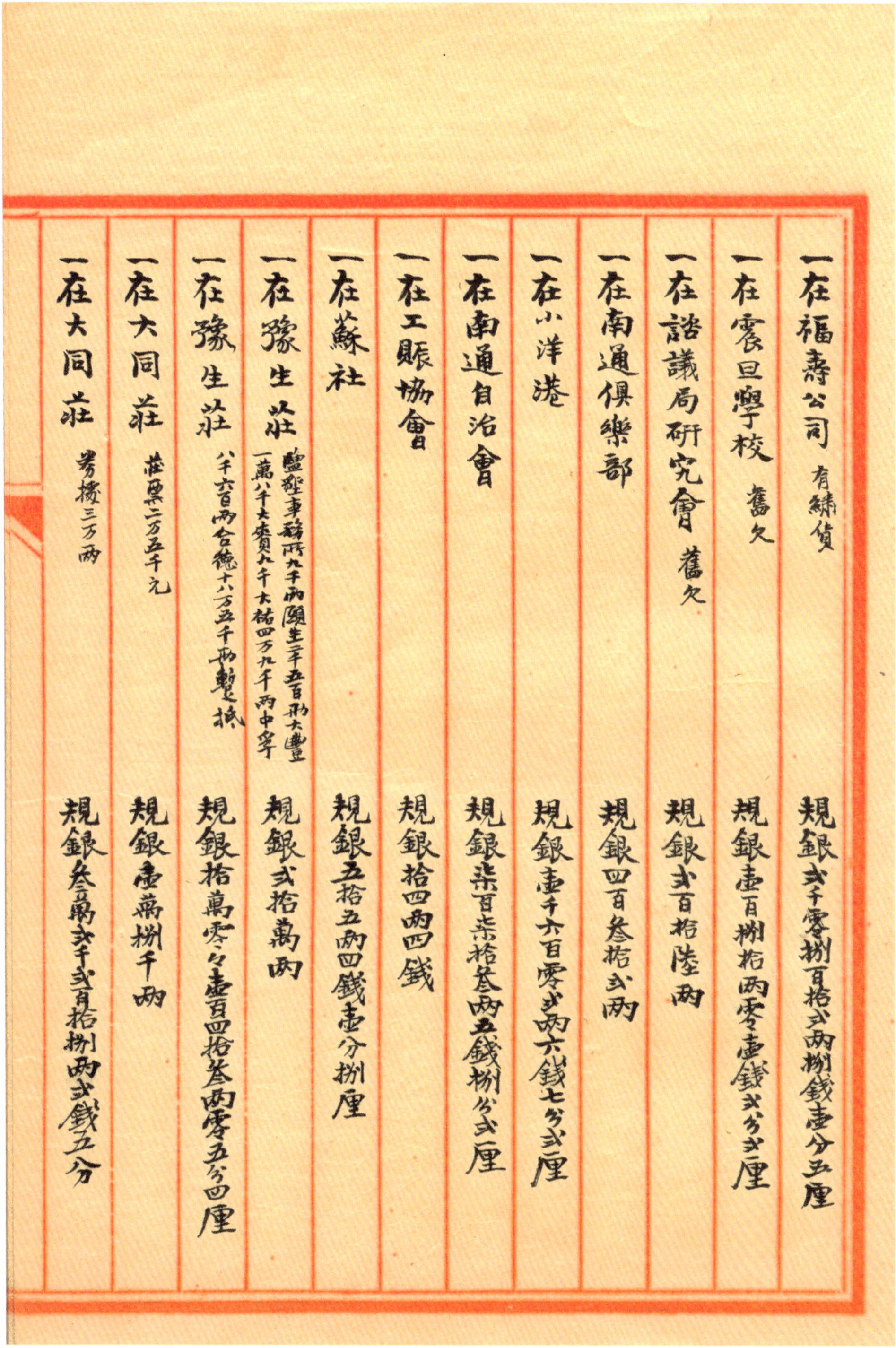

一在福壽公司　有綉貨　規銀貳千零捌百拾貳兩捌錢壹分五厘
一在震旦學校　舊欠　規銀壹百捌拾兩零壹錢貳分貳厘
一在諮議局研究會　舊欠　規銀貳百拾陸兩
一在南通俱樂部　規銀四百叁拾貳兩
一在小洋港　規銀壹千六百零貳兩六錢七分貳厘
一在南通自治會　規銀柒百柒拾叁兩五錢捌分貳厘
一在工賑協會　規銀拾四兩四錢
一在蘇社　規銀五拾五兩四錢壹分捌厘
一在豫生莊　鹽墾事務所九千兩　頤生二千五百兩　大豐一萬八千　大賚九千　大祐四萬九千兩　中孚　規銀貳拾萬兩
一在豫生莊　八千六百兩　合德十八万五千兩　暫抵　規銀拾萬零壹百四拾叁兩零五分四厘
一在大同莊　莊票二万五千元　規銀壹萬捌千兩
一在大同莊　劳據三万兩　規銀叁萬貳千貳百拾捌兩貳錢五分

『七旬千纸落江湖』

——鬻字善举

鬻字，是张謇运用个人的特长和名望，为公益慈善事业做贡献的特殊方式。张謇 1908 年 1 月 31 日起草《张謇鬻字字婴启》解释原因："仆字本不鬻钱，有时借逃人役则鬻，有时营实业乏旅资则亦鬻，年来鲜暇，不复为。今发起通州新育婴堂……而以鬻字之钱当所育婴。"张謇鬻字初衷是解决其创办的慈善机构经费不足的问题，其批量鬻字一直持续到 1924 年 9 月 29 日，张謇"鬻字告终以诗记之"。

上海是当时中国的经济和文化中心，相对来说鬻字的市场空间比较大，价格也会比他处高。况且上海有强大的辐射力，发达的传媒和人们的口口相传，使得鬻字的潜在客户增多。1908 年开始，张謇以类似公司运作的组织形式进行鬻字。主要是在上海刊登启事，由大生沪所专人收取润笔费后，根据客户的要求，把所需撰写的内容和纸张送到南通，张謇写好后递送到上海，再转交客户。1908 年大生沪所《同人杂户》账目的"鬻字字婴"分项，是替张謇代收和拨付鬻字款项的记录。大生沪所《杂户》账目，一直到 1925 年始终保留有张謇鬻字款的分项。

大生沪所的《宣统二年啬翁鬻字》，是该年（1910）大生沪所经手的鬻字细账。开头两页是"书例"，涵盖楹联、屏、堂轴、横轴、榜书、册页、手卷、扇、名刺的润例，此外志铭、碑表、盖额另议。后面的 11 页，记载每笔鬻字的形制、数量、书体、上款、交办人、润格，已经交款的加盖"付讫"章并注明时间，共 99 号。其中 8 号为"换赔"，39 号送给朵云轩老板，84 号则"墨污减润"。《宣统二年啬翁鬻字》反映的是大生沪所在上海接受鬻字订单的过程。

《丁巳沪帐房致濠南别业讯底（鬻字信底）》提供了更多大生沪所与南通之间就鬻字事宜的沟通细节。尽管这本信底的封面写着丁巳年（1917），其实内容还包括戊午年（1918），涉及己未年（1919）。讯底和信底，即号信的留底。号信是以年为时间单位的两个通讯者之间的往来信件，大生沪所与大生纱厂之间的经营管理事宜，很多就是通过号信来沟通的。大生沪所一般将来往的号信抄录一份留底。濠南别业是张謇在南通的住所之一，大生沪所把鬻字需求连同书写的纸张一并寄到濠南别业，由濠南别业的管家再具体安排。张謇写好后，由濠南别业寄大生沪所转交客户。

丁巳年的元号信是在1917年2月5日从上海寄出的，信中首先提到："今寄上三百六十一号至三百六十四号对纸，并根条四纸，至祈詧收。"这是上个农历年（丙辰，1916）尚未及寄到南通的订单。2月9日的第2号信揭示，沪所收到濠南别业寄来的号信以及随信的一包鬻例。沪所在第2号信中提到："鬻例当登申、新报三天。前寄三百六十四号三尺屏四条，此屏乃东洋人所求，三月须应东京书画展览会之用，望早寄下为祷。"沪所对元号信寄去的第364号订单做了说明，希望早日书写寄发，由客户来源可见张謇书法的爱慕者不局限于国内。2月14日3号信提及，大生沪所通过"大德"轮船，把丁巳年（1917）的"元、2号对，根条二纸"带到南通。

南通市档案馆保存着大生沪所代张謇收取鬻字润金和墨费的印制的格式收条，落款是"上海九江路大生沪事务所黄光益代收"。所谓九江路大生沪事务所，指上海南通房产公司于1920年在九江路建成的南通大厦，大生沪所于5月18日迁入其中的二楼办公。因此这批收条不早于1920年出现。收条写明，钱款收清后，"俟南通挨号书成寄沪后凭条取件"。

1908年后张謇鬻字，总体分为三个阶段，分别是1908年至1909年、1915年至1919年、1922年至1924年。

第一阶段鬻字，主要是为新育婴堂筹款。《张謇鬻字字婴启》刊登不久，1908年3月28日，张謇作《鬻字改例启》，主要内容为："鬻字字婴，始意也。通州师范学校附属之博物苑购求陈列品，亦苦无资，又有从求留学费者，不知仆负任之力固已尽也。无已，则倍鬻以济之。春季所鬻，得已逾千，人事卒卒鲜暇，顷姑截收夏季。”在补助新育婴堂的同时，张謇又需要资助南通博物苑和帮助准备留学的学生筹措学费，无奈社会负担太重，只能加倍鬻字，来应付各方面的求援。

张謇鬻字第二阶段，主要是为南通残废院、盲哑学校和其他公益事业筹款。1912年8月9日晚上，张謇乘坐“大和”号轮船从上海回南通，这天的日记里记载有“规建医院、残废院、盲哑学校”。残废院和盲哑学校是张謇在南通规划的慈善公益事业的重要组成部分。残废院和盲哑学校选址狼山东北麓，建筑为一个院落，南半部为残废院，北半部为盲哑学校。这个阶段鬻字，从乙卯年（1915）开始，一直到己未年（1919），登报则始于丙辰年（1916）。1916年1月8日起，张謇在南通《通海新报》连载《张謇为残废院盲哑学校鬻字启》：“仆于前清光绪三十二年，曾鬻字字婴矣。鬻之二年，人事大冗乃辍。今残废院、盲哑学校，建筑甫竣而开办费绌，豫计岁支前三年亦需五六千元，旦旦而救人之助，不足济缓急也。而仆之力用于教育慈善事者，又以途多而分。无已，惟再鬻字。”

第三阶段鬻字，开始于张謇在1922年7月12日《申报》头版刊登的《张謇鬻字》，启事提到：“南通前年歉，去年灾，农饥商疲，而金融滞。下走岁入大觳，而所负地方慈善公益之责，年费累巨万，无可解除，亦无旁贷也。求助于人必无济，无已，惟求诸己。往者尝以慈善事一再鬻字，有例矣。鬻字犹劳工也，忽忽十余年，今政七十，宁复胜劳？然无如何！”鬻字收件处为大生沪所。1923年6月24日《申报》、1924年5月25日《通海新报》上刊登的鬻字广告中，收件处均为大生沪所。

1924年9月29日，71岁高龄的张謇终于放下鬻字之笔，并作诗一首纪念鬻字告终：“大热何尝困老夫，七旬千纸落江湖。墨池径寸蛟龙泽，满眼良苗济得无。”

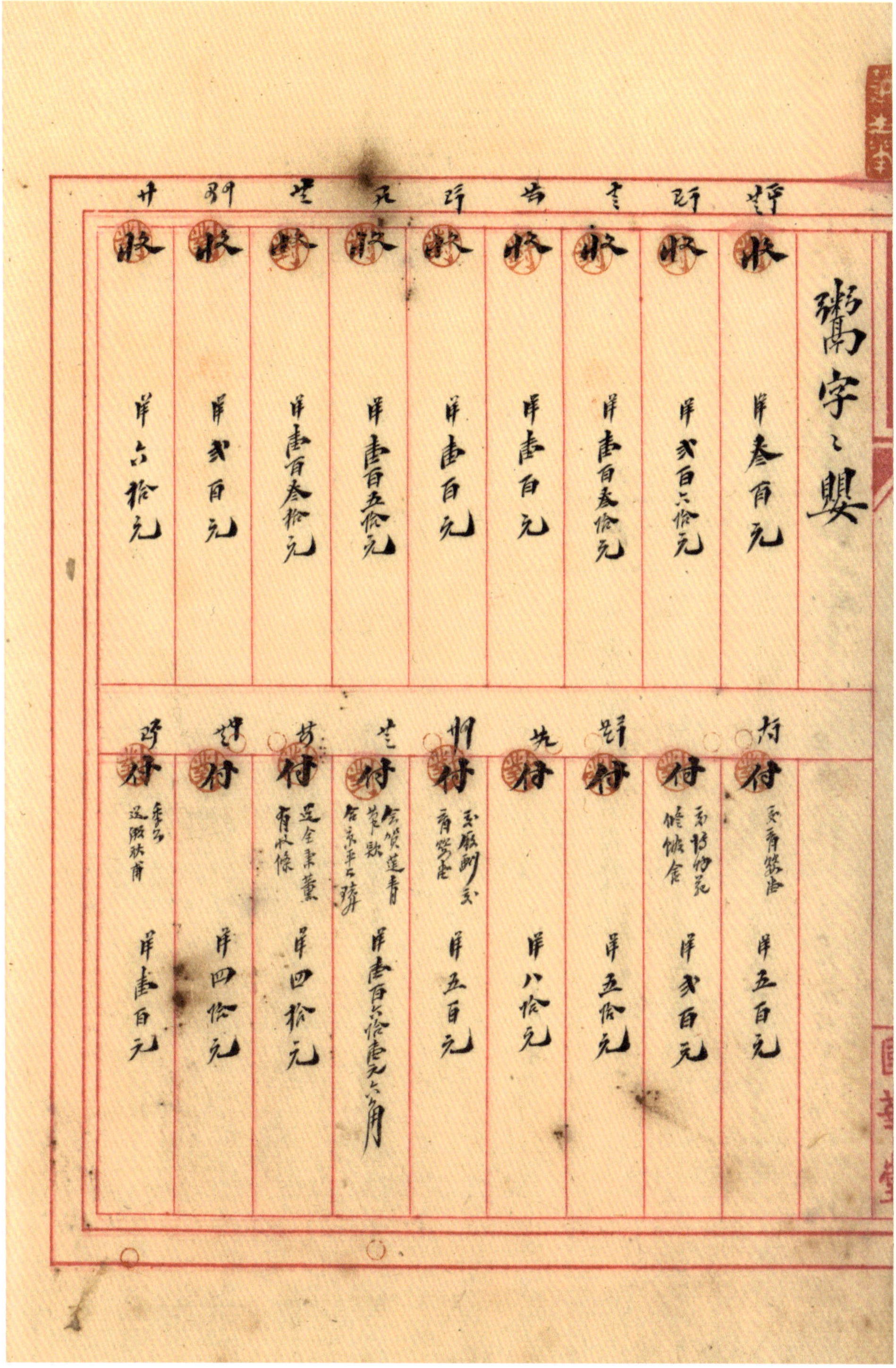

1908 年大生沪所《同人杂户》账目的张謇《鬻字字婴》分项。

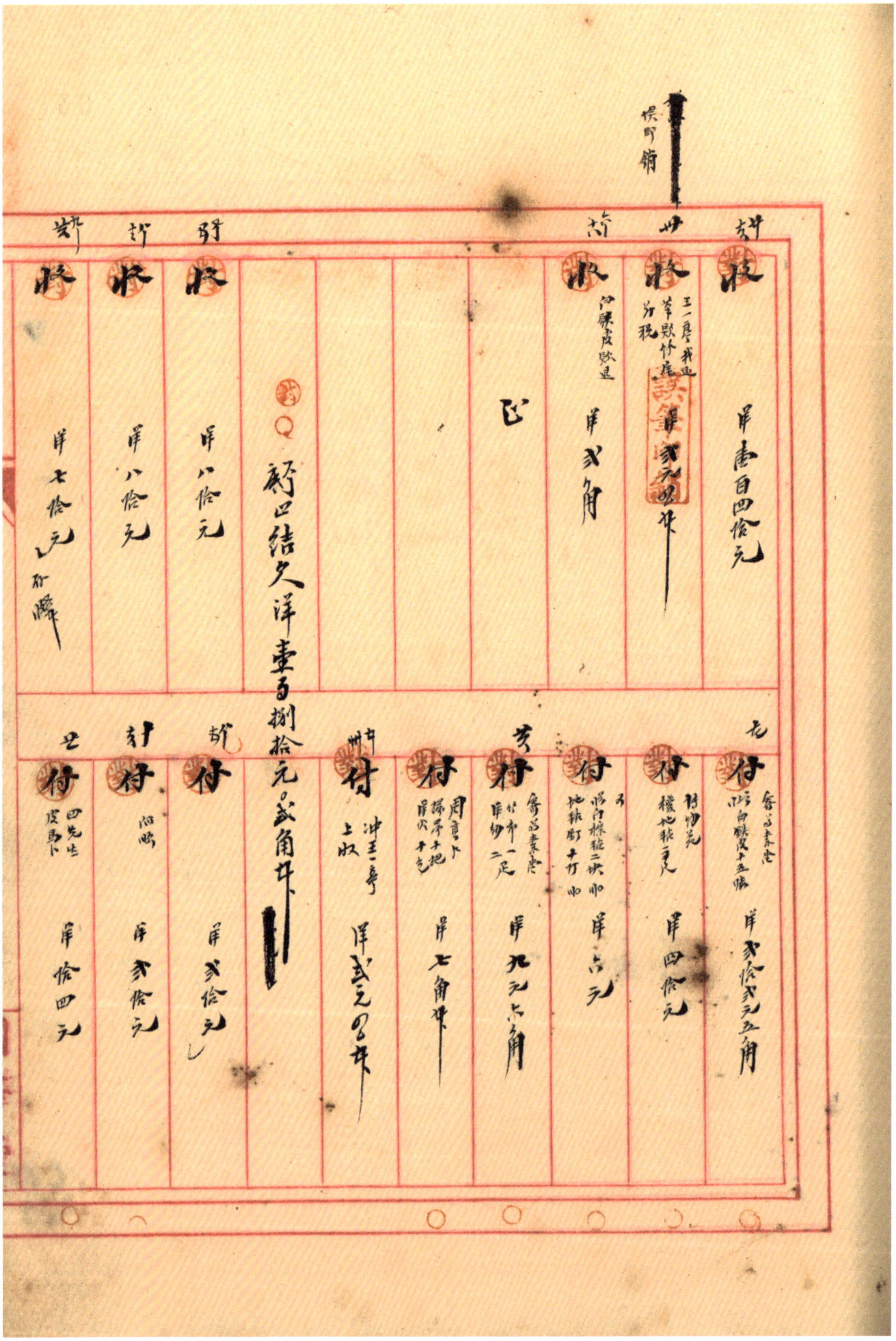

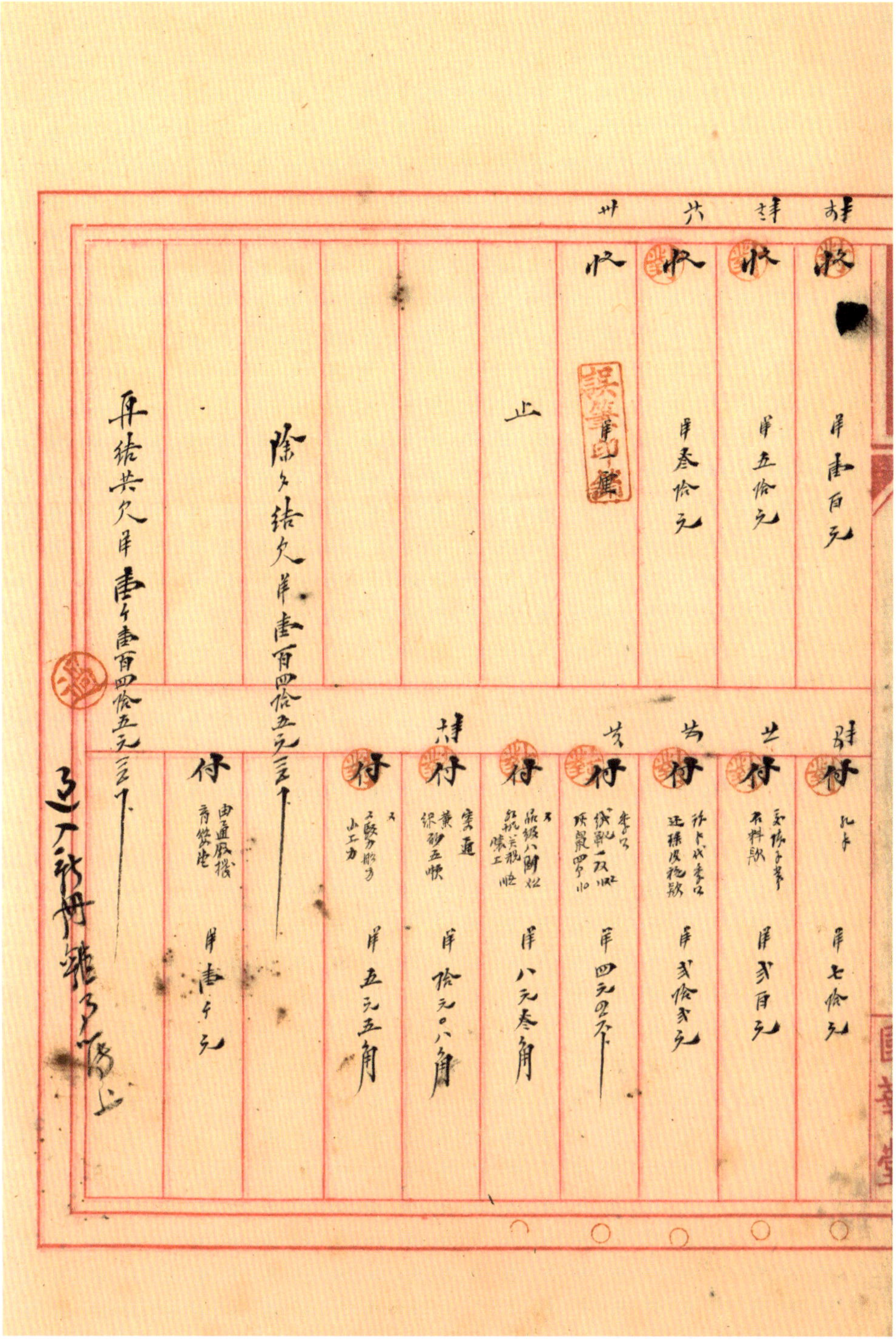

收 洋壹百元

收 洋五拾元

收 洋叁拾元

收 误笔作废

止

除夕结欠洋壹百四拾五元

再结共欠洋壹千壹百四拾五元

付 洋七拾元

付 洋贰百元

付 洋贰拾贰元

付 洋四元

付 洋八元叁角

付 洋拾元〇八角

付 洋五元五角

付 洋壹千元

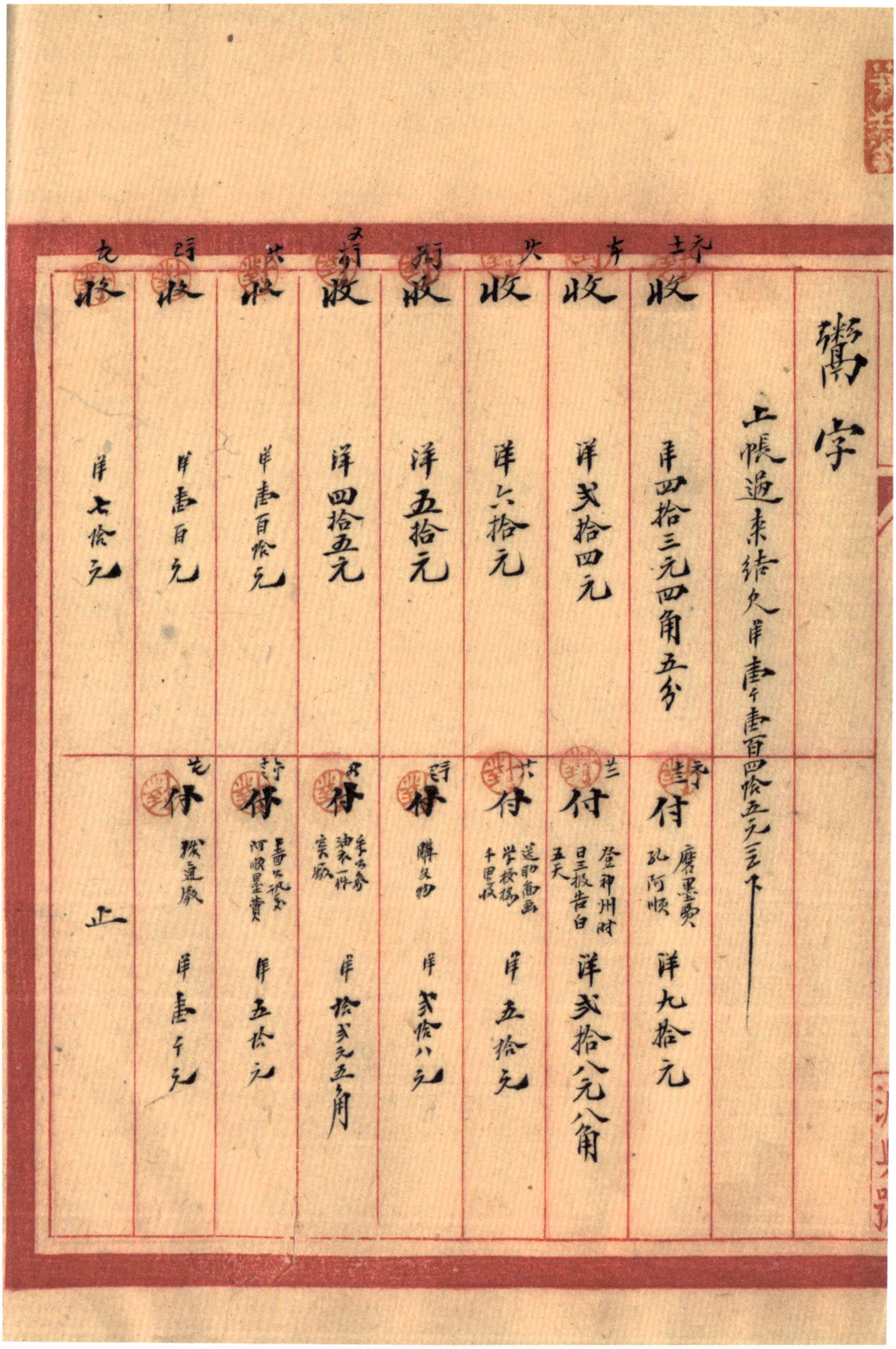

1909 年大生沪所《杂户》账目的张謇《鬻字》分项。

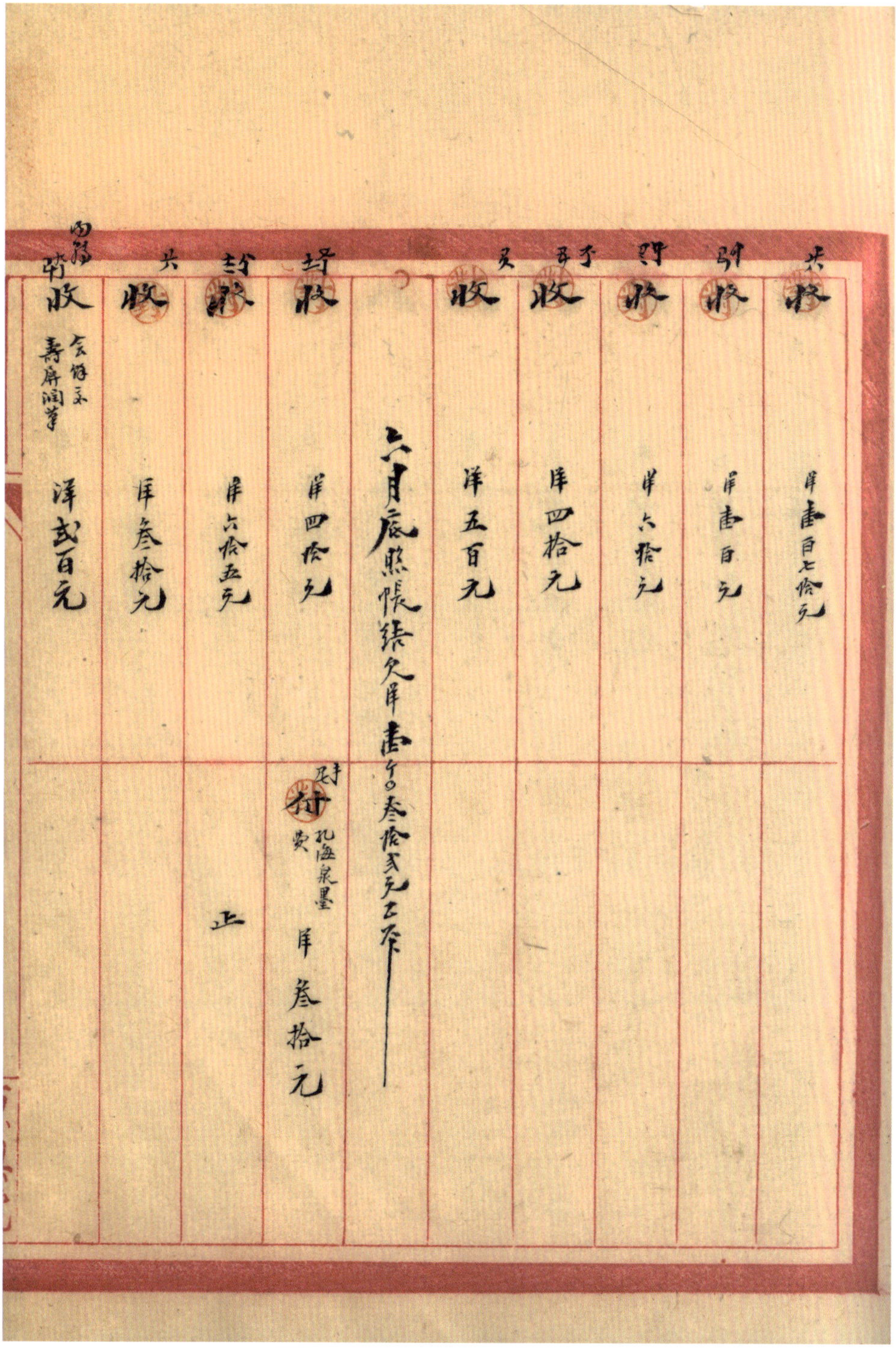

收 洋壹百七拾元
收 洋壹百元
收 洋六拾元
收 洋四拾元
收 洋五百元
六月底照帐结欠洋壹千〇叁拾贰元五角
收 洋四拾元
收 洋六拾五元
收 洋叁拾元
收 会馆承 寿屏润笔 洋贰百元
付 孔海泉墨费 洋叁拾元
止

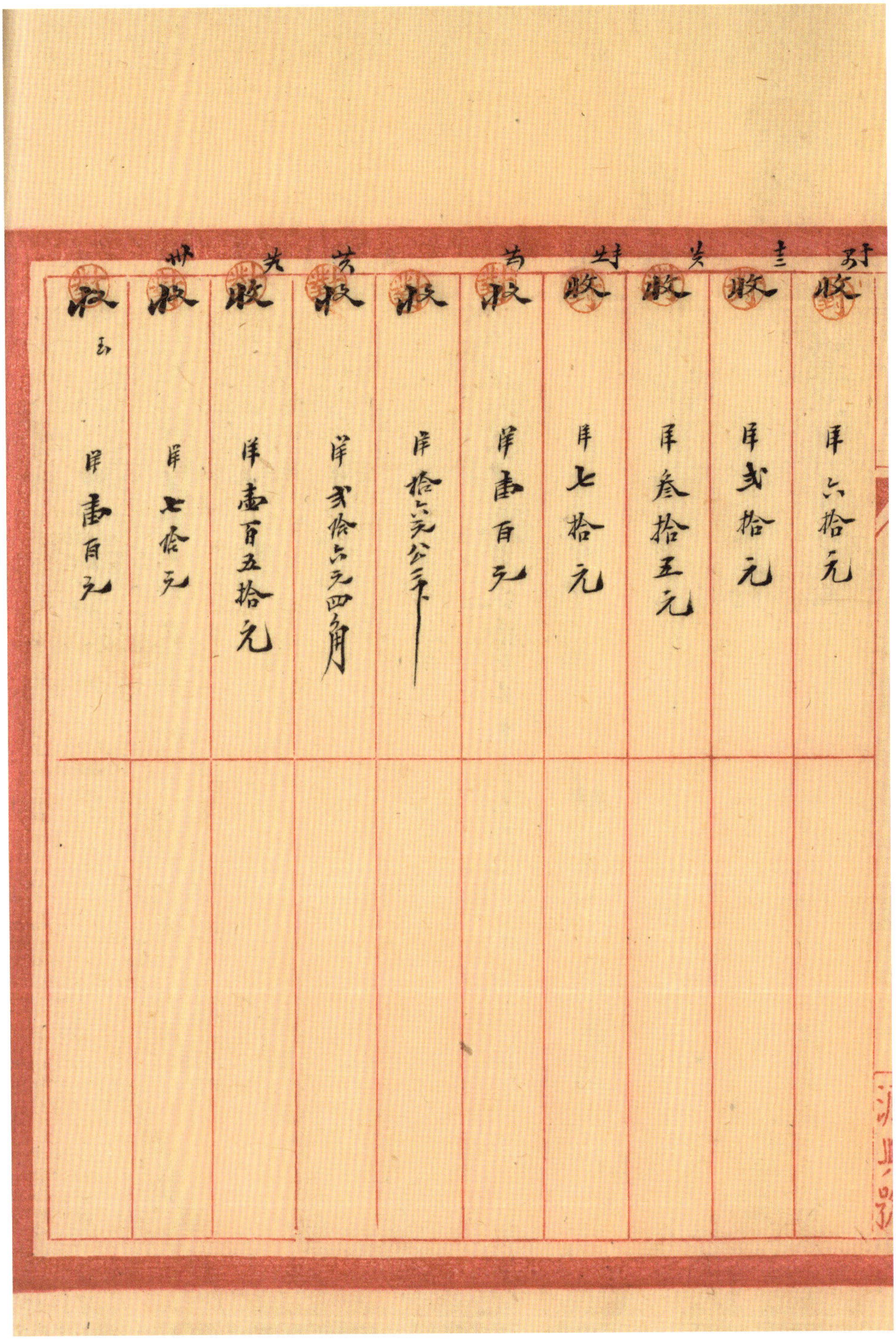

收 洋六拾元
收 洋贰拾元
收 洋叁拾五元
收 洋七拾元
收 洋壹百元
收 洋拾六元
收 洋贰拾六元四角
收 洋壹百五拾元
收 洋七拾元
收 洋壹百元

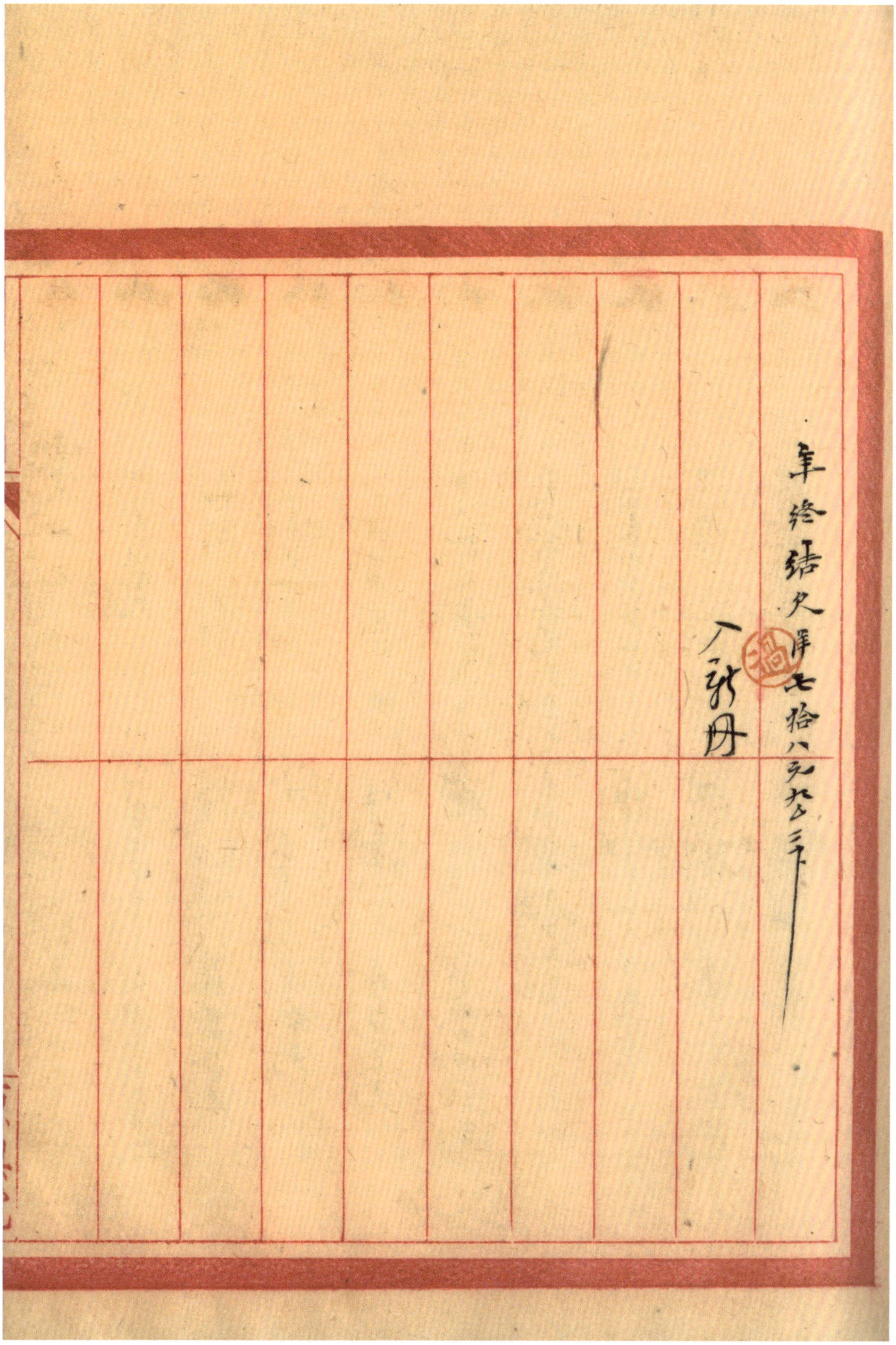

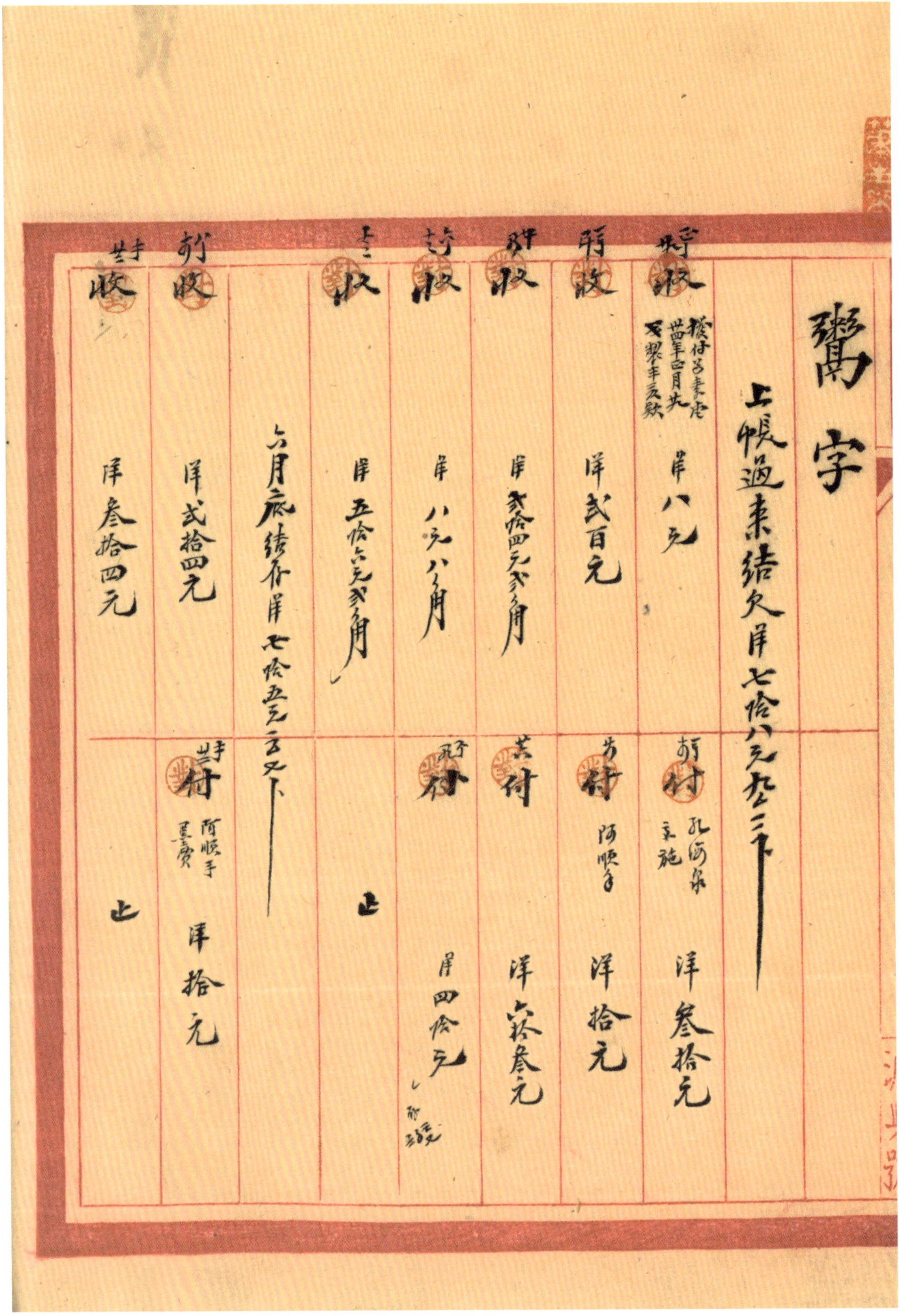

1910年大生沪所《杂户》账目的张謇《謇字》分项。

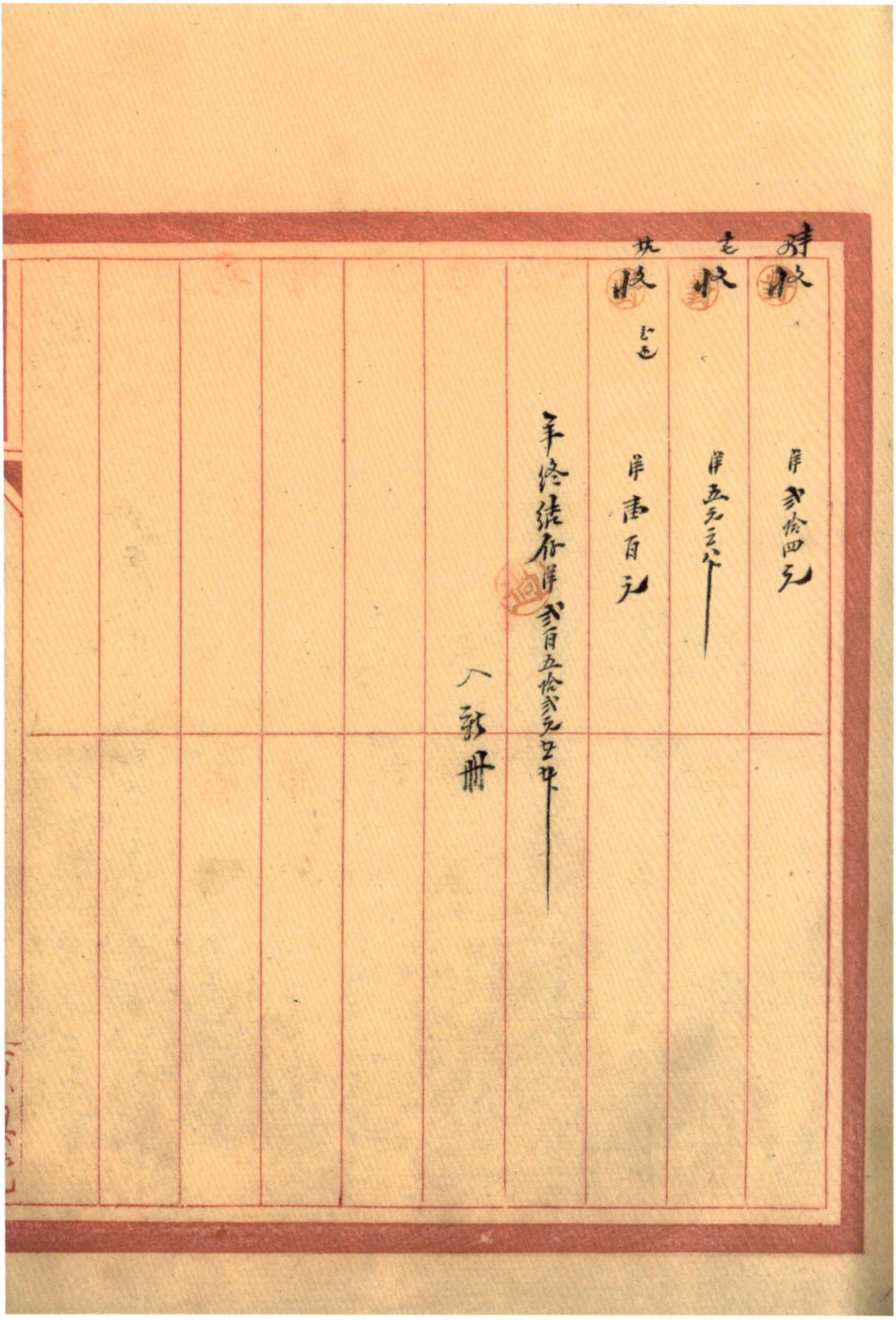

肆收　洋叁拾四元

七收　洋五元三角

共收　洋壹百元

年终结存洋贰百五拾贰元五角

入新册

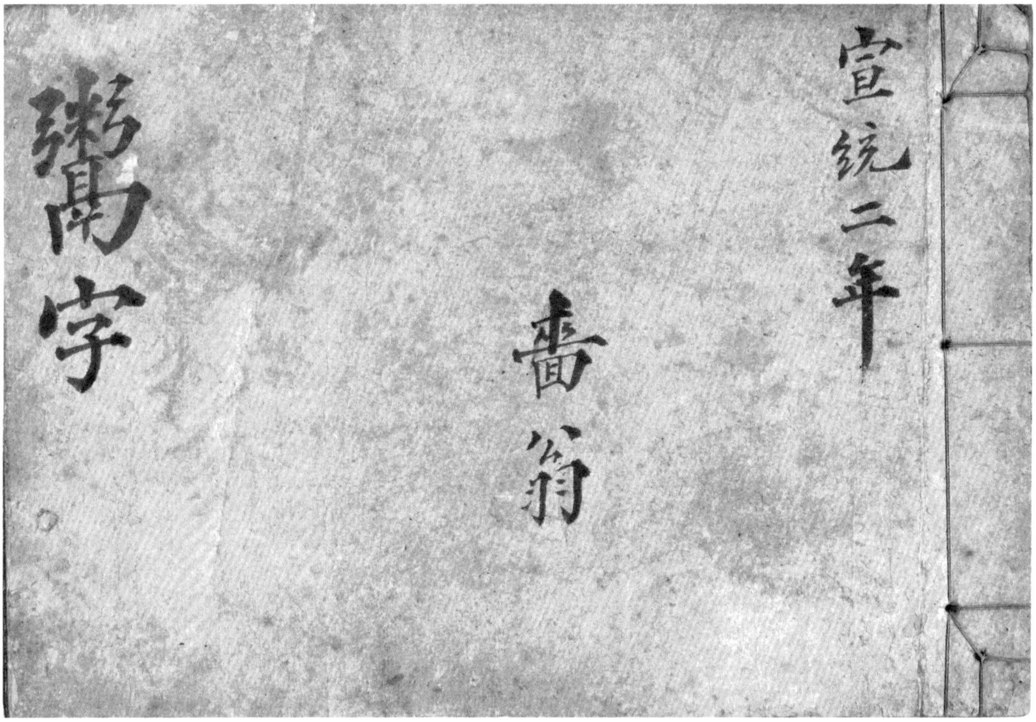
宣统二年
啬翁
鬻字

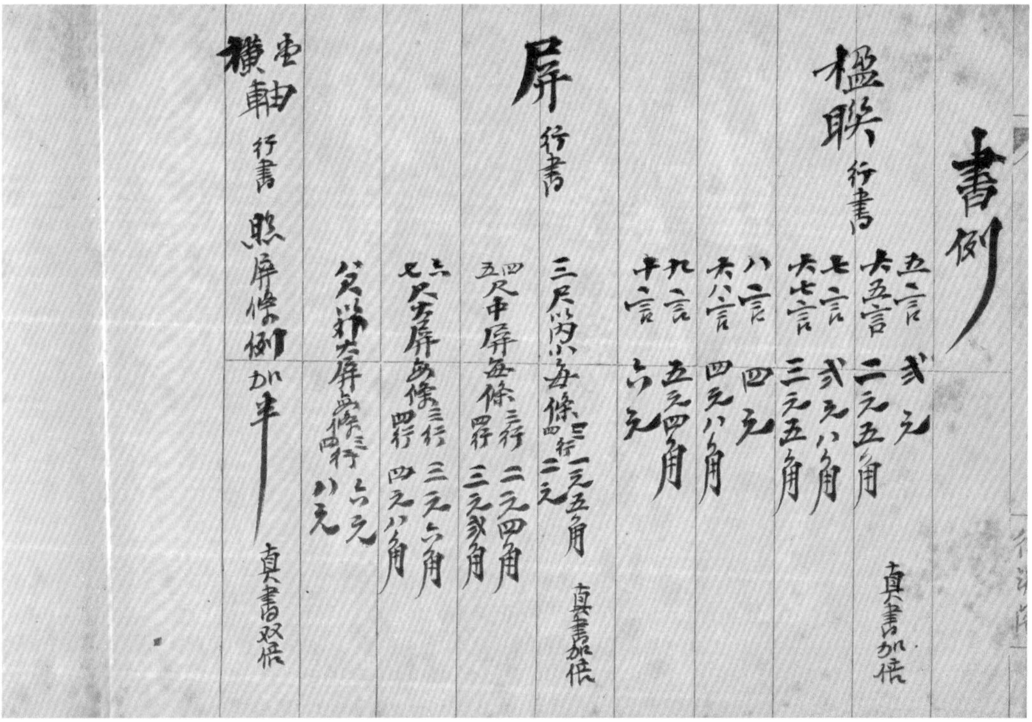
書例
楹聯
行書
五言 弍元
大五言 二元五角
七言 弍元八角
大七言 三元五角
八言 四元
大八言 四元八角
九言 五元
十言 六元
真書加倍
屏
行書
真書加倍
橫軸
行書
真書双倍

1910 年张謇鬻字清册中记载的鬻字润例。

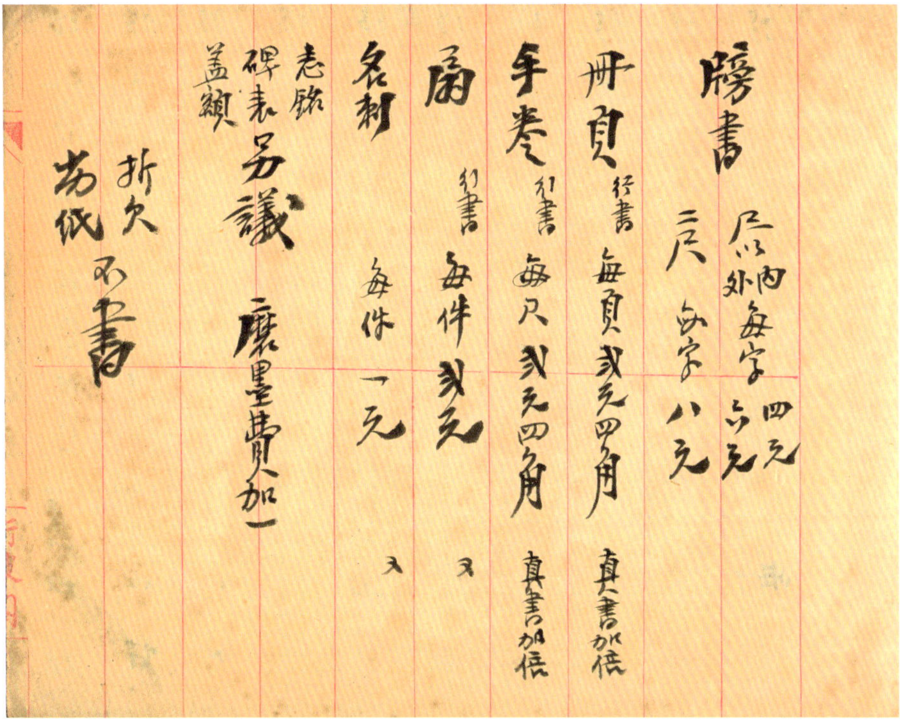

榜書 尺以内每字四元 尺以外每字六元
二尺 每字八元
册頁 行書每頁貳元四角 真書加倍
手卷 行書每尺貳元四角 真書加倍
扇 行書每件貳元 又
名刺 每件一元 又
碑表志銘盖額另議 磨墨費加一
折欠不書
劣紙

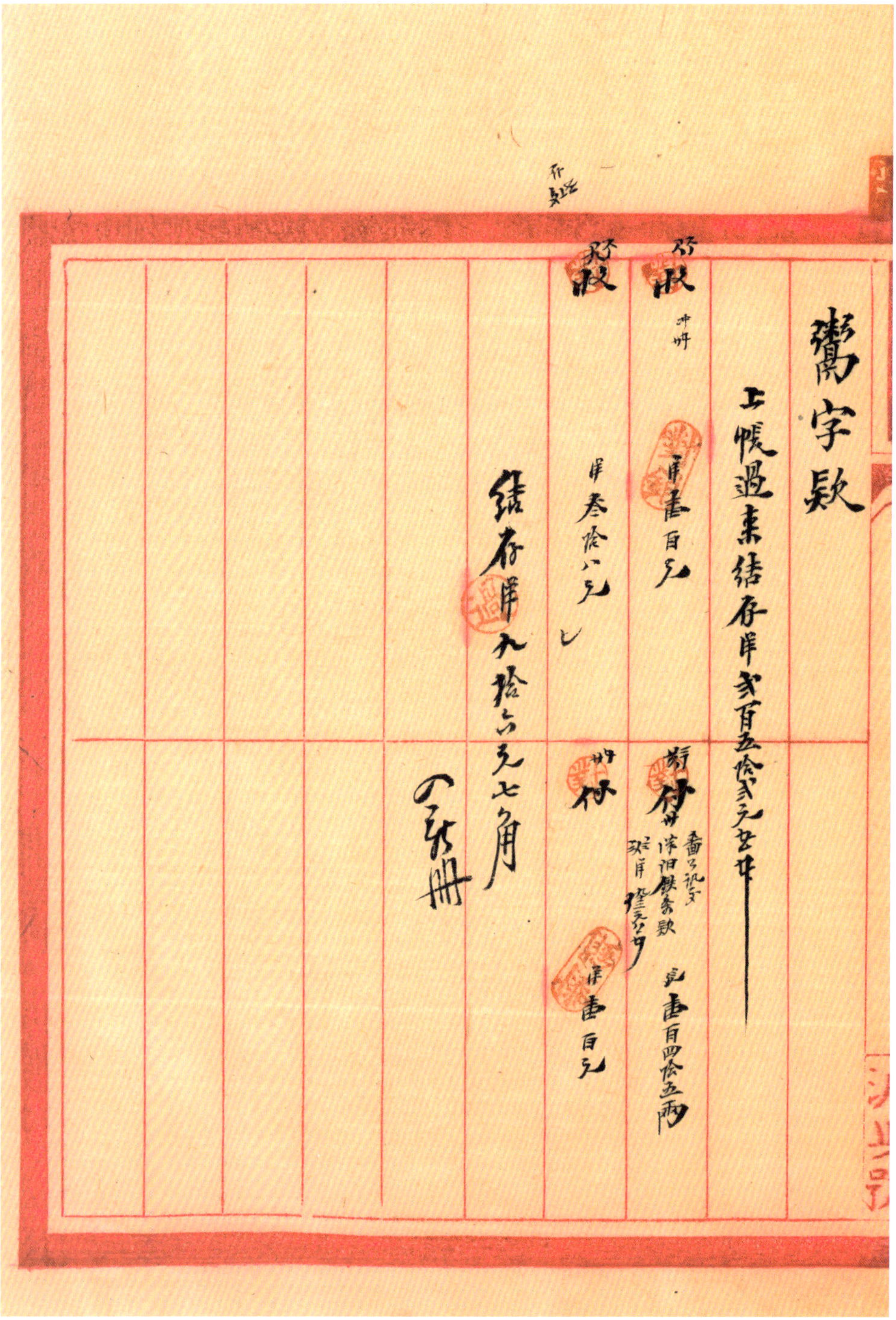

1911 年大生沪所《杂户》账目的张謇《鬻字》分项。

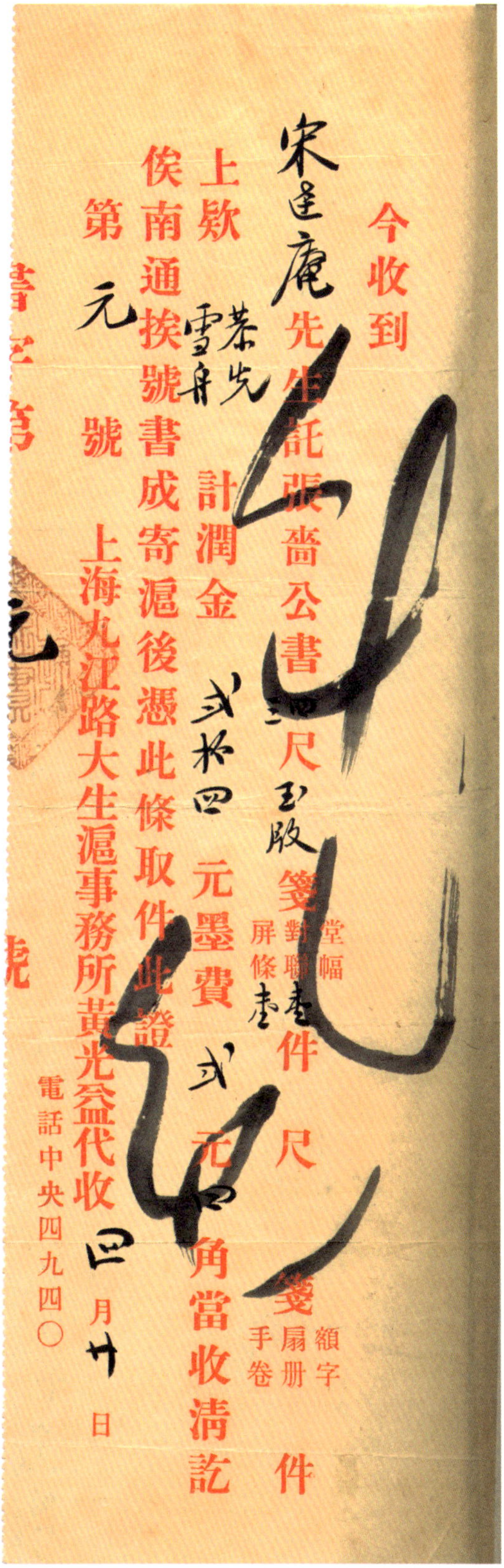

今收到
宋達庵先生託張嗇公書四尺玉版箋（堂幅、對聯、屏條）壹件 尺箋（額字、扇冊、手卷）件
上款恭先雪舟 計潤金貳拾四元墨費貳元四角當收清訖
俟南通揆號書成寄滬後憑此條取件此證
第元號 上海九江路大生滬事務所黃光益代收 四月廿日
電話中央四九四〇

黄光益出具的收到宋达庵支付张謇鬻字润笔费的收条。

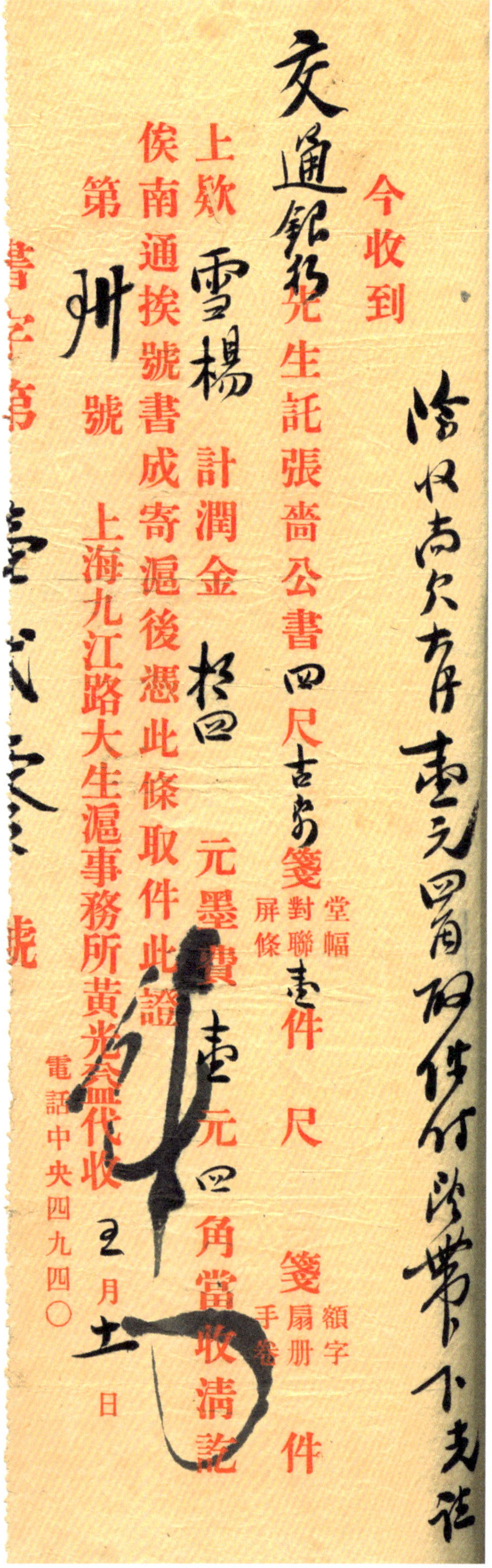
今收到
交通銀行先生託張謇公書四尺古宋箋 堂幅 對聯 屏條 壹件 尺箋 額字 扇冊 手卷 件
上欵 雪楊 計潤金 拾四 元 墨費 壹元四角 當收清訖
俟南通挨號書成寄滬後憑此條取件此證
第 卅 號 上海九江路大生滬事務所黃光益代收 三月十一日
電話中央四九四〇

黄光益出具的收到交通银行支付张謇鬻字润笔费的收条。

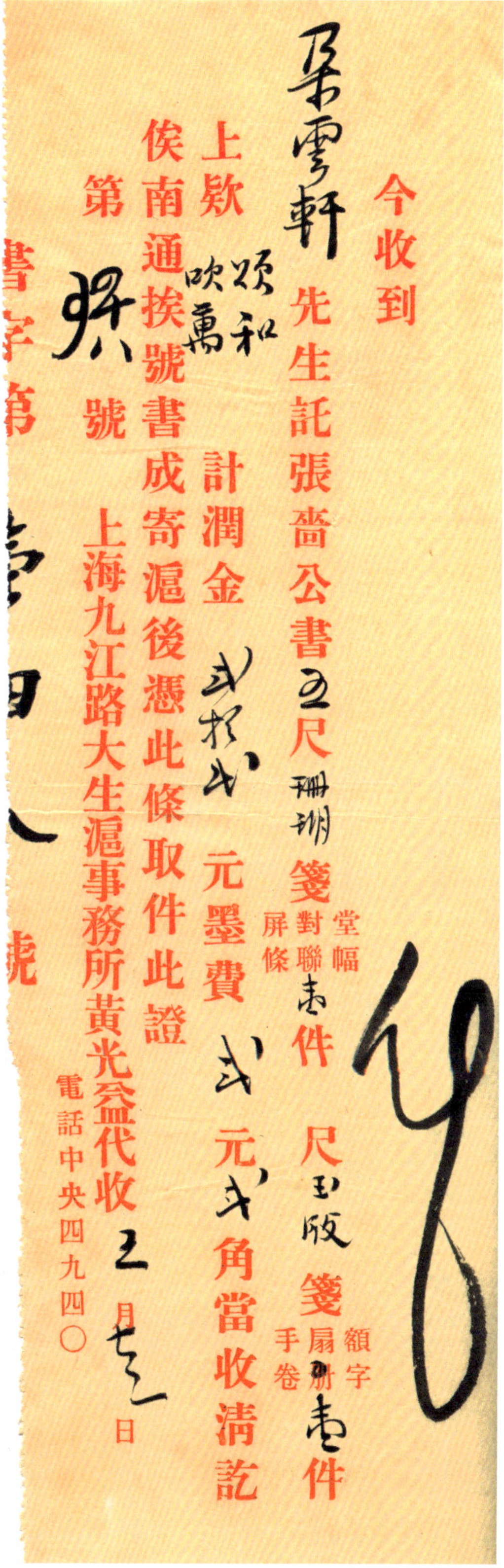
今收到
朵雲軒先生託張嗇公書五尺珊瑚箋堂幅對聯屏條壹件尺玉版箋額字扇冊手卷壹件
上款頌和吹萬計潤金貳拾貳元墨費貳元元貳角當收清訖
俟南通挨號書成寄滬後憑此條取件此證
第八號上海九江路大生滬事務所黃光益代收三月廿一日
電話中央四九四〇

黄光益出具的收到朵云轩支付张謇鬻字润笔费的收条。

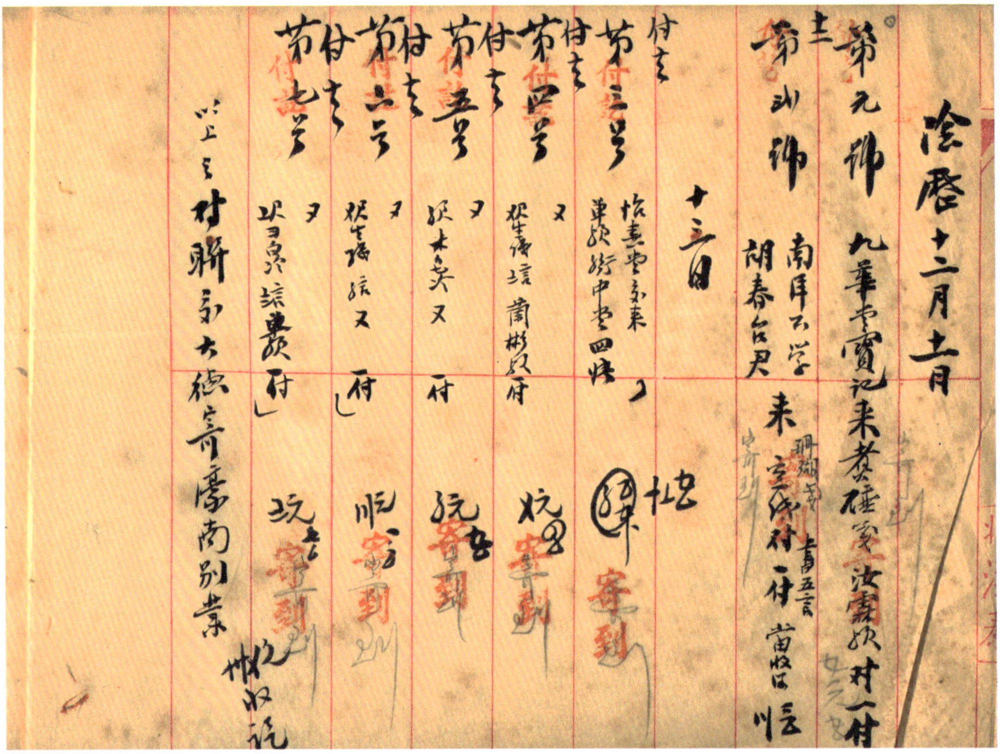

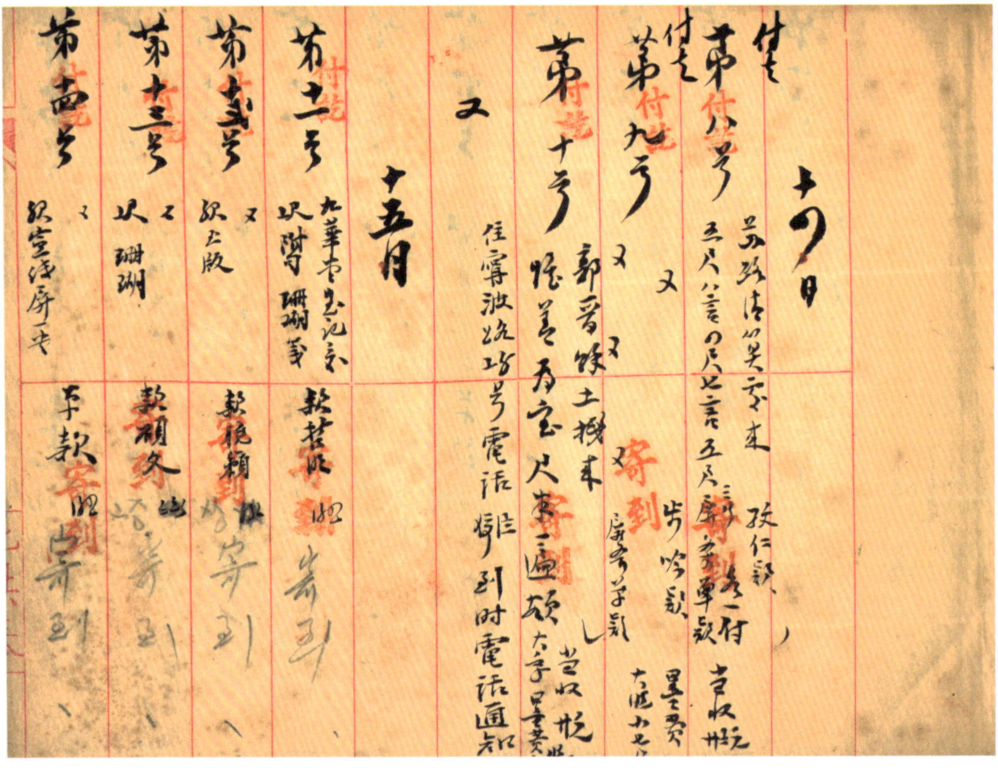

1916年张謇鬻字清册（局部）。

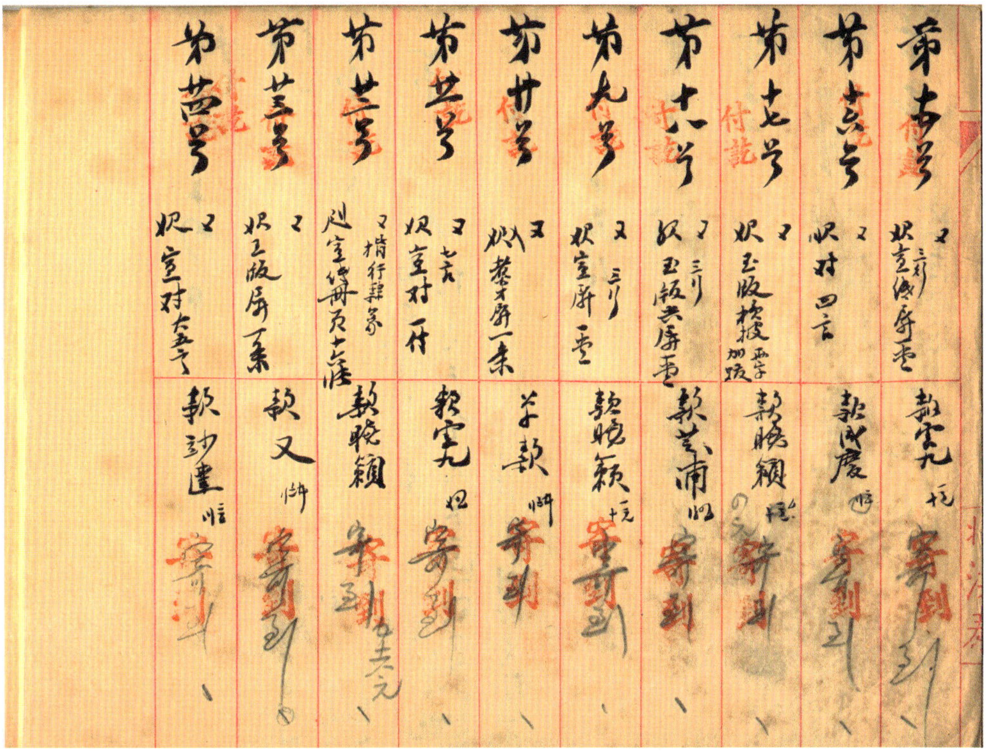

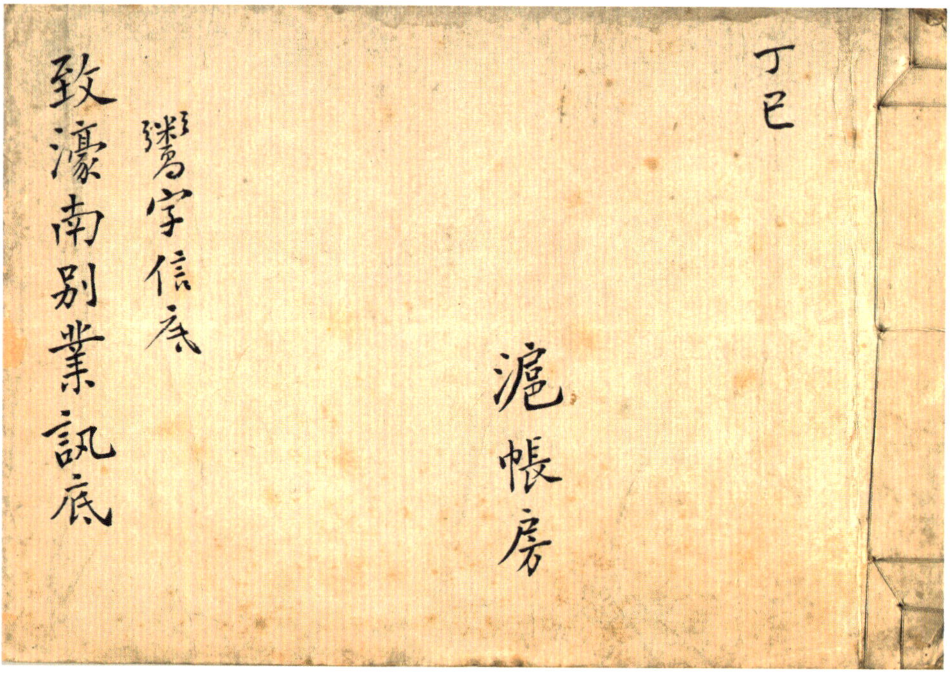

丁巳

滬帳房

鬻字信底

致濠南别業訊底

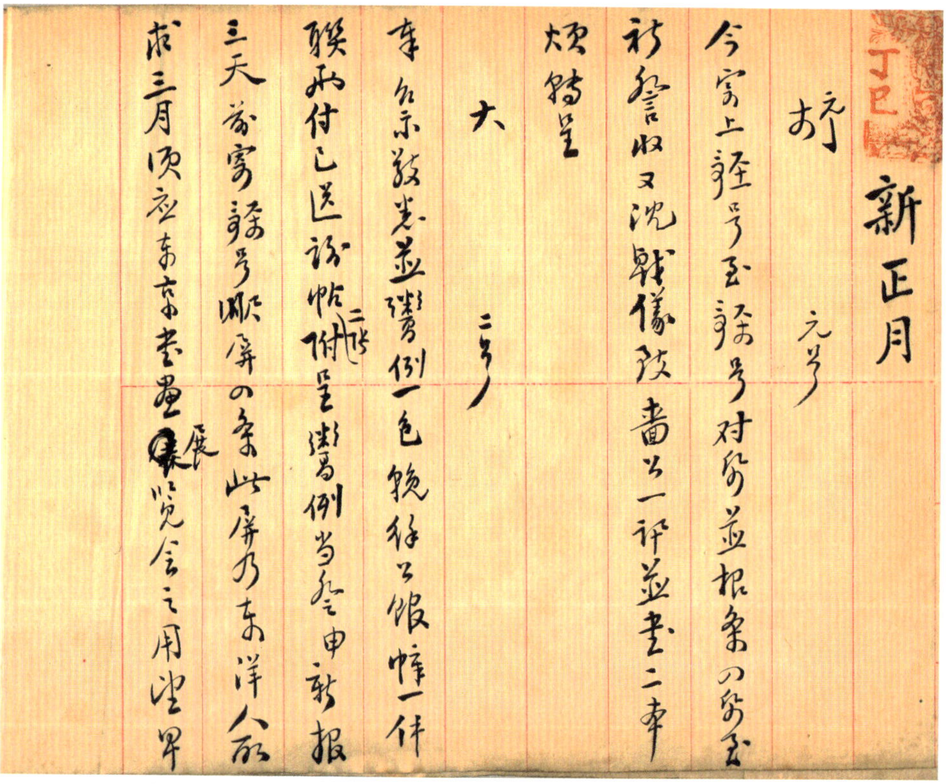

丁巳

新正月

1917 年，大生沪所就张謇鬻字事宜致南通濠南别业号信的底稿（局部）。

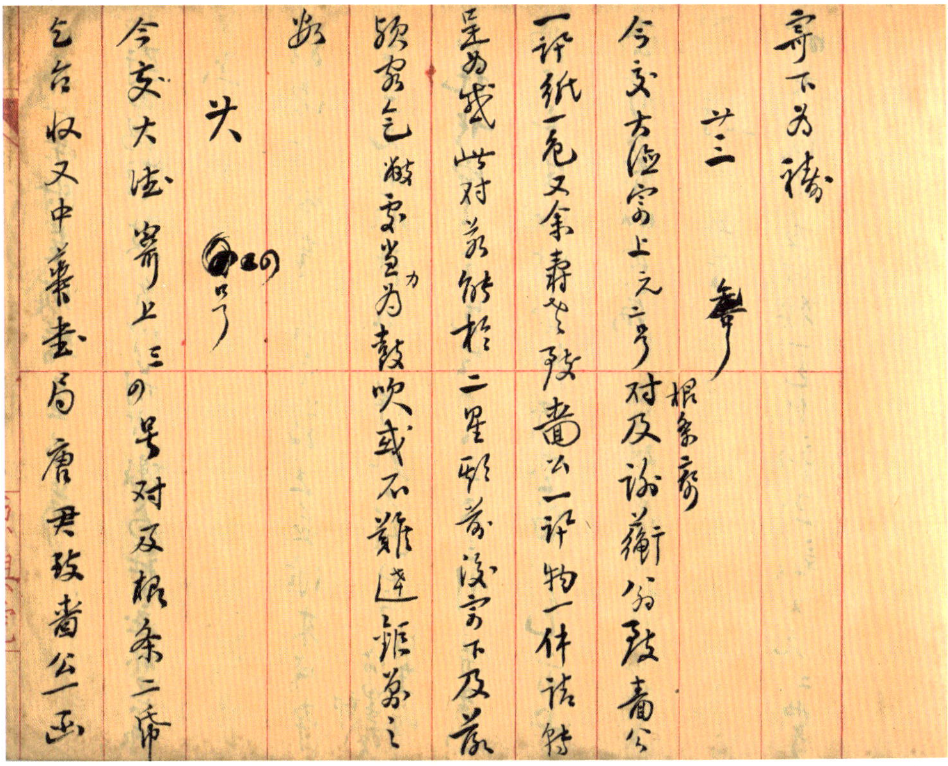

寄下为祷

廿三 鹭

今交大洋寄上之二号对及谢衡翁段啬公 根条寄

一评纸一包又余寿段啬公一评物一件请转

呈为感此对若能于二星期前后寄下及最

须寄包邮票当为数吹或不难达距离之

款

大 鹭

今交大洋寄上三の号对及根条二幅

包台收又中华书局唐君致啬公一函

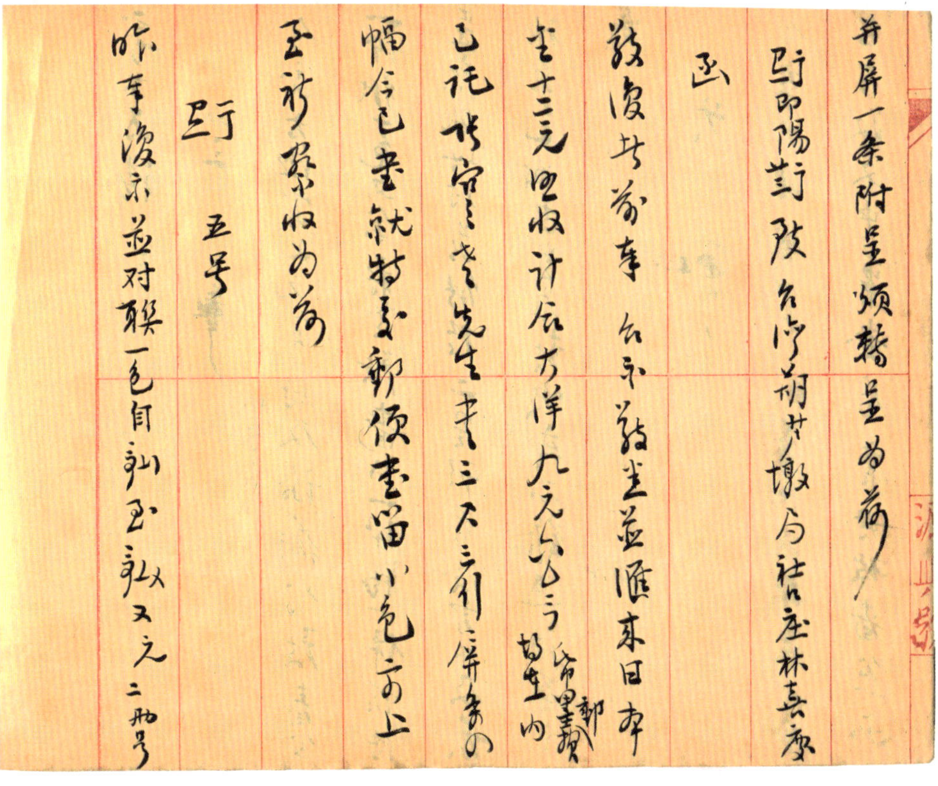

并屏一条附呈烦转呈为荷

盯即阳盯 段 名字湖廿墩与社座林喜庆

函

敬复者前奉 台示敬悉并汇来日本

金十二元照收计合大洋九元六角三分 余邮票内

已托张宗之先生书三尺之对屏条の

幅今已书就特交邮便书留小包寄上

至祈察收为荷

盯 五号

昨奉复示并对联一包自弘函弘文之二册号

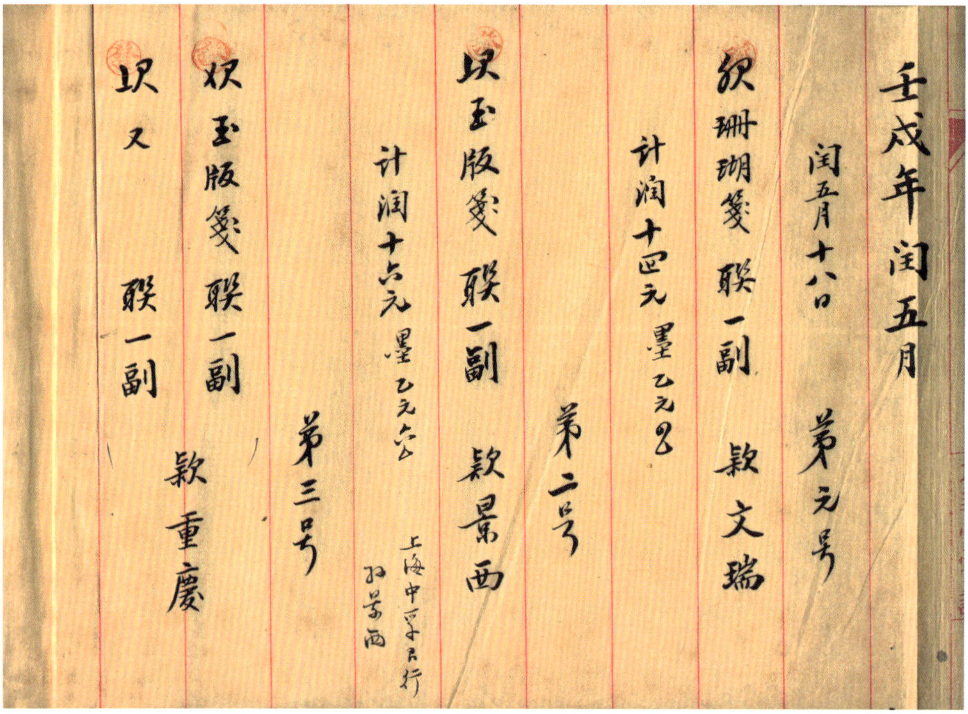

壬戌年闰五月

闰五月十八日　第元号

织珊瑚笺　联一副　款文瑞

计润十四元　墨乙元

第二号

织玉版笺　联一副　款景西

计润十六元　墨乙元

第三号

织玉版笺　联一副　款重庆

织　又　联一副

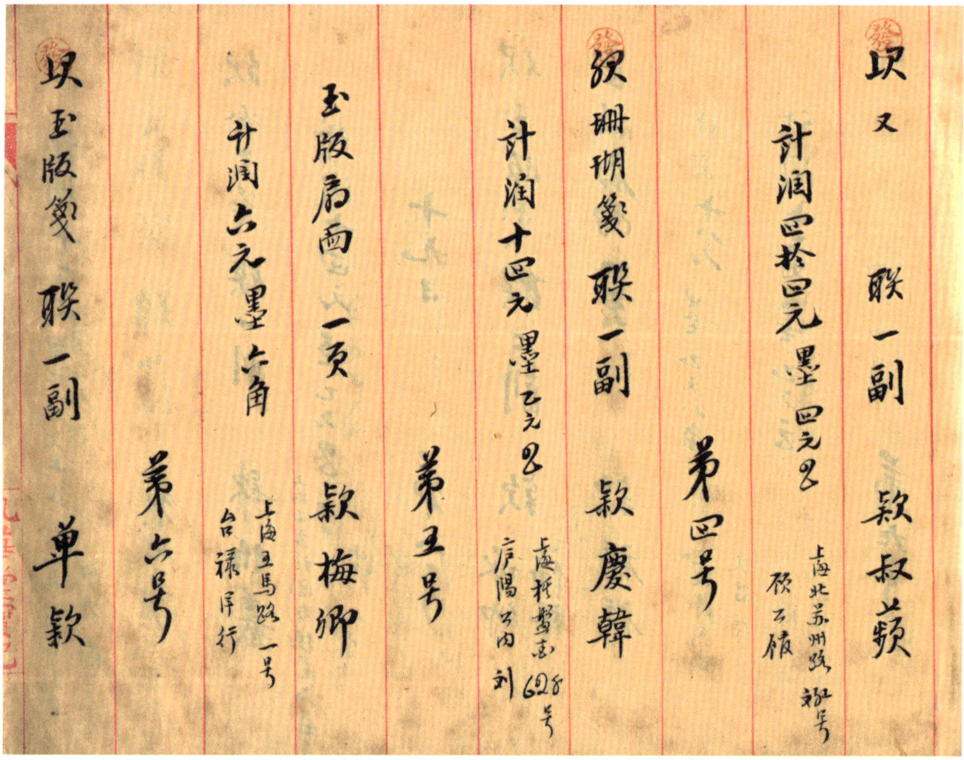

织　又　联一副　款叔蘋

计润四拾四元　墨四元

第四号

织珊瑚笺　联一副　款庆韩

计润十四元　墨乙元

第五号

玉版扇面　一页　款梅卿

计润六元　墨六角

第六号

织玉版笺　联一副　单款

1922 年张謇鬻字清册（局部）。

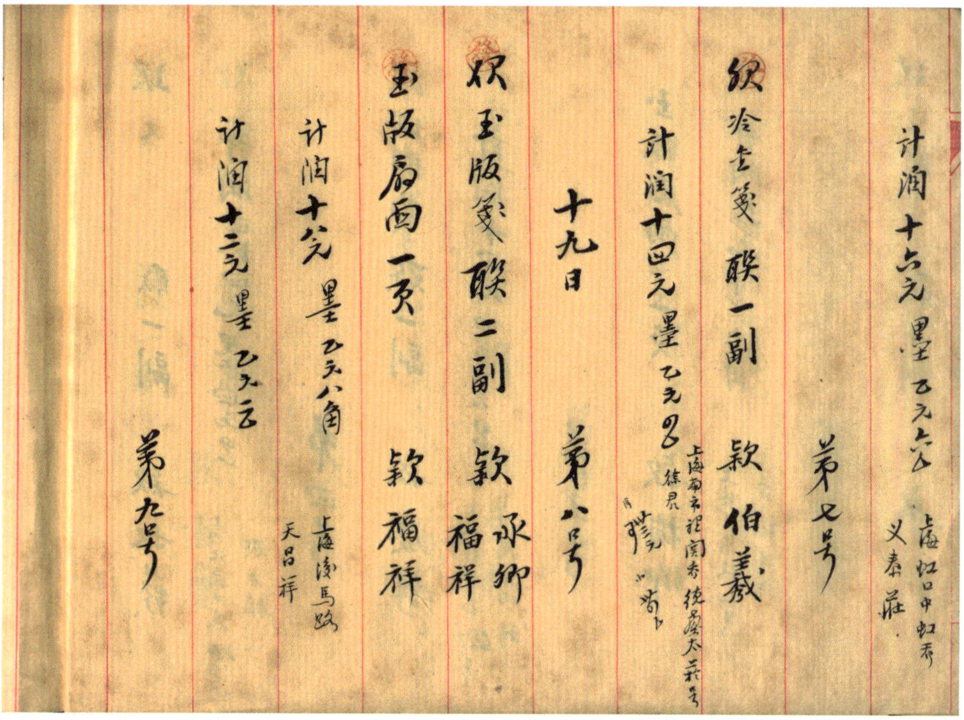
计润十六元 墨乙元六角
上海虹口中虹桥 义泰庄
第七号
织冷金笺联一副 款伯羲
计润十四元 墨乙元四角
十九日
第八号
织玉版笺联二副 款承卿
玉版扇面一页 款福祥
计润十元 墨乙元八角
上海洋马路 天吕祥
计润十二元 墨乙元二角
第九号

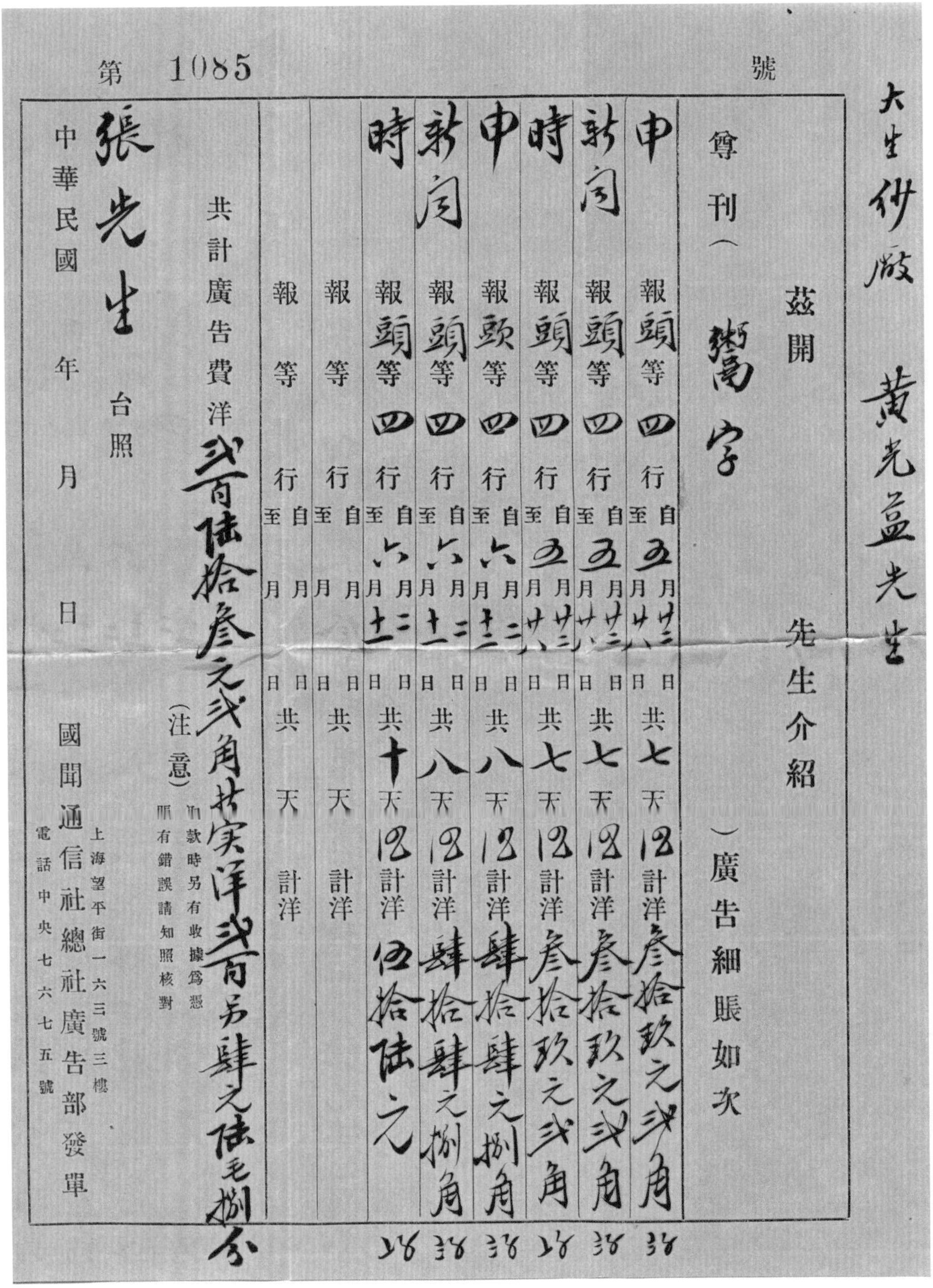
第 1085 號

大生紗廠 黃先益先生

茲開 先生介紹

尊刊（鬻字）廣告細賬如次

申報頭等四行 自五月廿三日至 月廿八日 共七天 12 計洋叁拾玖元貳角

新聞報頭等四行 自五月廿三日至 月廿八日 共七天 12 計洋叁拾玖元貳角

時報頭等四行 自五月廿三日至 月廿八日 共七天 12 計洋叁拾玖元貳角

申報頭等四行 自六月二日至 月十二日 共八天 12 計洋肆拾肆元捌角

新聞報頭等四行 自六月二日至 月十二日 共八天 12 計洋肆拾肆元捌角

時報頭等四行 自六月二日至 月十二日 共十天 12 計洋伍拾陸元

報 等 行 自 月 日至 月 日 共 天 計洋

報 等 行 自 月 日至 月 日 共 天 計洋

共計廣告費洋貳百陸拾叁元貳角 折實洋貳百另肆元陸毛捌分

（注意）付款時另有收據爲憑 賬有錯誤請知照核對

張先生台照

中華民國 年 月 日

國聞通信社總社廣告部發單

上海望平街一六三號三樓

電話中央七六七五號

1924年6月10日，国闻通信社总社广告部出具的在《申报》《新闻报》《时报》代理刊登张謇鬻字广告的收费明细和收据。

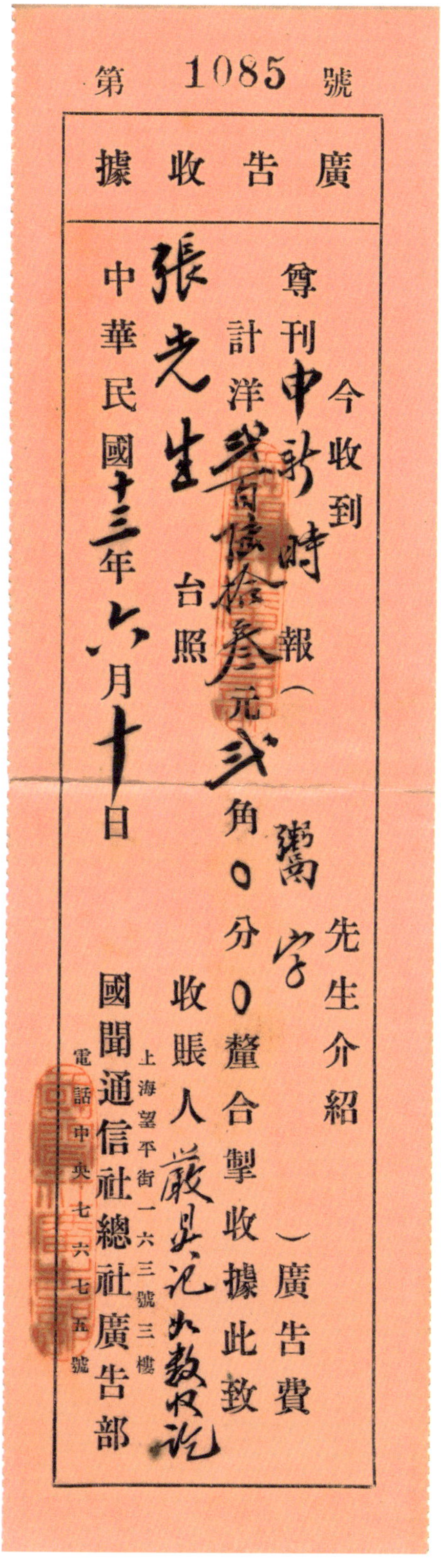

第 1085 號

廣告收據

今收到 先生介紹

尊刊中新時報（鬻字）廣告費

計洋叁百伍拾叁元貳角〇分〇釐合掣收據此致

張先生台照

收賬人 嚴具記如數收訖

國聞通信社總社廣告部

上海望平街一六三號三樓

電話中央七六七五號

中華民國十三年六月十日

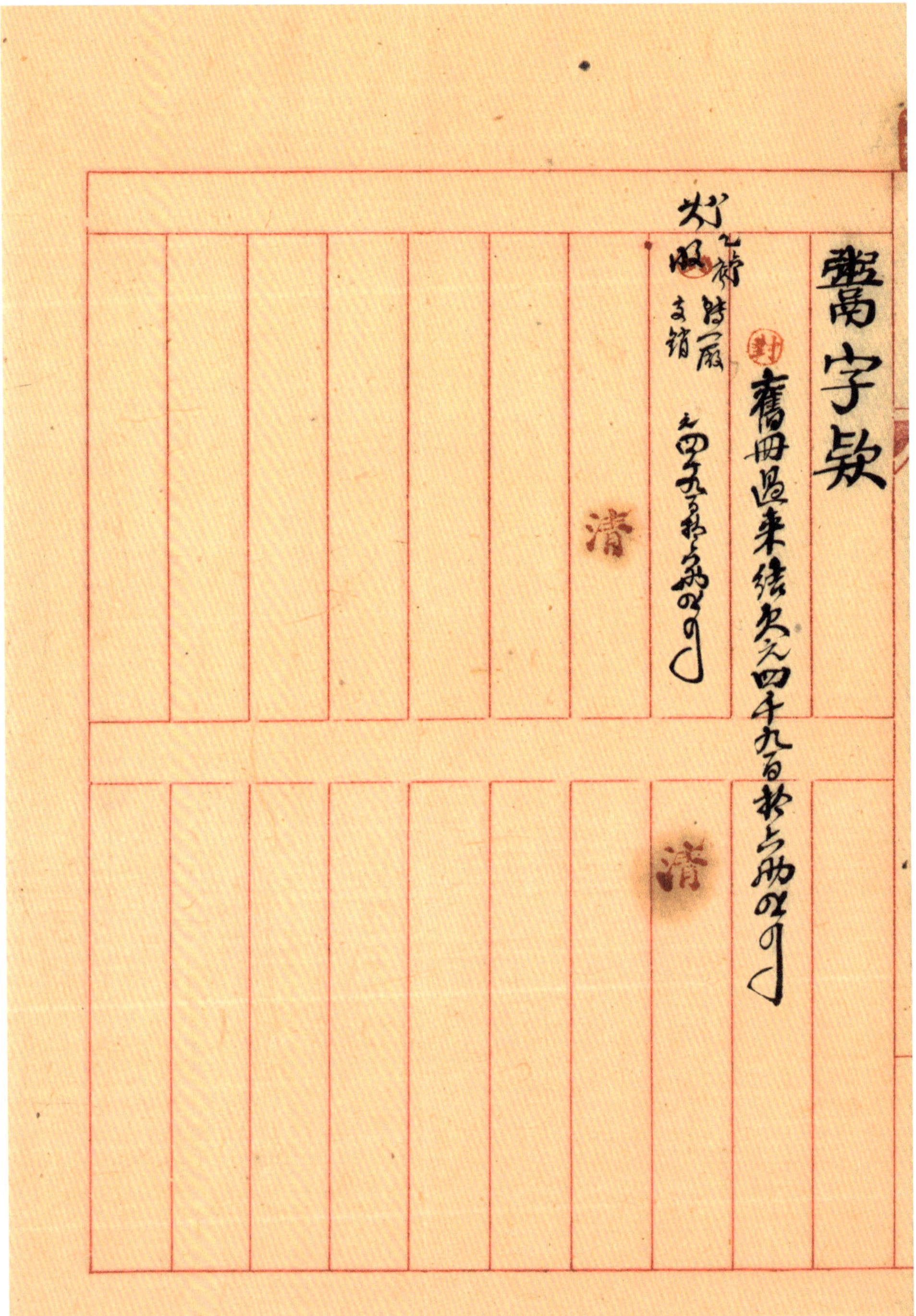
鬻字欵

1925 年大生沪所《杂欠》账目的张謇《鬻字》分项。

『吴淞为吾国第一口岸』

——开发吴淞

吴淞位于宝山东部，黄浦江口西岸。张謇认为："吴淞为吾国第一口岸，于水为长江门户，于陆为铁路终点，而又位于上海租界之前，宜为世界所瞩目。"张謇对吴淞情有独钟，吴淞是南通之外张謇探索中国早期现代化的又一个重要基地。

1903 年，张謇与两江总督魏光焘会晤时，提到渔业公司关系领海主权，南方与北方地区都应该设立，如果财力有限，则重点在江苏、浙江、直隶和山东等地推动，实在不行的话，就从江浙起步。

1904 年，张謇筹建江浙渔业公司。直接的动因是上一年冬天，胶州湾的德国商人设立的所谓"中国渔业有限公司"在上海招股，计划招股 170 万，先向外国人募集，不足再允许华商附入。根据"中国渔业有限公司"的章程，该公司计划在东亚地区的海滨用拖船捕捞海鱼，拟用渔轮 6 艘、运鱼船 1 艘。张謇认为此举"侵我国之海权，夺我国之渔利，上下受损，名实俱亏"。张謇设立渔业公司，目的在于"首保海权，次保渔利"。

1903 年冬，"中国渔业有限公司"已经从德国开来一艘名为"万格罗"的小型渔船，在胶州湾附近海面试捕。该船于 1895 年在德国建造，载重 631 吨。"万格罗"号斩获不少，但在青岛销售不畅，于是转向上海兜售，但没有鱼行愿意包销，导致渔获大部分腐败。于是"中国渔业有限公司"准备出售"万格罗"号，委托上海捷成洋行代售，捷成洋行转交荣华洋行经手。

在上海道的支持下，江浙渔业公司以 4.5 万两买下"万格罗"号，改名"福海"号。连同派人往来青岛查看的旅费、江浙渔业公司开办经费 5000 两，合计 5 万两全部由官府垫资。鉴于浙江渔业发达，所以江浙渔业公司的筹备工作，张謇主要依靠浙江人士，并聘请宁波帮商人樊时勋为江浙渔业公司总董。江浙渔业公司开辟了中国现代化渔业之路。

张謇在发展实业的同时，欲进军国际贸易市场。1920 年 12 月，张謇在给华义银行上海分行李国芝的信中提及:“海外贸易，今行已迟迟，乃益不可缓，但必枢纽于航业。”吴淞背靠上海，滨江临海，是发展国际航运业的理想场所。张謇先后在吴淞创办海外航业公司(初名中比航业公司)、海通贸易公司和左海公司，尽管无功而返，但在中国航运史写下了开创性的一页。

创办海外航业公司和海通贸易公司来自梁启超的倡议。1919 年，旅欧考察的梁启超在比利时与该国政府部门会晤时，得知比利时方面拟组织中比合资的航业公司和贸易公司，希望梁启超牵线中方愿意投资合办的人士。1920 年梁启超回国后，找到张謇商议此事。张謇认为商业上绝对不能闭关自守，但中国自从五口通商以来，远洋航运与对外贸易被外国人控制，巨大的经济利益也为外国人所攫取，中国人必须能够直接进行对外贸易，因此极力推动合资企业的成立。

据《创办海外航业股份有限公司、海通贸易股份有限公司说明及招股简章》，拟议中的合资航业公司“以直航中国与欧洲之间，中国以青岛、上海为终点，欧洲则经过法国之马赛、比国之昂维斯、荷兰之劳特但姆，而至德国之亨堡”。海通贸易公司“以中国土货输往欧美，而以欧美货物输入中国。运销欧洲之货，尽先用航业公司之船输运”。

1920 年 8 月，张謇联合荣宗敬、金其堡等人，承领吴淞的衣周塘滩地，组织左海公司，规划开辟轮埠、建设工厂(先筹办电厂，再筹划机器铁厂)、经营航业。但海外航业公司、海通贸易公司和左海公司，最后都没能如愿进行如此大规模的投资和开发。

张謇还参与了中国第一家民族纺织机器企业中国铁工厂的创立。中国铁工厂由聂云台倡议设立，主要股东为张謇、荣宗敬、徐静仁、穆藕初等，实收股金 30 万元。张謇任董事长，聂云台为总经理。1921 年在吴淞建厂。产品供应上海、汉口、天津等地纺织厂。由于民族棉纺织业不景气，中国铁工厂开工后经营不利。1932 年“一·二八”遭炮击，损失惨重，不久宣告清理倒闭。

1920 年 11 月 4 日，张謇受北京政府委任，督办吴淞商埠事宜。1921 年 2 月 12 日，吴淞商埠局开局，张謇发表了就职讲话。时年 68 岁的张謇说，经营地方事业是从这三方面考虑的：有益于百姓、对一个县也有好处的事，他会积极推动；不利于百姓、对一个县有危害的事，尽量避免；有利于社会，但是一个县的力量做不到，或者不是十分迫切的事，暂缓从事。20 多年来，他在南通很多事都力不从心，很难顾得上南通之外的事。至于督办江苏运河工程，是因为政府和百姓的信任，也因为他对于运河治理有过几十年的研究、十多年的测绘和筹备，算是得偿所愿，也避免了读书人喜欢空谈的弊病。这次督办吴淞开埠，是时势所迫，尽管他垂垂老矣，作为国民义不容辞，也就不考虑江南和江北的地域之别了。

吴淞商埠局在吴淞镇原来的提督行辕办公，根据张謇 1921 年 2 月 19 日报送给外交总长颜惠庆的吴淞商埠局组织规程，吴淞商埠局有六项职能：建筑工程之规划及核定事项；官地、民地之调查登记及收用事项；规定土地之等第事项；经理土地及房屋之租赁事项；筹办警察事项；征收杂捐事项。

张謇统领的吴淞商埠局，对于吴淞开埠是从两方面入手的。一方面是进行测绘，在测绘的基础上确定埠界。1922 年 9 月 15 日，张謇与江苏省长韩国钧咨行外交部，所附的埠界图明确东至以黄浦为界，西至以宝山南北县道为界，南至以沈金港、葛家嘴、虬江为界，北至以宝山东西县道、马路塘、采淘港为界。

另一方面，在测绘的基础上，张謇认为“水利、交通，为最要之政。一面于沿江筹建公共码头堆栈，以期运输之便；一面区划各工厂聚业之所”。吴淞口从谈家浜往西，经剪淞桥至杨树泓，拥有 6400 米的深水岸线，可以建设码头，张謇设想剪淞桥之东岸线建海轮码头，其西则用于建江轮码头。此外计划疏通蕴藻浜，既便利与内地的水路运输，也有利于太湖的泄水。至于吴淞的内部交通，张謇计划修筑一条环形轨道交通线路，以及一条与轨道线走向相同略微偏西的电车线路，两者都与上海的铁路和电车衔接。

张謇对于吴淞开埠，有着全面细致的计划，在1923年元旦《申报》发表的《吴淞开埠计画概略》里，有着详尽的说明。张謇精心设计全埠街道、码头、水陆交通、公共事业、模范市街的建设方案。

张謇把吴淞商埠范围的街道规划为方格形，南北长而东西短。商埠划分为六个区，各区设一个中点，各中点以斜路互联。中点的土地均收归公有，供市政、司法、警察、消防、税务等机关办公；学校、医院、图书馆等，则位于住宅区僻静之处。公园，除了在各区中点各设一处外，斜直两路交叉的地方、所留的三角地、高低不平之处、原有树木之处，因地制宜设为公园，或者作为菜市场，方便各区居民在十分钟内到达。张謇的吴淞市政规划，充分体现以人为本的理念。

张謇吴淞开埠的目标为“以自辟商埠之先声，为改良港务之张本”，可惜的是1924年江浙战争爆发，吴淞成为主战场，第二次吴淞开埠失败。

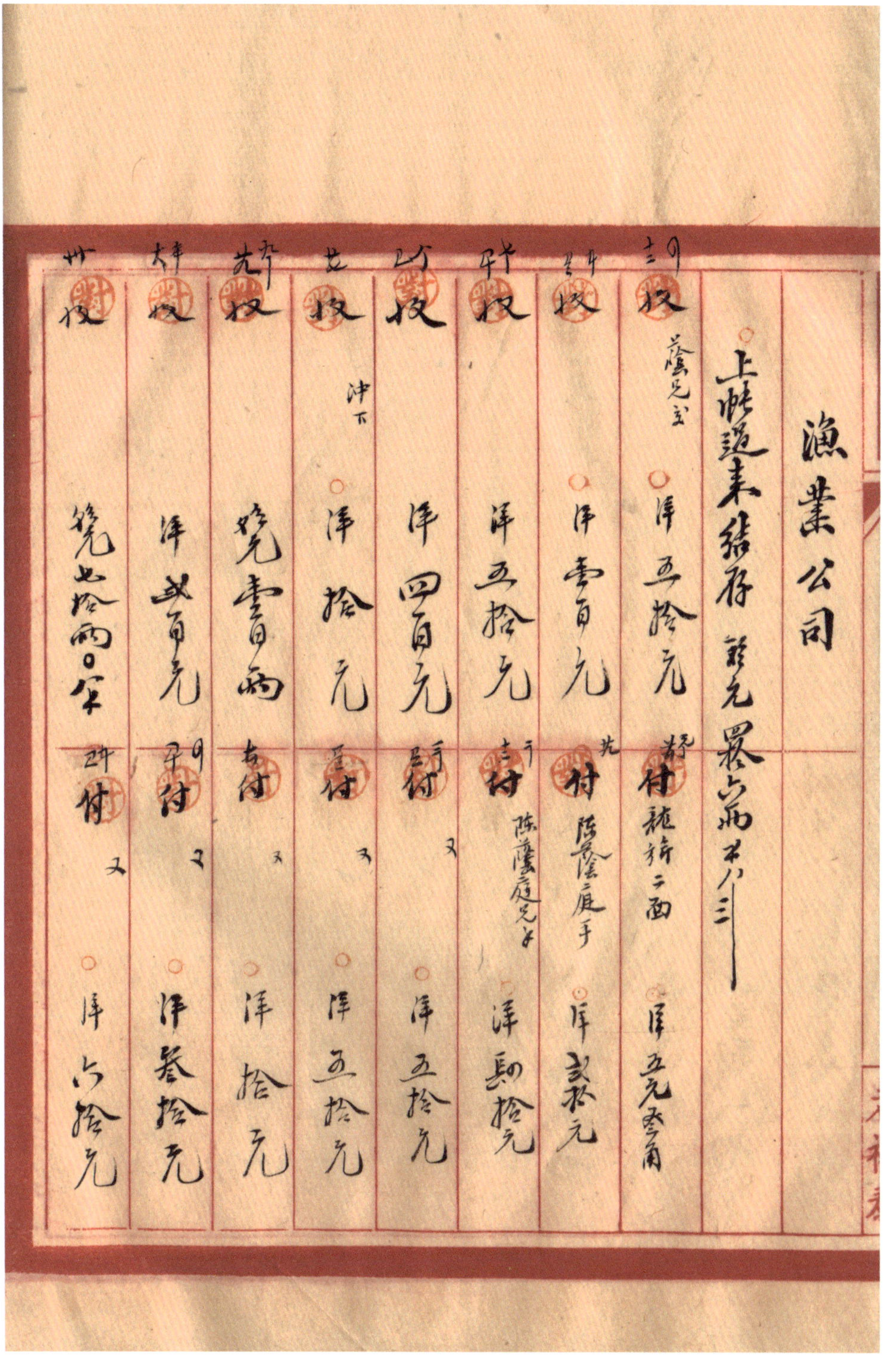

1905 年大生沪所《总录》中的《渔业公司》分项。

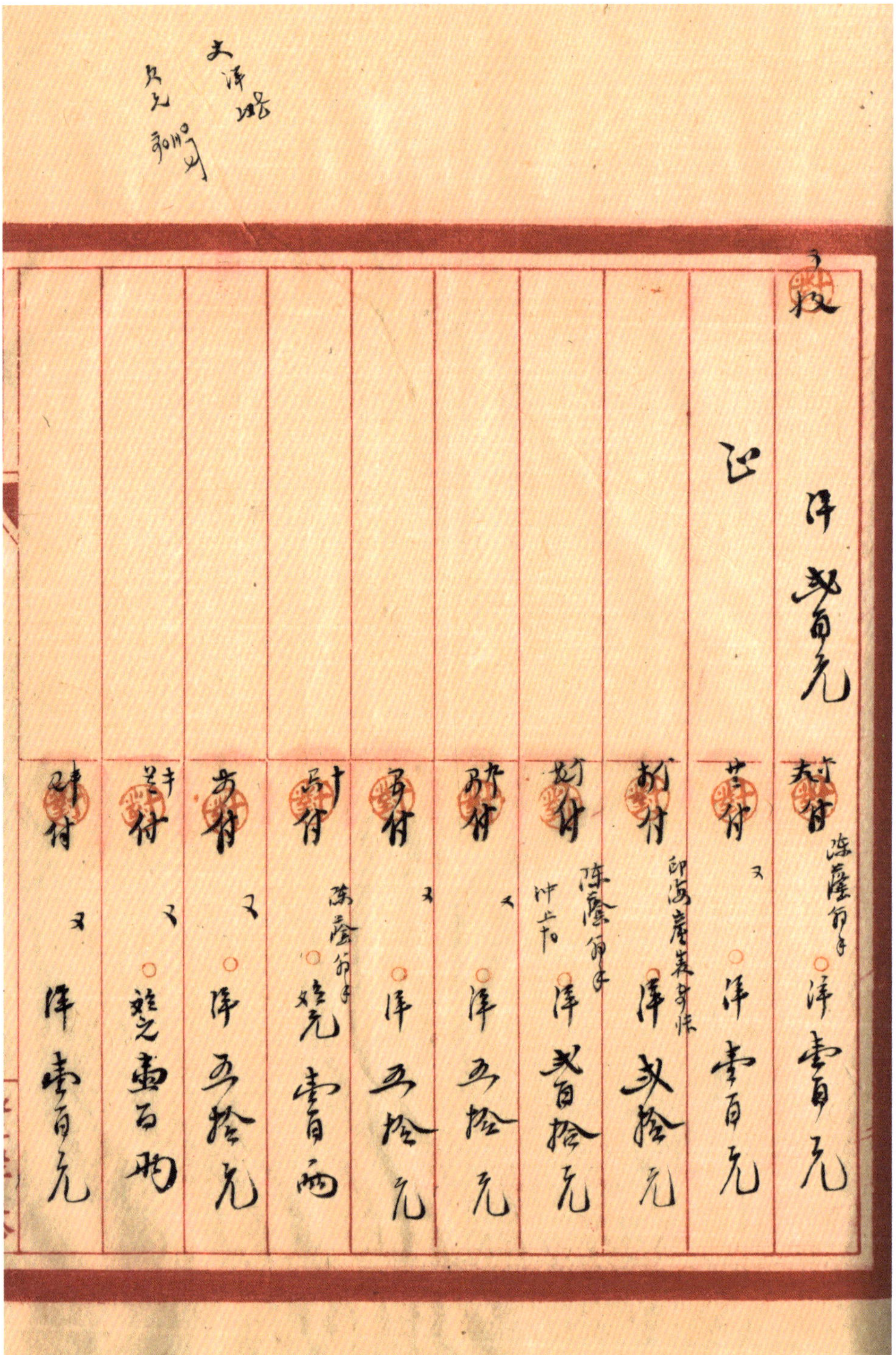

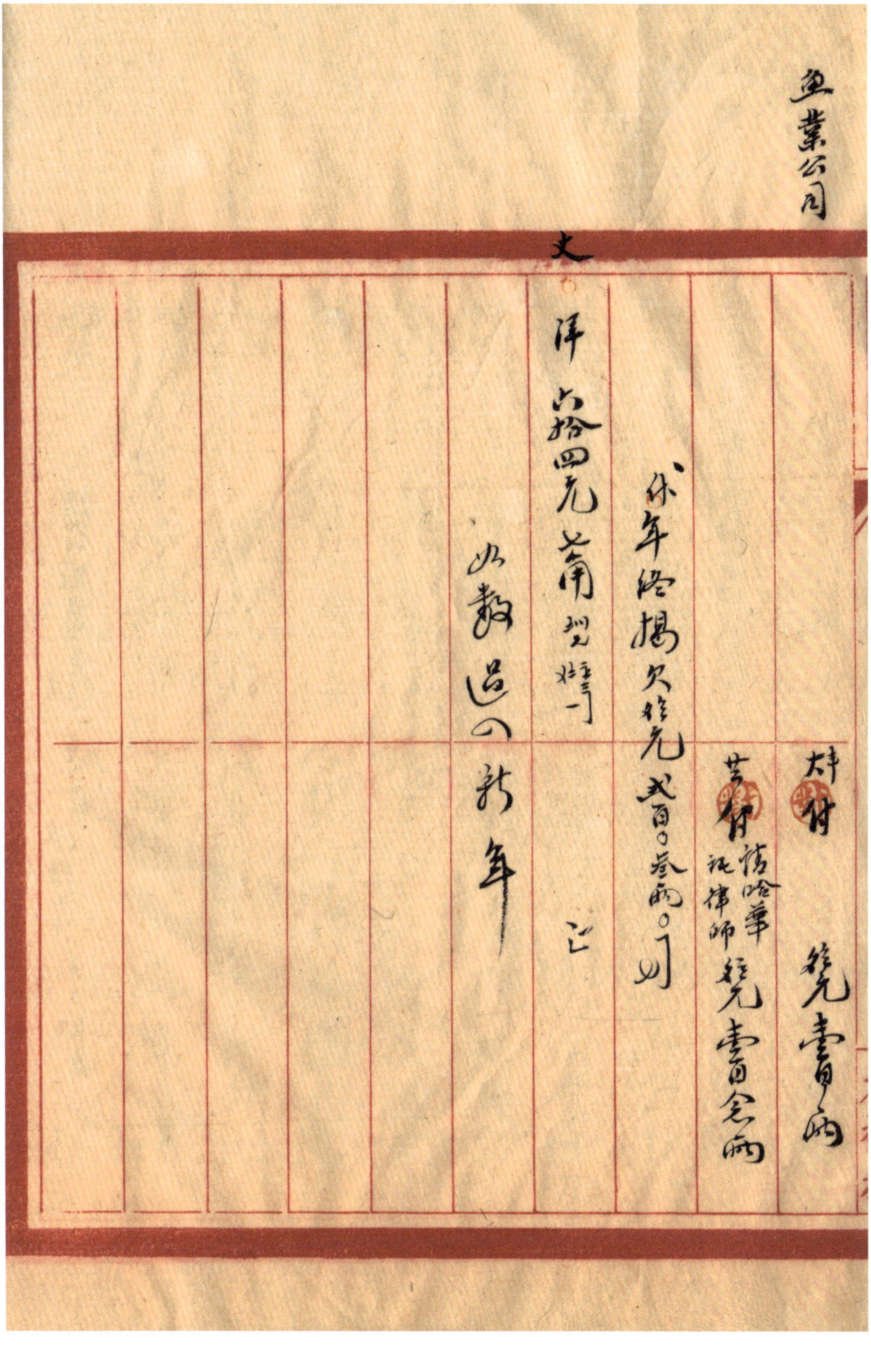

漁業公司
大付 洋壹百兩
芸付 請哈華託律師洋壹百念兩
除年終揭欠洋貳百叁兩○外
洋六拾四元七角
以敷過新年

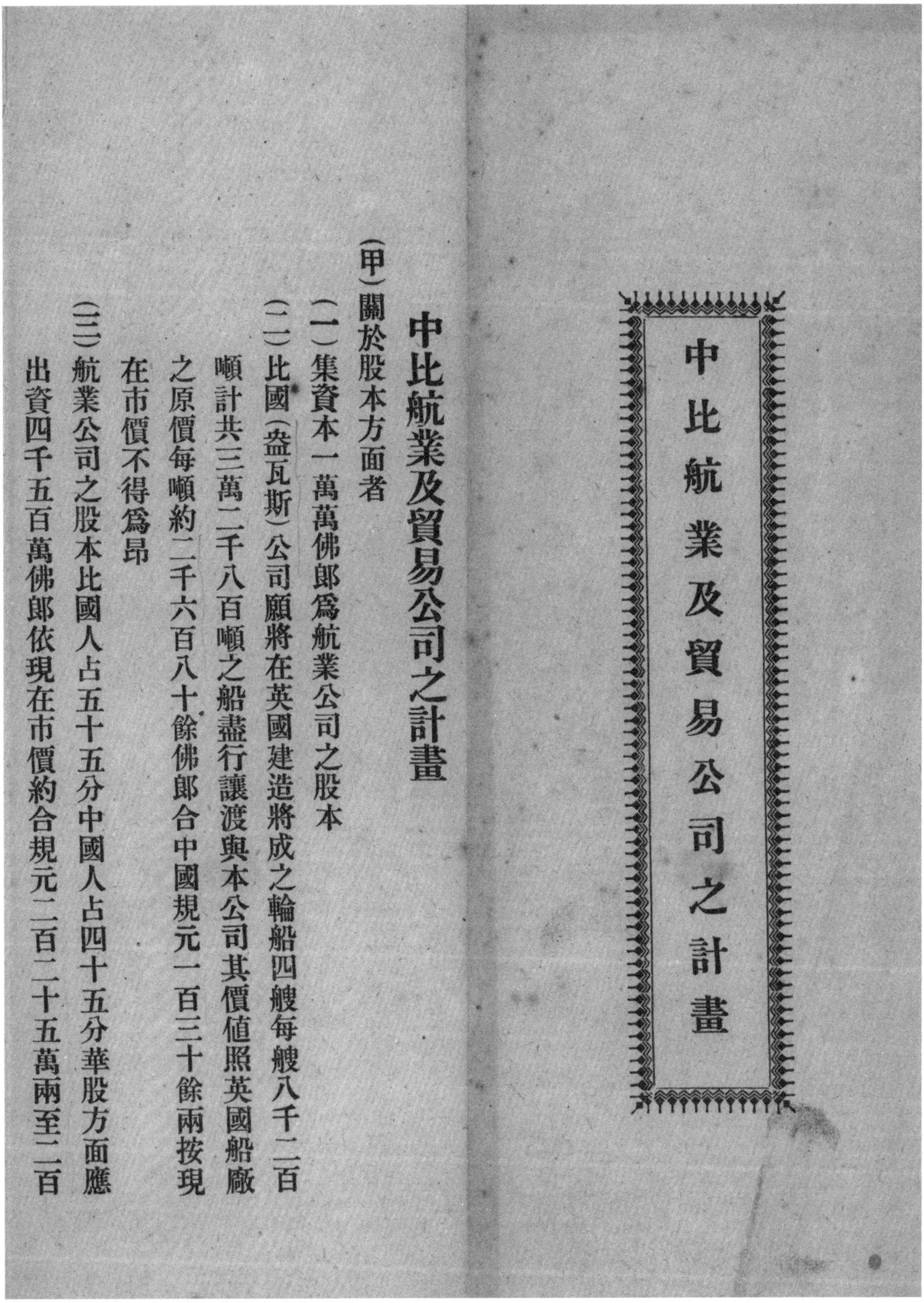

中比航業及貿易公司之計畫

中比航業及貿易公司之計畫

(甲)關於股本方面者

(一)集資本一萬萬佛郎爲航業公司之股本

(二)比國(盎瓦斯)公司願將在英國建造將成之輪船四艘每艘八千二百噸計共三萬二千八百噸之船盡行讓渡與本公司其價值照英國船廠之原價每噸約二千六百八十餘佛郎合中國規元一百三十餘兩按現在市價不得爲昂

(三)航業公司之股本比國人占五十五分中國人占四十五分華股方面應出資四千五百萬佛郎依現在市價約合規元二百二十五萬兩至二百

《中比航业及贸易公司之计画》。

五十萬兩

(四)貿易公司股本額定一千萬佛郎華比各半華股方面應占五百萬佛郎合上海規元二十五萬兩至二十八萬兩

(五)航業貿易兩公司中國方面應出股本五千萬佛郎約合規元二百五十萬兩至二百八十萬兩北京方面暨山東專做出口之某富商等已認二十五分之七餘二十五分之十八歸南通方面完全擔任

(乙)關於航業方面者

(一)該輪四艘在中國方面兩艘以青島爲終點兩艘以上海爲終點惟航行青島者經過上海時仍須停泊

(二)歐洲方面經過法國比國而至德國以德國之亨堡爲終點

(三)僅有航行歐洲之遠洋船而中國沿江沿海無輪船以爲之輔則土貨之輸出與外貨之輸入不能逕達仍足爲貿易之障礙現擬由徐君靜仁擔任將利淮公司之海輪兩艘專駛北洋天津營口等埠此海輪或作價售與公司或與公司訂立特別契約均俟將來雙方協商再由大達公司設法添置江輪兩艘專駛漢口將來亦與中比航業公司訂立特別契約中比公司凡有洋貨之輸入揚子江流域者或向漢口等處採辦土貨輸出海外者均由大達公司承裝如此則內海外洋長江脈絡貫通微特於航業有益且足發達國際之貿易也

（丙）關於貿易公司者

（一）中國土貨出口在北方則草帽牛皮羊毛繭綢雜糧等爲大宗漢口則以牛皮茶葉藥材爲大宗此項貨物貿易公司皆可自己經理并可代中國內地商人代運至外洋銷售而取其相當之佣金

（二）通海布疋向以營口爲大宗銷路第以運輸不靈所有權利幾爲外人攘奪中比成立後北至營口南至南洋等埠不獨運輸便利亦且消息靈通棉質品之銷路必日可推廣於通海實業關係至巨

（三）比國銷售中國之貨物種類不多故航業之終點在德國之亨堡爲中歐諸國之中心如奥國匈牙利捷克司拉大等國現在皆缺乏船隻我公司應特派深通商業之人往各國調查其工廠凡其出品能行銷中國者一一承攬之而代其在中國銷售

（四）德國之電機及其他機器顏料五金鋼針等貨在歐戰前行銷中國最廣今德國船隻已悉數被協約國沒收彼正苦無法運銷中國我如派人前往接洽擔任代爲經理必爲彼所歡迎因我既有船於彼必甚便我也

（五）比國德國奥國匈牙利捷克司拉夫等國皆缺乏食品及原料我應派人前往調查彼國所需要於我國者爲何種貨物并預約彼國商家爲我公司之經理貨物一到即可銷售

（丁）關於銀行匯兑方面者

(一)銷售土貨及販運洋貨全恃銀行爲樞紐雖比國已有華比銀行之設立但彼國金融近頗艱困現擬商由上海商業銀行金城銀行及將來設立之淮海實業銀行公共組織一國外匯兑機關凡中比航業貿易公司所到之處均設立匯兑所或代理所

(二)中國內地土貨出產之地亦應分設銀行並代販運土貨之客商經理運輸保險押匯之事將來外國購買土貨我之機關種種完備則各種貿易可占優勝地位

以上計畫不過大概一切情形應請詳細研究辦理

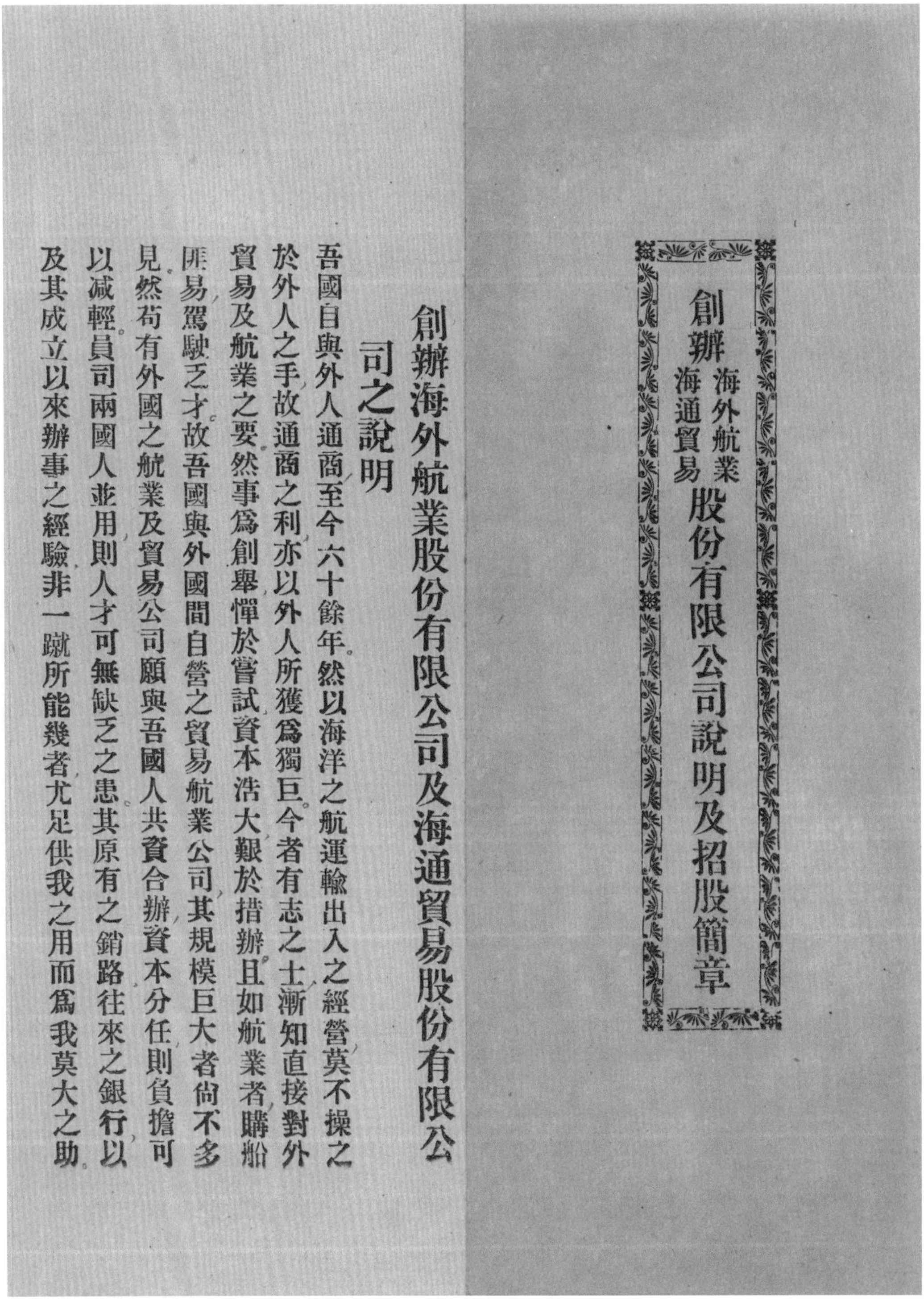

創辦海外航業
海通貿易股份有限公司說明及招股簡章

創辦海外航業股份有限公司及海通貿易股份有限公司之說明

吾國自與外人通商至今六十餘年。然以海洋之航運輸出入之經營，莫不操之於外人之手，故通商之利亦以外人所獲為獨巨。今者有志之士漸知直接對外貿易及航業之要，然事為創舉，憚於嘗試，資本浩大，艱於措辦，且如航業者購船匪易，駕駛乏才。故吾國與外國間自營之貿易航業公司，其規模巨大者尚不多見。然苟有外國之航業及貿易公司願與吾國人共貲合辦，資本分任，則負擔可以減輕；員司兩國人並用，則人才可無缺乏之患。其原有之銷路、往來之銀行，以及其成立以來辦事之經驗，非一蹴所能幾者，尤足供我之用，而為我莫大之助

《创办海外航业、海通贸易股份有限公司说明及招股简章》(局部)。

際此經營直接對外貿易及航業發軔之時循此折中之道似不得謂非善策也
比利時素爲工業之國壤地雖小而富庶爲各國之冠其投巨資於吾國以興辦鐵路礦業銀行公司爲人所共知已歐戰之時比國爲德人所佔然境內戰事甚暫損失之額尚不爲巨休戰以後恢復之速凡美國人士之游歷歐洲各國者莫不許爲第一如礦業玻璃造紙紡織固已漸復戰前之舊即受創最深之鋼鐵機器各業亦已恢復至六七成矣比人於復國之後慘淡經營於恢復舊業之外抑且力謀新事業之發展以吾國爲天產饒富之區將來必爲世界經濟之重鎮乃謀闢與吾國直通之航綫又以德國之商業勢力經歐戰而大受懲創非數年間所可恢復乃欲於擴充中比商業之中更寓繼承德國代起而興之志昂維斯爲比國之大商港其戰前之位置僅亞於英國之倫敦德國之亨堡其地之比國航業公司既抱增闢中國航綫之願復知吾國有經營遠洋航業之志因願將其在英國新造之船四艘每艘八千二百噸共計三萬二千八百噸以原價轉讓與我國人合辦一航業公司以直航中國與歐洲之間中國以青島上海爲終點歐洲則經過法國之馬賽比國之昂維斯荷蘭之勞特但姆而至德國之亨堡即以亨堡爲終點昂維斯又有殖民商業信用銀行擬與中國人合辦一貿易公司以中國土貨輸往歐美而以歐美貨物輸入中國運銷歐洲之貨儘先用航業公司之船輸運運銷美國之貨則由太平洋現有之各船公司裝運也
以上兩事表面雖係分立以兩公司辦兩種事然暗中實相輔而行蓋外國貿易

之與航業原有脣齒相依之勢有船以後而我國土貨可以逕運出洋而我國之採辦外國貨物者亦不至以無船可裝聽人操縱矣。右稱之貿易公司定名爲海通貿易股份有限公司資本額定一千萬佛郎中比方面各居五成航業公司定名爲海外航業股份有限公司資本額定一萬萬佛郎中國方面占百分之四十五比國方面占百分之五十五招股簡章謹列左方。

海外航業股份有限公司及海通貿易股份有限公司招股簡章

第一條　今與比利時國昂維斯地方之比國航業公司合辦一航業公司定名爲海外航業股份有限公司又與昂維斯之殖民商業信用公司合辦一貿易公司定名爲海通貿易股份有限公司

第二條　海外航業股份有限公司資本額定一萬萬佛郎分二百萬股每股爲五十佛郎海通貿易股份有限公司資本額定一千萬佛郎分二十萬股每股爲五十佛郎

第三條　海外航業股份有限公司資本中國方面攤出百分之四十五比國方面攤分百分之五十五海通貿易股份有限公司資本中比方面各出百之五十計兩公司資本中國方面共出五千萬佛郎

第四條　海外航業股份有限公司以經營中國與歐洲間之航綫爲目的有船四艘每艘八千二百噸計共三萬二千八百噸

海通貿易股份有限公司以經營中國與歐洲及美洲間之進出口貿易爲目的

第五條　兩公司在比國註冊中國立案

第六條　兩公司之總辦事處中國設於上海歐洲設於昂維斯

第七條　兩公司董事監事中比兩方按照認股成數攤選董事局設於昂維斯但在上海設董事分局

第八條　兩公司辦事人中比兩國人並用權限平等

第九條　兩公司之年限各爲三十年滿期得延長之

第十條　中國方面股欵以中國人認購爲限

第十一條　購股者於兩公司之股份按照海外九分海通一份分購設如購股一萬佛郎即作爲認購海外九千佛郎海通一千佛郎

第十二條　購股者應於民國九年八月一日至三十一日之內繳付第一次欵十分之一先行掣取收條俟後換給股票其餘股欵之交付日期應俟公司籌備處通知之

第十三條　股票爲記名式如有轉讓抵押等事應通知公司籌備處

第十四條　後開各銀行爲兩公司之收股機關

上海　上海商業儲蓄銀行　浙江興業銀行

北京　中國銀行　匯豐銀行

青島　山東銀行　東萊銀行

第十五條　兩公司之中國方面籌備處設於上海九江路二十二號

創辦人
周扶九　袁南生
鄧君翔　范季美
張嗇庵　蔣孟蘋
張退庵　徐靜仁　等公啓
張乾若　陳光甫
徐振飛　劉聚卿
劉厚生　吳寄塵
榮宗敬　榮德生

海外航業公司說畧

凡事無不有過去現在與未來論事者能記憶過去時之情狀便得其眞作事者能審慎未來時之情形所失即鮮航業之發起在歐戰時輪値之巨輪租之昂全球震駭商業無論大小均受影響南通實業關係甚巨比時適新會梁任公先生自海外歸爲中比航業投資之介紹而又値大生連年獲利過母之時於是大生有除發正息八厘餘利四分二厘現金外建提欵經營航業之議案經過而與政府購德奧船亦有成約後微聞美有帆船搆置歐美輪租之價微平因愼審其事復派員至歐美調查知時機已過遂未舉辦僅徵受調查費與保證金之息銀損失而已此過去之情形股東當可記憶嗣國人迫季弟謇督理吳淞商埠知濬浦局六國技術委員會議決將商港郵船碼頭地點定在吳淞季弟爲保國家主權計因用航業股欵與寶山士紳會商將吳淞豫計所須地約八十畝購定現有人出價過倍曾於今年夏曆六月二十日提交大生董事會核議董事中有知此地郵船碼頭無可替代之地未

海外航業公司說畧　一

庚申年（1920）四月至乙丑年（1925）底，海外航业公司说略、帐略。

允照售就航業論地值已漲未用之銀仍存大生毫無損失惟大生値此全國淪於俶擾之中營業年年虧耗現欵暫提不出所有該項股本若股東念其本由大生餘利項下撥來今大生處紡織業公共困難之年或將此項股本加息並將所收吳淞地照時値售脫收入航業帳一併改發大生股票或輕息存單作爲股東維持公司之用照票面計股本十兩者可加六兩有奇是否可行應請股東討論決之

張退盦

海外航業公司帳畧 自庚申四月至乙丑年底止

收欵項下

一收售法郎餘　元伍萬柒仟壹伯叁拾兩零零貳分伍釐

一收通廠股欵貼息　五十萬兩庚申五月朔至辛酉五月朔年息六厘　元叁萬兩

一收通廠往來息　辛酉五月朔至年底年息六厘　元壹萬叁仟壹伯叁拾叁兩玖錢伍分柒釐

一收　又　壬戌全年年息六厘　元壹萬柒仟伍伯拾玖兩零伍分柒釐

一收　又　癸亥全年年息六厘　元壹萬玖仟貳伯拾陸兩伍錢肆分玖釐

一收　又　甲子全年年息六厘　元貳萬伍仟伍伯肆拾陸兩捌錢叁分貳釐

一收　又　乙丑全年年息六厘　元貳萬捌仟伍伯叁拾陸兩壹錢捌分伍釐

一收崇廠股欵貼息　十二萬兩庚申五月朔至辛酉五月朔年息六厘　元柒仟貳伯兩

一收崇廠　又　十二萬兩辛酉五月朔至年終止年息八厘　元柒仟陸伯捌拾兩

一收　又　十二萬兩壬戌全年年息六厘　元柒仟貳伯兩

一收　又　十二萬兩癸亥全年年息六厘　元柒仟貳伯兩

一收　又　十二萬兩甲子全年年息六厘　元柒仟貳伯兩

一收　又　十二萬兩乙丑全年年息六厘　元柒仟貳伯兩

一收新通股份貼息　二百〇八天九千一百十七元八角　元陸仟陸伯貳拾陸兩叁錢陸分壹釐

一收新通股息　二十萬元至十二年六月底　長年七厘半洋一萬五千元　元壹萬零捌伯肆拾伍兩

一收　又　二十萬元至十三年六月底（十二萬五千至十三年五月十二）長年五厘九千一百六十元〇九角八分　元陸仟陸伯叁拾伍兩壹錢陸分壹釐

一收左海公司墊欵息　壬戌全年年息六厘　元貳仟玖伯柒拾肆兩玖錢貳分壹釐

一收　又　癸亥全年年息六厘　元叁仟壹伯伍拾叁兩肆錢壹分陸釐

一收　又　甲子全年年息六厘　元叁仟叁伯肆拾貳兩陸錢貳分壹釐

一收又 乙丑全年年息六厘 元叁仟伍伯肆拾叁兩壹錢柒分捌釐

一共收元貳拾柒萬壹仟捌伯捌拾叁兩貳錢陸分叁釐

一支欵項下

一支施簣徐三君調查航業費 元壹萬叁仟貳伯貳拾玖兩貳錢捌分伍釐

一支酬許翥屏 洋五千元 元叁仟陸伯兩

一支購船保證金息 元壹萬貳仟玖伯伍拾伍兩叁錢捌分

一支滬事務所 元肆仟玖伯伍拾陸兩肆錢玖分柒釐

房租自十年六月至十二年十月止 元貳仟伍伯拾柒兩

生財器具 元伍伯柒拾兩零玖錢壹分壹釐

印刷文件 元貳伯貳拾陸兩叁錢

道契挂號及地捐 元肆伯貳拾柒兩捌錢捌分

薪工自十年七月至十二年二月止 元肆伯陸拾陸兩陸錢玖分叁釐

酬應 元壹伯捌拾陸兩貳錢陸分玖釐

郵電雜支 元伍伯陸拾壹兩肆錢肆分肆釐

共支元叁萬肆仟柒伯肆拾壹兩壹錢陸分貳釐

收支兩抵淨存元貳拾叁萬柒仟壹伯肆拾貳兩壹錢零壹釐

存欵項下

一存股本 元柒拾貳萬玖仟兩

一存歷屆餘欵 元貳拾叁萬柒仟壹伯肆拾貳兩壹錢零壹釐

共存元玖拾陸萬陸仟壹伯肆拾貳兩壹錢零壹釐

在欵項下

一在入新通股 洋七萬五千元 元伍萬肆仟捌伯叁拾柒兩伍錢

一在吳淞地價 元貳拾壹萬柒仟叁伯陸拾玖兩貳錢捌分壹釐

一在左海公司墊欵 元陸萬貳仟伍伯玖拾陸兩壹錢伍分伍釐

一在大生通廠　元肆拾陸萬柒仟陸伯伍拾玖兩壹錢陸分伍厘

一在大生崇廠　元拾陸萬叁仟陸伯捌拾兩

共在元玖拾陸萬陸仟壹伯肆拾貳兩壹錢零壹釐

海外航業公司帳畧

五

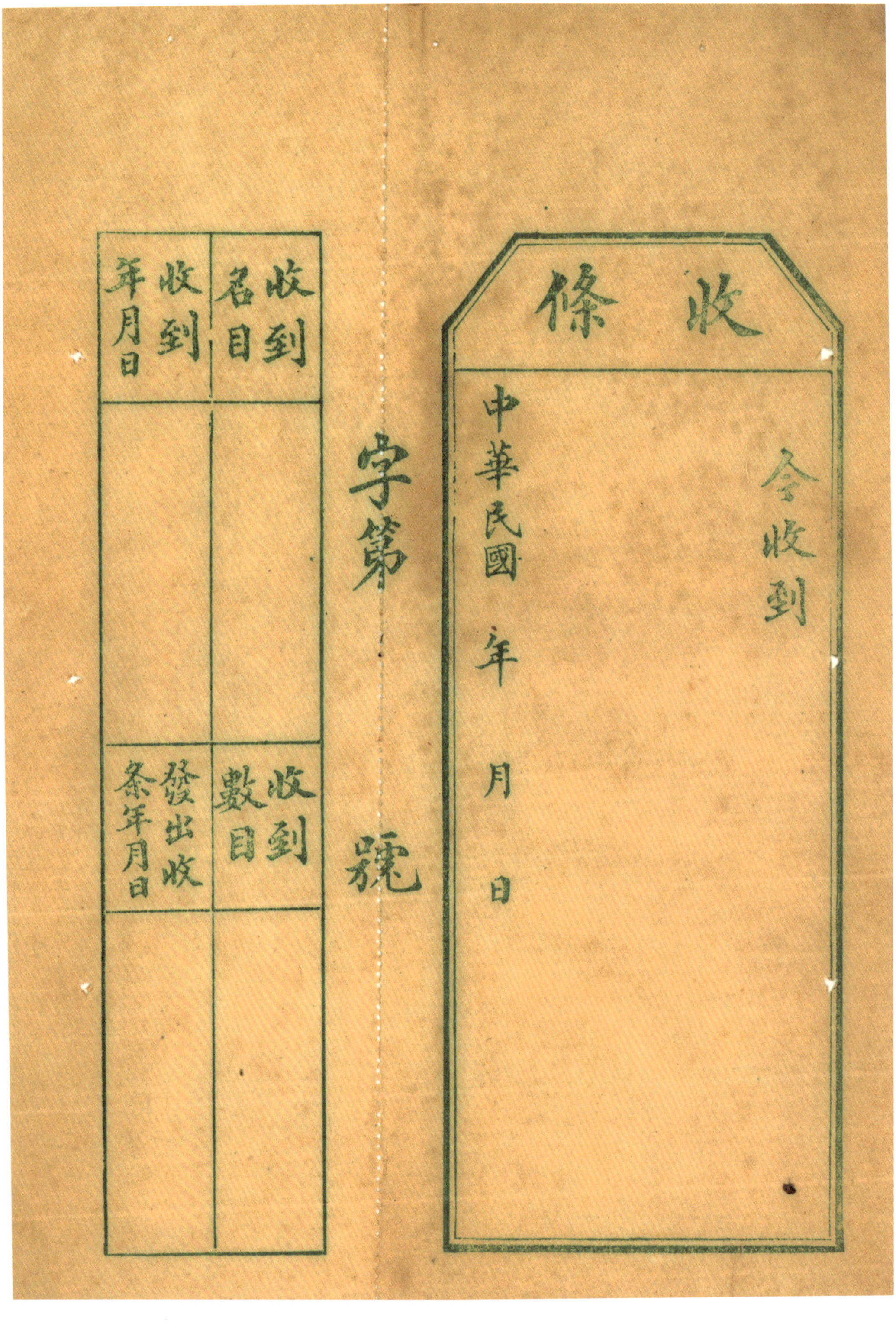

收條

今收到

中華民國 年 月 日

字第 號

收到名目

收到年月日

收到數目

發出收条年月日

海外航业公司股金收据。

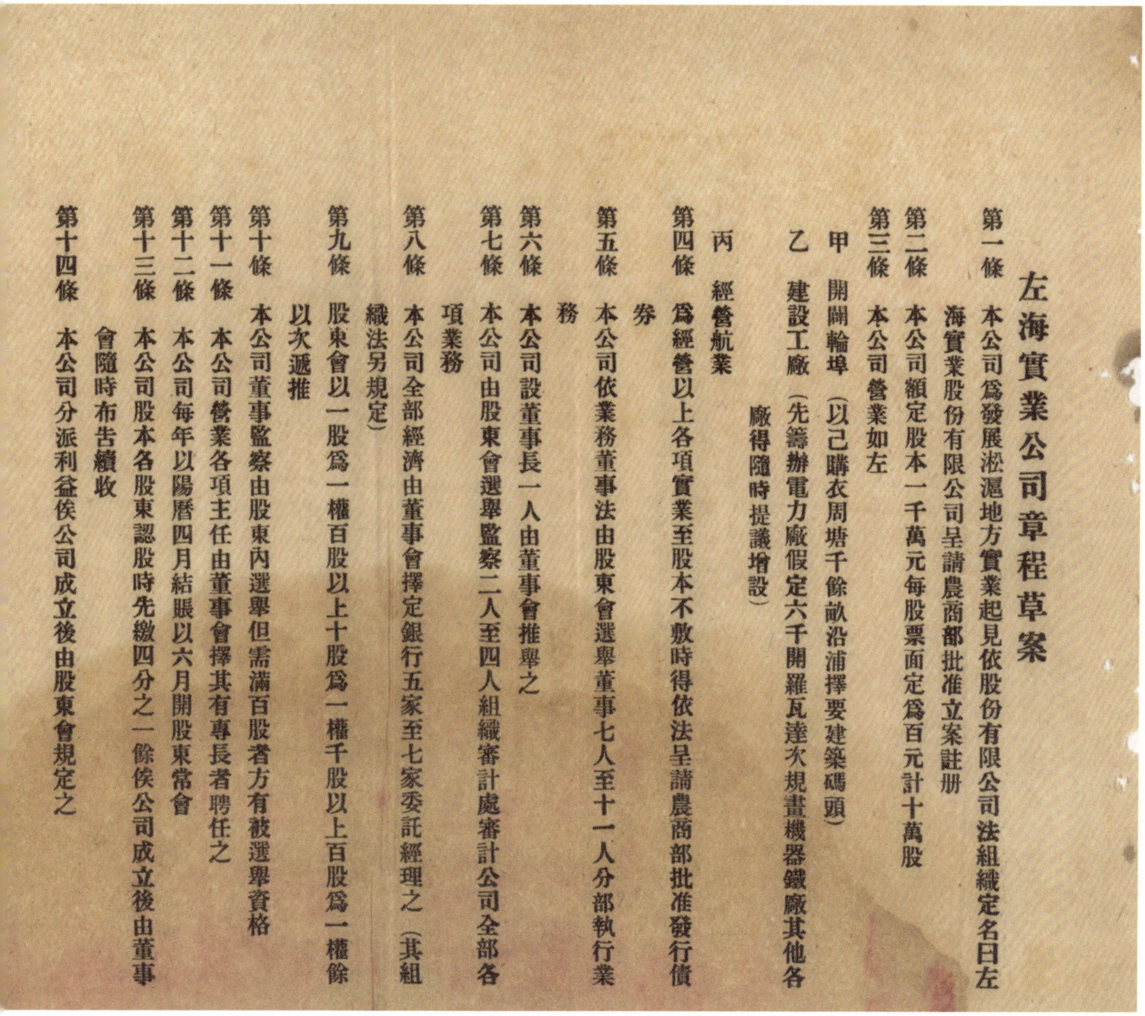

左海實業公司章程草案

第一條　本公司爲發展淞滬地方實業起見依股份有限公司法組織定名曰左海實業股份有限公司呈請農商部批准立案註册

第二條　本公司額定股本一千萬元每股票面定爲百元計十萬股

第三條　本公司營業如左

甲　開闢輪埠（以己購衣周塘千餘畝沿浦擇要建築碼頭）

乙　建設工廠（先籌辦電力廠假定六千開羅瓦達次規畫機器鐵廠其他各廠得隨時提議增設）

丙　經營航業

第四條　爲經營以上各項實業至股本不敷時得依法呈請農商部批准發行債券

第五條　本公司依業務董事法由股東會選舉董事七人至十一人分部執行業務

第六條　本公司設董事長一人由董事會推舉之

第七條　本公司由股東會選舉監察二人至四人組織審計處審計公司全部各項業務

第八條　本公司全部經濟由董事會擇定銀行五家至七家委託經理之（其組織法另規定）

第九條　股東會以一股爲一權百股以上十股爲一權千股以上百股爲一權餘以次遞推

第十條　本公司董事監察由股東內選舉但需滿百股者方有被選舉資格

第十一條　本公司營業各項主任由董事會擇其有專長者聘任之

第十二條　本公司每年以陽曆四月結賬以六月開股東常會

第十三條　本公司股本各股東認股時先繳四分之一餘俟公司成立後由董事會隨時布告續收

第十四條　本公司分派利益俟公司成立後由股東會規定之

《左海实业公司章程草案》。

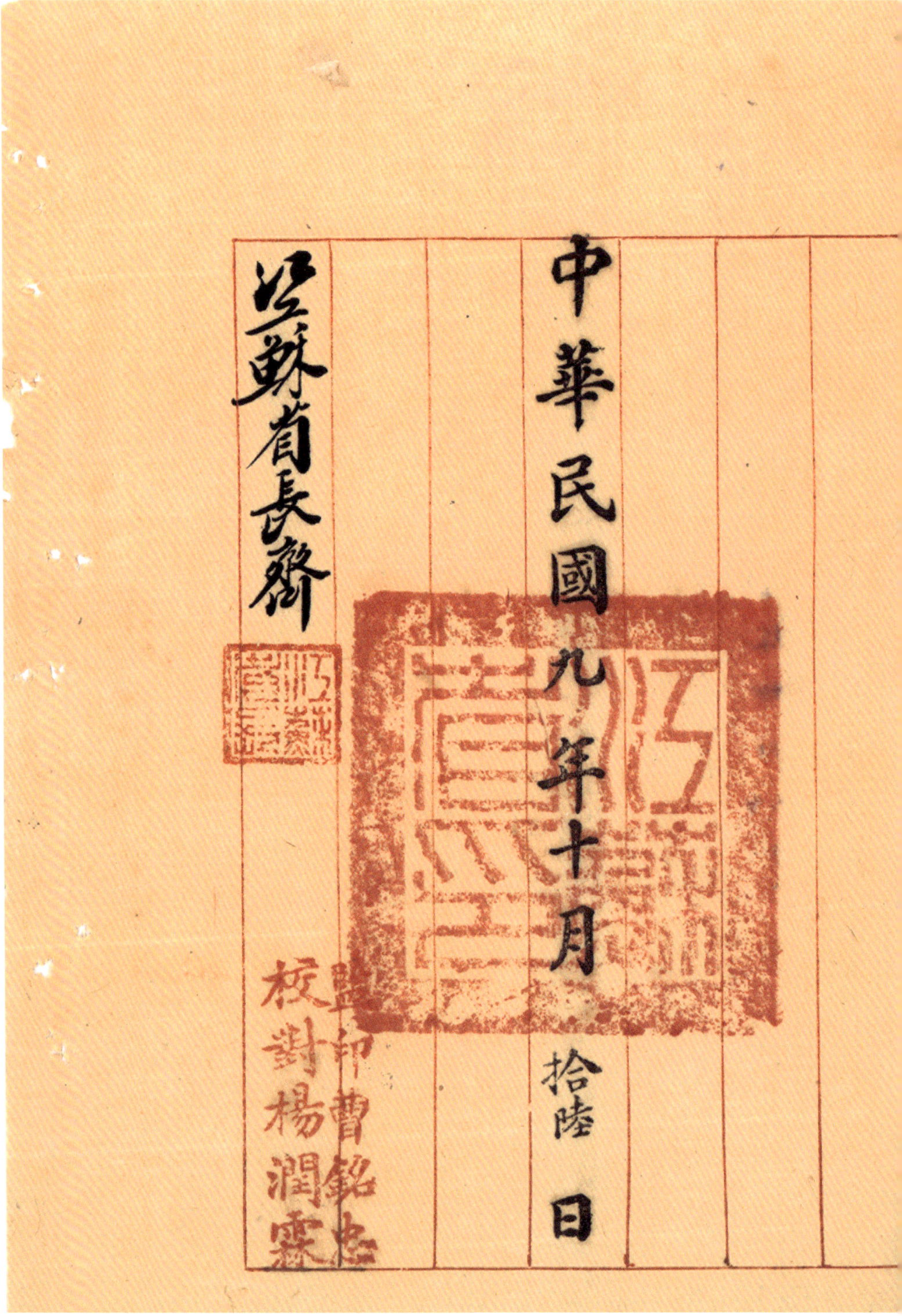
中華民國九年十月拾陸日

江蘇省長齊

監印曹銘忠

校對楊潤霖

江苏省长公署关于张謇等人承领衣周塘滩地缴纳照册费数目事宜的第1738号批。

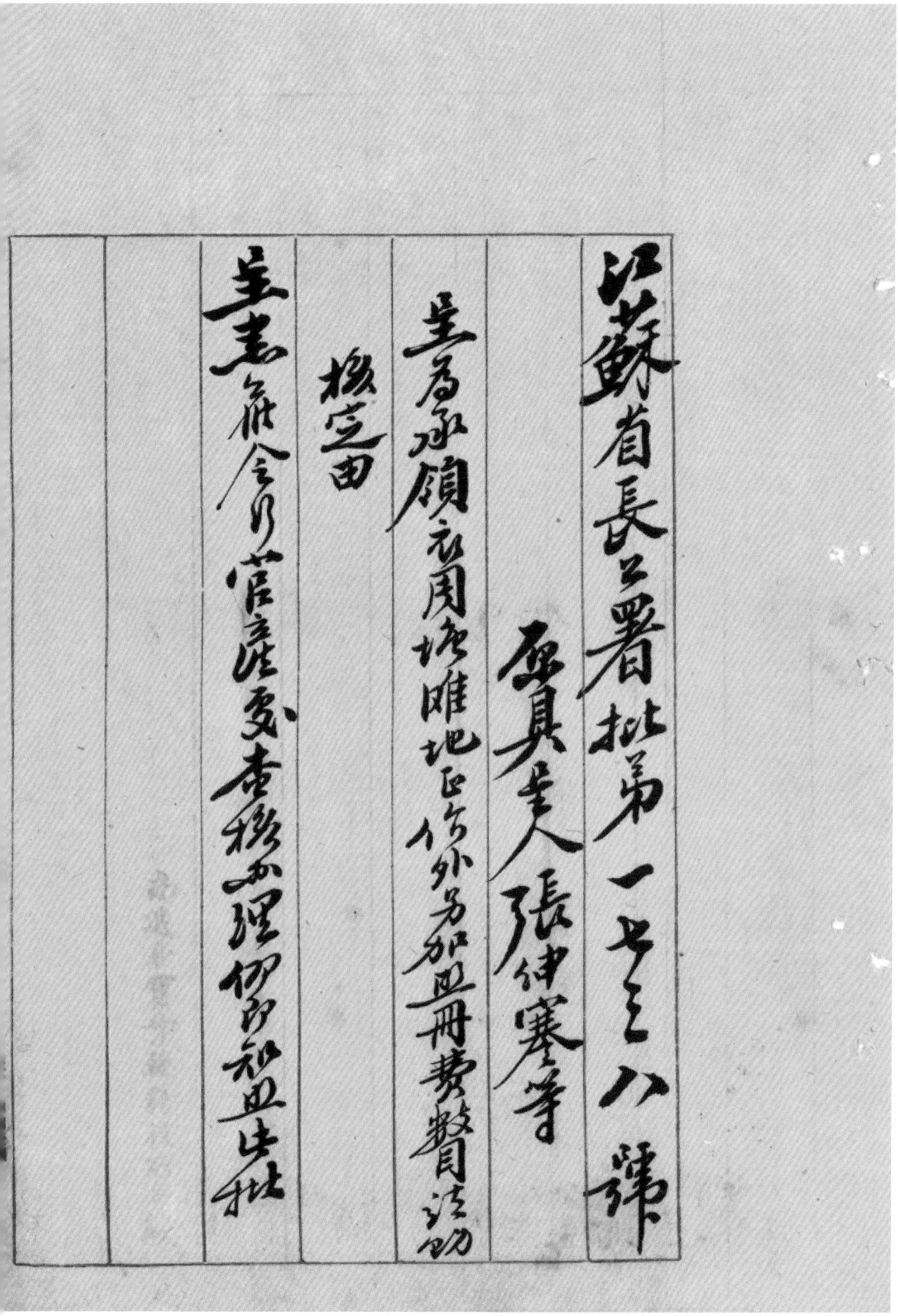
江蘇省長公署批第一七三八號

原具呈人張仲寰等

呈為承領公有塘灘地段除外另加照冊費數目請明

核定由

呈悉。所稱公司管業區域，查核辦理，仰即知照。此批

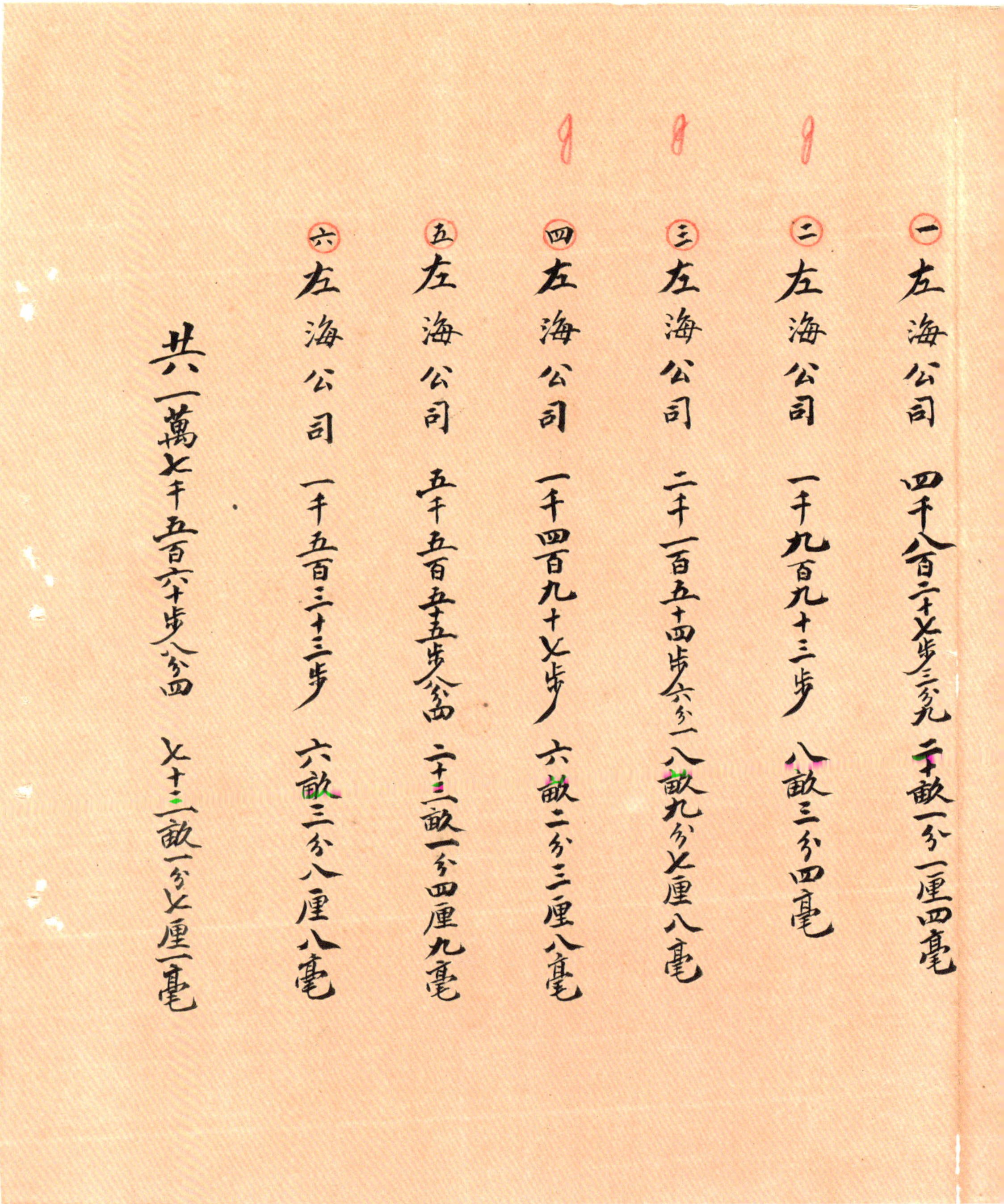
一 左海公司 四千八百二十七步二分九 二十畝一分一厘四毫
二 左海公司 一千九百九十三步 八畝三分四毫
三 左海公司 二千一百五十四步六分一 八畝九分七厘八毫
四 左海公司 一千四百九十七步 六畝二分三厘八毫
五 左海公司 五千五百五十五步八分四 二十三畝一分四厘九毫
六 左海公司 一千五百三十三步 六畝三分八厘八毫
共一萬七千五百六十步八分四 七十三畝一分七厘一毫

左海公司衣周塘地亩“衣二图（外天第十一号）”。

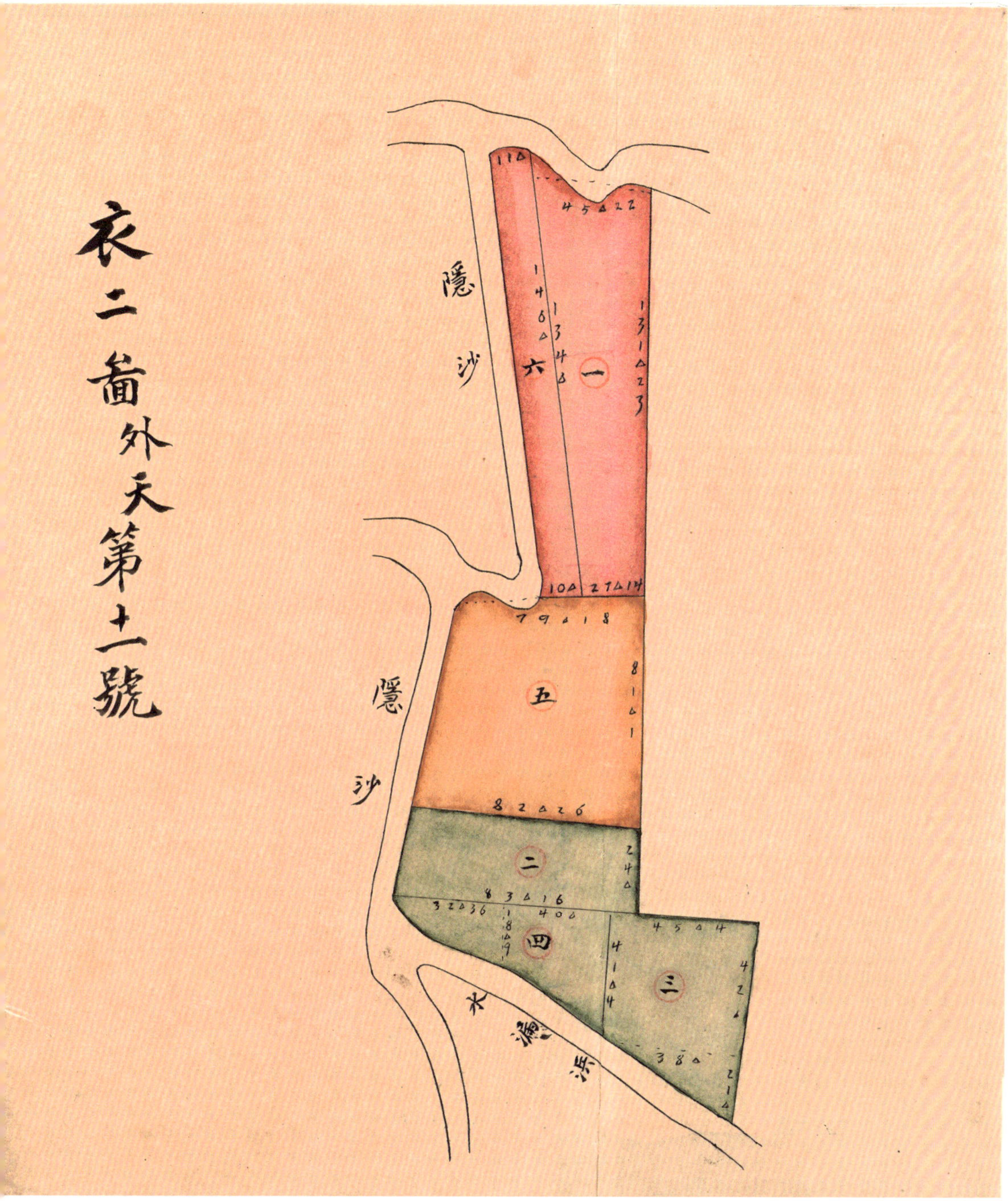
衣二畨外天第十一號
隱沙
隱沙
一
二
三
四
五
六

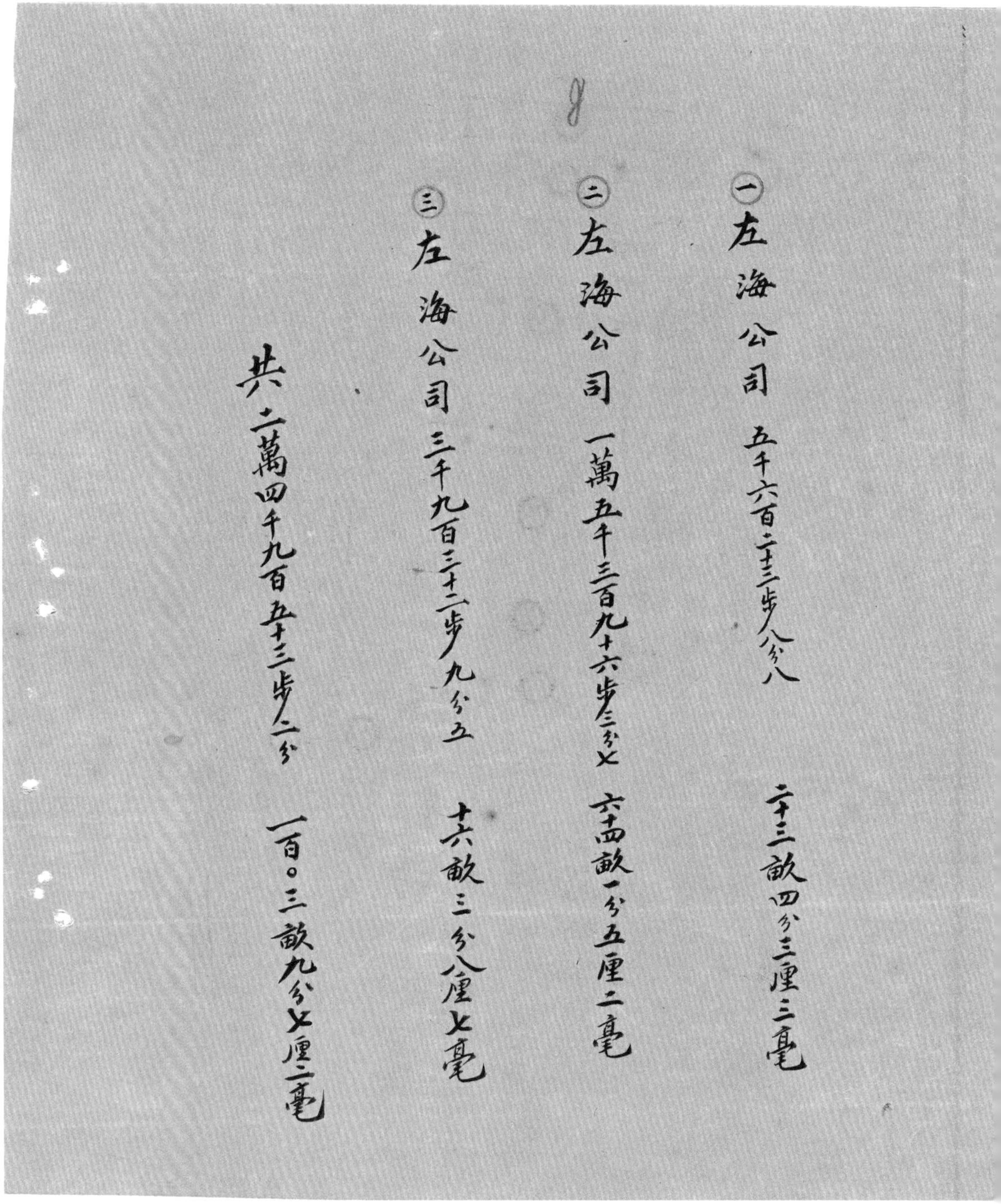

一 左海公司 五千六百二十三步八分八 二十三畝四分三厘三毫

二 左海公司 一萬五千三百九十六步三分七 六十四畝一分五厘二毫

三 左海公司 三千九百三十二步九分五 十六畝三分八厘七毫

共二萬四千九百五十三步二分 一百〇三畝九分七厘二毫

左海公司衣周塘地亩“周十一（东宿第五号）”。

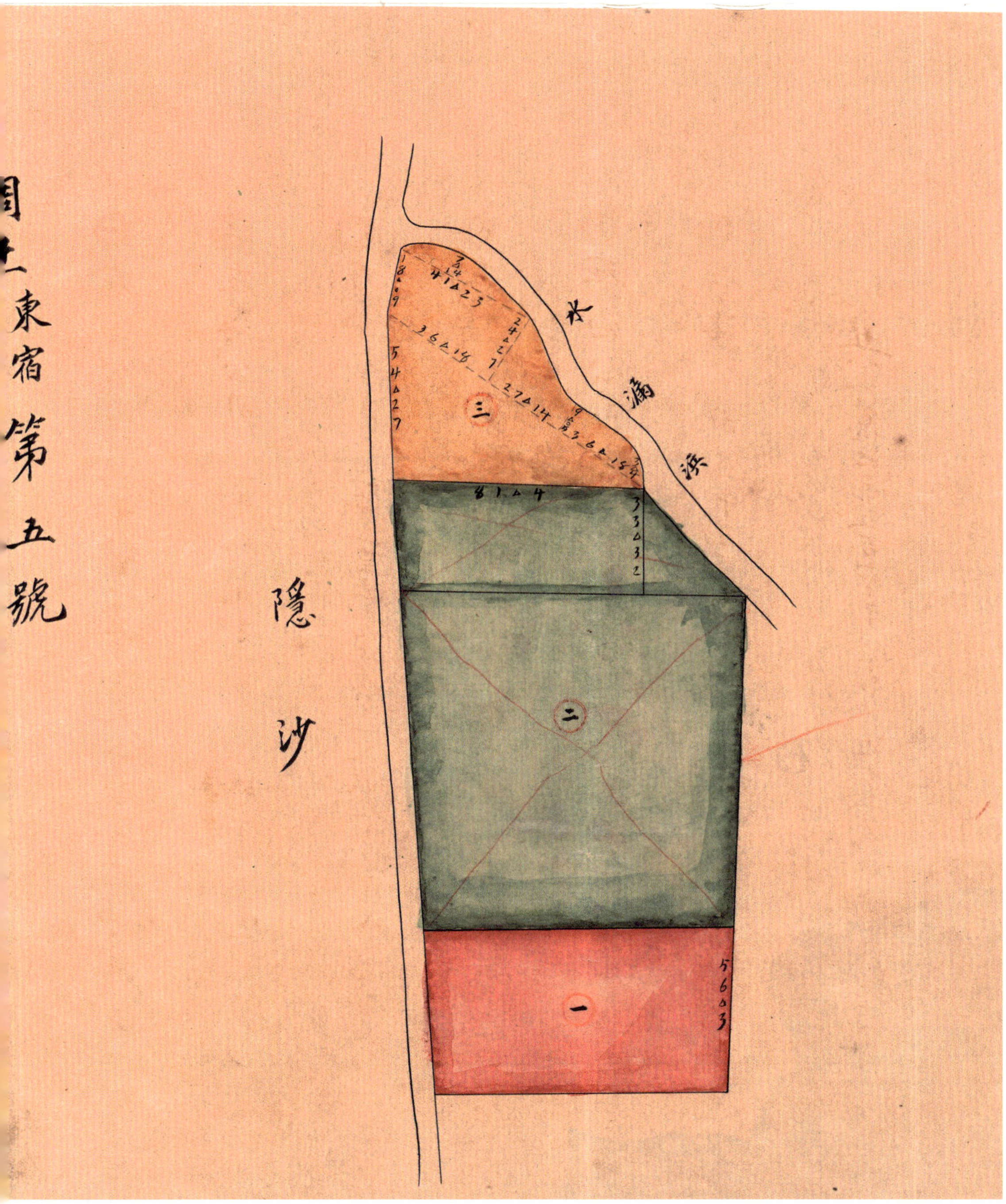
東宿第五號
隱沙
水滿浜
三
二
一

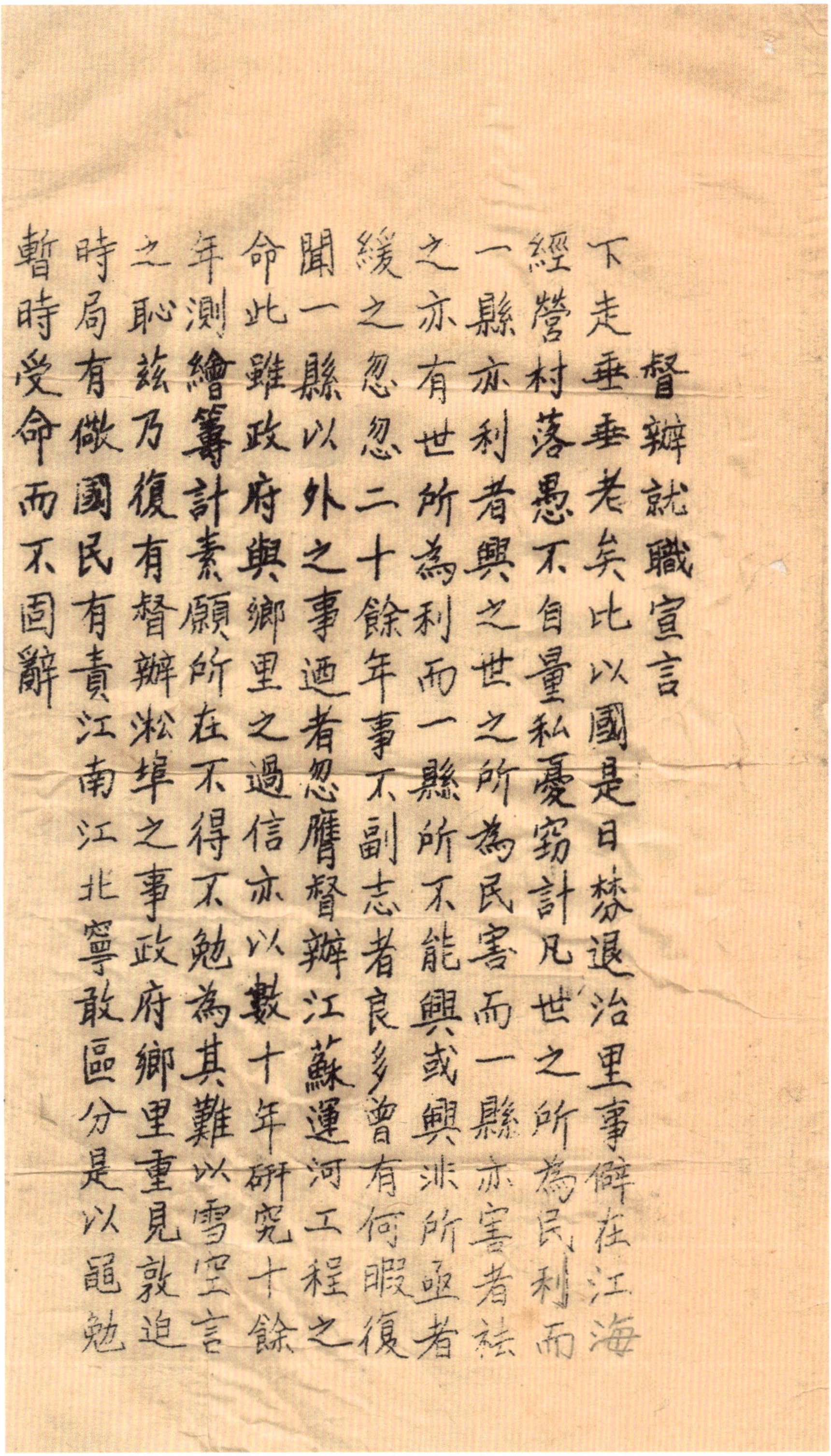
督辦就職宣言
下走垂垂老矣比以國是日棼退治里事僻在江海
經營村落愚不自量私憂竊計凡世之所為民利而
一縣亦利者興之世之所為民害而一縣亦害者祛
之亦有世所為利而一縣所不能興或興非所亟者
緩之忽忽二十餘年事不副志者良多曾有何暇復
聞一縣以外之事迺者忽膺督辦江蘇運河工程之
命此雖政府與鄉里之過信亦以數十年研究十餘
年測繪籌計素願所在不得不勉為其難以雪空言
之恥茲乃復有督辦淞埠之事政府鄉里重見敦迫
時局有儆國民有責江南江北寧敢區分是以黽勉
暫時受命而不固辭

1921 年 2 月 12 日，吴淞商埠局开局，张謇发表的就职宣言。

自歐戰停後世界商戰將在中國中國形便必在上海十餘年來世變倣擾避地之人日益受廛之所無多海客以拓界為容民地主乃羣嫌於逼處既非主客相安之道應有供求適劑之謀[redacted]吳淞壤地相接足以自圖設更遲迴行嗟何及故商埠為江蘇今日重要問題吳淞闢商埠清季固嘗設局矣卒不果行近年中西人士以為淞口攔江淤沙不能容二萬噸以上駛入之舟又有主張闢杭州灣為商港之說又有議就淞海岸築堤逼江潮南趨以其力冲刷攔江淤沙俾巨艦將來可以駛入者二說聚訟有待實地測驗顧世界商埠有可合商港為一有不必與商港合一者是

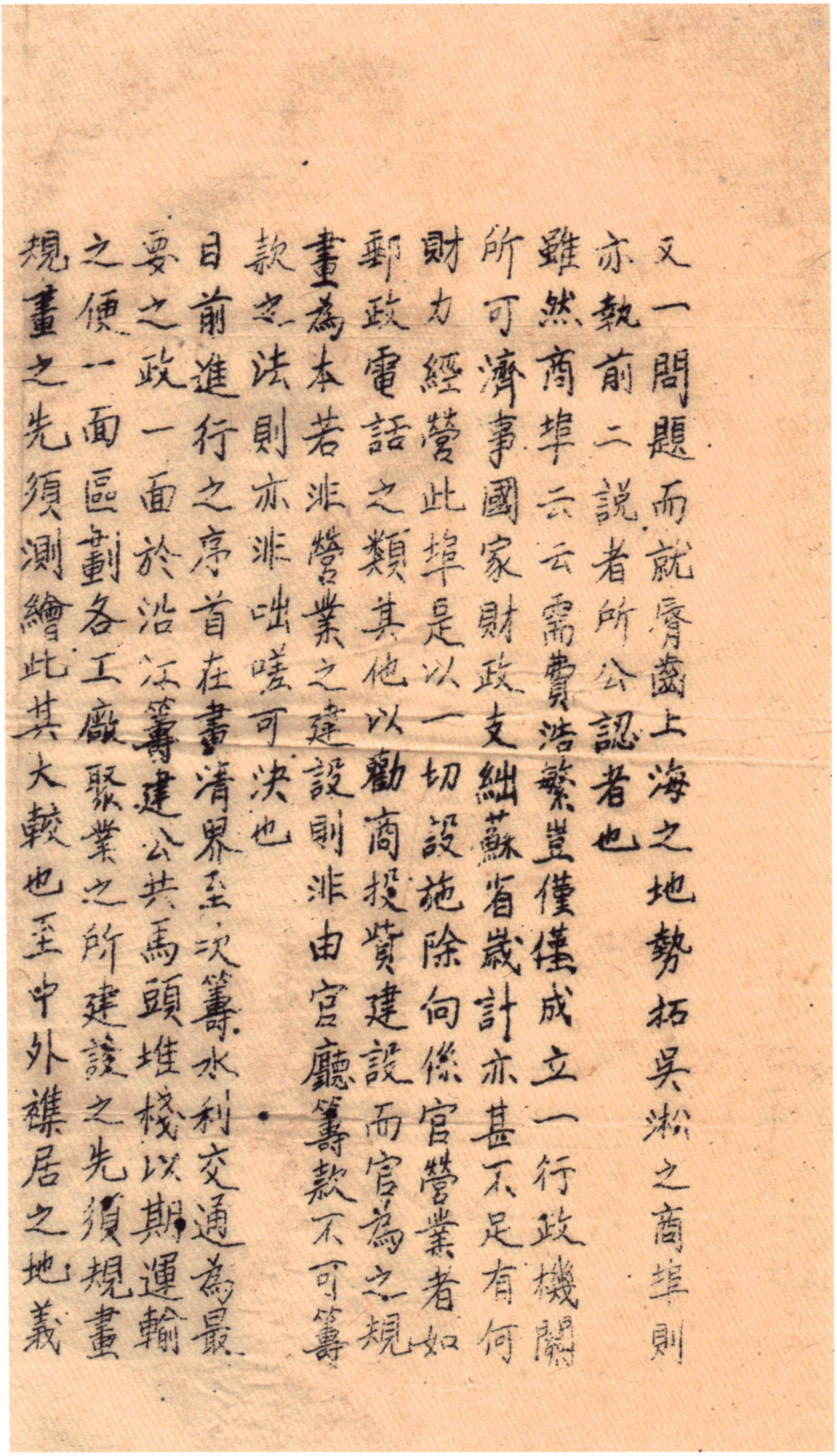
又一問題而就脣齒上海之地勢拓吴淞之商埠則
亦執前二説者所公認者也
雖然商埠云云需費浩繁豈僅僅成立一行政機關
所可濟事國家財政支絀蘇省歲計亦甚不足有何
財力經營此埠是以一切設施除向係官營業者如
郵政電話之類其他以勸商投資建設而官為之規
畫為本若非營業之建設則非由官廳籌款不可籌
款之法則亦非咄嗟可決也
目前進行之序首在畫清界至次籌水利交通為最
要之政一面於沿江籌建公共馬頭堆棧以期運輸
之便一面區劃各工廠聚業之所建設之先須規畫
規畫之先須測繪此其大較也至中外襍居之地義

當以前清舊案寶山縣界為根據以一切公平待遇
係持治安為主旨期於主客不欺供求不忒本埠局
當開誠竭慮特訂規章施行
要言之則今日之局雖成立固仍為籌備時代耳建
設之規畫求其當規畫之測繪求其詳循序以進當
另具計畫書商告國人廣求教益若內部事務則下
走性不宜友館生平所矢惟公誠而已公不自利誠不
自欺所願在局諸君同此競業一朝一夕必慎獨知
一事一為必使共見所願海內君子同此監助助規
畫者企充分之理由助覺察者企備具之證據十手
十目毋吝其嚴是則下走所深感企者也

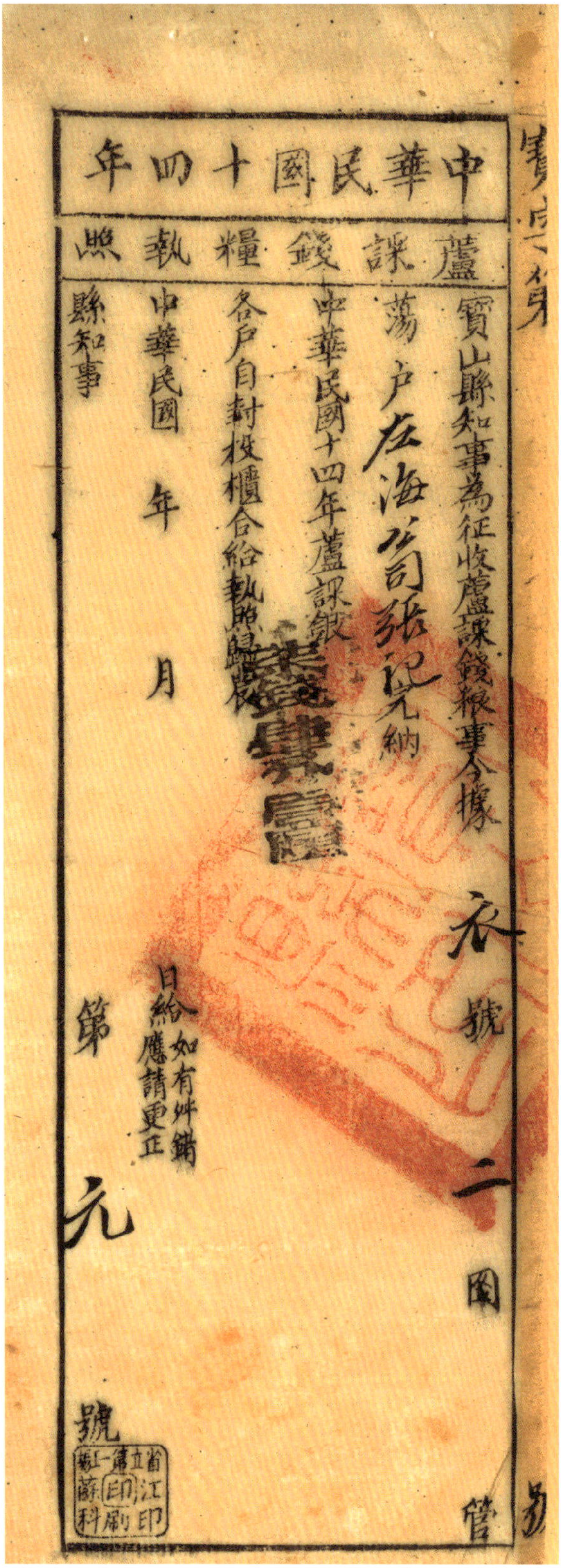
中華民國十四年
蘆課錢糧執照
寶山縣知事為征收蘆課錢糧事今據 衣號二图
蕩户左海公司張記完納
中華民國十四年蘆課錢
各戶自封投櫃合給執照
中華民國 年 月 日給 如有舛錯應請更正
縣知事 第 元 號 管

1925 年，左海公司张记缴纳衣号二图的芦课钱粮执照。

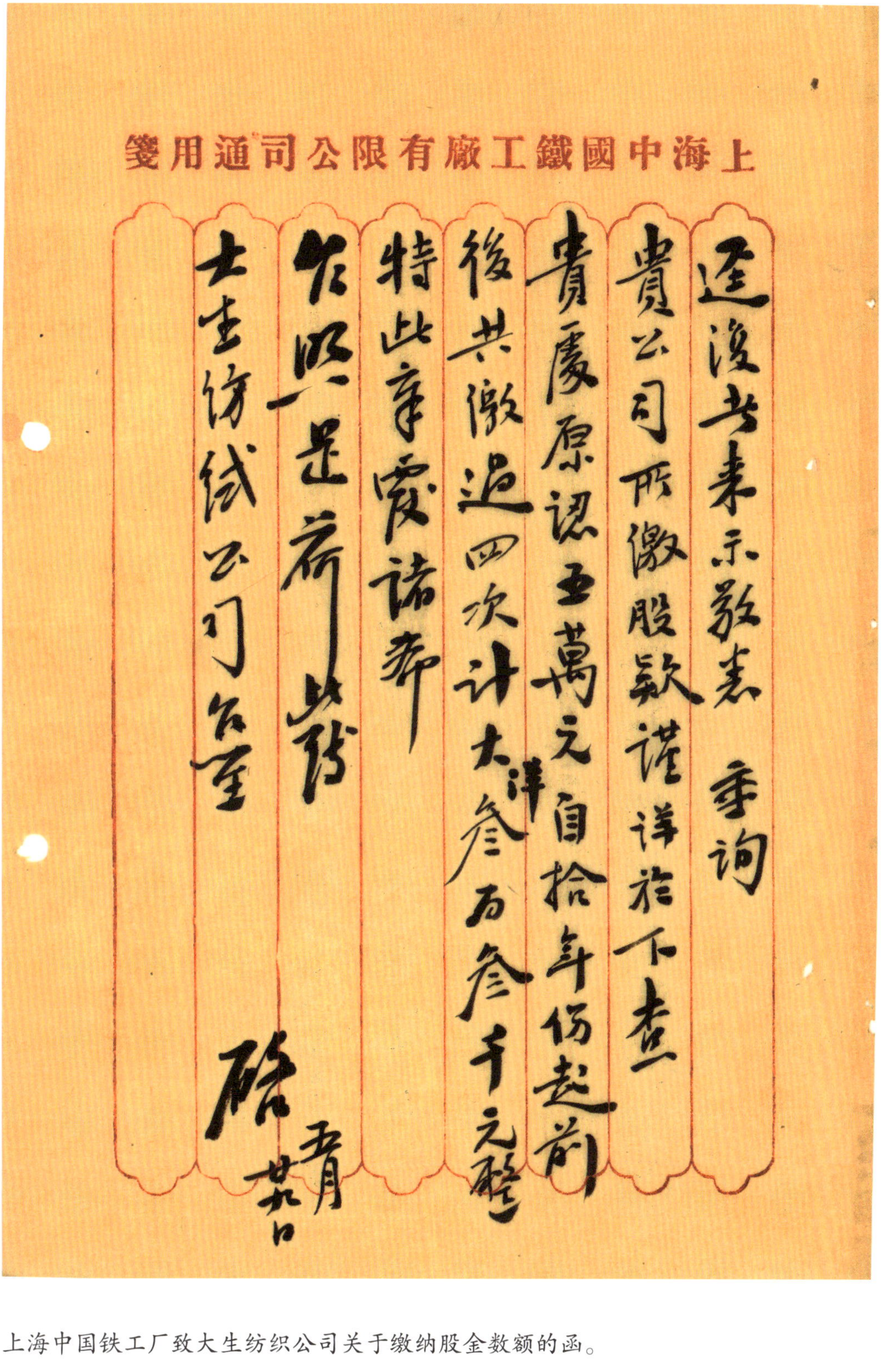
上海中國鐵工廠有限公司通用箋

逕復者：來示敬悉。承詢
貴公司所繳股款，謹詳於下：查
貴處原認五萬元，自拾年份起前
後共繳過四次，計大洋叁萬叁千元整。
特此奉覆，諸希
台照是荷。此致
大生紡織公司台鑒
啟 五月廿日

上海中国铁工厂致大生纺织公司关于缴纳股金数额的函。

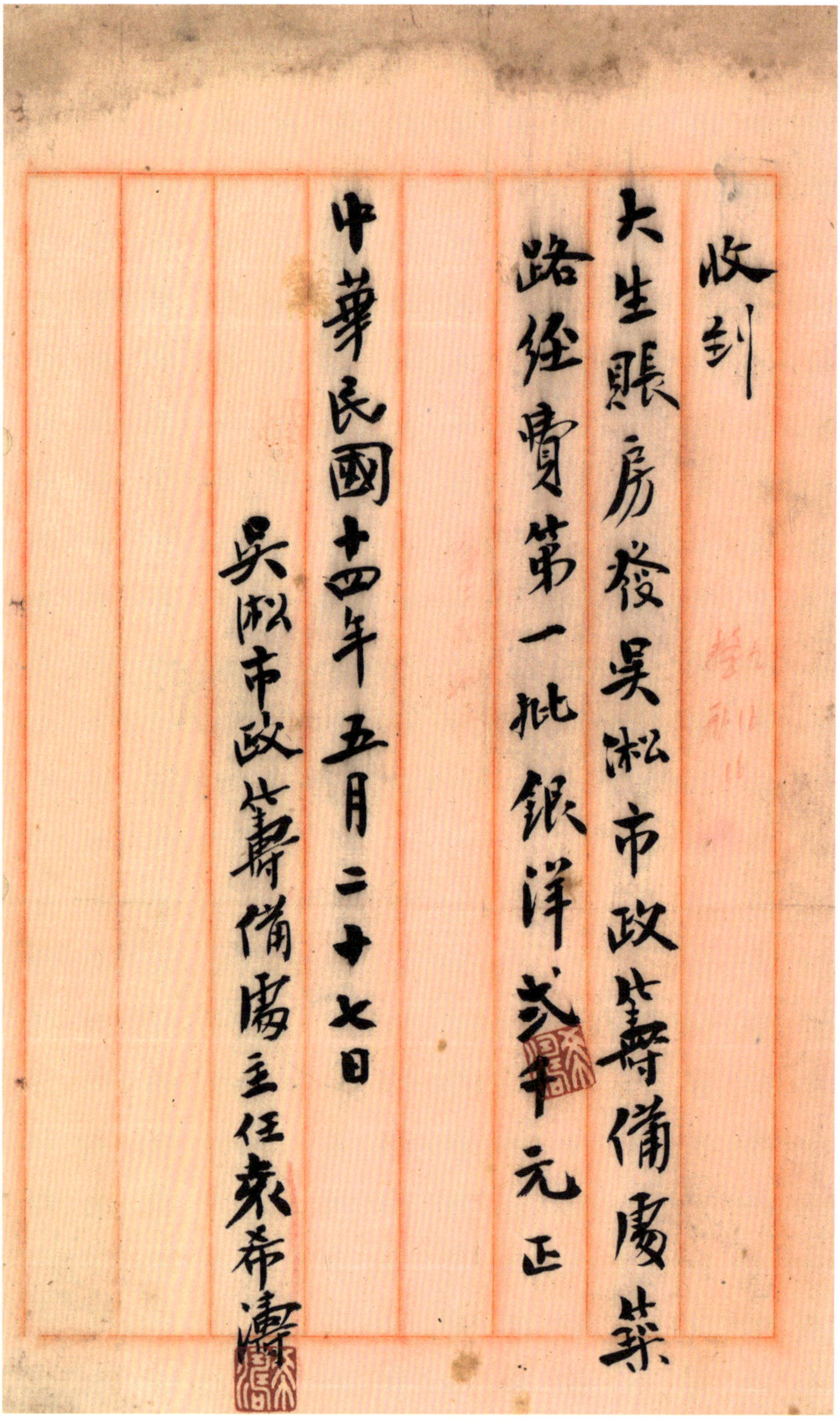

收到
大生賬房發吳淞市政籌備處築
路經費第一批銀洋貳千元正
中華民國十四年五月二十七日
吳淞市政籌備處主任袁希濤

1925 年 5 月 27 日，吴淞市政筹备处主任袁希涛收到筑路经费洋 2000 元后给大生沪所的收条。

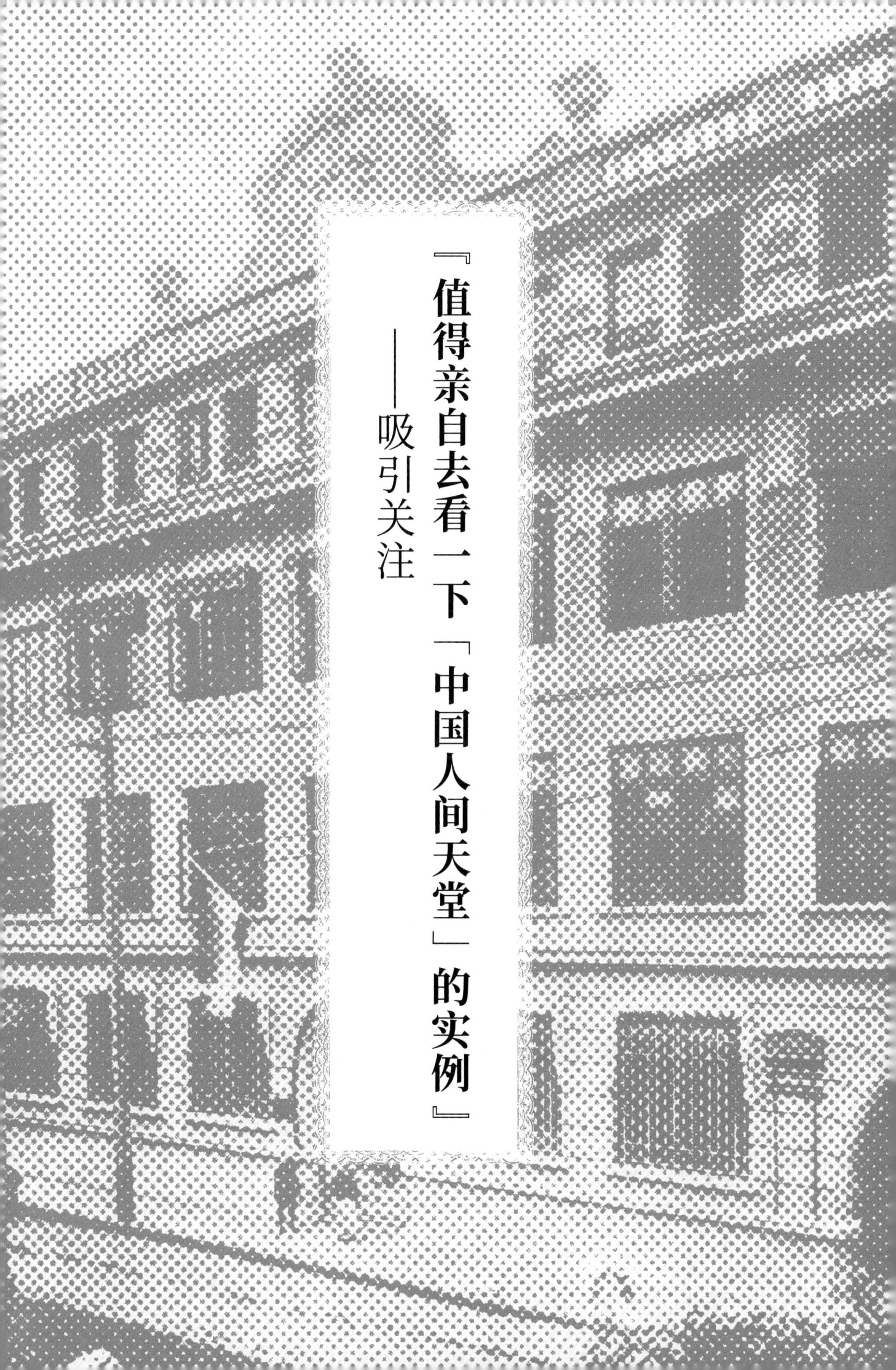

『值得亲自去看一下「中国人间天堂」的实例』

——吸引关注

张謇是晚清民初新闻媒体，特别是上海的媒体关注的人物。一方面是地缘的因素，张謇社会活动的核心区域在上海和南通，取得的成效也主要在两地；另一方面跟张謇的宣传意识有关，张謇希望通过媒体的报道，让自己的理念为更多的人接受。除了《申报》《时报》等中文媒体，《密勒氏评论报》《字林西报》《大陆报》等外文媒体也对张謇有诸多的关注，其中《密勒氏评论报》是个典型。

《密勒氏评论报》是美侨在上海出版的英文周刊，1917 年由密勒（Thomas F. Millard）创办，1953 年停刊。《密勒氏评论报》见证了时代风云。1936 年美国记者斯诺赴陕北苏区采访，与毛泽东的对话内容，最早就是在《密勒氏评论报》发表。张謇与《密勒氏评论报》保持着良好的互动关系，《密勒氏评论报》持续关注张謇和近代南通的发展，其特点是报道视角独特，内容翔实又有深度。

《密勒氏评论报》对张謇最早的报道，是刊登在 1919 年 8 月 9 日《中国名人录》（Who's Who in China）栏目里对张謇的介绍。该文采用了张謇着西装像，并标注为“中国杰出的实业领袖张謇阁下”。认为张謇是中外人士公认的中国最为杰出的实业领袖，成功地将落后的故乡转变为一座现代化的工业城镇。

1920 年，张謇等人发起成立苏社，以推动江苏地方事业，特别是实业、教育、水利、交通的发展。《密勒氏评论报》主编鲍威尔应邀与会，他与上海美国商会的 6 位代表下榻桃之华旅馆。5 月 11 日至 13 日，南通方面在苏社成立会议前后的参观安排，使得鲍威尔有机会全面地接触南通的企业、学校、公益慈善机构，也游览了闻名遐迩的五山风景区。南通之行给鲍威尔留下深刻印象，他在 5 月 22 日《密勒氏评论报》发表《不受日本影响的南通天堂》，对张謇及其带领下的南通给予高度评价：

南通现在以“模范城市”而著称，而它所在的区域被称为“模范地区”。这一地区的现代发展归功于张謇以及他的兄弟张詧，两位多年苦心经营，推动了这一长三角重点地区的进步。不可能以只言片语表述这一地区的生动图景，只有通过现实的造访与观察才能获得。从上海前往南通的旅程大约需8到10个小时，然而仍然值得亲自去看一下“中国人间天堂”的实例。

1920年6月12日的《密勒氏评论报》，刊登以《南通——中国模范城》（NANTUNGCHOW——The Model City of China）为题的整版广告。《南通——中国模范城》首先介绍南通的地理和人口情况：“南通地处长江北岸，距离上海100英里[1]，位于富饶的长江三角洲的核心地带。南通城区人口15万，全县人口150万。”接着枚举11项南通的发展成就：

——“通州棉”的出产中心，其质量冠绝华夏，年产超过100万包。

——拥有50多英里长的新式马路，大部分是石子路面。

——多个棉、蚕种养实验基地和学校。

——一所现代农业学校，126名学生在具有留学经历的教师指导下，从事实务操作。

——散布的334所学校接纳20000余名学生。

——2座现代化的棉纺厂，共有60000纱锭、500织布机和3000工人。

——1个现代化的棉籽油加工企业，产能可供出口。

——5家银行和8个钱庄。

——火柴厂、面粉厂、缫丝厂、铸铁厂、电灯公司各一。水运线路直达上海等地。

1　1英里≈1.61千米。

——在上海拥有一座现代办公楼，内设银行。

——在纽约第五大街开设中国绣品商店。

对于南通的经济发展前景，广告做了如此展望："南通方兴未艾的事业包括：总投资超过 30 万元的数百英里筑路计划，新建 7 个棉纺织厂，新建发电厂，保障工业发展的煤矿开采，对长江泥沙淤积形成的成千上万英亩[1]土地的开垦。"

广告的最后，向境内外的各界人士发出了邀请："南通欢迎四方宾朋。这里有两家舒适的旅馆。境内五座圣山之一的狼山，风景美不胜收。数百座庙宇和一座宝塔构成了无双的东方胜景。需要了解更多南通情况的人士，可与南通商会联系。"

《南通——中国模范城》与其说是广告，不如讲是对南通城市形象的宣传。《南通——中国模范城》既是张謇和南通自信的体现，也是一种希望，希望其发展的成果能为更多人所接受，希望南通经验在更大的范围推广，希望能有更多的资源注入南通。这个广告从 1920 年 6 月 12 日到 9 月 18 日共刊载 15 次。1921 年元旦，在原来广告内容的基础上，又增加大达轮船公司上海至南通的航行信息，并且陆续刊登到 1922 年 4 月 15 日。

《密勒氏评论报》对于南通的评价，不仅在当时，甚至放在现在，都不失其独到之处。《密勒氏评论报》强调南通的经济、文化和城市建设的成果，是中国人自主经营的结果。《不受日本影响的南通天堂》里提及："南通的现代发展完全是一项中国成就，除了那些通过各领域的归国学生所取得的成果，可谓完全不受外国的影响。"

1921 年 3 月 26 日，裴德生在《密勒氏评论报》上发表的《张謇：

1　1 英亩≈ 4046.86 平方米。

中国的城市建造师》对此阐述得更深入，在他的眼里，“创造天才不分国界与种族，勿论背景与阶层，可以在任何地方展现才华。从上海沿扬子江往上 100 英里，创造天分体现在中国最伟大的工业领袖与资本家张謇身上。通过南通这个模范城市的建造，他为中国未来的工业化树立了里程碑。孤立于那些受外国影响的城市之外，没有铁路带来的便捷，也没有走商业发展的寻常路线。南通成为张謇与其同僚和亲属（包括其子张孝若与其兄张詧）行政才能、视野与组织能力的不朽作品”。

1923 年 3 月 17 日，《密勒氏评论报》刊登《中国实业之进步观——中国模范城南通州》一文的中英文两个版本，文章指出：“此城为完全中国人所经营，无外人营业于此，而居留之外国人，仅限于传教师及教育家而已。以其为中国人所经营之商埠，故年来变化之速，革新之进步，实堪为吾人注意也，而有中国模范城之称。观此城，亦可表率中国人建造革新之能力。”

《密勒氏评论报》不仅洞察了南通在近代中国城市发展中，与以上海、天津等为代表的条约口岸城市的区别，还分析了张謇与南通城市规划和建设的关系。《张謇：中国的城市建造师》中认为，“张謇所拥有的经验与远见，并非西方国家所赋予。没有哪所西方的技术学校，能够光荣宣称他为自己的校友。中国的传统文化，讲求内省与精神追求而非工业扩张，有着深厚传统根基的张謇，他人生的前 40 年与此后的 29 年很难调和”。但是，张謇却显示了迥异于中国传统文人的特质与雄心：“24 年以前，张謇的梦想，是在南通古城墙外兴建一个工业城市，不仅作为工业中心，同时也是慈善事业与教育汇集之地。”随着各项实业取得迅速发展，“以实业为核心，张謇开始了他的梦想之城——南通模范城的建造”。因此，裴德生认为：

南通可以视作这位中国最伟大的城市建造者之一的自传。25 年间，南通在长三角北冀平原迅速崛起，兴旺发达。它的影响力与发明创造在过去数年间成为公众关注的焦点，带来了国际声誉。

通过南通，张謇成为了建造优良道路的先驱。

南通见证了中国近代教育的发展。

张謇在其同僚的协助下，为年青一代的中国人提供了范例，如果薪火相传的话，将会使这个国家走向世界最伟大的工业国家的前列。每个年轻的中国人都有必要花费一些时间，在南通城吸取它的精神，学习它的内部建设，从而培养未来的城市与国家建造者。南通对于外国游客也是令人愉悦的体验，它的好客让人回想起美国南部地区传统的礼貌。

毕竟，南通令人最为印象深刻的特性，它极大的活力以及活泼进取的精神，在于这一切诞生于中国最伟大的学者之一——张謇的脑海中。

值得一提的是，《密勒氏评论报》于1922年10月7日举办“中国当今十二位大人物”（Who Are the Twelve Greatest Living Chinese？）读者投票选举活动。在10月14日发布的中文公告这样明确选举的目的：“论中国政事经济者，每谓中国乏强有力之领袖人物。盖国中出类拔萃之人才，昔已凋谢。而自共和创始以来，各方之领袖人物，尚未产出也。夫中国今日岂乏此项人才乎？为解决此问题起见，阅者之意，以中国何人具有此项资格，可选出十二人。”公告要求“投票者所举之人物，须于各方事业中，择其名望素著，堪为一业中之代表者”。投票截止期为1923年1月1日，每周在报纸上刊登选票。1923年1月6日，《密勒氏评论报》公布了投票结果：孙中山、冯玉祥、顾维钧等12人入选，张謇名列第8位。尽管《密勒氏评论报》读者面有一定的局限，主要是在中国的外国人以及中国的年轻知识分子，但张謇在这次民意投票中入选，至少表明他在这部分人心目中的地位。

living in China. Twenty years or so ago $6 was a rather good salary for an able school teacher.

An Anti-Cigarette Society has been inaugurated by the Piece-Goods Dealers' Guild whose members will conduct a campaign against smoking. They declare that the cigarettes consume more money of China than opium does, the cigarette smoking habit being by far more easily spread than opium smoking. According to their investigation, one-third of the income of the wharf coolies goes to pay for this curse.

The Anfu Club in Changsha is endeavoring to crush the People's Union and held a meeting last week to advocate the dissolution of that organization. They came into an open clash with the representatives of the Student's Union. Prior to this, the arrest of many newspaper men was effected through their efforts and the people of Hunan are complaining under their supremacy.

Arthur V. Perry and E. G. Byrne, two old residents of Hankow, returned to the port safe and sound on Thursday evening, July 31, from the front in France. When in France Mr. Perry served in the motor establishment of a large section of the front, while Mr. Byrne was connected with the Labor Battalion.

An official has been despatched by the government of Hupeh to Ichang to arrest the spread of the opium smoking habit that has already gained a headway in that port. The smuggling of opium is carried on peacefully by the merchants who cooperated with the soldiers there. This trade is so flourishing in that center that in order to eradicate the curse an anti-opium campaign has to be carried on over again.

The boycott has not yet ended in Hunan, according to a report from Pingkiang. The students have organized a campaign to educate and inform the ignorant concerning the dangers threatening the country. One special feature in their activities is the New Dramatic Club, a deputation of which is touring the country places, giving dramatic displays which are calculated to stimulate patriotic feeling among the people.

There is a steady demand for white vegetable and animal tallow, quite abnormal for the time of the year. In the absence of further supplies, the quotations for sessamum seed have appreciated again and any arrivals are quickly snapped up. Sessamum oil has been purchased considerably for America and the local price has soared up. Wood oil is steady and bean oil firmer with no sellers at present. Available supplies of second quality cowhides find a ready sale, but the amount is insignificant.

The following is a list of current quotations in taels per picul of some important articles of export in Hankow: 2nd quality cowhides 44; white China grass, hemp or ramie, 13; vegetable tallow, white 51° titre 16.40, green 52° titre 13.80; gallnuts, usual shape 24.80; gallnuts plum 26.75; cotton, Liho 28; Shensi 31; Hankow bristles, riflings 129; steamed 140; sessamum seeds, white and yellow 8.05; yellow beans 2.50; broad beans 2.15; white peas 2.20; sessamum seed oil 16.20; wood oil 16.35; tea oil 13.50; bean oil 12.20; hen albumen 111; hen yolk, liquid, 2 per cent boracic 29. Antimony crude Tls. 47 and antimony regulus Tls. 98 per ton.

The Peking-Hankow Railway Company makes the following announcement concerning the temporary arrangement of trains: The 1st and 2nd trains of this line have to be suspended for the time being, as the railway bridges on the Hsinlo River are under water. From July 26 until further notice all the other trains keep the usual times as scheduled, but run up to the north and south banks of the above named river only. Porters are employed by the company for transportation purposes at the spot. The time for the 1st and 2nd trains, however, is to be changed as follows, to enable them to come up to the connection in daytime and to facilitate transport:— The 1st train leaves Peking at 12 midnight arriving at the north banks of the Hsinlo River at 6.15 a.m.; the connecting train leaves the south bank 10 a.m. arriving at Hankow at 12.50 p.m. the next day. The 2nd train leaves Hankow at 7 a.m. arriving at the south bank of the Hsinlo River at 9.20 a.m. the next morning; the connecting train leaves the north bank at 1 p.m. arriving at Peking at 8.15 p.m.

Hankow, August 1, 1919.

Who's Who in China

Hon. Chang Chien, China's Great Industrial Leader

張謇

Chang Chien is recognized by both Chinese and foreigners as the greatest industrial leader in China. He is now 67 years of age, and was born at Tungchow, Kiangsu. After years of hard labor, he has succeeded in transforming his wretched birthplace into a modern industrial town where there is not a single beggar and where everyone is prosperous.

Mr. Chang is a noted Hanlin scholar (Optimus), and in the Tsing dynasty declined to take any executive office, except that of Adviser to the Board of Commerce in 1904, in order to devote his energies to the fostering of industry and commerce. During his viceroyship of Liang Kiang, Chang Chih-tung appointed Chang Chien to organize a spinning and weaving mill, the capitalization of which was Tls. 1,000,000. This mission the Tungchow scholar carried out with success. Later he organized the Fuhsin Flour Mill, the Kwangsheng Oil Mill, the

1919 年 8 月 9 日，《密勒氏评论报》对张謇的介绍。

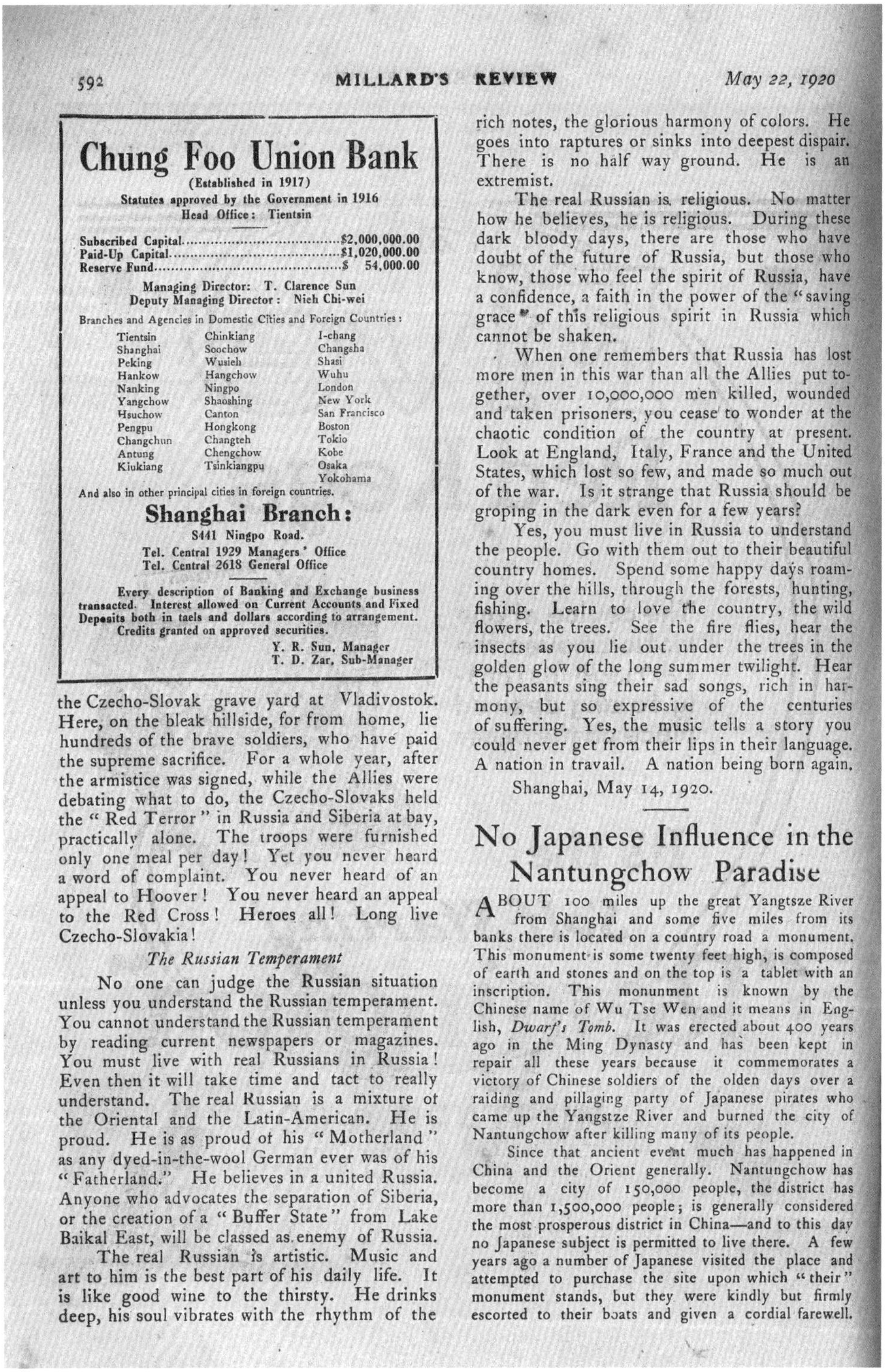

592 MILLARD'S REVIEW May 22, 1920

the Czecho-Slovak grave yard at Vladivostok. Here, on the bleak hillside, for from home, lie hundreds of the brave soldiers, who have paid the supreme sacrifice. For a whole year, after the armistice was signed, while the Allies were debating what to do, the Czecho-Slovaks held the "Red Terror" in Russia and Siberia at bay, practically alone. The troops were furnished only one meal per day! Yet you never heard a word of complaint. You never heard of an appeal to Hoover! You never heard an appeal to the Red Cross! Heroes all! Long live Czecho-Slovakia!

The Russian Temperament

No one can judge the Russian situation unless you understand the Russian temperament. You cannot understand the Russian temperament by reading current newspapers or magazines. You must live with real Russians in Russia! Even then it will take time and tact to really understand. The real Russian is a mixture of the Oriental and the Latin-American. He is proud. He is as proud of his "Motherland" as any dyed-in-the-wool German ever was of his "Fatherland." He believes in a united Russia. Anyone who advocates the separation of Siberia, or the creation of a "Buffer State" from Lake Baikal East, will be classed as enemy of Russia.

The real Russian is artistic. Music and art to him is the best part of his daily life. It is like good wine to the thirsty. He drinks deep, his soul vibrates with the rhythm of the rich notes, the glorious harmony of colors. He goes into raptures or sinks into deepest dispair. There is no half way ground. He is an extremist.

The real Russian is religious. No matter how he believes, he is religious. During these dark bloody days, there are those who have doubt of the future of Russia, but those who know, those who feel the spirit of Russia, have a confidence, a faith in the power of the "saving grace" of this religious spirit in Russia which cannot be shaken.

When one remembers that Russia has lost more men in this war than all the Allies put together, over 10,000,000 men killed, wounded and taken prisoners, you cease to wonder at the chaotic condition of the country at present. Look at England, Italy, France and the United States, which lost so few, and made so much out of the war. Is it strange that Russia should be groping in the dark even for a few years?

Yes, you must live in Russia to understand the people. Go with them out to their beautiful country homes. Spend some happy days roaming over the hills, through the forests, hunting, fishing. Learn to love the country, the wild flowers, the trees. See the fire flies, hear the insects as you lie out under the trees in the golden glow of the long summer twilight. Hear the peasants sing their sad songs, rich in harmony, but so expressive of the centuries of suffering. Yes, the music tells a story you could never get from their lips in their language. A nation in travail. A nation being born again.

Shanghai, May 14, 1920.

No Japanese Influence in the Nantungchow Paradise

ABOUT 100 miles up the great Yangtsze River from Shanghai and some five miles from its banks there is located on a country road a monument. This monument is some twenty feet high, is composed of earth and stones and on the top is a tablet with an inscription. This monunment is known by the Chinese name of Wu Tse Wen and it means in English, *Dwarf's Tomb*. It was erected about 400 years ago in the Ming Dynasty and has been kept in repair all these years because it commemorates a victory of Chinese soldiers of the olden days over a raiding and pillaging party of Japanese pirates who came up the Yangstze River and burned the city of Nantungchow after killing many of its people.

Since that ancient event much has happened in China and the Orient generally. Nantungchow has become a city of 150,000 people, the district has more than 1,500,000 people; is generally considered the most prosperous district in China—and to this day no Japanese subject is permitted to live there. A few years ago a number of Japanese visited the place and attempted to purchase the site upon which "their" monument stands, but they were kindly but firmly escorted to their boats and given a cordial farewell.

1920年5月22日，《密勒氏评论报》发表的《不受日本影响的南通天堂》。

Ten years ago a prominent official of the district visited Tokyo and in a museum found many swords, flags and trophies, all captured from China at one time or another by Japanese conquerors and invaders and now displayed with much pride in the capital of Nippon. When this Chinese official returned to his ancestral home of Nantungchow, it is reported, he immediately set a new force of laborers to work repairing the monument of *Wu Tse Wen*.

Nantungchow is now known at the "Model City," and the district tributary to it is known as the "Model District." It is the home of Hon. Chang Chien, China's former Minister of Commerce and Agriculture and captain of modern industry in China, and from this city is now radiating a new influence that has as its object the making of Kiangsu, the province in which Shanghai is located, a model province of China. On May 11, 12 and 13, a meeting of influential Chinese business men, bankers and industrial leaders was held in this city and there was formed an organization known as the Kiangsu Association, the purpose of which is to uphold right principles, seek knowledge for the benefit of the locality, maintain local order, develop local self-government, study modern industries and education, and to develop conservancy and communications. About 300 prominent men attended the meeting, forty of whom were from Shanghai. An annual meeting will be held on Lang-shan mountain and there will be monthly meetings of the board of directors.

When we call Nantungchow a "model district," we mean just that and a party of American business men from Shanghai who recently visited the place are ready to place their certification upon the statement. Some of the elements that contribute toward the making of Nantungchow a model city are:

1—Some 50 miles of modern roads upon which a motor car (there are six in the place) may travel at 50 miles an hour if desired.
2—A Cotton and Sericulture Experimentation Station and Schools.
3—334 Schools with 21,382 students.
4—A modern theater where only high class plays are given, many of which are of the "modern" variety.
5—No beggars or poverty of any kind.
6—An agricultural college with 126 students who do their own agricultural development work with their own hands.
7—Two modern cotton mills with 60,000 spindles, 500 looms and 4,000 employes.
8—A modern cotton seed oil mill that provides for the local consumption and a surplus which is sold abroad.
9—Five modern banks and eight native style banks.
10—One match factory, one flour mill, one silk filiature, one iron foundry, one electric light plant and a direct river steamer line to Shanghai and other points.
11—The district produces annually about 1,000,000 bales of cotton which is the best quality produced in China.
12—Proposals for the future include hundreds of miles of good roads, seven new cotton mills, a new electric light and power plant, a coal mine to supply the industries of the district, extensive conservancy work that will reclaim thousands of acres of land from the overflow of the Yangtsze River.

A view of the Nantung countryside, showing the modern road which has been constructed between the city and Lan Shan Mountain.

Hon. Chang Chien, and his son Chang Chien, Jr.

The credit for the modern development of the district belongs to Mr. Chang Chien and to his brother Mr. Chang Cha, both of whom have labored long and effectively in improving this important section of the Yangtsze valley. Mr. Chang Cha, the elder brother has never been in official life, but has devoted most of his eighty years and more to his district. Mr. Chang Chien, also a noted Hanlin scholar, was Minister of Agriculture and Commerce in 1913 and has a reputation for his constructive endeavors that extend all over the Orient and has even received attention in American magazines. He has been offered many high positions in the Chinese government, one being the premiership; but has always declined to serve. Now that his son, Chang Chien, Jr., an American returned student, is gradually taking over the active affairs of his father, there is hope in many liberal circles that Mr. Chang will enter active political affairs in this present hour of China's darkness. Many leaders think he has qualifications for occupying the highest position in the land, after His Excellency, Hsu Shih Chang, retires from the presidency.

The modern foreign style residence of Chang Chien, Jr. The building was constructed by his father, but has been occupied by the son since his marriage to a graduate of the French Siccawei Institution, Shanghai.

It is practically impossible to convey in a few words an effective picture of this district—that only may be acquired by an actual visit and inspection. In the first place there has been constructed on the banks of the river modern docking and godown facilities for river steamers. From this dock stretch out in all directions modern roads and canal transportation lines. The factory district is located on the river while the city, schools, banks and business houses are located some six miles inland.

The most striking development that the foreign visitor notes are the modern roads, most of which are now being hard surfaced. There are probably forty miles of good roads with modern bridges and the present appropriation for road construction is $300,000. There are about a half dozen motor cars already in the city, one of them being a passenger truck recently constructed in Shanghai that accommodates twenty persons. As soon as the road connecting the city and the river has been rock surfaced, it is planned to connect the places with a regular truck service. It would seem that Shanghai motor car dealers are neglecting a fine field in not pushing their business at this interior city which already has more country roads than Shanghai.

Of the manufacturing enterprises the cotton weaving and spinning mills are most interesting. Together they have 60,000 spindles, 500 looms and 4,000 operators. The average daily wage for adults is forty cents, for children apprentices twenty cents. The machinery in the cotton mill as well as in the cotton seed oil mill is of English manufacture. Orders have just been placed for new machinery which will double the capacity of the oil mill and Mr. Chang Chien now has definite plans for seven cotton mills for the district, this number being considered necessary to make the section independent of foreign, or in other words, Japanese products.

A group of American returned students who are assisting in the industrial, educational and social development of Nantungchow.

A volume could be written on the educational development of Nantungchow and vicinity, there being 334 separate institutions with more than 20,000 students in regular attendance. Literally it may be said that this is one district of China in which every child has an opportunity to acquire an education. There is a medical college, normal school, agricultural school, commercial school, and numerous primary and intermediate institutions. Among the novel innovations is a school of embroidery with about 100 young women students. Several of the productions of this institution have been awarded first prizes abroad and there is one retail estalishment in New York City that takes practically the entire output. Another unusual educational institution is a school for actors, this being an attempt by Mr. Chang, and probably the first in China to elevate the Chinese stage. A large sericulture school is now in process of construction. Women receive instruction in the girl's normal school. In addition to the eductional institutions there is a public library, a botanical and zoological garden, a museum containing objects from old China in porcelain, bronze, embroidery, animal life, old literary productions, models of machinery and so on. There is a large public park, a model prison and a people's factory. Water for a fountain in the botanical park is supplied from a deep well by an American windmill. Upon one of the "five mountains" is an observatory and at the foot of another mountain pleasantly located is an infirmary and a school for the blind and dumb children.

The wisteria arbor in the Botannical Gardens at Nantungchow. The group consists of a number of American business men from Shanghai and American returned students of Nantungchow. Chang Chien, Jr., is in the center.

And then there is Lan Shan Mountain, a hill of some six hundred feet rising abrupt from the river plain and about five miles inland from the river bank. It is difficult to describe the mountain scenery and refrain from poetry, especially in the spring. In the distance is the Yangstze River that fades into the sky with junks in the breeze that remind the visitor of mammoth birds. Around the mountain on all sides spreads the level plain with fields in geometrical designs with canals as borders. The modern road back to the city appears as a silver ribbon in the picture. The mountain has a special significance to Americans since it is the ancestral home of the *Lang Shang* chicken, a brand of poultry of black feathering that is common to almost every American farm yard. There are probably more than a hundred temples and shrines and one nunnery on the mountain. Some idea of the wealth of the district may be gained from the fact that the priests receive more than $300,000 annually in copper and cash offerings. Several years ago Mr. Chang educated under his personal supervision several of the boy candidates for the priesthood and these men are now leaders in the religious community and are said to have "elevated" the profession considerably. In connection with Lan Shan Mountain mention should also be made of the afforestation work that has been carried on until the hill is completely covered with trees, many being of imported varieties. There is a nursery and experimental orchard where seedlings are produced for replanting along the country roads and canals. The cotton experiment station at the foot of the mountain is said to be producing excellent results from American varieties of cotton.

The modern development of Nantungchow is entirely a Chinese accomplishment, no foreign influence entering into the work except through the returned students who are everywhere. With one or two exceptions the returned students are from American universities, the leaders in the various lines being Messrs. Alex. Y. Lee, Huang Yu-lang, Lai Ping-ling, Y. M. Tseng, Hsu Kung-che, S. Z. Kwauk, K. M. Loo, B. Y. Lee, and Mr. Ho. Most of these men are graduates of courses in agriculture, engineering, textile work and chemistry.

To make the trip from Shanghai to Nantungchow requires from eight to ten hours, and it is well worth the effort to see this example of "Paradise on Earth in China." Chang Chien and his brother Chang Cha and Chang Chien, Jr., literally are monarch of all they survey and probably have no counterpart outside of the fiction of childhood where the benevolent ruler ministers to his subjects as he does to his own children, for in truth that is what they are at Nantungchow.

J. B. P.

News from North China

The Law College in Peking has enlisted 120 students and teachers for free night schools.

Captain Watson the Naval Attache of the American Embassy in Tokyo, and Mrs. Watson, are spending a few days in Peking.

Major W. C. Philoon, Assistant Military Attache at the American legation here, has left for a two or three weeks' trip in Manchuria.

J. Paul Jameson has been appointed first American Consul at Kalgan and will leave Washington in the near future to take up the new duties.

The engagement has been announced of V. Reinhardt, chief accountant of Andersen, Meyer and Company, to Miss Edith Pearson, Tientsin.

A concert will be given to-night at the Peking Y. M. C. A. auditorium by the Tsing Hua College students. The proceeds will be devoted to charity.

A recital under the auspices of the School of Music was given by Mme de Sigalas, pianist, Mrs. Dunlap, mezzo contralto, and Mme Megret, mezzo-soprano, at the American legation, Wednesday.

General Chiang Kuei-ti, Lieutenant-General of Jehol, makes an announcement in the *Government Gazette* that he is in no way connected with the Sino-Italian Bank nor is he a promoter of the institution.

The Ministry of Communications has appointed Messrs. Rouse, Poullain and Wang Chung-yi to act as attaches to the Chinese Plenipotentiary Delegate to the International Postal Convention to be held in Madrid.

"Midsummer Nights' Dream" which was to have been presented on May 14, by the students of the Anglo-Chinese Girls' School in English, at the Y. M. C. A. auditorium in Tientsin, has been postponed to June 4.

Sidney Barton, C. M. G., Chinese Secretary of the British legation in Peking, who has been on a year's home leave, is expected to be back at his post in ten days. During his absence, H. I. Harding has acted as Chinese secretary.

The oratorical contest between Tsing Hua, Peking Higher Normal and Peking Academy, which was postponed becauses of the American College

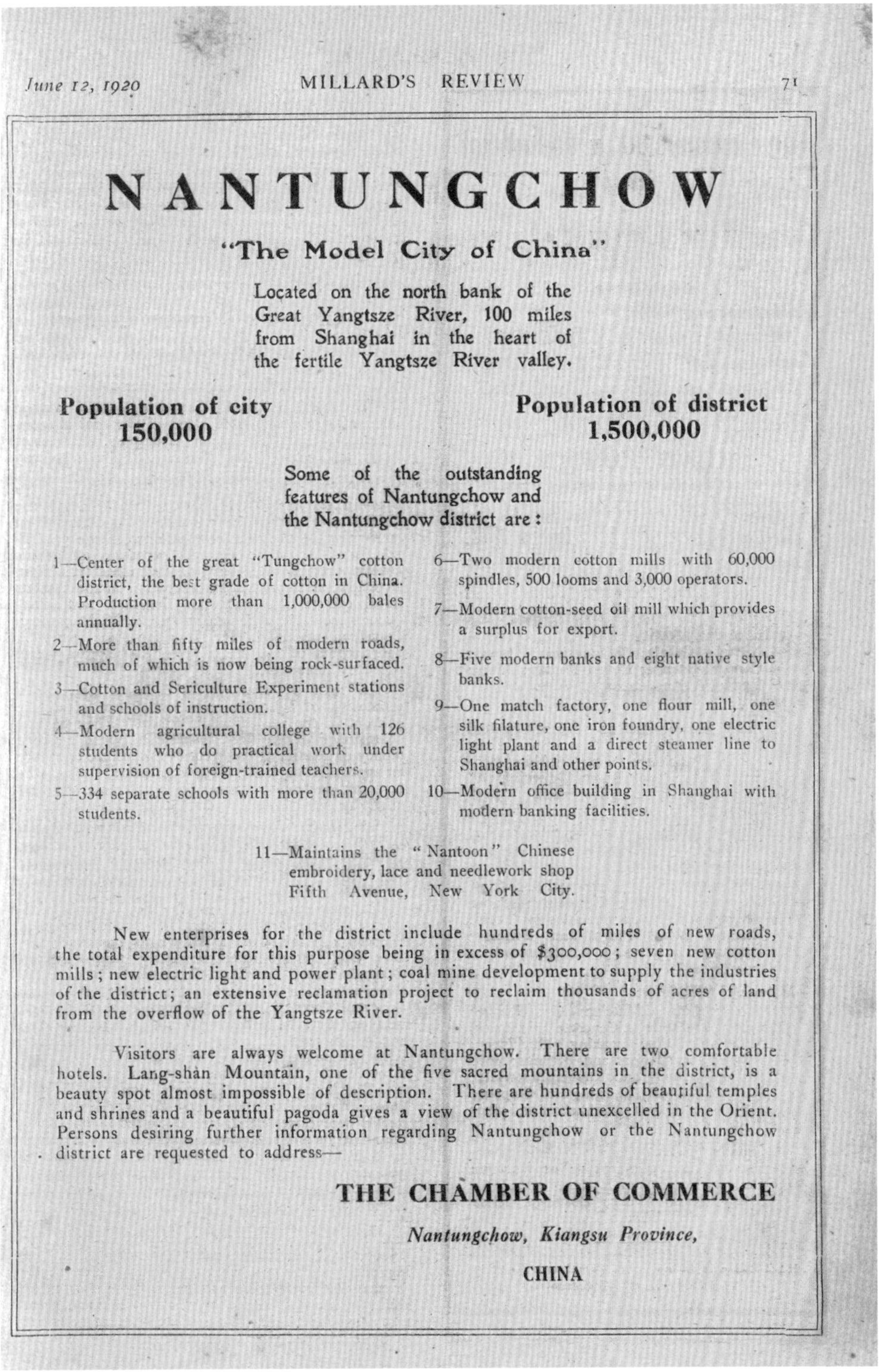
June 12, 1920 MILLARD'S REVIEW 71

NANTUNGCHOW

"The Model City of China"

Located on the north bank of the Great Yangtsze River, 100 miles from Shanghai in the heart of the fertile Yangtsze River valley.

Population of city 150,000

Population of district 1,500,000

Some of the outstanding features of Nantungchow and the Nantungchow district are:

1—Center of the great "Tungchow" cotton district, the best grade of cotton in China. Production more than 1,000,000 bales annually.

2—More than fifty miles of modern roads, much of which is now being rock-surfaced.

3—Cotton and Sericulture Experiment stations and schools of instruction.

4—Modern agricultural college with 126 students who do practical work under supervision of foreign-trained teachers.

5—334 separate schools with more than 20,000 students.

6—Two modern cotton mills with 60,000 spindles, 500 looms and 3,000 operators.

7—Modern cotton-seed oil mill which provides a surplus for export.

8—Five modern banks and eight native style banks.

9—One match factory, one flour mill, one silk filature, one iron foundry, one electric light plant and a direct steamer line to Shanghai and other points.

10—Modern office building in Shanghai with modern banking facilities.

11—Maintains the "Nantoon" Chinese embroidery, lace and needlework shop Fifth Avenue, New York City.

New enterprises for the district include hundreds of miles of new roads, the total expenditure for this purpose being in excess of $300,000; seven new cotton mills; new electric light and power plant; coal mine development to supply the industries of the district; an extensive reclamation project to reclaim thousands of acres of land from the overflow of the Yangtsze River.

Visitors are always welcome at Nantungchow. There are two comfortable hotels. Lang-shan Mountain, one of the five sacred mountains in the district, is a beauty spot almost impossible of description. There are hundreds of beautiful temples and shrines and a beautiful pagoda gives a view of the district unexcelled in the Orient. Persons desiring further information regarding Nantungchow or the Nantungchow district are requested to address—

THE CHAMBER OF COMMERCE

Nantungchow, Kiangsu Province,

CHINA

1920年6月12日，《密勒氏评论报》刊登《南通——中国模范城》。

266 MILLARD'S REVIEW July 3, 1920

learning to Chinese youths, and allow them as much freedom as they allow to their own students, and not to put them in a place especially set apart. If a Sino-French University is established for the benefit of French scholars, that is another matter.

The arrival at Peking of M. Painleve, Chief of the French Industrial Mission, on June 22, will further promote the friendly relationship between France and China. M. Painleve, as former Prime Minister of France, is wielding a tremendous influence with his countrymen at home, and whatever messages he will have for them about China upon his return to France will carry greater weight. For a time, the former French Prime Minister will act as adviser to the Ministry of Communications, and enlighten that Ministry upon the question of the improvement of the railway system in China. Those who accompanied M. Painleve in this trip are: M. Borrel, director of the Normal School of Paris, who during the war was General Secretary of War and President of the Council; M. Germain Martin, well known French legislator, professor of law in the University of Paris and former collaborator with Premier Alexander Ribot; M. Abel Bonnard, literary man, poet and distinguished novelist, representing the Ministry of Foreign Affairs. Educational institutions throughout China will be the particular object of their visit. Upon their return to France, these French educationalists and novelists will be able to interpret Chinese thoughts and ideals to their own people in an effective way such as has never been done before. Views of M. Painleve on China and the object of his mission have already been given in a press interview while passing through Japan. They are full of interest and sympathy toward the Chinese. Part of the interview is given here:

"The young Chinese republicans are turning with sympathy toward the older sister republics, France and America. We know the influence and the attraction which Anglo-Saxon America exercises upon the imaginations of the Chinese. All of the Great Powers, the governments of which have understood the importance of peaceful penetration into China, seek to create sympathy and strong support for their nations there.

"France must not fail, at this time, when China, seeking to modernize herself, is calling for intellectual guides and technical counsellors, to answer that call. Anything that fails to present French culture to China leaves the way open for German Kultur to stifle.

"The peace of the world has nothing to gain from an Americanized or an Anglicized China. Without in any way meaning to offend our friends or allies, we feel that to the French belongs the moral obligation to encourage and develop the intellectual, scientific and technical relations which exist already between China and France.

"My journey to China has no other aim. I am invited by the President of the Chinese Republic, Hsu Shih-chang, to be his guest and I go with the approval and bearing instructions from the Chinese world—which represents a third of all humanity, which has countless riches still unexplored and which possesses prodigious power for the advance of civilization—in order that they may become better known to the French intellectuals and men of action.

"Above all I shall make it my aim to guide the Chinese who are seeking a higher education toward France, where Chinese students are already going in increasing numbers every year. I count as much on gaining the friendship of the republicans of the south as that of the people of the north. I think I will be able to rally for China the effective sympathy of the whole of France."

Peking, June 26.

John Dewey in China

BY C. F. REMER

JOHN Dewey has been in China for more than a year; and this fact needs to be more widely and more fully appreciated than it is. Dewey is not known to most Americans either in China or in America. He "is not famous like W. J. Bryan or Charlie Chaplin" as a recent writer remarks. The results of his work do not appear before the world in the form of a Panama canal; he has brought about no changes in American government or in American laws; he has invented no mechanical devices; he has lead no armies; he has not made millions of dollars. He has done nothing more spectacular during most

Two Great Scholars of China and America

Dr. John Dewey, Columbia University, and Hon. Chang Chien, Nantungchow, China

of his life than teach school, lecture in college class-rooms and write a number of books and magazine articles. Nevertheless John Dewey is a great man. He has changed the attitude of mind toward education of more teachers than any other one thinker of modern America; he, with William James and some others, has done much toward making a philosophy out of modern experimental science and modern democracy; he has given that turn to the thinking of America which is growing to be characteristic of the country; and, during the years of the late war, he more than any other single man, except perhaps Woodrow Wilson, made it clear to America

1920年7月3日，《密勒氏评论报》登载的《杜威在中国》一文，配图是张謇与杜威的合影。

188 MILLARD'S REVIEW September 25, 1920

New Nantung Building, Shanghai Home of Nantung Industries

Modern office structure on Kiukiang Road, the ground floor of which is occupied by the Hwei Hai Industrial Bank, Ltd.

Hwei Hai Industrial Bank Opens Shanghai Branch

The Hwei Hai Industrial Bank., Ltd., opened its Shanghai branch with a public reception on September 17 and at the close of the day deposits had been received to the amount of $2,000,000. The bank occupies its own building, being a part of the interests of the Nantung Industries, who have recently completed a modern office building on Kiukiang Road, Shanghai, to be their home in this city. The Nantung Industries under the direction of Chang Chien, Chang Cha and Chang Chien, Jr., are coming to be known as one of the greatest, modern commercial factors in China. A complete list of the activities of the corporation may be found in the advertisement of Nantungchow, the home of the industries, in this issue of the *Review*. The head office of the Hwei Hai Industrial Bank is at Nantungchow.

The new bank was organized by Chang Cha and Chang Chien and is headed by Chang Chien, Jr., adviser to the military and civil governors of Kiangsu and auditor-in-chief of the Administrative Board of Nantung Industries, as president. The manager of the Shanghai branch is S. S. Yang, former manager of the Salt Industrial Bank of Yangchow, who has been identified with banking in China for more than thirty years. C. C. Hsu, M. A. of Columbia University, auditor of the Administrative Board of Nantung Industries and secretary to Chang Chien, is sub-manager of the branch. The general secretary is C. Chu, Ph. D., of Columbia University, professor of economics at the Nanking Teachers' College, author of "The Tariff Problem in China" and an editor of *The Eastern Times*.

The foreign department will be in charge of C. P. Chow, B. S., a graduate of the Wharton School of Finance and Commerce, who also received the degree of M. B. A. from the Graduate School of Business Administration of Harvard. Mr. Chow is especially fitted to occupy this post having studied American and foreign banking systems and procedure at first hand. For three years prior to his arrival in Shanghai last August, he was a member of the staff of J. P. Morgan and Company, New York. Y. H. Wu will be chief accountant of the new branch and S. P. Li, T. F. Liu, and V. P. Hsi members of the business department.

Among the guests at the opening of the bank were: Tong Shao-yi, Dr. C. T. Wang, K. P. Chen, manager of the Shanghai Commercial and Savings Bank, Y. Hsu, commissioner of foreign affairs, U. Y. Hsu, deputy managing director of the Chinese-American Bank of Commerce, Y. M. Chien, manager of the Bank of Communications, Y. D. Wei, manager of the Russo-Asiatic Bank, H. Y. Moh, Y. C. Tong, Fu Siao-En, manager of the Commercial Bank of China, Chu Pao-san, J. J. Bleeker, manager Nederlandsch Indische Handelsbank, Junkichi Matsushima, manager of Sumitomo Bank, Wang Keng Ting, Taoyin of Shanghai, Kai Fu Shah of the Han-yeh-ping Iron and Coal Co., and Sung Han-chang, manager of the Bank of China.

1920年9月25日，《密勒氏评论报》对南通大厦和淮海实业银行上海分行的报道。

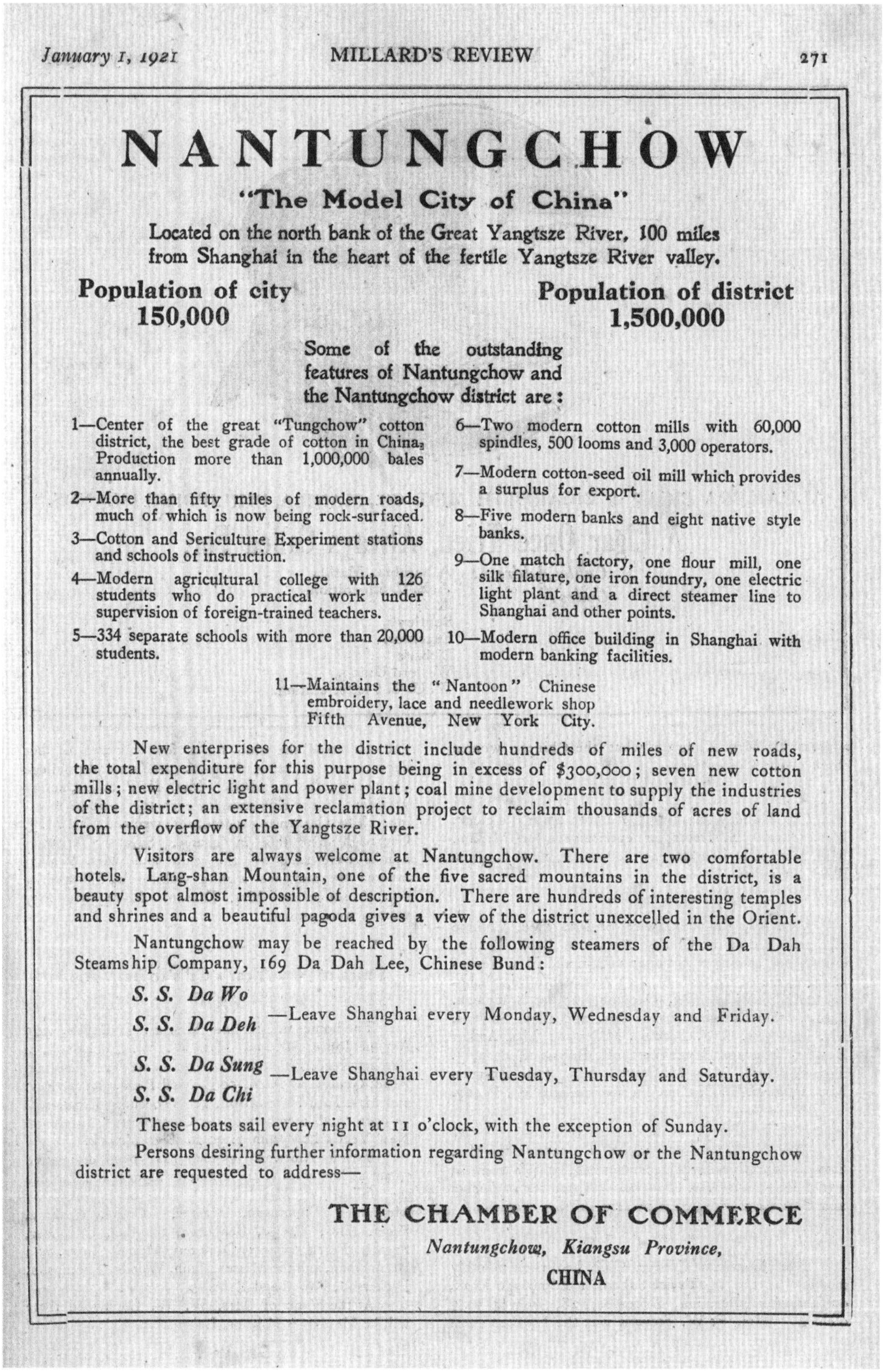
January 1, 1921 MILLARD'S REVIEW 271

NANTUNGCHOW

"The Model City of China"

Located on the north bank of the Great Yangtsze River, 100 miles from Shanghai in the heart of the fertile Yangtsze River valley.

Population of city 150,000

Population of district 1,500,000

Some of the outstanding features of Nantungchow and the Nantungchow district are:

1—Center of the great "Tungchow" cotton district, the best grade of cotton in China. Production more than 1,000,000 bales annually.

2—More than fifty miles of modern roads, much of which is now being rock-surfaced.

3—Cotton and Sericulture Experiment stations and schools of instruction.

4—Modern agricultural college with 126 students who do practical work under supervision of foreign-trained teachers.

5—334 separate schools with more than 20,000 students.

6—Two modern cotton mills with 60,000 spindles, 500 looms and 3,000 operators.

7—Modern cotton-seed oil mill which provides a surplus for export.

8—Five modern banks and eight native style banks.

9—One match factory, one flour mill, one silk filature, one iron foundry, one electric light plant and a direct steamer line to Shanghai and other points.

10—Modern office building in Shanghai with modern banking facilities.

11—Maintains the "Nantoon" Chinese embroidery, lace and needlework shop Fifth Avenue, New York City.

New enterprises for the district include hundreds of miles of new roads, the total expenditure for this purpose being in excess of $300,000; seven new cotton mills; new electric light and power plant; coal mine development to supply the industries of the district; an extensive reclamation project to reclaim thousands of acres of land from the overflow of the Yangtsze River.

Visitors are always welcome at Nantungchow. There are two comfortable hotels. Lang-shan Mountain, one of the five sacred mountains in the district, is a beauty spot almost impossible of description. There are hundreds of interesting temples and shrines and a beautiful pagoda gives a view of the district unexcelled in the Orient.

Nantungchow may be reached by the following steamers of the Da Dah Steamship Company, 169 Da Dah Lee, Chinese Bund:

S. S. Da Wo
S. S. Da Deh —Leave Shanghai every Monday, Wednesday and Friday.

S. S. Da Sung
S. S. Da Chi —Leave Shanghai every Tuesday, Thursday and Saturday.

These boats sail every night at 11 o'clock, with the exception of Sunday.

Persons desiring further information regarding Nantungchow or the Nantungchow district are requested to address—

THE CHAMBER OF COMMERCE

Nantungchow, Kiangsu Province,

CHINA

1921年元旦，《南通——中国模范城》广告在原有内容的基础上，增加大达轮船公司上海至南通段的航班信息。

closing for lack of funds, the Ministry of Communications is starting many new educational institutions. In some of these which are already in operation, not only the teachers' salaries and the operating expenses are guaranteed, but also a monthly subsidy of twelve dollars is given each student.

The teachers of the National University and the other national schools, he declared, have no desire to prevent the establishment of new schools. Rather they favor moves in that direction. But, they ask, if the government have sufficient funds to finance such new educational institutions, which are not provided for in the national budget, why can they not demand a similar support for the educational institutions which are already established, which are truly national in character and which have been given a place in the budget?

Dr. Hu then emphasized the point that the question of salary payments was of secondary importance. The real issue is as to whether the incomes of all the departments shall be nationalized. The teachers felt that they should be. As a first step toward this essential reform, therefore, he proposed —and the faculty and administrative officers of the National University unanimously agreed—that the demand be made for the payment, from the proceeds of the national railways, of arrears of salaries and of the funds allowed by the national budget for the administrative expense of the schools, and that a guarantee on these same proceeds be given for the payment of the budgeted administrative expenses and the salaries in the future.

"The reprinting of the Four Imperial Libraries," he said in conclusion, "may very well be postponed. The purchase of aeroplanes may well be reduced. But these few national educational institutions must go on. And in order that these institutions may go on, their legitimate expenses, which have been approved by the national government and included in the national budget, must be paid."

The resolution as amended by Dr. Hu was unanimously adopted, and a committee representative of all the departments of the National University was appointed, with power to carry on the strike and to undertake negotiations with the other schools and with the government.

The wording of this resolution is as follows: "Resolved, that we temporarily suspend work at the National University and ask the government to secure funds from the proceeds of the national railways from which to pay the arrears in salaries and administrative expenses and to guarantee the prompt payment of salaries and administrative expenses in the future."

Another important resolution also was adopted: "Resolved, that all members of the National University staff who also teach in other national schools should suspend their work in these other institutions." The significance of this resolution shows National University are on from the fact that many of the teachers in the faculties are also on the faculties of various other schools. The Higher Normal School will be especially effected.

The six schools that up to tonight have formally become involved in the strike are the National University, the National Technical College, the National Law School, the National Agricultural College, the National Art School and the Women's Higher Normal School. The other two schools which will unquestionably follow suit as soon as meetings can be held are the National Medical College and the Peking Higher Normal School. Whether the movement will spread outside of Peking is still uncertain, though the schools throughout the country have been suffering from the same shortage of funds which was the immediate cause of the present crisis in the Capital.

However that may be, when the three schools have joined the five—which will be in a day or two at most—at least eight hundred administrative officers and teachers and six thousand students will be effected.

All of the schools are following the lead of the National University in raising the question of the nationalization of the incomes of the government departments, and in insisting on a satisfactory settlement of this question as a basis for the settlement of the strike. The students, also, are preparing to organize in support of the teachers.

Peking, March 14, 1921.

Chang Chien, China's City Builder

BY DON D. PATTERSON

CREATIVE genius knows no land or race, recognizes no school or caste, but finds expression wherever situated. One hundred miles up the Yangtse River from the city of Shanghai, creative genius embodied in China's greatest industrial leader and capitalist, Chang Chien, is building a milestone in the industrial future of the nation in the model city of Nantungchow. Isolated from cities affected by foreign influence, untouched by railways and comparatively inaccesible along the beaten paths of commerce, Nantungchow stands as a monument to the executive ability, vision, and power of organization of this man and his associates, who include his son, Chang Chien, Jr., and his brother, Chang Cha.

Hon. Chang Chien

1921 年 3 月 26 日，《密勒氏评论报》登出《张謇：中国的城市建造师》一文。

No contact with Western lands has brought about the experience and foresight with which His Excellency Chang Chien is gifted, no Western technical school has the honor of claiming him as an alumnus, rather the opposite. Until more than forty years of age Chang Chien was one of the leaders of the old schools of China and a noted Hanlin scholar. With such a foundation of ancient learning, whose traditions counseled seclusion and mental pursuits rather than industrial expansion, it is difficult to reconcile the first forty years of the life of Chang Chien with the past twenty-nine.

Twenty-four years ago Chang Chien dreamed of an industrial city rising just outside of the walls of the ancient town of Nantungchow, his birthplace, which would be not only an industrial center but a place of benevolent happiness and a mecca of education. With a zeal, unprecedented in the history of modern China, he began his task, the immediate impetus being a commission to organize a spinning and weaving mill of $1,000,000 capitalization. The work of organization and construction was successfully accomplished, to be followed by the Fuhsin Flour Mill, the Kwangsheng Oil Mill, the Tse-sheng Iron Works, the Fousheng Silk Filature and the Da Dah Steam Navigation Company.

Hon. Chang Cha

With these enterprises as a nucleus, Chang Chien began the construction of his dream city, the model town of Nantungchow. Appreciating the value of contentment among his workers, his first work was that of the laying out of a public park for the center of his city with attractive artificial lagoons. This having been completed, he next turned his attention to the building of a modern theater with a seating capacity of 1, 200. Being one of the greatest modern day students and patrons of the Chinese drama, he gathered about him many of the most famous actors of the nation and with the amusement of his people cared for, he began the development work.

Nantungchow stands as the autobiography of one of the greatest of China's city builders. Within twenty-five years it has risen out of the level plain of the north Yangtse Valley growing rapidly and waxing increasingly prosperous. Its ramifications and innovations have brought it into the lime light of publicity within the past few years and have given it an international fame.

The district of Tungchow is the region of production of the highest quality of Chinese cotton and the weaving looms of the country turn out the choicest of the nation's cotton cloth. Two modern cotton mills are now in operation and their ranks are being swelled by the addition of seven more. Supplementing this work, the Nantung College of Agriculture, organized by Chang Chien and directed by Alex. Y. Lee, assisted by S. Z. Kwauk and two other American returned students, is carrying on experimental work with the view to improving the cotton culture and production. Working in conjunction with the mills, the Nantung Textile School, also under the guidance of American returned students, is giving instruction in all phases of cotton milling and weaving. The district has a production of 1,000,000 bales of cotton annually.

To the oil mill has been added a refinery, capable of producing the finest cotton seed oil adapted to household uses, and a hardening process to turn out a cooking compound. Increasing demands have brought the necessity for the construction of a new flour mill, which will be completed within a few months and will be equipped with the most modern machinery.

The other industries of the city include a silk filature, an iron foundry, one electric light and power plant, with a second under construction to cost $1,000,000, a newly organized shop for the production of hair nets and laces, a soap factory and a match making plant. Projected are a caustic soda plant and a paper mill. Added to these are the Da Dah Steamship Company, operating a river line from Shanghai to Nantungchow, and the Chino-Belgian Steamship Company, which will soon inaugurate a service from Shanghai to various ports in Europe, Great Britain and America.

Chang Chien through Nantungchow has become a pioneer in the construction of good roads. The city and district now has more than fifty miles of motor roads, most of which are rock surfaced or paved, and a planned expansion of more than 700 li. The country is made accesible by ten modern motor buses, the city proper being four miles from the river landings, which operate along regular routes according to schedule. This line is to be increased by the additional of several more specially built cars within a short time. In addition to this, the district has approximately thirty private motor cars, all of the most modern American makes. The road building has been a cooperative offort, the farmers furnishing both the land and the labor where the routes have traversed the country districts.

Nantungchow is a revelation in the development of modern education in China having in addition to its agricultural college, and textile school, 332 other separate schools, which include a commercial college, an embroidery school, whose products are being sold in the United States and elsewhere, a girl's normal school, and most unique of all an actor's school. The latter school has been established for the study of the Chinese drama and its production. Boys are admitted at an early age, taught the histronic art of the Chinese stage, playwriting and, the classics under the director of Eu-yung Yu Chien, who is said to be China's most accomplished actor and who is a graduate of the law school, of Waseda University. In addition to his duties with the, school Eu-yung is the playwriter, director, producer and star of the Nantung theater.

There are no pinched faces in Nantungchow, no beggars and a general air of business, happiness and contentment fill the place, The benevolent institutions that have been established are: the Nantung Orphanage, the Door of Hope, the Nantung Hospital, the Deaf and Dumb School, the old Peoples Home, the Blind School, the Cripple's Home, the People's Trade School, and the Beggar's Home. In the majority of these institutions, the dwellers there are given the benefit of a semi-technical training which will make them self-supporting.

Chang Chien, Jr.

There's a building boom in Nantung. The Nantung Club has recently been finished and provides all of the comforts and attractions of a Western institution of its kind. It is being added to now in order to provide housing facilities for the entertainment of visitors to the city of Nantung. A new modern hotel and a $160,000 executive building for the Nantung Chamber of Commerce are nearing completion. The building for the College of Agriculture, with modern laboratories and other facilities will be finished by fall as will the new flour mill, the new cotton mill, the power station, the many new shops and the new building for a textile school.

The district has become self-governing and under the guidance of Chang Chien. Jr., who is the speaker, a district assembly has been instituted and a building for its housing is under way.

Chang Chien, in addition to building his city, is also bringing up industrial leaders to carry on after his own work and that of his brother, Chang Cha, is finished, The most prominent of these is Chang Chien, Junior, who now takes a majority of the executive responsibility off the shoulders of his father and who is looked upon by the people as an able successor to him. Chang Chien, Junior, is a graduate of a commercial school in the United States. Surrounding him, Chang Chien has a number of younger Chinese supervising the educational and industrial work, all of whom are fired with the same ideals, the same ambitions and the same qualifications for putting them into effect.

An increased amount of cooperation is being introduced in the community and the workers are being urged to put their money into the industries of the district. A movement is now on foot for the raising of bonds among the people of the district for the financing of various projects. The dwellers in the Nantung district are proud of their city, its leader and its accomplishments. Their pride has made it China's cleanest city. The Chang family holds infinite power over the district, containing 1,500,000 people and 7,435 square li of land, but exercise it in a most benevolent and patriotic manner.

But now that Nantung is well under way, the compelling creative desire in Chang Chien is turning his efforts in other directions. A modern bank and office building in Shanghai to house his industrial offices has been recently built. An embroidery and lace store, known as the Nantoon Shop, on Fifth Avenue, New York, acquaints the Americans with the model city of China and at the same time keeps the city out here informed on the latest industrial developments. Conservation work along the Yangtze Coast extending from the Nantung district north along the Pacific shore which will reclaim millions of mow of land for cotton growing is also another Chang Chien project.

The longing of the city builder for expression in a greater way has been responsible for his acceptance of the direction of the new project for the construction of an international port city under Chinese guidance at Woosung, a distance of twelve miles from Shanghai. Here will be constructed a more magnificient city—Nantung having served to give experience—one that with Shanghai will become one of the best known ports of the world. With his inherent ability and providing that his physical condition will permit, there is no question of the success of Chang Chien in this undertaking.

Chang Chien, with the assistance of his associates, is handing down to the younger generation of Chinese an example which if followed will bring the country to the forefront as one of the greatest industrial nations of the world. It should be made compulsory for every young man of China to spend a time in the city of Nantungchow imbibing its spirit and studying its inner workings, in order that future city and nation builders may be trained. Nantungchow is a delightful revelation to the foreign visitor and its hospitality reminds one of the traditional courtesy of the Southern section of the United States.

But after all the most impressive feature of Nantungchow, with its multitudinous activities and its alert, progressive spirit, is that it was born in the mind of one of China's greatest scholar, Chang Chien.

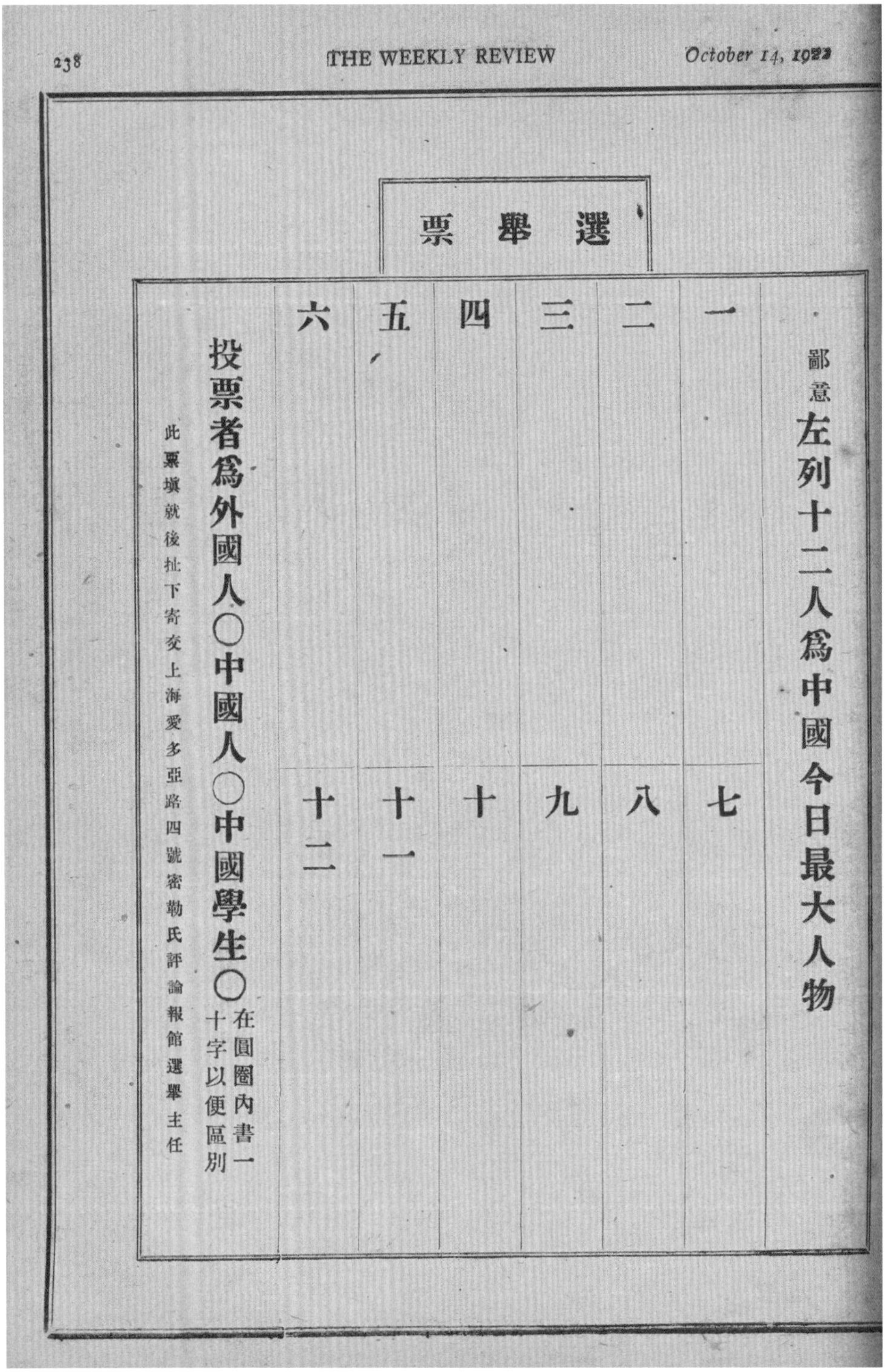

238 THE WEEKLY REVIEW October 14, 1922

選舉票

鄙意左列十二人爲中國今日最大人物

一
二
三
四
五
六
七
八
九
十
十一
十二

投票者爲外國人○中國人○中國學生○在圓圈內書一十字以便區別

此票塡就後扯下寄交上海愛多亞路四號密勒氏評論報館選舉主任

《密勒氏评论报》于1922年10月7日举办“中国当今十二位大人物”读者投票选举活动。图为10月14日刊登的选票。

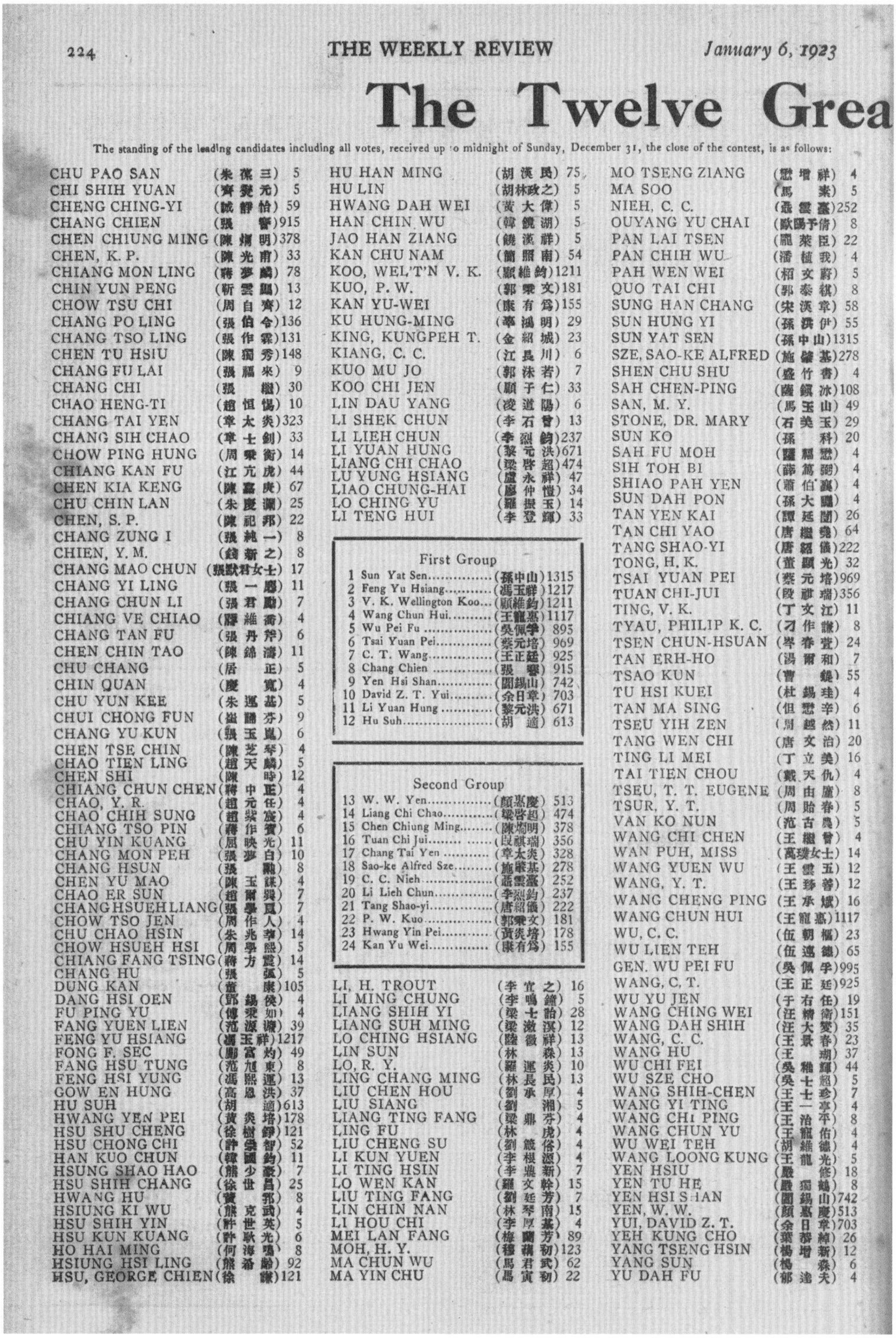

224 THE WEEKLY REVIEW *January 6, 1923*

The Twelve Grea

The standing of the leading candidates including all votes, received up to midnight of Sunday, December 31, the close of the contest, is as follows:

CHU PAO SAN (朱葆三) 5
CHI SHIH YUAN (齊燮元) 5
CHENG CHING-YI (誠靜怡) 59
CHANG CHIEN (張　謇) 915
CHEN CHIUNG MING (陳炯明) 378
CHEN, K. P. (陳光甫) 33
CHIANG MON LING (蔣夢麟) 78
CHIN YUN PENG (靳雲鵬) 13
CHOW TSU CHI (周自齊) 12
CHANG PO LING (張伯令) 136
CHANG TSO LING (張作霖) 131
CHEN TU HSIU (陳獨秀) 148
CHANG FU LAI (張福來) 9
CHANG CHI (張　繼) 30
CHAO HENG-TI (趙恒惕) 10
CHANG TAI YEN (章太炎) 323
CHANG SIH CHAO (章士釗) 33
CHOW PING HUNG (周秉衡) 14
CHIANG KAN FU (江亢虎) 44
CHEN KIA KENG (陳嘉庚) 67
CHU CHIN LAN (朱慶瀾) 25
CHEN, S. P. (陳祀邦) 22
CHANG ZUNG I (張純一) 8
CHIEN, Y. M. (錢新之) 8
CHANG MAO CHUN (張默君女士) 17
CHANG YI LING (張一麐) 11
CHANG CHUN LI (張君勱) 7
CHIANG VE CHIAO (蔣維喬) 4
CHANG TAN FU (張丹斧) 6
CHEN CHIN TAO (陳錦濤) 11
CHU CHANG (居　正) 5
CHIN QUAN (慶　寬) 4
CHU YUN KEE (朱運基) 5
CHUI CHONG FUN (崔聰芬) 9
CHANG YU KUN (張玉崑) 6
CHEN TSE CHIN (陳芝琴) 4
CHAO TIEN LING (趙天麟) 5
CHEN SHI (陳　時) 12
CHIANG CHUN CHEN (蔣中正) 4
CHAO, Y. R. (趙元任) 4
CHAO CHIH SUNG (趙紫宸) 4
CHIANG TSO PIN (蔣作賓) 6
CHU YIN KUANG (屈映光) 11
CHANG MON PEH (張夢白) 10
CHANG HSUN (張　勳) 8
CHEN YU MAO (陳玉謀) 4
CHAO ER SUN (趙爾巽) 7
CHANG HSUEH LIANG (張學良) 7
CHOW TSO JEN (周作人) 4
CHU CHAO HSIN (朱兆莘) 14
CHOW HSUEH HSI (周學熙) 5
CHIANG FANG TSING (蔣方震) 14
CHANG HU (張　弧) 5
DUNG KAN (董　康) 105
DANG HSI OEN (鄧錫侯) 4
FU PING YU (傅秉如) 4
FANG YUEN LIEN (范源濂) 39
FENG YU HSIANG (馮玉祥) 1217
FONG F. SEC (鄺富灼) 49
FANG HSU TUNG (范旭東) 8
FENG HSI YUNG (馮熙運) 13
GOW EN HUNG (高恩洪) 37
HU SUH (胡　適) 613
HWANG YEN PEI (黃炎培) 178
HSU SHU CHENG (徐樹錚) 121
HSU CHONG CHI (許崇智) 52
HAN KUO CHUN (韓國鈞) 11
HSUNG SHAO HAO (熊少豪) 7
HSU SHIH CHANG (徐世昌) 25
HWANG HU (黃　郛) 8
HSIUNG KI WU (熊克武) 4
HSU SHIH YIN (許世英) 5
HSU KUN KUANG (許耿光) 6
HO HAI MING (何海鳴) 8
HSIUNG HSI LING (熊希齡) 92
HSU, GEORGE CHIEN (徐　謙) 121

HU HAN MING (胡漢民) 75
HU LIN (胡林政之) 5
HWANG DAH WEI (黃大偉) 5
HAN CHIN WU (韓鏡湖) 5
JAO HAN ZIANG (饒漢祥) 5
KAN CHU NAM (簡照南) 54
KOO, WEL'T'N V. K. (顧維鈞) 1211
KUO, P. W. (郭秉文) 181
KAN YU-WEI (康有為) 155
KU HUNG-MING (辜鴻明) 29
KING, KUNGPEH T. (金紹城) 23
KIANG, C. C. (江長川) 6
KUO MU JO (郭沫若) 7
KOO CHI JEN (顧子仁) 33
LIN DAU YANG (凌道陽) 6
LI SHEK CHUN (李石曾) 13
LI LIEH CHUN (李烈鈞) 237
LI YUAN HUNG (黎元洪) 671
LIANG CHI CHAO (梁啓超) 474
LU YUNG HSIANG (盧永祥) 47
LIAO CHUNG-HAI (廖仲愷) 34
LO CHING YU (羅振玉) 14
LI TENG HUI (李登輝) 33

First Group

1 Sun Yat Sen..............(孫中山) 1315
2 Feng Yu Hsiang..........(馮玉祥) 1217
3 V. K. Wellington Koo...(顧維鈞) 1211
4 Wang Chun Hui.........(王寵惠) 1117
5 Wu Pei Fu.................(吳佩孚) 895
6 Tsai Yuan Pei............(蔡元培) 969
7 C. T. Wang...............(王正廷) 925
8 Chang Chien..............(張　謇) 915
9 Yen Hsi Shan.............(閻錫山) 742
10 David Z. T. Yui..........(余日章) 703
11 Li Yuan Hung............(黎元洪) 671
12 Hu Suh.....................(胡　適) 613

Second Group

13 W. W. Yen.................(顏惠慶) 513
14 Liang Chi Chao...........(梁啓超) 474
15 Chen Chiung Ming.......(陳炯明) 378
16 Tuan Chi Jui...............(段祺瑞) 356
17 Chang Tai Yen............(章太炎) 328
18 Sao-ke Alfred Sze........(施肇基) 278
19 C. C. Nieh.................(聶雲臺) 252
20 Li Lieh Chun..............(李烈鈞) 237
21 Tang Shao-yi..............(唐紹儀) 222
22 P. W. Kuo.................(郭秉文) 181
23 Hwang Yin Pei...........(黃炎培) 178
24 Kan Yu Wei...............(康有為) 155

LI, H. TROUT (李宜之) 16
LI MING CHUNG (李鳴鐘) 5
LIANG SHIH YI (梁士詒) 28
LIANG SUH MING (梁漱溟) 12
LO CHING HSIANG (陸徵祥) 13
LIN SUN (林　森) 13
LO, R. Y. (羅運炎) 10
LING CHANG MING (林長民) 13
LIU CHEN HOU (劉承厚) 4
LIU SIANG (劉　湘) 5
LIANG TING FANG (梁鼎芬) 4
LING FU (林　虎) 4
LIU CHENG SU (劉箴俗) 4
LI KUN YUEN (李根源) 4
LI TING HSIN (李鼎新) 7
LO WEN KAN (羅文幹) 15
LIU TING FANG (劉廷芳) 7
LIN CHIN NAN (林琴南) 15
LI HOU CHI (李厚基) 4
MEI LAN FANG (梅蘭芳) 89
MOH, H. Y. (穆藕初) 123
MA CHUN WU (馬君武) 62
MA YIN CHU (馬寅初) 22

MO TSENG ZIANG (默增祥) 4
MA SOO (馬　素) 5
NIEH, C. C. (聶雲臺) 252
OUYANG YU CHAI (歐陽予倩) 8
PAN LAI TSEN (龐萊臣) 22
PAN CHIH WU (潘植我) 4
PAH WEN WEI (柏文蔚) 5
QUO TAI CHI (郭泰祺) 8
SUNG HAN CHANG (宋漢章) 58
SUN HUNG YI (孫洪伊) 55
SUN YAT SEN (孫中山) 1315
SZE, SAO-KE ALFRED (施肇基) 278
SHEN CHU SHU (盛竹書) 4
SAH CHEN-PING (薩鎮冰) 108
SAN, M. Y. (馬玉山) 49
STONE, DR. MARY (石美玉) 29
SUN KO (孫　科) 20
SAH FU MOH (薩福懋) 4
SIH TOH BI (薛篤弼) 4
SHIAO PAH YEN (蕭伯巖) 4
SUN DAH PON (孫大鵬) 4
TAN YEN KAI (譚延闓) 26
TAN CHI YAO (唐繼堯) 64
TANG SHAO-YI (唐紹儀) 222
TONG, H. K. (董顯光) 32
TSAI YUAN PEI (蔡元培) 969
TUAN CHI-JUI (段祺瑞) 356
TING, V. K. (丁文江) 11
TYAU, PHILIP K. C. (刁作謙) 8
TSEN CHUN-HSUAN (岑春萱) 24
TAN ERH-HO (湯爾和) 7
TSAO KUN (曹　錕) 55
TU HSI KUEI (杜錫珪) 4
TAN MA SING (但懋辛) 6
TSEU YIH ZEN (周越然) 11
TANG WEN CHI (唐文治) 20
TING LI MEI (丁立美) 16
TAI TIEN CHOU (戴天仇) 4
TSEU, T. T. EUGENE (周由廑) 8
TSUR, Y. T. (周詒春) 5
VAN KO NUN (范古農) 5
WANG CHI CHEN (王繼曾) 4
WAN PUH, MISS (萬璞女士) 14
WANG YUEN WU (王雲五) 12
WANG, Y. T. (王琇善) 12
WANG CHENG PING (王承斌) 16
WANG CHUN HUI (王寵惠) 1117
WU, C. C. (伍朝樞) 23
WU LIEN TEH (伍連德) 65
GEN. WU PEI FU (吳佩孚) 995
WANG, C. T. (王正廷) 925
WU YU JEN (于右任) 19
WANG CHING WEI (汪精衛) 151
WANG DAH SHIH (汪大燮) 35
WANG, C. C. (王景春) 23
WANG HU (王　瑚) 37
WU CHI FEI (吳稚輝) 44
WU SZE CHO (吳士超) 5
WANG SHIH-CHEN (王士珍) 7
WANG YI TING (王一亭) 4
WANG CHI PING (王治平) 8
WANG CHUN YU (王寵佑) 4
WU WEI TEH (胡維德) 4
WANG LOONG KUNG (王龍光) 5
YEN HSIU (嚴　修) 18
YEN TU HE (嚴獨鶴) 8
YEN HSI SHAN (閻錫山) 742
YEN, W. W. (顏惠慶) 513
YUI, DAVID Z. T. (余日章) 703
YEH KUNG CHO (葉恭綽) 26
YANG TSENG HSIN (楊增新) 12
YANG SUN (楊　森) 6
YU DAH FU (郁達夫) 4

1923 年 1 月 6 日，《密勒氏评论报》公布“中国当今十二位大人物”投票结果：孙中山、冯玉祥、顾维钧等 12 人入选，张謇名列第 8 位。

st Living Chinese

Brief Biographical Notes regarding Those Who Received the Highest Votes in the Competition for the Twelve Greatest Living Chinese.

(*Compiled by Francis Zia*)

SUN YAT-SEN: Founder and Executive Head of the Kuomintang; President of the Provisional Government at Nanking after the overthrow of the Manchu Imperial regime; President of the Constitutional Government of the South.

At present: living in retirement in Shanghai.

FENG YU-HSIANG: Ex-Tuchun of Honan; popularly known as the "Christian General" whose troops are kept under strict discipline.

At present: Inspecting Commissioner of the Ministry of War in command of troops stationed in the metropolitan area for the defence of the capital.

V. K. WELLINGTON-KOO: Ph. D. in Law, Columbia University; Minister at Washington till 1920 when he was transferred to London as Minister there; a member of the Chinese Delegation at the Paris Peace Confererence and at the Washington Conference; Minister of Foreign Affairs of the Wang Chung hui Cabinet.

At present: Chairman of the Society for the Investigation of National Financial Problems; now residing in Peking.

WANG CHUN-HUI: Barrister-at-law, D. C. L.; Minister of Foreign Affairs in Nanking Provisional Government and Minister of Justice in the first Republican Cabinet; President, Law Codification Commission; Chief Judge, Supreme Court; Member of Chinese Delegation to Washington Conference; Premier of Cabinet after retirement of Dr. W. W. Yen.

At present: living in retirment in Peking.

WU PEI-FU: Hsiu-tsai (B.A.) at 21; graduate of Kai Ping Military Academy near Tientsin; noted for bravery in military campaigns in Shansi, Szechuen and Honan since the Republic; Commander of 3rd Division under Tsao Kun; regarded as leading military strategist in recent Chihli-Fengtien conflict in which he vanquished Chang Tso-lin.

At present: living in Loyang with the dual rank of Vice-Inspecting General of Chihli, Shantung and Honan and Inspecting General of Hupeh and Hunan.

TSAI YUAN-PEI: A specialist in educational methods; made extensive studies in Germany; Minister of Education of the first Republican Cabinet; President of the Peking National University; a staunch scholar of the modern school.

At present: President of the Peking University.

C. T. WANG: Studied law in America; Vice-Minister of Commerce and Industry in the first Republic Cabinet; Vice-President of the Senate; member of Chinese Delegation at Paris Peace Conference, representing Southern Government; chief Promoter of National Good Roads Movement.

At present: Minister of Foreign Affairs, Acting Premier and Director-General of Rehabilitation of Shantung Rights.

CHANG CHIEN: A Hanlin scholar (Optimus); Director-General, Huaiho Conservancy; Director-General, National Conservancy Bureau; Minister of Industry and Commerce and temporary Minister of Agriculture and Forestry.

At present: absorbed in industrial enterprises in Nantungchow reputed as the "Model City" of China. Also Director of the Woosung Commercial Development Bureau, and managing director of the Bank of Communications.

YEN HSI-SHAN: Graduate of Military Staff School in Japan; member of the Tung Meng Hui; espoused revolutionary cause when the Revolution broke out; Tutuh of Shansi; led in army reduction by disbanding more than 30,000 troops; popularly known as the "model Tuchun."

At present: Civil and Military Governor of Shansi.

DAVID Z.T. YUI: Studied in St. John's University, Shanghai and in America where he received the M. A. degree; received doctor's degree from St. John's University when its 40th anniversary was celebrated; one of the two "People's Delegates" sent to Washington Conference; actively connected with the national campaign for raising the needed funds to redeem the Shantung Railway.

At present: General Secretary of the National Committee of the Y. M. C. A.

LI YUAN-HUNG: Studied at Peiyang Naval College, and fortification at Japan; appointed by the late Viceroy Chang Chih-tung to organize the modern troops at Hupeh; took command of the revolutionary troope on the outbreak of the Revolution at Wuchang; Vice-President of the Republic; Chief of General staff and Tutuh of Hupeh; President of the Republic on the death of Yuan Shih Kai.

At present: President of the Republic following the retirement of Hsu-Shih-chang.

HU SUH: B. A. Cornell University and Ph. D., Columbia University; Professor of Philosophy at the Government University of Peking; Champion of the movement to introduce the popular spoken language in lieu of the *wen-li* in order to make the written language easily intelligible; regarded as one of the younger philosophers of the new school.

At present: teaching at the Government University of Peking.

DR. W. W. YEN: Studied in University of Virginia, receiving degree of B. A. and LL. D. Minister to Germany and Denmark:, Minister of Foreign Affairs; Acting Premier; appointed to head Chinese Delegation at Washington Conference but did not leave China; author of Standard Chinese-English Dictionary.

At present: living in retirement, frequently mentioned as prospective head of Ministry of Foreign Affairs or new cabinet.

LIANG CHI CHAO: Studied under Kang Yu-wei; noted for his versatile literary powers in modernized writings; advocate of limited monarchy in pre-republican days; Vice-Minister of Justice in Yuan Shih-kai's first cabinet and Minister of Finance in Tuan Chi-jui cabinet; figured in campaign opposing Yuan Shih-Kai's imperial regime; editor of several periodicals of modern thought.

At present: writing a history of Chinese civilization from the cultural standpoints and also lecturing.

(*Continued on page 226*)

THE WEEKLY REVIEW 37

INDUSTRIAL PROGRESS IN CHINA

NANTUNGCHOW (MODEL CITY OF CHINA)

IV

THE impulse toward industrial development started in Shanghai, but has now spread to nearby cities in the Yangtze delta country. The two most notable instances are Nantungchow (also called Nantung and Tungchow) and Wusih. Nantung is situated on the northerly side of the Yangtze about seventy miles from Shanghai by steamer. The transformation which has taken place there within recent years is of special interest inasmuch as Nantung is not open to foreign trade and residence. The few foreigners are engaged in mission or educational work. Consequently the developments which have won for Nantung the title, "Model City of China," stand as a monument to Chinese accomplishment.

Twenty-five years ago, Nantung was much like any other small walled town located in a richly productive agricultural area. Then came Chang Chien the son of a well to do farmer in the Nantung district. His Excellency had achieved the highest scholastics honors and today he is counted as one of China's great scholars. Nevertheless he was of a practical turn of mind and set about to improve agriculture in his native district and establish modern industries. He avoided public office although at one time he served in the cabinet as minister of agriculture and commerce. He has served as chairman or president of many public and semi-public boards such the Hwai River Conservancy Bureau, National Agricultural Association, Central Educational Association and many others.

Mr. Chang's influence is national but his

Scene in reclamation district, easterly of Nantungchow.

Long Shan hill and pagoda near Nantung.

1923 年 3 月 17 日，《密勒氏评论报》刊登《中国实业之进步观——中国模范城南通州》一文的中英文两个版本。

Motor busses in service in the vicinity of Nantung.

Interior of new cotton mill, Nantungchow.

Nantung steamers and wharf, Shanghai.

intensive energies have been centered in the Nantungchow district. On the economic side he has established industries, reclaimed lands, built roads, canals, wharves and organized steamship and steam launch services. He has transformed Tungchow into a modern city with wide, well paved streets and substantial business houses.

In the sphere of public service and altruistic work he has forwarded and financially assisted primary and middle schools, normal, agricultural commercial, industrial and engineering schools and colleges, also a girl's vocational school, orphanages, old peoples' homes and hospitals have been founded. It is a long and splendid record and at the age of 70 Mr. Chang is still active in the furtherance of these and new activities, local and national.

INDUSTRIAL

Nantung and adjoining districts are famous for their production of cotton. Quite naturally one of the first industries started by Mr. Chang was a cotton spinning mill, The Dah Sung Cotton Spinning & Weaving Co., Mill No.1, established in 1899. Another mill is located at Haimen in a neighboring district and a third on Tsung Ming Island near the mouth of the Yangtze river. Tsung Ming Island is famous for the quality of cotton grown thereon. A new mill at Nantungchow is nearly completed and The Dah Sung Company is planning other mills, two at Nantungchow and one at Shanghai.

A few power looms have been installed, but most of the cotton goods woven in the Nantung district are the product of hand looms in thousands of homes.

In addition to the cotton mills, there is a flour mill, vegetable oil mill, iron works and machine shop and electric light plant. A new central power house is under construction on the banks of the Yangtze river from which it is proposed to transmit electric energy to the new cotton mills. The array of industries is not large when compared with Shanghai, but it is notable in view of the fact that it has all

Nantung General Chamber of Commerce Building

Nantung Building, Shanghai

A typical building to house a primary school of Nantungchow district

Nantung Club Building on the left, Nantung Hotel on the right

Textile School

ABOVE—The building which houses the School of Commerce of Nantung. As may be judged from the appearance of this building, much attention is given to keeping the schools up to the standard of the pace set in other lines of progress.

LEFT—One of the modern type of cotton mills which give the Nantung district its distinctive appearance and which attract attention for the district.

been accomplished in a country district very largely as a result and inspiration of one man.

PUBLIC UTILITIES

Hand in hand with the industrial expansion at Nantungchow, public utility developments have been fostered by Mr. Chang. A modern city has been constructed outside the old walled town. Motor cars are frequently seen on the well-paved streets, the public and semi-public buildings are creditable and the parks attractive.

Recently upon the occasion of the public celebration of Mr. Chang's 70th birthday, the city was

Street Scene—Nantung in the new business section outside the old walled town.

brilliantly lighted with electric displays and festoons of lights much as would be done in an American city on a special occasion. Between two and three hundred miles of motor roads have been built in the Nantung and Haimen districts, approximately thirty miles are hard surfaced while the dirt roads are usable for motor traffic except in wet weather. Motor bus and truck lines are operated between important points and between the city and the steamer landing several miles distant. Altogether, with parks, public schools, good roads, streets, electric

Group of visitors at the Hon. Chang Chien's home. Mr. Chang in center.

lights, telephone and motor bus services, Nantungchow is on a par with the most progressive cities in China and leads most of them.

LAND RECLAMATION

Along the seacoast northeasterly of Nantungchow there are extensive areas of what might be called a "no man's land." That is low lying ground built up by river deposits, potentially fertile but not properly drained nor fully reclaimed from the influence of salt sea. With a view to increasing the cotton production of the district Mr. Chang as early

Control gates and drainage canal near the sea, easterly of Nantung.

as 1899 organized the Tung Hai (East Sea) Land Reclamation Co. Drainage canals and roads were built and about 10,000 acres of land reclaimed. Showing fairly good results in the way of harvest, subsequently other reclamation companies were formed and altogether approximately 50,000 acres have been reclaimed or are in process of relcamation. Settlers have been located on the land who cultivate it on a share basis. Incidentally it may be noted that the land companies have established primary schools throughout the reclaimed areas so that these districts together with Nantungchow are famous in China for the progress made in educational work.

TRANSPORTATION

Realizing the necessity of adequate transportation if his enterprises were to be successful Mr. Chang organized the Dah Ta steamship company which operates a line of steamers between Shanghai, Nantungchow and other points on the lower Yangtze river. Wharves and godowns have been constructed at Nantungchow landing and at Shanghai also an Inland navigation company operates steam launches on the numerous canals radiating inland from Nantungchow.

BANKING AND COMMERCIAL

The Chinese are probably the oldest bankers in the world, but the so called "Native Banks," do not meet the modern industrial and commercial requirements. This led to the organization at Nantungchow of the Hwei Hai Industrial Bank, with branches at Shanghai and several of the cities in the lower Yangtze river country. The Shanghai branch is located in the Nantung Building which is also used for the offices of Mr. Chang's various industrial enterprises and the Nantung Company maintains a branch in New York City, having to do with marketing also purchasing of supplies and equipment.

中國實業之進步觀

（其四） 中國模範城南通州

中國實業發展之動力初以上海爲起點今已逐漸擴張而及揚子江口岸各城鎮其最顯著者爲南通及無錫兩處南通爲揚子江北岸之商埠距上海七十哩有輪船往來其間此城爲完全中國人所經營無外人營業於此而居留之外國人僅限於傳教師及教育家而已以其爲中國人所經營之商埠故年來變化之速革新之進步實堪爲吾人注意也而有中國模範城之稱觀此城亦可表率中國人建造革新之能力玆將此城進步情形於下文略述之

沿　革

廿五年前南通情形與其他小城無異而位置於膏腴之地此城之居民中有張君季直者脫穎而出爲此城改革之重要人物張君生於小康之家於前清科舉時代得最高學位爲中國今日有名文學家雖爲文學家而竟能注意於發展農業建造工廠等事其對於宦途頗漠視之嘗爲農商總長一次而已至關於農實各業之機關則不辭勞瘁竭力贊助故於各官商合辦機關彼每位列首席如淮海濬河局督辦全國農會會長中央教育會監督等張君之名望爲全國所欽仰然其精神則多注意於南通毗鄰區域其經濟方面之事業則建設工廠墾殖築路濬河建築碼頭創船公司等故南通經其經營而成爲新商埠埠中路政寬坦商業殷實此沿革大略也至於張君對於公衆慈善事業之贊助擘畫亦大有可觀如各級學校以及師範農業商務工藝工程等學校外尚有女子職業學校孤兒院養老院醫院等皆爲張君手創其對於社會服務事業昭然在人耳目且歷久不惓雖年及古稀不但孜孜於增進其舊有事業且對於地方及全國各新事業仍進行不已

工　業

南通毗鄰境地爲有名之產棉區域故張君手創之第一工廠爲棉織廠卽大生第一紗織廠是也該廠創於一千八百九十九年另一紗廠設於毗鄰之海門鎮復一廠設於近揚子江口之崇明島島中所產之棉質良物美有名於時尚有一廠設於南通該廠尚在建造中不日可完成而大生紗織廠尚擬再建三廠其中二廠將建於南通其一則建於上海至於織布事業則有動力織機數具已裝配而在運用中其餘多用手搖織機故南通所出之布疋多爲織戶之手搖織機所織成者此紗織業大概也除紗廠外有麪粉廠榮油廠鐵廠機械廠電燈廠尚有在建築中之中央電力廠建於揚子江岸專供各新造紗廠發動電流之用南通實業工廠其數尚不及上海之多然以一人之力於鄉村區域其所造就者已非易得也

公衆便利事業

南通工業之發展既如上文所言而張君對於公衆利便事業亦鋭意經營其所計畫而已實行者如南通城外之新市場其中街道平廣可行駛汽車而公私建築物亦齊整悅目去歲市民爲張君慶祝七十壽辰城中以各種電燈點綴入夜但見燈光照耀五光十色其美麗與美國逢舉行祝典時之點綴相埒誠美觀也南通至海門之路線長約二三百哩有三十哩爲堅結之路餘者以泥土鋪成有汽車往來惟遇陰雨則不便於行駛至於往來各重要地點以及距城數哩之輪渡碼頭則有裝貨及公衆乘客汽車往來運送頗稱便利城中之公園公學道路電燈電話汽車種種公衆便利事業與中國其他各新進城市所設者相頡頏有時且較他處爲優美

墾殖荒地

南通東北隅海濱之區有未經開墾之荒地極廣爲揚子江河道所淤漬者膏腴之地也因其常有海水灌入而無排洩水道不合種植故無人耕耘成爲一片荒地張君乃於一千八百九十九年組織東海拓殖公司開墾荒地種植棉種以增南通毗鄰區域之棉產於是開河築路經公司經營開墾者約一萬英畝每年出產成效頗佳於是有數公司起而效之故今日已耕耘或在開墾中之地已佔五萬英畝耕種之農戶多移居於此而農戶所得之利則按其所耕之地每年出產若干與公司按份均分此種墾殖公司且於開墾區域設立蒙學以便農家子女就近入學故南通及其毗鄰墾殖區域在中國爲教育最有進步之區

運　輸

張君知欲使其各種事業得良好效果必有便利之運輸於是乃組織大達輪船公司其所置之輪船專行駛申通間而兩處皆設碼頭貨棧至於內河之交通則有內河小輪公司其輪船行駛於南通各河道往來內地各城鎮而以南通爲中心點

商務及金融

世界之有銀行當推中國最早然老式錢莊不合近今商務之需用南通乃有淮海實業銀行之組織其分行則設於上海及揚子江下遊各城鎮其上海分行設於南通大廈張君各實業公司及南通公司皆設辦公處於此大廈中南通公司且設分行於美國之紐約城專事銷售中國貨物及購辦各種需要器械此南通城大略情形也

『皆有公牍私函可据』

——积累档案

1899 年 11 月 17 日，张謇致函两江总督刘坤一，在全面报告大生纱厂从 1895 年筹办到 1899 年开车的 44 个月艰苦历程后写道："以上各节，皆有公牍私函可据，撮要备采。"张謇有很强的档案意识，所创企业的规章中都有关于档案管理的规范。张謇与其创业团队，以及他们的事业继承者，在兴办实业、倡导教育、捐资公益事业等方面，为后人留下近万卷大生档案，这些档案主要形成于大生沪所，现在保存在江苏省南通市档案馆，是中国档案文献的瑰宝。

张謇的档案意识，跟他幕僚生涯有很大的关系。张謇年轻时，曾先后在原通州知州、后来负责江宁发审局的孙云锦和庆军统领吴长庆处当幕僚。幕僚相当于私人秘书，既处理文书，也管理档案，因此可以视作兼职的档案管理员。

张謇十分重视档案的形成与积累，他的儿子张孝若所作的《南通张季直先生传记》"自序"中说："我父有许多实在的事业，他一生几乎没有一件事没有一篇文字的。"大生纱厂最早的有关档案管理的制度，体现在 1899 年 10 月张謇制定的《厂约》中。《厂约》明确了大生纱厂档案管理的负责人："入储卖纱之款，出供买花之款，备给工料，备支杂务，筹调汇画，稽查报单，考核用度，管理股票、公文、函牍，接应宾客，银钱账目董事之事也。"银钱账目董事相当于总理的副手，在大生纱厂地位显赫，作为文书和档案管理的负责人，可以确保文书和档案工作的正常开展。银钱账目董事还需在每年年底"另刊账略，分别咨商务局寄各股东"。

张謇 1900 年制定的《大生纱厂章程》里，档案管理制度有了细化的规定。如《银钱总帐房章程》规定，"沪帐房逐日所来信件，凡与厂事有关者，各处阅后，均应送总帐房存查""沪帐房逐日寄到洋厘报单，进出货处阅后录簿，原单送存总帐房备核"。这里主要涉及银钱总帐房与大生沪所来往文件的归档，可以推测大生沪所的档案管理制度应该是与银钱总帐房相一致的。而大生沪所保存下来的档案，就是大生档案的主要部分。

大生企业留存档案的目的，主要是维护自身的利益。大生纱厂早期的股份中，以官机作价的官股占实收资本额的56.17%。1899年5月23日大生纱厂开车前，禀请南洋大臣刘坤一，要求派员到大生纱厂，实地查验官机的破损情况。同时请江宁商务局的崔鼎，把瑞记洋行、地亚士洋行在湖北承办这批纺纱机器的原始合同拿到大生纱厂来，用合同上的机器清单与实物核对。1893年瑞记洋行、地亚士洋行承办纱机合同规定，“全厂机器备齐，零用物件配足六个月用，不得短少”“如机器物料照来单有短少损坏，均由瑞记等行认赔”。后来根据现场勘察，以及通过与负责指导机器装配的英国工程师汤姆斯的交流，张謇在10月19日给刘坤一的咨呈中认为，“似此项分领之机，因锈损而缺，非原单所缺”，至于应该添配的机件，先由大生纱厂垫办。另据前往大生纱厂查验的候补道林志道致刘坤一的禀文，官机合同的原件存江南筹防局，大生纱厂的沈燮均和高清建议林志道把点验的官机清单交给江南筹防局，让其与合同原单逐项对比。

大生纱厂是否、何时借到官机合同，或者江南筹防局是否有替大生纱厂核对缺损情况，没有史料说明。但大生档案里确实保存着这份官机合同的抄件，张謇在首页上批注，“存沪帐房备查”，说明大生纱厂最终取得合同的复本。通过核对官机合同，一方面避免机器的缺少，另一方面也验证锈损的机器的数量，作为向官府获取补偿的依据。

大生沪所最早是大生纱厂的驻沪办事机构。张謇在南通所办的企业、文化和慈善机构，大都是在大生纱厂盈利之后，通过已有企业注资、个人捐资、社会集资等方式发展起来的。大生沪所起到筹集资金、购买物料、招聘人员等推动及协助作用。作为孵化器的大生沪所，自然形成和保存与其有关联的大生系统单位的档案。

由于社会动荡，特别是战争的原因，大生系统的核心企业，如大生纱厂、通海垦牧公司，其原始档案，特别是早年的股东会议记录、董事会记录、合同、往来函件等原件，已经不知所终。幸好张謇注重编纂档案汇编，使得大量的大生档案通过档案汇编的形式得以保存。

张謇继承了先辈的做法，把诸如账略、说略、股东会议录、重要文件等，通过编纂有关档案汇编，分发给社会各界。如企业每年度的账略和说略，在当时既是对股东的交代，也是向社会的宣传，客观上起到复制原件内容、增加副本数量的作用。

张謇编纂的大生企业文献中，《通州大生纱厂本末章程帐略》无疑占据重要的地位。它是张謇最早编纂的大生企业文献汇编。大生纱厂筹划于 1895 年，1899 年 5 月 23 日开车。张謇在《通州大生纱厂本末章程帐略》的“后序”中提及，“光绪二十六年（1900）二月，编次本末章程帐略既竟”——光绪二十六年二月《通州大生纱厂本末章程帐略》就已经编纂完成，说明编纂工作在大生纱厂开车之后很快就展开。

《通州大生纱厂本末章程帐略》第二至第四部分，分别是“商办本末”“官商合办本末”和“绅领商办本末”。张謇其实是把大生纱厂的筹办时期划分成三个阶段，这样的划分也为后来的研究者沿用。第五部分“一切开办章程”，包括《厂约》和各部门的规章。第六和第七部分，则是“开机以前帐略”和“开机以后帐略”。《通州大生纱厂本末章程帐略》收入的文献，基本是当时形成的，可以视为大生纱厂的原始档案。

大生档案 1953 年从上海运到南通后，在大生纱厂进行了初步分类整理和重新装箱。1960 年南京大学历史系师生对部分大生档案进行了整理，拟写案卷题名，编制档号，并对每卷档案的内容做了简要说明，共整理成 1203 卷。

1962 年 1 月，江苏人民出版社副社长蔡暹和扬州师范学院历史系教师祁龙威、姚能等人到访南通，与时任南通市副市长曹从坡商谈，建议由扬州师范学院历史系师生利用假期时间，来南通整理大生档案，编成资料，由江苏人民出版社出版。这个提议虽没有得以落实，但曹从坡提出把大生档案集中到南通市档案馆。

同年 3 月，鉴于大生纱厂缺乏良好的保管条件，在曹从坡的主持下，存放在大生纱厂的大生档案首先移交至南通市档案馆；5 月，其余暂存上海的大生档案也运回南通，直接入藏南通市档案馆。这两次档案进馆，奠定了大生档案的基本内容框架。从此，大生档案也从企业的资产转化为社会的共同记忆。20 世纪 80 年代初，南通市档案馆再次启动大生档案整理工作，到 20 世纪 90 年代初基本完成，并开始对外开放查阅。

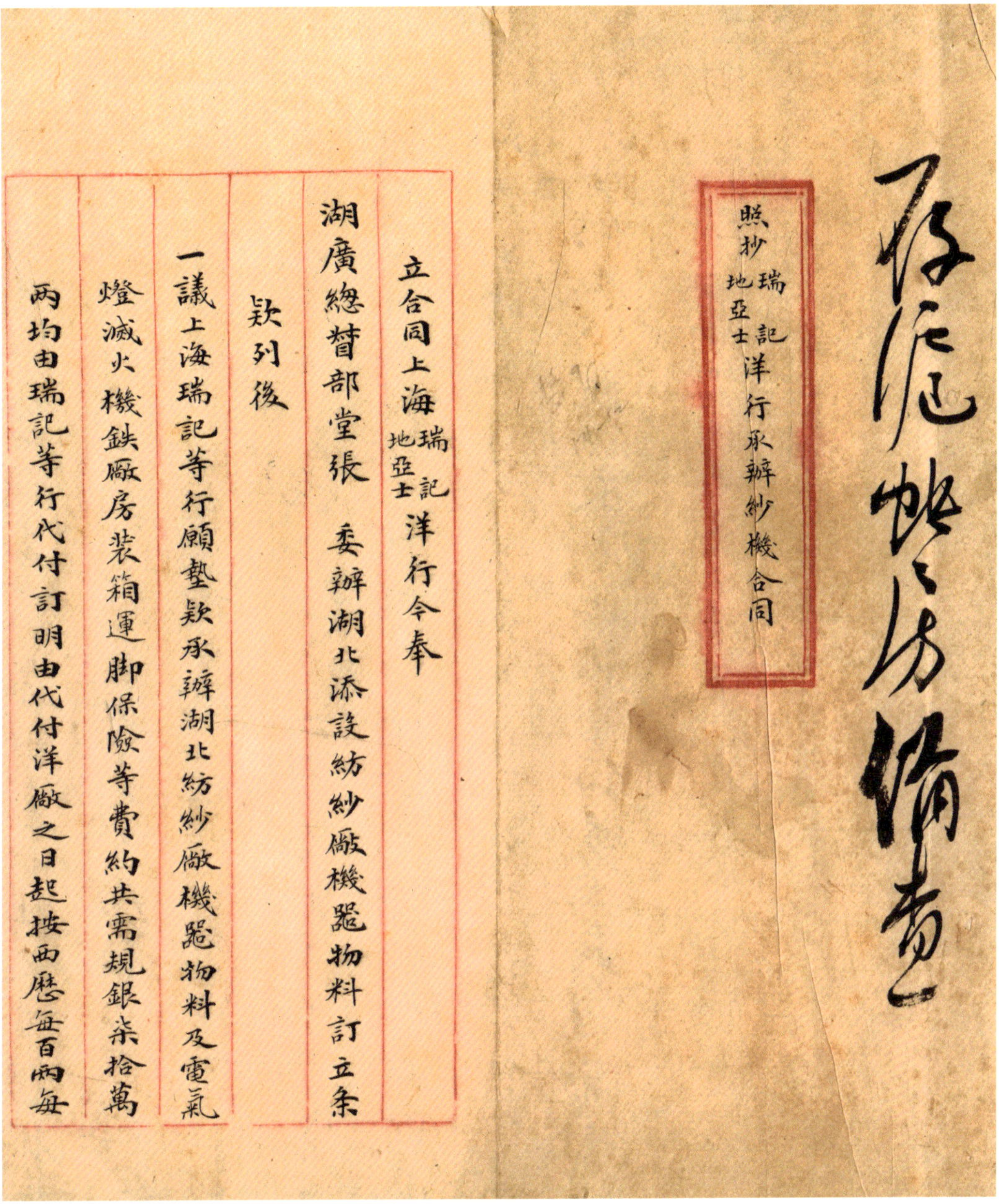
存沪帐房备查

照抄瑞記地亞士洋行承辦紗機合同

立合同上海瑞記地亞士洋行今奉

湖廣總督部堂張 委辦湖北添設紡紗廠機器物料訂立条

欵列後

一議上海瑞記等行願墊欵承辦湖北紡紗廠機器物料及電氣

燈滅火機鉄廠房裝箱運脚保險等費約共需規銀柒拾萬

兩均由瑞記等行代付訂明由代付洋廠之日起按西歷每百兩每

1893 年瑞记洋行、地亚士洋行承办湖北纺纱厂纱机合同抄件（局部），上有张謇的批注“存沪帐房备查”。

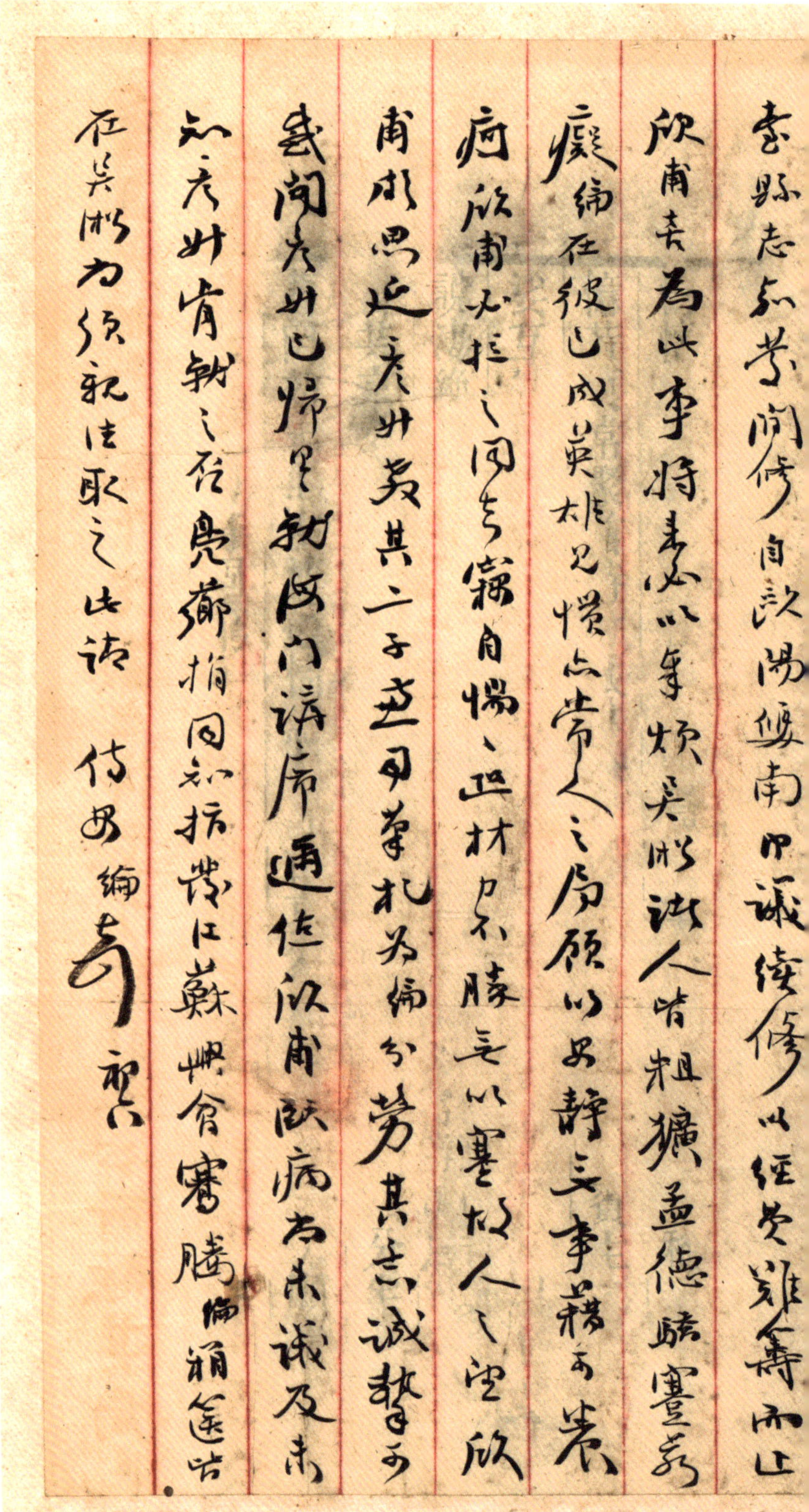

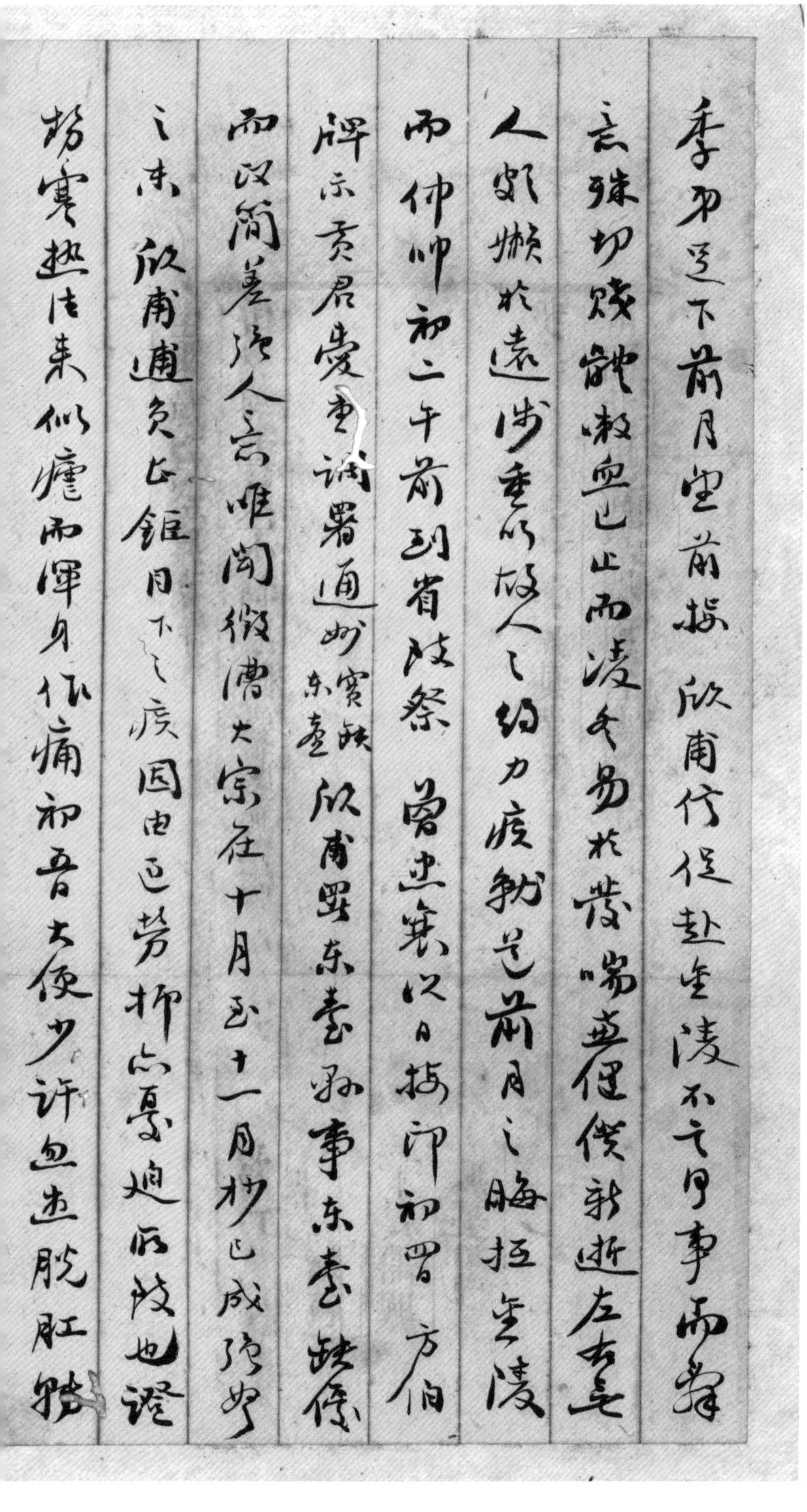

吴汝纶致张謇函。

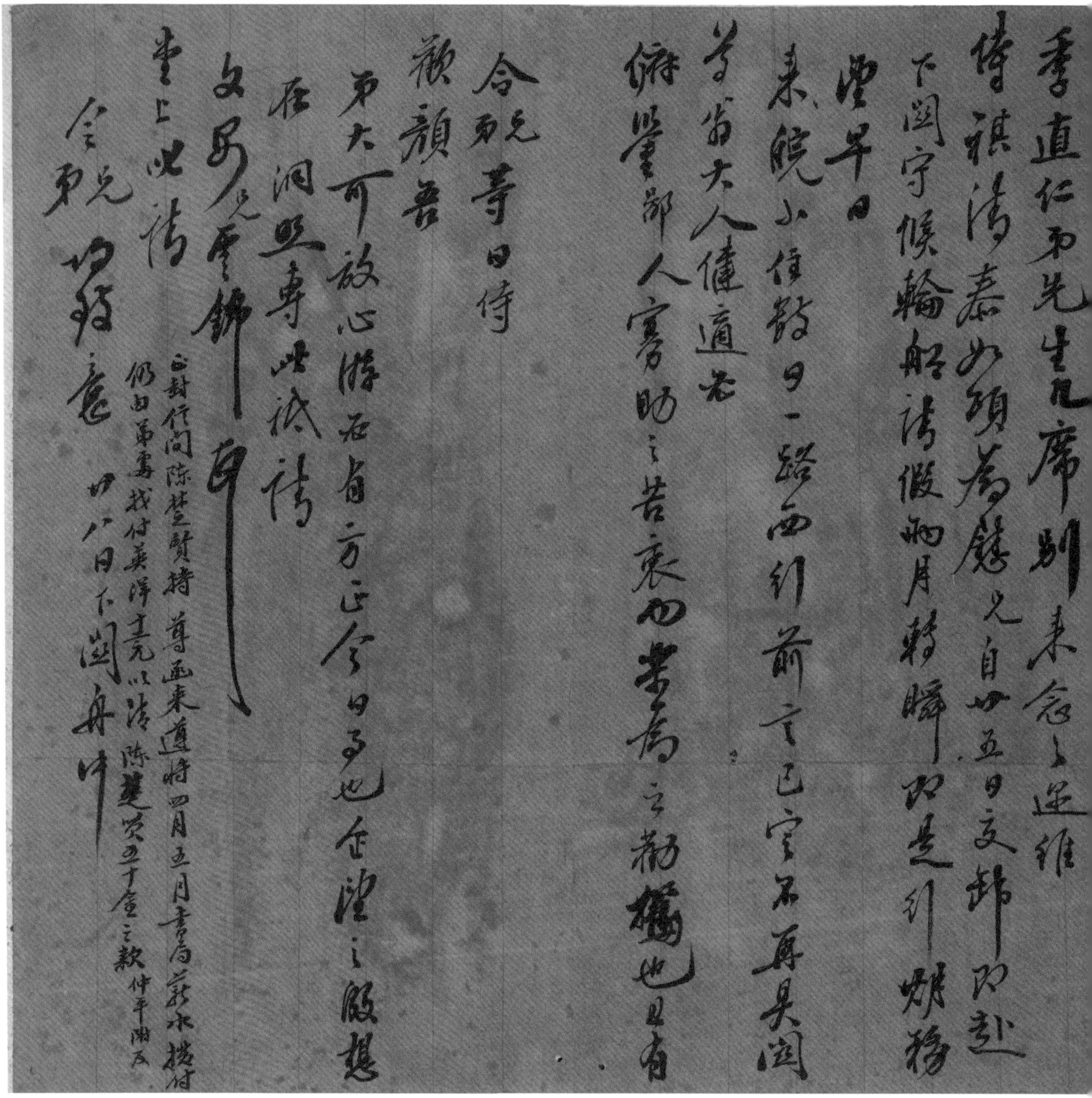

孙云锦致张謇函。

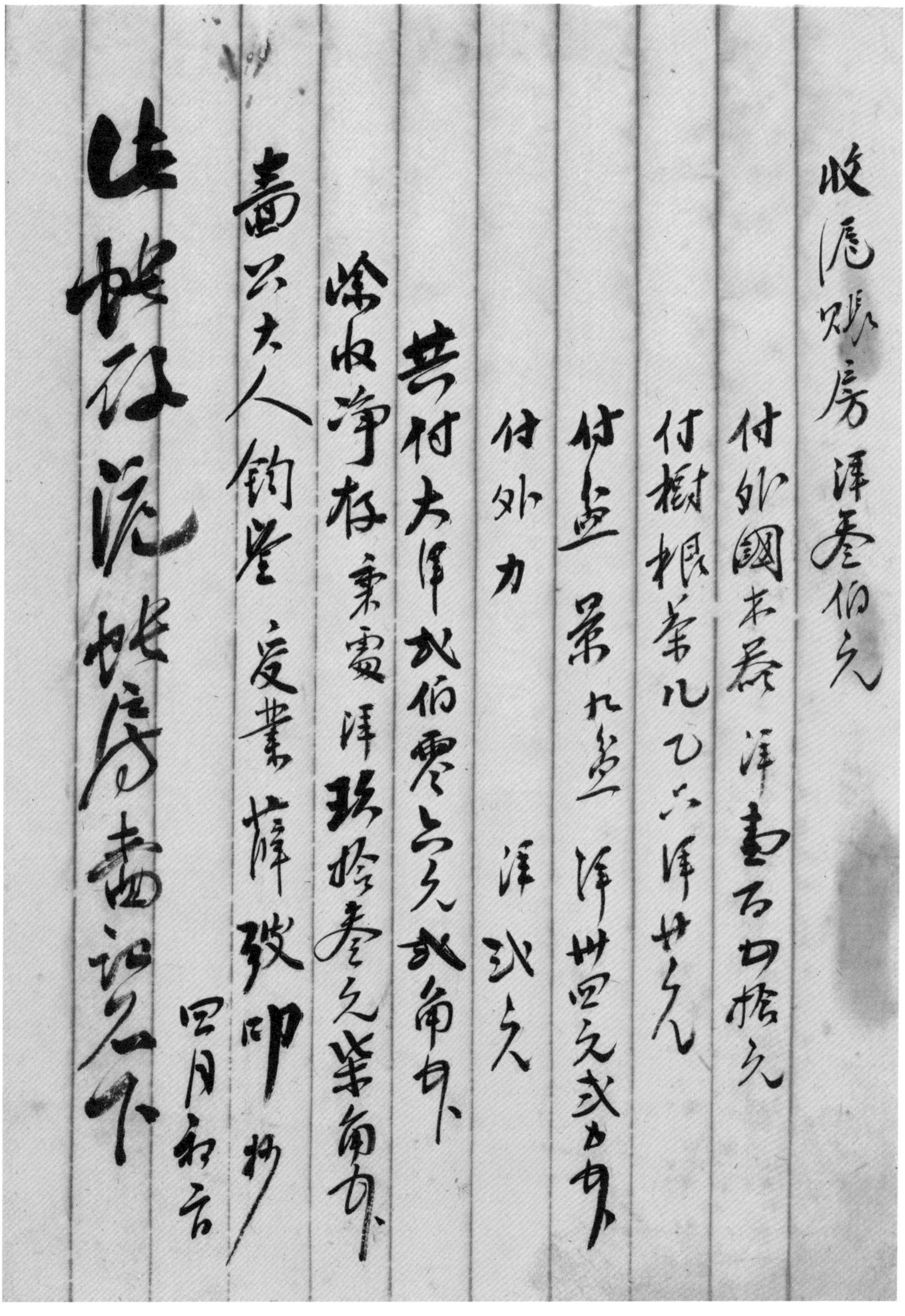

薛弢致张謇有关购物清单的函，张謇批注“此帐存沪帐房啬记名下”。

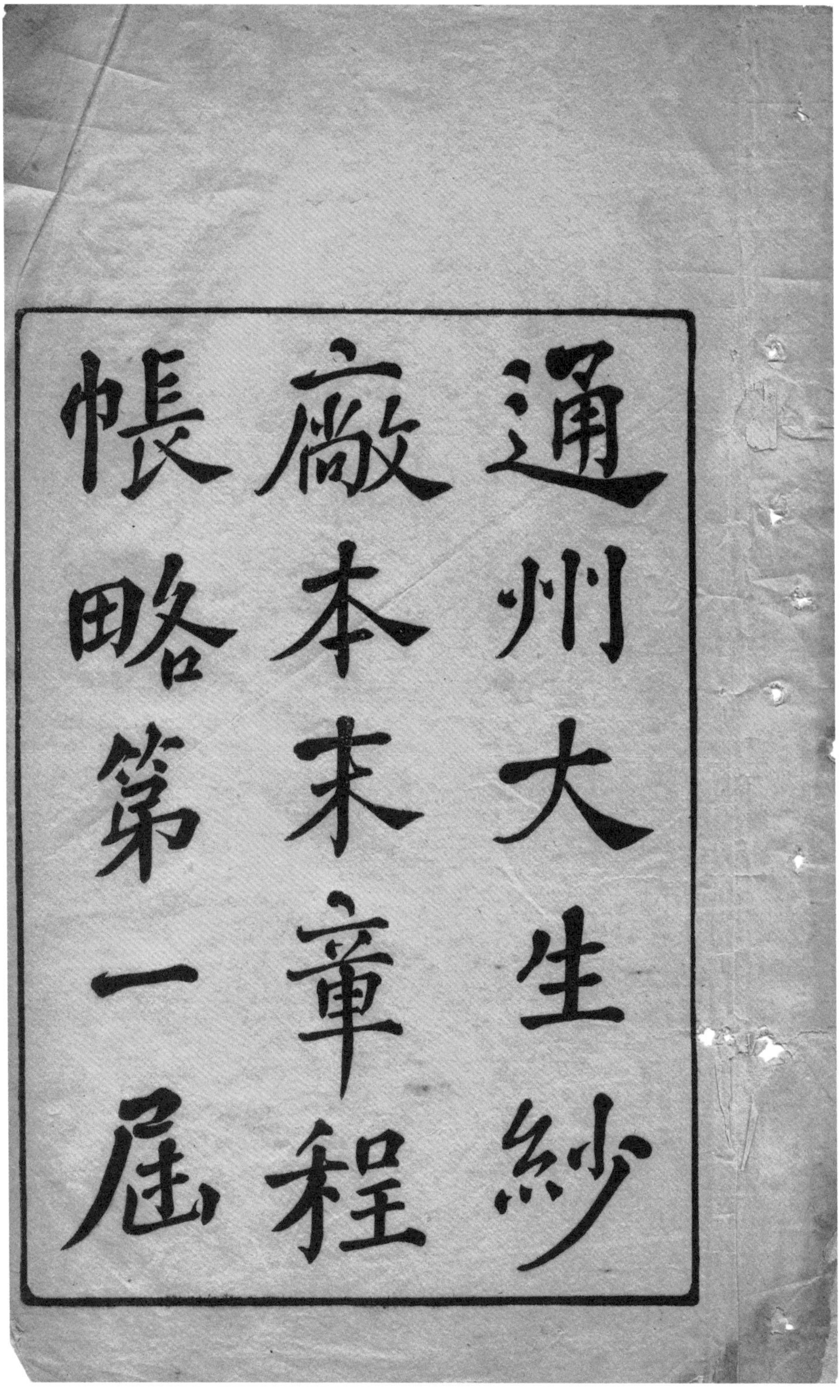
通州大生紗
廠本末章程
帳略第一屆

《通州大生纱厂本末章程帐略（第一届）》收录大生纱厂早期的文献，包括《厂约》。

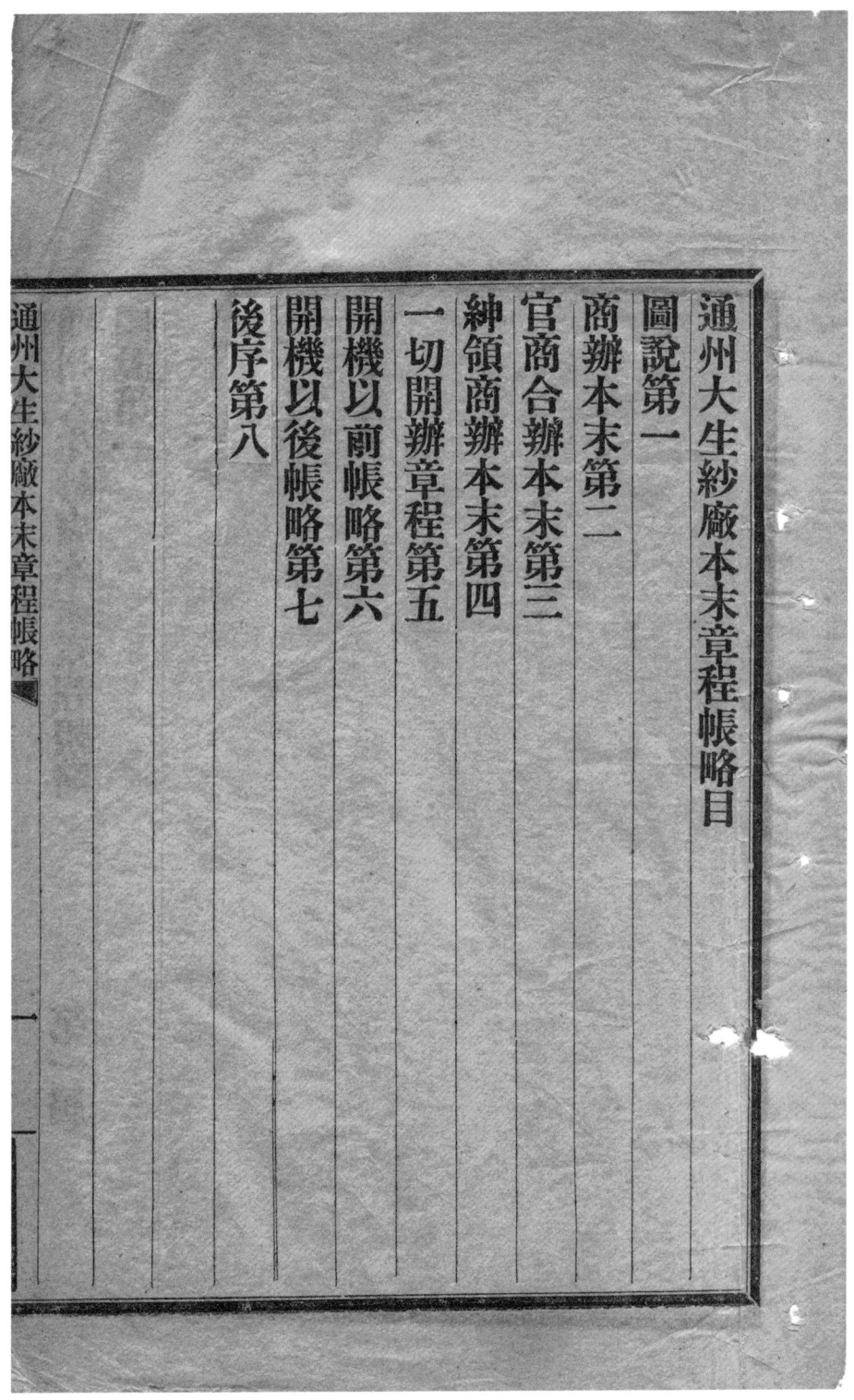

通州大生紗廠本末章程帳略目

至二十五年四月火食津貼川貲訊力雜費及洋匠酬勞火食等項共用二萬餘兩今詳細通盤核算分類剔清開辦經費實止用規元銀一萬四千四百九十四兩五錢三分九釐合并聲明須至咨呈者

一切開辦章程第五

廠約

通州之設紗廠爲通州民生計亦即爲中國利源計通產之棉力韌絲長冠絕亞洲爲日廠之所必需花往紗來日盛一日捐我之產以資人人即用資於我之貨以售我無異瀝血肥虎而袒肉以繼之利之不保我民日貧國於何賴下走寸心不死稍有知覺不忍並蹈於淪胥是以二十一年冬南皮督部既 奏

入儲賣紗之款出供買花之款備給工料備支雜務籌調匯畫稽查報單考核用度管理股票公文函牘接應賓客銀錢帳目董事之事也銀錢帳目執事之功過皆其功過董事執事皆住總辦事處每月月終彙記各執事之功過每四禮拜彙記花紗出入盈虧之細數單年終核明結總開具清摺另刋帳略分別咨商務局寄各股東

進貨出貨有通有滬事重而繁舉正董一人駐滬幫董一人廠工雜務銀錢帳目各舉董一人可省之日酌量省併

凡行廠及各帳房棧所應如何明定章程便於辦事便於查察由各董詳思博采與各執事約各執事詳思博采自爲約擬約核定書揭於版懸各處所此後或有續議變通更改之條隨時擬開核定再行

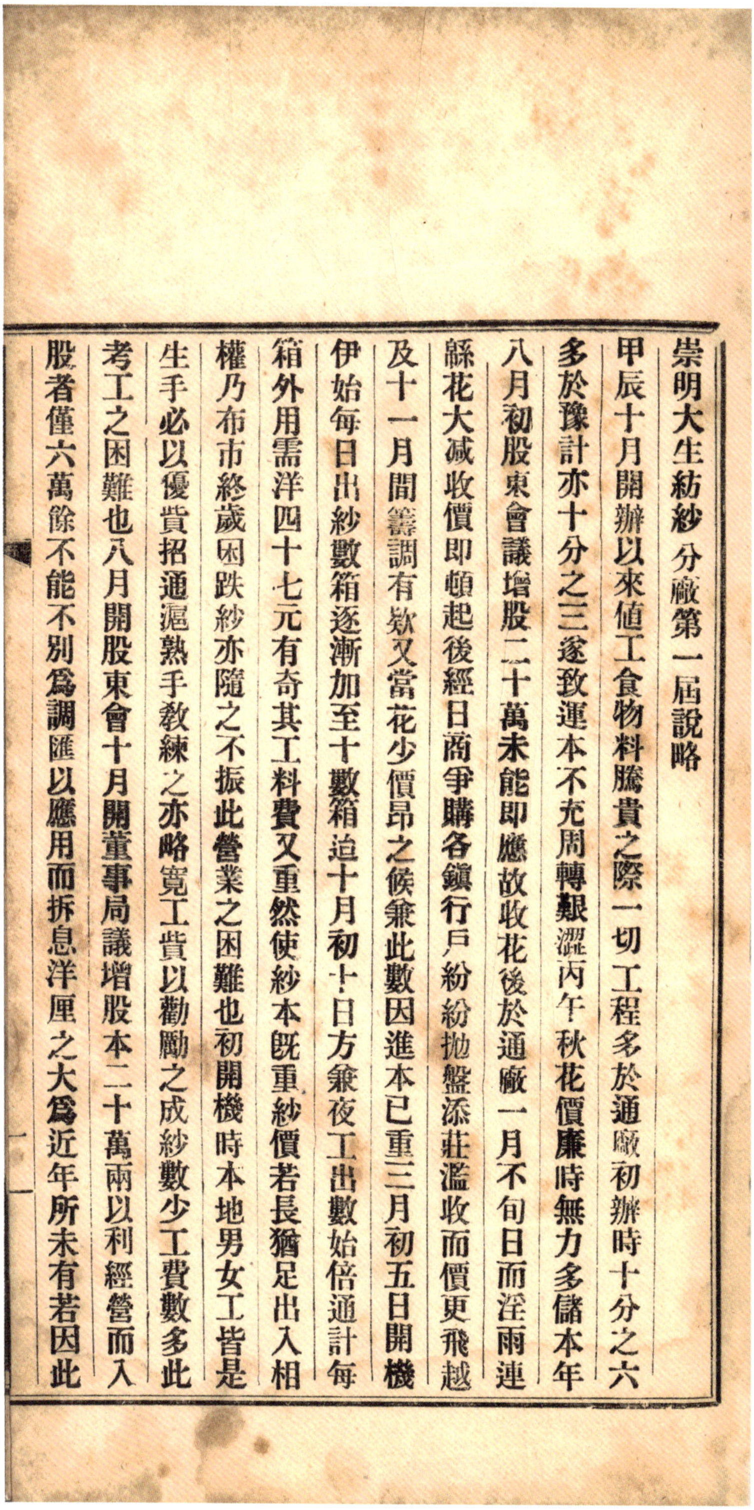
崇明大生紡紗分廠第一屆說略

甲辰十月開辦以來値工食物料騰貴之際一切工程多於通廠初辦時十分之六多於豫計亦十分之三遂致運本不充周轉艱澀丙午秋花價廉時無力多儲本年八月初股東會議增股二十萬未能即應故收花後於通廠一月不旬日而淫雨連緜花大減收價即頓起後經日商爭購各鎭行戶紛紛抛盤添莊濫收而價更飛越及十一月間籌調有欵又當花少價昂之候兼此數因進本已重三月初五日開機伊始每日出紗數箱逐漸加至十數箱迨十月初十日方兼夜工出數始倍通計每箱外用需洋四十七元有奇其工料費又重然使紗本既重紗價若長猶足出入相權乃布市終歲困跌紗亦隨之不振此營業之困難也初開機時本地男女工皆是生手必以優貲招通滬熟手教練之亦略寬工貲以勸勵之成紗數少工費數多此考工之困難也八月開股東會十月開董事局議增股本二十萬兩以利經營而入股者僅六萬餘不能不別爲調匯以應用而拆息洋厘之大爲近年所未有若因此

大生分厂第一届说略和帐略。

縮手不調則更非工商營業之法然求利實窘此會計之困難也具此三困難雖有
進花出紗回息各餘所得不足以償失凡本廠出入大概之可言者如此

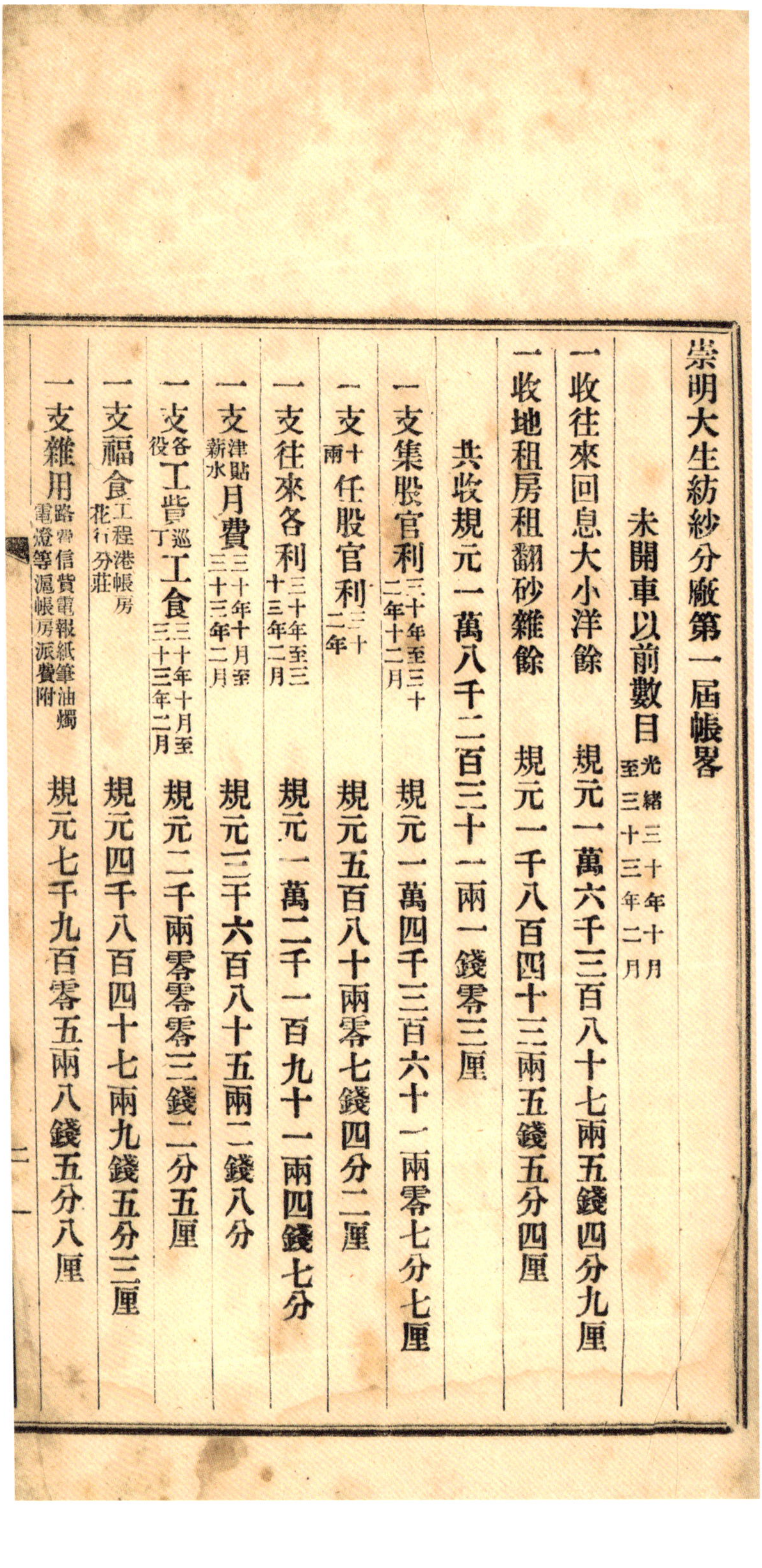

崇明大生紡紗分廠第一屆帳畧

未開車以前數目 光緒三十年十月至三十三年二月

一收往來回息大小洋餘 規元一萬六千三百八十七兩五錢四分九厘

一收地租房租翻砂雜餘 規元一千八百四十三兩五錢五分四厘

共收規元一萬八千二百三十一兩一錢零三厘

一支集股官利三十年至三十二年十二月 規元一萬四千三百六十一兩零七分七厘

一支十兩任股官利三十二年 規元五百八十兩零七錢四分二厘

一支往來各利三十年至三十三年二月 規元一萬二千一百九十一兩四錢七分

一支津貼薪水月費三十年十月至三十三年二月 規元三千六百八十五兩二錢八分

一支各役工資巡丁工食三十年十月至三十三年二月 規元二千兩零零零三錢二分五厘

一支福食工程港帳房花行分莊 規元四千八百四十七兩九錢五分三厘

一支雜用路費信資電報紙筆油燭電燈等滬帳房派費附 規元七千九百零五兩八錢五分八厘

二一

共支規元四萬五千五百七十二兩七錢零五厘

一續支集股官利（三十二年以前） 規元四萬九千零二十五兩二錢三分二厘

一續支（十兩）任股官利（三十二年） 規元三千六百零五兩零五分八厘

一續支集股官利（三十三年正二月） 規元八千一百二十六兩六錢六分七厘

一續支（十兩）任股官利（三十三年正二月） 規元八百三十八兩

一續支津貼（補酬章吳畬若君經董事局議准有案） 規元一千九百五十二兩六錢零四厘

一續支滬帳派拖駁費 規元五千六百五十五兩一錢五分

共續支規元六萬九千二百零二兩七錢一分一厘

以上兩抵淨支規元九萬六千五百四十四兩三錢一分三厘

開車以後數目（三十三年三月始）

一收進花出紗核餘 規元六萬八千零七十二兩六錢六分三厘

一收售飛花棉子餘 規元五千九百五十八兩三錢二分三厘

一收往來回息大小洋餘　規元四千七百六十三兩四錢八分八厘

一收地租房租翻砂雜餘　規元三千三百六十八兩三錢二分二厘

共收規元八萬二千一百六十二兩七錢九分六厘

一支集股官利（三月至十二月）　規元四萬零六百三十三兩三錢三分三厘

一支續股官利（三十三年）　規元一千三百九十九兩一錢二分六厘

一支（十兩）任股官利（三月至十二月）　規元四千一百九十兩

一支（廿兩）任股官利（三月至十二月）　規元八千三百二十九兩九錢一分七厘

一支往來調滙利　規元二萬六千六百五十六兩四錢七分二厘

一支花紗釐捐　規元一萬二千一百四十八兩九錢五分

一支修理機器鐵件　規元六百零三兩五錢八分九厘

一支煤斤物料　規元三萬四千七百零三兩四錢五分四厘

一支機匠（男女大小）工費　規元三萬七千五百九十三兩三錢一分二厘

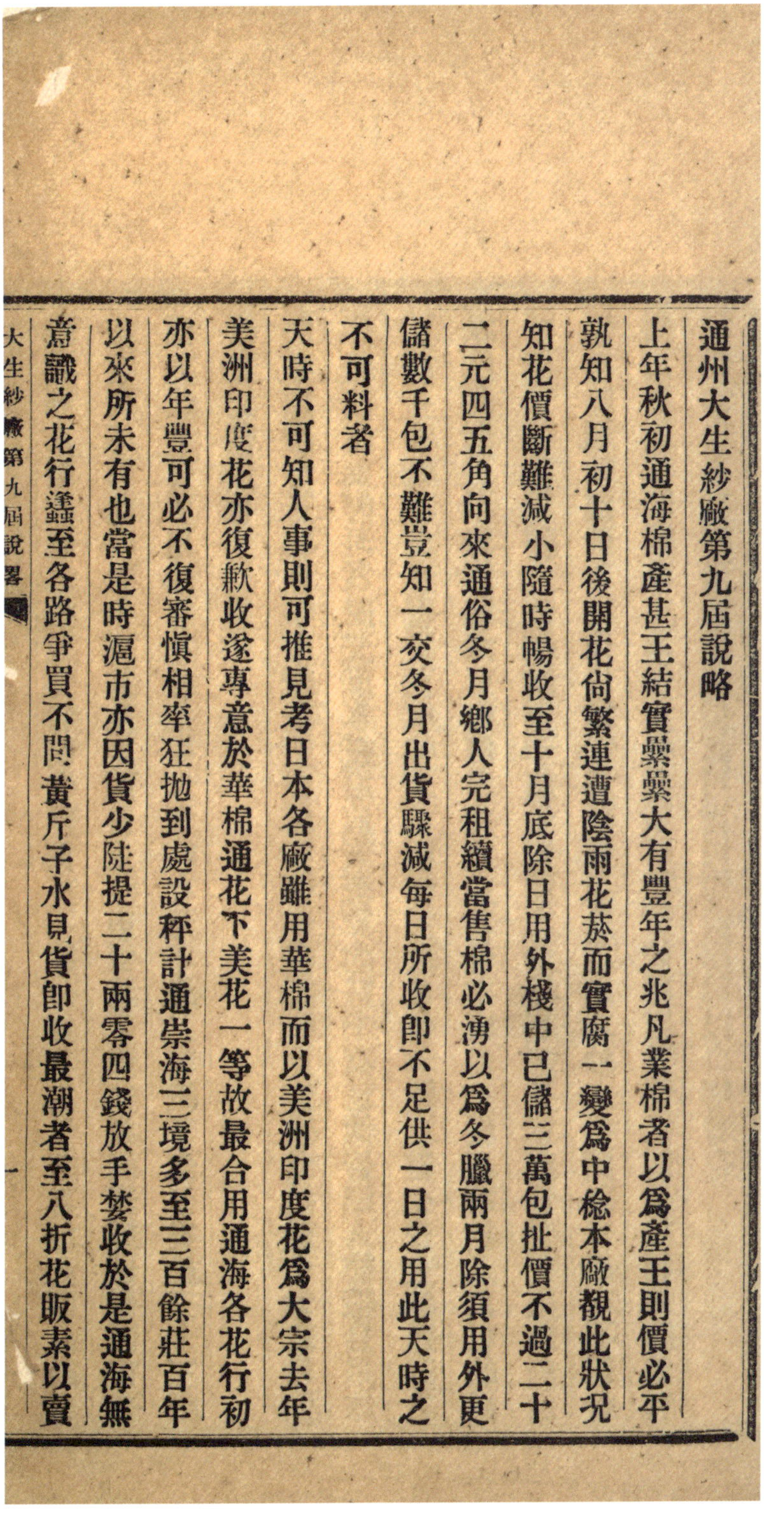

通州大生紗廠第九屆說略

上年秋初通海棉產甚王結實纍纍大有豐年之兆凡業棉者以爲產王則價必平孰知八月初十日後開花尙繁連遭陰雨花菸而實腐一變爲中稔本廠覩此狀況知花價斷難減小隨時暢收至十月底除日用外棧中已儲三萬包扯價不過二十二元四五角向來通俗冬月鄉人完租續當售棉必湧以爲冬臘兩月除須用外更儲數千包不難豈知一交冬月出貨驟減每日所收即不足供一日之用此天時之不可料者

天時不可知人事則可推見考日本各廠雖用華棉而以美洲印度花爲大宗去年美洲印度花亦復歉收遂專意於華棉通花下美花一等故最合用通海各花行初亦以年豐可必不復審愼相率狂抛到處設秤計通崇海三境多至三百餘莊百年以來所未有也當是時滬市亦因貨少陡提二十兩零四錢放手婪收於是通海無意識之花行蠭至各路爭買不問黃斤子水見貨卽收最潮者至八折花販素以賣

大生紗廠第九屆說畧　一

大生纱厂第九届说略。

潮爲利本廠收花之價較他行明大兩圓亦不願以好花來售若再加大則牽於布市有所不可此時軋手更甚及至臘月上海市面雖平無如通海底貨已稀門市來源更絀逐日所用惟有在棧抽提年底結存乃不過二萬四千餘包矣此三十三年營業之情形也

向來通崇海三境每年由新花上市起至明年接新時止運滬者約計十六萬包此外運往山東內河者四五萬本廠用八萬統計約三十萬包餘皆鄉人紡織自用故凡前一年廠花或未辦足至次年二月開秤三數萬包不難收辦今查上年運滬之花已共到三十萬包運山東內河者約二三萬包本廠與分廠所收約八萬包總計已四十一萬包較之往年溢出十萬包底貨之少已可想見本廠尚需花兩萬餘包惟有陸續補進營業所長自當妥爲籌畫至於所出之紗去年因營口布市不振紗無去路而花既難收成本較大紗益不可積滯故議以貶價抵制外紗倒灌雖無利可餘亦尚不至因積滯而虧損此可比例他廠而稍以自解者也

修機項下上屆較往歲多支而本屆所添配之機件較上屆尤多蓋官機未歸大生廠時堆擱漚灘日久本非新機可比鋼絲布螺軔等物易於損壞隨壞隨脩支欵甚巨

老新兩廠之地板上經磨擦損闕下受汽濕腐爛屋面之青鉛及墻壁亦多剝損故本屆修理費較上屆更多

七月二十三日股東會前刊印之帳收欵是照七月十五日停機之日爲止開支是按上半年六個月核算且此時折舊退隱費等之名目尚無故特列表以明界畫仍復折舊第一次會場議決退隱及總理公費五所長薪水是八月初六日董事局議決均見議事錄及議案

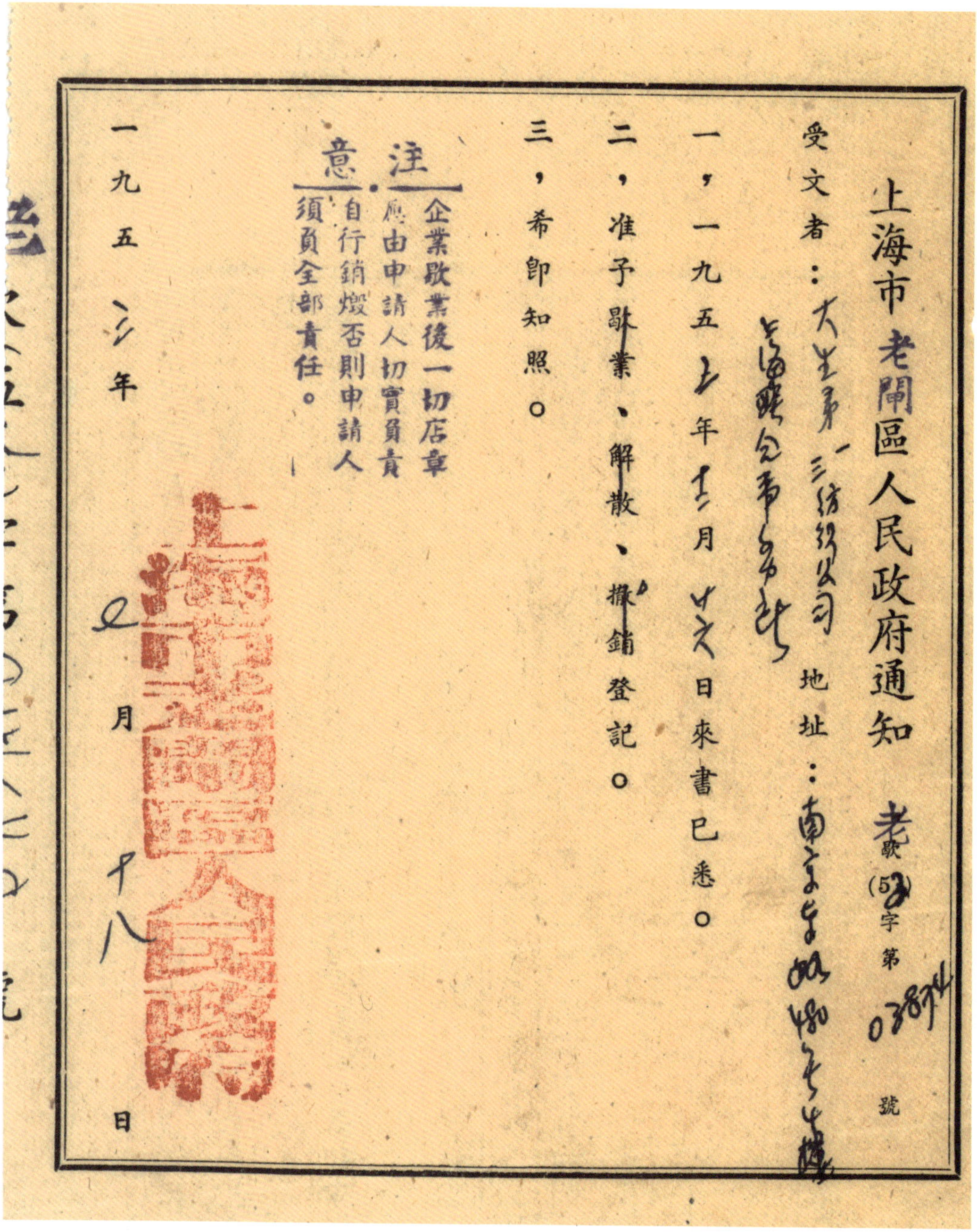

上海市老閘區人民政府通知

老歇（53）字第[illegible]號

受文者：大生第一、三紡織公司上海聯合事務所　地址：南京東路[illegible]

一、一九五三年七月十六日來書已悉。

二、准予歇業、解散、撤銷登記。

三、希即知照。

注意：企業歇業後一切店章應由申請人切實負責自行銷燬否則申請人須負全部責任。

上海市老閘區人民政府

一九五三年七月十八日

1953 年 7 月 18 日上海市老闸区人民政府同意大生第一、第三纺织公司上海联合事务所（大生沪所）撤销的通知。

1953 年大生档案从上海回归南通，存放于大生纱厂公事厅。

滬所文卷目錄
一九五三年九月

1953 年 9 月，大生档案初步整理后形成的《沪所文卷目录》(局部)。

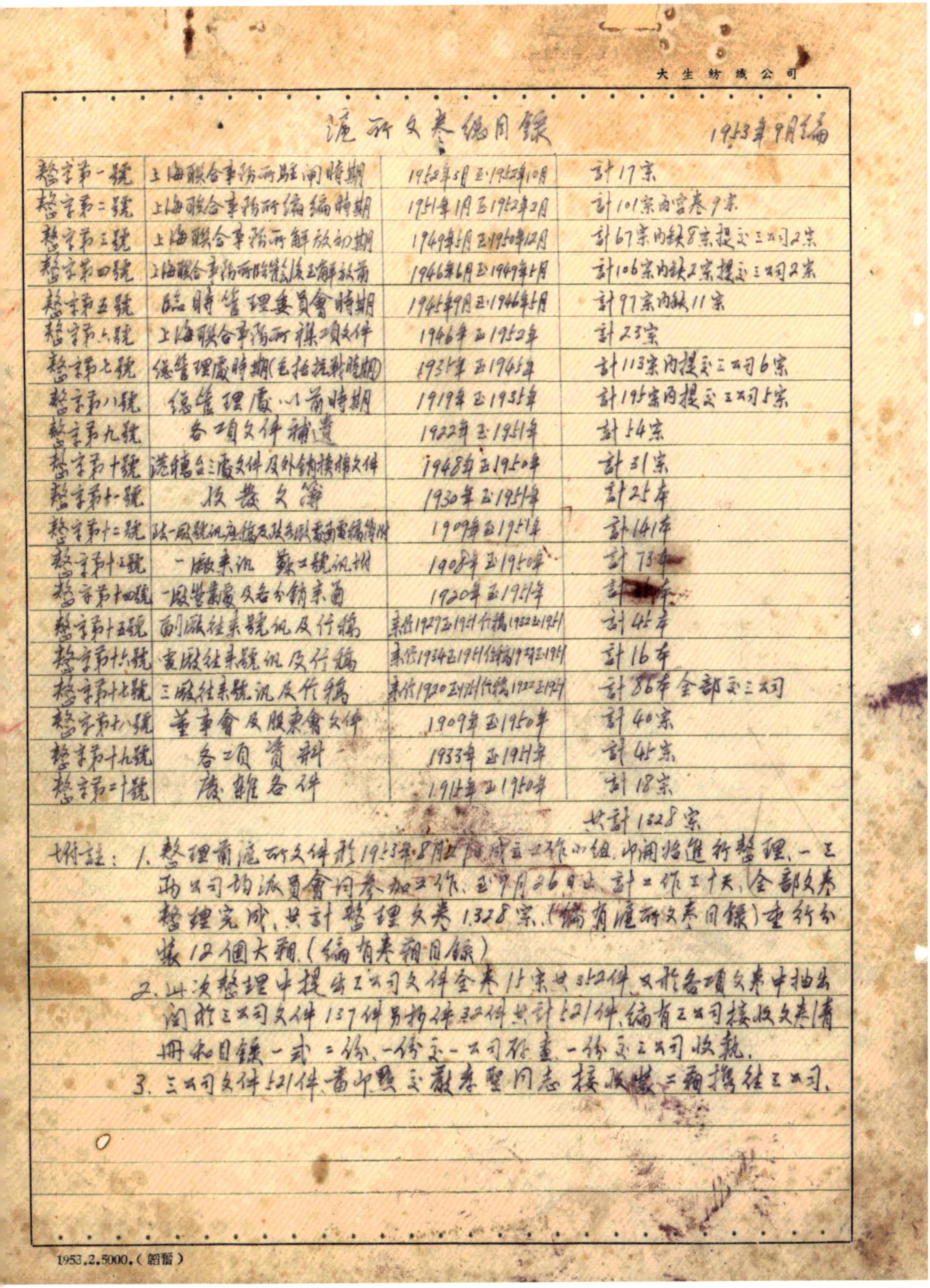

大生紡織公司

滬所文卷總目錄　　1953年9月編

整字第一號	上海聯合事務所駐滬時期	1952年5月至1952年10月	計17宗
整字第二號	上海聯合事務所統編時期	1951年1月至1952年2月	計101宗內密卷9宗
整字第三號	上海聯合事務所解放初期	1949年5月至1950年12月	計67宗內缺8宗提交三公司2宗
整字第四號	上海聯合事務所勝利後至解放前	1946年6月至1949年5月	計106宗內缺2宗提交三公司2宗
整字第五號	臨時管理委員會時期	1945年9月至1946年5月	計97宗內缺11宗
整字第六號	上海聯合事務所雜項文件	1946年至1952年	計23宗
整字第七號	總管理處時期（包括抗戰時期）	1935年至1945年	計113宗內提交三公司6宗
整字第八號	總管理處以前時期	1919年至1935年	計195宗內提交三公司5宗
整字第九號	各項文件補遺	1922年至1951年	計54宗
整字第十號	滬總台三處文件及外銷積欠文件	1948年至1950年	計31宗
整字第十一號	收發文簿	1930年至1951年	計25本
整字第十二號	致一廠號訊底稿及致各廠處函電稿簿冊	1909年至1951年	計141本
整字第十三號	一廠來訊　蘇廠號訊冊	1908年至1950年	計73本
整字第十四號	一廠營業處及各分銷來函	1920年至1951年	計[illegible]本
整字第十五號	副廠往來號訊及底稿	來信1927至1951 底稿1932至1951	計45本
整字第十六號	實廠往來號訊及底稿	來信1934至1951 底稿1932至1951	計16本
整字第十七號	三廠往來號訊及底稿	來信1920至1951 底稿1922至1951	計86本全部交三公司
整字第十八號	董事會及股東會文件	1909年至1950年	計40宗
整字第十九號	各項資料	1933年至1951年	計45宗
整字第二十號	廢雜各件	1915年至1950年	計18宗

共計1328宗

附註：1. 整理前滬所文件於1953年8月2?日成立工作小組，即開始進行整理，一、三兩公司均派員會同參加工作，至9月26日止，計工作五十天，全部文卷整理完成，共計整理文卷1328宗，（編有滬所文卷目錄）重行分裝12個大箱（編有卷箱目錄）。

2. 此次整理中提出三公司文件全卷15宗共352件，又於各項文卷中抽出關於三公司文件137件，另抄件32件，共計521件，編有三公司接收文卷清冊和目錄一式二份，一份交一公司存查，一份交三公司收執。

3. 三公司文件521件當即點交嚴孝豐同志接收，裝二箱攜往三公司。

1953.2.5000.（紹晉）

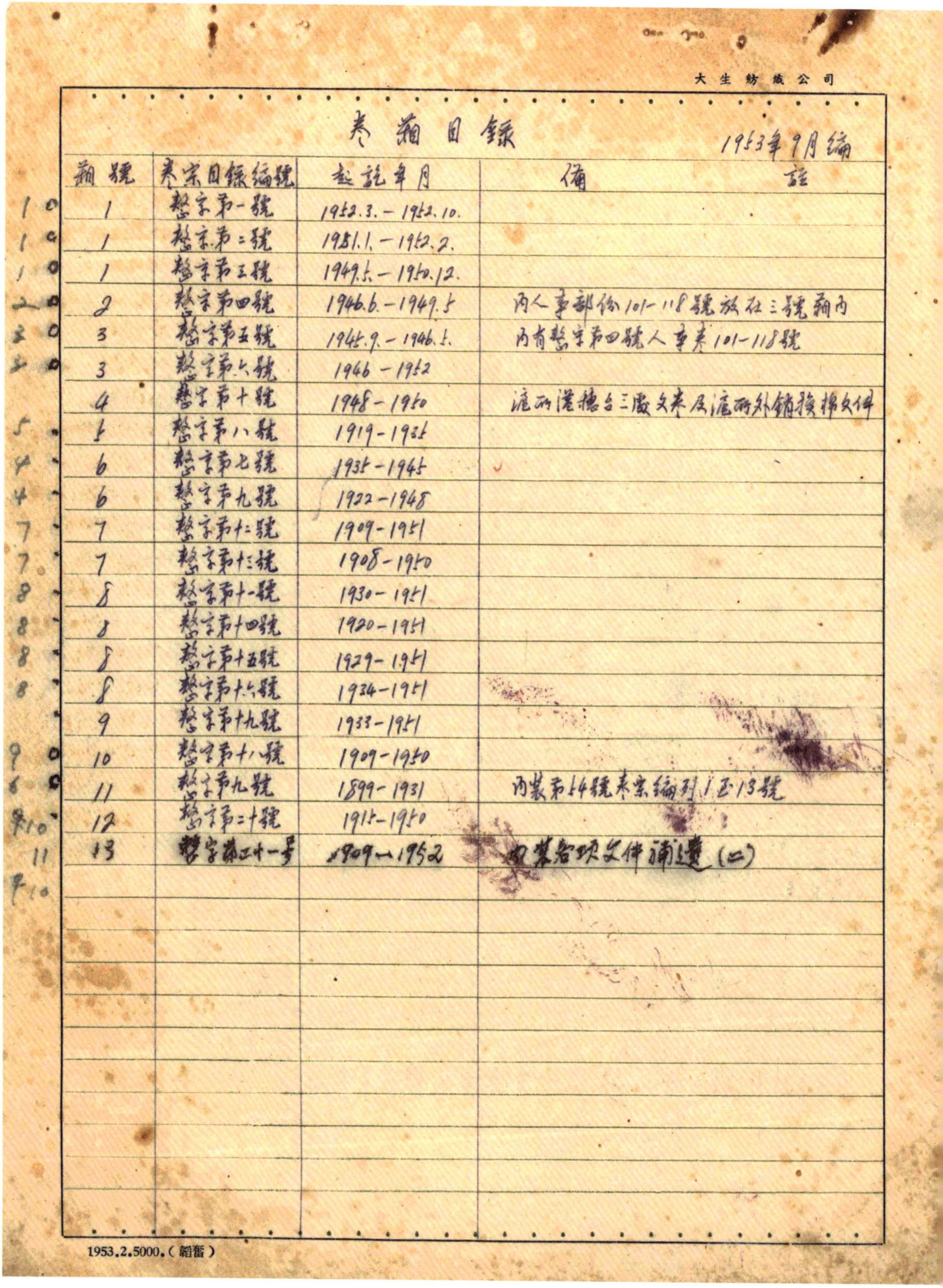

大生紡織公司

卷箱目錄　　　1953年9月編

箱號	卷宗目錄編號	起訖年月	備註
1	整字第一號	1952.3.－1952.10.	
1	整字第二號	1951.1.－1952.2.	
1	整字第三號	1949.5－1950.12.	
2	整字第四號	1946.6.－1949.5	內人事部份101－118號放在三號箱內
3	整字第五號	1945.9.－1946.5.	內有整字第四號人事類101－118號
3	整字第六號	1946－1952	
4	整字第十號	1948－1950	滬所灌穗台三廠文卷及滬所外銷換棉文件
5	整字第八號	1919－1935	
6	整字第七號	1935－1945	
6	整字第九號	1922－1948	
7	整字第十二號	1909－1951	
7	整字第十三號	1908－1950	
8	整字第十一號	1930－1951	
8	整字第十四號	1920－1951	
8	整字第十五號	1929－1951	
8	整字第十六號	1934－1951	
9	整字第十九號	1933－1951	
10	整字第十八號	1909－1950	
11	整字第九號	1899－1931	內裝第54號卷宗編列1至13號
12	整字第二十號	1915－1950	
13	整字第二十一号	1909－1952	內幕名映文件補遺（二）

1953.2.5000.（縮舊）

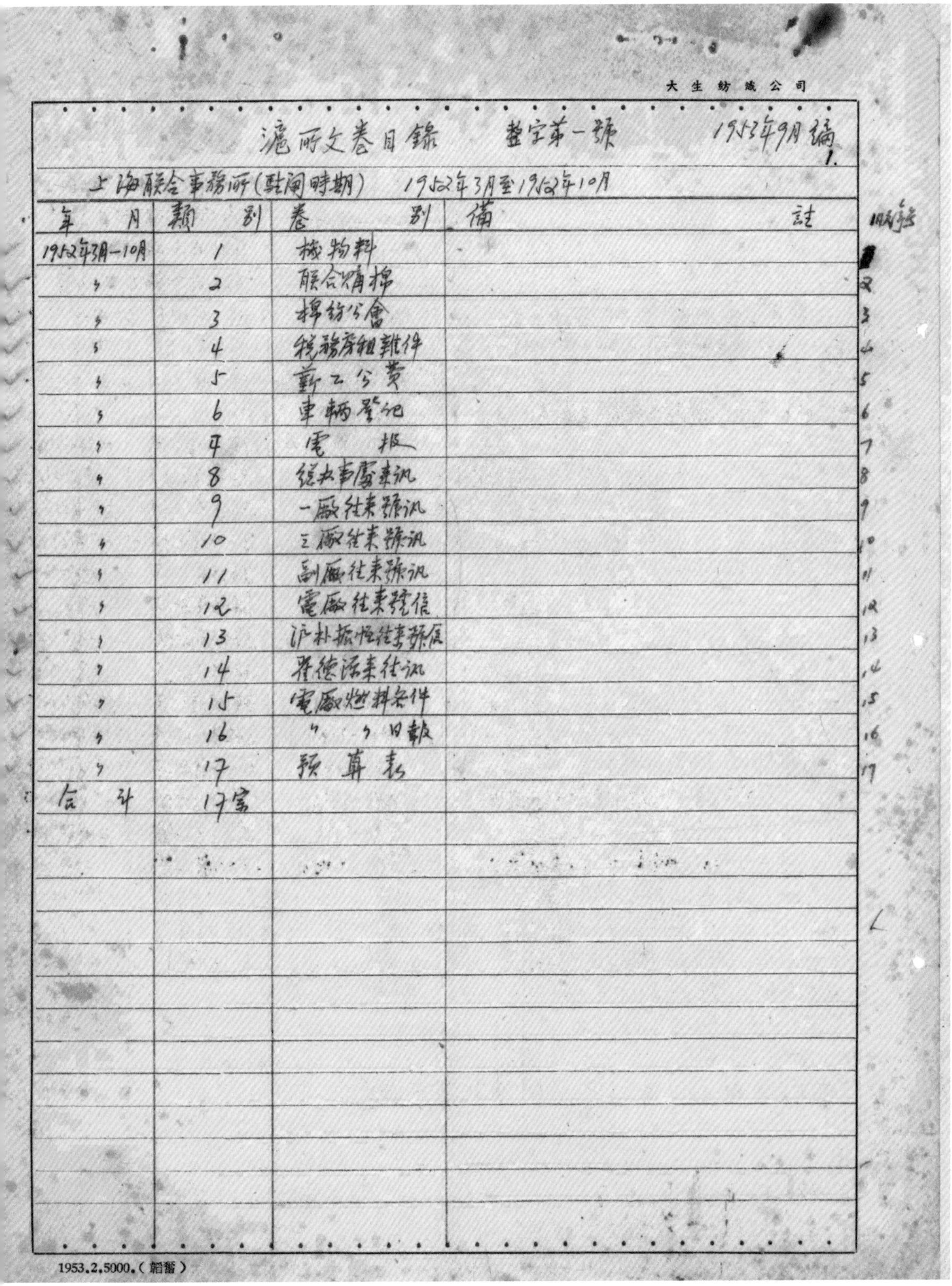

大生紡織公司

滬所文卷目錄　整字第一號　1953年9月編

1.

上海聯合事務所（駐滬時期）　1952年3月至1952年10月

年　月	類　別	卷　別	備　註
1952年3月—10月	1	機物料	
〃	2	聯合購棉	
〃	3	棉紡公會	
〃	4	稅務房租雜件	
〃	5	薪工公費	
〃	6	車輛登記	
〃	7	電　報	
〃	8	總辦事處來訊	
〃	9	一廠往來號訊	
〃	10	三廠往來號訊	
〃	11	副廠往來號訊	
〃	12	電廠往來號信	
〃	13	滬杭振恆往來號信	
〃	14	群德源來往訊	
〃	15	電廠燃料各件	
〃	16	〃 〃 日報	
〃	17	預算表	
合計	17宗		

1953.2.5000.（韜奮）

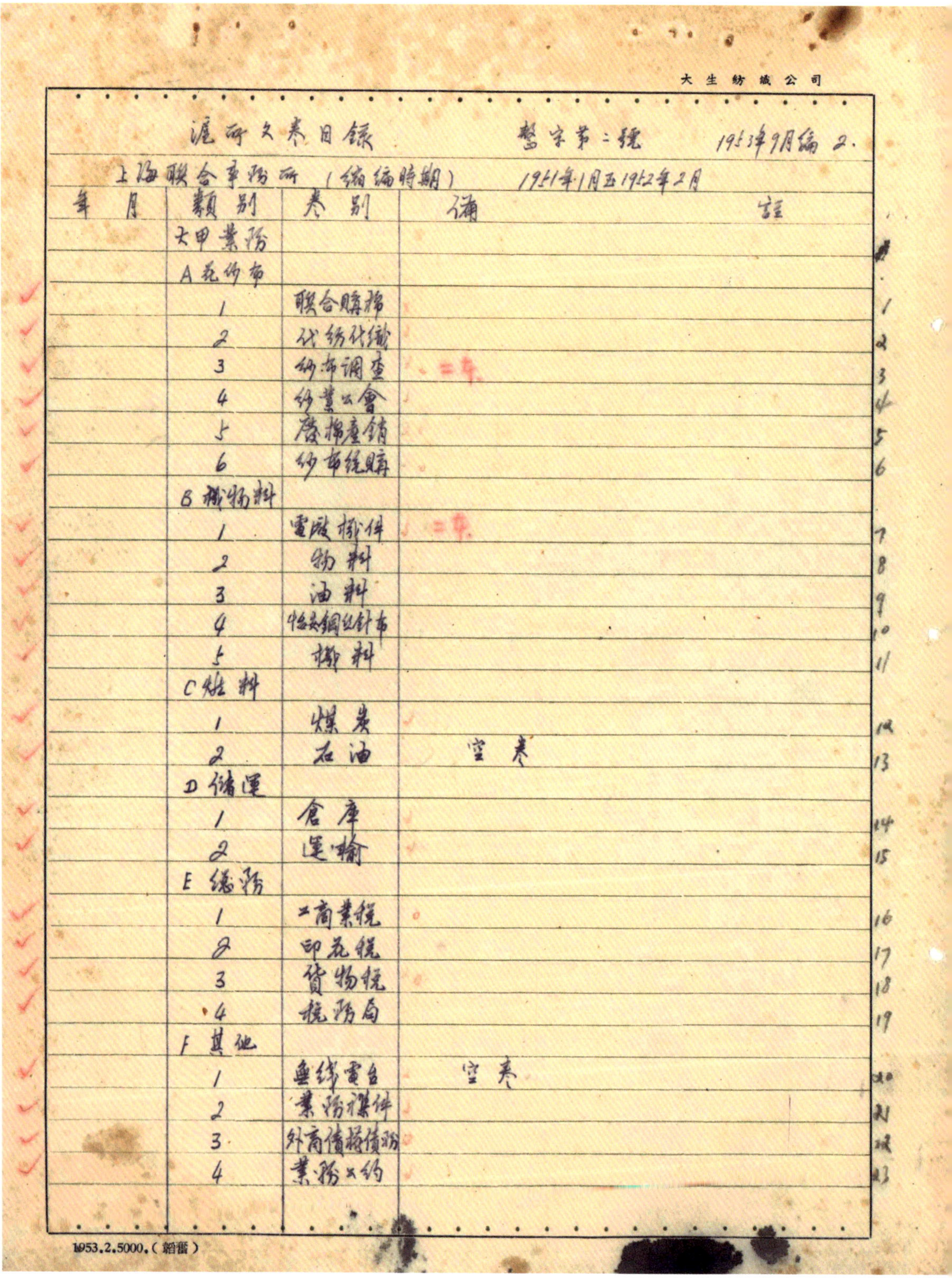

大生紡織公司

滬所文卷目錄　　整字第二號　　1953年9月編 2.

上海联合事務所（結編時期）　1951年1月至1952年2月

	年月	類别	卷别	備註	
		甲業務			
		A 花紗布			
✓		1	聯合購棉		1
✓		2	代紡代織		2
✓		3	紗布調查	二本	3
✓		4	紗業公會		4
✓		5	廢棉產銷		5
✓		6	紗布統購		6
		B 機物料			
✓		1	電廠機件	二本	7
✓		2	物料		8
✓		3	油料		9
✓		4	帆布鋼絲針布		10
✓		5	機料		11
		C 燃料			
✓		1	煤炭		12
✓		2	石油	空卷	13
		D 儲運			
✓		1	倉庫		14
✓		2	運輸		15
		E 稅務			
✓		1	工商業稅		16
✓		2	印花稅		17
✓		3	貨物稅		18
✓		4	稅務局		19
		F 其他			
✓		1	無線電台	空卷	20
✓		2	業務雜件		21
✓		3	外商債權債務		22
✓		4	業務契約		23

1953.2.5000.（韜奮）

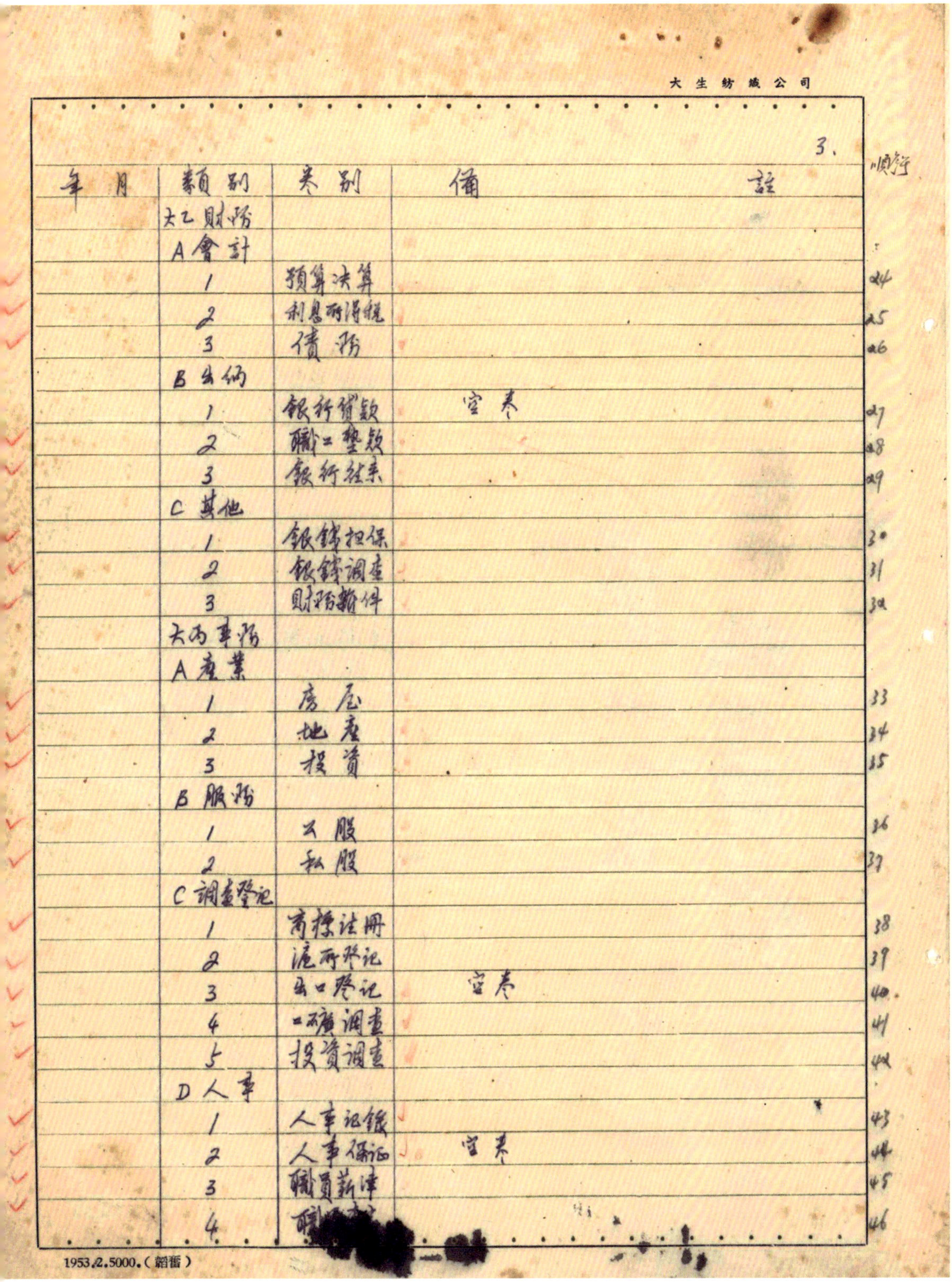
大生紡織公司

3、

年月	類別	類別	備註	順序
	大乙 財務			
	A 會計			
	1	預算決算		24
	2	利息所得税		25
	3	債務		26
	B 出納			
	1	銀行貸款	空卷	27
	2	職工墊款		28
	3	銀行往來		29
	C 其他			
	1	銀錢担保		30
	2	銀錢調查		31
	3	財務雜件		32
	大丙 事務			
	A 產業			
	1	房屋		33
	2	地產		34
	3	投資		35
	B 股務			
	1	公股		36
	2	私股		37
	C 調查登記			
	1	商標註冊		38
	2	滬所登記		39
	3	出口登記	空卷	40
	4	工礦調查		41
	5	投資調查		42
	D 人事			
	1	人事記錄		43
	2	人事保證	空卷	44
	3	職員薪津		45
	4	職[illegible]		46

1953.2.5000.（紹番）

大生紡織公司

4

年月	類別	类别	備註	
	5	工友工資		47
	6	工友車宿		48
	7	職工值班		49
	8	職工假曠		50
	9	職工獎金		51
	10	職工福利		52
	11	醫藥津貼		53
	12	救濟金		54
	13	工會經費		55
	14	人事雜件		56
	15	勞動保險		57
	16	職工退職養老補助金		58
	17	重估財產		59
	18	勞資協商會議		60
	E 號訊			
	1	通處號訊		61
	2	一廠來訊		62
	3	副廠來訊		63
	4	電廠來訊		64
	5	三廠來訊		65
	6	致通處訊		66
	7	致一廠訊		67
	8	致副廠訊		68
	9	致電廠訊		69
	10	致三廠訊		70
	F 電報			
	1	來電		71
	2	發電		72
	G 庶務			
	1	生財器具	空表 單冊另存	73
	2	房捐房租		74
	3	水電電話		75

1953.2.5000.（韜奮）

5.

年月	類別	卷別	備註	
	4	慈善募捐		76
	5	膳食		77
	6	宿舍		78
	H 其他			
	1	工商聯會	二本	79
	2	棉紡工會		80
	3	各級工會	空卷	81
	4	各項章則		82
	5	證明文件		83
	6	事務雜件	二本	84
	7	同業公會執監會		85
	8	同業公會專门委員會	廠務	86
	8	〃	計劃	87
	8	〃	組織	88
	8	〃	勞資	89
	8	〃	稅務	90
	8	〃	文教	91
	9	一公司計劃委員會		92
	10	工時改制		93
	生甲	股東會		
	A	名冊	冊存股務部门	94
	B	章程		95
	C	函件	空卷	96
	D	帳略	〃	97
	生乙	董監會		
	A	名冊		98
	B	章程		99
	C	函件		100
	D	議案		101
	E	工資		102
	F 1	清理公股公產		103
	F 2	整理股權		104

1953.2.5000.(韜奮)

大生紡織公司

6.

年月	類別	卷別	備註
	F 3	清估資產	105
	F 4	清估委員會	106
			共計 101 宗(内空卷9宗)

1953.2.5000.(韜奮)

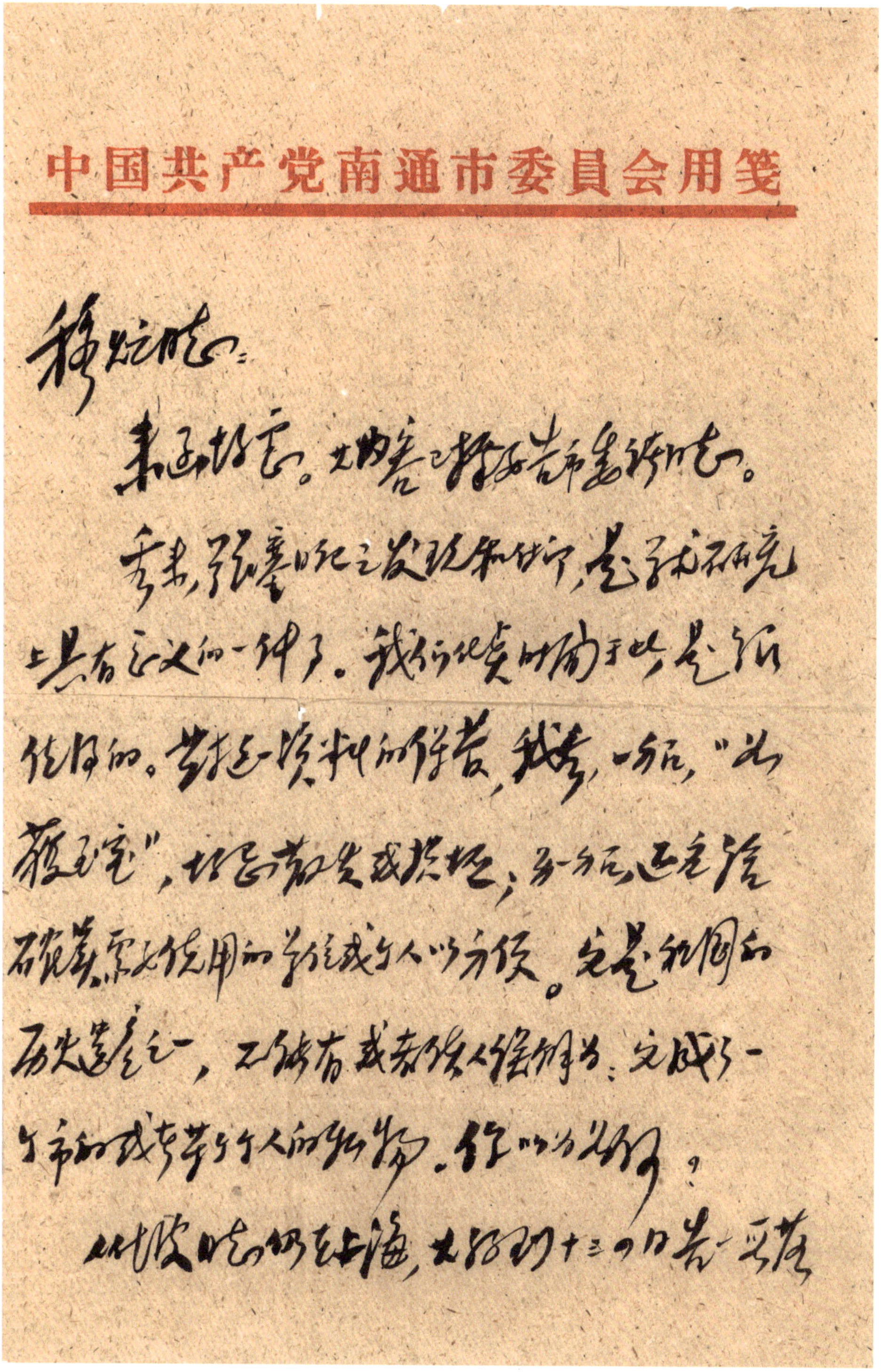
中国共产党南通市委员会用笺

1962 年 3 月 12 日南通市委秘书长朱剑致穆烜的函，涉及大生档案移交南通市档案馆事宜。

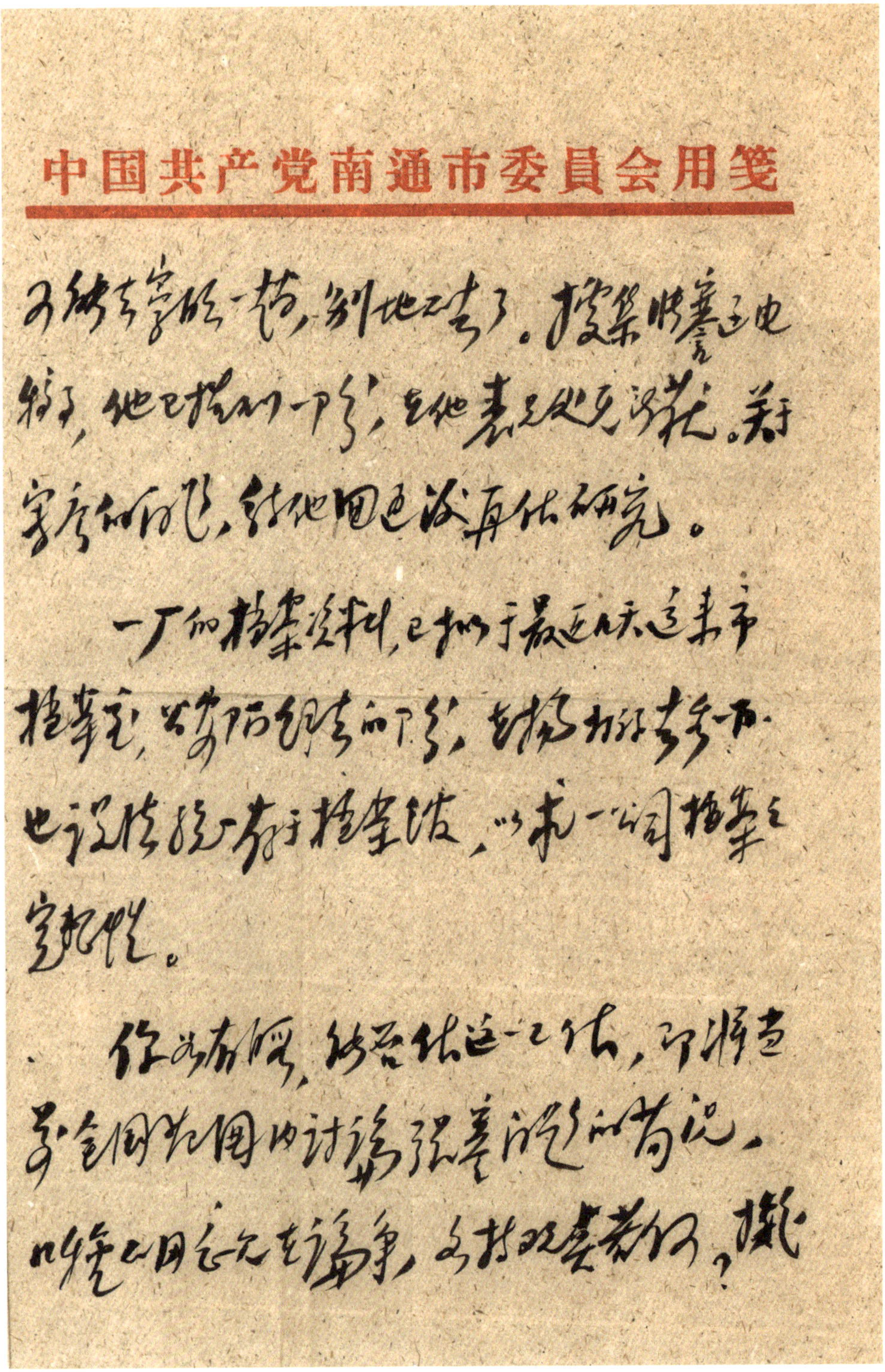

中国共产党南通市委员会用笺

不能去掌握一些，别地已去了。据梁怀謇之史稿，他已接到一部分，其他素之处更没有。关于家庭的问题，待他回通后再作研究。

一厂的档案资料，已于最近几天送来市档案室，此外随组传的一部分，已移打纺专学中，也设法接收存于档案馆，以求一定档案之完整性。

你如有暇，能否做这一工作，即将去年全国范围内讨论张謇问题的简况，以笔记用之文字之综合，不知能否赶得？撰

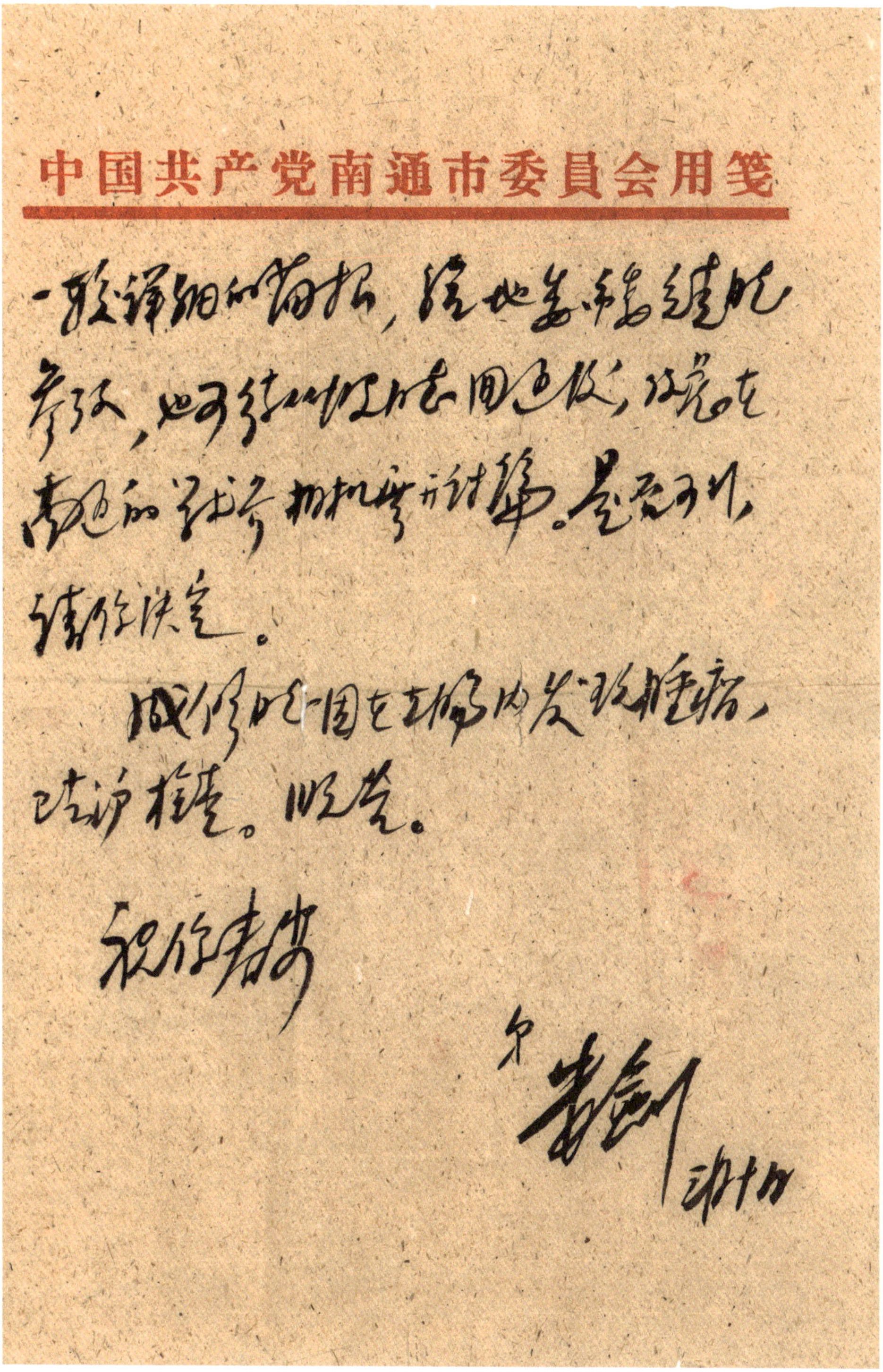

中国共产党南通市委员会用笺

一般详细的答复，请他每年编选建议参考，也可经以时候回通报，以免在南通的地方机关要计算。是否可以，请你决定。

我们此间在去年内发现张謇遗稿，已清理清楚。此覆。

祝你春安

弟 [illegible] [illegible]

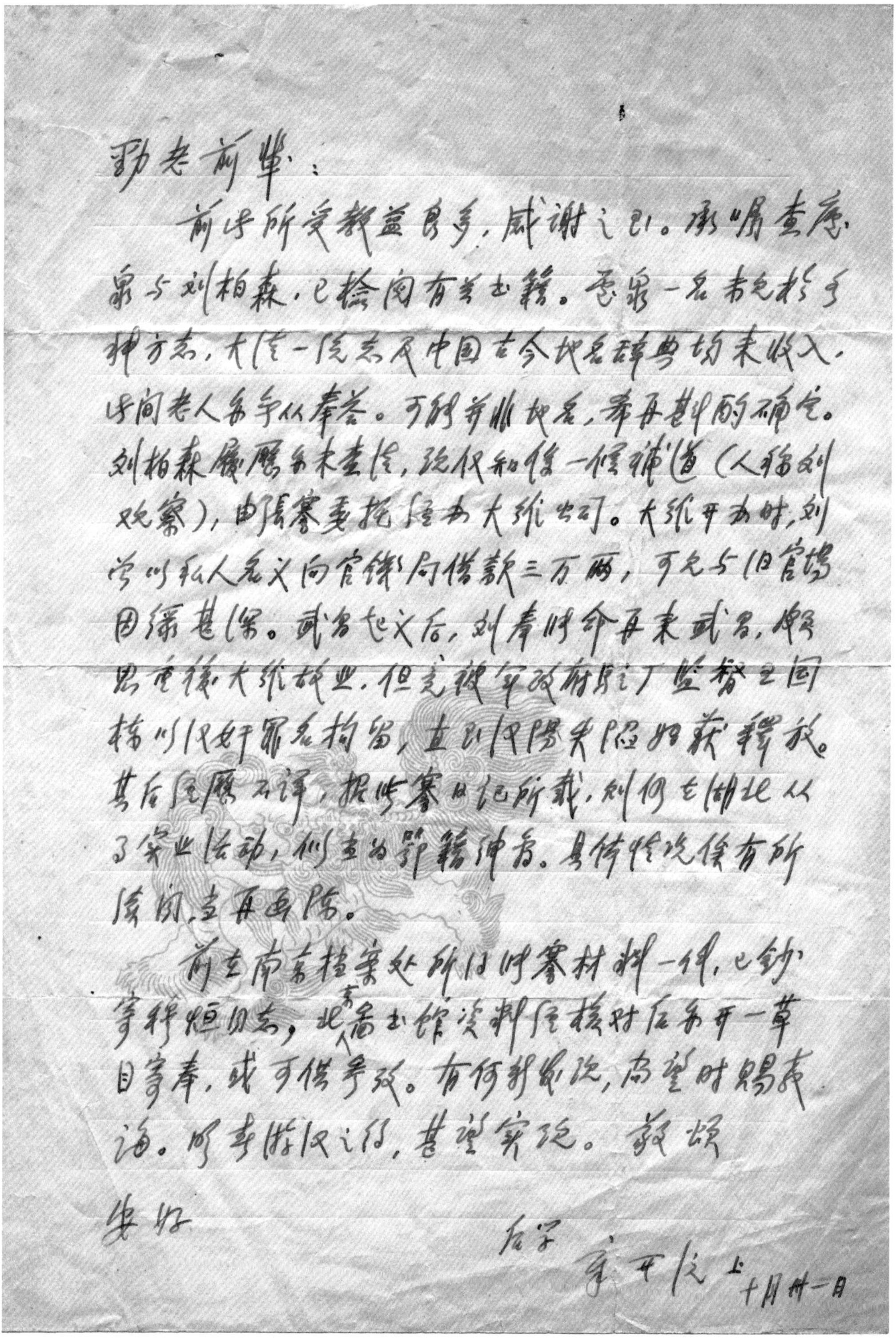
勁老前辈：

前时所受教益良多，感谢之至。承嘱查意象与刘柏森，已检阅有关书籍。意象一名未见于各种方志，大清一统志及中国古今地名辞典均未收入，此间老人亦无从奉答。可能并非地名，希再斟酌确定。刘柏森履历尚未查清，现仅知系一候补道（人称刘观察），由张謇委托经办大维公司。大维开办时，刘曾以私人名义向官钱局借款三万两，可见与旧官场因缘甚深。武昌起义后，刘奉时命再来武昌，思重振大维纱业，但竟被军政府派人监督之，旋以汉奸罪名拘留，直至汉阳失陷始获释放。其后经历不详，据张謇日记所载，刘仍在湖北从事实业活动，似当为鄂籍绅商。另待检阅后有所续闻，当再函陈。

前在南京档案处所借张謇材料一件，已钞寄祥烜同志，北京图书馆资料经核对后再开一草目寄奉，或可供参考。有何新发现，尚望时赐教诲。所幸游从之役，甚望实现。敬颂

安好

后学 章开沅上 十月卅一日

1962 年 10 月 31 日，华中师范学院教师章开沅致南通管劲丞的信。

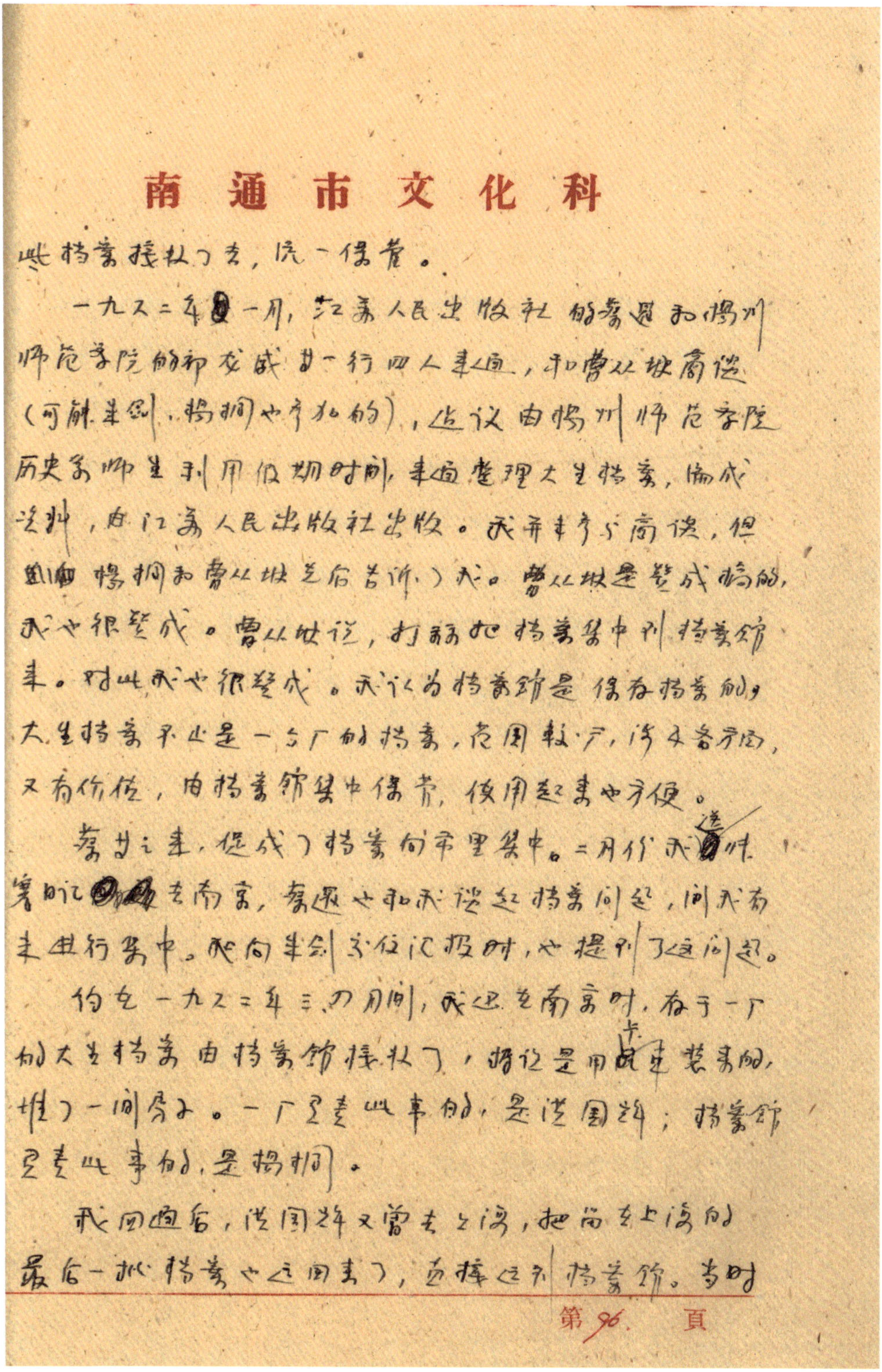

南通市文化科

些档案接收了去，统一保管。

一九六二年一月，江苏人民出版社的李遐和扬州师范学院的祁龙威等一行四人来通，和曹从坡商谈（可能张桐也参加的），建议由扬州师范学院历史系师生利用假期时间，来通整理大生档案，编成资料，由江苏人民出版社出版。我开头参加商谈，但张桐和曹从坡先后告诉了我。曹从坡是赞成的，我也很赞成。曹从坡说，打算把档案集中到档案馆来。对此我也很赞成。我认为档案馆是保存档案的，大生档案不止是一个厂的档案，范围较广，涉及各方面，又有价值，由档案馆集中保管，使用起来也方便。

李遐之来，促成了档案向市里集中。二月份我送[illegible]时去南京，李遐也和我谈起档案问题，问我有未进行集中。我向市委会议汇报时，也提到了这问题。

约在一九六二年三、四月间，我还在南京时，存于一厂的大生档案由档案馆接收了，据说是用卡车装来的，堆了一间房子。一厂负责此事的，是张国祥；档案馆负责此事的，是张桐。

我回通后，张国祥又曾去上海，把尚在上海的最后一批档案也运回来了，直接送到档案馆。当时

第96页

1966年，就职革命史料编辑室的穆烜有关大生档案的回忆（局部）。

检验合格
检验员 35